World Economic and Financial Surveys

WORLD ECONOMIC OUTLOOK
October 2007

Globalization and Inequality

International Monetary Fund

Production: IMF Multimedia Services Division
Cover and Design: Luisa Menjivar and Jorge Salazar
Figures: Theodore F. Peters, Jr.
Typesetting: Choon Lee

World economic outlook (International Monetary Fund)
World economic outlook: a survey by the staff of the International Monetary Fund.—1980– —Washington, D.C.: The Fund, 1980–

v.; 28 cm.—(1981–84: Occasional paper/International Monetary Fund ISSN 0251-6365)
Annual.
Has occasional updates, 1984–
ISSN 0258-7440 = World economic and financial surveys
ISSN 0256-6877 = World economic outlook (Washington)
1. Economic history—1971– —Periodicals. I. International Monetary Fund. II. Series: Occasional paper (International Monetary Fund)

HC10.W7979 84-640155
338.5'443'09048—dc19
AACR 2 MARC-S

Library of Congress 8507

Published biannually.
ISBN 978-1-58906-688-5

Price: US$57.00
(US$54.00 to full-time faculty members and students at universities and colleges)

Please send orders to:
International Monetary Fund, Publication Services
700 19th Street, N.W., Washington, D.C. 20431, U.S.A.
Tel.: (202) 623-7430 Telefax: (202) 623-7201
E-mail: publications@imf.org
Internet: http://www.imf.org

CONTENTS

Tables

Figures

ASSUMPTIONS AND CONVENTIONS

A number of assumptions have been adopted for the projections presented in the *World Economic Outlook*. It has been assumed that real effective exchange rates will remain constant at their average levels during August 22–September 19, 2007, except for the currencies participating in the European exchange rate mechanism II (ERM II), which are assumed to remain constant in nominal terms relative to the euro; that established policies of national authorities will be maintained (for specific assumptions about fiscal and monetary policies in industrial countries, see Box A1); that the average price of oil will be $68.52 a barrel in 2007 and $75.00 a barrel in 2008, and remain unchanged in real terms over the medium term; that the six-month London interbank offered rate (LIBOR) on U.S. dollar deposits will average 5.2 percent in 2007 and 4.4 percent in 2008; that the three-month euro deposits rate will average 4.0 percent in 2007 and 4.1 percent in 2008; and that the six-month Japanese yen deposit rate will yield an average of 0.9 percent in 2007 and of 1.1 percent in 2008. These are, of course, working hypotheses rather than forecasts, and the uncertainties surrounding them add to the margin of error that would in any event be involved in the projections. The estimates and projections are based on statistical information available through end-September 2007.

The following conventions have been used throughout the *World Economic Outlook:*

. . . to indicate that data are not available or not applicable;

— to indicate that the figure is zero or negligible;

– between years or months (for example, 2005–06 or January–June) to indicate the years or months covered, including the beginning and ending years or months;

/ between years or months (for example, 2005/06) to indicate a fiscal or financial year.

"Billion" means a thousand million; "trillion" means a thousand billion.

"Basis points" refer to hundredths of 1 percentage point (for example, 25 basis points are equivalent to ¼ of 1 percent point).

In figures and tables, shaded areas indicate IMF staff projections.

Minor discrepancies between sums of constituent figures and totals shown are due to rounding.

As used in this report, the term "country" does not in all cases refer to a territorial entity that is a state as understood by international law and practice. As used here, the term also covers some territorial entities that are not states but for which statistical data are maintained on a separate and independent basis.

FURTHER INFORMATION AND DATA

This report on the *World Economic Outlook* is available in full on the IMF's Internet site, www.imf.org. Accompanying it on the website is a larger compilation of data from the WEO database than in the report itself, consisting of files containing the series most frequently requested by readers. These files may be downloaded for use in a variety of software packages.

The following changes have been made to streamline the Statistical Appendix of the *World Economic Outlook*. Starting with this issue, the printed version of the *World Economic Outlook* will carry only Part A Tables in the Statistical Appendix section.

Part A contains Tables 1, 2, 3, 6, 7, 8, 11, 20, 25, 26, 31, 35, 43, and 44 from the previous issues of the *World Economic Outlook;* Tables 1.2 and 1.3, which used to be in the main text of the report; and a new table on private capital flows. Tables in Part A present summary data for both advanced economies and emerging market and developing countries in the categories of Output, Inflation, Financial Policies, Foreign Trade, Current Account Transactions, Balance of Payments and External Financing, Flow of Funds, and Medium-Term Baseline Scenario.

Part B of the Statistical Appendix contains the remaining tables. The complete Statistical Appendix, which includes both Part A and Part B Tables, will be available only via the Internet at www.imf.org/external/pubs/ft/weo/2007/02/index.htm.

Inquiries about the content of the *World Economic Outlook* and the WEO database should be sent by mail, electronic mail, or telefax (telephone inquiries cannot be accepted) to:

World Economic Studies Division
Research Department
International Monetary Fund
700 19th Street, N.W.
Washington, D.C. 20431, U.S.A.
E-mail: weo@imf.org Telefax: (202) 623-6343

PREFACE

The analysis and projections contained in the *World Economic Outlook* are integral elements of the IMF's surveillance of economic developments and policies in its member countries, of developments in international financial markets, and of the global economic system. The survey of prospects and policies is the product of a comprehensive interdepartmental review of world economic developments, which draws primarily on information the IMF staff gathers through its consultations with member countries. These consultations are carried out in particular by the IMF's area departments together with the Policy Development and Review Department, the Monetary and Capital Markets Department, and the Fiscal Affairs Department.

The analysis in this report has been coordinated in the Research Department under the general direction of Simon Johnson, Economic Counsellor and Director of Research. The project has been directed by Charles Collyns, Deputy Director of the Research Department, and Tim Callen, Division Chief, Research Department.

The primary contributors to this report are Roberto Cardarelli, Kevin Cheng, Selim Elekdag, Florence Jaumotte, Ben Jones, Michael Keen, Ayhan Kose, Toh Kuan, Subir Lall, Valerie Mercer-Blackman, John Norregaard, Chris Papageorgiou, Hossein Samiei, Alasdair Scott, Martin Sommer, Nikola Spatafora, Jon Strand, Natalia Tamirisa, and Petia Topalova. Sergei Antoshin, Gavin Asdorian, To-Nhu Dao, Stephanie Denis, Nese Erbil, Angela Espiritu, Patrick Hettinger, Susana Mursula, Murad Omoev, Allen Stack, Bennett Sutton, and Ercument Tulun provided research assistance. Mahnaz Hemmati, Laurent Meister, and Emory Oakes managed the database and the computer systems. Sylvia Brescia, Celia Burns, Jemille Colon, and Sheila Tomilloso Igcasenza were responsible for word processing. Other contributors include Andrew Benito, Luis Catão, Gianni De Nicolò, Hamid Faruqee, Thomas Helbling, Michael Kumhof, Tim Lane, Douglas Laxton, Gian-Maria Milesi-Fer retti, Emil Stavrev, Thierry Tressel, and Johannes Wiegand. External consultants include Nancy Birdsall, Menzie Chin, Gordon Hanson, Massimiliano Marcellino, and Carlos Végh. Archana Kumar of the External Relations Department edited the manuscript and coordinated the production of the publication.

The analysis has benefited from comments and suggestions by staff from other IMF departments, as well as by Executive Directors following their discussion of the report on September 17 and 24, 2007. However, both projections and policy considerations are those of the IMF staff and should not be attributed to Executive Directors or to their national authorities.

FOREWORD

Throughout a turbulent summer, the World Economic Outlook *team at the IMF has worked hard to stay ahead of developments, to refine our analytical work, and to keep our forecasts up to date. Led by Charles Collyns and Tim Callen, the World Economic Studies division has worked closely with other IMF staff to produce a* WEO *that is close to current developments while providing some much-needed longer-term perspective. We hope that it will help you both understand what has happened in the past few months as well as reflect on what might be in store for the next 15 months.*

The world economy has entered an uncertain and potentially difficult period. The financial turmoil of August and September threatens to derail what has been an excellent half-decade of global growth. The problems in credit markets have been severe, and while the first phase is now over, we are still waiting to see exactly how the consequences will play out.

Still, the situation at present is one with threats rather than actual major negative outcomes on macroeconomic aggregates. At this point, we expect global growth to slow in 2008, but remain at a buoyant pace. Growth in the United States is expected to remain subdued. Problems in the housing sector are more intense than previously expected, and the disruption of credit is likely to have further impact. We expect some slowing in Japan, where the second quarter was disappointing, and in Europe, where banks were involved to a surprising degree with instruments and vehicles exposed to the U.S. subprime sector.

The good news is that emerging market and developing countries weathered the recent financial storm and are providing the basis for strong global growth in 2008. For the first time, China and India are making the largest country-level contributions to world growth (in purchasing-power-parity terms; see the figure). China is also making the largest contribution at

Emerging Markets Now the Major Engine of Global Growth
(Percent of world growth)

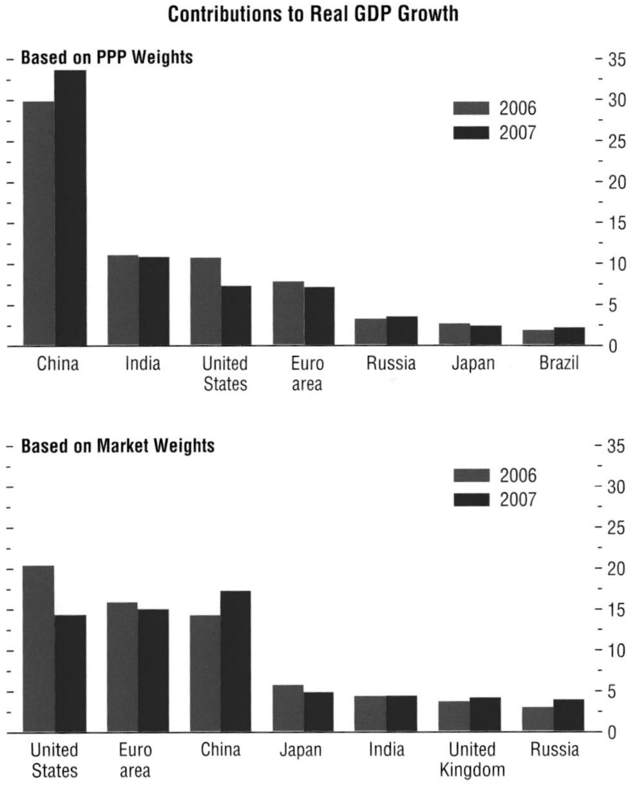

Source: IMF staff calculations.

market prices. More generally, emerging market and developing countries are reaping the benefits of careful macroeconomic management over the past decade. While there are some potential vulnerabilities, and there is no room for complacency going forward, emerging markets should remain strong in the foreseeable future.

In terms of global risks, we see most of these as being on the downside for growth, that is, unexpected developments are more likely to push growth down rather than push it up. Our growth fan chart shows probabilities both above and below our forecast, based on our previous forecast errors, but the skewness of the chart—based on our reading of what could push the global economy away from our central forecast—is almost entirely to the downside.

Some of these risks have received considerable attention, including those in housing markets and financial sectors. But some are more surprising, including the fact that oil prices remain high and that sharp food price increases are contributing to inflation concerns in emerging market and developing countries. A key unknown is what will happen in Europe. Until the events of this summer, Europe was in the upswing of its cycle, with Germany in particular emerging as a driver of growth, moving beyond the long, difficult process of reunification. But the serious disruptions in the market for interbank liquidity and the difficulties experienced by some European banks in recent months were largely unexpected. Quite how these developments will affect the real economy remains to be seen.

I would also stress that the implications for global imbalances remain uncertain. It seems likely that the U.S. current account deficit will decline relative to GDP, in part because the dollar has depreciated further since the summer—its value is down more than 20 percent from its recent peak in 2002. Fortunately, we have in place a framework for cooperative actions by the key countries involved with imbalances; this was a major outcome of the IMF's Multilateral Consultation this year. Oil producers continue to scale up their spending on infrastructure and investments. China remains determined to rebalance its demand so as to lower its current account surplus. Europe and Japan continue with the process of structural reform, which should help with restructuring and boost domestic demand. We expect that this framework will facilitate the gradual decline of imbalances and reduce risks of disruptive changes in exchange rates, but this situation requires continued careful attention.

Turning to our analytical chapters, Chapter 3 highlights a major challenge for many emerging market and developing countries—how to manage large capital inflows. These inflows slowed this summer, but recent indications are that they are again picking up. The chapter assesses what we can learn from recent episodes of capital inflows around the world, and it looks at what kinds of macroeconomic policies help to ensure that growth post-inflows remains strong. It turns out that intervening in exchange markets, either with or without sterilization, has not been successful in limiting real exchange rate appreciation or avoiding a deceleration in post-inflow growth. What really helps is being careful with fiscal spending. The lesson here is not that a country needs to cut spending when there are inflows, but rather that it needs to exercise fiscal restraint. The greater caution of some leading emerging markets in this regard since the late 1990s is commendable and has definitely contributed in part to their resilience today. I hope other countries will learn the same lesson.

Chapter 4 takes a longer-term perspective and looks at what has happened to inequality around the world, particularly during the recent surge in various forms of globalization. While we have written extensively, including in the April 2007 *World Economic Outlook*, about the benefits of globalization, the findings in this chapter should be seen as more cautionary. In almost all countries, inequality has increased in recent years. The authors find that increased trade is not the culprit. Rather, it seems likely that the spread of new technology around the world, both in general and through foreign direct investment, has disproportionately benefited people who are better educated. The implication, of course, is not to try to prevent the adoption of new technology—such an approach would be sure to derail growth. Rather the policy objective should be to provide the education and other social services (such as affordable health care, a reasonable-cost pension system, and so on) to ensure that as many people as possible can find and keep high-productivity jobs. It would be unwise to ignore the issue of growing inequality; globalization is a key source of rising world prosperity, but more effective policy actions are needed to make sure that these benefits are well shared.

Chapter 5 offers hope but also some caution regarding the longer-term prospects of the global economy. Looking back as far as possible with comparable data (which takes us to around 1960), it is clear that the past half-decade has seen the strongest and most broadly based run of global growth since the 1960s. This was not a fluke, but rather the result of improved frameworks for both monetary and fiscal policies, as well as serious institutional improvements in many middle- and lower-income countries. At the same time, there was some luck involved—inflation has been low, globally, in part because of low-cost manufactured goods (part of the globalization process) and because private capital flows have been relatively stable. It would be unwise to expect that there will not be shocks going forward, and the chapter makes recommendations that should help ensure that these shocks do not have major repercussions.

In sum, the main message of this *World Economic Outlook* is that, as long as policy fundamentals remain strong and institutions are not undermined, the global economy should grow rapidly, with the continued involvement of almost all countries. Events of the past few months have been a major test of global financial stability, and some unexpected weaknesses have emerged. As long as those remain contained within a few industrial countries and are addressed in a timely fashion, the impact on world growth should be small.

The key, in the years ahead, is to make sure that emerging market and developing countries can continue to grow rapidly and without major disruptions. Macroeconomic stability is necessary but not sufficient for economic growth. We have to continue the process of trade liberalization, allow capital to flow to more productive opportunities in poorer countries, and—most important—make sure that the benefits of growth are widely shared across all countries and by as many people as possible within countries. We would do well to anticipate further serious shocks, both downside and upside, and to work harder to make sure that the policies and institutions in place can withstand these shocks.

Simon Johnson
Economic Counsellor and Director, Research Department

EXECUTIVE SUMMARY

The global economy grew strongly in the first half of 2007, although turbulence in financial markets has clouded prospects. While the 2007 forecast has been little affected, the baseline projection for 2008 global growth has been reduced by almost ½ percentage point relative to the July 2007 World Economic Outlook Update. *This would still leave global growth at a solid 4¾ percent, supported by generally sound fundamentals and strong momentum in emerging market economies. Risks to the outlook, however, are firmly on the downside, centered around the concern that financial market strains could deepen and trigger a more pronounced global slowdown. Thus, the immediate focus of policymakers is to restore more normal financial market conditions and safeguard the expansion. Additional risks to the outlook include potential inflation pressures, volatile oil markets, and the impact on emerging markets of strong foreign exchange inflows. At the same time, longer-term issues such as population aging, increasing resistance to globalization, and global warming are a source of concern.*

Global Economic Environment

The global economy continued to expand vigorously in the first half of 2007, with growth running above 5 percent (Chapter 1). China's economy gained further momentum, growing by 11½ percent, while India and Russia continued to grow very strongly. These three countries alone have accounted for one-half of global growth over the past year. Robust expansions also continued in other emerging market and developing countries, including low-income countries in Africa. Among the advanced economies, growth in the euro area and Japan slowed in the second quarter of 2007 after two quarters of strong gains. In the United States, growth averaged 2¼ percent in the first half of 2007 as the housing downturn continued to apply considerable drag.

Inflation has been contained in the advanced economies, but it has risen in many emerging market and developing countries, reflecting higher energy and food prices. In the United States, core inflation has gradually eased to below 2 percent. In the euro area, inflation has generally remained below 2 percent this year, but energy and food price increases contributed to an uptick in September; while in Japan, prices have essentially been flat. Some emerging market and developing countries have seen more inflation pressures, reflecting strong growth and the greater weight of rising food prices in their consumer price indices. The acceleration in food prices has reflected pressure from the rising use of corn and other food items for biofuel production and poor weather conditions in some countries (Appendix 1.1). Strong demand has kept oil and other commodity prices high.

Financial market conditions have become more volatile. As discussed in the October 2007 *Global Financial Stability Report* (GFSR), credit conditions have tightened as increasing concerns about the fallout from strains in the U.S. subprime mortgage market led to a spike in yields on securities collateralized with such loans as well as other higher-risk securities. Uncertainty about the distribution of losses and rising concerns about counterparty risk saw liquidity dry up in segments of the financial markets. Equity markets initially retreated, led by falling valuations of financial institutions, although prices have since recovered, and long-term government bond yields declined as investors looked for safe havens. Emerging markets have also been affected, although by relatively less than in previous episodes of global financial market turbulence, and asset prices remain high by historical standards.

Prior to the recent turbulence, central banks around the world were generally tightening monetary policy to head off nascent inflation pressures. In August, however, faced by mounting market disruptions, major central banks injected liquidity into money markets to stabilize short-term interest rates. In September, the Federal Reserve cut the federal funds rate by 50 basis points, and financial markets expect further reductions in the coming months. Expectations of policy tightening by the Bank of England, Bank of Japan, and European Central Bank have been rolled back since the onset of the financial market turmoil. Among emerging markets, some central banks also provided liquidity to ease strains in interbank markets, but for others the principal challenge remains to address inflation concerns.

The major currencies have largely continued trends observed since early 2006. The U.S. dollar has continued to weaken, although its real effective value is still estimated to be above its medium-term fundamental level. The euro has appreciated but continues to trade in a range broadly consistent with fundamentals. The Japanese yen has rebounded strongly in recent months but remains undervalued relative to medium-term fundamentals. The renminbi has continued to appreciate gradually against the U.S. dollar and on a real effective basis, but China's current account surplus has widened further and its international reserves have soared.

Outlook and Risks

In the face of turbulent conditions in financial markets, the baseline projections for global growth have been marked down moderately since the July *World Economic Outlook Update,* although growth is still expected to continue at a solid pace. The global economy is projected to grow by 5.2 percent in 2007 and 4.8 percent in 2008—the latter forecast is 0.4 percentage point lower than previously expected. The largest downward revisions to growth are in the United States, which is now expected to grow at 1.9 percent in 2008; in countries where spillovers from the United States are likely to be largest; and in countries where the impact of continuing financial market turmoil is likely to be more acute (see Chapter 2).

The balance of risks to the baseline growth outlook is clearly on the downside. While the underlying fundamentals supporting growth are sound and the strong momentum in increasingly important emerging market economies is intact, downside risks emanating from the financial markets and domestic demand in the United States and western Europe have increased. While the recent repricing of risk and increased discipline in credit markets could strengthen the foundations for future expansion, it raises the near-term risks to growth. The extent of the impact on growth will depend on how quickly more normal market liquidity returns and on the extent of the retrenchment in credit markets. The IMF staff's baseline forecast is based on the assumption that market liquidity is gradually restored in the coming months and that the interbank market reverts to more normal conditions, although wider credit spreads are expected to persist. Nonetheless, there remains a distinct possibility that turbulent financial market conditions could continue for some time. An extended period of tight credit conditions could have a significant dampening impact on growth, particularly through the effect on housing markets in the United States and some European countries. Countries in emerging Europe and the Commonwealth of Independent States region with large current account deficits and substantial external financing inflows would also be adversely affected if capital inflows were to weaken.

Several other risks could also have an impact on the global outlook. While downside risks to the outlook from inflation concerns have generally been somewhat reduced by recent developments, oil prices have risen to new highs and a further spike in prices cannot be ruled out—reflecting limited spare production capacity. Risks related to persistent global imbalances still remain a concern.

Policy Issues

Policymakers around the world continue to face the immediate challenge of maintaining strong noninflationary growth, a challenge heightened by recent turbulent global financial conditions. In the advanced economies, after a period of tightening that has brought monetary stances close to or above neutral, central banks have addressed the recent drying up of market liquidity and associated financial sector risks while continuing to base monetary policy decisions on judgments about the economic fundamentals. In the United States, signs that growth was likely to continue below trend would justify further interest rate reductions, provided that inflation risks remain contained. In the euro area, monetary policy can stay on hold over the near term, reflecting the downside risks to growth and inflation from financial market turmoil. However, as these risks dissipate, further tightening eventually may be required. In the event of a more protracted slowdown, an easing of monetary policy would need to be considered. In Japan, while interest rates will eventually need to return to more normal levels, such increases should await clear signs that prospective inflation is moving decisively higher and that concerns over recent market volatility have waned.

In due course, lessons will need to be drawn from the current episode of turbulent global financial market conditions. One set of issues concerns the various approaches that central banks have used to provide liquidity to relieve financial strains and the linkage of this liquidity support with financial safety nets. A series of regulatory issues will need to be addressed, as discussed in the October 2007 GFSR. Greater attention will need to be given to ensuring adequate transparency and disclosure by systemically important institutions. It will also be relevant to examine the regulatory approach to treating liquidity risk, the relevant perimeter around financial institutions for risk consolidation, the approach to rating complex financial products, and whether the existing incentive structure ensures adequate risk assessment throughout the supply chain of structured products.

Substantial progress has been made toward fiscal consolidation during the present expansion in advanced economies, but more needs to be done to ensure fiscal sustainability in the face of population aging. Much of the recent improvement in fiscal positions has reflected rapid revenue growth driven by strong growth in profits and high-end incomes, and it is not clear to what extent these revenue gains will be sustained. Further, current budgetary plans envisage limited additional progress in reducing debt ratios from current levels over the next few years. Governments should adopt more ambitious medium-term consolidation plans, together with reforms to tackle the rising pressures on health and social security spending, although in most countries there is scope to let the automatic fiscal stabilizers operate in the event of a downturn.

A number of emerging markets still face overheating pressures and rising food prices, and further monetary tightening may be required. Moreover, notwithstanding recent financial market developments, strong foreign exchange inflows are likely to continue to complicate the task of policymakers. As discussed in Chapter 3, there is no simple formula for dealing with these foreign exchange inflows. Countries need to take a pragmatic approach, finding an appropriate blend of measures suited to their particular circumstances and longer-term goals. Fiscal policy is likely to play a key role. While fiscal positions have improved, this reflects strong revenue growth generated by high commodity prices that may not be sustained. At the same time, government spending in many countries has accelerated, which has added to the difficulties of managing strong foreign exchange inflows. The avoidance of public spending booms, particularly in emerging Europe but also in Latin America, would help both in managing inflows and in continuing to reduce public debt levels. In fuel-exporting countries, however, there is scope to further increase spending, subject to absorptive capacities and the cyclical position of the economy. A tightening of prudential standards in financial systems and steps to liberalize controls on capital outflows can all play useful roles. In some cases, greater exchange rate flexibility would provide more room for better monetary control. Specifically for China, further upward flexibility of the renminbi, along with measures to reform the exchange rate regime and boost consumption, would also contribute to a necessary rebalancing of demand and to an orderly unwinding of global imbalances.

Across all countries, a common theme is the need to take advantage of the opportunities created by globalization and technological advances, while doing more to ensure that the benefits of these ongoing changes are well distributed across the broad population. A key part of this agenda is to make sure that markets work well, with priorities being to boost productivity in the financial and service sectors in Europe and Japan; resist protectionist pressures in the United States and Europe; and improve infrastructure, develop financial systems, and strengthen the business environment in emerging market and developing countries.

Globalization is often blamed for the rising inequality observed in most countries and regions. Chapter 4 of this report finds that technological advances have contributed the most to the recent rise in inequality, but increased financial globalization—and foreign direct investment in particular—has also played a role. Contrary to popular belief, increased trade globalization is actually associated with a decline in inequality. It is important that policies help ensure that the gains from globalization and technological change are more broadly shared across the population. Reforms to strengthen education and training would help to ensure that workers have the appropriate skills for the emerging "knowledge-based" global economy. Policies that increase the availability of finance to the poor would also help, as would further trade liberalization that boosts agricultural exports from developing countries.

Chapter 5 of this report examines the current global expansion from a historical perspective. It finds that not only has growth been stronger than in other recent cycles, but also the benefits are being more widely shared across the world and economic volatility has been lower. Indeed, better monetary and fiscal policies, improved institutions, and increased financial development mean that it is likely that business cycles will be of longer duration and lesser magnitude than in the past. Nevertheless, the prospects for future stability should not be overstated, and recent increased financial market volatility has underlined concerns that favorable conditions may not continue. The abrupt end to the period of strong and sustained growth in the 1960s and early 1970s provides a useful cautionary lesson of what can happen if policies do not adjust to tackle emerging risks in a timely manner.

In some key areas, joint actions across countries will be crucial. The recent slow progress with the Doha Trade Round is deeply disappointing, and major countries should demonstrate leadership to re-energize the process of multilateral trade liberalization. Concerns about climate change and energy security also clearly require a multilateral approach. As discussed in Appendix 1.2, global warming may be the world's largest collective action problem where the negative consequences of individual activities are felt largely by others. It will be important that countries come together to develop a market-based framework that balances the long-term costs of carbon emissions against the immediate economic costs of mitigation. Energy policy should focus less on trying to secure national sources of energy and more on ensuring the smooth operation of oil and other energy markets, encouraging diversification of energy sources (for example, by reducing barriers to trade in biofuels), and paying greater attention to price-based incentives to curb the growth of energy consumption.

Welcome progress has been made toward developing a joint approach toward tackling global imbalances, and this now needs to be followed through. The IMF's Multilateral Consultation on Global Imbalances with key countries represents the first use of an innovative approach to addressing systemic global challenges. The Consultation provided a forum to strengthen mutual understanding of the issues, to reaffirm support for the International Monetary and Financial Committee (IMFC) Strategy of sustaining global growth while reducing imbalances, and for each country to indicate specific policies consistent with the Strategy. The result of the Consultation was a set of policy plans that, according to IMF staff analysis, will make a significant contribution toward the goals of the IMFC Strategy. With the agreement of the participants in the Consultation, the implementation of the policy plans will be the subject of regular IMF surveillance.

CHAPTER 1

GLOBAL PROSPECTS AND POLICIES

Although the global economy has sustained strong growth in recent quarters, turbulence in financial markets has clouded the prospects. The baseline projections for global growth in 2008 have been revised down by almost ½ percentage point relative to the July 2007 World Economic Outlook Update, *although growth would remain a solid 4¾ percent, supported by generally sound fundamentals and the strong momentum in the emerging market economies* (Figure 1.1). *However, risks to the outlook lie firmly on the downside, centering around the concern that financial market strains could continue and trigger a more pronounced global slowdown. Thus, the immediate task for policymakers is to restore more normal financial market conditions and safeguard the continued expansion of activity. Additional risks to the outlook include potential inflation pressures, volatile oil markets, the impact on emerging markets of strong capital inflows, and continued large global imbalances. Key longer-term issues relate to addressing obstacles to sustained growth from population aging and the increasing resistance to globalization.*

Strong Global Growth Is Being Confronted by Turbulent Financial Conditions

Global growth remained above 5 percent in the first half of 2007. China's economy gained momentum, growing 11½ percent and, for the first time, making the largest contribution to global growth evaluated at market as well as purchasing-power-parity (PPP) exchange rates. India continued to grow at more than 9 percent and Russia at almost 8 percent. These three countries alone accounted for one-half of global growth over the past year, but other emerging market and developing countries have also maintained robust expansions. Rapid growth in these countries counterbalanced continued moderate growth in the United States, which grew at about 2¼ percent in the first half, as the

Figure 1.1. Global Indicators[1]

(Annual percent change unless otherwise noted)

The global economy has been experiencing its strongest sustained period of growth since the early 1970s. The expansion is projected to remain above the long-term trend, notwithstanding recent financial market turbulence, with emerging market and developing countries leading the way. Inflation generally remains at low levels, while trade volumes continue to increase robustly, albeit at a slower pace than in 2006.

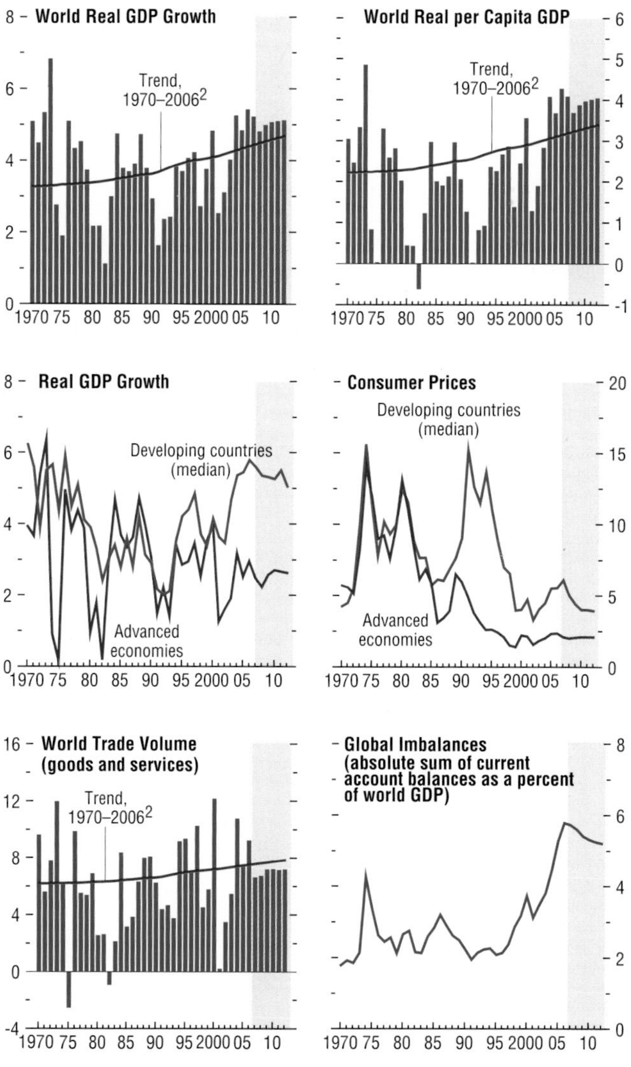

[1]Shaded areas indicate IMF staff projections. Aggregates are computed on the basis of purchasing-power-parity (PPP) weights unless otherwise noted.

[2]Average growth rates for individual countries, aggregated using PPP weights; the aggregates shift over time in favor of faster-growing countries, giving the line an upward trend.

Figure 1.2. Global Inflation

(Twelve-month change of the consumer price index unless otherwise noted)

Inflation has been contained in the advanced economies, but it has moved up in emerging markets as oil prices have rebounded and food prices have accelerated.

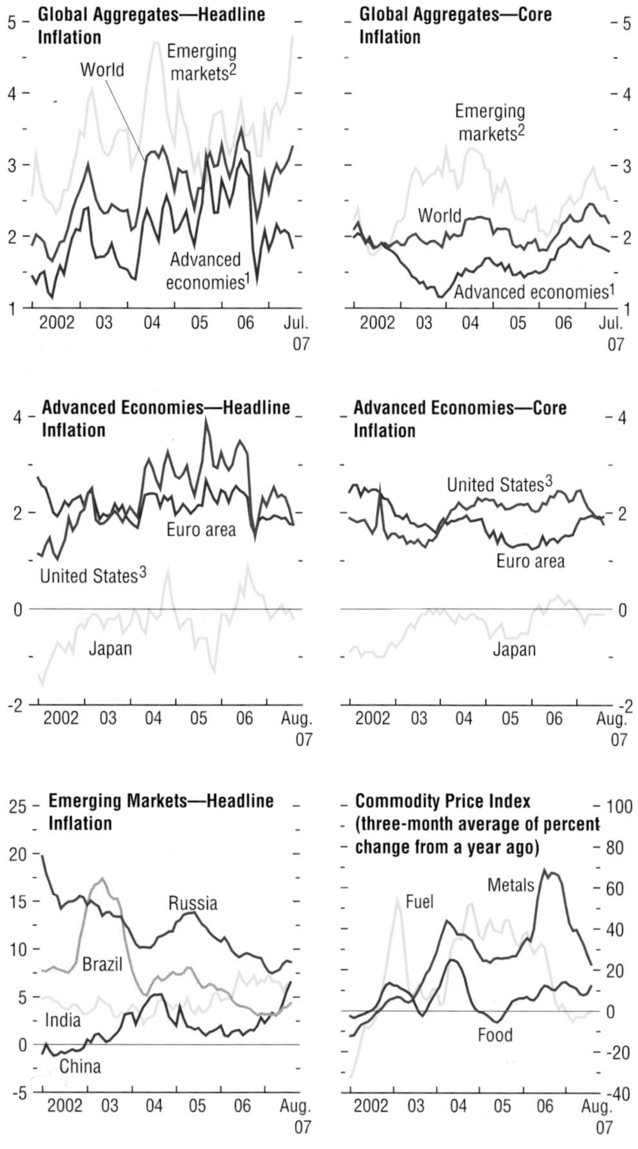

Sources: Haver Analytics; and IMF staff calculations.

[1]Australia, Canada, Denmark, euro area, Japan, New Zealand, Norway, Sweden, the United Kingdom, and the United States.

[2]Brazil, Bulgaria, Chile, China, Estonia, Hong Kong SAR, Hungary, India, Indonesia, Korea, Malaysia, Mexico, Poland, Singapore, South Africa, Taiwan Province of China, and Thailand.

[3]Personal consumption expenditure deflator.

housing correction continued to apply considerable drag. Growth in the euro area and Japan slowed in the second quarter, after two quarters of strong gains.

Inflation has been contained in the advanced economies in recent months, but rising food prices have contributed to heightened pressures elsewhere (Figure 1.2). In the United States, core inflation has gradually subsided to below 2 percent in significant part because of slowing shelter cost increases. In the euro area, inflation has generally remained below 2 percent this year, although energy and food price increases contributed to an uptick in September; whereas in Japan, prices have essentially been flat. However, inflation has picked up in a number of emerging market and developing countries, reflecting strong growth of domestic demand and the greater weight of rising food prices in the consumer price index. The acceleration in food prices has reflected pressure from increasing use of corn and other food items for biofuel production as well as poor weather conditions and supply disruptions in a number of countries (Box 1.1). Meanwhile, oil prices have recently rebounded to new highs, owing to stronger growth of demand than initially projected in the face of lower production by the Organization of Petroleum Exporting Countries (OPEC), a smaller-than-expected rise of non-OPEC output, and continuing geopolitical concerns (Appendix 1.1).

Global credit market conditions have deteriorated sharply since late July as a repricing of credit risk sparked increased volatility and a broad loss of market liquidity. Initially, rising delinquencies on U.S. subprime mortgages led to a spike in yields on securities collateralized with such loans and to a sharp widening in spreads on structured credits, particularly in the United States and the euro area (Figure 1.3; see also detailed discussion in the October 2007 *Global Financial Stability Report,* or GFSR). From mid-August, rising uncertainty about the amount and distribution of associated valuation losses and concerns about the off-balance-sheet exposures of financial institutions have added to market strains. The result has been a drying up of high-yield corporate bond issues, a sharp contraction in the asset-backed commercial paper market, a dramatic disruption of liquidity in the interbank market, and stress on institutions funded through short-term money markets. Yields on government paper declined sharply as investors looked for safe havens and as expectations about future monetary policy were revised. Toward the end of September, some of these strains started to ease, following a 50 basis point cut in the federal funds rate, but credit market conditions still remain under stress with wider spreads and low issuance of riskier assets. Equity markets in the advanced economies also retreated from highs in August, led by falling valuations of financial institutions, although prices have since recovered (Figure 1.4).

Emerging markets have also been affected by these developments, with sovereign spreads widening, stock markets falling, and capital flows being scaled back (Figure 1.5). Overall, however, the impact has been less than in previous episodes of global financial turbulence, and emerging market equity prices are again reaching record highs. This resilience reflects two sets of factors. First, the turbulence has been related to setbacks in markets for innovative credit instruments and in institutional structures that are less prevalent in emerging markets. Second, most emerging market countries have reduced external vulnerabilities by strengthening their public balance sheets and policy frameworks. That said, certain countries that have received heavy short-term capital inflows experienced pressures in interbank markets as these flows started to reverse.

Prior to the recent turbulence, central banks around the world were generally pushing up policy rates to head off nascent inflationary pressures. However, in August, faced by mounting market disruptions, central banks in the major advanced economies injected liquidity through open market operations on a scale not seen since the Long-Term Capital Management (LTCM)/Russian default crisis in 1998 to stabilize overnight interest rates. They also

Figure 1.3. Developments in Mature Credit Markets

(Interest rates in percent unless otherwise noted)

Credit market conditions have deteriorated sharply since late July as rising fallout from problems in the U.S. subprime mortgage sector led to a spike in yields on high-risk investments. In this context, interest rates on government securities have declined, reflecting a flight to quality and changing expectations about the path of monetary policy.

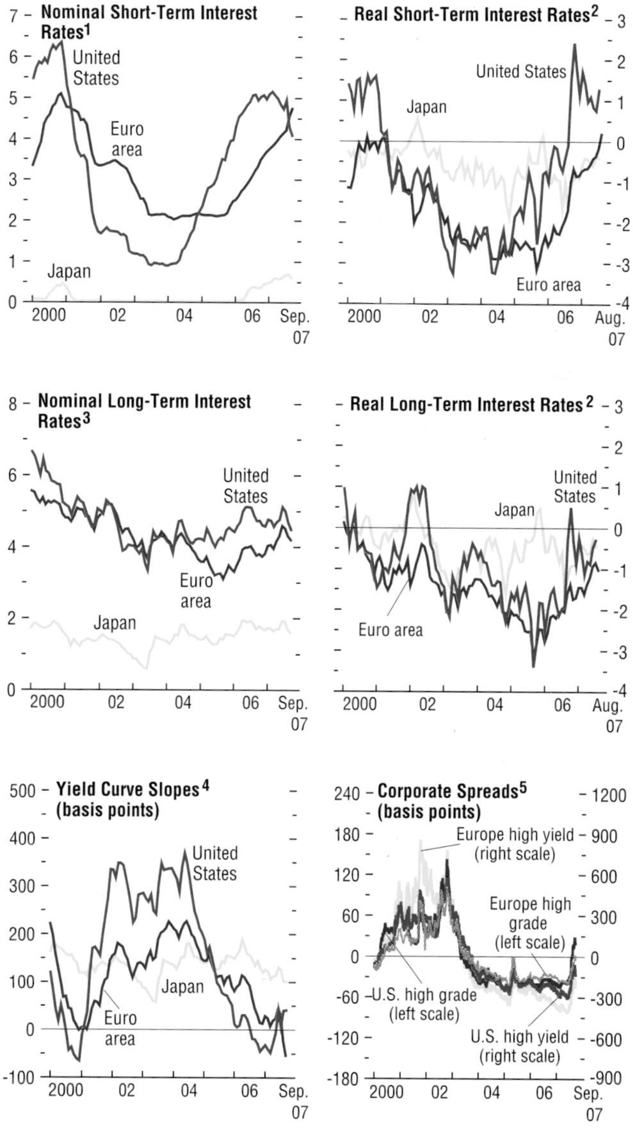

Sources: Bloomberg Financial Markets, LP; Merrill Lynch; and IMF staff calculations.
[1]Three-month treasury bills.
[2]Relative to headline inflation. Measured as deviations from 1990–2007 (August) average.
[3]Ten-year government bonds.
[4]Ten-year government bond minus three-month treasury bill rate.
[5]Measured as deviations from 2000–07 (September) average.

Figure 1.4. Mature Financial Market Indicators

Equity markets were initially affected by turbulent conditions in credit markets, with volatility increasing sharply. However, equity prices have regained ground in recent weeks.

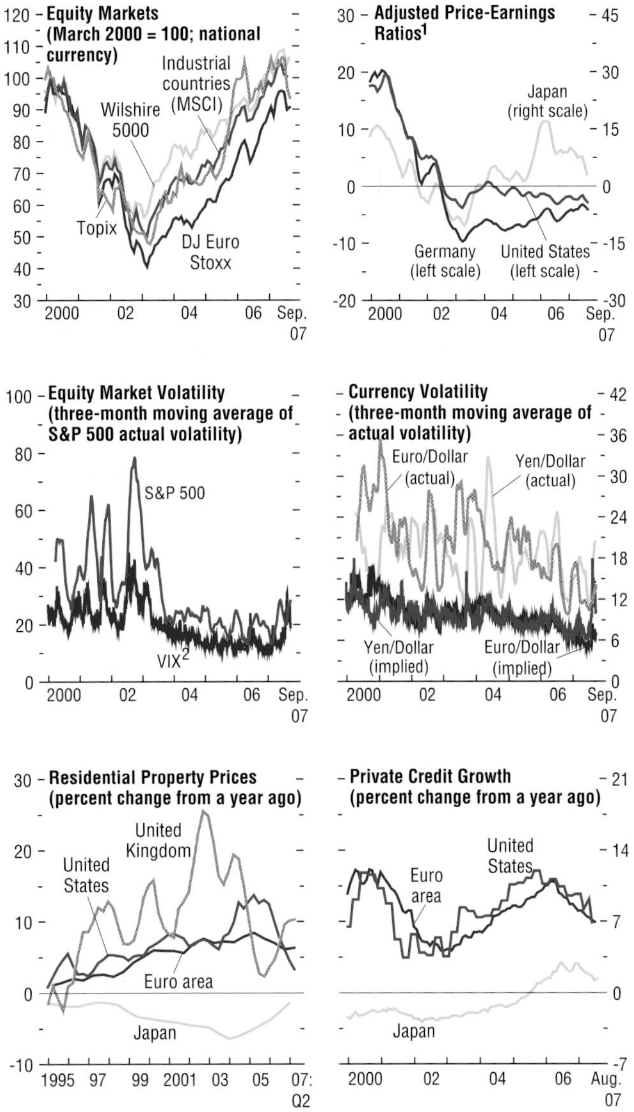

Sources: Bloomberg Financial Markets, LP; Datastream; CEIC Data Company Limited; Haver Analytics; IMF, *International Financial Statistics*; OECD, *Economic Outlook*; and IMF staff calculations.

[1]Adjusted price-earnings ratios are the ratio of stock prices to the moving average of the previous 10 years' earnings, adjusted for nominal trend growth. Adjusted price-earnings ratios are measured as three-month moving average of deviations from 1990–2007 (September) average.

[2]VIX is the Chicago Board Options Exchange volatility index. This index is calculated by taking a weighted average of implied volatility for the eight S&P 500 calls and puts.

facilitated access to their discount windows, and in the United Kingdom, the authorities extended deposit insurance coverage to reassure depositors after a bank experienced difficulties. In September, the Federal Reserve reacted to rising risks to growth by lowering the federal funds rate by ½ percentage point, and market participants expect further reductions in the coming months. Moreover, expectations of policy tightening by the European Central Bank (ECB) and the Bank of Japan (BoJ) have been rolled back. Central banks in a number of emerging market countries (e.g., Argentina, Kazakhstan, and Russia) also provided liquidity to relieve strains in interbank markets, but for others the principal challenge has continued to be addressing inflation concerns (Chile, China, and South Africa have all raised interest rates since August).

The U.S. dollar temporarily regained some ground in August in the context of recent financial turbulence, but has since resumed a weakening trend, against the background of a wide current account deficit, a slow-growing economy, and the cut in the federal funds rate (Figure 1.6). In the IMF staff's view, the dollar remains overvalued relative to medium-term fundamentals.[1] Although the euro has strengthened in effective terms, it continues to trade in a range broadly consistent with medium-term fundamentals. The pound sterling and the Canadian dollar have also appreciated in real effective terms; the pound is viewed as overvalued relative to fundamentals and the Canadian dollar to be broadly in line with fundamentals. The yen depreciated somewhat more rapidly through June, despite Japan's rising current account surplus, as continued low interest rates and a waning home bias of Japanese investors encouraged capital outflows. However, it has rebounded since then, as heightened market volatility has prompted some unwinding of yen carry trades, although the yen still remains undervalued relative to medium-term fundamentals.

[1]Various approaches for assessing an exchange rate's valuation relative to medium-term fundamentals are described in IMF (2006).

The renminbi has continued to appreciate gradually against the U.S. dollar, and its real effective exchange rate has risen modestly in recent months (Figure 1.7). Nevertheless, China's current account surplus has widened further, and its international reserves have continued to soar, reaching $1.4 trillion at end-August. Other emerging market countries have also faced strong foreign exchange inflows from both current and capital accounts, reflected in significant exchange rate appreciations in a number of countries and a rapid accumulation of international reserves that has driven strong domestic credit growth. Emerging market currencies generally weakened in July and August, in the context of turbulent global financial markets, but have since regained ground.

The Baseline Outlook Has Been Marked Down Moderately—And Downside Risks Have Intensified

In the face of turbulent financial conditions, the baseline projections for the global economy have been marked down moderately since the July 2007 *World Economic Outlook Update*, but growth nonetheless is expected to continue at a solid pace. According to the latest IMF forecast, global growth would slow to 5.2 percent in 2007 and 4.8 percent in 2008, down from the 5.4 percent rate registered in 2006 (Table 1.1 and Figure 1.8). The largest downward revisions to growth are in the United States and countries where financial and trade spillovers from the United States are likely to be largest (particularly Canada, Mexico, and parts of emerging Asia).

In the United States, growth is now projected to remain at 1.9 percent in 2008, a mark-down of almost 1 percentage point below the previous projections. Ongoing difficulties in the mortgage market are expected to extend the decline in residential investment, while higher energy prices, sluggish job growth, and weaker house prices are likely to dampen consumption spending. In the euro area, growth has been marked down to 2.1 percent in 2008, 0.4 percentage point lower than in July, reflecting lagged effects

Figure 1.5. Emerging Market Financial Conditions

Financial flows to emerging markets and private credit growth continued to be strong in the first half of 2007. Since July, more turbulent global financial market conditions have prompted some widening of bond yield spreads and a weakening of equity prices, but, generally, emerging market asset valuations remain near historic highs.

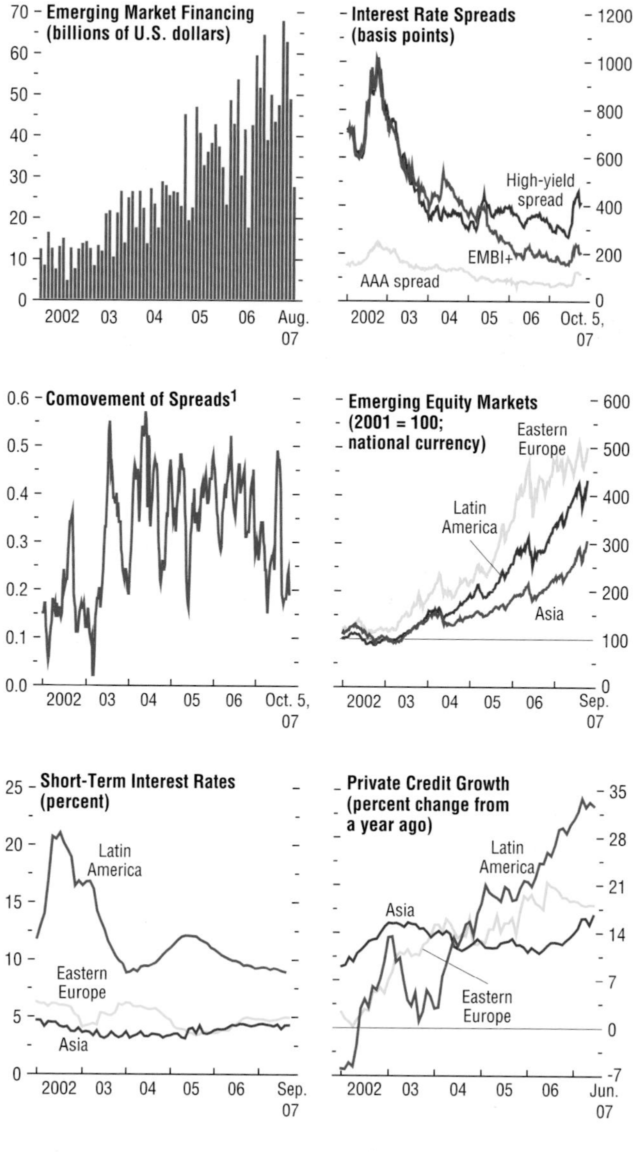

Sources: Bloomberg Financial Markets, LP; Capital Data; IMF, *International Financial Statistics*; and IMF staff calculations.

[1]Average of 30-day rolling cross-correlation of emerging market debt spreads.

Figure 1.6. External Developments in Selected Advanced Economies

The U.S. dollar has continued to depreciate, while the U.S. current account deficit has come down moderately in recent quarters but remains close to 6 percent of GDP. The yen rebounded in August as turbulent financial conditions led to some reversal of carry trade flows. The euro has remained on an appreciating trend.

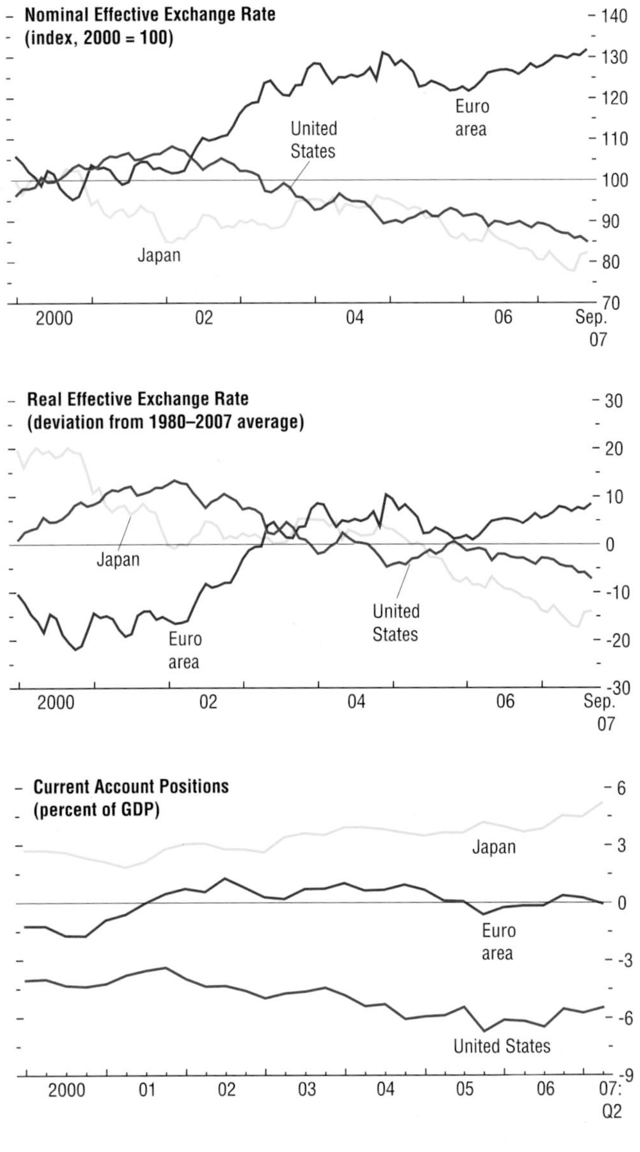

Sources: Haver Analytics; and IMF staff calculations.

of euro appreciation, trade spillovers from the United States, and more difficult financing conditions. In Japan, the growth projection has been reduced to 2 percent in 2007 and 1.7 percent in 2008 (0.6 and 0.3 percentage points lower than in July), reflecting the weaker-than-expected second quarter GDP outturn, slower global growth, and a somewhat stronger yen. Among emerging market and developing countries, growth is expected to remain very strong. The Chinese economy is now expected to grow by 10 percent in 2008, some 0.5 percentage point lower than in the July update.

The baseline projections assume that market liquidity is gradually restored in coming months and that the interbank market reverts to more normal conditions, although wider spreads would persist on riskier assets following a prolonged period of exceptionally low spreads, and lending standards would be tighter. These assumptions are consistent with experience following previous episodes of financial turbulence (Box 1.2). The baseline also assumes that the Federal Reserve cuts interest rates by a further 50 basis points by the end of the year, and the ECB and BoJ refrain from further interest rate increases through the end of the year.

On this basis, the IMF staff assessment is that sound fundamentals would continue to support solid global growth. In the advanced economies, sources of resilience include the strong balance sheets and capital positions of core financial institutions at the beginning of the recent episode, the high profitability and generally low leverage of the corporate sector, and the healthy situation in labor markets and household net wealth. Moreover, strong domestic demand growth in emerging market economies should continue to be a key driver of global growth, with more robust public balance sheets and policy frameworks providing scope for most countries to weather some weakening in external demand (Figure 1.9). Indeed, somewhat slower capital inflows from the torrid pace of the first half of 2007 may serve to ease concerns about excessive currency appreciation or too rapid credit growth.

However, the risks to the baseline forecast are distinctly to the downside. As shown in the fan chart in the upper panel of Figure 1.10, the IMF staff envisages a 1 in 6 chance of global growth falling to 3½ percent or less in 2008. The main sources of the increase in the downside risk since the July 2007 update come from deteriorating financial conditions and from the uncertain prospects for domestic demand in the United States and Europe, as shown in the lower panel of Figure 1.10. Risks to domestic demand in western Europe and Japan are now seen as somewhat to the downside and risks in emerging markets are seen as broadly balanced—previously the balance of risks in these economies was viewed as positive. By contrast, risks to the outlook from inflation concerns and oil market volatility are now somewhat less negative, as supply constraints and commodity market pressures would be reduced by some moderation in the pace of global growth. Risks related to persistent global imbalances remain a concern.

Financial Market Risks

Previous issues of the *World Economic Outlook* and the GFSR have expressed concern that heightened volatility and a widening of risk spreads from exceptionally low levels could have a significant dampening impact on economic activity. The manifestation of such risks in the recent period of financial turbulence is now reflected in some lowering of the baseline forecast. Nonetheless, financial market conditions remain a major source of downside risks to the global outlook. While the baseline assumes a return to more normal market conditions after a repricing of risk, there remains the distinct possibility that recent turbulent conditions could continue for some time and generate a deeper "credit crunch" than envisaged in the baseline scenario, with considerably greater macroeconomic impact.

As discussed in more detail in the October 2007 GFSR, recent financial market developments represent an inevitable return to greater market discipline after a period of very low

Figure 1.7. External Developments in Emerging Market and Developing Countries

Exchange rates in emerging market and developing countries have tended to appreciate, in the face of strong foreign exchange inflows and despite heavy intervention that has pushed reserves up to record levels.

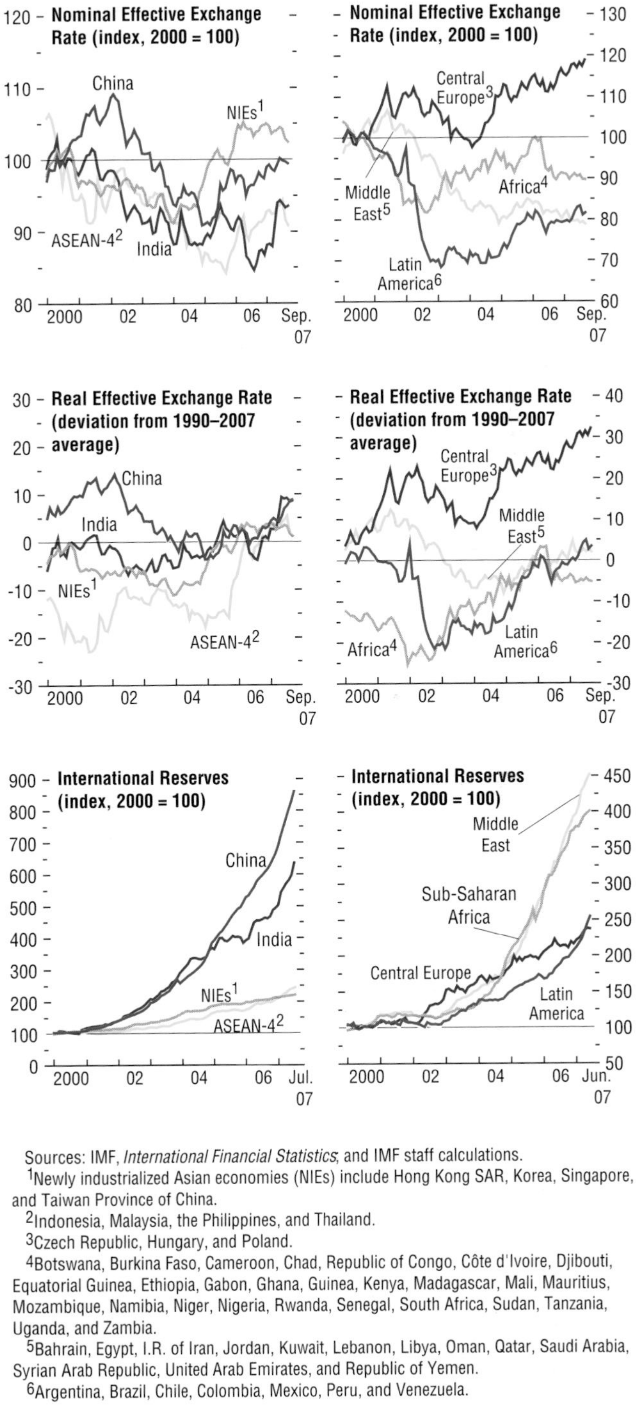

Sources: IMF, *International Financial Statistics*; and IMF staff calculations.

[1]Newly industrialized Asian economies (NIEs) include Hong Kong SAR, Korea, Singapore, and Taiwan Province of China.

[2]Indonesia, Malaysia, the Philippines, and Thailand.

[3]Czech Republic, Hungary, and Poland.

[4]Botswana, Burkina Faso, Cameroon, Chad, Republic of Congo, Côte d'Ivoire, Djibouti, Equatorial Guinea, Ethiopia, Gabon, Ghana, Guinea, Kenya, Madagascar, Mali, Mauritius, Mozambique, Namibia, Niger, Nigeria, Rwanda, Senegal, South Africa, Sudan, Tanzania, Uganda, and Zambia.

[5]Bahrain, Egypt, I.R. of Iran, Jordan, Kuwait, Lebanon, Libya, Oman, Qatar, Saudi Arabia, Syrian Arab Republic, United Arab Emirates, and Republic of Yemen.

[6]Argentina, Brazil, Chile, Colombia, Mexico, Peru, and Venezuela.

Table 1.1. Overview of the *World Economic Outlook* Projections

(Annual percent change unless otherwise noted)

			Current Projections		Difference from July 2007 WEO Update	
	2005	2006	2007	2008	2007	2008
World output	**4.8**	**5.4**	**5.2**	**4.8**	**—**	**–0.4**
Advanced economies	2.5	2.9	2.5	2.2	–0.1	–0.6
United States	3.1	2.9	1.9	1.9	–0.1	–0.9
Euro area	1.5	2.8	2.5	2.1	–0.1	–0.4
Germany	0.8	2.9	2.4	2.0	–0.2	–0.4
France	1.7	2.0	1.9	2.0	–0.3	–0.3
Italy	0.1	1.9	1.7	1.3	–0.1	–0.4
Spain	3.6	3.9	3.7	2.7	–0.1	–0.7
Japan	1.9	2.2	2.0	1.7	–0.6	–0.3
United Kingdom	1.8	2.8	3.1	2.3	0.2	–0.4
Canada	3.1	2.8	2.5	2.3	—	–0.5
Other advanced economies	3.9	4.4	4.3	3.8	0.1	–0.3
Newly industrialized Asian economies	4.7	5.3	4.9	4.4	0.1	–0.4
Other emerging market and developing countries	7.5	8.1	8.1	7.4	0.1	–0.2
Africa	5.6	5.6	5.7	6.5	–0.7	0.3
Sub-Sahara	6.0	5.7	6.1	6.8	–0.8	0.4
Central and eastern Europe	5.6	6.3	5.8	5.2	0.1	–0.2
Commonwealth of Independent States	6.6	7.7	7.8	7.0	0.2	–0.1
Russia	6.4	6.7	7.0	6.5	—	–0.3
Excluding Russia	6.9	9.8	9.4	8.1	0.6	0.3
Developing Asia	9.2	9.8	9.8	8.8	0.2	–0.3
China	10.4	11.1	11.5	10.0	0.3	–0.5
India	9.0	9.7	8.9	8.4	–0.1	—
ASEAN-4	5.1	5.4	5.6	5.6	0.2	–0.1
Middle East	5.4	5.6	5.9	5.9	0.5	0.4
Western Hemisphere	4.6	5.5	5.0	4.3	—	–0.1
Brazil	2.9	3.7	4.4	4.0	—	–0.2
Mexico	2.8	4.8	2.9	3.0	–0.2	–0.5
Memorandum						
European Union	2.0	3.2	3.0	2.5	–0.1	–0.3
World growth based on market exchange rates	3.3	3.8	3.5	3.3	–0.1	–0.4
World trade volume (goods and services)	**7.5**	**9.2**	**6.6**	**6.7**	**–0.5**	**–0.7**
Imports						
Advanced economies	6.1	7.4	4.3	5.0	–0.3	–1.0
Other emerging market and developing countries	12.1	14.9	12.5	11.3	–0.3	0.2
Exports						
Advanced economies	5.8	8.2	5.4	5.3	–0.1	–0.9
Other emerging market and developing countries	11.1	11.0	9.2	9.0	–1.5	–0.2
Commodity prices (U.S. dollars)						
Oil[1]	41.3	20.5	6.6	9.5	7.4	1.7
Nonfuel (average based on world commodity export weights)	10.3	28.4	12.2	–6.7	–2.3	1.1
Consumer prices						
Advanced economies	2.3	2.3	2.1	2.0	0.1	–0.1
Other emerging market and developing countries[2]	5.2	5.1	5.9	5.3	0.5	0.6
London interbank offered rate (percent)[3]						
On U.S. dollar deposits	3.8	5.3	5.2	4.4	–0.2	–0.9
On euro deposits	2.2	3.1	4.0	4.1	0.2	0.4
On Japanese yen deposits	0.1	0.4	0.9	1.1	0.1	–0.1

Note: Real effective exchange rates are assumed to remain constant at the levels prevailing during August 22–September 19, 2007. See the Statistical Appendix for details on groups and methodologies.

[1]Simple average of prices of U.K. Brent, Dubai, and West Texas Intermediate crude oil. The average price of oil in U.S. dollars a barrel was $64.27 in 2006; the assumed price is $68.52 in 2007 and $75.00 in 2008.

[2]Excludes Zimbabwe; see Table 2.7 for more details.

[3]Six-month rate for the United States and Japan. Three-month rate for the euro area.

risk spreads and lax credit conditions, which should ultimately strengthen the foundations of global growth. However, the correction has been extremely turbulent because of uncertainties about the distribution of valuation losses and the drying up of money market liquidity. As markets work their way through the repricing and the uncertainties are reduced, the initial strong capital and profitability of core financial institutions and the dispersion of losses across investors should limit systemic risks. Thus, the most likely outcome built into the baseline scenario is a gradual return to more normal market conditions after a repricing of credit risk and a tightening of credit standards. Some financial market segments are likely to shrink very substantially—notably the subprime mortgage market and riskier forms of asset-backed securitization—while risk spreads for nonprime corporate borrowing are likely to be persistently higher. However, the impact on interest rates for lower-risk borrowers may be quite limited. It is noteworthy that amid the turmoil, the effect on interest rates for conforming mortgage loans and high-grade corporate borrowers has been small, as some widening in spreads has been at least partly offset by lower benchmark government bond yields.

Nevertheless, at the time of writing, conditions in financial markets remain volatile, and the stress in credit markets may continue despite efforts by central banks to ensure adequate market liquidity and calm market sentiment. A key element of uncertainty is the extent to which a drying up of demand for securitized assets could drive the reintermediation of credit into the banking system, limiting capacity for new credit growth. Moreover, continued stress in interbank and other short-term funding markets could add to pressure on bank liquidity and profitability. Such an outturn could imply not only a sustained setback for riskier market segments, but also tighter credit conditions for even high-grade borrowers in the household and corporate sectors. Although the impact would likely be greatest in the United States and western Europe—where the use of, and investor exposure to, structured credits has been most

Figure 1.8. Global Outlook

(Real GDP; percent change from a year ago)

While projections have been marked down moderately to reflect the impact of recent financial market turbulence, output growth is still expected to be well sustained over 2007–08. Emerging market countries in Asia continue to lead the way, but all regions are expected to share in the strong performance.

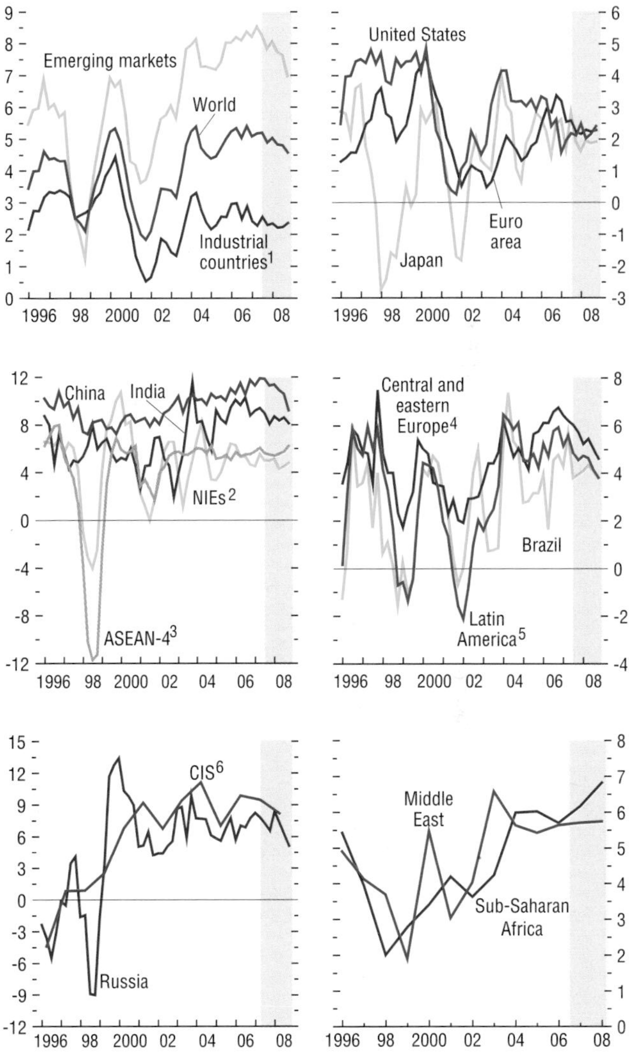

Sources: Haver Analytics; and IMF staff estimates.
[1]Australia, Canada, Denmark, euro area, Japan, New Zealand, Norway, Sweden, Switzerland, the United Kingdom, and the United States.
[2]Newly industrialized Asian economies (NIEs) include Hong Kong SAR, Korea, Singapore, and Taiwan Province of China.
[3]Indonesia, Malaysia, the Philippines, and Thailand.
[4]Czech Republic, Estonia, Hungary, Latvia, Lithuania, and Poland.
[5]Argentina, Brazil, Chile, Colombia, Mexico, Peru, and Venezuela.
[6]Commonwealth of Independent States.

Figure 1.9. Current and Forward-Looking Indicators
(Percent change from a year ago unless otherwise noted)

Industrial production and trade growth have moderated since 2006 as growth in the advanced economies has eased. Business and consumer confidence indicators have dipped recently but remain generally positive. Domestic demand continues to grow robustly in the emerging market economies.

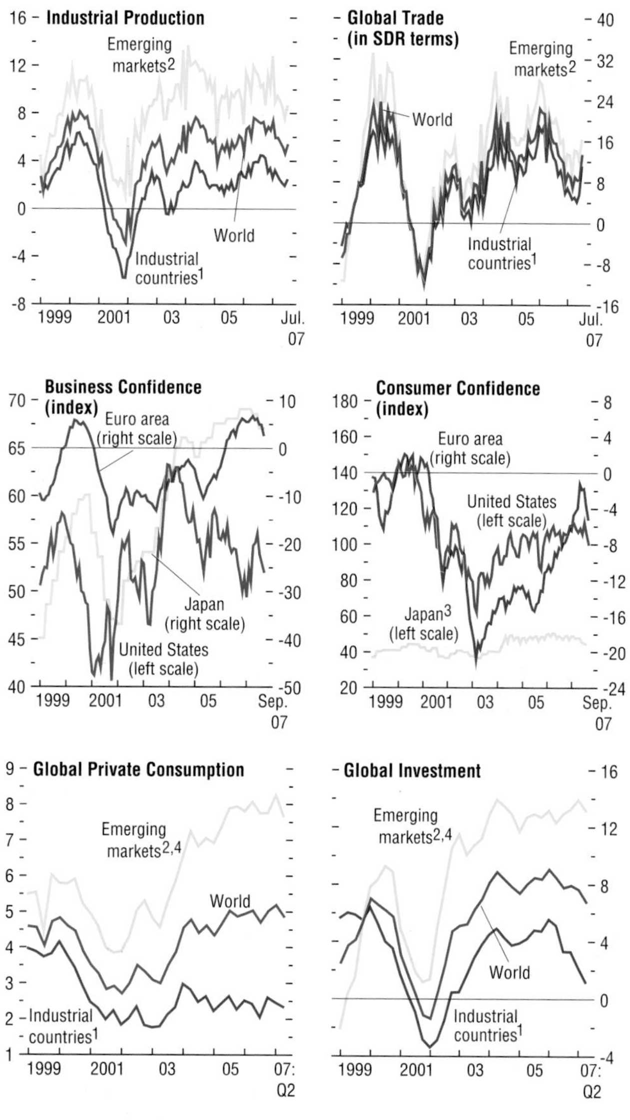

Sources: Business confidence for the United States, the Institute for Supply Management; for the euro area, the European Commission; and, for Japan, Bank of Japan. Consumer confidence for the United States, the Conference Board; for the euro area, the European Commission; for Japan, Cabinet Office; and, for all others, Haver Analytics.

[1]Australia, Canada, Denmark, euro area, Japan, New Zealand, Norway, Sweden, Switzerland, the United Kingdom, and the United States.

[2]Argentina, Brazil, Bulgaria, Chile, China, Colombia, Czech Republic, Estonia, Hong Kong SAR, Hungary, India, Indonesia, Israel, Korea, Latvia, Lithuania, Malaysia, Mexico, Pakistan, Peru, the Philippines, Poland, Romania, Russia, Singapore, Slovak Republic, South Africa, Taiwan Province of China, Thailand, Turkey, Ukraine, and Venezuela.

[3]Japan's consumer confidence data are based on a diffusion index, where values greater than 50 indicate improving confidence.

[4]Data for China, India, Pakistan, and Russia are interpolated.

extensive—the effects could be felt more widely, given growing cross-border linkages across the global financial system.

Moreover, other sources of financial risk could be exposed by sustained volatile conditions. So far, emerging markets have generally been less affected by recent turbulence in the advanced economies than in past episodes beyond a few countries that were affected by a reversal of short-term flows. However, a number of countries have become dependent on large external financing inflows, including some emerging European and Commonwealth of Independent States (CIS) countries. In these countries, promising growth prospects have generated large foreign direct investment (FDI) inflows, but also bank flows and international bond issuance often denominated in foreign currencies, which have been used to finance credit booms and rapid growth in consumption. These flows could be jeopardized by a fuller repricing of risk and tightening of lending standards, and a general increase in risk aversion in the context of continued turbulent conditions.

Risk to Domestic Demand in the United States

In the baseline projections, the U.S. economy is now expected to maintain only moderate growth through the end of 2008. However, the balance of risks to domestic demand has shifted further to the downside, as recent financial developments have raised the risk of more protracted problems in the housing sector that could start having a deeper impact on the rest of the economy.

The correction in the U.S. housing sector, which has now been under way for two years, has been a major drag on activity as the drop in residential investment alone has taken nearly 1 percentage point off GDP growth in the past year. The baseline forecast for the U.S. economy already envisages that the housing correction will continue well into 2008. Inventory-to-sales ratios remain exceptionally high; conditions for mortgage financing have now tightened beyond the subprime sector, including for Alt-A and jumbo prime mortgages; and delinquency rates are expected to continue rising as interest rates on adjustable rate mortgages are reset upward. However, although consumption will be slowed, it is projected to remain resilient, provided that key supports—low unemployment and high household wealth—remain in place.

However, downside risks to U.S. domestic demand have clearly risen. The concern is that tightening credit availability would affect a broader range of households and further curtail effective demand for housing, while also adding to the supply as foreclosures rise and sales fall through. The baseline projections already build in a further 5 percent decline in house prices, but the decline could be sharper, adding to difficulties of refinancing and weakening household balance sheets, with a dampening impact on consumption as well as residential investment. A more general deterioration in labor market conditions or a sustained drop in the stock market would also make it more difficult for households to absorb the impact of housing-related difficulties. Against this background, risks of a recession have risen, although the Federal Reserve would be expected to respond quickly by easing monetary policy further in the face of signs of rising weakness, and the more likely outcome would seem to be a more prolonged period of subpotential growth.

Risk to Domestic Demand in Western Europe and Japan

Notwithstanding the downward revision to the baseline forecast, risks to domestic demand in western Europe and Japan have now shifted to the downside, particularly in the event of continuing financial turbulence. Western Europe has been impacted directly by contagion from the turmoil in the U.S. subprime mortgage sector, as a number of banks have been affected by their involvement in the housing sector, including through off-balance-sheet vehicles supported by backup lines of credit and difficulties in funding markets. Although actions by the ECB and the Bank of England have helped to address

Figure 1.10. Risks to the Global Outlook

Risks to the global outlook have moved squarely to the downside. The largest adverse risks relate to global financial conditions and domestic demand in the United States and western Europe.

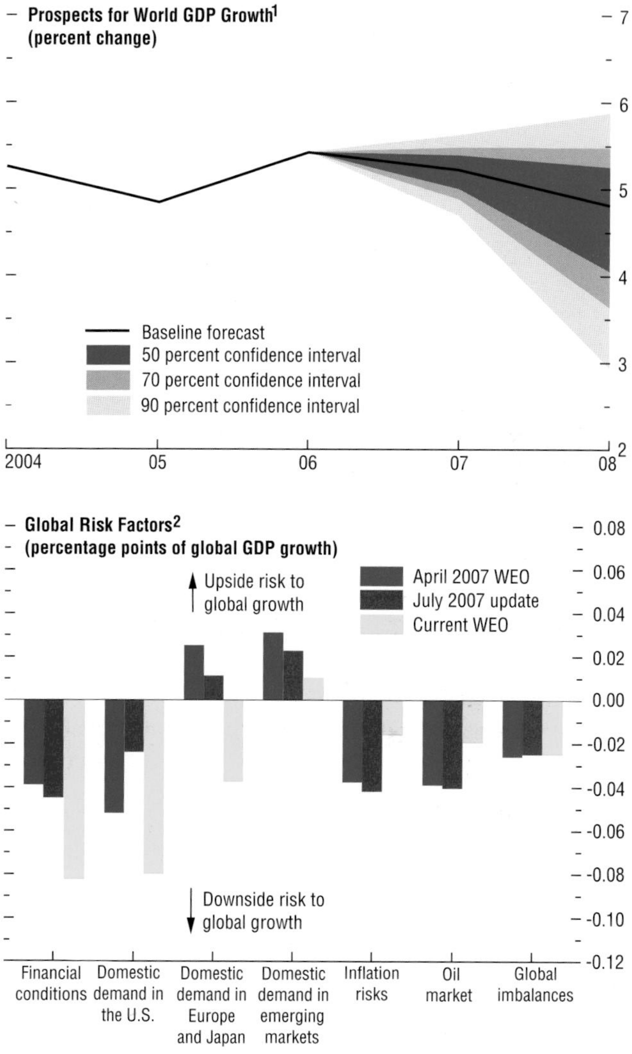

Source: IMF staff estimates.

[1]The fan chart shows the uncertainty around the *World Economic Outlook* (WEO) central forecast with 50, 70, and 90 percent probability intervals. As shown, the 70 percent confidence interval includes the 50 percent interval, and the 90 percent confidence interval includes the 50 and 70 percent intervals. See Box 1.3 in the April 2006 *World Economic Outlook* for details.

[2]The chart shows the contributions of each risk factor to the overall balance of risks to global growth, as reflected by the extent of asymmetry in the probability density for global GDP growth shown in the fan chart. The balance of risks is tilted to the downside if the expected probability of outcomes below the central or modal forecast (the total "downside probability") exceeds 50 percent (Box 1.3 in the April 2006 *World Economic Outlook*). The bars for each forecast vintage sum up to the difference between the expected value of world growth implied by the distribution of outcomes (the probability density) shown in the fan chart and the central forecast for global GDP growth. This difference and the extent of asymmetry in the probability density in the fan chart also depend on the standard deviation of past forecast errors—which, among other factors, varies with the length of the forecasting horizon. To make the risk factors comparable across forecast vintages, their contributions are rescaled to correct for differences in the standard deviations.

Box 1.1. Who Is Harmed by the Surge in Food Prices?

Over the past year, prices of some food products—notably corn, soybeans, and wheat—have risen substantially. The boom in nonfuel commodity prices, including food, was discussed in the September 2006 issue of the *World Economic Outlook*. This box reexamines the impact of the food price surge in light of the increased use of some food items as a source of fuel (see Box 1.6)—a development that could substantially alter the structure of demand for food products. These developments are of particular significance for low-income countries, given the large exposure of their populations to fluctuations in food prices.[1] Specifically, this box aims at

- identifying the factors behind the recent rise in food prices,
- gauging the impact on net trade and inflation across different regions, and
- providing some policy assessment.

Impact on Trade Balances

For many economies, food represents a significant share of export receipts or import payments. Thus, higher food prices can have a significant impact on a country's net trade balances.[2] A number of food-exporting countries in the Western Hemisphere—such as Argentina, Bolivia, and Chile—and in southern Africa—such as South Africa, Namibia, and Swaziland—have benefited from higher food prices since 2002. However, many of the poorer regions of Africa—for example, Benin, Cape Verde, Ghana, and Niger—and a number of countries in Asia—including Bangladesh, China, Nepal, and Sri Lanka—as well as in the Middle East are net losers. Among advanced economies, Canada, the United States, Australia, and New Zealand are among the gainers from higher prices.

Headline, Food, and Nonfood Inflation

(Twelve-month percent change, January 2005–April 2007)

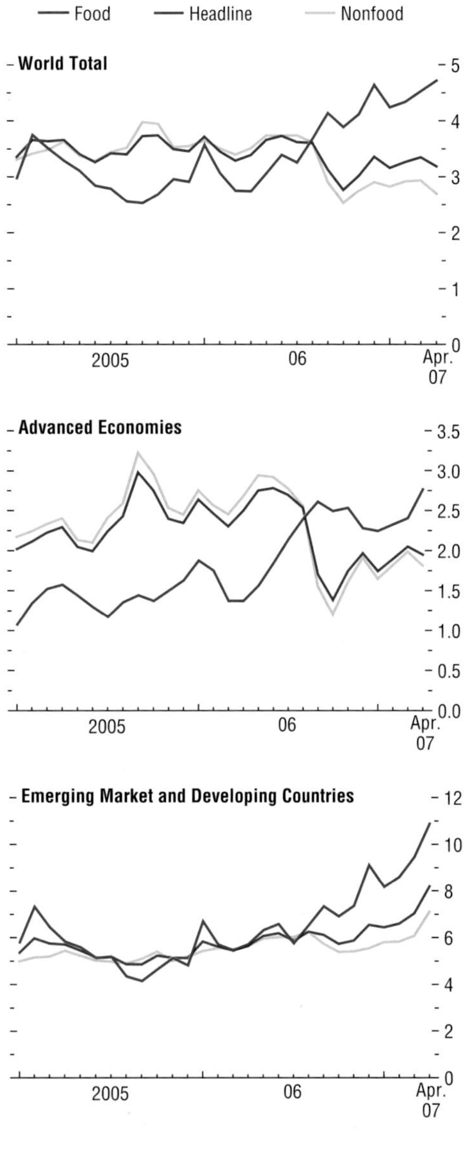

Source: IMF staff calculations.

Note: The authors of this box are Kevin Cheng and Hossein Samiei. Research assistance was provided by Murad Omoev.

[1]Factors underpinning the recent food price boom are discussed in Appendix 1.1.

[2]Based on commodity weights obtained from COMTRADE, the exercise calculates the first-round cumulative impact of movements in food prices on trade balances relative to the base year (2002), assuming that trade patterns remain unchanged.

Per Capita Income and Food Weight in Total CPI[1]

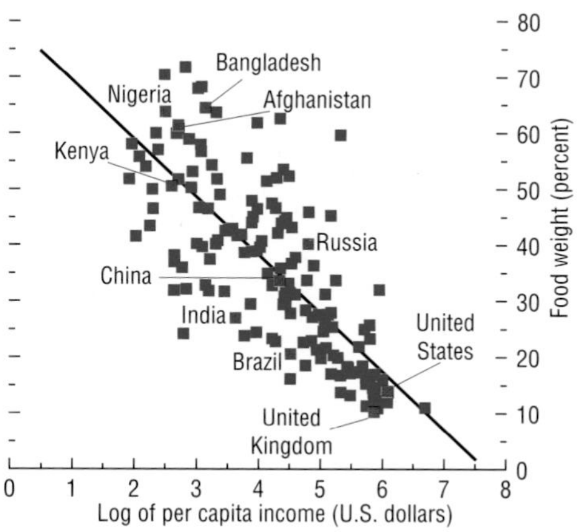

Source: IMF staff calculations.
[1]Equation: Food weight = 79.8 – 10.4 x per capita income; with R^2 = 0.5835 and *t*-ratio = –14.59.

Impact on Inflation

Higher international food prices put upward pressure on the cost of living, both directly and through their potential impact on nonfood prices. Average domestic food price inflation (defined as the purchasing-power-parity-weighted aggregate of an individual country's domestic food price inflation) rose to about 4½ percent in the first four months of 2007 from about 3 percent over the same period in 2006 (first figure). The figure is more than 9 percent for developing countries (excluding Zimbabwe and other countries with insufficient data).

To analyze the impact of food prices on headline inflation across regions, two methodologies are followed: inflation accounting to calculate the direct impact and econometric analysis to estimate the indirect impact through spillovers to nonfood prices.

Direct effect. For many developing countries, food accounts for a significant share of total consumer expenditure and the headline CPI. Indeed, the share across countries tends to be negatively correlated with income levels (second figure). For example, the weight of food in the consumption basket averages more than 60 percent in sub-Saharan Africa, whereas it is about 30 percent in China, and only 10 percent in the United States.[3]

Direct Impact of Food Prices on Headline Inflation

	2000–06 Contribution (percent)	2007[1] Contribution (percent)
World	26.6	36.4
Advanced economies	14.2	18.4
Africa	46.5	37.9
CIS	41.3	26.9
Developing Asia	34.1	55.9
Central and Eastern Europe	29.9	33.0
Middle East	37.4	52.2
Western Hemisphere	25.6	37.2

Sources: Country authorities; and IMF staff calculations.
[1]January–April.

The direct first-round contribution of food to inflation[4] for the world as a whole has risen from about ¼ in 2000–06 to more than ⅓ in the first four months of 2007 (table and map). It has risen quite drastically in developing Asia, with the contribution in China, at more than ¾, being among the largest. The contribution has also risen in most other developing regions. In Africa it has fallen, but remains high, in part reflecting earlier price hikes associated with adverse weather conditions—for example, in East Africa in 2006.

Indirect effect. Food prices could also increase headline CPI indirectly by raising nonfood prices—for example, through a wage response to higher food prices—especially in poorer countries in which food accounts for a sizable share of total household expenditure. A VAR

[3]These weights may overestimate the true consumption of food in some countries, owing to the time it takes to revise them.

[4]The contribution is calculated as the share of food in the CPI multiplied by food price inflation divided by headline inflation. In calculating the contribution, food price and headline inflation were first aggregated across regions. The direct contribution assumes no change in consumption patterns in response to changes in prices.

Box 1.1 *(concluded)*

Contribution of Food Inflation to Headline Inflation (January–April 2007, Year on Year)

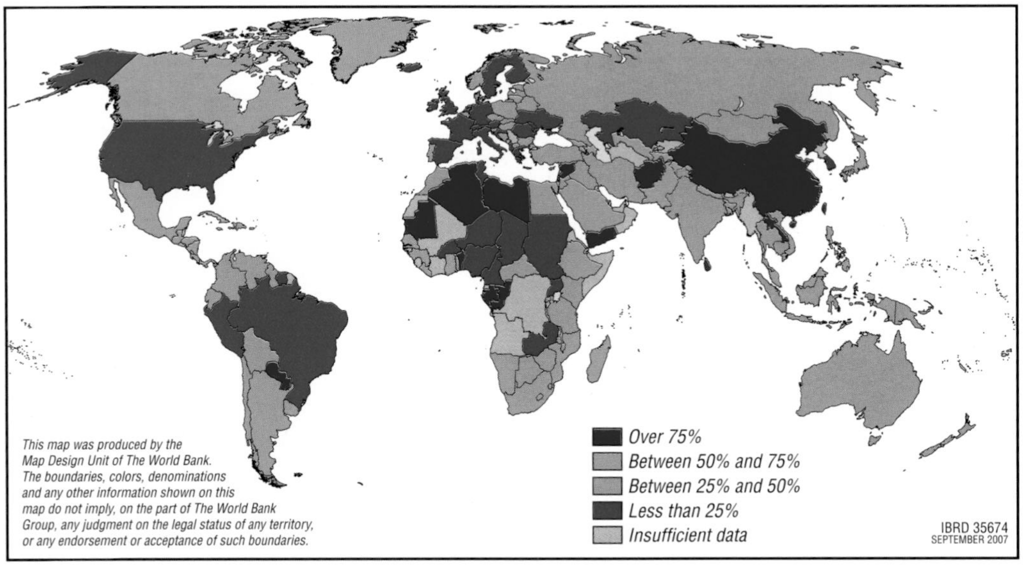
This map was produced by the Map Design Unit of The World Bank. The boundaries, colors, denominations and any other information shown on this map do not imply, on the part of The World Bank Group, any judgment on the legal status of any territory, or any endorsement or acceptance of such boundaries.
Over 75%
Between 50% and 75%
Between 25% and 50%
Less than 25%
Insufficient data
IBRD 35674
SEPTEMBER 2007

model is estimated using monthly data to illustrate the indirect effect for 10 selected countries from different income groups: Switzerland, the United Kingdom, and the United States for advanced economies; Brazil, China, India, and Russia for emerging markets; and Kenya, Tanzania, and Uganda for low-income countries. The models consist of three endogenous variables: domestic food and nonfood annual price inflation, and annual rate of change in broad money; and two exogenous variables: international food and energy annual price inflation. The idea is to capture the impact of food prices on nonfood prices after controlling for other possible factors (for which monthly data are available):[5]

- for the three advanced economies, based on the generalized impulse response functions, food price inflation does not appear to have a discernible impact on nonfood inflation;
- for the four emerging market economies, except for India, the results suggest a significant impact: a 1 percentage point temporary increase in food price inflation may raise nonfood price inflation in the range of 0.1–0.6 percentage point, with the effect disappearing only after six months to a year; and
- similarly, for the three low-income economies, food prices appear to be a significant determinant of nonfood inflation. A 1 percentage point temporary increase in food price inflation may raise nonfood price inflation in the range of 0.1–0.9 percentage point, with the effect sustained up to a year.

These results illustrate the likely impact of higher food prices on nonfood prices across different regions, but—given the small number of countries in the sample and the simple model used—further research is needed to provide more solid global evidence.

[5]The models use monthly observations for January 1995–April 2007. Optimal lags are chosen based on the Schwarz Information Criteria. We use Pesaran's generalized impulse responses, which do not require an ordering of the endogenous variables. The estimation results and impulse responses for the 10 countries will be available on the *World Economic Outlook* website.

Other Effects

Higher food prices could have other macroeconomic and distributional effects.

- An inflation-targeting central bank may have to curb inflationary pressure from higher food prices when the effect on nonfood prices is significant. As noted above, this is likely to be a more serious problem for developing countries, where feed-through to nonfood prices is more pronounced. For example, interest rates have been raised recently in China (in August), Mexico (in May), and Chile (in July) in part to preempt the potential impact of higher food prices. In China, soaring domestic meat prices have further boosted food price inflation, pushing up headline inflation to 6.5 percent in August.
- Higher food prices are also likely to adversely affect income distribution within a net-food-importing economy, because food tends to absorb a greater share of expenditure for poorer people. Indeed, the World Food Program recently warned that, as a result of the increases in food prices, its purchasing costs have risen by almost 50 percent in the past five years, thereby making it difficult to afford to feed the same number of people that it has helped in the past.

Concluding Remarks and Policy Implications

The use of food as a source of fuel may have serious implications for the demand for food if the expansion of biofuels continues: income elasticity of demand will likely increase; and although supply will respond to the surge in demand, the catch-up period may be prolonged.[6] Technological advances in both food and biofuel production will mitigate the long-term effects on food supply-demand balances, but the developments already warrant a reexamination of policy frameworks and may call for coordination at the international level:

- One country's policy to promote biofuels while protecting its farmers could increase another (likely poorer) country's import bills for food and pose additional risks to inflation or growth. This impact would be mitigated if the United States and the EU biofuel-producing countries reduced barriers to biofuel imports from developing countries (such as Brazil) where production is cheaper, more efficient, and environmentally less damaging (see Box 1.6). Such a shift in policies could also provide opportunities for other developing countries with potential comparative advantage in producing biofuels to enter the industry.
- In many countries, monetary policy decisions focus on core inflation, because food price movements are often erratic, supply driven, and have transient effects on overall inflation. However, central banks—particularly in developing countries where food prices do significantly affect nonfood prices—will need to monitor food prices carefully and respond quickly if food price movements are threatening achievement of inflation goals.

[6]In the case of sugar production in Brazil, supply responded strongly to higher demand for ethanol production in 2005–06, which led to a subsequent fall in prices.

systemic concerns, credit spreads have widened, uncertainty has increased, and the impact on domestic demand could turn out to be substantially larger than already incorporated in the revised baseline forecasts.

One particular area of downside risk relates to the housing market in western Europe. Housing markets have boomed in a number of fast-growing economies, most notably Ireland, Spain, and the United Kingdom, with rapid price rises and sharp increases in residential investment relative to GDP exceeding even those observed during the U.S. housing boom (see Box 2.1 in Chapter 2). The steady increase in policy interest rates has already contributed to some cooling of these housing booms, and recent developments are likely to have a further dampening impact, particularly if credit

Box 1.2. Macroeconomic Implications of Recent Financial Market Turmoil: Patterns from Previous Episodes

How could the recent period of financial turmoil affect global growth? This box aims to shed some light on this issue by comparing current events with four previous episodes of financial market stress: the U.S. stock market crash of 1987; the Russian debt default and collapse of Long-Term Capital Management (LTCM) in 1998; the "dotcom" crash of 2000; and the aftermath of the September 11, 2001, terrorist attacks. The obvious similarity across all of these episodes is a sudden and widespread increase in uncertainty and difficulty of judging risks. Also, often, but not always, these episodes were accompanied by a drying up of liquidity. But the fundamental causes of these episodes, the policy reactions to them, and their impact on growth and employment show significant differences.

Episodes of financial market turbulence can be analyzed by tracing the evolution of key variables around these events (first figure).[1] At first glance, the current episode appears similar to previous episodes, with an increase in investor risk aversion, characterized by heightened market volatility and a flight to safer assets. In some ways, market movements have been more limited in this episode. Despite an increase in volatility in equity markets, the declines in equity prices in the United States and the rest of the world have, so far, been smaller than in previous episodes. Spreads on high-yield corporate paper and mortgage-backed securities have risen, but have remained at or below historical averages. Spreads on emerging market sovereign bonds have been less affected than in other episodes, reflecting the origin of the current distress and reduced external vulnerabilities of emerging market countries.

It is more worrying, however, that the disruption to money markets and interbank operations seems more severe than in recent episodes. This is displayed in the sharp rise in the TED spread—the difference between the eurodollar rate, the rate at which banks lend to each other in the eurodollar market, and the risk-free treasury bill rate, particularly at three-month maturity. There has also been a large rise in the spread between monetary policy rates and interbank lending rates. This disruption, which has persisted despite heavy liquidity injections by major central banks, seems to reflect a combination of banks' desire to hoard their own liquidity in the face of possible calls on their lending capacity and heightened perceptions of counterparty risk in the context of continuing uncertainty about the distribution of losses from the financial turbulence.

A key question is how the turbulence in financial markets is likely to spill over into the wider economy. Two channels appear to be at work during crisis episodes: a first whereby households and firms face a higher cost of and/or restrictions on financing activity, and a second "confidence" channel, which may suppress aggregate demand because of greater caution about the future.

Evidence from previous episodes suggests that increases in spreads and restrictions on credit are likely to be persistent, and could have a moderating influence on consumption and investment. There are two particular factors in this episode that could increase the macroeconomic impact. The first is the potential for a rolling back of the rapid rise in securitization seen in recent years as investors took on more risk in a "search for yield."[2] Second, the banking system's capacity to re-intermediate credit

Note: The main author of this box is Alasdair Scott.

[1]In the figures in this box, the 1987 crash is centered on October 19, 1987, when the Dow Jones Industrial average fell dramatically; the Russian default/LTCM episode is centered on August 17, 1998, the day of the Russian default and devaluation; the dotcom crash is centered on March 13, 2000, the day after the peak of the NASDAQ index value; the 9/11 episode is centered on September 11, 2001; and the current episode is centered on July 26, 2007, the first major fall in stock markets worldwide.

[2]For example, between 2000 and 2006, assets under management by hedge funds increased by over 250 percent. Issuances of credit derivatives, collateralized debt obligations, and mortgage- and asset-backed securities have experienced even greater growth in this period, all consistent with a rise in leverage in a quest for yield. See the April 2007 *Global Financial Stability Report*, pp. 50–57.

Recent Market Volatility in Perspective[1]

(Months before and after event on x-axis)

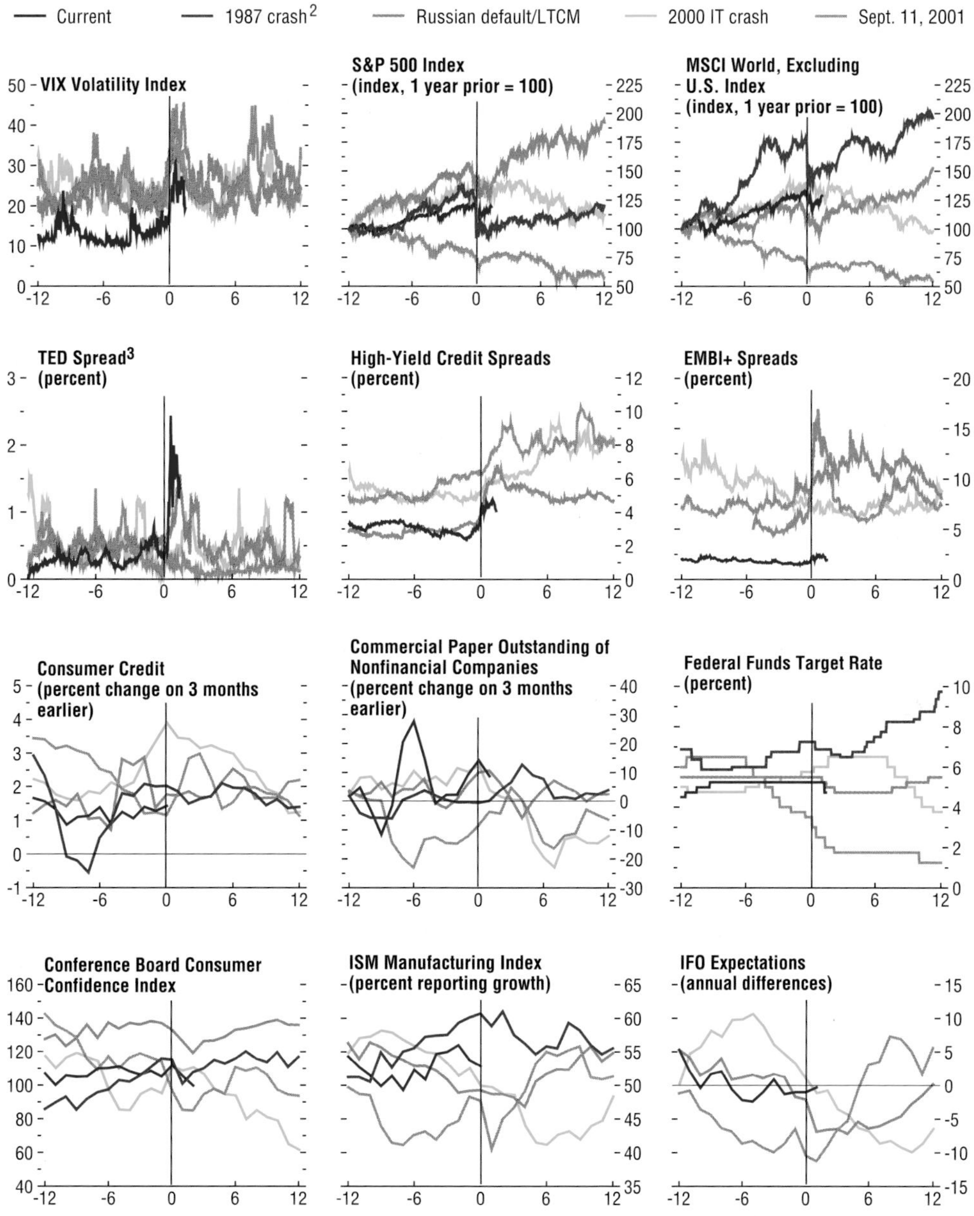

Sources: Bloomberg LP; Haver Analytics; and IMF staff calculations.

[1]All series for the United States, except the MSCI World stock index, the EMBI+ emerging markets index, and the German IFO business expectations series. IT = information technology.

[2]Not all data series are available for this episode.

[3]Defined as the difference between rates on three-month eurodollar deposits and on three-month treasury bills.

Box 1.2 *(concluded)*

flows onto its balance sheets may be limited by constraints on bank capital and by losses already incurred in the present turbulence. For both of these reasons, the impact on economy-wide credit availability may go considerably beyond the repricing of risk.

Consumer and business confidence in the United States has typically fallen following previous episodes of financial turbulence, and measures of foreign confidence often follow U.S. measures. But previous episodes also show that such indicators can recover quickly, such as during the stock market crash of 1987 and the Russian default/LTCM case. In most cases, an important factor helping to bolster confidence was swift action by the central bank to ease the monetary stance. The exception was in 2000 when the Fed continued to raise interest rates for another six months after the NASDAQ peaked, and only started to ease the rates nine months later; confidence measures did not pick up until approximately one year later. This time, the Fed has cut interest rates by 50 basis points, and financial markets expect interest rates to be cut by a further 50 basis points by early next year.

What then were the effects of previous episodes of financial market turbulence on activity? Output growth in the United States actually picked up after the 1987 and 1998 episodes, and was largely unaffected in 2001 (second figure). In 1987, 1998, and 2001, the Fed cut interest rates quickly. Moreover, the events of 1998 and 2001 were initiated by events outside the U.S. financial system. By contrast, the bursting of the information technology bubble in 2000 preceded a short recession and a long bear market, perhaps because the financial turbulence was related to a fundamental reevaluation of prospects for profitability; notwithstanding the eventual application of strong monetary and fiscal stimulus, it took some time for demand to regain momentum and asset values to return to more typical ratios to earnings.[3]

Real Output Growth During Previous Episodes
(Percent)

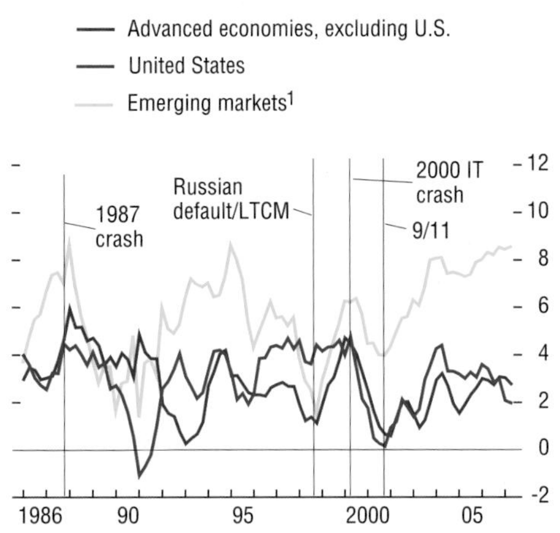

Sources: IMF staff calculations.
[1]Aggregate comprises 27 emerging market and developing countries.

In summary, with the exception of disruption to money markets, recent financial market turbulence has not been unusually large compared with previous episodes. Moreover, past periods of financial retrenchment have not always presaged slower economic activity—in three out of the four previous episodes considered here, growth accelerated, helped by easier monetary policy. However, there are at least three reasons why the macroeconomic implications of recent events may yet be larger than what these earlier experiences suggest.

[3]Activity in the rest of the world has generally followed that in the United States. The IMF staff analysis in the April 2007 *World Economic Outlook* found significant spillovers from growth rates of U.S. output to those in the rest of the world. Moreover, previous work has noted that U.S. house price movements lead world house prices—see the September 2004 *World Economic Outlook*, p. 87. Recent work by IMF staff has identified financial conditions as the major conduit for the transmission of shocks from the United States to the rest of the world. (See Bayoumi and Swiston, 2007, who argue that short-term interest rates are the most important factor in the spillover mechanism, but real equity prices and nominal government bond yields are also important.)

First, recent financial developments have been associated with, and may exacerbate, an ongoing correction in the U.S. housing market, which could continue to exert substantial drag on the economy. Second, continuing uncertainty and loss of confidence in structured credits could lead to a sustained retrenchment in securitization. Third, the current turbulence has placed strains on banking systems in the United States and elsewhere, which could further exacerbate constraints on the availability of credit.

availability were to be tightened. Given that rapid increases in some countries have raised concerns about possible excesses, some cooling seems desirable, if it does not go too far too fast. But could a housing correction in western Europe be as deep as in the United States? The analysis in Box 2.1 suggests that the extent of house price overvaluation may be considerably larger in some national markets in Europe than in the United States, and there would clearly be a sizable impact on the housing markets in the event of a widespread credit crunch. Nevertheless, there are moderating factors. First, housing markets in western Europe have generally avoided subprime mortgage origination and the deterioration of lending standards observed in the United States. Second, a number of country-specific structural factors, including strong immigration and supply constraints, are likely to continue to support housing sectors in particular national markets.

In the case of Japan, the direct financial exposure to the U.S. subprime mortgage sector is much more limited. However, recent indicators of activity suggest a weakening of momentum, and consumption and investment could be affected if the recent global financial turmoil intensifies and undermines confidence.

Risks to Emerging Market Countries

Risks to domestic demand growth in emerging market countries are now viewed as being modestly to the upside overall. China and India maintained a strong growth momentum in the first half of 2007, but further upside surprises remain possible. In particular, it remains unclear to what extent policy tightening in both countries will prove effective in cooling robust demand growth that has raised concerns about overinvestment (particularly in China) and overheating (particularly in India).

Nevertheless, there are considerable downside risks in some countries. The main one is that continued turbulence in global financial markets could disrupt financial flows to emerging markets and trigger problems in domestic markets. As already mentioned, countries in emerging Europe and the CIS with substantial current account deficits and reliance on bank-related inflows for financing would seem to be at particular risk, especially given concerns that credit booms have fueled a deterioration in credit quality and run-ups in house prices. Elsewhere, emerging market countries in Asia and Latin America would generally seem much less vulnerable than in the past to tighter conditions in international credit markets, given their high levels of international reserves, stronger public sector balance sheets, and improved macroeconomic management. However, growth in these countries would be vulnerable to spillover effects from slower aggregate demand growth in the advanced economies, including through the dampening effect on prices of commodity exports. Other downside risks relate to supply constraints in specific countries—such as emerging energy shortages in Argentina and production problems in a number of oil exporters, such as Nigeria.

Inflation Pressures

Recent buoyant global activity and rising commodity prices raise the concern that tightening resource constraints could put upward pressure on inflation and prompt central banks to tighten monetary conditions more aggressively than has been built into the projections. Such concerns have taken a backseat in the advanced economies since the recent bout of financial market turbulence, but even under a somewhat slower growth track than previously envisaged, the assessment of the extent of inflationary risks remains a key factor affecting central banks' judgments in setting the policy stance. In the emerging market and developing countries, inflation risks are more immediate.

Commodity markets have been the most obvious source of recent upward pressure on prices. Strong growth of demand has kept oil and metals prices at high levels since 2006, while food prices have also spiked upward. Despite recent financial turbulence, supplies remain tight, and this area remains an important source of risk. The concern is particularly acute in emerging market and developing countries where food often represents 35–40 percent of consumption baskets and the credibility of monetary policy regimes is less well established, increasing the likelihood that rising food and energy costs could affect inflation expectations and feed into other prices and wages.

A second source of inflationary pressures comes from closing output gaps more broadly. Product markets for manufactured goods were a disinflationary force until recently, as rapid productivity growth, especially in East Asian exporters, and spare capacity that opened up after the global downturn in 2000–01 led to declining nonfuel import prices in the advanced economies. However, over the past three years, this tide has reversed, as sustained growth has closed output gaps, not only in the advanced economies but also in emerging market countries (Figure 1.11).[2] As a result, a number of emerging market countries are facing overheating risks, which could also affectinflation pressures in the advanced economies coming from rising nonfuel import prices. However, such risks would clearly be alleviated in the event of a significant global slowdown.

Another concern is that labor market pressures could intensify in the advanced economies if a combination of sluggish productivity and rising compensation led to an acceleration of unit labor costs. So far in the present cycle, such concerns have been focused on the United States—which is further along the cycle and where productivity growth has come down to its slowest pace since the early 1990s (Figure 1.12). While much of this slowdown is likely to be cyclical, part of the recent performance may reflect some moderation in the burst of productivity growth from the application of new information technologies from the 1990s onward. At the same time, employee compensation has risen. Thus, overall unit labor costs have accelerated, although not yet to the point of posing a serious threat, given that U.S. growth is likely to remain moderate and that high corporate profit margins provide firms some leeway to limit feed-through of rising costs to price increases. In the euro area and Japan, meanwhile, unit labor costs have been contained, because productivity performance has been favorable, particularly in the euro area, and compensation has shown few signs of acceleration, despite declines in unemployment rates to cyclical lows. Thus, concerns about labor cost pressures at this point are still largely forward looking, related to the possibility of accelerating wage growth if labor markets continue to tighten.

Tight Oil Markets

Global oil markets remain very tight, and with spare capacity still limited, supply shocks or heightened geopolitical concerns could

[2]Output gaps are notoriously difficult to measure, except with the benefit of considerable hindsight. Figure 1.11 shows a simple aggregate measure of the output gap, based on a Hodrick-Prescott times series technique for estimating potential output. It also shows alternative measures of the gap based on estimates of the nonaccelerating inflation rate of unemployment (NAIRU) and of capacity utilization in the manufacturing sector.

lead to further price spikes that could quickly translate into higher headline inflation (see Appendix 1.1). The subsequent impact on output may be more subdued than in the 1970s, because economies are less energy intensive and greater monetary policy credibility has anchored inflation expectations more securely (see discussion in Box 1.1 of the April 2007 *World Economic Outlook*). Thus far, the global economy has been able to absorb the sustained run-up in oil prices over the past five years without major impact. Nevertheless, while OPEC's capacity has expanded (in particular in Saudi Arabia) and the Gulf states are embarking on massive investments, the overall supply response to the recent higher level of prices has been sluggish so far, in part because rising demand has pushed up the price of investment in new capacity in the oil sector and because of uncertainties about the investment climate in certain oil producers. Moreover, demand for oil products has continued to rise, especially in fast-growing emerging market countries, and shortages of refining capacity are an increasing constraint. Thus, the dip in oil prices in the second half of 2006 proved temporary, and prices rose to new highs by the summer of 2007. At this point, markets are expecting that prices will remain around their current level through the end of 2008, but uncertainty remains high, and options prices suggest a 1 in 6 chance of prices rising above $95 a barrel over this period.

Global Imbalances

Persistent large global imbalances remain a worrisome downside risk for the global economy. The U.S. current account deficit is projected to decline slightly to 5½ percent of GDP this year and next, as it benefits from recent real effective depreciation of the U.S. dollar and a more balanced pattern for global demand growth. Nevertheless, assuming no further changes in real effective exchange rates and with current policies, the U.S. deficit would still remain close to this level in 2012—equivalent

Figure 1.11. Measures of the Output Gap and Capacity Pressures[1]

Various measures of the output gap suggest that the gap has been closing in both advanced and emerging market economies. Another indicator of supply pressures is that commodity prices have been sustained at high levels.

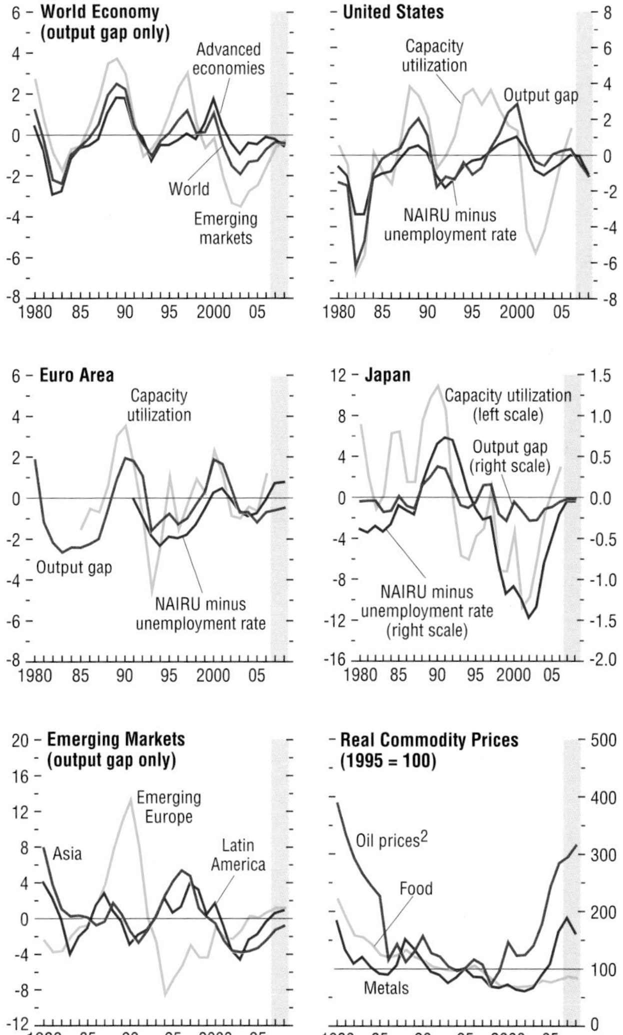

Sources: OECD, *Economic Outlook;* and IMF staff estimates.

[1]Estimates of the nonaccelerating inflation rate of unemployment (NAIRU) come from the OECD. Estimates of the output gap, expressed as a percent of potential GDP, are based on IMF staff calculations. Capacity utilization measured as deviations from 1980–2006 averages for the United States (percent of total capacity) and Japan (operation rate index for manufacturing sector), and deviations from 1985–2006 for euro area (percent of industry capacity).

[2]Simple average of spot prices of U.K. Brent, Dubai Fateh, and West Texas Intermediate crude oil.

Figure 1.12. Productivity and Labor Cost Developments in Selected Advanced Economies[1]

(Percent change from four quarters earlier)

Labor productivity has slowed in the United States, but performance has improved in the euro area and Japan. Unit labor costs have accelerated in the United States, but in the euro area and Japan, with little upward trend in compensation growth, unit labor costs have remained largely contained.

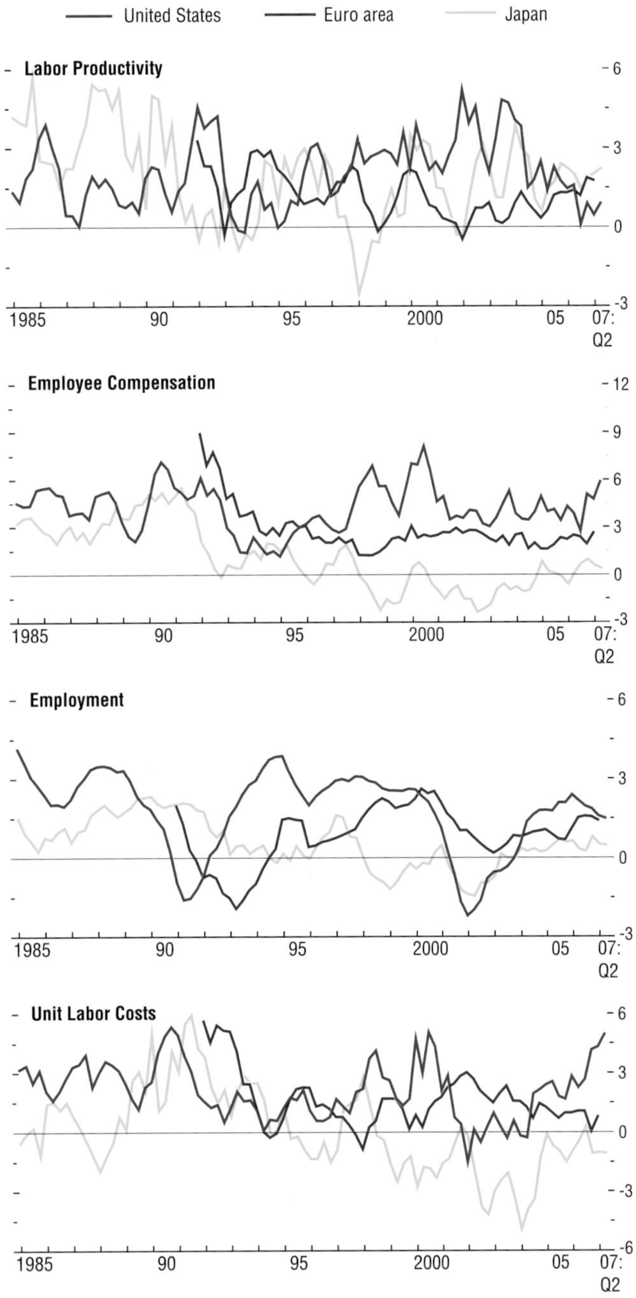

Sources: Haver Analytics; OECD, *Economic Outlook;* and IMF staff calculations.
[1]Estimates are for the nonfarm business sector for the United States, and the whole economy for the euro area and Japan.

to 1.5 percent of global GDP (Figure 1.13). The current account surpluses of the oil exporters are projected to come down as these countries ramp up spending. However, China's current account surplus has widened sharply in recent quarters, and it is now projected at 12 percent of GDP in 2008 and to remain at a high level through the medium term. Accordingly, emerging Asia's projected current account surplus in 2012 has been marked up to 1¼ percent of global GDP.

Persistent large imbalances raise two principal concerns. First, the necessary financing flows for the U.S. current account deficits may become less easily obtained, triggering a disorderly adjustment—a low-probability but high-cost event. Second, sustained large trade imbalances could prompt rising protectionist pressures.

One open question at this point is how recent financial market developments have affected risks of a disorderly adjustment. In recent years, the U.S. economy has benefited from large capital inflows, attracted by the apparent sophistication and security offered by the U.S. financial system, as well as the underlying strength of the U.S. economy itself. Under an "orderly adjustment," the U.S. current account deficit would be lowered gradually through a combination of demand rebalancing and further exchange rate movements, and would be smoothly financed. However, investors in the United States have been earning lower returns on their assets than elsewhere in recent years—as a result of both dollar depreciation and slower rates of asset price appreciation than in other markets. As a consequence, the composition of inward flows to the United States had shifted over time toward higher-return, higher-risk vehicles.[3] During recent market turmoil, foreign investors presumably shifted away from collateralized debt obligations, and back toward more secure and more liquid U.S. government bonds. What remains

[3]It is noteworthy that in recent quarters, a high share of net capital flows to the United States have come from official sources. Some official investors are also adopting more aggressive investment strategies, such as shifting reserves into sovereign wealth funds.

to be seen are the longer-term consequences of recent events. One possibility is that disillusion with asset-backed credit structures could prompt a more sustained shift in investor preferences away from U.S. assets, which would raise risks of a disorderly unwinding of imbalances.

A separate concern is that persistently large trade imbalances could be a source of protectionist pressures, particularly where domestic industry does not adjust successfully in the face of import competition, contributing to a sense that the growth benefits of an open economy are not being adequately shared among different social groups. Protectionist sentiment could be exacerbated by perceptions of unfair use of exchange rate policy for competitive advantage. The recent lack of progress with negotiations on the Doha Round and increasing recourse to a proliferation of bilateral trade treaties are an indication of an increased focus on national interest on the trade front. Pressures for increased trade restrictions or retaliatory measures have so far been largely resisted, but protectionist risks associated with large trade imbalances would be substantially increased in the context of a global slowdown with rising levels of unemployment.

Against this background, some welcome progress has been made toward developing a joint approach toward global imbalances. The Multilateral Consultation held by the IMF represents the first use of an innovative approach to addressing systemic challenges. It has provided a forum for discussion with key countries to strengthen mutual understanding of the issues and to reaffirm support for the International Monetary and Finance Committee (IMFC) Strategy, and for each country to indicate specific policies consistent with the Strategy that together should allow for a substantial reduction in imbalances in the years ahead (see Box 1.3).

Figure 1.13. Current Account Balances and Net Foreign Assets
(Percent of world GDP)

The U.S. current account deficit is projected to come down only slowly relative to world output and still be close to 1.5 percent of global GDP in 2012. This trajectory implies a continuing buildup in U.S. net foreign liabilities, with the main counterpart being a steady rise in net assets of emerging Asia.

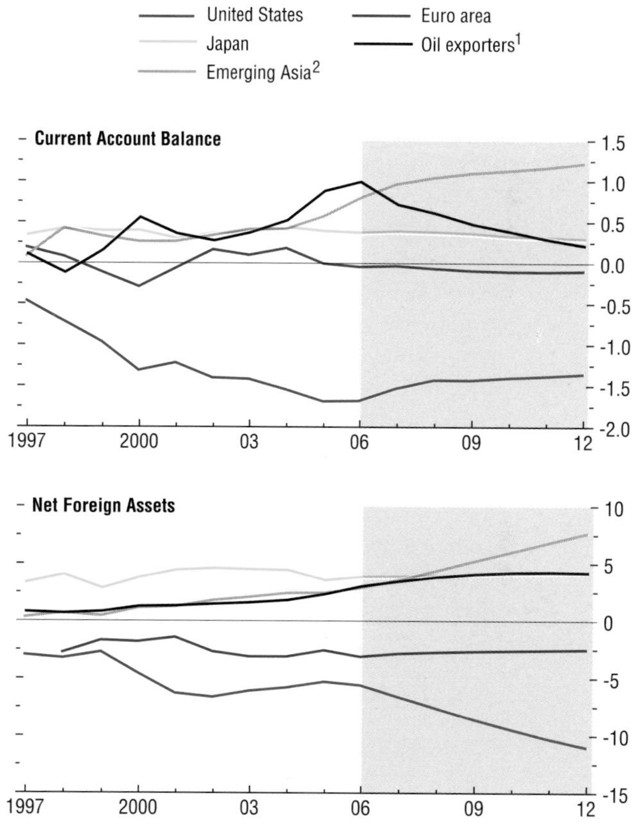

Sources: Lane and Milesi-Ferretti (2006); and IMF staff estimates.
[1]Algeria, Angola, Azerbaijan, Bahrain, Republic of Congo, Ecuador, Equatorial Guinea, Gabon, I.R. of Iran, Kuwait, Libya, Nigeria, Norway, Oman, Qatar, Russia, Saudi Arabia, Syrian Arab Republic, Turkmenistan, United Arab Emirates, Venezuela, and the Republic of Yemen.
[2]China, Hong Kong SAR, Indonesia, Korea, Malaysia, the Philippines, Singapore, Taiwan Province of China, and Thailand.

Two Downside Scenarios

In discussing the various risks to the global economy, it is clear that many of these risks are interrelated, with the evolution of financial

Box 1.3. Multilateral Consultation on Global Imbalances

What Was the Multilateral Consultation and Why Was It Needed?

On June 5, 2006, the IMF initiated its first-ever Multilateral Consultation (MC)—a new tool of multilateral surveillance—with a focus on addressing global current account imbalances in a manner supportive of global growth. Five countries or regions agreed to participate—China, the euro area, Japan, Saudi Arabia, and the United States. This group of participants was chosen either because they were a direct party to the existing imbalances (through their current account deficits or surpluses) or because they represented a very large share of global output and could contribute to sustaining world growth as demand and saving patterns adjusted.

The central issue at hand was that, despite widespread agreement on which policies were needed to help support a global rebalancing process—as communicated in the IMF's International Monetary and Financial Committee (IMFC) Strategy,[1] progress in implementing policies was relatively slow, and imbalances remained wide. This suggested the need to develop new avenues for achieving the goal. Thus, a central objective of the first MC was to facilitate a dialogue and, ultimately, foster policy actions by participants that could make a significant contribution toward global rebalancing—that is, sustaining global growth while reducing imbalances—and reducing the associated risks of a disorderly adjustment.

To this end, the Consultation began with bilateral discussions with senior policymakers from each of the participant countries or regions, followed by joint meetings of senior officials from all participating countries or regions with IMF staff. The open and constructive consultations contributed to an improved understanding of the issues and of each other's positions. Participants reaffirmed that reducing global imbalances was a multilateral challenge, and that resolving them in a manner compatible with sustained growth was a shared responsibility. They also stressed that an orderly unwinding of imbalances was in the interest of the world economy more generally, because, among other reasons, sustained imbalances could add to protectionist pressures.

What Did the MC Deliver?

During the Consultation, the participants reiterated their support for the IMFC Strategy to reduce imbalances through policies that were in each individual country's interest as well as desirable from a multilateral perspective. The Consultation culminated with the publication of policy plans by each participant, which included substantive steps in all key areas of the IMFC Strategy.[2] When implemented, these policy plans could significantly reduce global risks. The agreement to publish these plans also provided a clear roadmap to assess progress toward policy implementation. In its April 2007 Communiqué,[3] the IMFC welcomed the report from the group, noting that the policy plans set out by the participants represented further progress in the implementation of the IMFC Strategy.

Note: The main authors of this box are Hamid Faruqee and Gian Maria Milesi-Ferretti.

[1]Since April 2004, the IMFC has set out in each Communiqué its views on the measures needed to foster an orderly resolution of global imbalances—the so-called IMFC Strategy. While the IMFC Strategy has evolved somewhat over time, reflecting the changing nature of the imbalances, in September 2006, the Committee called for steps to boost national saving in the United States, including fiscal consolidation; further progress on growth-enhancing reforms in Europe; further structural reforms, including fiscal consolidation, in Japan; reforms to boost domestic demand in emerging Asia, together with greater exchange rate flexibility in a number of surplus countries; and increased spending consistent with absorptive capacity and macroeconomic stability in oil-producing countries.

[2]See IMF, "IMF's International Monetary and Financial Committee Reviews Multilateral Consultation," Press Release No. 07/72, April 14, 2007.

[3]See IMF, "Communiqué of the International Monetary and Financial Committee of the Board of Governors of the International Monetary Fund," Press Release No. 07/71, April 14, 2007.

The Executive Board's review of the experience with the process in July 2007 reached a similar assessment.[4]

Will It Make a Difference?

While a precise quantification of the effects of the proposed policy package on global imbalances is difficult, IMF staff estimates based on simulations from the Global Economic Model[5] and other empirical evidence suggest that, when fully implemented, the package could reduce the U.S. current account deficit by 1–1¾ percent of GDP over the medium term, and hence limit the accumulation of U.S. external liabilities. Surpluses would decline correspondingly elsewhere, and particularly in China and Saudi Arabia. For the purpose of these calculations, IMF staff assumed an increase in exchange rate flexibility in China, with a real appreciation consistent with current market expectations as embedded in forward rates and Consensus Forecasts, as well as financial market reforms; the implementation of growth-enhancing structural reforms in the euro area and Japan; a substantial increase in investment in line with policy plans in Saudi Arabia; and a fiscal adjustment of about 2 percent of GDP (consistent with the target of a balanced federal budget) and measures to stimulate private saving in the United States.

It should be stressed, however, that an orderly adjustment in global imbalances accompanied by sustained growth does not depend solely on the participants' policies. In particular,

- *Other countries have an important part to play.* Higher expenditures by other oil exporters, together with greater exchange rate flexibility and higher investment in other parts of emerging Asia, could reduce the U.S. current account deficit by a further ¼–½ percent of GDP, matched by reduced surpluses in these regions, assuming broadly comparable efforts to those by MC participants.
- *Changes in private sector balances can also be expected to play a key role in reducing current account imbalances,* including through an increase in household savings in the United States and strengthened private domestic demand in surplus countries. Although the size of this adjustment could be significant, its pace is uncertain, not least because it depends on variables that are difficult to forecast—such as house prices in the United States. These uncertainties, as well as other imponderables such as oil prices, reinforce the case for early public policy adjustment, especially since this is also consistent with the domestic interests of the countries concerned.

Where Do We Go from Here?

The key now is implementation. Since the consultation discussions and the report, each participant has made some progress toward implementing its policy intentions, but much remains to be done. Specifically,

- In the *United States,* the federal deficit has narrowed more rapidly than expected, and Congress has adopted the administration's balanced budget objective by FY2012. But consensus has not emerged on how to achieve this objective while providing adequately for war funding and the alternative minimum tax relief, and there are political obstacles to deeper entitlement reform.
- In *China,* the renminbi has appreciated in real effective terms by about 6 percent over the past year, and the currency band for daily exchange rate fluctuations against the dollar has been widened from 0.3 percent to 0.5 percent. However, China's current account surplus has widened further, reflecting continued strong export performance. More rapid appreciation of the renminbi would help provide the right price signals for investment and, together with additional steps toward rebalancing domestic demand, help to contain China's current account surpluses

[4]See IMF, "IMF Executive Board Discusses Multilateral Consultation on Global Imbalances," Public Information Notice No. 07/97, August 7, 2007.

[5]The Global Fiscal Model was used to calibrate the effects of fiscal policy on the current account. See Faruqee and others (2007); Appendix 1.2 in the September 2005 *World Economic Outlook*; and Box 1.3 in the September 2006 *World Economic Outlook*.

Box 1.3 *(concluded)*

over time. At the same time, it would provide greater scope for monetary policy to focus on slowing lending and investment growth.

- In the *euro area*, some progress is being made with respect to the structural reform agenda, including improving the efficiency of clearing and settlements in EU financial markets. Looking forward, raising competition, productivity, and growth will require further reforms in product, labor, and financial markets—such as, for example, an effective implementation of the Services Directive in all member states.
- In *Japan*, recent progress on the structural reform agenda includes advances on job placement and training and on liberalization of foreign direct investment inflows. Looking forward, further action is needed to strengthen competition and thereby raise productivity, particularly in the nontradables sectors.
- In *Saudi Arabia*, public spending in 2007 was increased in three key areas—oil sector investment, social projects, and infrastructure—as planned. Massive public-private partnership-based investment programs are also continuing, although there is still a long way to go to meet the medium-term targets.

Thus, the Multilateral Consultation on Global Imbalances represents the first use of an innovative approach to addressing systemic challenges. Working with the endorsement of the IMF's global membership, a relevant subset of IMF members—with the participation of IMF staff and management—conducted a series of focused, constructive, and confidential discussions. The result was a set of mutually consistent policy plans that have been welcomed by the IMF. With the agreement of the participants in the Consultation, the implementation of these policy plans will be the subject of regular IMF surveillance. According to IMF staff analysis, these plans will—as implemented—make a significant contribution toward the achievement of the goals of the IMFC Strategy of sustaining global growth while reducing imbalances.

market conditions having important consequences for the range of other domestic and external risk factors. In principle, financial disturbances—even large ones such as the recent credit market turmoil—could be absorbed without major consequences for global activity, provided markets stabilize, prices adjust in an orderly way, and losses are recognized. Indeed, some previous episodes of financial market dislocation—prominently the stock market drop in 1987 and the events in 1998 surrounding the collapse of LTCM and the Russian default—have had only a limited and temporary effect on global activity. Nevertheless, the interaction between a deterioration in financial conditions with other vulnerabilities in advanced and emerging market economies could lead to a deeper and more prolonged slowdown in global activity than envisaged in the baseline projections. Such an episode would have more in common with the lengthy global slowdown following the 2000 equity market crash, where a correction in equity market valuations interacted with a reassessment of the returns to high-tech investment not just in the United States but also in Europe and Asia. In present circumstances, the core vulnerability would seem to be the possibility that a tightening of credit constraints could interact with the housing market corrections in the United States and other countries where house prices have risen rapidly in recent years.

Figure 1.14 shows the results of a macroeconomic modeling exercise aimed at simulating the impact of a financial shock originating in the United States on three key counterparts of the global economy: the United States, other advanced economies, and emerging market countries. With a temporary shock—which starts to be reversed after two quarters—the impact on GDP would be relatively small, and largely confined to the United States itself. With a sustained

Figure 1.14. Simulated Effect of a Financial Disturbance on the Global Economy

(Deviation from baseline)

A persistent large financial disturbance centered on the United States (involving a 10 percent decline in house prices, a 10 percent drop in equity prices, and a 50 basis point widening in the term premium, all relative to baseline) would have a substantial adverse impact on global activity, with spillovers from the U.S. economy through trade and financial channels, including by inducing corrections in housing markets, around the world. Monetary policy easing would help to cushion the downward impact. By contrast, a disturbance of the same initial magnitude that was quickly reversed would have a much smaller macroeconomic impact.

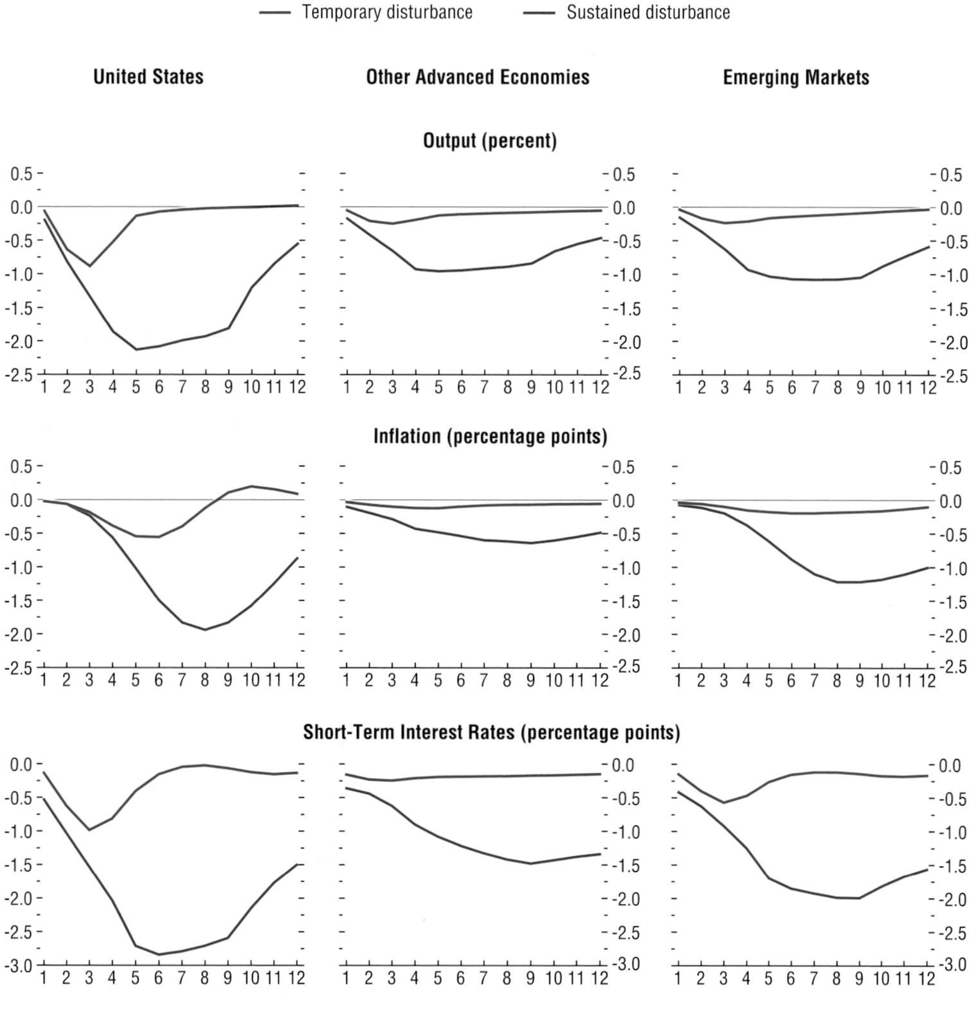

Source: IMF staff estimates.

Figure 1.15. Private Capital Flows to Emerging Markets
(Billions of U.S. dollars)

Gross private flows to emerging markets have risen rapidly in recent years, while net flows have been sustained at historically high levels. Although foreign direct investment has risen, portfolio flows and other investment flows have risen more steeply, especially to emerging Asia, emerging Europe, and the Commonwealth of Independent States (CIS).

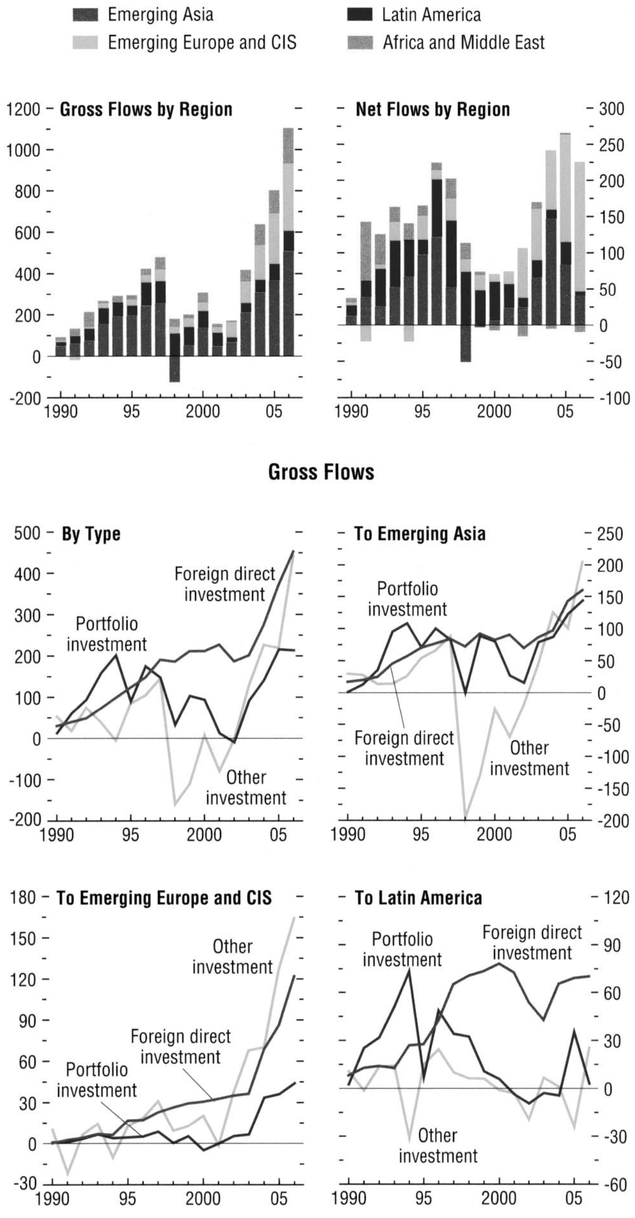

Sources: IMF, World Economic Outlook database; and IMF staff calculations.

shock—lasting eight quarters—the impact on output in the United States would be much greater, however, as wealth effects start to kick in and depress consumption, and the Federal Reserve would be prompted to cut interest rates aggressively to stabilize output and inflation. Moreover, the spillover effects on other countries are substantially larger—housing markets around the world would weaken on top of the impact of slower trade growth, weaker equity prices, and higher risk premiums. This scenario is consistent with the finding in the April 2007 *World Economic Outlook* that spillovers are more than proportionately greater in the context of a downturn than in a mild slowdown in activity. With this combination of events, the global economy could slow sharply.

Living with Heavy Foreign Exchange Inflows

Over the past year, many emerging market and developing countries have experienced historically high levels of net foreign exchange inflows, through both current and capital accounts. The recent rise in private capital flows to emerging markets has been particularly dramatic. As shown in Figure 1.15, in dollar terms, gross flows have risen sharply in the past few years—to levels twice as high as at the previous peak in 1996, just before the Asian crisis. In part, the gross flow number reflects the continuing process of cross-border financial diversification. The rise in net flows to emerging markets has been somewhat less steep, but nevertheless capital has flown at record levels over 2005–06, picked up further in the first half of 2007, and is projected to be maintained at high levels in the aggregate, notwithstanding recent financial market turbulence.

An abundance of foreign exchange resources provides an enormous opportunity for boosting long-term growth if used prudently. However, countries also face substantial short-term macroeconomic challenges in managing heavy foreign exchange inflows. If exchange rate flexibility is limited, a surge in net foreign exchange inflows can quickly generate rapid credit growth, strong increases in domestic asset prices, an overheated economy, and eventual pressure on inflation. Allowing the exchange rate to appreciate provides a greater degree of monetary control, but also can lead to a loss of competitiveness and limit export opportunities. There is also the related challenge of avoiding a buildup in vulnerabilities to a sudden reversal of the inflows—a concern underlined by the recent turbulence in global financial markets.

While these challenges are general ones, different groups of countries are facing different external and domestic situations, affecting policy trade-offs (Figure 1.16). Across a variety of different situations, how have countries responded and what lessons can be learned from their experience? Chapter 3 of this report investigates countries' experiences with surges in capital flows since the late 1980s. One general finding in Chapter 3 is that in recent years, countries have shifted to more flexible exchange rate regimes and allowed more upward movement in exchange rates, although resistance to appreciation through intervention remains generally high. Thus, significant exchange rate appreciations have occurred both in inflation targeters in Latin America (Brazil, Chile, and Colombia) and in emerging Asian countries (India, Korea, and Thailand are good examples). Allowing more exchange rate flexibility has the advantages of increasing direct control over the monetary base, and thus credit growth, and helping reduce one-way bets and thus incentives for carry trade capital inflows to arbitrage interest rate differentials. However, in the face of very strong capital inflows, countries have also continued to intervene heavily, building up reserves in an attempt to limit the extent of real exchange rate appreciation, although the results obtained in Chapter 3 suggest that such intervention has not generally been successful over extended periods.

One strong conclusion from the experience reviewed in Chapter 3 is that fiscal restraint in the face of strong capital inflows helps reduce pressures on the real exchange rate and the

Figure 1.16. Current and Capital Account Flows to Selected Emerging Market and Developing Countries
(Percent of GDP)

The buildup in reserves in most Asian emerging markets and Middle East oil-exporting countries has been driven mainly by large current account surpluses (India being an exception). In emerging Europe, large net capital inflows have financed substantial current account deficits.

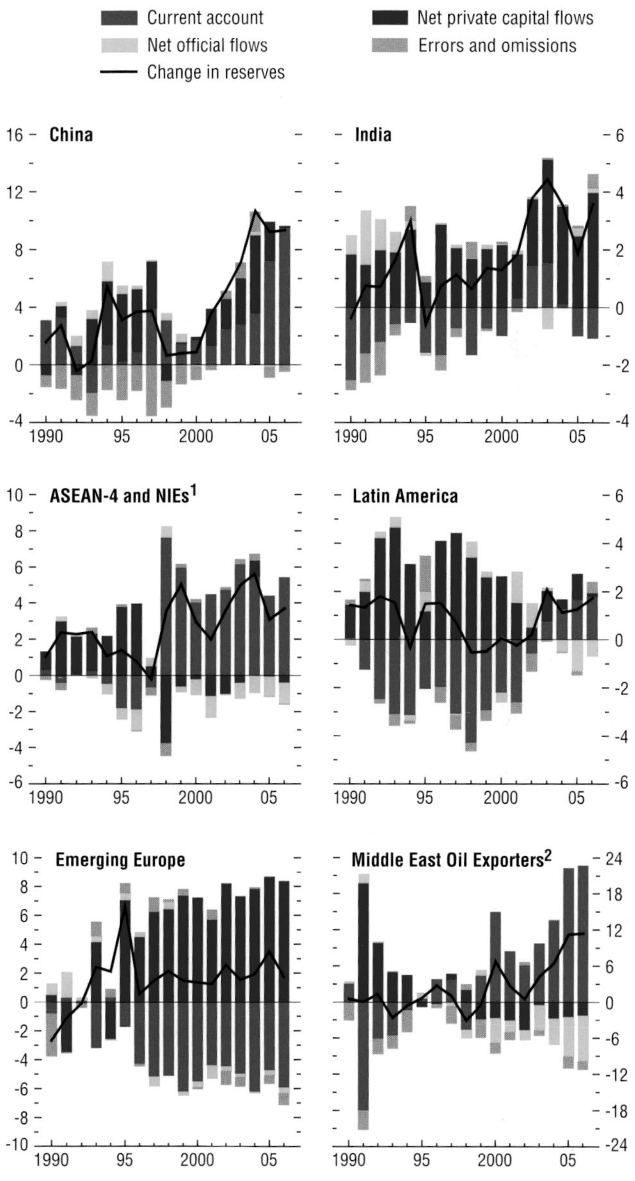

Source: IMF staff calculations.
[1]ASEAN-4 countries include Indonesia, Malaysia, the Philippines, and Thailand. Newly industrialized Asian economies (NIEs) include Hong Kong SAR, Korea, Singapore, and Taiwan Province of China.
[2]Bahrain, I.R. of Iran, Kuwait, Libya, Oman, Qatar, Saudi Arabia, Syrian Arab Republic, United Arab Emirates, and the Republic of Yemen.

risk of a hard landing when the inflows slow or reverse. There are well-known limits to the use of discretionary fiscal policy for fine-tuning purposes that apply particularly in this context, because capital flows are volatile, hard to predict, and have an uncertain macroeconomic impact, while frequent short-term modification to fiscal policy instruments would reduce transparency and predictability. That said, the evidence suggests that countries facing overheating pressures in the context of strong output growth and capital inflows would benefit from greater fiscal restraint, by saving a larger share of buoyant revenues, rather than allowing public spending to soar or prematurely cutting taxes. This is a lesson that is particularly relevant for countries in emerging Europe and the CIS with large current account deficits, where vulnerabilities are particularly salient, and where government spending has grown rapidly.

Moving beyond macroeconomic policy instruments, a number of countries have imposed measures to restrict or discourage capital inflows. Notably, Chile in the 1990s and, more recently, Argentina (since 2005), Thailand (since 2006), and Colombia (since May 2007) have set unremunerated reserve requirements on certain types of capital inflows, effectively applying a tax on short-term inflows. Other countries, such as Brazil, Kazakhstan, and Korea, have recently introduced other specific measures aimed at curbing short-term inflows through the banking system, and India has recently placed new restrictions on external commercial borrowing. Experience suggests that such measures tend to have a diminishing impact over time, as ways are found to elude the controls, and can, if sustained, also have negative consequences for financial system development.[4] Consistent with this assessment, Chapter 3 finds that capital controls have not had much impact on the macroeconomic outcomes from capital inflows.

Alternatively, liberalization of restrictions on capital outflows can help ease foreign exchange market pressures while also encouraging greater cross-border portfolio diversification for domestic investors and integration with international markets. East Asian countries have been most successful in following this approach, as evidenced by the high and rising capital outflows from these countries, and similar reforms have continued over the past year across a wide spectrum of countries, including Brazil, China, Colombia, India, Malaysia, Morocco, Peru, and Thailand. However, the timing and magnitude of the impact of such reforms is hard to quantify with any precision, qualifying their value for short-term macroeconomic management.

A final set of approaches seeks to offset the domestic side effects of capital inflows. First, countries have tightened regulatory and supervisory guidelines related to bank lending, to limit the risk of increasing balance sheet vulnerabilities. Second, countries have used tax and other measures to cool down domestic equity and property markets, such as China's recent increase in stamp duty on stock market transactions and Singapore's increased property redevelopment charge. Third, countries have used fiscal incentives to offset some of the implications of exchange rate appreciation, such as Brazil's introduction of import tariffs on certain sectors. Care must be taken in using such fiscal measures to make sure that they do not have adverse microeconomic or political economy consequences. A more productive approach would be to advance initiatives to increase an economy's ability to adapt to exchange rate movements, including, for example, labor market reforms and improvements in the business environment.

Overall, recent experience and the findings of Chapter 3 are consistent with the view that there is no single universal formula for dealing with the short-term macroeconomic

[4]In Thailand, the controls were initially set very broadly, including to apply to FDI-related inflows; had a strong negative impact on equity and currency markets; and were quickly narrowed in scope. In Argentina and Colombia, the requirements were set more narrowly and seem to have had a limited impact.

consequences of heavy foreign exchange inflows. Instead, countries need to take a pragmatic approach, finding an appropriate blend of measures suited to their particular circumstances and longer-term goals. So far, most countries have been largely successful in averting exchange rate appreciations that leave exchange rates substantially overvalued, but overheating concerns are a continuing issue. A number of countries would find monetary control and inflation objectives easier to achieve by allowing somewhat more flexible exchange rates. There would also seem to be scope for more restrained fiscal policy approaches, saving rather than spending a larger portion of strong revenue growth; for further steps toward liberalization of capital account outflows; and for tighter regulatory and prudential frameworks to limit possible balance sheet vulnerabilities from too rapid growth of domestic credit.

Sustaining Robust Growth

The current global expansion has been the period of strongest growth since the early 1970s (Figure 1.17). The recent experience is also remarkable in other ways. First, with the rapid growth of world trade, openness has risen by more than 10 percentage points since 2001, and financial openness has also risen rapidly. Second, emerging market and developing countries now account for a high share of growth: more than ⅔ compared with about ½ in the 1990s. Third, the success is not being enjoyed only by a few dynamic countries; in fact, most countries and regions are doing well by their own past standards, as reflected in the decline in the dispersion of growth rates relative to trend. And, fourth, the volatility of growth has declined substantially.

Chapter 5 of this report provides a longer-term perspective on the current expansion, asking how much of the changing dynamics of the global business cycle reflects good policies and how much is good luck. It presents evidence that a number of structural changes—including higher-quality monetary policy, reduced fiscal

Figure 1.17. Perspectives on Global Growth

More than two-thirds of global growth is being contributed by emerging market and developing countries. These countries also account for a rising share of world trade, and they show lower growth dispersion and growth volatility.

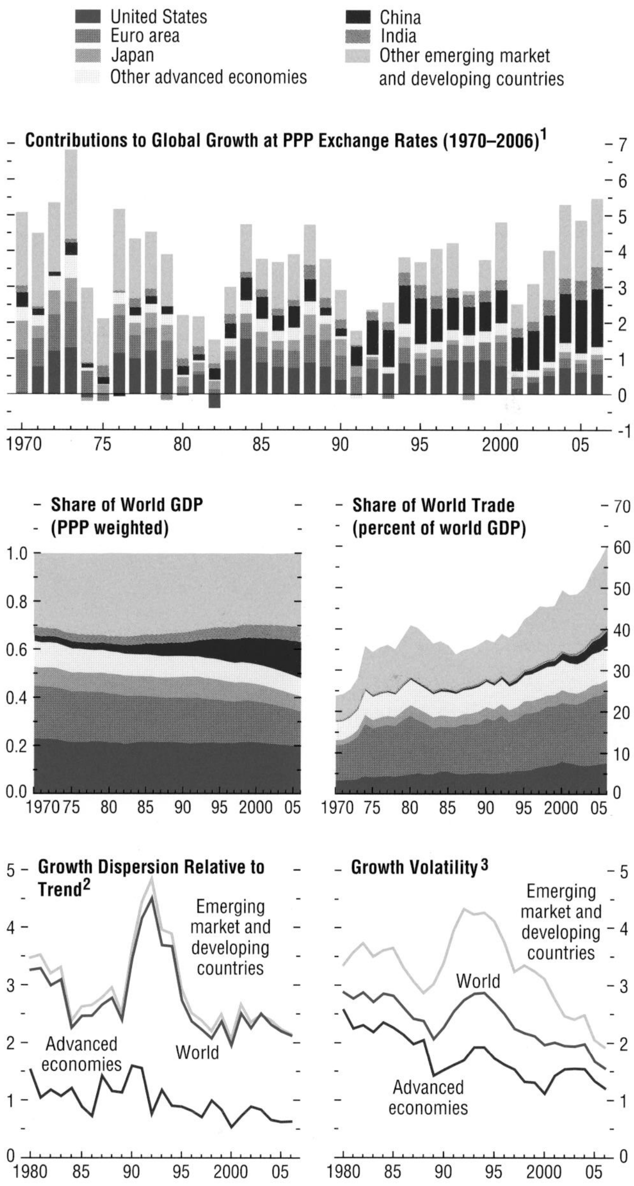

Source: IMF staff calculations.
[1]Exchange rates based on purchasing power parity (PPP).
[2]Standard deviation of current year growth minus average growth in 1970–2006.
[3]Measured as weighted averages for countries' standard deviation of growth over rolling seven-year periods.

policy volatility, improved institutions, and greater financial development—imply that business cycles are likely to be of longer duration and lesser magnitude than in the past.

However, the chapter warns that the business cycle is by no means dead, and concludes on a cautionary note that the present period shares a number of characteristics with the 1960s and early 1970s—a period of strong sustained global growth but followed by a period of greater turbulence punctuated by the collapse of the prevailing monetary policy anchor (the Bretton Woods system of fixed exchange rates), large supply shocks, and inflationary surges. Recent increased financial market volatility has underlined concerns that benign conditions may not be sustained. But, going beyond such considerations, there are also a number of deeper-rooted concerns, which, if not adequately addressed, could pose serious challenges to the continued success of the current expansion.

First, while most countries are doing well at the aggregate level, there are rising concerns about the distribution of the gains. Rapid technological progress and continuing globalization of trade and finance have been enormously growth enhancing and have helped reduce poverty, but they have also contributed to increasing concentrations of income and wealth, both in the advanced economies and the emerging market and developing countries. Owners of capital and of scarce skills have been amply rewarded, but less-skilled workers and those with limited access to jobs or finance have seen more limited gains. Rising inequality has already led to resistance to globalization and contributed to recent setbacks in the process of multilateral trade liberalization, but the protectionist backlash could become yet more virulent. And beyond welfare and political economy concerns, inequality also has real economic costs, because it implies that human resources are not being productively used, as a high share of the world's population continues to have inadequate access to education, health care, and economic and financial opportunities.

Chapter 4 of this report looks in more detail at the relationship between globalization and income inequality. It finds that technological progress is by far the largest factor behind rising inequality, because of the associated income gains to highly skilled workers. Globalization has offsetting effects on income distribution: trade, and particularly exports by developing countries, has in fact tended to reduce inequality, whereas financial globalization, including foreign direct investment, has increased inequality, in part because it is closely related to the diffusion of new technologies. These results yield a number of policy lessons, including the importance for developing countries to achieve their export potential, particularly in agriculture; the value of extending access to education and financial resources to ensure that lower-income groups have the skills and resources needed to benefit from opportunities created by new technologies and globalization; and the need to ensure adequate safety nets for groups adversely affected by the new environment.

A second possible trend that would affect growth dynamics is that over time global savings may well become more scarce, putting upward pressure on real interest rates. In recent years, the global expansion has been supported by the ready availability of external financing at relatively low interest rates. In part, this reflected very easy monetary policy in the advanced economies after the 2000–01 downturn to head off deflationary concerns, but this source of liquidity has been progressively tightened (Box 1.4). Abundant credit has also been related to financial market innovations that have improved liquidity and the distribution of risk, which, notwithstanding recent market volatility, should provide permanent gains. A third factor is the pattern of global saving and investment, which created what Federal Reserve Chairman Ben Bernanke has called a "savings glut" but is perhaps more accurately characterized as low rates of investment (outside China) and a very high rate of saving in China.

However, the global pattern of saving and investment is likely to shift over time. Surpluses of the oil-exporting countries are projected to decline quite rapidly as they increase their absorption to match the earnings potential implied by higher export price trajectories. In the advanced economies and in some middle-income countries too, population aging will tend to increase consumption rates as rising shares of the population retire from the labor force. In China, in particular, consumption rates are likely to rise substantially from current low levels (only 35 percent of GDP), as precautionary savings are reduced and the financial system becomes better adapted to providing credit to households, supported by government policies to rebalance domestic demand and in a context in which the population is aging fast.

Third, more resources may be required for investment and for addressing climate change. Current rapid growth has been achieved with relatively low rates of global investment, driven by productivity gains from trade and financial globalization and application of new information technologies. However, the impetus from globalization and new technology may dwindle, especially if distributional issues are not adequately addressed. Moreover, the need to reduce the rate of global warming is increasingly accepted, which will require new investments to control carbon emissions, for example, in power generation. Recent estimates suggest that mitigation efforts could cost about 1 percent of GDP. Appendix 1.2 looks in more detail at the macroeconomic consequences of climate change and the policy challenges it generates.

Overall, then, a number of medium-term trends may contribute to slowing productivity, rising interest rates, and conditions less conducive to rapid global growth. Financing may become less readily available, and the global economy may become more susceptible to financial reversals and crises. One large question mark in such a context would be the continuing ability of the United States to fund a large current account deficit at a reasonable cost, particularly as surpluses come down in other countries and as financial systems elsewhere develop and are better able to compete in terms of scarcity, liquidity, and range of products. Emerging market and developing countries that have become reliant on external savings—such as those in emerging Europe—could also find themselves facing tighter external financial constraints.

Policy Challenges

Policymakers around the world face the immediate challenge of safeguarding the continued expansion of activity in the face of risks posed by recent turbulent global financial conditions, while remaining alert to inflation pressures. At the same time, greater progress is needed to tackle the deeper obstacles to continued global prosperity.

After a period of tightening that has brought monetary stances to close to or above neutral in most advanced economies, central banks have had to address the recent dramatic drying up of market liquidity and associated financial strains. They have acted as needed to ensure the orderly functioning of financial markets while continuing to base decisions on the monetary policy stance on judgments about economic fundamentals. The concern is to avoid perceptions that central banks would automatically respond to financial distress by taking actions to curtail losses, which could raise moral hazard, reduce credit discipline, and impart an inflationary bias to policy setting.

Looking forward, policy choices will be contingent on the consequences of recent volatility becoming clearer. In the United States, signs that growth was likely to continue below trend would justify further interest rate reductions, provided that inflation remains contained. In the euro area, monetary policy can stay on hold over the near term, reflecting the downside risks to growth and inflation from financial market turmoil. However, as these risks dissipate, further tightening eventually may be required. In the event of a more protracted slowdown, an easing of monetary policy would

Box 1.4. What Is Global Liquidity?

In recent years, a great deal of attention has been paid to the concept of liquidity. Declines in risk premiums across various asset classes; buoyant prices in equity, bond, and real estate markets; low long-term real interest rates; and rising cross-border flows of capital have been interpreted as signs of "excess liquidity" in the global economy. At the same time, however, major central banks around the world have been in a tightening mode for some time. And in mid-August, liquidity dried up suddenly in several money markets and spreads on a number of risky asset classes widened markedly, prompting a significant injection of funds by central banks to stabilize short-term interest rates. What definition of liquidity can reconcile these facts?

The term excess liquidity is rarely well defined. In fact multiple definitions of liquidity, seldom carefully distinguished, are often used. One definition associates excess liquidity with low interest rates or easy borrowing conditions created by an unusually accommodative monetary policy stance across major central banks. Another focuses on market liquidity, associated with structural trends toward financial innovation, deepening, and integration. This box assesses recent trends in simple indicators of global liquidity related to these alternative notions of liquidity and considers how far these are drivers of the global decline in risk premium.

Measures of the Global Monetary Policy Stance

A simple proxy of the monetary policy stance is given by the evolution of *real policy rates.* A monetary policy stance can be termed *strongly accommodative* if real policy rates are negative. The first figure depicts the evolution of real policy rates for the euro area, Japan, and the United States. The U.S. monetary policy stance was indeed strongly accommodative between 2003:Q1 and 2005:Q3, but rates are now close to neutral. Moreover, even during the expansionary phase, the degree of accommodation was less than that observed in the late 1970s and

Note: The authors of this box are Gianni De Nicolò and Johannes Wiegand.

Measures of the Global Monetary Policy Stance

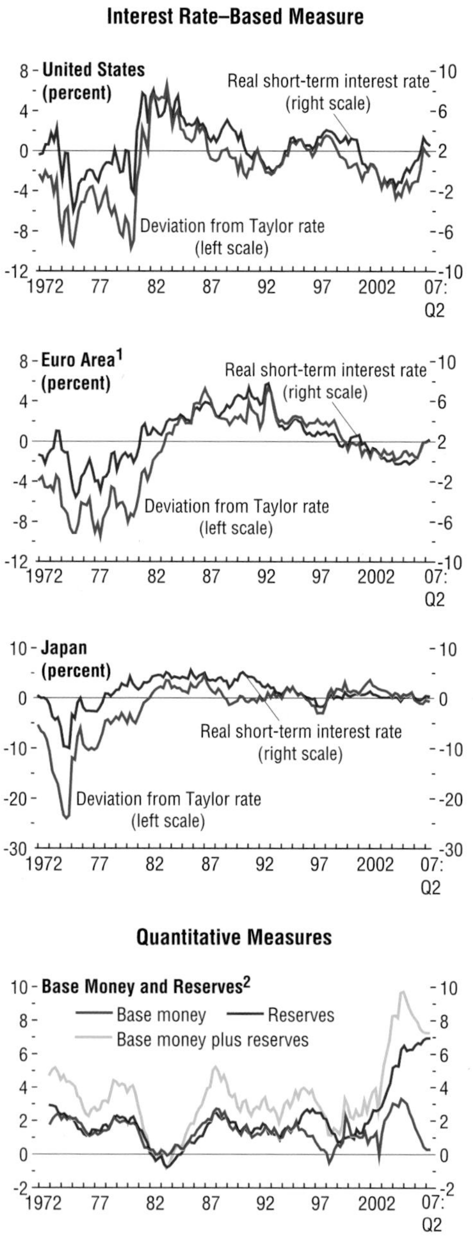

Source: IMF staff calculations.
[1]Before 1998, purchasing-power-parity-weighted average across euro area member countries.
[2]Change over three years for the United States, euro area, and Japan, denominated in U.S. dollars, scaled with GDP.

early 1980s. A similar, albeit less pronounced, pattern characterizes the monetary policy stance of the European Central Bank (ECB) since 1999. In Japan, a strongly accommodative monetary policy stance shows up only in 1997–98.

Another proxy measure of monetary policy stance, also shown in the first figure, is the deviation of a nominal short-term interest rate from a "Taylor rate," obtained by estimating a Taylor rule, or monetary reaction function that relates the policy interest rate to the inflation rate and the economy's cyclical position. A short-term nominal interest rate that is lower than the Taylor rate can be seen as reflecting aggressive monetary accommodation.[1] Overall, this measure provides very similar results to the real policy rate, showing aggressive monetary accommodation between 2002 and end-2006 in the United States and—to a lesser extent—Europe. More recently, however, rates have moved back in line with those implied by the Taylor rule as a result of policy tightening.

An alternative to interest rate measures of the global monetary policy stance is a quantitative measure. A global monetary aggregate based on the growth of base money in the major advanced economies, shown in the bottom panel of the first figure, generally confirms monetary accommodation in the early 2000s, which exceeded in scope even that of the 1970s. The expansion peaked in 2002–04, but it has since reversed. This index is sometimes broadened by adding on the global accumulation of international reserves, the latter being a proxy for monetary expansion by central banks of countries with external surpluses, many of them emerging markets. Using this measure, "global liquidity" shows elevated growth rates until very recently. However, this measure mixes different sorts of indicators, and it is difficult to draw firm conclusions based on it.

[1]The Taylor rate depends positively on (1) the neutral real rate of interest, which, in turn, is a function of (time-varying) potential output growth, (2) the deviation of consumer price inflation from the inflation target, and (3) the output gap. For the exact parameterization of the index, see Chapter 2 of the September 2004 *World Economic Outlook.*

Notwithstanding the reversion to a neutral monetary policy stance in the United States and the euro area, real long-term interest rates on government securities in advanced economies have remained low compared with their historical average. One factor that is likely to have affected long-term interest rates is the global pattern of saving and investment. In particular, the abundance of global savings relative to investment may have contributed to, among other things, an increase in demand for longer-term securities. In this context, large current account surpluses in oil-exporting and Asian countries and the associated capital outflows may have also contributed to the decline of long-term interest rates.[2]

Financial Market Liquidity

The monetary policy measures discussed so far do not capture the implications for market liquidity of the rapid financial deepening and innovation that has characterized global financial markets in the past decade.[3]

Standard monetary and finance theory views liquidity as an attribute of an asset. The degree of liquidity of an asset is higher the lower the expected costs incurred in converting it into cash—by definition the most liquid asset—at any point in time. Liquidation costs can be reduced by borrowing to spread asset sales over time, but the ability to borrow and its cost will depend on the extent to which other market participants are able and willing to provide financing.[4] This suggests that the

[2]See Warnock and Warnock (2006).

[3]A simple illustration of this is provided by a decomposition of changes in M2/GDP between changes in the ratio of liquid assets to total assets in the economy—the ratio of M2 to an economy's total financial assets—and the ratio of total financial assets to GDP, as an indicator of financial deepening. Data over the past decade show that the aggregate liquidity ratio has *decreased* whereas financial deepening has increased.

[4]This ability can be temporarily enhanced by central banks' *money injections.* However, money injections do not as such increase the liquidity of the market as defined, but just increase the ability of market participants to obtain funding to carry out and settle certain transactions.

Box 1.4 *(concluded)*

degree of liquidity of an asset *cannot* be defined independently from the liquidity of its market. Moreover, market liquidity can dry up rapidly as a result of market participants' reassessment of counterparty risk. This point is underscored by recent events when major central banks have temporarily injected large amounts of funds to support liquidity in the interbank market.

One important point to stress is that the *risk premium of an asset incorporates a liquidity premium.* The degree of liquidity of a tradable asset has value and therefore carries a price. Thus, higher market liquidity can reduce the risk associated with a given asset portfolio (Longstaff, 2001). An important implication of this is that a larger portion of investors' wealth may be invested in "risky" assets, even though risk tolerance has not changed.

Three indicators of a financial-markets-based concept of liquidity are illustrated in the second figure.[5] The first such indicator is the yield differential between less frequently traded (off-the-run) and more frequently traded (on-the-run) three-month U.S. treasury bonds, which is a proxy measure of the liquidity premium in the short-term U.S. government bond market. The second indicator is based on a return-to-volume ratio[6] introduced by Amihud (2002), which captures two dimensions of market liquidity—*depth* or the volume of trades (order flows) that can be executed without significantly affecting prices and *resiliency* or the speed at which price fluctuations resulting from trading dissipate. Specifically, it tracks the liquidity of global equity markets—measured by a market-capitalization-weighted average of the inverse of the daily return-to-volume ratios of equity markets in advanced economies and emerging market countries. As constructed, an increase in this indicator denotes improved liquidity. The third

[5]In its April 2007 *Financial Stability Report,* the Bank of England constructs a similar indicator relevant to the market in which U.K. banks are active.

[6]The return-to-volume ratio is given by the daily absolute return on the equity market divided by the ratio of traded volume over market capitalization.

Global Market Liquidity Indicators

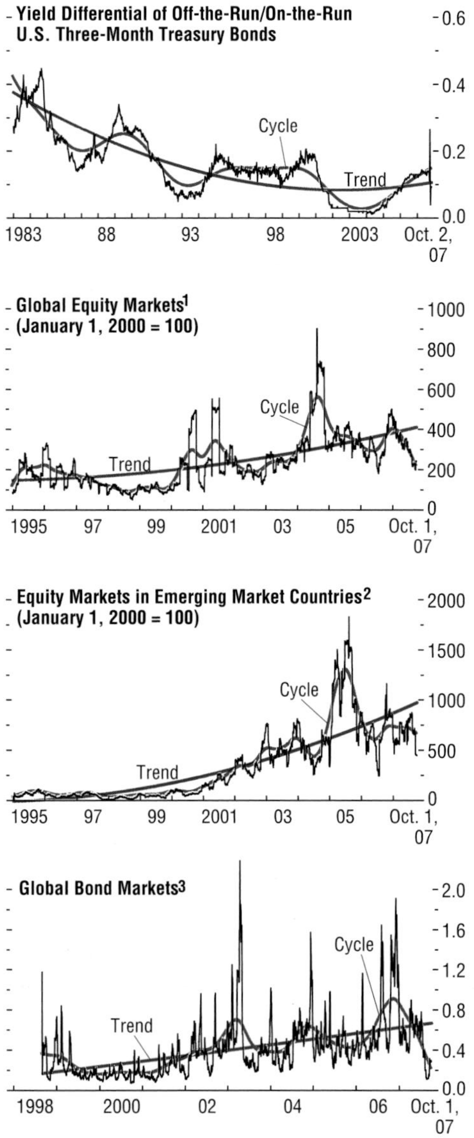

Sources: Datastream; Federal Reserve Board; and IMF staff calculations.

[1]Market-capitalization-weighted average of daily return-to-volume ratios of equity markets in advanced and emerging market countries.

[2]Market-capitalization-weighted average of daily return-to-volume ratios of equity markets in emerging market countries.

[3]Market efficiency ratio of the JPMorgan Global (All Maturities) Bond Index.

indicator tracks the liquidity of global bond markets—measured by a version of the so-called market efficiency ratio (MEC) introduced by Hasbrouck and Schwartz (1988), which equals the ratio of volatility of bond market returns for a five-day horizon divided by the volatility of daily returns multiplied by the length of the horizon (five days).[7] This indicator should be closer to 1 in more *resilient* markets, because in such markets the short-term volatility due to price discovery, measured in the denominator, dissipates quickly, making the volatility of returns in a buy-and-hold strategy for a given investment horizon comparable with the daily-return volatility multiplied by the length of the horizon.

As shown in the second figure, liquidity in the U.S. Treasury market has risen sharply since the early 1980s. The liquidity of global equity markets has also increased substantially since the mid-1990s, with the rise in emerging market economies being particularly impressive. Likewise, liquidity in global bond markets has also risen substantially, as seen by the increasing closeness of the MEC indicator to unity both from below and from above.

All three of these market liquidity indicators exhibit cycles, but the cycle is only weakly related to movements in real policy rates and is unrelated to quantitative measures of the global monetary policy stance, suggesting that secular factors underlie improvements in global market liquidity.[8] Overall, this evidence is strongly suggestive of an implied historical decrease in liquidity premiums, likely contributing to the overall decline in risk premium.

Against the backdrop of worsening subprime woes in the United States, in mid-August, liquidity in money markets in several advanced countries became scarce. In this context, the global equity and bond liquidity indicators recorded a sharp decline, although market liquidity has remained higher than the low levels recorded in the late 1990s. Liquidity in bond markets, however, declined more sharply than in equity markets, reflecting the greater impact on the former of the drying up of liquidity in money markets.

Conclusion

Notwithstanding recent market events, long-term interest rates and spreads across a broad range of assets are still at low levels relative to their long-term averages. This seems, however, no longer associated with aggressive monetary accommodation. In particular, measures of the global monetary policy stance confirm a period of generally accommodative policies in industrial countries in the early 2000s, but this has ended. At least part of the increase in global liquidity and the associated decrease in risk premium is likely the result of a structural, and possibly enduring, component related to improvements in the liquidity of financial markets. These improvements are a result of financial globalization; financial innovation, such as securitization and the growth of derivatives markets; and increased market participation. Even in the context of the recent market turmoil, these improvements do not appear to have been completely reversed. However, money markets are yet to return to normal and this could still have a further bearing on global liquidity. At the same time, low long-term interest rates may also reflect the impact of global savings-investment imbalances, which are likely to correct over the medium term.

[7]The MEC has been computed for a global bond market return index, the JPMorgan Global (All Maturities) Bond Index.

[8]An estimate of the cycle of the liquidity premium in the short-term U.S. government bond market and of global equity and bond market liquidity indicators is obtained by filtering daily data at standard business cycle frequencies using a Hodrick-Prescott filter. Estimates of a vector autoregression (VAR) with global equity and bond market liquidity indicators and U.S. real policy rates yield a negative but statistically insignificant relationship between current U.S. real policy rates and future market liquidity, while there is no such relationship when quantitative measures of the monetary policy stance replace U.S. real policy rates in the VAR. However, a thorough analysis of the relationship between market liquidity and monetary policy stance is left for future research.

need to be considered. In Japan, given the muted outlook for prices, monetary policy should remain supportive. The return to a more neutral stance should proceed in tandem with a firming of inflation prospects and a reduction of concerns about the consequences of recent financial volatility.

Despite the weaker growth prospects for advanced economies, a number of emerging market economies still face overheating pressures and rising food prices, and further monetary tightening may be required to contain inflation. Moreover, notwithstanding recent financial developments, strong foreign exchange inflows from current account surpluses as well as continuing net capital inflows are likely to continue to complicate the policymakers' task. In some cases, greater exchange rate flexibility would help provide more room for monetary control. Specifically for China, further upward flexibility of the renminbi, along with measures to reform the exchange rate regime and boost consumption, would also contribute to a necessary rebalancing of demand and to an orderly unwinding of global imbalances. More generally, policymakers in emerging market countries should be pragmatic in managing the trade-offs between excessive credit growth driven by rapid reserve accumulation and concerns about competitiveness from exchange rate appreciation, but should be careful to avoid measures that could bring microeconomic inefficiencies and other longer-term costs. Greater restraint over growth of government spending, a tightening of prudential standards in financial systems, and steps to liberalize controls on capital outflows could all play useful roles.

In due course, lessons will need to be drawn from the recent experience of turbulent market conditions to reduce vulnerabilities to future strains, lessons that would be relevant in both advanced and developing economies. One set of issues concerns the various approaches central banks have used to provide liquidity to relieve financial strains and linkage with broader financial safety nets. For some countries, stronger deposit insurance systems and bank resolution mechanisms may provide more scope to take a disciplined approach to providing liquidity to individual institutions that minimizes moral hazard without generating systemic risk. There are also a series of regulatory issues that will need to be addressed, as discussed in more detail in the October GFSR. First, greater attention will need to be given to ensuring adequate transparency over risks, including off-balance-sheet exposures, to ensure that the market is able to price risk properly in a world where financial instruments have become more complex, particularly with increasing reliance on securitization. Second, there is a need to strengthen checks and balances throughout the supply chain of structured products to ensure that loan originators have appropriate incentives to assess repayment capacity. Third, the approach taken to rating of complex financial products should be reviewed to ensure that investors are alerted to liquidity and market risks, in addition to credit risks. Fourth, financial institutions should be encouraged to improve liquidity risk management. And fifth, the relevant perimeter for risk consolidation for banks may need to be widened to recognize that banks may be forced under adverse circumstances to step in to support their affiliates.

The advanced economies have made significant progress toward fiscal consolidation during the present expansion, but need to do more to advance plans to ensure fiscal sustainability in the face of population aging, although automatic stabilizers should be allowed to work in most countries in the event of a downturn. General government structural deficits have been lowered substantially across the major economies since 2003, and further progress is expected in 2007. However, prospects through 2012 show limited further consolidation, implying little reduction in net debt to GDP from current levels. Moreover, much of the consolidation that has occurred in recent years has reflected rapid revenue growth driven by the rising share of profits and high-end incomes, and it is not clear to what extent these revenue gains will be sustained. Governments should adopt more ambitious medium-term consolidation plans, together with reforms to tackle the rising pressures from government health and social security spending (see Box 1.3 of the April 2007 *World Economic Outlook*).

- In the *United States*, the newly adopted goal of balancing the federal budget by 2012 is a step forward, but the policies to achieve this objective are not yet in place, and a more ambitious medium-term target—such as balancing the budget without relying on Social Security revenues—would better prepare for the coming buildup in spending pressures and contribute to current account adjustment.
- In the *euro area*, the Eurogroup ministers have committed to achieving country-specific medium-term objectives (MTOs) by 2010. Although this commitment is welcome, it will be important that countries that fall short of their MTOs adjust by at least ½ percentage point of GDP a year—a goal that according to current plans does not look likely to be met in some countries in 2007.
- In *Japan*, net debt is projected to continue to rise despite continuing consolidation efforts, and faster progress than currently envisaged would buy policy insurance against shocks and help meet the challenges of population aging.

The emerging market and developing countries have also generally taken advantage of recent buoyant conditions to advance fiscal consolidation goals, which has contributed importantly to reduce balance sheet vulnerabilities. But, as with the advanced economies, there are concerns that much of the recent improvement reflects strong revenue growth—for example, generated by high commodity prices and strong profits—which may not be sustained. Moreover, in many countries, government spending has been allowed to accelerate, which has added to overheating concerns. Most countries face a long list of fiscal reform challenges—to improve the structure of taxation, to strengthen the allocation of spending, and to consolidate the overall framework for fiscal management—and should do more to tackle these challenges.

More broadly, countries must continue their efforts to advance reforms that allow their economies to take full advantage of the opportunities created by globalization and technological advances. A key part of this agenda are initiatives to make sure that markets work well, with priorities being liberalization of financial and service sectors in western Europe and Japan and a broad range of reforms in emerging market and developing countries to improve infrastructure, develop financial systems, and strengthen the business environment.

It is increasingly recognized that more is needed to ensure that the benefits of globalization and technological advances are well distributed, with rewards accruing not only to the well-off and well positioned but also to the broader population. As emphasized in the analytical chapters of the April 2007 *World Economic Outlook* and in this report, a range of policies are relevant here across advanced and developing economies. Reforms to strengthen education and training would help to ensure that workers have the appropriate skills to compete and contribute in the emerging knowledge-based global economy. Labor market reforms are needed to ensure that jobs are created flexibly in the most dynamic sectors. And social safety nets should be enhanced to provide greater protection for those who may be adversely affected by the process of change, without impeding the changes themselves.

In some key areas, joint actions across countries will be crucial. The recent slow progress with the Doha Trade Round is deeply disappointing, and major trading countries should show leadership to find a way to reenergize the process of multilateral trade liberalization. The continuing proliferation of bilateral trade treaties is a concern. Although such treaties can bring benefits to the countries involved, they also have negative externalities, and a code of conduct is sorely needed that would help reduce trade diversion and contain the complexities from multiple sets of rules of origin and other regulations.

Concerns about climate change and energy security also clearly require a multilateral

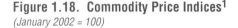

Figure 1.18. Commodity Price Indices[1]
(January 2002 = 100)

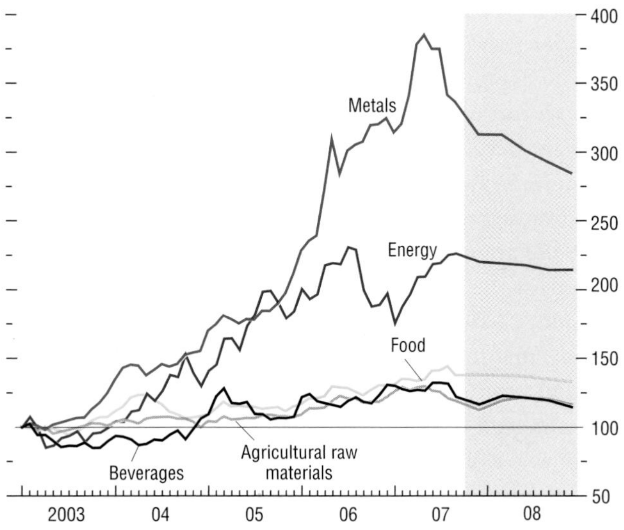

Source: IMF staff estimates.
[1]Shaded area denotes projections.

approach. Global warming may be the world's largest collective action problem with the negative consequences of individual activities felt largely by others. It is to be hoped that countries can come together to develop a market-based framework that balances the long-term costs of carbon emissions against the immediate economic costs of mitigation, which can attract broad country participation while providing a fair distribution of the costs involved. Approaches to energy security must be consistent with greater attention to environmental consequences, involving reduced focus on the autarkic strategy of developing national sources of energy, often with considerable associated environmental damage, and more attention to price-based incentives to containing growth of energy consumption and steps to encourage international diversification of energy sources (for example, by reducing barriers to trade in biofuels).

Finally, joint actions toward ensuring a smooth unwinding of global imbalances remains an important task. Following up on the IMF's Multilateral Consultation, the key now is consistent implementation by participating countries of the policy plans that have been announced, which, according to IMF staff analysis, will make a significant contribution toward the reduction of imbalances while sustaining growth. With the agreement of participants in the Consultation, implementation will be monitored by the IMF, including through future issues of the *World Economic Outlook.*

Appendix 1.1. Developments in Commodity Markets

The authors of this appendix are Kevin Cheng, Valerie Mercer-Blackman, and Hossein Samiei, with contributions from Nese Erbil and To-Nhu Dao.

Commodity markets have generally been tight since the beginning of 2007, notwithstanding the recent financial turmoil. The IMF commodities and energy price index rose by 21 percent in the first eight months of the year, dominated by a resurgence in oil prices and supported by rising metals and food prices (Figure 1.18). Oil prices rose to all-time highs in September, largely resulting from solid demand growth in the face of tight supply. Metals prices have remained strong, despite some losses amid sell-offs during the recent financial turmoil, and food prices have been boosted by strong demand—particularly for biofuel production—and supply shortfalls. Looking forward, with continued geopolitical and supply risks coupled with stronger demand—especially from China, the Middle East, and the United States—oil prices are likely to remain high in the absence of a further change in OPEC's quota policies or a major global slowdown. Metals prices are expected to soften further from recent highs, although rising production costs will limit the decline. Food prices should also moderate over the medium term, although demand for biofuels and from emerging markets could provide continued support.

Surging Oil Prices Reflect Robust Demand amid Tight Supply

Record-high crude oil prices. Following a dip in January, the average petroleum spot price (APSP) has remained strong since late March. Despite OPEC's announced quota increase of 0.5 million barrels a day (mbd) starting in November and some softening in August amid the subprime turmoil, the APSP set an all-time record high in mid-September, with the West Texas Intermediate (WTI) reaching beyond \$83 and Dubai beyond \$75; the Brent price has also reached a record high of almost \$80 in late September (Figure 1.19, top panel). Long-term futures prices have risen much less than spot prices: since early July, the crude oil forward curve has moved from partial contango at the front end (where futures prices are higher than the spot price) to full backwardation (the opposite situation) for the first time in three years (Figure 1.19, upper-middle panel). This development suggests that market concerns are focused on the current availability of oil in the context

Figure 1.19. Crude Oil and Gasoline Prices

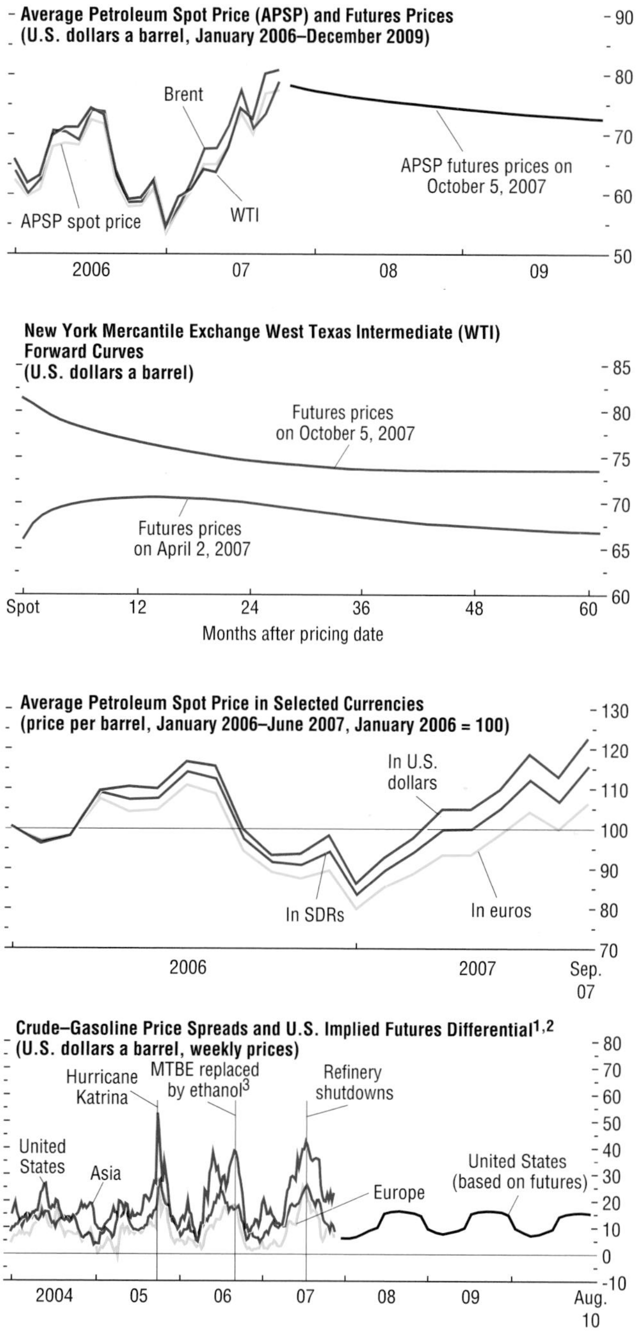

Sources: Bloomberg Financial Markets, LP; and IMF staff estimates.
[1]Differentials are West Texas Intermediate prices and 93 octane gasoline for the United States; Brent and 95 octane gasoline for Europe; and Dubai and 95 octane gasoline for Asia.
[2]Futures crack margins are as of September 19, 2007.
[3]MTBE is methyl tertiary-butyl ether.

Figure 1.20. Developments in Oil Consumption and Production

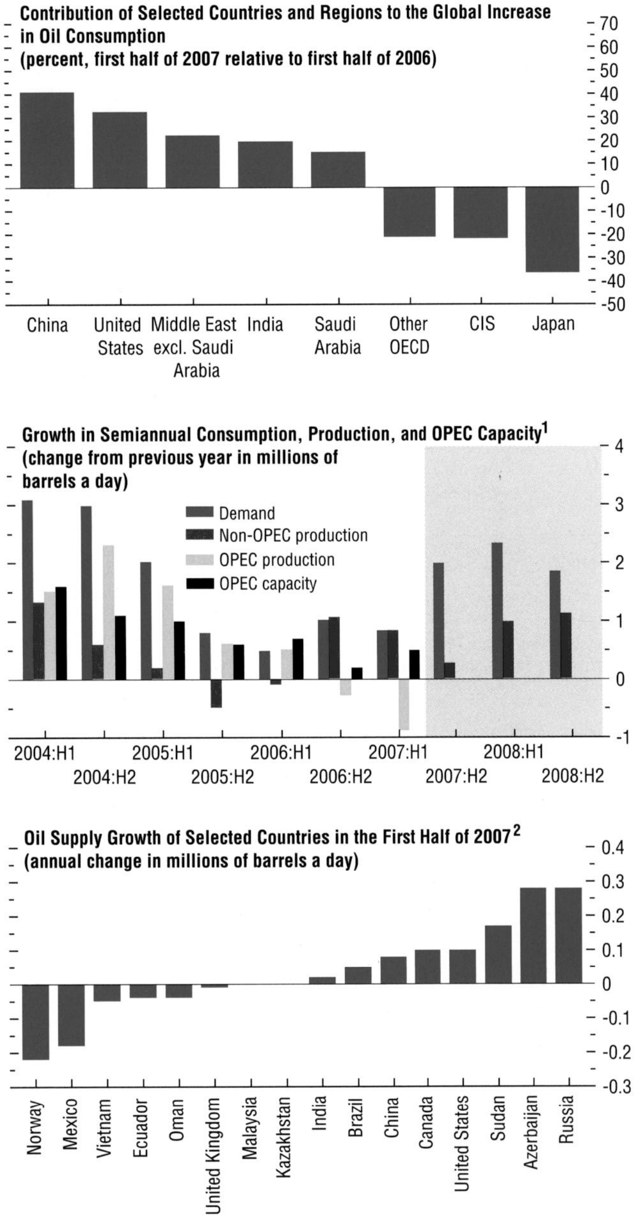

Sources: International Energy Agency; and IMF staff estimates.

[1]Non-OPEC supply and demand projections are from the International Energy Agency. Projections are not available for OPEC production and capacity.

[2]Includes crude oil and synthetic crude oil from tar sands, oil shale, and others.

of increased supply uncertainty and declining crude inventories.[5] The weakening of the U.S. dollar—by lowering real prices for consumers and producers—may have also contributed to higher dollar prices: in terms of the euro and the SDR, oil prices have not risen as sharply (Figure 1.19, lower-middle panel).

Gasoline price spike. Refinery bottlenecks pushed U.S. retail gasoline prices to a record high in late May, but prices have since eased somewhat (Box 1.5). While the long-term gasoline price trend is determined by crude oil prices, over shorter periods changes in refinery availability can cause crude and gasoline price movements to diverge.[6] Indeed, the gasoline crack spread spike in May 2007 followed two major spikes within a span of less than two years,[7] likely reflecting an increased susceptibility of gasoline prices to supply shocks in the face of increasing refinery bottlenecks. Refinery problems in the United States have spilled over to other regions, in part through higher demand for imports of refined products—particularly in the United States and the Middle East—resulting in a rise in crude-gasoline price differentials in all major markets in the second quarter (Figure 1.19, lower panel). Refinery bottlenecks also depressed the price of WTI—the U.S. reference crude—relative to other crudes, particularly Brent, as crude inventories built up, waiting to be refined in the central United States. As refinery problems in the U.S. Midwest eased, WTI recovered and rose above Brent in late July.

[5]In general, the futures price equals the spot price plus costs of carry (such as cost of interest, cost of storage, and insurance) minus benefits of carry (or the "convenience yield"). When the spot market is tight, the benefits (or convenience) of having the commodity available on hand may offset costs of carry, pushing futures prices below the spot price.

[6]In addition, gasoline demand has a strong seasonal component that could cause large crude-gasoline differentials.

[7]The first spikes took place when Hurricane Katrina damaged Gulf of Mexico refineries and the second when ethanol was introduced as a gasoline additive.

Buoyant consumption. Global oil demand accelerated in the first half of 2007, growing at about 1 percent year on year, compared with about ½ percent during the same period in 2006. Demand has been subdued in many OECD countries, with consumption falling in Europe and Japan in the first half of 2007, as warm winter temperatures reduced demand for heating oil. Demand also weakened in the United States in the early part of 2007 but ended up increasing as a whole by about 1¼ percent year on year in the first half of 2007 as a result of strong consumption of transportation fuels, particularly diesel. Weak overall OECD demand, however, has been more than offset by robust demand growth in non-OECD countries—led by buoyant demand from China, India, and the Middle East (Figure 1.20, top panel; and Table 1.2). The strong non-OECD consumption growth, despite high prices, reflects rapid income growth in emerging market countries and below-market prices (especially in the Middle East), coupled with a weakening U.S. dollar that makes oil more affordable in local currencies.

Supply and inventories. Notwithstanding robust demand growth, overall output was unchanged in the first half of 2007 relative to the same period last year, and inventories were flat. The rise in non-OPEC production (1.0 mbd) was offset by a decline in OPEC production (0.9 mbd) (Figure 1.20, middle panel), reflecting quota cuts as well as shutdowns in Nigeria. Non-OPEC production growth was also lower than expected, reflecting a fall in production in Alaska, Mexico, and Norway, despite strong growth in Russia and Azerbaijan (Figure 1.20, lower panel). Preliminary estimates suggest global supply fell by 0.4 mbd in August owing to hurricane outages in Mexico and maintenance work in the North Sea. OECD commercial oil and product inventories have remained flat in the first half of 2007. U.S. gasoline inventories fell precipitously starting in February 2007 and are now decisively below their five-year average. Crude inventories began to decline in the third quarter of 2007—losing 10 percent of the stock—but still remain comfortable (Figure 1.21, top panel). No comprehensive data are available on non-OECD inventories.

Table 1.2. Global Oil Demand by Region

	Demand			Annual Change		
	2005	2006	2007*	2005	2006	2007*
	Millions of Barrels a Day			*Percent*		
OECD	49.67	49.23	49.41	0.6	–0.9	0.4
North America	25.50	25.26	25.66	0.5	–0.9	1.6
of which						
United States	20.80	20.67	20.92	0.3	–0.6	1.2
Europe	15.61	15.56	15.38	0.8	–0.3	–1.2
Pacific	8.57	8.40	8.38	0.8	–1.9	–0.3
Non-OECD	34.05	35.27	36.56	3.2	3.6	3.6
of which						
China	6.69	7.16	7.58	4.2	6.9	5.9
Other Asia	8.79	8.87	9.11	1.9	0.9	2.8
Former Soviet Union	3.80	3.98	3.92	1.2	4.7	–1.5
Middle East	5.99	6.28	6.58	4.6	4.8	4.7
Africa	2.94	2.93	3.06	6.1	–0.3	4.4
Latin America	5.13	5.31	5.49	2.9	3.6	3.5
World	83.75	84.50	85.92	1.7	0.9	1.7

Source: International Energy Agency, *Oil Market Report,* September 2007.
Note: OECD = Organization for Economic Cooperation and Development.
*Projections.

Increased OPEC spare capacity. OPEC crude oil production capacity increased by 0.5 mbd in the first half of 2007 relative to the same period in 2006. This, together with previous production cuts, has increased spare capacity to more comfortable levels. While this could in principle mitigate upward pressures on prices by reducing concerns about potential future supply disruptions, its impact on current prices has been more than offset by lower OPEC production (Figure 1.21).

Outlook. Looking forward, demand growth is expected to outstrip non-OPEC supply growth in 2007 and 2008. The International Energy Agency's (IEA's) revised forecasts point to a tighter market than envisaged earlier. On the supply side, growth is expected to be limited, with non-OPEC supply growth remaining lackluster at 0.6 mbd in 2007 (slightly higher than the increase in 2006), reflecting a proliferation of project delays and higher output declines than earlier expected in maturing fields (particularly in Norway, the United Kingdom, and Mexico). OPEC envisages a more optimistic supply scenario, projecting a rise in non-OPEC

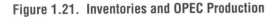

Figure 1.21. Inventories and OPEC Production

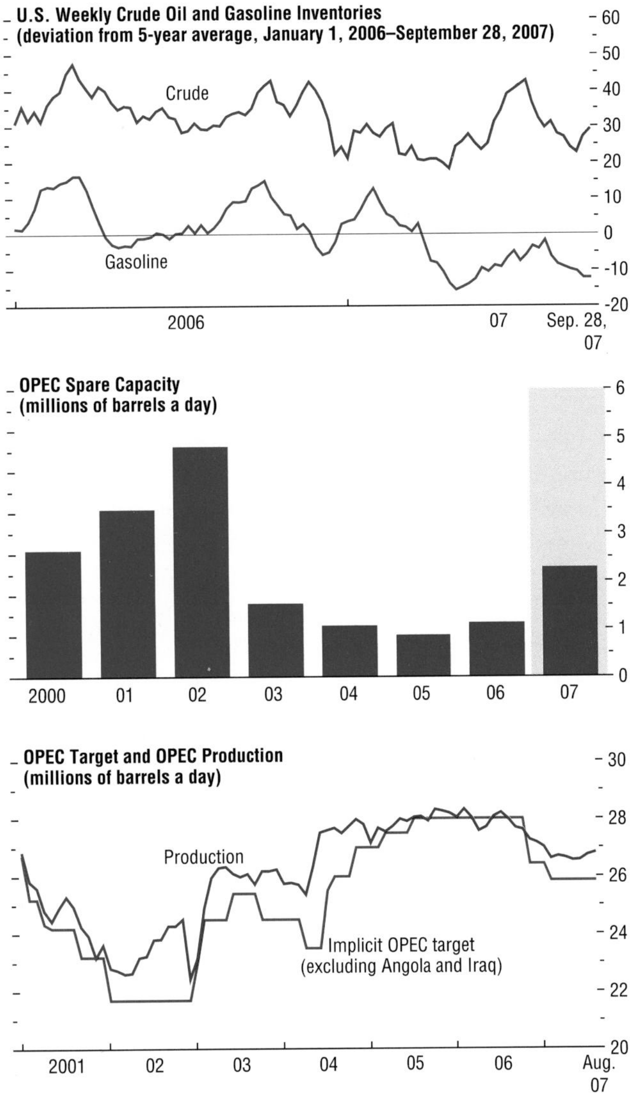

Sources: Bloomberg Financial Markets, LP; Energy Information Agency, U.S. Department of Energy; International Energy Agency; and IMF staff estimates.

production of about 0.8 mbd in 2007. Rapid growth of the biofuels supply will raise the supply of transportation fuel, but biofuels still account for just over 1 percent of total fuel use (Box 1.6). The impact of biofuels on oil prices should be small—although they are having a tangible impact on food prices.

In contrast, on the demand side, the IEA expects consumption to grow by 1.4 mbd, driven by emerging market economies, in particular China, India, and the Middle East, as well as the United States—despite a slight downward revision to U.S. demand growth in the wake of the credit turmoil in August 2007. Furthermore, OECD demand for nontransportation fuels—which is more sensitive to the weather—is expected to pick up in the second half of 2007, assuming that temperatures revert to more normal levels from a relatively mild 2006. OPEC's forecasts point to a somewhat smaller increase in global consumption (1.3 mbd in 2007).

As a result, although oil prices currently lie at the upper end of their historical range and modest declines are possible, upward pressures remain. An important characteristic of the recent price surge is that—unlike last year's price peak in August—there has been no apparent intensification of geopolitical risks in the wake of the surge. Therefore, further upward price pressure could materialize in the event of renewed geopolitical concerns. The extent of upward pressures will in part depend on OPEC's quota policies, dollar exchange rate movements, and global activity, but the direction and magnitude of these pressures remain uncertain. OPEC has indicated that it would consider increasing supply further in 2007:Q4, if necessary, as its assessment (as outlined above) is consistent with an implicit price target in the $60–$70 range. While OECD economic activity is expected to weaken somewhat, oil demand will be significantly affected only if the slowdown spills over to emerging markets where oil consumption growth is the most prominent.

As of October 5, futures and options markets indicate that oil prices will average over $77 a barrel in the remainder of 2007 and $76 a barrel in 2008, with a 50 percent probability that Brent crude prices will be between $69 and $87 by January 2008 (Figure 1.22, top panel).

Over the medium term, the IEA expects tight market conditions to persist and possibly intensify by 2012, assuming strong GDP growth continues. Average global demand in the 2007–12 period would remain strong, increasing by 1.9 mbd a year—slightly above the average annual increase during 2002–07: a period of rising prices, spurred by accelerating non-OECD demand. OPEC's capacity is expected to increase by an average of 0.8 mbd a year and non-OPEC capacity by only 0.5 mbd a year over the same period (compared with 0.7 mbd in the previous five years), as rising investment costs and prolonged project delays, together with high decline rates of major fields, create a drag on capacity expansion plans. With the increase in capacity likely falling short of the increase in demand, medium-term upward pressure on prices may continue in the absence of a global slowdown.

Natural Gas and Coal Markets

Natural gas prices have followed different trends across the Atlantic (Figure 1.22, middle panel). In the United States, after rising in the first quarter of 2007, prices have weakened—amid record-high inventory accumulation and the financial turmoil, although it strengthened somewhat in September. By contrast, after a dip in late April, U.K. prices largely followed an upward trend, reflecting some storage maintenance problems amid strong weather-related demand. Russian gas export prices have weakened somewhat over the past year. Average international coal prices rose by more than 32 percent during the first eight months of 2007, and demand is expected to strengthen further, with China emerging as a net importer for the first time in April.

Nonenergy Commodities

The IMF nonenergy index rose by 7 percent during the first eight months of 2007. Metals

Figure 1.22. Oil Futures Prices, and Selected Energy and Metals Prices

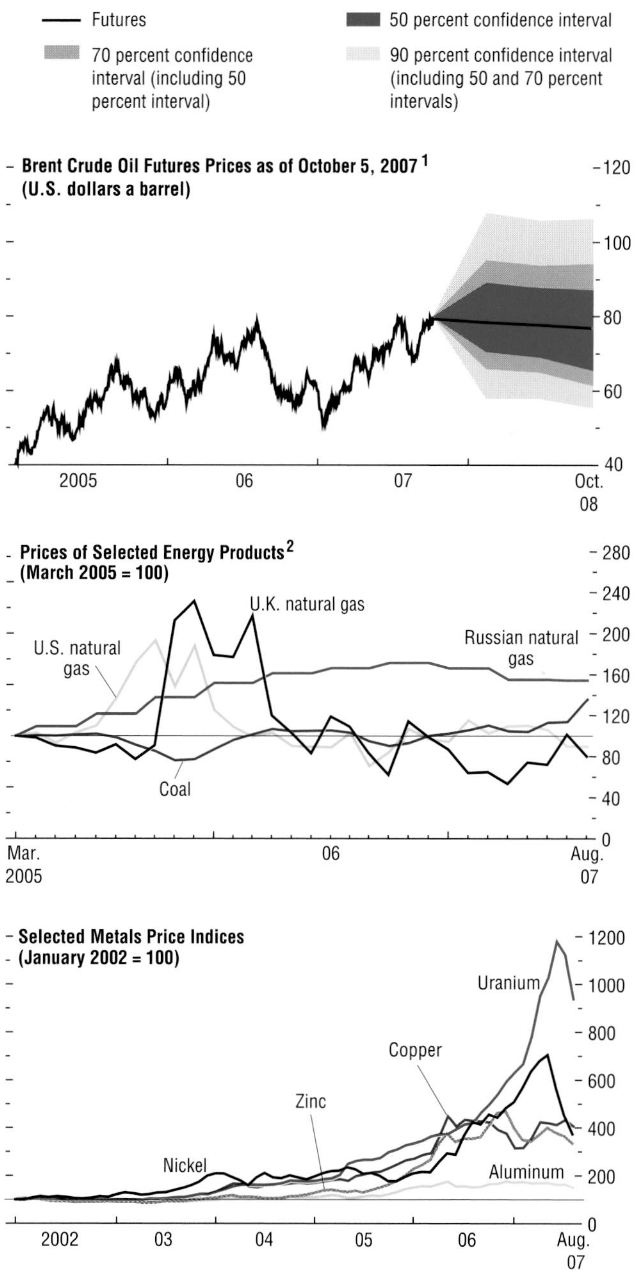

Sources: Bloomberg Financial Markets, LP; and IMF staff calculations.
[1]From futures options.
[2]U.K. natural gas price data begin on March 11, 2005.

Box 1.5. Refinery Bottlenecks

Gasoline and diesel prices in the United States and elsewhere rose sharply in May 2007, with "crack spreads" (premium over crude oil prices) reaching levels close to those seen following Hurricane Katrina. The rise in spreads stemmed from refinery outages in the United States, owing to delayed maintenance and unexpected factors, which, combined with tight global refinery capacity, resulted in a drawdown in product stocks just before the peak summer demand period for transport fuels. Spreads have since come down (see Figure 1.19, bottom panel).

Refinery problems are not new in the United States. Refining capacity has lagged behind consumption growth, implying greater dependence on gasoline imports over the years (top panel of figure).[1] New investment has been hampered by strict environmental regulations, which can vary considerably by locality and thus add to uncertainty, as well as by a depressed oil market throughout the 1990s (which kept refining profit margins low). No new refineries have been built in the United States since the late 1970s. While notional capacity has increased somewhat through expanding capacity at existing refineries and enhancing efficiency, this process is limited by aging distillation units and increasingly strict fuel specifications, which have led to more required downtime and longer processing periods.

There is also a mismatch between the type of crude available and the refining capabilities at a more global scale. The majority of refineries cannot process heavy or sour oil[2] (which is in relatively greater supply globally) into high-quality distillates such as gasoline and low-sulfur diesel (which are in relatively greater demand, and increasingly so) (bottom panel of figure).

In part reflecting these global mismatches, OPEC (2007) projects that growth of trade in refined products will exceed growth of trade in crude by 2020, with much of the growth coming from trade in products refined from sour oil (abundant in the Middle East) and directed mostly toward Asian markets. Planned refinery investment in the coming years should

Gasoline Consumption and Refining Capacity

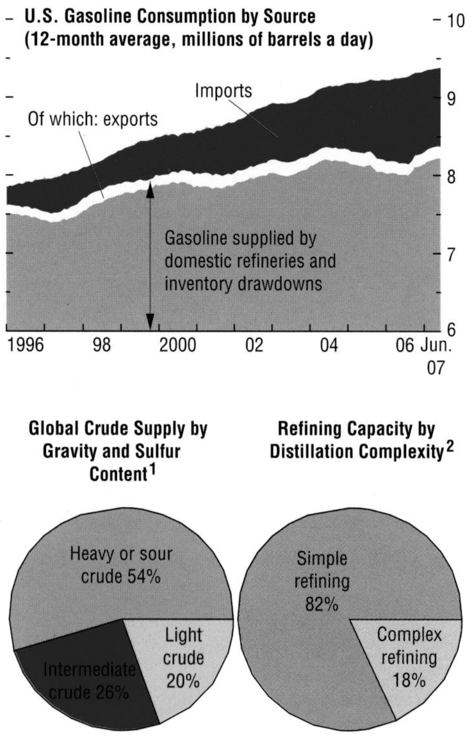

Sources: HPI Consultants; International Energy Agency; Platt's Haverly Crude Assay Library; and IMF staff calculations.

[1]Crude quality is defined by its density and sulfur content. It is classified as heavy if its API gravity is below 30 degrees, intermediate if it is between 30 and 40 degrees, and light otherwise. It is sour if its sulfur content is greater than 0.05 parts per million.

[2]Simple refining is defined as a process of simple distillation or reforming. Complex refining is defined as catalytic cracking or thermal cracking, including upgrading capacity.

Note: The author of this box is Valerie Mercer-Blackman.

[1]Refinery capacity problems also exist in Europe and in Japan, but unlike in the United States, consumption has stabilized in these regions.

[2]Heavy oil refers to a crude type that is relatively dense or has a high gravity per volumetric unit. Sour crude refers to a crude type that has relatively high sulfur content per volumetric unit. Both properties mean that the crude requires additional and more complex distillation to turn it into a unit of light, low-sulfur product.

expand capacity, albeit slowly. The International Energy Agency predicts that most of the new distillation capacity additions will be in emerging markets: out of the almost 11 million barrels a day (mbd) capacity expansions planned globally over the next five years, Asia and the Middle East are expected to contribute about 7 mbd.

The risks to these projections, however, are on the downside. Rising costs of materials and a chronic lack of skilled labor may delay or constrain projects. In addition, uncertainties arising from environmental concerns and efforts to switch to cleaner alternatives, in part through stricter regulations to control emissions, will likely raise costs for potential refinery investors.

prices extended their strong price run-up of recent years, while some food prices rose sharply. Agricultural raw materials and beverage prices increased more slowly. Looking forward, the index is expected to decline somewhat as supply responds to increased demand, although short-term downside price risks to food prices should be limited by the strong biofuel demand.

Robust metals prices reflecting supply problems. While prices suffered losses amid sell-offs during the recent credit crunch, they have remained strong, largely reflecting supply problems. Overall, prices rose by about 8¾ percent during the first eight months of 2007, led by lead—which set new record highs during the period—as well as copper and tin (Figure 1.22, lower panel). Nickel and uranium, however, suffered major losses more recently after both reached record highs in the early summer. While demand has been buoyant—for example, for copper, reflecting increased Chinese demand for restocking, and for uranium (during the first half of 2007), owing to increased demand for nuclear energy—supply factors appear to have been the main driver of higher prices. Labor disputes in copper mines in Chile, Mexico, and Peru continued to disrupt production, while the ensuing wage increases have increased the long-term cost of production. In addition, certain restrictive government policies—such as Indonesia's tightened tin export regulation—have reduced supply. Finally, industry consolidation has reduced the number of plants against the background of delays in new projects. Consequently, inventories have been low for most metals, thereby reducing the safety cushion in the event of supply disruptions. Looking forward, prices are expected to soften from recent highs, but they are expected to be supported by increasing costs over the longer term, reflecting intense competition for skilled labor and equipment and energy costs.

Buoyant food prices amid robust biofuel demand. Food prices rose by 10½ percent during January–August, led by soybean, edible oils, and wheat prices, and have remained relatively immune to the recent financial turmoil. Expansion of biofuel production has increased demand for corn, soybeans, and edible oils. Although corn prices fell by 8½ percent during the first eight months of 2007—as a result of production growth of 15 percent relative to 2006 in response to high prices—they are still about 50 percent higher than in the same period in 2006. Wheat prices reached their highest level since the mid-1990s in mid-July, reflecting adverse weather amid historically low inventories. Meat prices rose by more than 8 percent, reflecting the increased cost of feed. Higher prices have been accompanied by generally tighter demand-supply balances, as manifested in declining stock-to-consumption ratios for corn, wheat, and meat, as well as the projected decline for soybeans. In contrast, sugar prices have weakened significantly over the past year, owing to the strength of supply in Brazil and limited export opportunities for Brazilian sugar-based ethanol.

Box 1.6. Making the Most of Biofuels

High oil prices in recent years, together with generous policy support, have led to a surge in biofuel use as a supplement to transportation fuels in advanced economies.[1] In 2005, the United States overtook Brazil to become the world's largest producer of ethanol, while the European Union is the largest biodiesel producer. This box examines this development, assessing whether the strong push toward biofuels production makes sense in a global context, from both an economic and an environmental perspective.

What Are the Costs and Benefits of Biofuels?

There are important disagreements among policymakers and analysts on the viability of biofuels as a supplement to transportation fuels. Part of the disagreement stems from the difficulty of measuring their net benefit. Average production costs and net greenhouse gas emissions can vary substantially according to location, labor intensity, feedstock prices, production scale, and available infrastructure. Moreover, rapid advances in some biofuels production technology are rendering early estimates obsolete.

Subject to these limitations, the table shows indicators of costs and benefits of producing a unit of biofuel. Only Brazilian ethanol derived from sugarcane is less costly to produce than gasoline and corn-based ethanol (about 15 percent and, in energy-equivalent terms, 25 percent less, respectively). Furthermore, sugarcane ethanol produces 91 percent fewer greenhouse gas emissions per kilometer traveled than gasoline. Soaring palm oil prices since 2006 have recently eliminated the relative cost advantage Malaysian biodiesel had compared with diesel, but it is still cheaper to produce than other types of biodiesel. According to some estimates, Jatropha-based biodiesel that is developed in India may be cheaper to produce than diesel, but some inefficiencies remain. All biofuels do less environmental damage than gasoline or diesel, but the relative benefits of corn- and wheat-based ethanol are small. Second-generation biofuels have substantially greater environmental benefits but are costlier to produce.[2]

In addition to these quantifiable aspects of biofuels' production, there are other, indirect, costs that would quickly escalate if first-generation biofuels were used more intensively than they are now. First, the growing use of grains and oils as feedstock in biofuel production could further boost food prices beyond current levels. Second, feedstock planting on a greater scale—particularly for biodiesel—would exert additional stress on already highly exploited land and water resources worldwide. A study by LMC International (2006) finds that raising biofuels production sufficiently to provide 5 percent of global fuel needs by 2015 would require expanding planted land acreage of all cultivated land by 15 percent. Finally, substantial fixed costs would be required to build the infrastructure and vehicles necessary for the distribution of ethanol on a larger scale.[3]

On the other hand, there are also potentially significant indirect benefits, particularly for commodity-producing developing countries. First, biofuels allow for the diversification of energy sources and thus lower a country's exposure to oil price volatility. They also hold the promise of contributing to rural development by creating jobs in the production of the feedstock and the relatively simple manufacture of biofuels. Given their negligible tailpipe

Note: The author of this box is Valerie Mercer-Blackman.

[1]Ethanol accounts for over 80 percent of global biofuel use; it can be blended with gasoline and is produced from corn, wheat, and sugar. Biodiesel can substitute for diesel fuel and is produced from edible oils (soy, palm, rapeseed) and other fats.

[2]Global biofuels research aimed at developing biofuels that use waste vegetable products as inputs instead of foods (known as second-generation biofuels) is ongoing, but is expected to take at least five years to become commercially viable.

[3]Conventional gasoline-powered vehicles can only use fuel with up to about 15 percent ethanol without costly alterations.

Costs and Benefits of Biofuels Production
(2007 or latest available figures)

Fuel	Cost Indicators: Cost of production per liter in dollars[1]	Cost Indicators: Share of feedstock cost in total production cost (in percent)	Indicators of Environmental Benefits: Life cycle analysis of GHG emissions[2] (in percent)	Indicators of Environmental Benefits: Net renewable energy creation relative to petroleum-based fuels[3]
Ethanol				
First generation				
Sugarcane-based Brazilian	0.23–0.29	37	–91	1.7
Corn-based U.S.	0.40	39–50	–18	1.22
Wheat-based European	0.59	68	–47	1.1
Sugar beet–based European	0.76	34	–35	1.7
Second generation				
Ethanol from cellulosic waste	0.71	90	–88	8.2
Gasoline in energy-value terms (U.S. market)[4]	0.34	73	0	1.0
Biodiesel				
First generation				
Palm oil Malaysian	0.54	80–85	–70 to –110[6]	5.1
Soybean oil-based, U.S.	0.66	80–85	–70	3.8
Rapeseed oil-based, Europe	0.87	80–85	–21 to –38	3.8
Second generation				
Jatropha-based, India[5]	0.40–0.65	80–85	–100 to –120	7.3 (e)
Diesel in energy-value terms (U.S. market)[4]	0.41	75	0	1.0

Sources: Kojima, Mitchell, and Ward (2007); Energy Charter Secretariat (2007); Larson (2006); Farrell and others (2006); USDA Foreign Agricultural Service (2007); U.S. Department of Agriculture (2006); Sheehan and others (1998); World Wildlife Fund (2007); Renewable Energy (2007); European Biomass Association; and IMF staff estimates.

[1]Costs are highly sensitive to feedstock prices. Average prices between 2006:Q1 and 2007:Q2 were used for estimates, where crude oil prices averaged about $65. Subsidies and transport costs are not considered in the cost estimates.

[2]Defined as the change in life cycle greenhouse gas (GHG) emissions per kilometer traveled by replacing fossil fuels with biofuels in conventional vehicles. Life cycle means that the emissions are measured over the production cycle of the respective fuel.

[3]Defined as the new energy created relative to the energy input in the production, distribution, and retailing of biofuels. Measured relative to the new energy created in the production of the respective fossil fuel (measured in megajouls/megajouls).

[4]Ethanol gives about a third less energy per liter than gasoline in conventional autos, while biodiesel gives about 8 percent less than diesel. Gasoline and diesel costs have been correspondingly adjusted downward to make them comparable with biofuels' costs.

[5]Jatropha is a drought-resistant oil-producing tree that does not compete with food for arable land and water. It is being developed in India and, to a lesser extent, in Africa and Central America as a biodiesel feedstock. (e) = estimate.

[6]This estimate assumes best practices in land management and does not account for potential emissions caused by rain forest deforestation suggested by some environmental groups.

emissions, they can help reduce local pollution from agents such as sulfur particles—particularly when vehicle fleets are old. Finally, a producer from a Kyoto-Protocol-signatory developing country can earn carbon credits through the clean development mechanism for every unit of renewable energy created (Appendix 1.2).

On balance, therefore, some biofuels are economically and environmentally beneficial at modest blends. Whether the net benefits are realized, and how they are distributed, depends crucially on the policy context under which they are instituted.

What Are the Likely Effects of the Current U.S. and EU Biofuels Policies?

A number of countries have adopted policies to promote domestic biofuels production in an effort to reduce their dependence on petroleum imports.[4] The most generous incentives

[4]In addition to the EU countries and the United States, tax benefits for consumers exist in Australia, Canada, Brazil, and India. Moreover, many countries have adopted targets—some mandatory—as well as research tax incentives for increasing biofuels production. Among them are Argentina, Canada, Brazil, India, Thailand, Malaysia, the Philippines, Colombia, China, and Japan.

Box 1.6 *(concluded)*

are offered by the United States and the EU countries.

- *In the United States,* blenders receive tax credits of $0.51 and $1, respectively, per gallon of ethanol and biodiesel sold against their income tax. There is also a $0.54 a gallon ($0.14 a liter) tariff on ethanol imports (none on biodiesel).[5] In several states, a 10 percent ethanol blend must be added to gasoline as an oxygenate (to make it burn more efficiently) as of May 2006; other states have additional tax incentives. At the federal level, the 2005 Energy Policy Act set a goal that renewable fuels reach 7.5 billion gallons by 2012 (about 10 percent of the total expected gasoline use). Most of the target is expected to be met by domestically produced corn-based ethanol. A bill that would almost quintuple the biofuels target, to 35 billion gallons by 2022, is under consideration.
- *In the European Union,* most countries offer fuel tax exemptions for biofuels (a large benefit, given high fuel taxes) and research subsidies. The average tariff on ethanol imports is $0.19 a liter, whereas biodiesel feedstocks have tariffs of up to 6.5 percent. Countries' official targets vary, but most converge to the EU current voluntary and somewhat ambitious target of biofuels comprising 5.75 percent of total fuels by 2010. The European Union also has a legally binding target of 10 percent by 2020.

To illustrate the effect of U.S. and EU policies, a hypothetical yet politically unlikely alternative scenario was simulated to 2012. The scenario illustrates the impact of removing biofuels tax credits and tariffs in the United States and European Union on global biofuels production and on net commodity exports. Many important interactions are ignored, and so the analysis should be considered as illustrative of the likely effects rather than as predictive. The baseline forecast for production and consumption volume of biofuels by country is based on the International Energy Agency's medium-term projections, whereas baseline commodity price projections are those of the IMF. Total demand for biofuels in 2012 and its distribution across countries is assumed to remain exactly the same under both scenarios, and still largely dictated by targets and mandates. Retail prices for mostly first-generation biofuels continue to be determined by domestic fuel prices as a result of their negligible share in total transportation fuels. Therefore, the only changes relative to baseline in the analysis are the geographical distribution of production, and feedstock prices.

Under this scenario, production using other, more expensive, feedstocks in the United States and European Union would become unprofitable and shut down as supply increasingly came from lower-cost importers (see figure). By 2012 ethanol would be produced largely by Brazil and other Latin American countries, and biodiesel by Asian countries (using Jatropha for the case of India).[6] There is also an indirect effect through commodity prices. The ensuing higher demand for sugarcane and palm oil raises their price by 15 percent and 20 percent, respectively, while lower demand for corn, wheat, soybean oil, and rapeseed oil (the main biofuels feedstocks in the United States and the European Union) reduces their prices by 10 percent

[5]However, the United States and European Union both have tariffs on the oils used as feedstock for biodiesel, which at the outset ironically puts domestic producers at a disadvantage relative to importers. This is offset by the $1.00 a gallon blender credit (in the United States) and tax exemptions for biodiesel (in Europe); these distortions have given rise to "subsidy arbitrage" across countries.

[6]In the alternative scenario, countries are assumed to produce ethanol and biodiesel in proportion to their expected 2007 sugarcane and palm oil exports, respectively, using U.S. Department of Agriculture (USDA) data. This is because the production technology is fairly simple. At projected consumption levels, there would not yet be significant constraints on land use. Moreover, the market for Indian Jatropha-based biodiesel is expected to open up in the alternative scenario, as it is already being developed but does not have a large enough impetus in the baseline scenario.

Net Gain in 2012 Biofuels Production and Net Exports over Trade—Selected Countries and Regions[1]
(Percent change relative to baseline forecast)

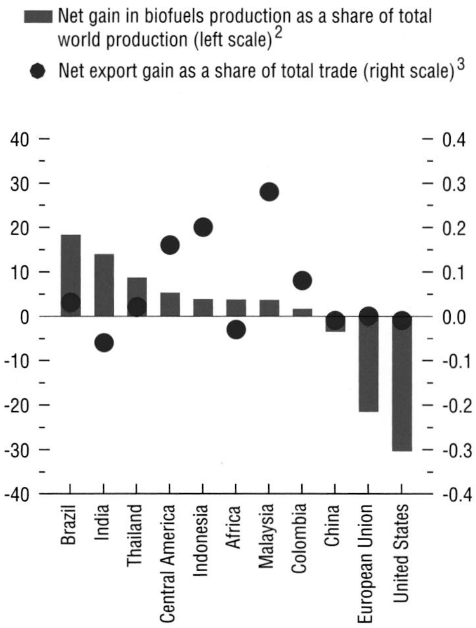

Sources: International Energy Agency; and IMF staff estimates.
[1]In the alternative scenario, ethanol is produced exclusively from sugarcane, and biodiesel from palm oil (jatropha in India).
[2]Refers to the percent change in ethanol and biodiesel produced in 2012 relative to the baseline forecast.
[3]Refers to the change in net exports in the alternative scenario relative to baseline divided by projected 2012 trade, where trade is defined as exports plus imports of goods (IMF estimates). In the alternative scenario, corn, wheat, and soybean oil prices fall by 10 percent, and sugar and palm oil prices rise by 15 percent and 20 percent, respectively.

relative to baseline.[7] Net exports as a share of total projected trade in goods in 2012 would generally improve for biofuels producers (less so for net grain exporters). They would worsen slightly for net palm oil importers such as India and Africa, and by a negligible amount in the United States and the European Union (less than 0.01 percent of total trade). All in all, overall average global production costs and greenhouse gas emissions would decline as more efficient producers came in. Fiscal costs in the United States and the European Union would also fall, although by a very small percentage of their respective budgets.[8]

How Could Biofuels Policies Improve?

The analysis in this box illustrates how current policies in the United States and the European Union are sustaining inefficient production patterns. This does not mean that biofuel use should not be promoted as a supplement to regular fuel in small amounts; biofuels have some useful environmental benefits relative to petroleum-based fuels. Certain policies could be implemented to enhance these net benefits.

- The first-best policy would be to allow free trade in biofuels while levying a carbon tax on all fuels to reflect emissions costs. This way, the environmental benefits of biofuels would be fully maximized (see Appendix 1.2).
- A blending mandate with a clear time limit could be justified for biofuels as a means to overcome the transitional fixed costs of moving to a new technology.
- Research and development of renewables should be promoted. There is a legitimate role for governments to fund promising research on such activities, given their public good character, especially if the environmental impact is not being adequately priced.

[7]Price changes are based on USDA forecasts and IMF staff calculations based on historical elasticities. Sugar is highly protected in the United States and European Union, so there is considerable room for expansion of its cultivation worldwide (including in the highly productive southcentral Brazil). Consequently, unlike corn in the United States, prices do not have to rise too dramatically to incite a supply response.

[8]The main direct and indirect fiscal costs in the United States and European Union stem from agricultural policies, which are assumed to remain unchanged in the baseline and alternative scenarios. See the discussion on costs in Box 5.2 of the September 2006 *World Economic Outlook.*

Figure 1.23. Sources of Demand and Prices of Selected Fuel-Related Food Items

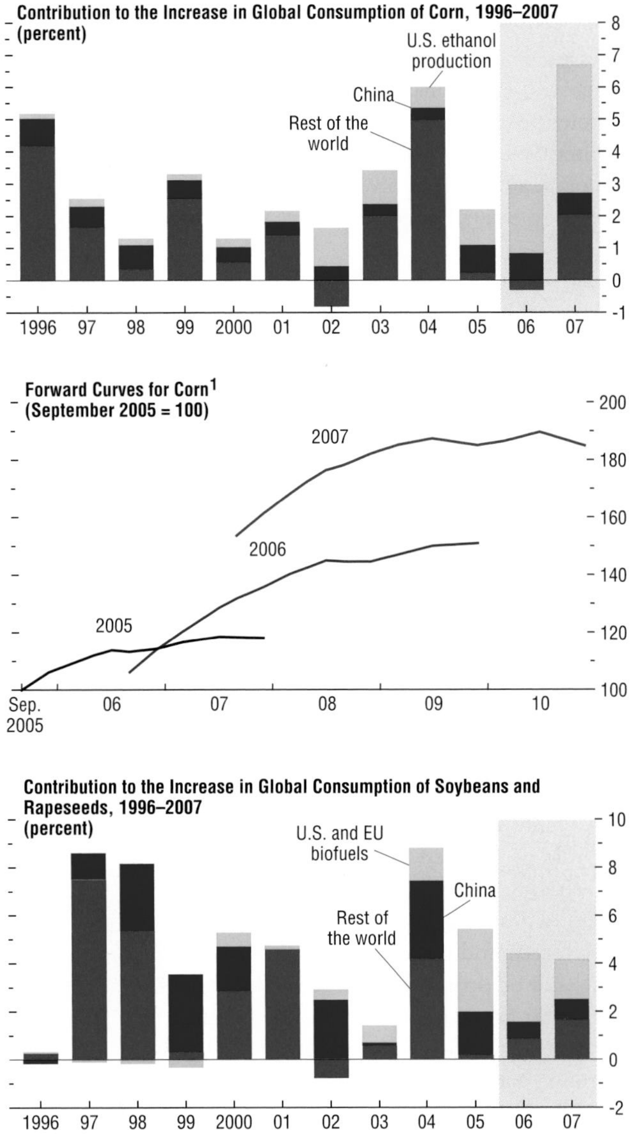

Sources: Bloomberg Financial Markets, LP; U.S. Department of Agriculture; and IMF staff estimates.
[1]Futures prices as of August 8 of each year.

Overall, the recent boom in food prices reflects a combination of factors:

- Strong demand for biofuel: higher ethanol production in the United States is projected to account for 60 percent of the global increase in corn consumption in 2007 (Figure 1.23, top panel). The impact on corn prices has been amplified by policy commitments to promote the use of ethanol further, which have pushed up futures prices (Figure 1.23, middle panel). According to the U.S. Department of Agriculture, the amount of corn used to produce ethanol in the United States is likely to increase from 14 percent of total U.S. production in 2005/06 to 30 percent by 2010/11. Similarly, increasing use of soybean and rapeseed oil in producing biofuels in the United States and the European Union has accounted for the bulk of demand growth for these crops in recent years (Figure 1.23, bottom panel). Strong expansion in biofuel production has also indirectly buoyed prices of other nonfuel-related food items by providing incentives for farmers to switch away from other crop plantings and by increasing the cost of livestock feed.
- Increased demand from emerging markets: China has been an important source of global food demand growth, accounting, for example, for 35–40 percent of the increase in global consumption of soybeans and meat. India's contribution to global demand for food, particularly meat, has also picked up recently. Although increased food consumption by emerging market economies has supported food prices, it is unlikely to have played a leading role in the recent surge, given that these economies' food demand began to increase strongly in the 1990s, long before the current run-up in prices.
- Adverse supply shocks: unfavorable weather conditions have reduced the global harvest for some food items. For example, the severe drought in Australia, a major wheat exporter, reduced the Australian wheat production by 60 percent in 2006. In addition, an outbreak of the "blue-ear disease" has significantly

reduced pork stocks in China and pushed up domestic meat prices by over 50 percent in August 2007 (year on year), raising annual food price inflation to over 16 percent.

Semiconductors. Global semiconductor sales revenue declined by more than 2 percent the first half of 2007 year on year, compared with growth of more than 9 percent during the same period in 2006. This reflected declining average selling prices, because of fierce competition in the microprocessor segment amid excess capacity in DRAM markets, fragile demand, and high inventories. Looking forward, this trend is expected to continue in the second half of 2007 and beyond, with the forecast for 2007 sales growth revised significantly downward to 1.8 percent from the 10 percent envisaged earlier.

Appendix 1.2. Climate Change: Economic Impact and Policy Responses

The authors of this appendix, including the boxes, are Ben Jones, Michael Keen, John Norregaard, and Jon Strand.

There is now a wide consensus that man-made climate change is occurring, will continue into the foreseeable future, and is likely to intensify (IPCC, 2007b).[8] The challenges for economic policy that this poses are substantial. Perhaps most fundamentally, climate change is a global externality: the social consequences of emitting the greenhouse gases (GHGs) that drive the process are not borne fully by those emitting the gases, but are shared across the world—with low-income countries likely to be most seriously affected. This raises significant problems of international coordination. These are compounded by the stock nature of the externality (harm arising not from the current flow but from the cumulated stock), which implies that much future damage reflects past emissions. Further conceptual and practical issues arise from the long lags in the process and from the considerable uncertainties that remain, including the risk (even if with relatively low probability) of extremely damaging events.

This appendix explores these challenges. It briefly lays out what is known about the science of climate change, to set the scene for a review of its economic impact. The appendix also discusses the economics of policy interventions to promote adaptation aimed at reducing the damage from climate change and of mitigation strategies to limit the atmospheric changes that cause it. These issues will be explored in greater depth in the April 2008 *World Economic Outlook.*

Outlining the Challenge

The main GHGs emitted by human activity are carbon dioxide (CO_2), contributing about 77 percent of total GHG emissions, and methane and nitrous oxide, each contributing about 14 and 8 percent, respectively.[9] The atmospheric concentration of GHGs (measured in CO_2 equivalents, CO_2e) has increased from about 300 parts per million (ppm) in 1750 to 430 ppm now, and is increasing by about 2 ppm a year.[10] The global average temperature increased by about 0.7°C between 1906 and 2005,[11] and existing GHG concentrations are expected to cause a further substantive temperature increase in the coming decades.[12]

[8]The Intergovernmental Panel on Climate Change (IPCC) was established by the United Nations Environment Programme (UNEP) and the World Meteorological Organisation to provide syntheses of research on climate change. There are, it should be noted, dissenting opinions on the relationships between human activities and increased atmospheric concentrations of greenhouse gases and between increased concentrations and observed and projected temperature changes: see, for example, Lindzen, Chou, and Hou (2001); and Carter and others (2007).

[9]Water vapor is the most abundant GHG, but human activities have only a small direct effect on its amount, and, unlike other GHGs, it has only a relatively short-lived climatic impact. References to GHGs henceforth exclude water vapor.

[10]Stern and others (2007).

[11]IPCC (2007b). The increase has not been monotonic, however.

[12]Model-based estimates are that even if atmospheric concentrations were held constant at 2000 levels, further warming of about 0.2°C would occur over the next 20 years (with a best estimate of cumulative warming of 0.6°C by the end of the century): IPCC (2007b).

Figure 1.24. Greenhouse Gas Emissions by Region

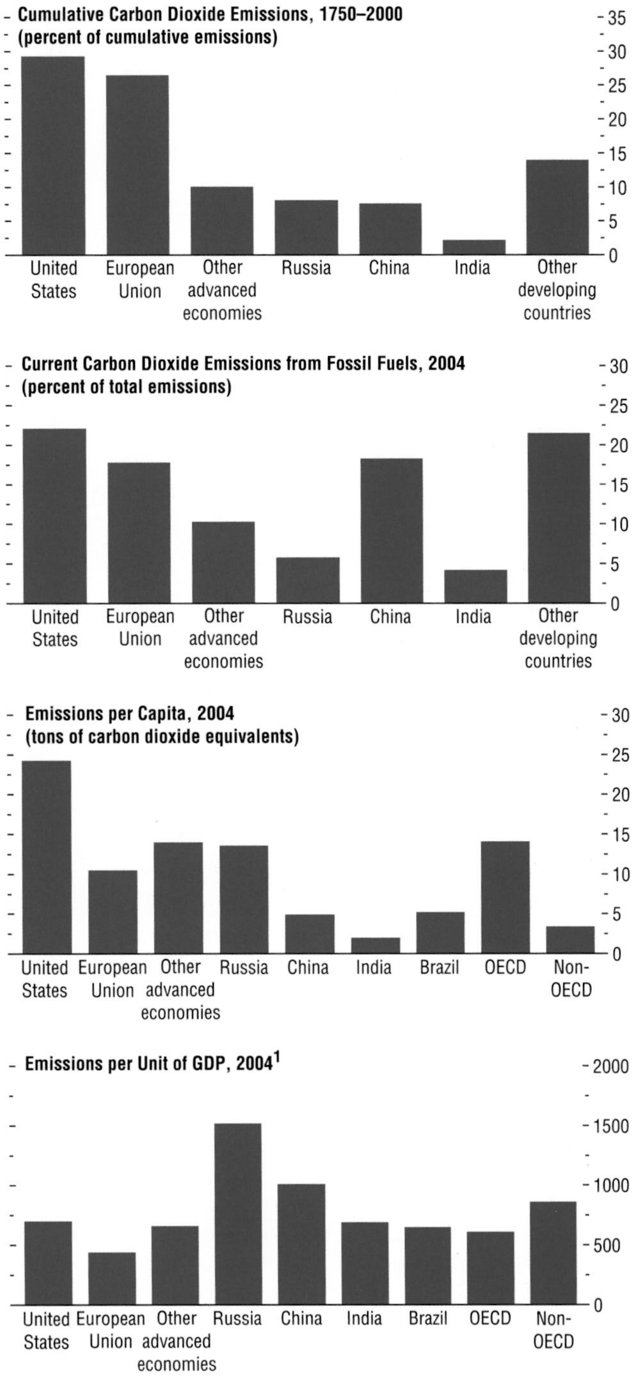

Sources: Baumert, Herzog, and Pershing (2005); and International Energy Agency (2006, 2007).

[1]Tons of carbon dioxide equivalents per million U.S. dollars, adjusted for purchasing power parity.

With no policy response, "business-as-usual" (BAU) emissions are projected by IPCC (2007b) to lead to average global temperature increases of between 1.1°C and 6.4°C (above preindustrial levels) by 2100.[13] As an indication of the potential significance of this projection, warming of 5°C would be roughly comparable to the difference between temperatures during the most recent ice age and today.

Although timing and geographical incidence are uncertain, a number of climatic effects are expected. The greatest increases in temperature are projected for the northern parts of North America, Europe, and Asia, with smaller (but still sizable) increases in tropical areas. The global pattern of rainfall is likely to change, with many already dry areas (including in Africa, Australia, South Asia, the Middle East, and the Mediterranean) expected to become even drier. There are further possible (but highly uncertain) effects on rainfall in many tropical zones (such as the Amazon region) as well as on seasonal patterns (of the Asian monsoon, for example), potentially affecting the sustainability of large human populations and critical natural resources. Flood risk is projected to increase by more intense rainfall and sea-level rise (from 0.2 to 0.6 meters in this century[14]—more with accelerated glacial melting). In addition, the frequency and/or severity of extreme weather events, including hurricanes, floods, heat waves, and droughts, are expected to increase, most seriously in Africa, Asia, and the Caribbean.

Beyond these effects, there may be "tipping points," which, if passed, would result in more dramatic and irreversible climate effects. These include the potential for rapid glacial

[13]IPCC (2007b) reports temperature projections for a series of scenarios, providing for each an upper and lower bound, with an 82 percent probability of temperature rise being between them: the range reported here is between the lowest and highest of these bounds. Underlying all these scenarios—and providing a simple, ready reckoner—is a common assumption that doubling CO_2 concentrations above preindustrial levels implies a 66 percent or higher chance of global average surface warming of 2°–4.5°C (with a best estimate of about 3°C).

[14]IPCC (2007a).

melting, reversal of the Gulf Stream (leading to dramatic climate change in northern Europe), and large-scale tundra thawing in Canada, China, and Russia, resulting in massive methane release. Although there is considerable uncertainty as to the precise location of these thresholds, many—such as irreversible melting of the Greenland ice sheet, contributing to several meters of sea-level rise—may lie within the range of temperature increases that are possible (even under some mitigation scenarios) in this century.

Sources of Greenhouse Gas Emissions

Climate change is caused by the accumulated *stock* of GHGs, while most policies to limit the risk can address only the flow of *emissions.*[15] The top two panels of Figure 1.24 show the sources of the stock of CO_2 (accumulated emissions since 1750) by region, together with annual emissions in 2004, both in percent of the total. Advanced economies account for about 75–80 percent of this stock, but a much greater proportion of current emissions stems from emerging market and developing countries (henceforth, "developing countries" includes emerging markets).

The bottom two panels in Figure 1.24 show that emissions per capita are about four times as high in OECD countries as elsewhere; relative to GDP, however, they are higher in developing countries. Reflecting this pattern of emission intensity, and prospective future growth, the share of developing countries in total emissions under BAU is expected to rise substantially from 2004 to 2050 (Figure 1.25).

Figure 1.25. Actual and Projected Fuel-Related Carbon Emissions Under "Business-as-Usual"
(Millions of tons of carbon per year)

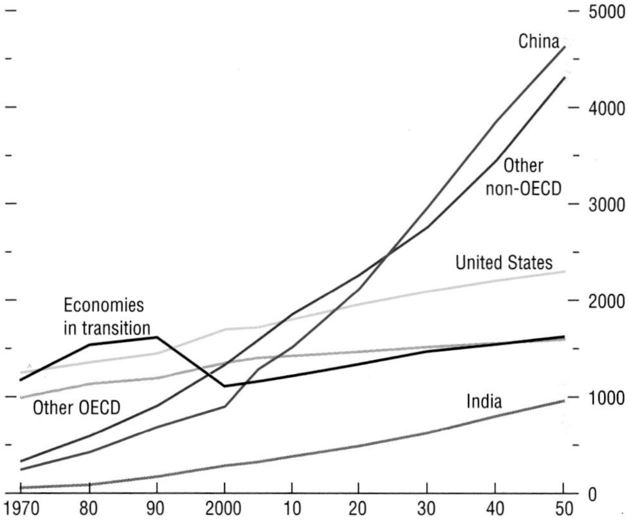

Sources: Baumert, Herzog, and Pershing (2005); and International Energy Agency (2007).

Macroeconomic and Fiscal Impact of Climate Change

The macroeconomic and fiscal impact of climate change is potentially substantial, and could include the following effects:

[15]There are geoengineering approaches that instead seek to limit the warming from a given atmospheric concentration by limiting incoming radiation from the sun: see, for instance, Schelling (2007).

- direct negative impact on output and productivity from long-term temperature change and more intense and/or frequent extreme weather events,[16] particularly in the agriculture, fisheries, and tourism sectors.[17] Agricultural effects are likely to differ by region, with reduced output in hotter (and generally poorer) regions, whereas northern (often more prosperous) areas may benefit from temperature increases of 1°–3°C;[18]
- costs from sea-level rise and increased severity of flooding. One study estimates that a one-meter increase would reduce GDP by close to 10 percent for several countries, including Bangladesh, Egypt, Mauritania, and Vietnam (Dasgupta and others, 2007). This degree of sea-level rise is some way above the consensus estimate, and the costs are likely to fall more than proportionately at lower levels of the rise, but the effects could be sizable. Some small island states, including Kiribati, the Maldives, the Marshall Islands, and Micronesia, are seen as particularly at risk, as are populations in coastal areas across a wider set of countries, including many rapidly expanding urban centers;[19]
- increased risk of widespread migration and conflict, resulting from long-term climate deterioration and greater damage from extreme weather events;
- deteriorating fiscal positions arising from weakening of traditional tax bases and/or increased expenditure on some aspects of mitigation and adaptation (as discussed below);
- more positively, there is potential revenue to be gained from mitigation schemes—a double dividend, with benefits to the public finances as well as to the environment, from reduced reliance on more distortionary taxes;
- costs arising from efforts to mitigate carbon emissions, including higher energy prices and increased investment, are becoming important in many (so far, largely the industrial) countries;
- balance of payments problems in some countries owing to reduced exports of goods and services (agricultural products, fish, and tourism) or increased need for food and other essential imports. Damage to transport infrastructure (ports and roads) may disrupt trade flows; and
- "nonmarket" effects associated with the loss of biodiversity and ecological systems, and the effects of climate change on human health and the quality of life.

Determining an effective response to climate change requires calibrating the nature, extent, and distribution of these effects. Climate scientists have naturally focused on the uncertainties associated with the complex nonlinear dynamics of the warming process. But there are also substantial uncertainties associated with estimating the associated economic and wider welfare effects. Key variables include rates of future population and productivity growth, especially the rate of convergence of economic growth across regions, the intensity of emissions through time and for different regions, and the rate of adoption of new technologies. Aggregating effects over time also requires a choice of discount rate, which, as discussed later, has been the focus of much recent discussion.

Several studies take on these challenges, using models that emphasize different linkages. The recent *Stern Review* (Stern and others, 2007) uses an "integrated" climate-macroeconomic model and a probabilistic welfare framework that included nonmarket effects as well as low-probability but very damaging extreme

[16]There is evidence of rapid increases in the economic costs of extreme events. For example, Munich Re (cited in "UN Finance Initiative CEO Briefing," 2006) reports that the infrastructure and some other costs of extreme weather events increased by an annual average of 6 percent between 1950 to 2005. A continuation of this trend would see expected losses of $800 billion by 2041, with peak-year losses of over $1 trillion.

[17]During the drought of 1991–92, to give just one example of the costliness of such events, agricultural output in Malawi fell by about 25 percent and GDP by 7 percent.

[18]However, this would depend largely on there being a strongly positive carbon fertilization effect, which remains uncertain.

[19]Twelve of the world's 16 megacities (more than 10 million inhabitants), all growing rapidly, are coastal ("UN Finance Initiative CEO Briefing," November 2006).

outcomes. Figure 1.26 shows the time path of expected damage (in percent of global GDP per capita) under Stern's three main scenarios, which differ in climate sensitivity and the valuation of nonmarket effects (such as reduced biodiversity). The shaded areas show the corresponding 90 percent confidence intervals. The projected potential losses rise substantially over time: the range of the central estimates is from 1 to 2 percent of GDP in 2050, 2 to 8 percent by 2100, and 5 to 14 percent by 2200.[20]

Other studies that assess the macroeconomic effects of climate change at different levels of warming include Mendelsohn and others (2000); Nordhaus and Boyer (2000); Hope (2006); and Tol (2005). Figure 1.27 presents some of these results alongside the central estimates of the three *Stern Review* scenarios referred to above. These results span a wide range of possible economic costs ranging from negligible (even positive at low levels of warming) to output losses of about 10 percent for average global warming of 6°C (possible, but unlikely by 2100, according to the IPCC).

Why are the estimates of the economic impact of climate change so different? The Mendelsohn analysis is based on relatively narrow sector coverage and assumes a relatively high capacity for adaptation. Nordhaus and Stern include estimates of wider nonmarket effects, and at higher levels of warming their results are driven largely by more extensive allowance for the risks and costs of catastrophic impacts and economic disruptions. Nordhaus, Stern, and Tol look beyond aggregate effects, recognizing that the poorest countries are likely to be affected hardest and earliest, generally owing to greater exposure to physical climate change and weaker socioeconomic resilience.[21]

Figure 1.26. Time Profile of Aggregate Damages from Climate Change
(Percent loss in GDP per capita)

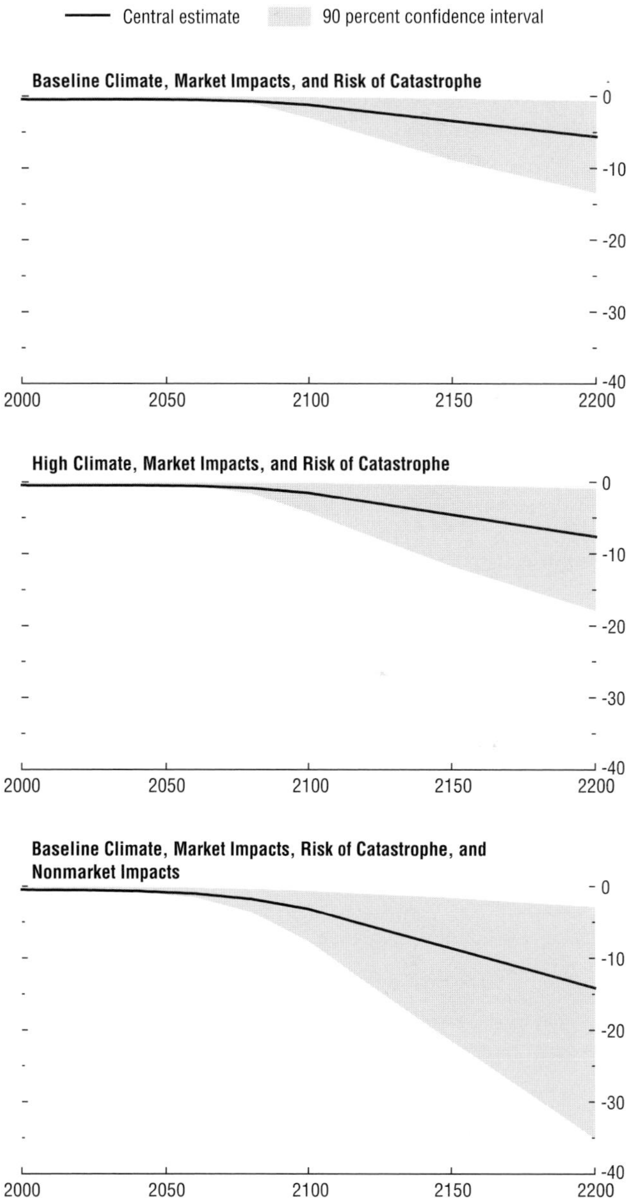

Source: Stern and others (2007).

[20]Rising to 20 percent in 2200 if account is taken of the disproportionately high burden of climate change borne by poorer parts of the world. This is not included in the scenarios of Figure 1.27.

[21]This often reflects lower income levels, greater economic dependency on agriculture and vulnerable ecosystems, food insecurity, and less-developed infrastructure and public services.

For example, at 2.5°C warming, Tol finds overall positive economic effects, reflecting output gains in rich countries, but he also finds (as does Nordhaus) GDP losses of about 4 percent in Africa. At higher levels of warming, similar distributional effects persist, although economic effects become universally negative (but with the range of uncertainty becoming wider). Allowing for these distributional aspects of climate change leads to larger effects than does focusing on total output. Differing choices of discount rate also powerfully affect the assessments that emerge from aggregating effects over time (see discussion below).

Figure 1.27. Mean per Capita GDP Losses at Different Levels of Warming

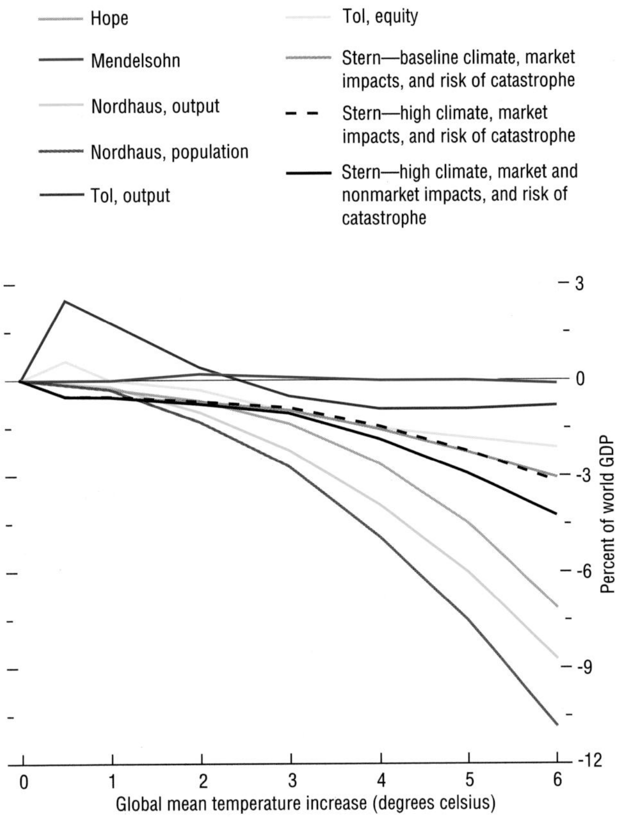

Sources: Hope (2006); and Stern and others (2007).

Policy Responses to Climate Change

Whereas views differ on the appropriate extent and urgency, there is broad consensus on the need for some action to reduce the high economic risks posed by expected levels of warming consistent with BAU projections. This can take the following two main forms, with action on both fronts now widely seen as needed:

- *adapting* behavior and investment to reduce the economic and social impact of climate change, for example, by constructing flood defenses in response to rising sea levels; and
- *mitigating* the extent of climate change by reducing GHG emissions through improved energy efficiency; carbon capture and storage; increased reliance on nuclear and renewable energy sources (wind, wave, tidal, geothermal and solar energy, hydroelectric power, and biomass for heat, electricity, and biofuels); and reduced deforestation.

While a number of policies bearing on climate change are in place (and some of them are discussed below), it is likely that their scale and coverage will need to be increased. The question of quite how much policy intervention would be desirable, however, has generated a lively debate, reflecting the differing assessments of the relative costs and benefits of action and inaction. The *Stern Review*, for example, argues for globally coordinated action to stabilize atmospheric concentration at about

450–550 ppm. This, the review proposes, would be achieved by substantial reduction in emissions (not merely relative to the large increase projected under BAU, but in absolute terms), beginning between 2020 and 2030 (Figure 1.28). This prescription reflects the *Stern Review's* conclusion that the potential costs of climate change under BAU are equivalent to a loss of between 5 and 14 percent of global per capita consumption, beginning now,[22] whereas the estimated mitigation costs consistent with stabilization (at around 500–550 ppm) are about 1 percent of GDP (the latter within a range of +/–3 percent).[23]

These results are heavily influenced by the use in the *Stern Review* of a low discount rate, reflecting a view that it is ethically inappropriate to attach less weight to the welfare of future generations than to our own. A low discount rate places a high weight on the benefits of mitigation, which largely come far in the future, relative to more immediate mitigation costs, thus warranting a high immediate mitigation effort. A fundamental problem in gaining broad support for mitigation policies is a lack of consensus on the appropriate discount rate to use in designing and evaluating alternative outcomes (Box 1.7).

Adaptation to Climate Change

Adaptation is the process by which adverse economic effects of climate change and variability are limited by changes in private behavior and public policies, reducing exposure to both extreme weather events and long-term climate deterioration. It encompasses two broad areas: (1) specific steps to reduce costs from climate change (such as planting more resilient crops or strengthening flood defenses) and (2) strengthening the capacity to respond to it (for example,

Figure 1.28. Greenhouse Gas Emission Paths Consistent with Alternative Concentration Targets

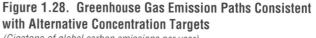

(Gigatons of global carbon emissions per year)

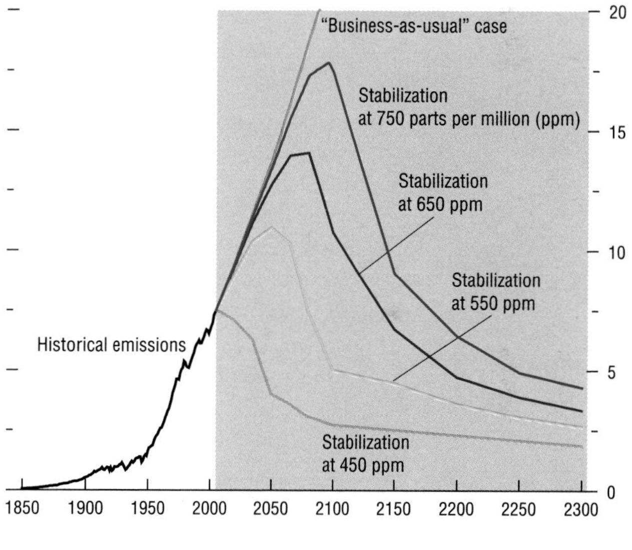

Source: Edmonds and others (2007).

[22]This rises to 20 percent when account is taken of the disproportionately high costs of climate change for poorer parts of the world. This is not taken into account in the scenarios of Figure 1.27.

[23]These cost assessments rise steeply (by a factor of three) with more aggressive abatement designed to stabilize emissions at 450 ppm.

Box 1.7. The Discounting Debate

The choice of discount rate is central to assessments regarding the timing and extent of many responses to climate change. Discussion has focused on the result that the appropriate rate to discount future consumption in a standard (Ramsey) growth models is given by

$$\rho \equiv \sigma + \eta . g,$$

where σ (the rate of pure time preference) is the rate at which future utility is discounted, g is the rate of growth of per capita consumption, and η is the elasticity of the marginal utility of consumption (which describes the rate at which society values the consumption of better-off generations relative to those less well off, and so captures aversion to inequality between the generations). The precise view taken of these parameters matters deeply because of the substantial mismatch in the timing of the costs incurred in limiting the damage from climate change (which would occur soon) and the benefits from doing so (occurring much later). The lower the discount rate, the greater the relative weight attached to future benefits, and so the stronger the case for action now.

Stern and others (2007) take $\sigma = 0.001$, $\eta = 1$, and $g = 1.013$, implying a discount rate ρ of 1.4 percent. The low value for σ reflects the view that equal weight should be given to the welfare of all current and future generations (with σ positive only to reflect the possibility of global catastrophe). Critics such as Nordhaus (2006) point out that this is not the only possible ethical position and does not appear to be a realistic description of many decisions people currently make (such as public investments in infrastructure). Reflecting the importance of the issue, raising the rate of pure time preference even to (a still modest) 1.5 reduces the range of expected damage costs from 5–20 percent to 1.4–6 percent of global consumption.

Views on the appropriate discount rate differ in other respects too. Dasgupta (2007) argues that a value of $\eta = 1$ is too low: it implies that a 10 percent reduction in the consumption of any future generation causes the same loss of social welfare as does a 10 percent reduction in current consumption—arguably, it should cause less of a loss, because growth means that future generations will have a higher level of consumption. Increasing the presumed value of this elasticity value from the Stern value of 1 to a modest 1.5 reduces the range of expected damage costs outlined above from 5–20 percent to 3–15 percent. As Stern and others (2007) point out, however, a greater aversion to inequality would also result in attaching more weight to the more immediate welfare losses in poorer countries, tending to strengthen the case for prompt action.

through improved weather forecasting or fuller planning for associated fiscal risks).

Significant adaptation is likely to occur through private market decisions, with no need for public policy interventions—one example being recent credit market innovations to create specialized weather derivatives and catastrophe bonds. Policy support is likely to be needed, however, in response to extensive market failures that impede efficient adaptation. These may include the following:

- an undersupply of information on the need and options for adapting to climate change, and on shifting patterns of variability;
- limited attention to the interests of future generations, leading to insufficient investment in reducing exposure to climate risk;
- credit market imperfections and insufficient access to capital, hampering adaptation that requires substantial investments, particularly in the poorest countries; and
- moral hazard problems that can arise when vulnerable households, firms, or governments are (or feel they are) protected against climate risks. For example, individuals may expect to be compensated for losses through insurance indemnities or government disaster responses, and governments

may anticipate foreign support if a natural disaster strikes.

Efficient adaptation will also require international coordination in the face of cross-border vulnerabilities, for example, to manage major river systems, such as the Ganges or the Nile, in response to new patterns of water stress. Similarly, governments may need to cooperate at a global or regional level to overcome the barriers to adaptation, for example, to improve regional weather forecasting or deliver disaster relief to migrating populations. Policy formation in this area is hampered, however, by a shortage of strong quantitative evidence on the likely scale of adaptation costs and benefits. One estimate puts the costs of adaptation to protect developing countries from climate change risks at between $3 billion and $37 billion each year—a very wide range (the higher figure being roughly ⅓ of total Official Development Assistance and concessional finance).

Mitigation of Greenhouse Gas Emissions

There are several feasible ways of achieving significant mitigation, and future technological advances are likely to further broaden the options. Putting them into effect, however, requires policies that are agreed on among major emitters and are in their own interests to actually implement. A crucial task for policymakers (including international institutions) is to design such policies, encourage and facilitate agreement on them, and ensure that they are implemented. A fundamental difficulty is overcoming the free-rider problem implied by the externalities involved: the harm caused by GHG emissions is felt by the entire global community, whereas the related costs of mitigation are borne fully by the emitter—so that each country may have a preference for mitigation by others rather than itself.[24]

[24]This does not mean there is no national incentive to mitigate: there may be local or national benefits from reducing local air pollution or energy insecurity. National and collective interests, however, remain potentially misaligned.

Core policy options for GHG mitigation are the following:

- taxes on GHG emissions, the first-best being a carbon tax applied uniformly across both emission sources and countries. Some existing tax instruments—notably, fuel excises—bear on emissions, but the approach is generally far from systematic;
- "cap-and-trade" schemes, which fix a total quantity of emissions while allowing trade in the associated rights to emit (such as the Emission Trading Scheme of the European Union, EU-ETS, discussed below);
- hybrid schemes, which combine elements of both tax and cap-and-trade schemes;
- energy efficiency standards for vehicles, buildings, and industrial processes, such as the U.S. Corporate Average Fuel Economy standards or the Japanese "top runner" program;
- subsidies to develop and deliver new and/or improved energy efficiency, energy storage, renewables, nuclear, and carbon sequestration technologies (such as expenditure in the European Union under the Framework Programme budget); and
- governance and incentive schemes to reduce deforestation and agricultural emissions (such as the payments to forest owners in Costa Rica and Mexico).

The first five of these are aimed at reducing fossil-fuel-related carbon emissions, which represent about 60 percent (and rising) of total GHG emissions. The last is relevant mainly in developing countries, where substantial scope for low-cost reductions in deforestation has been identified (see, for instance, Chomitz, 2007; and Grieg-Gran, 2006).

Policy should be designed to deliver mitigation efficiently, and with a distribution of the costs and benefits that is perceived as fair. In general, this requires policies that equalize marginal abatement costs across sectors and countries, with appropriate compensatory mechanisms to correct any undesirable distributional effects.

A key policy choice, likely to become central in discussions of climate policies beyond the

Kyoto Protocol period (2008–12), is between carbon taxes and cap-and-trade systems. Under ideal conditions—tradability and auctioning of emissions rights, perfect competition, and full certainty about abatement costs—a system of uniform GHG emission taxes is equivalent to a common cap-and-trade scheme: that is, they could lead to the same level of abatement, achieved at the same (minimized) total cost, and raise the same amount of revenue.

Under more realistic assumptions, however, the two instruments differ significantly. One key factor is uncertainty about the costs of reducing GHG emissions (see Box 1.8, based on Weitzman, 1974). In the case in which the marginal cost of reducing emissions increases only slowly with the level of reduction, while the marginal benefit from such abatement falls quickly, a cap-and-trade scheme is typically preferable to a tax scheme. Intuitively, a flat marginal cost curve means that surprises in the level of marginal costs will have a large impact on the realized level of mitigation under a tax scheme (compared with none, of course, under a cap-and-trade scheme) that, because of the steep marginal benefit curve, has a large impact on realized social benefit. By similar reasoning, a tax regime will tend to be preferable when the marginal cost curve is relatively steep and the damage function is relatively flat.

To see the implications of this in the climate change context, recall that the harm from global warming arises not from the flow but from the cumulative stock of emissions. This means that the expected damage function is relatively flat, because emissions over any relatively brief interval add relatively little to the accumulated GHG stock. This may lead to a preference for a tax instrument set over relatively short periods, but adjusted in its evolution over time by monitoring the associated emissions (and better informed, it is to be hoped, by increased understanding of the impact of alternative atmospheric concentrations).

Political economy considerations may also influence the choice between the two approaches. Proponents of cap-and-trade schemes argue that coordinating tax strategies across countries and jurisdictions is difficult. Moreover, caps can be allocated in a way that reduces the distributional consequences of mitigation and fosters interest in maintaining the scheme, thus reducing the risk that the scheme will be abandoned in the future. It may also be easier to explain a policy based explicitly on scientific guidance about appropriate emissions levels than a simple tax scheme. Others argue that taxation offers clearer and more stable signals about the future value of emissions reductions, or may be a more useful tool for importing countries faced with monopolistic supply,[25] while some trading schemes may be subject to substantial price volatility (price being more sensitive to demand shocks when total supply is fixed).

Hybrid schemes, combining features of both tax and cap-and-trade schemes, have been proposed to address some of the drawbacks of pure tax and cap-and-trade schemes. These involve, for example, selling extra permits at a fixed price so as to eliminate price spikes. However, these schemes have potential limitations, for example, by increasing the difficulty of devising mechanisms to link trading schemes.[26]

In practice, a controversial feature of cap-and-trade schemes has been a tendency for emissions rights to be partly or fully given away without charge to emitters, rather than auctioned to the highest bidders. This makes the introduction of the scheme more palatable to current emitters, but dissipates a potential source of government revenue. Under the EU-ETS (Box 1.9), at least 95 percent of emissions

[25]For example, Strand (forthcoming) shows that a tax has advantages for importers in giving a strategic advantage when fossil-fuel supply is monopolistic, since the exporter then tends to select a less aggressive pricing and/or supply strategy in the tax case. Put differently, a tax is in these circumstances a more effective device for importers to extract rent from exporters.

[26]McKibbin and Wilcoxen (2002), for instance, propose a scheme under which the short-run carbon price is determined by a cap-and-trade scheme with a ceiling price, but with no trading across countries.

Box 1.8. Taxes Versus Quantities Under Uncertainty (Weitzman, 1974)

The optimal level of emissions reduction is found where the marginal social benefit from such abatement (*MBA*) equals its marginal cost (*MCA*), which is at abatement level *A* in each panel of the figure. If it were known that the *MCA* curve would be exactly the unbroken line shown, that optimum could be achieved either by simply mandating abatement of *A* or by setting a tax on emissions at the level *T* (this being such that when the private sector equates the cost it would incur if it chose to reduce emissions slightly to the tax it would pay if it did not, it will abate exactly to *A*). The two instruments would thus be exactly equivalent. But suppose now that—after the policy instrument has been set and before it can be changed—abatement costs turn out to be higher, at *MCA′*. In this case, the ideal outcome would be the level of abatement at point *C*. With the tax fixed at *T*, however, abatement will actually be at *B*, to the left of *C*—that is, there will be too little abatement. Comparing the marginal benefits and costs associated with this policy error, there is an ex post welfare loss—relative to the ideal at *C*—given by the triangle *BDC*. The quantity restriction will also differ from the ex post optimum if marginal costs turn out to be *MCA′*: in this case, with quantity fixed at *A*, there will too much abatement, with a welfare loss given by the triangle *CEF*. Conversely, if marginal abatement costs turn out lower than expected, at *MCA″*, there is a welfare loss associated with too much abatement under the tax scheme, and a loss associated with too little abatement under the quantity scheme.

Comparing the upper and lower panels, whether the loss from the tax instrument is greater or less than that from quantity setting depends on the relative slopes of the *MBA* and *MCA* curves. Taxes are preferred in the lower panel, where *MBA* is relatively flat and *MCA* relatively steep.

Taxes Versus Quantities Under Uncertainty

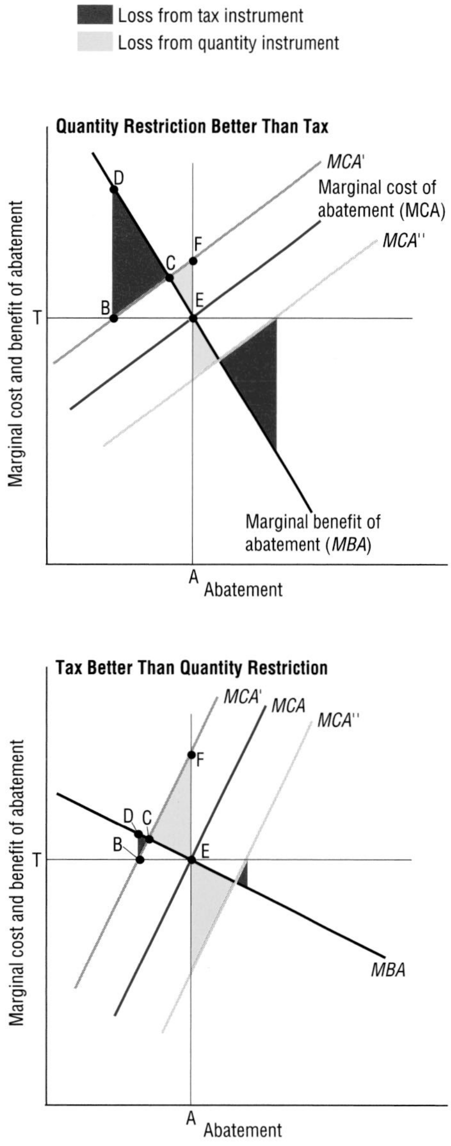

rights are currently given away to firms, based on their past emissions. GHG emissions taxes and plans to auction emissions rights faced strong resistance by powerful industry groups in the European Union, while cap-and-trade schemes with only limited auctioning met with far less resistance.

Efficiency standards are generally inferior to well-designed tax and cap-and-trade schemes, because they do not address the underpricing of

Box 1.9. Experience with Emissions Trading in the European Union

The EU-ETS, initiated in 2005, is a central policy instrument to meet the EU greenhouse gas emissions goals under the Kyoto Protocol. It aims at capping overall carbon dioxide emissions from electric power utilities and major industrial emitters representing about 40 percent of total EU carbon emissions. Emissions rights for Phases I and II (2005–07 and 2008–12) are allocated to individual installations, which are free to trade with other participants in the event of either surplus or insufficient permits to cover actual emissions levels.

The scheme is intended to promote economic efficiency in implementing a given overall emissions reduction, by enabling participating firms to reduce their emissions at the lowest marginal abatement costs. A number of design flaws, however, have reduced the scheme's effectiveness.

First, the total allocation has turned out to exceed actual emissions in the initial 2005–07 period, reflecting, among other things, informational difficulties and reduced demand for energy after the sharp run-up in oil prices. The current cap-setting process for Phase II (2008–12) is expected to generate some, rather limited, market scarcity, with emissions reduction in the region of 2.4 percent compared with BAU expected in 2010 (see Capoor and Ambrosi, 2007).

Second, the provision of free allocations to participating installations has created market expectations that free allocations in the future will be based on current emissions, thus limiting the current incentive to abate. Rigid exit and entry rules (whereby exiting units lose their free allocations, and new entering units in most cases obtain fully free allocations) add to these problems.

The EU-ETS is a pioneering example of coordinated international action on climate change. Progress is being made to improve its design and operations, with increased harmonization of allocations, monitoring, and compliance methodologies. Further reform is needed, however, to improve its economic efficiency, for example, in regard to the rules for allocating emissions rights, in total and within and across participating countries. Community-based, rather than national, cap-setting is another issue for consideration for the promotion of a more harmonized scheme.

emissions, cannot cater for variance in abatement costs at the firm level, and forgo potential revenue. Standards can, however, be useful when individuals are shortsighted in evaluating returns on investments. In addition, their use may be appropriate in markets where assessment of alternatives is constrained by substantial complexity or high transaction costs relative to the potential benefits, for example, in consumer electronics markets.[27]

The introduction of realistic carbon pricing, whether through tax or cap-and-trade schemes, can do much to provide appropriate incentives to develop alternative energy sources. Public subsidies to develop new, immature, or strategically important energy efficiency, energy storage, renewables, nuclear, and carbon sequestration technologies may nevertheless be a useful supplement to emissions taxes and cap-and-trade schemes if there are significant positive externalities related to their development and production. Private developers of new technologies may not reap the full social returns from developing new technologies (perhaps because they can be easily copied), which leads to underinvestment in the absence of subsidies. However, large-scale subsidies of this kind also have substantial drawbacks: they reduce the cost of production and thus may increase polluting output; in addition, tax-based incentives not only forgo revenue

[27]Spending on federal energy efficiency appliance standards in the United States of about $2 per household since 1978 is estimated to have delivered present-value savings of $1,270 per household (Meyers and others, 2002).

directly but can also create avoidance opportunities; finally, the correct levels of subsidy are difficult to determine. Given the revenue at stake, monitoring the cost and effectiveness of such subsidies is likely to become increasingly important.

Problems of Policy Coordination and Implementation

A core challenge is to reach agreement among major emitting countries on the implementation of policies to limit future GHG emissions. This is difficult for the following reasons:

- The negative externalities related to GHG emissions are global, so that countries' self-interest may not lead them to mitigate as much as their collective interest requires.
- Although abatement must start soon to have any significant future impact, the bulk of the prospective benefits arise relatively far in the future. Voters and policymakers may thus give too little emphasis to future benefits from current abatement.
- The considerable uncertainty that remains, including in relation to very damaging but low-probability events, calls for prudence—but may also imply some value, to a degree, in limiting costly actions now (recognizing that they might divert resources from alternative uses that have clear immediate benefit) while learning more about the problem and possible solutions.
- The potential future damage from climate change reflects past emissions, almost 80 percent of which originated in advanced economies (see Figure 1.24). This would suggest that they bear greater responsibility for the climate problem. On the other hand, however, more than half of current total emissions, and a much larger share of future emissions, are expected to be generated by less-advanced economies (see Figure 1.25).
- The effects of climate change are unevenly distributed across countries. Many tropical countries (most of which are poor) will sustain large losses from further global warming. Some currently cool countries (including Canada, Russia, and northern Europe) can instead expect to lose little, or even gain, from moderate climate change.
- Countries naturally fear disadvantaging their producers in world markets by raising energy prices unless their competitors do likewise.

Initial steps toward international cooperation—most notably the Kyoto Protocol—have had only limited success. Figure 1.29 shows emissions for major industrial countries effectively subject to emissions limitations under the Kyoto Protocol, both in 2004 and as projected for 2012 (when the Kyoto Protocol expires), together with their Kyoto Protocol targets. The United States, also included here, was assigned an emissions reduction under the Kyoto Protocol but did not ratify the Protocol and is thus not committed to it. Several ratifying countries are currently some way from achieving their commitments. The punishment for any such failure—tighter targets under any future agreement—is small and perhaps not credible.[28]

Early agreement on extension and development of mechanisms beyond the end of the Kyoto Protocol is critical, not least given the long lead time for many energy investments and the consequent need for reducing uncertainty about likely future carbon prices. It will also be a major policy challenge to broaden the coverage of a new mechanism to include major emitters in emerging market and low-income countries.

Some efforts to limit emissions currently undertaken by parties not bound by the Kyoto Protocol, notably Australia and the United States, have supported the development and diffusion of new technologies designed to promote energy efficiency. In addition, some non–Annex I countries have made efforts to reform energy pricing and reduce deforestation in order to increase energy security and reduce

[28]The punishment for not fulfilling emissions reductions committed to under the Kyoto Protocol is that quotas will be reduced by 130 percent of current shortfall in future (as yet unspecified) implementation periods.

Figure 1.29. Greenhouse Gas Emissions, Kyoto Targets, and Predicted Emissions
(Millions of tons of carbon dioxide)

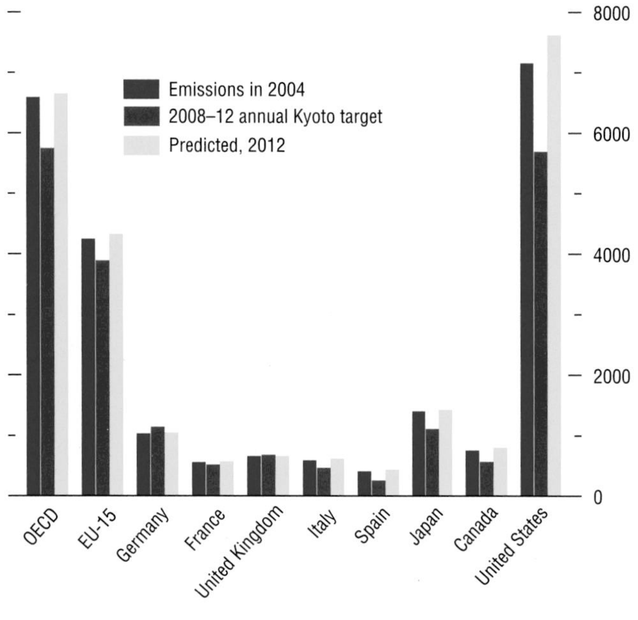

Sources: Capoor and Ambrosi (2007); and International Energy Agency (2006).

local air pollution. In each case, there have been important cobenefits in constraining the growth of GHG emissions.

A range of wider international frameworks and processes is being developed, which should help to reduce GHG emissions. These include collaborative efforts to promote technology cooperation, such as the Asia-Pacific Partnership, together with a joint project between the European Union and China designed to establish a carbon storage demonstration project, potentially an important precursor to more widescale diffusion of such technology. Finally, international cooperation in relation to the design and implementation of energy efficiency standards is raising the potential cost-effectiveness of energy savings across countries and strengthening incentives to innovate throughout the supply chain.

Concluding Remarks

Climate change resulting from man-made increases in atmospheric GHG concentrations presents a serious challenge to human welfare. Understanding of both the issue and potential policy responses has developed rapidly in recent years, but much remains to be learned, including the nature, extent, and likelihood of the macroeconomic and fiscal effects from climate change and alternative responses to it.

Dealing effectively with climate change requires international cooperation to manage risks and associated economic costs related to necessary reductions in GHG emissions and development of adaptive capacity. Existing cooperative mechanisms will need to be extended significantly in breadth, depth, and efficiency, while paying due regard to the need for equitable sharing of the burden, in order to meet this challenge.

References

Amihud, Yakov, 2002, "Illiquidity and Stock Returns: Cross-Section and Time-Series Effects, *Journal of Financial Markets*, Vol. 5, No. 1, pp. 31–56.

Baumert, Kevin, Timothy Herzog, and Jonathan Pershing, 2005, *Navigating the Numbers: Greenhouse Gas Data and International Climate Policy* (Washington: World Resources Institute).

Bayoumi, Tamim, and Andrew Swiston, 2007, "Foreign Entanglements: Estimating the Source and Size of Spillovers Across Industrial Countries," IMF Working Paper 07/182 (Washington: International Monetary Fund).

Capoor, Karan, and Philippe Ambrosi, 2007, "Carbon Call: State and Trends of the Carbon Market," seminar for the Center for Economic and Environmental Partnership, Inc., March 14.

Carter, Robert M., C.R. de Freitas, Indur M. Goklany, David Holland, and Richard S. Lindzen, 2007, "Climate Change: Climate Science and the Stern Review," *World Economics,* Vol. 8, No. 2, pp. 161–82.

Chomitz, Kenneth M., 2007, *At Loggerheads? Agricultural Expansion, Poverty Reduction, and Environment in the Tropical Forests* (Washington: World Bank).

Dasgupta, Partha, 2007, "Commentary: The Stern Review's Economics of Climate Change," *National Institute Economic Review,* Vol. 199 (January), pp. 4–7.

Dasgupta, Susmita, Benoit Laplante, Craig Meisner, David Wheeler, and Jianping Yan, 2007, "The Impact of Sea Level Rise on Developing Countries: A Comparative Analysis," Working Paper No. 4136 (Washington: World Bank).

Edmonds, James A., and others, 2007, "Global Energy Technology Strategy: Addressing Climate Change," Phase 2 findings from an international public-private sponsored research program (Battelle Memorial Institute).

Energy Charter Secretariat, 2007, *Driving Without Petroleum? A Comparative Guide to Biofuels, Gas-to-Liquids and Coal-to-Liquids as Fuels for Transportation* (Brussels).

European Biomass Industry Association, 2007, "Biodiesel." Available via the Internet: www.eubia.org.

Farrell, Alexander E., Richard J. Plevin, Brian T. Turner, Andrew D. Jones, Michael O'Hare, and Daniel M. Kammen, 2006, "Ethanol Can Contribute to Energy and Environmental Goals," *Science,* Vol. 311 (January 27), pp. 506–08.

Faruqee, Hamid, Douglas Laxton, Dirk Muir, and Paolo Pesenti, 2007, "Smooth Landing or Crash? Model-Based Scenarios of Global Current Account Rebalancing," in *G7 Current Account Imbalances: Sustainability and Adjustment,* ed. by Richard Clarida (Chicago: University of Chicago Press).

Grieg-Gran, Maryanne, 2006, "The Cost of Avoiding Deforestation," report prepared for the *Stern Review of the Economics of Climate Change* (London: International Institute for Environment and Development).

Hasbrouck, Joel, and Robert A. Schwartz, 1988, "Liquidity and Execution Costs in Equity Markets," *Journal of Portfolio Management* (Spring), pp. 10–16.

Hope, Chris, 2006, "The Marginal Impact of CO_2 from PAGE2002: An Integrated Assessment Model Incorporating the IPCC's Five Reasons for Concern," *Integrated Assessment Journal,* Vol. 6, No. 1, pp. 19–56.

Intergovernmental Panel on Climate Change (IPCC), 2007a, "Climate Change 2007: Impacts, Adaptation, and Vulnerability," Working Group II contribution to the *IPCC Fourth Assessment Report of the Intergovernmental Panel on Climate Change: Summary for Policymakers* (Geneva: IPCC).

———, 2007b, "Climate Change 2007: The Physical Science Basis," Working Group I contribution to the *IPCC Fourth Assessment Report of the Intergovernmental Panel on Climate Change: Summary for Policymakers* (Geneva: IPCC).

International Energy Agency (IEA), 2006, "CO_2 Emissions from Fossil Fuel Combustion On-Line Database," Version 2005–06 (Paris: OECD/IEA).

———, 2007, *International Energy Outlook* (Paris: OECD/IEA).

International Monetary Fund, 2006, "Methodology for CGER Exchange Rate Assessments," paper by the Research Department (Washington). Available via the Internet: www.imf.org/external/np/pp/eng/2006/110806.pdf.

Kojima, Masami, Donald Mitchell, and William Ward, 2007, "Considering Trade Policies for Liquid Biofuels," Renewable Energy Special Report No. 004/07, World Bank Energy Sector Management Assistance Program (Washington: World Bank).

Lane, Philip R., and Gian Maria Milesi-Ferretti, 2006, "The External Wealth of Nations Mark II: Revised and Extended Estimates of Foreign Assets and Liabilities, 1970–2004," IMF Working Paper 06/69 (Washington: International Monetary Fund).

Larson, Eric D., 2006, "A Review of Life-Cycle Analysis Studies on Liquid Biofuel Systems for the Transport Sector," *Energy for Sustainable Development,* Vol. X, No. 2 (June), pp. 109–26.

Lindzen, Richard S., Ming-Dah Chou, and Arthur Y. Hou, 2001, "Does the Earth Have an Adaptive Infrared Iris?" *Bulletin of the American Meteorological Society*, Vol. 82, No. 3, pp. 417–32.

LMC International, 2006, *A Strategic Assessment of the Impact of Biofuel Demand for Agricultural Commodities* (London: LMC International).

Longstaff, Francis A., 2001, "Optimal Portfolio Choice and the Valuation of Illiquid Securities," *The Review of Financial Studies*, Vol. 14, No. 2, pp. 407–31.

McKibbin, Warwick J., and Peter J. Wilcoxen, 2002, *Climate Change Policy after Kyoto: Blueprint for a Realistic Approach* (Washington: Brookings Institution Press).

Mendelsohn, Robert, Wendy Morrison, Michael E. Schlesinger, and Natalia Andronova, 2000, "Country-Specific Market Impacts of Climate Change," *Climate Change*, Vol. 45 (June), pp. 553–69.

Meyers, Stephen, James McMahon, Michael McNeil, and Xiaomin Liu, 2002, "Realized and Prospective Impacts of U.S. Energy Efficiency Standards for Residential Appliances," Lawrence Berkeley National Laboratory Report No. LBNL-49504 (Berkeley, California: University of California).

Nordhaus, William D., 2006, "The 'Stern Review' on the Economics of Climate Change," NBER Working Paper No. 12741 (Cambridge, Massachusetts: National Bureau of Economic Research).

———, and Joseph Boyer, 2000, *Warming the World: Economic Models of Global Warming* (Cambridge, Massachusetts: MIT Press).

Organization of Petroleum Exporting Countries, 2007, *World Oil Outlook* (Vienna).

Renewable Energy, 2007, "Jatropha for Biodiesel Figures." Available via the Internet: www.reuk.co.uk.

Schelling, Thomas C., 2007, "Climate Change: The Uncertainties, the Certainties, and What They Imply About Action," *The Economists' Voice*, Vol. 4, No. 3, pp. 1–5.

Sheehan, John, Vince Camobreco, James Duffield, Michael Gabroski, and Housein Shapouri, 1998, *An Overview of Biodiesel and Petroleum Diesel Life Cycles* (Golden, Colorado: National Renewable Energy Laboratories).

Stern, Nicholas, and others, 2007, *The Economics of Climate Change: The Stern Review* (London: HM Treasury).

Strand, Jon, forthcoming, "Importer and Producer Petroleum Taxation: A Geo-Political Model," IMF Working Paper (Washington: International Monetary Fund).

Tol, Richard S.J., 2005, "The Marginal Damage Costs of Carbon Dioxide Emissions: An Assessment of the Uncertainties," *Energy Policy*, Vol. 33 (November), pp. 2064–74.

U.S. Department of Agriculture, 2006, "The Economic Feasibility of Ethanol Production from Sugar in the United States," July (Washington).

———, Foreign Agricultural Service, 2007, "India Bio-Fuels Annual 2007," Global Agriculture Information Network Report No. IN7047 (Washington).

Warnock, Francis E., and Veronica Cacdac Warnock, 2006, "International Capital Flows and U.S. Interest Rates," NBER Working Paper No. 12560 (Cambridge, Massachusetts: National Bureau of Economic Research).

Weitzman, Martin L., 1974, "Prices vs. Quantities," *The Review of Economic Studies*, Vol. 41 (October), pp. 477–91.

World Wildlife Fund (WWF), 2007, *Rain Forest for Biodiesel? Ecological Effects of Using Palm Oil as a Source of Energy* (Frankfurt: WWF Germany).

CHAPTER 2 COUNTRY AND REGIONAL PERSPECTIVES

Against the background of the global outlook outlined in Chapter 1, this chapter analyzes prospects and policy issues in the major advanced economies and in the main regional groupings of emerging market and developing countries. A consistent theme is that policymakers around the world face the immediate challenge of maintaining strong noninflationary growth in the face of recent turbulent global financial conditions. They also need to continue to push forward with reforms necessary to ensure continued strong growth in the future.

United States and Canada: Uncertainties About the U.S. Outlook Have Risen

Following a weak start to 2007, the U.S. economy rebounded strongly in the second quarter, growing by 3.8 percent (annualized rate). Net exports and business investment provided a significant boost to growth, although private consumption growth slowed markedly in the face of rising gasoline prices, and residential investment continued to exert a significant drag on growth (Figure 2.1). Recent data, however, have painted a weaker picture of the U.S. economy going forward, reflecting in part the impact of the recent turmoil in financial markets. While personal consumption spending, employment, and nonresidential construction data have been solid, housing market indicators have been very weak, and consumer sentiment, the ISM business surveys, and durable goods orders all declined in the most recent readings.

Against this background, the projection for U.S. growth in 2007 as a whole is unchanged at 1.9 percent, but has been lowered by 0.9 percentage point (relative to the July *World Economic Outlook Update*) to 1.9 percent in 2008 (Table 2.1). Ongoing difficulties in the mortgage market are expected to extend the decline in residential investment, while house price declines are likely to encourage households to

Figure 2.1. United States: Indicators of Investment

(Percent change from a year earlier unless otherwise stated)

Weak investment spending, particularly in the residential sector, has been at the heart of the U.S. economic slowdown. Against the background of recent financial market turbulence, the investment outlook remains very uncertain.

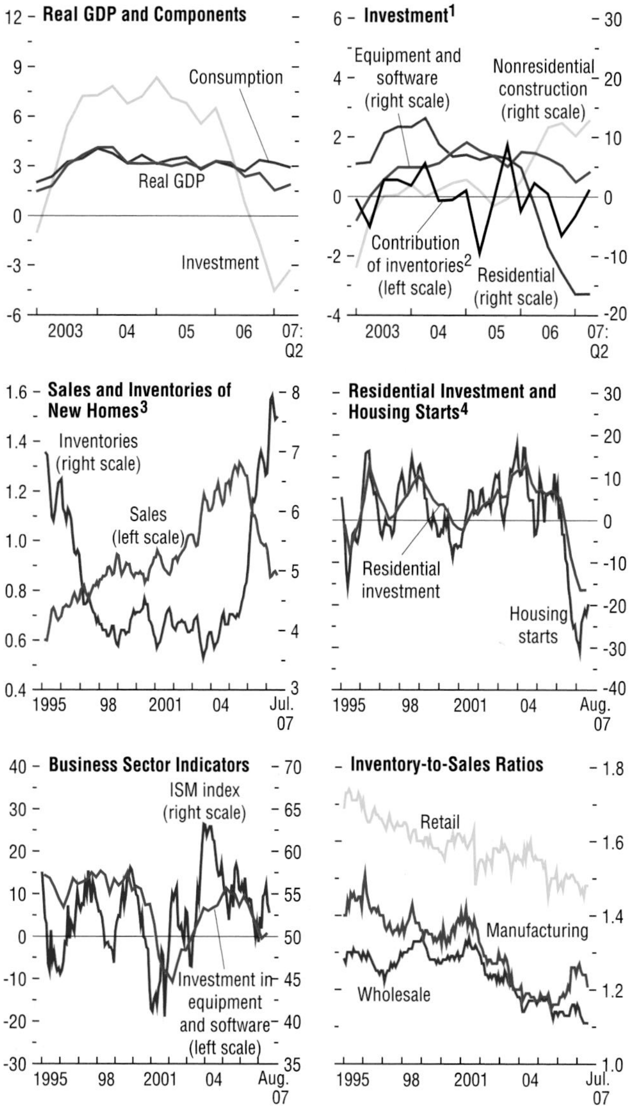

Sources: Bloomberg Financial Markets, LP; Haver Analytics; and IMF staff calculations.
[1]Investment in equipment and software, residential investment, and nonresidential construction measured as percent change from four quarters earlier.
[2]Contribution of change in real private inventories to GDP growth.
[3]Three-month moving averages of million units of sales, and months of supplies of inventories.
[4]Private housing starts measured as three-month moving averages of percent change from a year earlier.

Table 2.1. Advanced Economies: Real GDP, Consumer Prices, and Unemployment
(Annual percent change and percent of labor force)

	Real GDP				Consumer Prices				Unemployment			
	2005	2006	2007	2008	2005	2006	2007	2008	2005	2006	2007	2008
Advanced economies	**2.5**	**2.9**	**2.5**	**2.2**	**2.3**	**2.3**	**2.1**	**2.0**	**6.0**	**5.6**	**5.3**	**5.5**
United States	3.1	2.9	1.9	1.9	3.4	3.2	2.7	2.3	5.1	4.6	4.7	5.7
Euro area[1]	1.5	2.8	2.5	2.1	2.2	2.2	2.0	2.0	8.6	7.8	6.9	6.8
Germany	0.8	2.9	2.4	2.0	1.9	1.8	2.1	1.8	9.1	8.1	6.5	6.3
France	1.7	2.0	1.9	2.0	1.9	1.9	1.6	1.8	9.7	9.5	8.6	8.0
Italy	0.1	1.9	1.7	1.3	2.2	2.2	1.9	1.9	7.7	6.8	6.5	6.5
Spain	3.6	3.9	3.7	2.7	3.4	3.6	2.5	2.8	9.2	8.5	8.1	8.2
Netherlands	1.5	3.0	2.6	2.5	1.5	1.7	2.0	2.2	4.7	3.9	3.2	3.1
Belgium	1.4	3.0	2.6	1.9	2.5	2.3	1.8	1.8	8.4	8.2	7.6	7.6
Austria	2.0	3.3	3.3	2.5	2.1	1.7	1.9	1.9	5.2	4.8	4.3	4.2
Finland	2.9	5.0	4.3	3.0	0.8	1.3	1.5	1.8	8.4	7.7	6.7	6.5
Greece	3.7	4.3	3.9	3.6	3.5	3.3	3.0	3.2	9.9	8.9	8.5	8.5
Portugal	0.5	1.3	1.8	1.8	2.1	3.0	2.5	2.4	7.6	7.7	7.4	7.1
Ireland	5.9	5.7	4.6	3.0	2.2	2.7	2.5	2.1	4.4	4.4	4.7	5.5
Luxembourg	4.0	6.2	5.4	4.2	2.5	2.7	2.2	2.2	4.2	4.4	4.4	4.6
Slovenia	4.1	5.7	5.4	3.8	2.5	2.5	3.2	3.1	6.5	6.0	6.0	6.0
Japan	1.9	2.2	2.0	1.7	–0.3	0.3	—	0.5	4.4	4.1	4.0	4.0
United Kingdom[1]	1.8	2.8	3.1	2.3	2.0	2.3	2.4	2.0	4.8	5.4	5.4	5.4
Canada	3.1	2.8	2.5	2.3	2.2	2.0	2.2	1.9	6.8	6.3	6.1	6.2
Korea	4.2	5.0	4.8	4.6	2.8	2.2	2.6	2.7	3.7	3.5	3.3	3.1
Australia	2.8	2.7	4.4	3.8	2.7	3.5	2.3	2.8	5.1	4.8	4.4	4.3
Taiwan Province of China	4.1	4.7	4.1	3.8	2.3	0.6	1.2	1.5	4.1	3.9	3.9	4.0
Sweden	2.9	4.2	3.6	2.8	0.8	1.5	1.9	2.0	5.8	4.8	5.5	5.0
Switzerland	2.4	3.2	2.4	1.6	1.2	1.0	1.0	1.0	3.4	3.3	2.4	2.7
Hong Kong SAR	7.5	6.9	5.7	4.7	0.9	2.0	2.0	3.2	5.7	4.8	4.2	4.0
Denmark	3.1	3.5	1.9	1.5	1.8	1.9	1.9	2.0	5.7	4.5	3.6	3.9
Norway	2.7	2.8	3.5	3.8	1.6	2.3	0.8	2.5	4.6	3.4	2.8	2.9
Israel	5.3	5.2	5.1	3.8	1.3	2.1	0.5	2.5	9.0	8.4	7.5	7.2
Singapore	6.6	7.9	7.5	5.8	0.5	1.0	1.7	1.7	3.1	2.7	2.6	2.6
New Zealand[2]	2.7	1.6	2.8	2.3	3.0	3.4	2.4	2.7	3.7	3.8	3.8	4.3
Cyprus	3.9	3.8	3.8	3.7	2.6	2.5	2.0	2.4	5.3	4.5	4.0	4.0
Iceland	7.2	2.6	2.1	–0.1	4.0	6.8	4.8	3.3	2.1	1.3	2.0	3.2
Memorandum												
Major advanced economies	2.3	2.6	2.1	1.9	2.3	2.3	2.1	1.9	6.0	5.6	5.3	5.7
Newly industrialized Asian economies	4.7	5.3	4.9	4.4	2.3	1.6	2.0	2.3	4.0	3.7	3.5	3.4

[1]Based on Eurostat's harmonized index of consumer prices.
[2]Consumer prices excluding interest rate components.

raise their saving rate out of current incomes and thereby dampen consumption spending. Exports, however, are expected to grow robustly, benefiting from the continued decline in the dollar and solid growth in partner countries, and healthy corporate balance sheets should support business investment.

Risks to this outlook, however, are on the downside. While the recent further weakening of the U.S. dollar could lead to more vigorous export growth than in the baseline forecast, three downside risks are particularly apparent.

- First, while the turmoil in the financial markets appears to have eased, at this stage it is unclear to what extent the cost and availability of credit across the broader economy will be affected. The reintermediation of credit onto the balance sheets of banks as they absorb off-balance-sheet entities that are experiencing financial difficulties could curtail new lending, while difficulties among specialized mortgage lenders will reduce the availability of housing finance. Spreads in high-yield markets are also likely to remain elevated, affecting the investment outlook. A significant pullback in lending by financial institutions would clearly have negative implications for the growth outlook.
- Second, there are significant downside risks from the housing market. With inventories of unsold homes high, rising delinquencies

and tighter credit conditions in the subprime mortgage market, and the cost of some other types of higher-quality mortgages rising, a deeper and more protracted housing downturn than assumed in the current baseline is a risk. Not only would this extend the decline in residential investment, but deeper falls in house prices would put additional pressure on household finances and consumption, particularly if the labor market were to continue to weaken (see Box 2.1 for a discussion of the effects of house prices on growth).

- Third, at this stage it is unclear to what extent the recent sharp slowdown in productivity growth is attributable to structural, as opposed to cyclical, factors. Reflecting the view that the slowdown is indeed partly structural, IMF staff estimates of medium-term potential growth have been marked down to 2¾ percent. But, if underlying productivity growth is weaker than now estimated, this would feed through into expectations of future incomes, thus reducing consumption and investment spending.

With the economy weakening, inflation pressures have moderated. As measured by the core personal consumption expenditure deflator, 12-month inflation has come down below 2 percent. Pressures on core inflation are expected to continue to ease in the coming months against the backdrop of slowing growth in shelter costs (which have been an important driver of core inflation over the past year) and modest growth, although the depreciation of the dollar could add to import prices.

Against the background of the changing balance of risks to growth and inflation, the Federal Reserve cut the federal funds rate by 50 basis points to 4.75 percent at its September meeting. Looking forward, signs that growth was likely to continue below trend would justify further interest rate reductions, provided that inflation remains contained. At this stage, markets expect the Fed to cut rates by a further 50 basis points in the coming months.

The current account deficit is projected to narrow, reaching 5.5 percent of GDP in 2008 compared with 6.2 percent of GDP in 2006, assuming that the real effective value of the U.S. dollar remains at its current level (Table 2.2). Strong export growth and weaker import demand are expected to more than offset the impact of higher oil prices and lower net investment income. Despite the large external borrowing needed to finance the deficit, valuation gains from the depreciating U.S. dollar in recent years and the underperformance of the U.S. equity markets relative to those overseas have meant that the net foreign liability position of the United States actually

Table 2.2. Advanced Economies: Current Account Positions

(Percent of GDP)

	2005	2006	2007	2008
Advanced economies	**–1.3**	**–1.4**	**–1.3**	**–1.4**
United States	–6.1	–6.2	–5.7	–5.5
Euro area[1]	0.3	—	–0.2	–0.4
Germany	4.6	5.0	5.4	5.1
France	–1.1	–1.2	–1.6	–1.8
Italy	–1.5	–2.4	–2.3	–2.2
Spain	–7.4	–8.6	–9.8	–10.2
Netherlands	7.7	8.6	7.4	6.7
Belgium	2.6	2.0	2.5	2.5
Austria	2.1	3.2	3.7	3.7
Finland	4.9	5.2	5.0	5.0
Greece	–6.4	–9.6	–9.7	–9.6
Portugal	–9.7	–9.4	–9.2	–9.2
Ireland	–3.5	–4.2	–4.4	–3.3
Luxembourg	11.1	10.6	10.5	10.3
Slovenia	–1.9	–2.5	–3.4	–3.1
Japan	3.6	3.9	4.5	4.3
United Kingdom	–2.5	–3.2	–3.5	–3.6
Canada	2.0	1.6	1.8	1.2
Korea	1.9	0.7	0.1	–0.4
Australia	–5.8	–5.5	–5.7	–5.6
Taiwan Province of China	4.5	6.8	6.8	7.1
Sweden	7.0	7.2	6.0	5.7
Switzerland	13.5	15.1	15.8	15.0
Hong Kong SAR	11.4	10.8	11.2	9.5
Denmark	3.8	2.4	1.3	1.3
Norway	15.5	16.4	14.6	15.1
Israel	3.3	5.6	3.7	3.2
Singapore	24.5	27.5	27.0	25.4
New Zealand	–8.6	–8.7	–8.5	–8.6
Cyprus	–5.6	–5.9	–5.5	–5.6
Iceland	–16.1	–27.3	–11.6	–6.0
Memorandum				
Major advanced economies	–2.0	–2.2	–1.9	–1.9
Euro area[2]	—	–0.2	–0.1	–0.3
Newly industrialized Asian economies	5.5	5.6	5.4	4.9

[1]Calculated as the sum of the balances of individual euro area countries.

[2]Corrected for reporting discrepancies in intra-area transactions.

Box 2.1. What Risks Do Housing Markets Pose for Global Growth?

Following a long run-up, house prices in the United States have decelerated sharply since mid-2005, and the subsequent drop in residential investment has been a substantial drag on the economy over the past year. Housing markets in many other countries—in both advanced and emerging market economies—have experienced boom conditions in recent years, and some of these have also recently shown signs of softening. So far, these moderations have occurred without the deep correction seen in the United States, but there remains the concern that the U.S. experience might presage steep housing downturns in other countries that have also experienced a rapid rise in house prices, with associated risks for output growth.

Recent financial turbulence has raised the risk of more drawn-out difficulties in the U.S. housing sector that could have a deeper impact on the broader economy. Tightening credit conditions could affect a broader range of households and further curtail effective demand for housing. And house prices could decline more sharply than currently expected with implications for residential investment and consumer spending. At the same time, credit conditions may also tighten in some of the western European countries—because of their large exposures to asset-backed commercial paper and continuing strains in short-term funding markets—and this could have a significant bearing on the housing market in these countries.

The Run-Up in House Prices

Traditional valuation measures, ratios of both house price to income and house price to rent, have risen steeply in several Organization for Economic Cooperation and Development (OECD) and emerging market countries in recent years (first figure). Specifically,

- Relative to incomes and rents, many industrial economies have witnessed even larger run-ups

Note: The main author of this box is Andrew Benito. Sergei Antoshin provided research assistance.

Housing Price Developments
(Percent change)

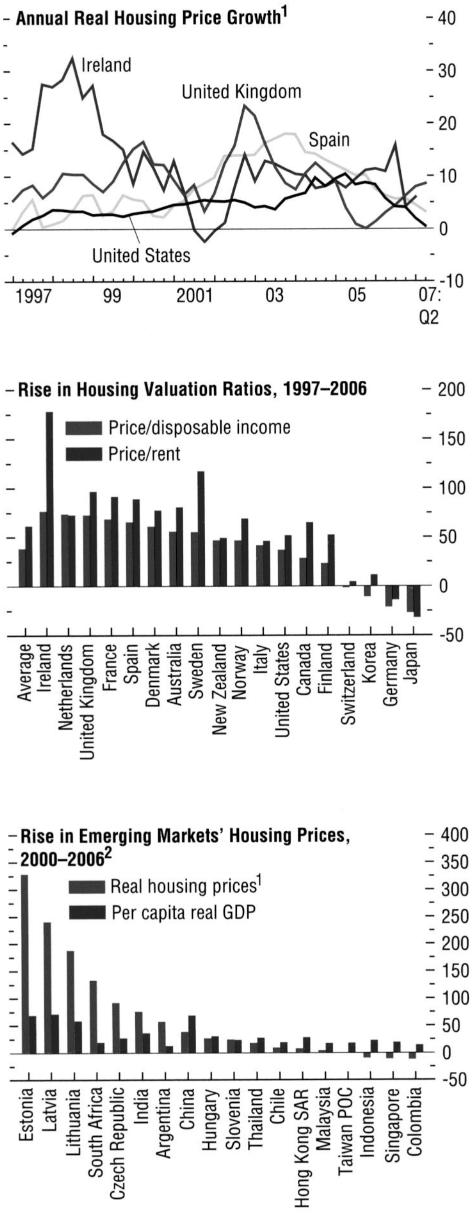

Sources: OECD; and IMF staff calculations.
[1]Deflated by CPI.
[2]Data for India cover 2000–05.

in house prices than the United States. For the OECD countries on average, the ratio of house price to income has risen by more than one-third, and the ratio of house price to rent by almost two-thirds, since 1997. The largest increases in house prices relative to incomes have been experienced by France, Ireland, the Netherlands, Spain, and the United Kingdom. By contrast, Germany and Japan have experienced falling house price valuation ratios over the past 10 years.

- Based on limited data, many emerging market economies have also experienced substantial house price run-ups since 2000, exceeding growth in per capita incomes. The largest increases were recorded in Estonia and Latvia (although data are only for the capital cities and are therefore likely to overestimate countrywide growth). Other large price rises, with real house prices almost doubling or more, were recorded in the Czech Republic, Lithuania, and South Africa. However, real house prices have declined in Colombia, Indonesia, and Singapore.
- In China, the increase in real house prices was less than real income growth over the same period, although there have been localized booms in fast-growing cities such as Beijing and Shanghai.

Risk of Weakening Housing Markets

The risk of a broader weakening in housing markets depends partly on how much of the previous price rise can be justified by changes in fundamental determinants of house prices, including interest rates, availability of financing, income growth, and demographics. It also depends on how those fundamentals, including long-term interest rates, evolve in the future. The assessment is likely to differ across countries, as will the time horizon over which the risk applies.[1]

[1]See, for example, Girouard and others (2006) and the collection of papers presented at the Jackson Hole Symposium on Housing, Housing Finance, and Monetary Policy, August 30–September 1, 2007.

The following analysis extends and updates an earlier IMF study that modeled house price inflation as a function of an affordability ratio (the lagged ratio of house prices to disposable incomes), the growth in disposable income per capita, short-term interest rates, credit growth, growth in the country's equity market index, and growth in the working-age population (see Terrones, 2004). The previous study is extended in two ways. First, long-term interest rates are included in addition to the variables considered in the previous study. This is generally found to be significant. Second, separate equations are estimated for each country, so that the role assigned to each factor is allowed to vary across countries, although the same variables are included for all countries. The equation is estimated for a group of 18 OECD countries for which adequate data are available, using quarterly data for the period 1970–2006.

The results indicate that almost three-quarters of the rise in real house prices over the period 1997–2006 can be explained on average by the estimated model, although this still leaves a significant unexplained component. For the United States, real house prices are assessed to have risen by about one-third more than explained by fundamentals (second figure). The unexplained share of house price increases is assessed to be still larger in a number of other countries, including Ireland, the Netherlands, and the United Kingdom. However, there is considerable uncertainty about these estimates, because local conditions that are not captured in the econometric analysis could play an important role. For example, migration patterns, supply constraints, and changes in the availability of mortgage financing—including to the subprime sector—could all be relevant. On the other hand, some of the increase in house prices that is explained by the model, such as through the role for credit growth, may not reflect solely economic fundamentals. Nevertheless, taken at face value, the estimates suggest that a number of advanced economies' housing markets outside the United States could be vulnerable to a correction.

Box 2.1 *(concluded)*

Risks to Output Growth, 1997–2006[1]

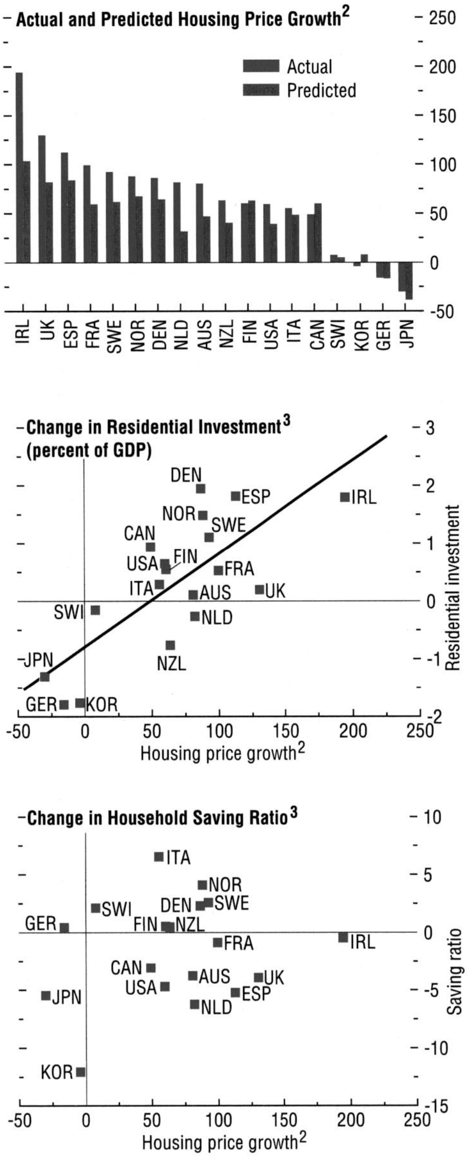

Source: IMF staff calculations.

[1]AUS: Australia; CAN: Canada; DEN: Denmark; ESP: Spain; FIN: Finland; FRA: France; GER: Germany; IRL: Ireland; ITA: Italy; JPN: Japan; KOR: Korea; NLD: Netherlands; NOR: Norway; NZL: New Zealand; SWE: Sweden; SWI: Switzerland; UK: United Kingdom; and USA: United States.

[2]Cumulative growth rate at constant prices.

[3]Difference over 1997–2006.

House Prices and the Broader Economy

The countries most at risk from a weakening housing sector are likely to be those that have experienced the largest increases in house-price-sensitive components of aggregate demand as well as those where the run-up in prices seems less easily explained by changes in fundamentals. Over the past decade, growth has been boosted across many OECD economies by strong residential investment, with the countries that experienced the largest run-up in house prices generally witnessing the strongest additional residential investment (see second figure). For example, in Ireland and Spain, the ratio of real residential investment to GDP rose by 1.8 percentage points compared with an increase of 0.6 percentage point in the United States over the same period, although part of the difference is accounted for by weakening U.S. residential investment in 2006.[2] Home builders' ability to respond to higher prices is, however, constrained in some countries, such as the Netherlands and the United Kingdom, by planning restrictions and land limits (Barker, 2004). This may help explain why housing demand pressures have raised prices more than has residential investment in these countries.

When home builders perceive the profitability of new housing investment to moderate, residential investment can decline rapidly, reversing some of the boost to output growth from housing investment. This has already been a significant feature of the housing correction in the United States. A number of other countries, such as Denmark, Ireland, and Spain, could also be subject to such a correction. However, the pace and depth of the corrections would depend on country-specific factors. In the United States, the correction has been exacerbated by the sharp reversal in the subprime mortgage market, a factor less relevant else-

[2]The spread of increases in residential investment is even larger in terms of nominal ratios of residential investment to GDP, reflecting the variation in the relative price of housing.

where, because subprime mortgages represent a much smaller share of lending.

A decline in house prices could also affect the broader economy through its impact on consumer spending. The strength of this link would again vary across countries and also depend on why house prices have changed. Weakening house prices would be expected to dampen spending of some households through a negative "wealth effect," although other households (such as renters planning to buy a home) are made better off by lower prices. Spending can also be affected through a collateral channel, because house price movements affect the value of home equity and the terms under which households can borrow from banks. This latter effect tends to be stronger in economies such as the United Kingdom and the United States, where financing of home equity withdrawal is more easily available.[3] The figure shows that the cross-country correlation between the household saving ratio and house prices is weak. Research also suggests that these links vary over time within a given country, depending on why house prices have varied.[4] For example, in the United Kingdom, house price rises were more strongly associated with rising income expectations in the mid- to late 1980s than during the recent run-up. This may help explain why the earlier period was associated with a more pronounced consumption boom.

Consumer spending is also influenced by many factors other than house prices. Relevant factors include current and expected incomes, financial market wealth, and retail lending conditions. During the recent U.S. housing correction, robust employment growth and solid equity market performance have supported consumption. The extent to which a weakening housing market is associated with weaker spending in other economies will also depend on the evolution of these factors.

In sum, after a period of remarkable house price growth, conditions have eased back in a number of advanced economies' housing markets. There is some risk to global output growth from these developments: economies that have experienced a larger unexplained increase in house prices than the United States account for almost 20 percent of the total output of advanced economies. These risks may have been exacerbated by recent market turmoil and by an associated repricing of risk. Furthermore, western European banks are exposed to the U.S. housing sector, and strains in short-term funding markets could restrain their lending activity and have an adverse impact on the housing market in these countries. The extent of these risks is, as yet, unclear. In general, residential investment is the component of demand most at risk to weaker housing market conditions, although consumption could also come under pressure in some countries. Spillovers from the U.S. housing market have also occurred through financial channels, and such links need to be carefully monitored.

[3]See the April 2002 *World Economic Outlook*, pp. 74–85; Klyuev and Mills (2006); and Carroll, Otsuka, and Slacalek (2006).

[4]See Benito and others (2006), pp. 142–54. Housing transactions also tend to be linked with spending durables, reflecting the number of households purchasing durable goods for their new homes.

improved slightly in 2006 for the third year running. Nevertheless, although the real effective U.S. dollar is still estimated to be above its medium-term fundamental value, valuation gains cannot be relied on to stabilize the liability stock going forward. It is therefore important that national savings increase in the coming years to support a reduction in the current account deficit.

Fiscal developments have remained favorable, with the federal government deficit now expected to come in at 1.2 percent of GDP in FY2007, less than half of that budgeted. This overperformance reflects both revenue buoyancy and lower-than-budgeted expenditures.[1] Going forward, the U.S. administration aims to balance the budget by FY2012 (a target also adopted by the U.S. Congress in its own budget resolution). Official projections, however, do not fully account for the alternative minimum tax relief or war costs in future years. The projections also assume spending restraint that may be difficult to achieve. Adjusting for these items, the IMF staff projects that the deficit will likely remain above 1 percent of GDP through FY2012. In the IMF staff's view, a more ambitious fiscal consolidation strategy than currently envisaged, combined with reforms to Social Security and Medicare, would better help ensure long-term fiscal sustainability, although automatic fiscal stabilizers should be allowed to operate in the event of a protracted downturn. Such a fiscal strategy should aim at achieving budget balance, excluding the Social Security surplus. Spending restraint is essential in this regard, but steps to increase revenues also may be considered.

The recent turmoil in financial markets has underscored the need for regulators and supervisors to increase their focus on several aspects of the U.S. financial system (see also the October 2007 *Global Financial Stability Report,* or GFSR). For example, greater transparency and disclosure by systemically important financial institutions, including of their links with off-balance-sheet vehicles, would help reduce uncertainties about counterparty risk that were at the center of the drying up of liquidity in some parts of the financial markets. It is also important to consider how securitization and financial innovation more generally have affected the incentive structure in financial markets. This would include looking at whether the incentives for loan originators to accurately assess risk have been diluted, and whether investors put excessive reliance on rating agencies in assessing risks rather than conducting their own due diligence.

In Canada, real GDP growth accelerated to over 3 percent in the first half of 2007. Strong domestic demand remained the main driver of growth, boosted by continuing gains in the terms of trade and strong credit and employment growth, while the inventory correction, which had been a significant drag on growth in late 2006, reversed. Nevertheless, the short-term outlook is clouded by weaker prospects in the United States and the recent global financial market turmoil, which has affected parts of the Canadian markets, and the growth forecast for 2008 has been marked down to 2.3 percent (0.5 percentage point lower than in the July *World Economic Outlook Update*). With core CPI inflation above the midpoint of the Bank of Canada's 1–3 percent target range despite the substantial appreciation of the Canadian dollar, the central bank raised its policy rate to 4½ percent in July (the first increase since May 2006), but has remained on hold since. The fiscal position remains strong, with the budget in surplus and the public debt ratio on a firm downward path.

Western Europe: How Resilient Is the Recovery?

The financial market turbulence has come at a time when western Europe has been enjoying its best economic performance for a decade. A long spell of robust global growth, healthy corporate balance sheets, accommodative financing conditions, and past reforms have laid the foundation for a strong upswing. The euro area economy has been expanding at about 3 percent (year on year) since the middle of 2006, although growth eased in the second quarter of 2007, partly owing to weather and holiday effects. Growth has been driven by a broad-based acceleration in investment spending, especially in Germany, in response to high regional and global demand for machinery and equipment, a pickup in construction, and robust exports. Private consumption softened in the first half of 2007, reflecting the

[1]Estimates suggest that 40 percent of the revenue increase during 2004–06 can be explained by corporate profits growing faster than GDP, 40 percent by the growth of capital gains, and much of the remaining 20 percent by stronger income growth at the upper end of the income distribution (which, given the progressive tax system, implies higher average tax rates). See Swiston, Mühleisen, and Mathai (2007).

German value-added tax (VAT) hike and pre-election uncertainty in France, but consumer confidence remained fairly robust until June, when it began to weaken. In the United Kingdom, the expansion has continued at a strong and steady pace, with growth of 3 percent (year on year) in the second quarter of 2007, led by consumption. In Norway, Sweden, and Switzerland, growth was also sustained above potential rates in the second quarter.

Recent data provide mixed signals about the likely growth performance of western European economies in the coming quarters, although the recent financial market turbulence and weaker growth in the United States are pointing to a likely slowdown. Euro area growth is now forecast to slow to about 2.5 percent in 2007 and 2.1 percent in 2008, while growth in the United Kingdom is now expected to ease from 3.1 percent in 2007 to 2.3 percent in 2008. Exports will be affected by weakening external demand, and the strength of the euro is likely to weigh on export prospects of countries lacking a sufficient cushion in competitiveness, including France, Portugal, and Spain. The tightening of global credit conditions is likely to lead to some cooling of European housing markets and dampening prospects for residential investment and household consumption. Growth is also likely to be affected by tighter availability of bank credit. A number of European banks have significant exposure to the U.S. housing market, particularly through off-balance-sheet vehicles supported by backup lines of credit, and the sector as a whole has been affected by the higher cost of funding and liquidity shortages. Responding to pressures in short-term interbank markets, the European Central Bank (ECB) and the Bank of England (BoE) stepped in to provide liquidity. On a more positive note, high capacity utilization and strong corporate profitability are projected to support investment, while recent improvements in the labor market should help to hold up consumer spending.[2]

[2]Recently approved tax cuts in France will also support activity in 2008.

The balance of risks to the outlook are to the downside. Deteriorating conditions in credit markets could further slow consumption and investment, particularly if banks sharply curtail lending in the coming quarters as they seek to improve their balance sheets in what still remains a volatile and uncertain environment. In countries where housing prices still seem elevated—France, Ireland, Spain, and the United Kingdom—growth dynamics will depend on the pace of adjustment in the housing sector in response to tightening credit conditions and, in some cases, changes in the fiscal treatment of housing investment. Other risks—mainly relating to volatile oil prices, a more protracted slowdown in the U.S. economy, and a disorderly unwinding of global imbalances—are also to the downside.

The euro area headline CPI has remained below 2 percent this year, but ticked up in September and is expected to temporarily exceed this threshold during the remainder of the year on account of higher energy and food prices (Figure 2.2). It is projected to hover around 2 percent in 2008 as tighter credit conditions, lower pressures of resources, as well as the unwinding of the German VAT increase are expected to offset rising energy costs. Despite continuing tightening in the labor markets, wage growth in the euro area is expected to remain moderate in the coming quarters, as the slowdown in activity, appreciation of the euro, and structural changes in the labor supply, including increased competition (partly due to the enlargement of the European Union) and large migration inflows, should continue to keep inflation in check (Box 2.2). In the United Kingdom, inflation temporarily overshot the BoE's 2 percent target, in part owing to the pass-through of energy price increases, but has recently fallen below the target.

The ECB and the BoE tightened monetary policy through June in the face of rising resource utilization and firming inflation, but have remained appropriately on hold since the onset of the financial market turmoil. In the euro area, considering the downside risks to growth and inflation from financial market turmoil,

Figure 2.2. Western Europe: What Is the Outlook for Inflation?

Inflation has been firming up in the euro area in tandem with rising resource utilization. Wages are not yet outpacing productivity, but structural changes in the labor supply are moderating the pickup in wages. Productivity improvements seem to have been concentrated in cyclical industries so far.

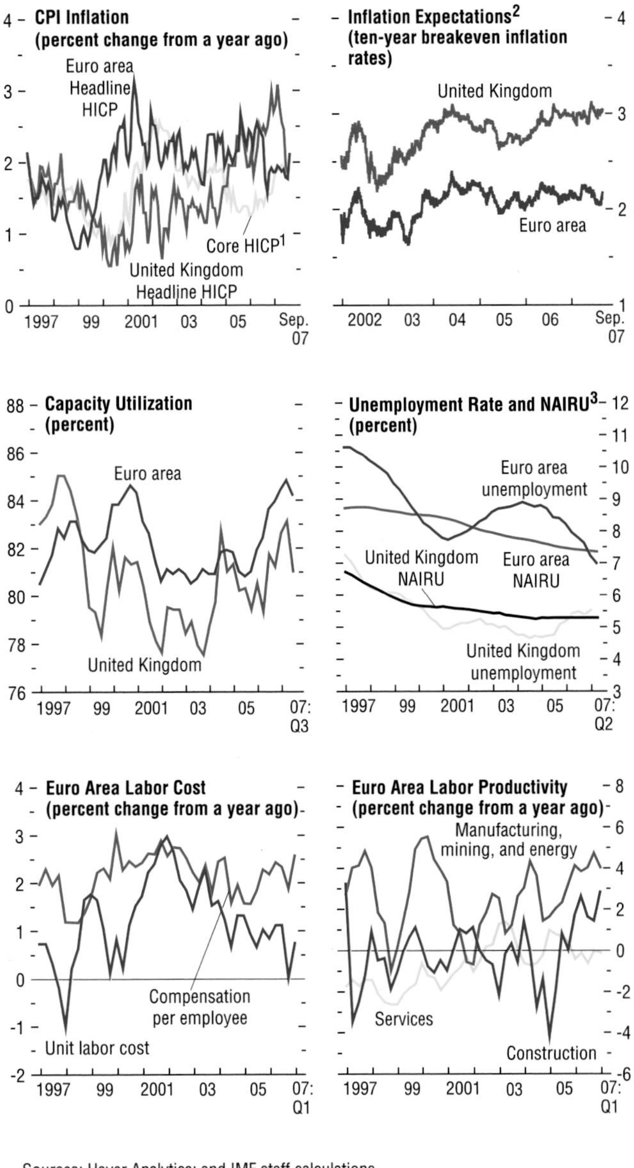

Sources: Haver Analytics; and IMF staff calculations.

[1]Core defined as headline, excluding energy, food, alcohol, and tobacco.

[2]Differences between inflation expectations from 10-year breakeven rates in the United Kingdom and the Bank of England's inflation target are, in part, because bonds are indexed to retail price inflation (RPI). The latter has tended to exceed the CPI in recent years, mainly because, in contrast to the CPI, the RPI includes interest rate payments on mortgages.

[3]NAIRU defined as nonaccelerating inflation rate of unemployment.

monetary policy can afford to stay on hold over the near term. However, as these downside risks dissipate, some further tightening may well be required. Conversely, in the event of a more protracted slowdown, an easing of monetary policy would need to be considered. In the United Kingdom, the monetary authorities will need to consider similar factors—with inflation, the exchange rate, the possible softening in domestic credit supply, and the U.S. outlook to be weighed against the strength of domestic demand.

Many, although not all, euro area countries took advantage of buoyant revenue growth in 2006 to advance fiscal consolidation. The euro area's cyclically adjusted fiscal deficit declined by almost 1 percentage point of GDP in 2006, led by reductions in Germany, France, and Italy (adjusting for one-off measures), and public debt declined relative to GDP. The challenge is to continue the progress on fiscal consolidation. Besides preparing for population aging, lower fiscal deficits would help create room for cutting distortionary taxes, laying the ground for a long-lasting improvement in economic performance. Under the reformed Stability and Growth Pact, most countries in the euro area are aiming for budget balance or even a small surplus over the medium term, and countries that have not yet reached their medium-term objectives are required to adjust by at least ½ percent of GDP a year. However, this goal seems unlikely to be met in a number of countries, including France (which has recently approved a package of tax cuts) and Italy (where the government has scaled back its fiscal adjustment in 2007–08, despite significant revenue overperformance).

The euro area's long-term prospects hinge on its ability to accelerate productivity and employment growth, as well as improve structural flexibility of member countries' economies. Employment performance has strengthened recently owing to past reforms and cyclical factors, but productivity performance remains lackluster. Although the euro area fares well on international comparisons of productivity in tradable goods sectors, its productivity in services, which tend to be more sheltered from competi-

Box 2.2. Labor Market Reforms in the Euro Area and the Wage-Unemployment Trade-Off

Labor Market Indicators for the Euro Area

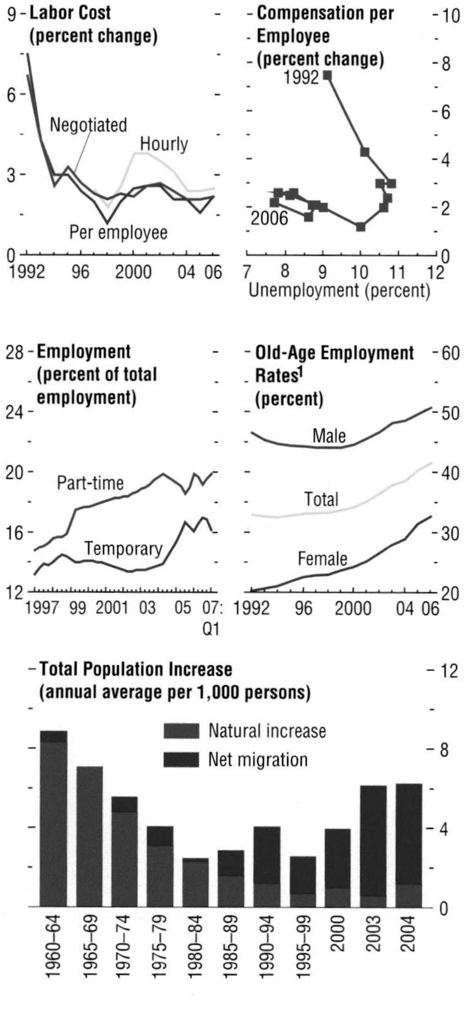

Sources: European Commission; Eurostat; and Haver Analytics.
[1]Ages 55 to 64 years.

Labor market performance in the euro area appears to have improved significantly over the past decade. During the 1970s, against the background of expanding welfare states, growing union assertiveness, and macroeconomic policy misjudgments, oil price and other shocks led to a sharp increase in unemployment and inflation and a decline in labor force participation. Experiences over the past few years could not have been more different: whereas oil and administrative prices grew rapidly, wages remained subdued and unemployment fell to a quarter-century low of 7 percent in mid-2007. This box examines the factors underlying the improved trade-off between wages and unemployment and concludes that labor market reforms have made an important contribution in this regard. Nonetheless, more work remains to be done to continue reducing unemployment on a sustainable basis and to boost the still relatively low labor force participation.

Background

Although unemployment has declined significantly over the past several years in the euro area, labor costs have not accelerated. Labor costs decelerated during 1992–97 and have moved sideways thereafter. Specifically, the rate of increase of compensation per employee and negotiated wages declined from about 7 percent in 1992 to about 2 percent in 1997 and has hovered between 1½ percent and 2½ percent a year since then, and real wage growth has also been declining (figure). Changes in national policies and union behavior as well as increased competition from emerging market countries were the key factors underlying these developments. Measures such as the exemption of small and medium-size enterprises from the 35-hour workweek in France increased scope for fixed-term and part-time contracts in Italy (under the so-called Biagi reforms), and flexible working-time agreements between employers and unions in various sectors in Germany have facilitated increased flexibility and have helped contain the growth of labor costs.

Analytical Framework

The labor supply (wage) curve proposed in Blanchflower and Oswald (1990) provides a framework for estimating the effect of labor market reforms on the supply of labor. In this

Note: The main author of this box is Emil Stavrev.

Box 2.2 *(concluded)*

framework, real wages adjusted for productivity changes are modeled as a function of the unemployment rate and supply-side factors:

$$ln\frac{W_t}{C_t A_t} = \alpha_t - \theta\ ln(u_t),$$

where W_t denotes wages, C_t is the consumer price index, A_t is the total factor productivity (scaled by the labor share), u_t is the unemployment rate, and α_t denotes the cumulative effect of factors that affect wage-setting behavior and thus shift the wage curve. These factors include changes in unemployment benefits, the tax wedge between earned wages and workers' purchasing power, and employment preferences of workers.

The cumulative effect of labor market reforms and changes in preferences toward employment, α_t, can be obtained as a residual from the above equation. Estimation of this equation for euro area data from 1992 to 2006 shows that α_t declined gradually by about 6 percent over this period, suggesting an improved trade-off between wages and unemployment, that is, lower unemployment for a given level of real wages.

Factors Behind Wage and Employment Developments

What are the factors that contributed to this improved trade-off between wages and unemployment in the euro area since the early 1990s?

- Structural reforms have helped increase the labor supply for any given real wage. Examples of such policies include the deregulation of part-time and "temp" work in Spain and France in the 1990s. As a result of such deregulation, the share of temporary employment in total employment increased significantly (see figure).[1]
- Participation rates of older workers have risen as a result of the phasing out of early retirement schemes. Similarly, female participation has continued to increase (see figure).
- Labor taxation has been reduced. Effective social security contribution rates declined in France, Germany, and Italy, and the tax wedge (the difference between wages and take-home pay) narrowed in France, Italy, and Spain in the second half of the 1990s.
- Greater emphasis has been given to employment by both unions and workers as their preferences have shifted toward job preservation and job creation, possibly in response to increased external competition, particularly from Asian emerging market countries.
- Higher net immigration has contributed to moderate wage growth (see figure). The employment of lower-cost immigrants in agriculture and other sectors has reduced overall inflation, allowing workers to have the same real wage growth for lower nominal wage increases. Also, by reducing skill mismatches and taking jobs that are difficult to fill, immigrants raise growth and welfare, increasing overall employment.

[1]European Central Bank (2007).

tion, is subpar. Improving contestability of services markets (particularly wholesale and retail trade and financial services) through deregulation and opening to foreign competition is critical for boosting long-term growth prospects. The Services Directive goes a long way in this direction, and the challenge now is to implement it in a meaningful way and possibly broaden it to additional sectors. Continued labor and product market reforms need to focus on strengthening incentives to work and on improving wage flexibility. The Lisbon Strategy holds promise in this regard, provided its full potential is unleashed. Further financial integration can facilitate sharing of risks relating to country-specific demand or supply shocks (Stavrev, 2007).

Industrial Asia: Deflation Is Not Yet Decisively Beaten in Japan

The Japanese economy contracted slightly in the second quarter of 2007, following two quarters of strong gains. The decline in real GDP in the quarter was driven largely by declines in investment and weaker consumption growth. Looking ahead, the September Tankan survey showed that business confidence remains solid, consistent with continued strong performance by large exporters, but some recent data on domestic demand, such as for household consumption, have been more mixed. Further, heightened global financial market volatility has clouded the near-term outlook, although the direct exposure of the Japanese financial system to the U.S. subprime mortgage market is limited.

Reflecting the weak second quarter outcome and other incoming information, the projection for real GDP growth has been marked down to 2 percent in 2007 and 1.7 percent in 2008 (0.6 and 0.3 percentage point lower than in the July *World Economic Outlook Update*). The tight labor market—the unemployment rate stood at 3.8 percent in August—is expected to underpin stronger income and consumption growth going forward, and robust profits and healthy balance sheets should provide support to corporate investment. Risks to the outlook appear tilted somewhat to the downside at this stage. While faster wage growth could boost consumption spending, growth would be dampened by a more significant downturn in the global economy, higher oil prices, or a further appreciation of the yen.

Despite four years of robust growth, deflation has yet to be decisively beaten (Figure 2.3). Indeed, after a period of rising consumer prices, the year-on-year changes in the headline and core CPI have once again turned modestly negative in recent months, although land prices are now rising. While the decline in consumer prices is likely to be reversed in the period ahead as higher energy prices feed into the CPI, prospects for a decisive move to positive inflation remain elusive. A number of factors seem to be limiting inflation. Corporate investment has been strong in recent years and, combined with structural reforms that have boosted productivity, this has likely increased the growth potential

Figure 2.3. Japan: Deflation Still Not Decisively Beaten

Sustained growth in recent years has not yet resulted in a decisive exit from deflation. With strong investment spending and improved productivity-boosting capacity, and inflation expectations remaining low, price increases are likely to remain limited in the near term.

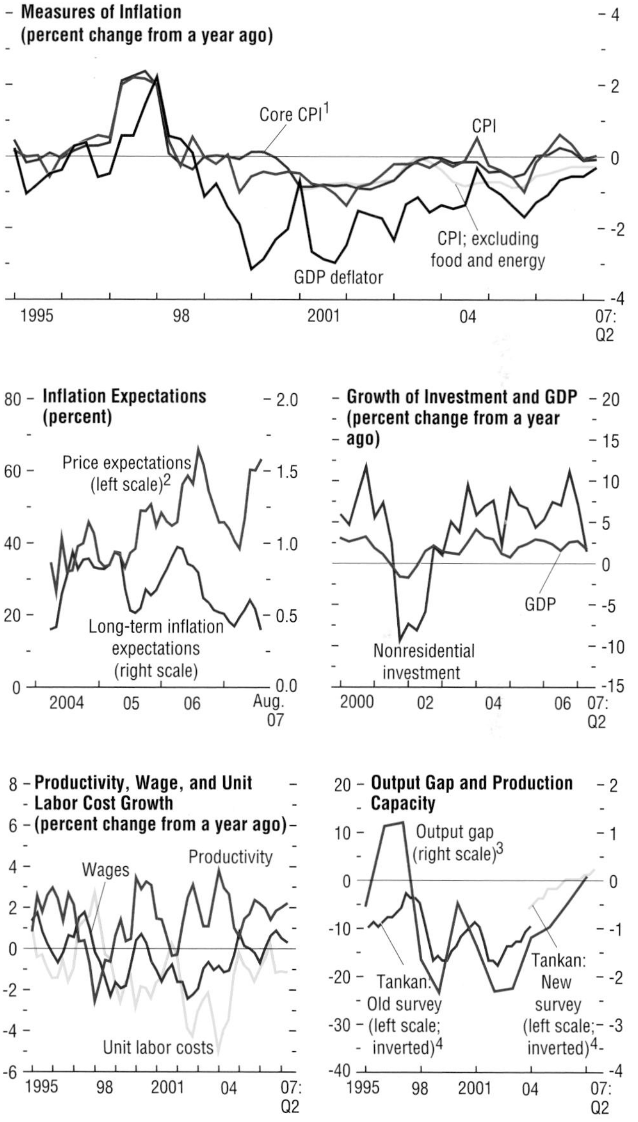

Sources: Cabinet Office, Government of Japan; CEIC Data Company Limited; Haver Analytics; OECD, *Economic Outlook;* and IMF staff calculations.

[1]All items, excluding fresh food.

[2]Respondents expecting prices to increase minus those expecting prices to decrease.

[3]Output gap expressed as a percent of potential GDP.

[4]Tankan, actual production capacity in diffusion index for all industries.

of the economy. Indeed, measures of capacity utilization have only recently begun to suggest that the economy is working at full capacity. In addition, wages have been held down by demographic changes that are seeing retiring older workers with high wages replaced by younger, lower-paid ones, and an increasing prevalence of new hires under temporary employment contracts who tend to have lower wages. Last, inflation expectations are anchored at low levels after many years of deflation. Although on some measures expectations have risen in recent months, consumers and investors are still apparently less certain about prospects for higher inflation than they were a year ago.

Against this background, the Bank of Japan has maintained an accommodative monetary stance, keeping its policy rate steady at about 0.5 percent since February. Although interest rates will eventually need to return to more normal levels, such increases should await clear signs that prospective inflation is moving decisively higher and that concerns over recent market volatility have waned. There is also scope for the Bank of Japan to help guide inflation expectations higher. A clearer indication from the Bank of Japan of its desired inflation rate and more forward-looking statements that inform financial markets about the central bank's views of the likely evolution of risks to growth and inflation and the likely future course of monetary policy would help.

With central banks in many other countries tightening monetary policy over the past year, interest rate differentials with Japan have widened. Until the recent increase in financial market volatility, this interest rate differential had contributed to strong capital outflows from Japan and a weaker yen. The yen carry trade—the practice of borrowing in yen to purchase higher-yielding assets in other currencies—was only one factor behind these outflows. Japanese investors have also increasingly turned to foreign investments to diversify their portfolios and earn higher returns, with retail investors (through mutual funds) and pension and life insurance companies being the main sources. Indeed, with the share of household financial assets held overseas still small, such outflows could be expected to continue going forward even if interest rate differentials narrow.

The yen depreciated on a real effective basis in the first half of 2007 to its weakest level in more than two decades, but it has regained ground recently as heightened financial market volatility has prompted some unwinding of yen carry trade capital outflows. Although the yen is undervalued relative to its medium-term fundamentals, it is appropriate for monetary policy to continue to focus on overcoming deflation and sustaining growth rather than on the level of the exchange rate. Indeed, a premature increase in policy rates could ultimately prove counterproductive by undermining growth, aggravating deflation, and working against the resolution of global imbalances. Nevertheless, as domestic economic fundamentals continue to improve and/or ongoing financial market volatility further discourages carry trade capital outflows, it would be expected that the yen will appreciate, and such upward pressures should not be resisted.

Considerable progress has been made in reducing the fiscal deficit in recent years on the back of buoyant corporate tax revenues and reduced outlays on public investment. Going forward, however, the pace of adjustment is set to slow. The IMF staff's assessment is that the structural budget deficit will decline by only about ¼ percent of GDP a year compared with about 1 percent of GDP a year over the past three years. Given the continued favorable outlook, a stronger fiscal adjustment would be desirable to help put the public debt ratio on a firmly declining path. In terms of specific measures, although there remains some scope for further reductions in public investment spending, a broad reform of the tax system that includes steps to widen the income tax base, raise the consumption tax rate, and strengthen tax administration would provide the basis for higher revenues. Fiscal consolidation would also be supported by further structural reforms to improve growth potential, particularly to increase labor utilization and promote greater market opening and deregulation in sheltered sectors of the economy.

The Australian and New Zealand economies are expanding strongly, although the global financial market turmoil could act to modestly dampen growth in the near term. While the impact has been more limited than in some other countries, financial markets in Australia and New Zealand have been affected by recent developments, with interbank interest rates and credit spreads increasing, and reduced liquidity among nonbank institutions. Nevertheless, at this juncture, the main short-term policy challenge in both countries continues to be to keep firm control on inflation in the face of strong domestic demand and tight labor markets. To this end, both central banks have recently raised their policy rates—to 6½ percent in Australia and to 8¼ percent in New Zealand. Flexible exchange rates and prudent fiscal policies have played central roles in managing the domestic impact of strong capital inflows and the improving terms of trade. Against this background, it is important that both governments continue to exercise fiscal restraint in the period ahead.

Emerging Asia: Successfully Managing Strong Foreign Exchange Inflows

Growth in emerging Asia remained exceptionally rapid in the first half of 2007. The regional expansion was led by China, where real GDP grew by 11½ percent (year on year) in the first half of 2007 as exports and investment accelerated, and by India, where gains in domestic demand, particularly investment, underpinned 9¼ percent (year on year) growth in the first half. Growth also accelerated in Singapore (where consumption and investment both strengthened), the Philippines (where record remittance inflows boosted consumption and government spending grew strongly), Korea (where the industrial sector rebounded), and Indonesia (where lower interest rates boosted domestic demand). In Thailand, political uncertainties continued to undermine confidence and domestic demand. Growth appears to have remained buoyant in the third quarter, with global financial market volatility having a limited impact on the region to date, although the weaker outlook for the advanced economies is likely to slow export growth going forward.

Against this background, growth projections have been revised downward modestly since the July *World Economic Outlook Update.* The regional economy is now expected to expand by 9.2 percent this year and 8.3 percent in 2008 (Table 2.3). Growth in China is projected at 11.5 percent in 2007, before slowing to 10 percent in 2008, while the Indian economy is expected to expand by 8.9 percent this year and 8.4 percent in 2008. The newly industrialized Asian economies are expected to be most affected by the weaker U.S. outlook, and growth for 2008 has been revised down to 4.4 percent (0.4 percentage point lower than in the July *World Economic Outlook Update*). Among the ASEAN-4 economies, some rebound in Thailand as confidence recovers is expected to offset modest slowdowns in Malaysia and the Philippines.

Risks to the outlook are broadly balanced at this stage. Slower demand for Asian exports, and electronic goods in particular, and the possibility of further global financial market turbulence are particular downside concerns. On the upside, the projected easing of growth in China may not materialize unless the authorities tighten monetary policy more decisively and allow a faster appreciation of the exchange rate. Faster growth in the near term, however, would come at the cost of increased downside risks related to overinvestment beyond the projection period. Growth in India could also be stronger than projected, particularly if robust corporate profits further boost investment spending.

Foreign exchange inflows to the region have been very strong (Figure 2.4). Current account transactions have accounted for much of the inflow, with the regional current account surplus expected at 6½ percent of GDP this year—the surplus in China is rising rapidly and that in

Table 2.3. Selected Asian Countries: Real GDP, Consumer Prices, and Current Account Balance
(Annual percent change unless noted otherwise)

	Real GDP				Consumer Prices[1]				Current Account Balance[2]			
	2005	2006	2007	2008	2005	2006	2007	2008	2005	2006	2007	2008
Emerging Asia[3]	**8.7**	**9.3**	**9.2**	**8.3**	**3.5**	**3.7**	**4.9**	**4.2**	**4.5**	**5.8**	**6.6**	**6.5**
China	10.4	11.1	11.5	10.0	1.8	1.5	4.5	3.9	7.2	9.4	11.7	12.2
South Asia[4]	**8.6**	**9.1**	**8.4**	**8.0**	**5.0**	**6.4**	**6.6**	**4.9**	**–1.0**	**–1.4**	**–2.3**	**–2.7**
India	9.0	9.7	8.9	8.4	4.2	6.1	6.2	4.4	–1.0	–1.1	–2.1	–2.6
Pakistan	7.7	6.9	6.4	6.5	9.3	7.9	7.8	7.0	–1.4	–3.9	–4.9	–4.9
Bangladesh	6.3	6.4	5.8	6.0	7.0	6.5	7.2	6.3	—	1.2	1.3	0.8
ASEAN-4	**5.1**	**5.4**	**5.6**	**5.6**	**7.3**	**8.2**	**4.0**	**4.2**	**2.1**	**5.2**	**4.7**	**3.7**
Indonesia	5.7	5.5	6.2	6.1	10.5	13.1	6.3	6.2	0.1	2.7	1.6	1.2
Thailand	4.5	5.0	4.0	4.5	4.5	4.6	2.0	2.0	–4.5	1.6	3.7	2.2
Philippines	4.9	5.4	6.3	5.8	7.6	6.2	3.0	4.0	2.0	4.3	3.8	2.6
Malaysia	5.2	5.9	5.8	5.6	3.0	3.6	2.1	2.4	15.3	17.2	14.4	13.3
Newly industrialized Asian economies	**4.7**	**5.3**	**4.9**	**4.4**	**2.3**	**1.6**	**2.0**	**2.3**	**5.5**	**5.6**	**5.4**	**4.9**
Korea	4.2	5.0	4.8	4.6	2.8	2.2	2.6	2.7	1.9	0.7	0.1	–0.4
Taiwan Province of China	4.1	4.7	4.1	3.8	2.3	0.6	1.2	1.5	4.5	6.8	6.8	7.1
Hong Kong SAR	7.5	6.9	5.7	4.7	0.9	2.0	2.0	3.2	11.4	10.8	11.2	9.5
Singapore	6.6	7.9	7.5	5.8	0.5	1.0	1.7	1.7	24.5	27.5	27.0	25.4

[1]Movements in consumer prices are shown as annual averages. December/December changes can be found in Table A7 in the Statistical Appendix.
[2]Percent of GDP.
[3]Consists of developing Asia, the newly industrialized Asian economies, and Mongolia.
[4]Includes Maldives, Nepal, and Sri Lanka.

Hong Kong SAR, Malaysia, Singapore, and Taiwan Province of China remains large. Net capital flows to the region, which in aggregate are dominated by foreign direct investment, have also picked up this year, although they remain below the 2004 level. Nevertheless, they are the predominant source of foreign exchange inflows for India, Korea, and Vietnam.

Large foreign exchange inflows present opportunities to boost investment and growth, but they also create short-term challenges. Policies have, however, generally steered a path between maintaining external competitiveness—regional exports continue to grow rapidly—limiting risks of overheating, and preparing for their possible reversals. In most countries, inflation remains low or has eased considerably following earlier upward pressures (Indonesia and the Philippines), while the pace of credit growth has slowed (Korea and Singapore are exceptions). In India, inflation has eased in recent months, but upside risks remain—core inflation is still elevated, credit growth remains rapid, and equity prices have risen sharply over the past 12 months. In China, surging food prices drove CPI inflation up to 6.5 percent in August (even though nonfood price inflation remains subdued), credit is expanding strongly, and there are concerns about overvaluation in equity prices.

The successful management of foreign exchange inflows into the region has been achieved through a pragmatic range of policy responses tailored to suit individual country circumstances.

- Exchange rate reforms have been introduced in some countries (China and Malaysia), and most currencies have appreciated in nominal and real effective terms over the past couple of years. Nevertheless, rapid reserve accumulation has continued.
- Restrictions on capital outflows have been eased. Regulatory reform has made it easier for private investors to acquire and hold foreign assets (China, Korea, Malaysia, and Thailand), and national pension funds have been permitted to invest an increasing share of their assets in foreign investments (Thai-

land). Foreign direct investment outflows from the region have also increased, as Asian firms have sought to increase their global presence and acquire natural resources overseas. In the case of Thailand, wide-ranging controls on capital inflows were introduced in December 2006, although most of these have now been removed, while in India restrictions on external commercial borrowing have been tightened.

- Declining inflation has allowed some central banks to cut interest rates (Indonesia, the Philippines, and Thailand), whereas others have recently tightened monetary policy (including China, India, and Korea). The restraint of government expenditures has also played a role in a number of countries, notably Hong Kong SAR, India, Malaysia, and Taiwan Province of China.

Looking forward, policymakers will need to respond flexibly to future foreign exchange flows. The continued liberalization of restrictions on capital outflows would be helpful, not only from a short-term demand management perspective if strong foreign exchange inflows continue, but also because of the broader diversification benefits that investors will gain. As discussed in Chapter 3, fiscal expenditure restraint can be an effective tool for managing large capital inflows and will need to play a role in the policy response. This is particularly the case in countries such as India and Pakistan, where further consolidation is still needed despite recent progress in reducing government deficits and debt levels. Strong financial sector supervision and the continued development of domestic financial markets will also be important (see the October 2007 GFSR). One concern in this respect is that corporates in some countries have increased their foreign currency borrowing, raising their exposure to any future exchange rate correction.

Greater exchange rate flexibility in some countries would also be helpful. In China, the large increase in reserves has been only partially sterilized and has added to already substantial liquidity in the banking system, threatening to

Figure 2.4. Emerging Asia: Managing Strong Foreign Exchange Inflows

Foreign exchange inflows into emerging Asia have been very strong, driven largely by current account surpluses. Policymakers have responded by letting exchange rates appreciate to some extent and liberalizing capital outflows, while continuing to accumulate reserves.

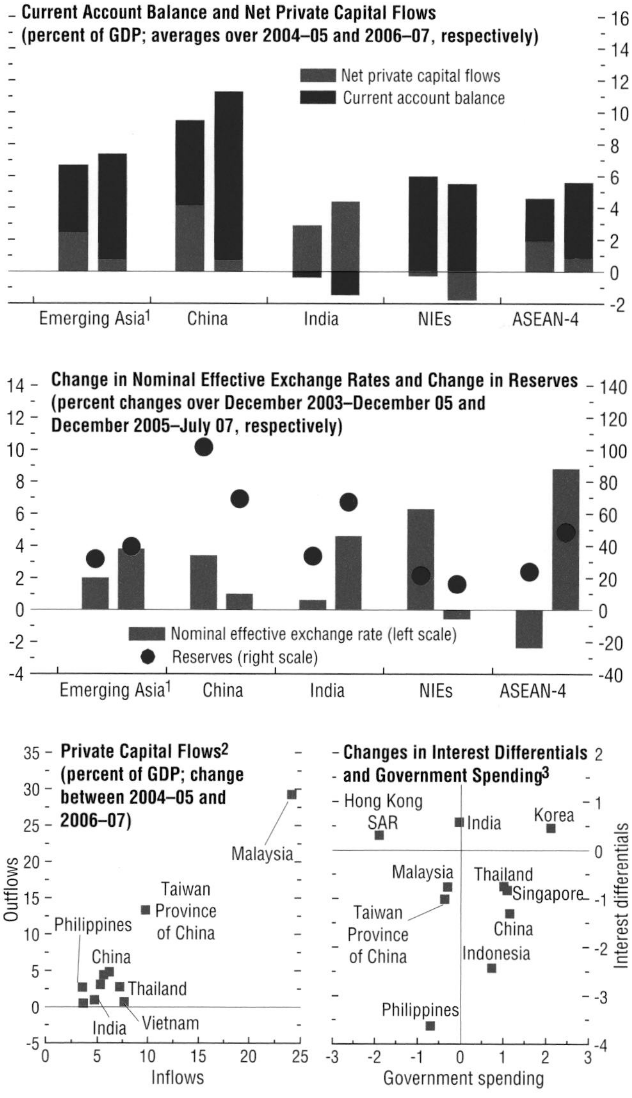

Source: IMF staff calculations.
[1]China, Hong Kong SAR, India, Indonesia, Korea, Malaysia, the Philippines, Singapore, Taiwan Province of China, and Thailand.
[2]Excludes Hong Kong SAR and Singapore, which are regional financial centers.
[3]Interest rate differential calculated as difference between country interest rate and U.S. interest rate. Change is measured as difference between the latest observation and the average of 2005. Changes in government spending, in percent of GDP, measured as difference between 2006–07 average and 2004–05 average.

Table 2.4. Selected Western Hemisphere Countries: Real GDP, Consumer Prices, and Current Account Balance

(Annual percent change unless noted otherwise)

	Real GDP				Consumer Prices[1]				Current Account Balance[2]			
	2005	2006	2007	2008	2005	2006	2007	2008	2005	2006	2007	2008
Western Hemisphere	**4.6**	**5.5**	**5.0**	**4.3**	**6.3**	**5.4**	**5.3**	**5.8**	**1.4**	**1.5**	**0.6**	**—**
South America and Mexico[3]	**4.5**	**5.4**	**4.9**	**4.2**	**6.2**	**5.2**	**5.2**	**5.8**	**1.7**	**1.8**	**0.8**	**0.2**
Argentina	9.2	8.5	7.5	5.5	9.6	10.9	9.5	12.6	1.9	2.5	0.9	0.4
Brazil	2.9	3.7	4.4	4.0	6.9	4.2	3.6	3.9	1.6	1.2	0.8	0.3
Chile	5.7	4.0	5.9	5.0	3.1	3.4	3.9	4.1	1.1	3.6	3.7	2.3
Colombia	4.7	6.8	6.6	4.8	5.0	4.3	5.5	4.6	–1.5	–2.1	–3.9	–3.5
Ecuador	6.0	3.9	2.7	3.4	2.1	3.3	2.1	2.3	0.8	3.6	2.4	2.5
Mexico	2.8	4.8	2.9	3.0	4.0	3.6	3.9	4.2	–0.6	–0.3	–0.7	–1.1
Peru	6.7	7.6	7.0	6.0	1.6	2.0	1.5	2.3	1.4	2.8	1.3	1.1
Uruguay	6.6	7.0	5.2	3.8	4.7	6.4	8.0	6.8	—	–2.4	–2.8	–2.8
Venezuela	10.3	10.3	8.0	6.0	16.0	13.7	18.0	19.0	17.8	15.0	7.8	4.1
Central America[4]	**4.5**	**5.9**	**5.4**	**4.9**	**8.4**	**7.0**	**6.5**	**6.0**	**–5.1**	**–5.0**	**–5.6**	**–5.8**
The Caribbean[4]	**6.5**	**8.4**	**6.0**	**4.4**	**6.7**	**8.0**	**6.4**	**5.3**	**–0.3**	**–0.4**	**–1.0**	**–0.6**

[1]Movements in consumer prices are shown as annual averages. December/December changes can be found in Table A7 in the Statistical Appendix.

[2]Percent of GDP.

[3]Includes Bolivia and Paraguay.

[4]The country composition of these regional groups is set out in Table F in the Statistical Appendix.

underpin a further surge in lending and investment growth. A more flexible exchange rate would give monetary policy more scope to focus on domestic objectives, particularly the need to slow lending and investment growth. Along with policies that reduce the need for precautionary savings (including increased spending on health care, pensions, and the social safety net), appreciation of the renminbi—which is undervalued relative to medium-term fundamentals—would also boost consumption by increasing household purchasing power. Together with reduced incentives for investment in the export sector, this would contribute to a narrowing of the very large current account surplus. Elsewhere, flexible exchange rate management will enable countries to adjust to evolving developments in global financial markets, while monetary policy has scope to respond to changes in the balance of risks to growth and inflation.

Latin America—Responding to Surging Foreign Exchange Inflows

Following 5½ percent growth in 2006, the pace of expansion in Western Hemisphere countries is projected to moderate to 5 percent in 2007 as a whole and to 4.3 percent in 2008 (Table 2.4). This easing would reflect in part spillovers from the slowdown of activity in the United States on Mexico and Central America, mainly through trade linkages as well as somewhat slower growth of remittances from migrant workers, and the end of a hotel construction boom in the Caribbean. In a number of commodity-exporting countries in South America—including Argentina, Colombia, Peru, Uruguay, and Venezuela—growth is expected to come down from very high rates in 2006, in part because of increasing supply constraints. Growth is picking up in Brazil in 2007, responding to monetary policy easing after inflation was brought on track with central bank objectives, but is also expected to slow in 2008.

The balance of risks to these projections for the region would seem to be moderately on the downside, arising principally from the possibility of continued turbulent conditions in global financial markets having spillover effects on Latin America through trade and financial channels. So far the impact of recent financial developments on Latin America has been relatively contained, because the strengthening of macroeconomic policy frameworks and public sector balance sheets has helped to anchor investor confidence. However, a weaker path for the U.S. economy would dampen demand for Latin American exports, with Mexico and Central America being most at risk because of greater trade linkages. Moreover, commodity exporters in South America would be affected by any softening in food, metals, or energy prices as a result of slower global demand growth. The impact through the financial channel would most likely be less dramatic than the "sudden stops" experienced in the past, given Latin America's stronger fundamentals, but nevertheless there would be a cooling influence from less-buoyant equity prices and from increases in borrowing spreads. On the other hand, there are also upside risks. Surging capital inflows in the first half of 2007 boosted local asset prices and credit growth, and further measures may still be needed to rein in growth of domestic demand in a number of countries in response to overheating concerns (Figure 2.5).

A key macroeconomic challenge for Latin America is how to handle foreign exchange inflows. Through 2006, these inflows were largely trade related, as strong foreign demand and high commodity prices boosted export earnings, and the regional current account surplus rose to a record 1.8 percent of GDP. In contrast, net capital inflows were on a declining trend, as governments took advantage of improved fiscal performance to repay foreign borrowing. However, these trends have reversed recently. Current account surpluses are moderating in 2007, as strong domestic demand has boosted import growth. In contrast, net capital inflows have risen rapidly since mid-2006, as portfolio and bank-related flows surged, particularly to Argentina, Brazil, and Colombia.[3] The recent turbulence in global financial markets has taken some of the momentum out of these flows, but the expectation is that Latin America

Figure 2.5. Latin America: Capital Inflows Are Complicating Macroeconomic Management

A number of Latin American countries are experiencing heavy capital inflows that are pushing up international reserves and contributing to rapid credit growth and rising equity prices. The degree of exchange rate movement in the face of foreign exchange inflows has varied across countries. Strong increases in government spending are adding to demand pressures.

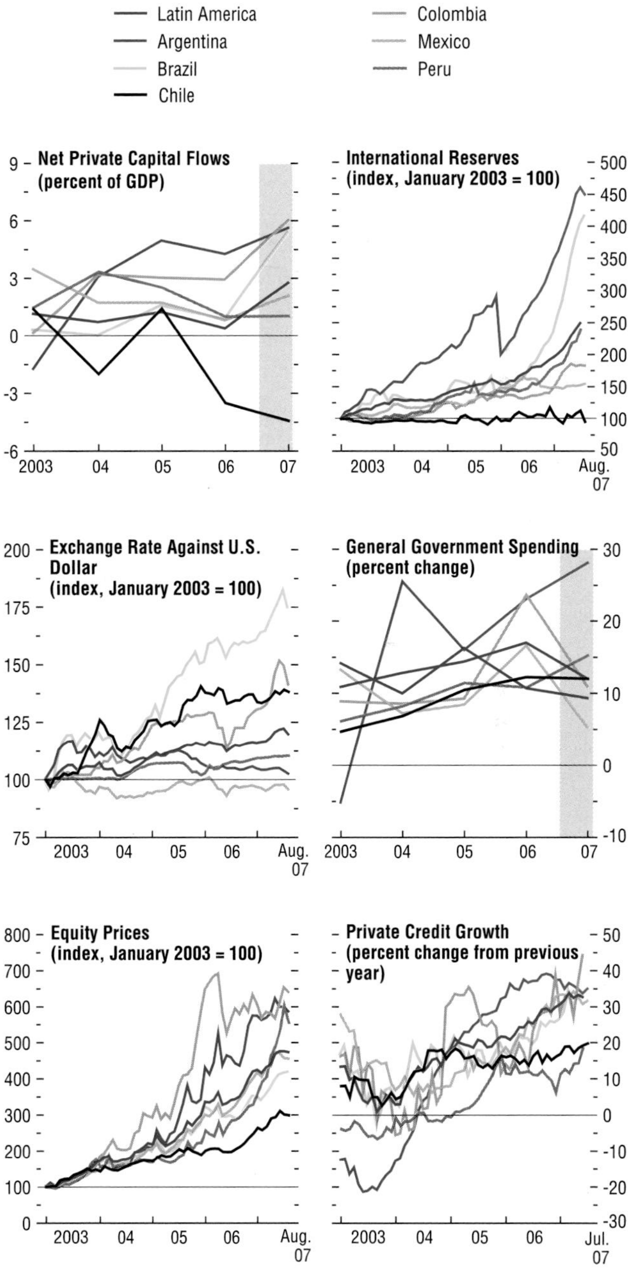

Sources: Haver Analytics; IMF, *International Financial Statistics;* and IMF staff calculations.

[3]See Chapter 2 of the IMF's *Regional Economic Outlook: Western Hemisphere* (October 2007).

will continue to receive sizable capital inflows in the period ahead, although countries should be prepared for the possibility of increased volatility.

Latin American economies have allowed exchange rates to move more flexibly than in the past, in response to shifts in exchange market pressures. Faced with strong inflows in the first half of 2007, exchange rates strengthened appreciably in a number of countries, including Brazil, Colombia, Paraguay, and Peru, notwithstanding continued intervention. In Brazil, foreign exchange inflows in the first half of 2007 were double their level in the same period of 2006, driving an appreciation of the real to its strongest level against the dollar in seven years, notwithstanding heavy intervention. The exchange rate appreciation has contributed to containing inflation, giving room to the central bank to continue to lower interest rates, thus reducing the wide interest differential with other countries. In July–August, market pressures turned, in the context of financial turbulence, and exchange rates initially weakened across the region, although they have recovered ground in recent weeks. In Argentina, the peso has fluctuated in a narrow range amid central bank interventions, and in Venezuela, the exchange rate has been kept unchanged for more than two years, and inflation has risen to about 20 percent.

Fiscal policy choices have affected the tradeoffs faced by Latin American countries in handling foreign exchange inflows. In Chile, fiscal policy has played a deliberately countercyclical role, as the budget has aimed at a structural surplus adjusted for variations in copper prices, a key determinant of revenues, and this approach has generated substantial capital outflows that have balanced upward pressure on the currency. Elsewhere, general government balances have mostly been kept in surplus or small deficit, helping to bring down the ratios of public debt to GDP. However, with fiscal revenues being boosted by strong growth and export performance, government spending has also been allowed to accelerate in a number of countries, providing a procyclical fiscal impulse and adding to overheating pressures. Such concerns are particularly salient in Argentina, where recent policy measures have added to fiscal stimulus, and in Venezuela.

Latin American countries have used various financial measures to try to discourage capital inflows, but the impact has been limited. For example, Colombia imposed a 40 percent unremunerated reserve requirement (URR) for six months on portfolio and bank-related inflows in May 2007—Argentina has had a similar mechanism (applying a 30 percent URR for one year) in place since 2005. However, these measures have generally had limited impact on market developments. Of greater long-term significance, countries have liberalized restrictions on capital outflows. For example, Argentina, Brazil, Chile, Colombia, and Peru have eased limits on holdings of foreign assets by local mutual funds and pension funds. Over time, such steps should help raise returns and diversify portfolios, while also easing pressures in the foreign exchange market.

A number of countries have also resorted to other microeconomic measures to contain domestic side effects of strong foreign exchange inflows or to contain the impact of strong growth in domestic demand on inflation. For example, Brazil has raised import tariffs on textiles, clothing, and footwear to protect labor-intensive domestic production from competition from Asian imports; both Brazil and Colombia have introduced cheap credit lines, and Argentina has maintained extensive administrative measures to contain increases in consumer prices, including limiting price adjustments in regulated industries, selective price agreements, and export restraints. Argentina's actions, if sustained, could exacerbate capacity constraints in key sectors and undermine the business climate.

From a longer-term perspective, Latin America's present expansion is its longest since the 1960s, and sustained growth has helped reduce external vulnerabilities. However, the region continues to be at the bottom of the

Table 2.5. Emerging Europe: Real GDP, Consumer Prices, and Current Account Balance
(Annual percent change unless noted otherwise)

	Real GDP				Consumer Prices[1]				Current Account Balance[2]			
	2005	2006	2007	2008	2005	2006	2007	2008	2005	2006	2007	2008
Emerging Europe	**5.6**	**6.3**	**5.8**	**5.2**	**4.9**	**5.1**	**5.1**	**4.1**	**–5.2**	**–6.6**	**–7.3**	**–7.5**
Turkey	7.4	6.1	5.0	5.3	8.2	9.6	8.2	4.6	–6.2	–7.9	–7.5	–7.0
Excluding Turkey	4.9	6.4	6.1	5.2	3.5	3.2	3.8	4.0	–4.8	–6.0	–7.3	–7.8
Baltics	**9.0**	**9.7**	**8.8**	**6.3**	**4.2**	**4.8**	**6.5**	**6.4**	**–9.4**	**–15.1**	**–18.3**	**–18.3**
Estonia	10.2	11.2	8.0	6.0	4.1	4.4	6.0	7.0	–10.0	–15.5	–16.9	–15.9
Latvia	10.6	11.9	10.5	6.2	6.7	6.5	9.0	8.9	–12.6	–21.1	–25.3	–27.3
Lithuania	7.6	7.5	8.0	6.5	2.7	3.8	5.2	4.6	–7.1	–10.9	–14.0	–12.6
Central Europe	**4.5**	**6.0**	**5.8**	**4.9**	**2.4**	**2.1**	**3.3**	**3.3**	**–3.2**	**–3.7**	**–4.1**	**–4.7**
Czech Republic	6.5	6.4	5.6	4.6	1.8	2.5	2.9	4.4	–1.6	–3.1	–3.4	–3.5
Hungary	4.2	3.9	2.1	2.7	3.6	3.9	7.6	4.5	–6.8	–6.5	–5.6	–5.1
Poland	3.6	6.1	6.6	5.3	2.1	1.0	2.2	2.7	–1.7	–2.3	–3.7	–5.1
Slovak Republic	6.0	8.3	8.8	7.3	2.8	4.4	2.4	2.0	–8.6	–8.3	–5.3	–4.5
Southern and southeastern Europe	**4.5**	**6.8**	**6.0**	**5.7**	**7.0**	**6.0**	**4.6**	**5.1**	**–8.7**	**–10.5**	**–13.6**	**–13.1**
Bulgaria	6.2	6.1	6.0	5.9	5.0	7.3	8.2	7.9	–12.0	–15.8	–20.3	–19.0
Croatia	4.3	4.8	5.6	4.7	3.3	3.2	2.3	2.8	–6.4	–7.8	–8.4	–8.8
Malta	3.3	3.3	3.2	2.6	2.5	2.6	0.6	2.0	–8.0	–6.1	–9.4	–8.2
Romania	4.1	7.7	6.3	6.0	9.0	6.6	4.3	4.8	–8.7	–10.3	–13.8	–13.2
Memorandum												
Slovenia	4.1	5.7	5.4	3.8	2.5	2.5	3.2	3.1	–1.9	–2.5	–3.4	–3.1

[1]Movements in consumer prices are shown as annual averages. December/December changes can be found in Table A7 in the Statistical Appendix.
[2]Percent of GDP.

world growth league, and governments should take advantage of present conditions to advance the reforms that are needed to support more rapid growth in investment and productivity. Impediments to improved performance include inefficient public sectors, limited financial intermediation, weak infrastructure, and high income inequality. One encouraging recent development has been progress with fiscal reforms in Mexico, including measures to contain the costs of civil service pensions and to broaden the tax base to replace declining oil revenues and provide additional funding for infrastructure and social spending.

Emerging Europe: Brisk Activity, Rising Imbalances

Growth in emerging Europe accelerated to 6.3 percent in 2006, and the pace moderated only slightly in the first half of 2007 (Table 2.5). Spending on new productive capacity and construction activity bolstered investment, while rising disposable incomes, improving labor markets, and easy access to credit, financed mainly through cross-border interbank loans, continued to buttress consumer spending and investment, especially in the Baltics and in southern and southeastern Europe. Exports benefited from an upswing in western Europe—the main trading partner—as well as increased integration of emerging Europe into regional production chains and the upgrading of the quality of export products. In particular, a pickup in exports helped support Turkey's economy, where domestic demand has slowed in the face of monetary tightening to reduce inflation after it spiked in mid-2006. Growth in Hungary continued to be weaker than in the rest of the region, reflecting in part the short-term impact of fiscal consolidation.

The recent strong performance, however, has been accompanied by rising concerns about widening external imbalances and overheating in the Baltics and southern and southeastern Europe, where booming credit has boosted

Figure 2.6. Emerging Europe: Rapid Credit Growth Is Fueling Domestic Demand

The brisk pace of credit growth in the Baltics and other areas of emerging Europe supports financial deepening, but it raises macroeconomic and prudential concerns. Credit growth bolstered domestic demand in these country groups, leading to a sharp deterioration in the external positions. Procyclical fiscal policies exacerbated imbalances in some cases. Current account deficits were financed largely through bank-to-bank and other borrowing rather than foreign direct investment, as in central Europe.

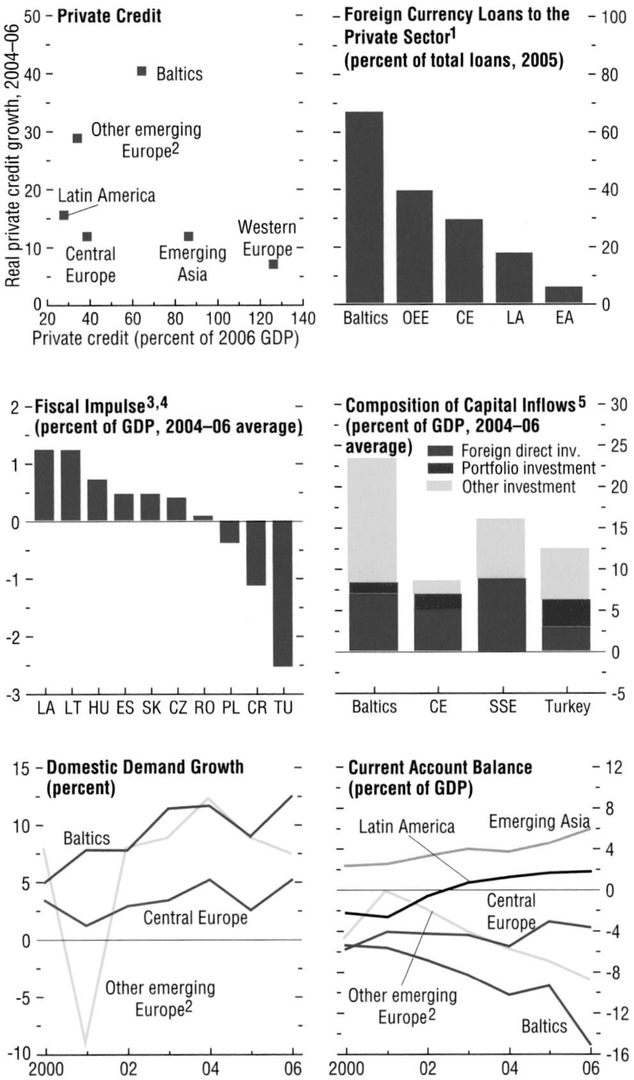

Sources: IMF, *International Financial Statistics;* and IMF staff calculations.

[1]CE: central Europe; OEE: other emerging Europe; EA: emerging Asia; LA: Latin America.

[2]Other emerging Europe includes Bulgaria, Croatia, Malta, Romania, and Turkey.

[3]LA: Latvia; LT: Lithuania; HU: Hungary; ES: Estonia; SK: Slovak Republic; CZ: Czech Republic; RO: Romania; PL: Poland; CR: Croatia; and TU: Turkey.

[4]Fiscal impulse is calculated as the first difference in structural balance, adjusted, where appropriate, to isolate the demand impact of fiscal policy by excluding EU grants and privatization receipts from revenues and excluding payments to the EU from expenditures.

[5]SSE: southern and southeastern Europe.

private domestic demand and elevated inflation and external deficits (Figure 2.6). In Latvia, the current account deficit widened to 21 percent of GDP in 2006, but deficits are also high, at 10–16 percent of GDP, in other Baltic countries, Bulgaria, and Romania. Credit booms in the Baltics and southern and southeastern Europe have been supported by readily available financing through foreign parent banks at low real interest rates and, in some cases, by procyclical fiscal policies (see Figure 2.6). A significant portion of credit in the Baltics and other emerging Europe has been denominated in, or indexed to, foreign currency (more so than in other emerging market regions) and directed to real estate, and the balance sheet mismatches such lending creates raise prudential and macroeconomic concerns. In central Europe, external positions have been stronger, in part because capital inflows there have tended to take the form of foreign direct investment in the tradable goods sectors, with the ensuing exports helping to keep current account deficits under control. Inflation has also been better contained in central Europe, owing in part to monetary policy independence in mostly inflation-targeting countries, past nominal currency appreciation, and the dampening effect of global competition on wages, although expanding demand is now starting to test resource constraints.[4]

Large external imbalances in the Baltics and southern and southeastern Europe are also raising concerns about possible real exchange rate overvaluation, although it is recognized that some part of the real exchange rate appreciation recently experienced by these countries has been consistent with improving fundamentals. Supporting factors include strong productivity growth in the tradables sector (the well-known Balassa-Samuelson effect); EU transfers to the new member states, which are projected to remain sizable in the coming years; and improvements in the quality of services. Moreover, part of the real appreciation is likely to

[4]The sharp increase in inflation projected in Hungary for 2007 reflects large increases in regulated prices.

have been a one-off level adjustment associated with, for example, the adoption of the EU acquis and the increased availability of foreign capital owing to the confluence of unusually benign global financial conditions and structural changes in the investor base for emerging markets. Speculative flows may also have contributed to real appreciation, but such factors are difficult to quantify. Emerging European countries, particularly those with large external financing needs and appreciable currency mismatches in private sector balance sheets, could thus be vulnerable to a change in investor sentiment.

Regional growth is forecast to soften to 5.8 percent in 2007 and further to 5.2 percent in 2008. Domestic demand will slow owing to monetary and fiscal tightening, but should remain strong, supported, among other things, by large inflows of EU transfers and the still significant incentives for outsourcing from western Europe. Tighter global credit conditions are likely to dampen growth of house prices and household consumption, with knock-on effects for construction and business investment.[5] Exports are also likely to slow as a result of weakening external demand from western Europe and, to a lesser extent, strong currencies and rising wage costs. However, the still significant wage differential vis-à-vis western Europe and strong productivity growth will continue to support the competitiveness. The slowdown of activity is expected to be most pronounced in the Baltics, where some cooling of demand would be welcome.

Risks to this outlook are tilted to the downside, largely owing to the possibility of a sharper-than-expected squeeze on credit. In addition, risks of a disorderly unwinding of large external imbalances are concentrated in some countries, with spillovers to the rest of the region mainly through contagion. Countries with large external imbalances—the Baltics, Romania, and Bulgaria—may be significantly affected by the increased cost of external financing and higher risk premiums, following recent financial market turbulence, although the strength of fiscal positions may mitigate the fallout in some cases. There is scope for financial market contagion, whereby a widening of the risk premium for one emerging European country may prompt investors to reassess sovereign risk of other countries in the region. The common-lender problem—a narrow group of predominantly European banks accounting for a significant portion of outstanding claims on emerging European banks and the private sector—is another potential channel for transmission of financial shocks across the region. The potential for spillovers from emerging Europe to western Europe through financial and trade channels exists, but is considerably smaller than within the emerging Europe region (Haas and Tamirisa, 2007).

Macroeconomic policies therefore need to focus on steering economies toward soft landings, while containing vulnerabilities and laying the foundation for sustainable long-term growth. Countries with fixed exchange rate regimes (for example, the Baltics and Bulgaria) or tightly managed floats (for example, Croatia) should rely more on fiscal restraint as they seek to rein in demand pressures. Countries with floating exchange rates (for example, Romania) can also raise interest rates as needed to stem inflationary pressures while reining in procyclical fiscal expansions. Since overall fiscal policy multipliers tend to be small in open emerging European economies, specific fiscal measures aimed at reducing tax and subsidy incentives for real estate borrowing are worth considering. The implementation of fiscal consolidation plans remains a priority in countries with long-term fiscal sustainability concerns, for example, the Czech Republic, Hungary, and Poland. Structural reforms to improve price and wage flexibility also need to be advanced in some countries.

Strong bank supervision, particularly of foreign currency and real estate lending, is critical for maintaining credit quality and bank capital in an environment of rapidly expanding balance sheets. Many countries have been tighten-

[5]The Swedish banks active in the Baltics have announced their intention to tighten the terms of credit, amid heightened concerns about the brisk pace of credit growth in the Baltics.

ing prudential and administrative regulations aimed at encouraging banks to strengthen risk management and/or to reduce the pace of credit growth, but the effectiveness of the latter measures seems to have been limited so far (Hilbers, Ötker-Robe, and Pazarbasioglu, 2007). A stronger prudential policy response is justified in countries where there are concerns about loan quality. In many countries, subsidiaries and branches of banks from advanced economies have been leading credit expansion, and the strength of their parent banks is reassuring, but these banks may have come to rely excessively on the strong profits of their emerging market offshoots (Tamirisa and Igan, 2006). This underscores the need for strong cross-border cooperation with foreign supervisors to ensure that any emerging signs of weaknesses are addressed in a timely and effective manner. Raising borrowers' awareness of risks and improving market infrastructure facilitating banks' risk assessment (for example, credit bureaus) are also a priority.

For the new members of the European Union that are committed to adopting the euro, the key challenge is to meet the necessary entry criteria and to enter the monetary union in positions that allow these countries to continue to perform well in the Economic and Monetary Union (EMU). The sustained real appreciation that accompanies rapid income convergence of the new EU member states, even in cases where the economies are not overheating, makes satisfying the inflation entry precondition particularly challenging (Haas and Tamirisa, 2007). The pursuit of consistent macroeconomic policies and further improvements in the structural flexibility of the economies are thus essential for the new member states to enter the euro area smoothly and to excel in the EMU. Especially in countries that are still far away from "prudent" medium-term fiscal targets, fiscal adjustment would help ease cyclical demand pressures, while putting public finances on a sustainable footing for the longer term and helping satisfy the Maastricht fiscal criteria with a margin. Clear communication of the new member states' euro-adoption prospects is also essential, as it would help households, businesses, and financial markets make appropriate decisions and perhaps facilitate the unwinding of the currency mismatches accumulated on earlier, more optimistic, expectations.

Commonwealth of Independent States: Tensions Between Inflation and Exchange Rate Objectives

The CIS region has not been immune to the recent financial turmoil, but this has come against the backdrop of the longest economic expansion since the beginning of transition. Although easing slightly, growth in the region remained strong in the second quarter of 2007. The Russian economy expanded by about 7¾ percent (year on year), and economic activity in other CIS countries has also remained buoyant. The robust expansion in the region has been underpinned by high commodity prices and strong capital inflows, as well as continuing productivity gains. Consumption has remained the main driver of growth, supported by rising real incomes and easy access to credit, but there are also incipient signs of rebalancing in the composition of demand, with investment picking up recently. Credit to the private sector has been expanding rapidly across the region, fueled by capital inflows, ample domestic liquidity, and structural improvements in the financial sector.

Against the backdrop of the global disruption to liquidity and pullback from risky assets, exchange rates in Kazakhstan and Russia came under some downward pressure in late August. In Kazakhstan, concerns that domestic banks could be vulnerable to global credit retrenchment contributed to depreciation pressures, while in Russia the repatriation of liquid ruble assets by nonresident investors was the primary factor behind the depreciation. As liquidity conditions in interbank markets deteriorated and banks experienced difficulties raising external funds and started to curtail their lending, the central banks of both countries

Table 2.6. Commonwealth of Independent States: Real GDP, Consumer Prices, and Current Account Balance
(Annual percent change unless noted otherwise)

	Real GDP				Consumer Prices[1]				Current Account Balance[2]			
	2005	2006	2007	2008	2005	2006	2007	2008	2005	2006	2007	2008
Commonwealth of Independent States (CIS)	**6.6**	**7.7**	**7.8**	**7.0**	**12.1**	**9.4**	**8.9**	**8.3**	**8.8**	**7.6**	**4.8**	**3.1**
Russia	6.4	6.7	7.0	6.5	12.7	9.7	8.1	7.5	11.1	9.7	5.9	3.3
Ukraine	2.7	7.1	6.7	5.4	13.5	9.0	11.5	10.8	2.9	–1.5	–3.5	–6.2
Kazakhstan	9.7	10.7	8.7	7.8	7.6	8.6	8.6	7.8	–1.8	–2.2	–2.2	–1.1
Belarus	9.3	9.9	7.8	6.4	10.3	7.0	8.1	10.0	1.6	–4.1	–7.9	–8.1
Turkmenistan	9.0	9.0	10.0	10.0	10.7	8.2	6.5	9.0	5.1	15.3	13.0	12.5
Low-income CIS countries	**12.0**	**14.6**	**15.7**	**13.4**	**8.4**	**10.0**	**12.1**	**11.7**	**2.2**	**7.5**	**13.7**	**19.1**
Armenia	14.0	13.3	11.1	10.0	0.6	2.9	3.7	4.9	–3.9	–1.4	–4.0	–4.2
Azerbaijan	24.3	31.0	29.3	23.2	9.7	8.4	16.6	17.0	1.3	15.7	31.4	39.9
Georgia	9.6	9.4	11.0	9.0	8.3	9.2	8.5	8.1	–9.8	–13.8	–15.7	–15.2
Kyrgyz Republic	–0.2	2.7	7.5	7.0	4.3	5.6	7.0	7.0	3.2	–6.6	–17.9	–15.1
Moldova	7.5	4.0	5.0	5.0	11.9	12.7	11.2	8.9	–10.3	–12.0	–8.0	–7.3
Tajikistan	6.7	7.0	7.5	8.0	7.3	10.0	9.9	12.6	–2.5	–2.9	–11.6	–12.6
Uzbekistan	7.0	7.3	8.8	7.5	10.0	14.2	12.2	9.8	13.6	18.8	21.1	21.0
Memorandum												
Net energy exporters[3]	7.1	7.7	7.9	7.3	12.1	9.7	8.5	7.9	10.0	9.2	6.3	4.4
Net energy importers[4]	4.5	7.7	7.2	6.0	12.0	8.5	10.4	10.3	1.4	–3.0	–5.4	–7.2

[1]Movements in consumer prices are shown as annual averages. December/December changes can be found in Table A7 in the Statistical Appendix.

[2]Percent of GDP.

[3]Includes Azerbaijan, Kazakhstan, Russia, Turkmenistan, and Uzbekistan.

[4]Includes Armenia, Belarus, Georgia, Kyrgyz Republic, Moldova, Tajikistan, and Ukraine.

injected liquidity to ensure stability in the banking systems.

Growth momentum is expected to ease from 7¾ percent in 2006–07 to 7 percent in 2008, largely owing to tightening credit conditions and a weakening external environment. High commodity prices and rising fiscal spending would continue to support activity in the net-energy-exporting countries (Azerbaijan, Kazakhstan, Russia, Turkmenistan, and Uzbekistan) (Table 2.6 and Figure 2.7). In the net-energy-importing countries (as a group), growth is expected to slow more rapidly, partly owing to rising oil prices, although growth in these countries will continue to be supported by the ongoing global commodity boom[6] and buoyant regional conditions, as manifested in strong external demand and large inflows of foreign direct investment and private remittances from the net-energy-importing countries.

Nevertheless, risks to growth are tilted to the downside, owing to a possible stronger impact of financial market turbulence on the availability of foreign and domestic financing, as well as the impact of slower global growth on commodity prices and export demand. If growth were to slow down significantly in Russia, demand for imports from smaller countries in the region (Armenia, Georgia, Moldova, the Kyrgyz Republic, and Tajikistan)[7] and flows of private remittances to these countries are likely to be adversely affected.

A long spell of robust demand growth in the region has tightened resource constraints, keeping inflation at high levels (9–10 percent). Unit labor costs are rising in some countries, reflecting higher labor utilization rates and tightening labor markets (Ukraine). Equipment shortages

[6]Many countries in the region export commodities: aluminum (Tajikistan), copper (Armenia and Georgia), cotton (Tajikistan and Uzbekistan), and ferrous and scrap metals (Georgia).

[7]These countries receive significant inflows of private remittances (15–35 percent of GDP).

Figure 2.7. Commonwealth of Independent States: Dealing with Capital Inflows

The CIS has benefited from inflows of direct, portfolio, and other investment, which supported financial deepening and economic expansion in the region. Yet large capital inflows have also presented macroeconomic challenges. Countries have to make a choice whether real appreciation should be effected mostly through inflation or nominal appreciation, a choice that is exacerbated by rapid demand growth, expansionary fiscal policies, and limited exchange rate flexibility in most CIS countries.

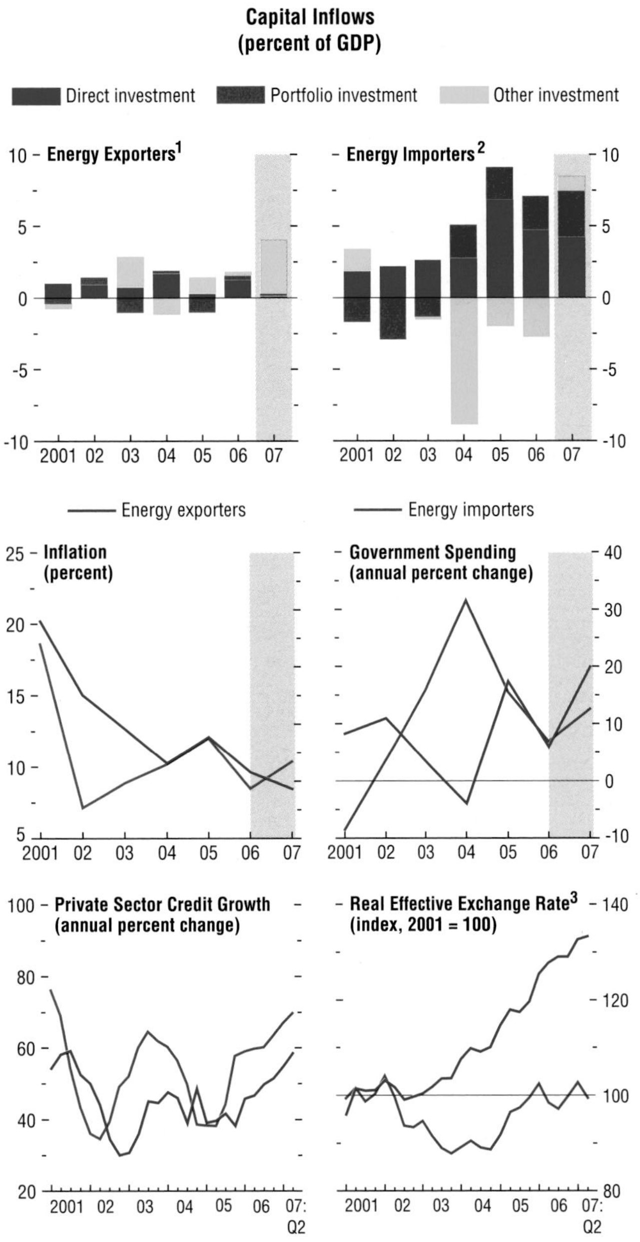

Sources: IMF, *International Financial Statistics;* and IMF staff estimates.
[1]Includes Azerbaijan, Kazakhstan, Russia, Turkmenistan, and Uzbekistan.
[2]Includes Armenia, Belarus, Georgia, Kyrgyz Republic, Moldova, Tajikistan, and Ukraine.
[3]An increase in the index represents a real appreciation whereas a decrease represents a real depreciation of a country's currency relative to that of its trading partners.

are also emerging, as indicated by rising imports of capital goods (Russia). In Azerbaijan, inflation is expected to rise to double digits in 2007 and 2008, as a large fiscal expansion is running up against supply constraints. Besides pushing up prices, robust demand growth in the region is also weakening the external current account positions, which nonetheless remain in a solid surplus in most energy-exporting countries. Competitiveness has suffered from rising prices in some countries, although many currencies in the region (notably, the Russian ruble) are still judged to be undervalued relative to medium-term fundamentals.

The region has attracted large inflows of foreign private capital in recent years. Foreign direct investment—reflecting privatization, mergers and acquisitions, as well as greenfield investment—has supported economic growth, especially in the net-energy-importing countries. Portfolio and other investment inflows have also been increasing over the years, including in the net-energy-exporting countries. This trend has been particularly pronounced in Russia and Kazakhstan, where external bank borrowing soared prior to the onset of the financial market turmoil.[8] High domestic interest rates and expectations of further ruble appreciation have prompted banks to switch to external funding of their domestic loan portfolios. More generally, limited flexibility in exchange rate policy in many CIS countries may have created perceptions of "one-way bets," encouraging speculative inflows. Prospects for continued bank and portfolio capital inflows are more uncertain following the onset of the financial market turmoil, but high oil and other commodity prices are likely to continue to attract capital to the region.

The increased reliance on bank borrowing and portfolio investment inflows for financing growth in the region has brought policy challenges in its wake. In contrast to commodity export revenues, which have been at least partly

[8]In the Kyrgyz Republic, Moldova, and Armenia, official financing has been an important contributor to growth.

sterilized in stabilization funds (for example, in Kazakhstan and Russia), capital inflows have largely fed through to boost domestic credit growth and have generated inflationary pressures. Nominal appreciation in response to capital inflows has been limited, as many countries are targeting nominal exchange rates. A decline in non-oil revenues and/or rapid growth of government spending have added to overheating problems (for example, in Armenia, Azerbaijan, Georgia, Russia, and Ukraine). More recently, concerns about a possible curtailment of external bank financing in the face of global market turmoil have highlighted potential problems that would arise if such flows were to reverse.

Some countries in the CIS region have responded to the large capital inflows and overheating pressures by broadening and tightening reserve requirements, and such approaches have helped mop up liquidity in the system. However, ultimately, greater exchange rate flexibility is required to improve inflation control (for example, in Kazakhstan, Russia, and Ukraine),[9] and preparations for moving to more flexible exchange rates need to be accelerated to prevent high-inflation expectations from becoming entrenched. Supporting this approach, further efforts are needed to develop market-based monetary instruments, deepen the domestic money market, and tighten financial regulations, particularly to ensure that foreign borrowing does not lead to bank or corporate balance sheet vulnerabilities. Growth of government spending should be kept in check, striking a balance between addressing still-significant social and infrastructure needs and excessively fueling inflation and appreciation pressures.

Beyond the near term, boosting savings and investment is critical to strengthening the region's growth outlook. Catch-up productivity gains are likely to diminish over time, while adverse demographic trends are weighing on long-term prospects. The rate of investment (at 21 percent of GDP in 2006 and projected to rise only slightly in 2007) remains lower than in other regions of the world, while the concentration of investment in extractive industries and construction points to the need to diversify the sources of growth. Whether private investment responds to this challenge will depend on further improvements in institutions and the business climate. Financial deepening and the development of arm's-length sources of finance would also strengthen long-term growth prospects. Additional strengthening of prudential regulations (for example, stricter provisioning and higher risk weights for particular categories of loans) and banking supervision would help improve the capacity of banks to manage risks and maintain credit quality in the environment of rapid loan growth.

Sub-Saharan Africa—Benefiting from Globalization

Sub-Saharan Africa (SSA) is enjoying another strong year, with overall growth in the region projected to rise from 5.7 percent in 2006 to 6.1 percent in 2007 and further to 6.8 percent in 2008 (Table 2.7). The growth acceleration reflects largely the coming onstream of new production facilities in oil-exporting countries, such as Angola and Nigeria. But most other countries in the region are projected to maintain relatively high rates of growth, while inflation would generally moderate (excluding Zimbabwe, which is expected to remain an outlier). Risks to the forecast are, however, tilted somewhat to the downside, reflecting mainly the possibility of a weaker global outturn, which would weaken demand for African commodity exports and tighten financial constraints, as well as risks from domestic political developments in individual countries.

Taking a longer-term perspective, SSA is clearly enjoying its best period of sustained growth since independence. While the oil-exporting countries are achieving the most rapid growth, most other countries are also growing strongly and outperforming historic

[9]The central bank let the Russian ruble appreciate by ½ percent vis-à-vis the dollar-euro dual currency basket on June 26 and again by 0.6 percent on August 9.

Table 2.7. Selected African Countries: Real GDP, Consumer Prices, and Current Account Balance
(Annual percent change unless noted otherwise)

	Real GDP				Consumer Prices[1]				Current Account Balance[2]			
	2005	2006	2007	2008	2005	2006	2007	2008	2005	2006	2007	2008
Africa	**5.6**	**5.6**	**5.7**	**6.5**	**6.6**	**6.3**	**6.6**	**6.0**	**2.0**	**3.1**	**—**	**0.6**
Maghreb	**4.1**	**5.2**	**4.3**	**5.6**	**1.5**	**3.1**	**3.6**	**3.4**	**11.7**	**14.6**	**10.4**	**9.7**
Algeria	5.1	3.6	4.8	5.2	1.6	2.5	4.5	4.3	20.7	25.6	19.4	18.4
Morocco	2.4	8.0	2.5	5.9	1.0	3.3	2.5	2.0	2.4	3.4	0.7	0.2
Tunisia	4.0	5.4	6.0	6.2	2.0	4.5	3.0	3.0	–1.1	–2.3	–2.6	–2.7
Sub-Sahara	**6.0**	**5.7**	**6.1**	**6.8**	**8.2**	**7.3**	**7.6**	**6.7**	**–0.9**	**–0.3**	**–3.0**	**–1.6**
Horn of Africa[3]	**9.3**	**10.5**	**10.9**	**10.2**	**7.7**	**9.3**	**12.0**	**10.3**	**–9.4**	**–13.5**	**–9.5**	**–7.3**
Ethiopia	10.2	9.0	10.5	9.6	6.8	12.3	17.8	15.9	–6.8	–10.4	–5.9	–3.0
Sudan	8.6	11.8	11.2	10.7	8.5	7.2	8.0	6.5	–10.7	–14.7	–10.7	–8.5
Great Lakes[3]	**6.2**	**5.6**	**6.3**	**7.0**	**11.5**	**10.3**	**9.6**	**6.5**	**–3.6**	**–5.2**	**–5.8**	**–7.5**
Congo, Dem. Rep. of	6.5	5.1	6.5	8.4	21.4	13.2	17.5	8.8	–10.6	–7.5	–8.1	–10.9
Kenya	5.8	6.1	6.4	6.5	10.3	14.5	6.9	7.2	–0.8	–2.4	–3.7	–5.1
Tanzania	6.7	6.2	7.1	7.5	4.4	7.3	5.6	5.0	–4.5	–8.6	–10.6	–10.8
Uganda	6.7	5.4	6.2	6.5	8.0	6.6	7.5	5.1	–2.1	–4.1	–2.4	–6.3
Southern Africa[3]	**6.5**	**7.2**	**9.2**	**11.0**	**11.7**	**10.4**	**9.0**	**7.3**	**4.4**	**10.9**	**3.6**	**2.6**
Angola	20.6	18.6	23.1	27.2	23.0	13.3	11.9	8.9	16.8	23.3	7.6	10.7
Zimbabwe[4]	–5.3	–4.8	–6.2	–4.5	237.8	1,016.7	16,170.2	. . .	–11.2	–4.0	–0.9	. . .
West and Central Africa[3]	**5.6**	**4.2**	**4.6**	**6.5**	**11.5**	**7.5**	**5.7**	**5.9**	**2.7**	**5.4**	**–0.4**	**1.8**
Ghana	5.9	6.2	6.3	6.9	15.1	10.9	9.4	8.8	–7.0	–9.7	–9.7	–7.7
Nigeria	7.2	5.6	4.3	8.0	17.8	8.3	5.3	7.4	9.3	12.2	1.8	6.0
CFA franc zone[3]	**4.5**	**2.2**	**4.6**	**5.3**	**4.4**	**3.6**	**3.1**	**3.1**	**–1.5**	**0.5**	**–0.7**	**–0.7**
Cameroon	2.0	3.8	3.8	5.3	2.0	5.1	2.0	2.7	–3.3	–0.7	–1.5	–3.1
Côte d'Ivoire	1.8	0.9	1.7	3.8	3.9	2.5	2.5	3.0	0.2	3.0	2.6	1.3
South Africa	**5.1**	**5.0**	**4.7**	**4.2**	**3.4**	**4.7**	**6.6**	**6.2**	**–4.0**	**–6.5**	**–6.7**	**–6.4**
Memorandum												
Oil importers	4.7	5.3	4.9	5.3	5.6	6.5	6.9	6.0	–3.2	–3.9	–4.5	–4.1
Oil exporters[5]	7.5	6.3	7.5	9.1	8.9	5.9	6.1	6.0	11.5	14.7	7.2	8.9

[1]For consumer price inflation, the composition of the regional groups excludes Zimbabwe. Movements in consumer prices are shown as annual averages. December/December changes can be found in Table A7 in the Statistical Appendix.

[2]Percent of GDP.

[3]The country composition of these regional groups is set out in Table F in the Statistical Appendix.

[4]Given recent trends, it is not possible to forecast inflation and nominal GDP with any precision and consequently no projection for 2008 is shown.

[5]Includes Chad and Mauritania in this table.

trends (Figure 2.8). Moreover, faster-growing countries in the region are making substantial progress in reducing poverty rates. This growth success reflects a potent combination of a favorable external environment (particularly, improving terms of trade), sound policy implementation, and the rising openness of SSA economies, achieved not only by oil and commodity exporters, but also by coastal and landlocked countries. While rising fuel and commodity-based exports have played a major role, African countries have also been able to expand nontraditional manufacturing exports and to diversify export destinations, especially to new destinations in Asia with strong demand for resource-based products.[10]

The combination of more open economies in a benign external environment, together with improved and more consistent policy implementation, reforms to strengthen the business environment, and official actions to reduce debt burdens, has allowed SSA countries to attract rising private capital inflows, as well as to benefit from some step-up in aid inflows and rising remittances. Foreign direct investment has

[10]See, for more detail, International Monetary Fund (2007).

been particularly strong to resource-rich countries, but also elsewhere, for example, to fund tourism projects. A smaller number of countries have also begun to attract interest from private portfolio investors—South Africa, with its well-developed financial structure, receives the bulk of these funds, but other countries, such as Ghana and Uganda, which have demonstrated increased policy credibility, have also been experiencing rising capital inflows. Official grants have not risen significantly at the aggregate level, despite commitments made at the Gleneagles Summit, but a number of countries have attracted rising aid inflows, particularly landlocked countries such as Lesotho, Malawi, and Rwanda.

SSA countries have so far experienced less severe trade-offs from the challenges of managing foreign exchange inflows than other parts of the developing world, but must be ready to face these issues. Most countries in the region have continued to run significant current account deficits; the buildup in international reserves has been welcome, but reserves remain quite low (outside the oil producers); and upward movements in the real effective exchange rate have been limited. The challenges are most pressing for oil exporters. Similar to other oil producers, the oil-exporting countries in Africa have made large terms-of-trade gains from recent fuel price increases, and international reserves have risen rapidly. These countries must be careful to spend oil windfall gains in a prudent manner, without straining domestic absorptive capacity, and saving appropriately for future generations. As discussed in IMF (2007), it will be important to combine well-targeted increases in government spending with measures to improve the supply-side response in the non-oil economy. Similar lessons also apply to considering how best to use stepped-up aid flows. Although such increased inflows would provide an important opportunity for poverty reduction, care will be needed to avoid crowding out other productive activities through upward pressure on scarce domestic resources (Box 2.3).

Figure 2.8. Sub-Saharan Africa: Benefiting from Globalization

Most African countries have grown robustly in recent years, helped by rising trade openness. Oil-exporting countries have grown particularly rapidly, with export revenues pushing up reserve levels fast. Net private inflows have risen, especially to coastal countries, while official flows have risen significantly to landlocked countries, financing rising current account deficits in both groups of countries.

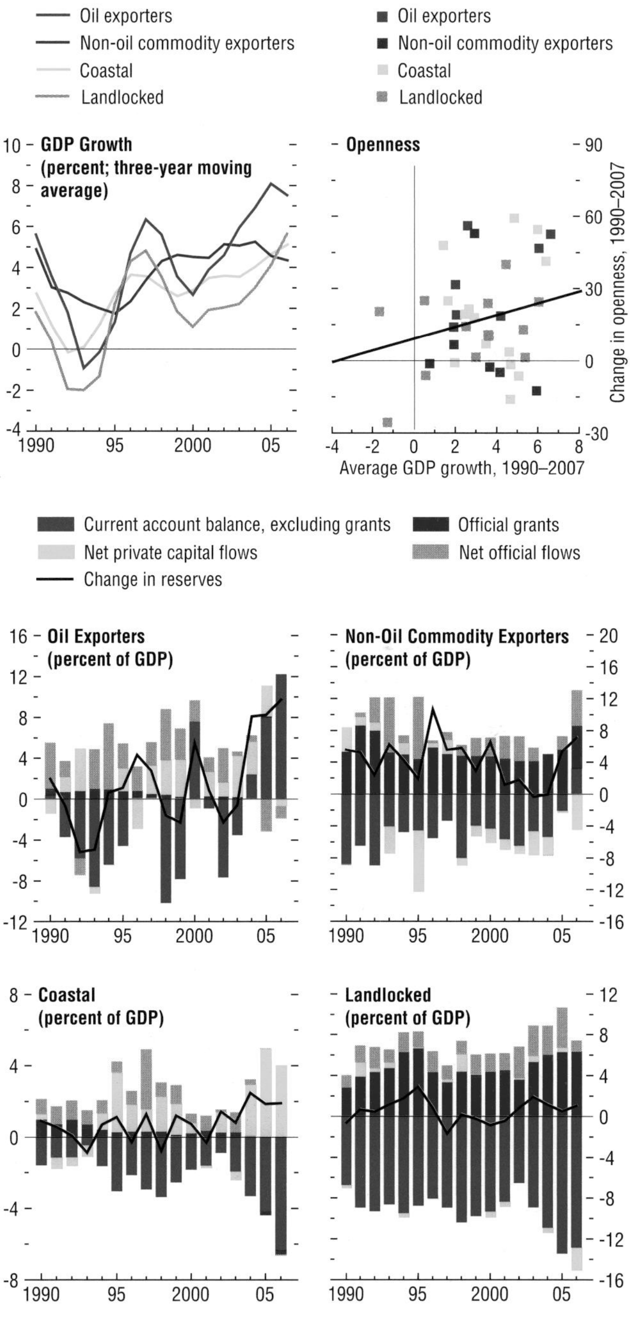

Source: IMF staff calculations.

Box 2.3. Managing the Macroeconomic Consequences of Large and Volatile Aid Flows

At the G-8 meeting in Gleneagles, Scotland, in 2005, world leaders pledged a large increase in official development assistance to low-income countries. The objective was to help poor countries achieve the Millennium Development Goals agreed upon at the Millennium Summit of the United Nations in 2000. The promised surge in aid flows is a unique opportunity to fight poverty on a large scale; however, it raises some macroeconomic challenges that need to be addressed to ensure that aid flows have the most beneficial impact.

Aid Flows Are Volatile

Aid flows to poor countries are often large and very volatile (Bulíř and Hamann, 2006). Between 1990 and 2005, about 40 poor countries experienced net aid inflows (excluding debt relief) above 10 percent of GDP (figure). This compares with net private capital flows to emerging markets, which in the past two decades have generally been less than 5 percent of GDP. Moreover, annual changes in net aid flows can be huge, easily exceeding 10 percent of GDP, and even more than 20 percent of GDP for a handful of countries. Moreover, recent research shows that aid is volatile and unpredictable even in countries that follow reasonable policies (Celasun and Walliser, forthcoming). Such volatility poses particular macroeconomic challenges to policymakers in low-income countries, which often suffer from weak public expenditure management, shortages of skilled workers, undiversified production structures, and shallow financial markets.

Variations in Aid Flows in Poor Countries, 1990–2005[1]
(Percent of GDP)

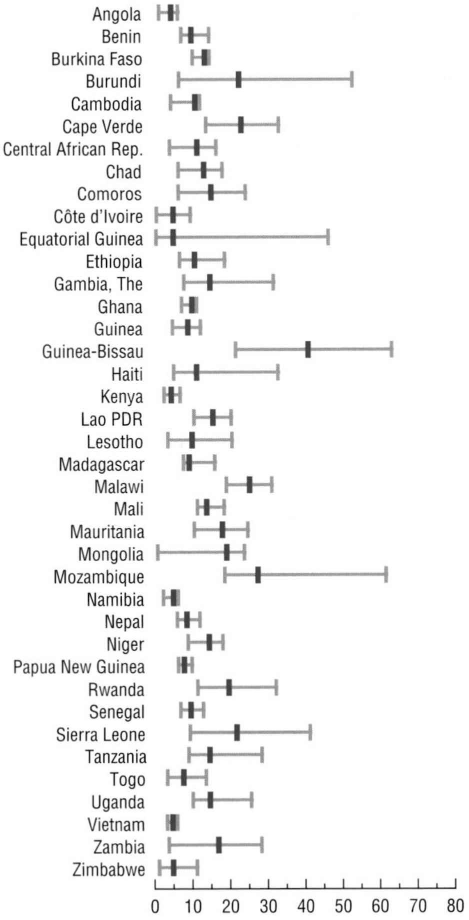

Source: IMF staff calculations.
[1]Chart displays minimum, median, and maximum aid flows over the period, excluding outliers.

Challenges in Macroeconomic Managing of Aid Flows

The problem of managing large aid inflows has several dimensions. First, the volatility and unpredictability of aid can complicate public expenditure management. It would be highly damaging if spending on recurrent expenditures (such as in the health and education sectors) had to be adjusted upward and downward on an annual basis because of aid fluctuations. Moreover, sustained periods of large aid inflows could weaken efforts in mobilizing domestic revenues, resulting in significant public financing gaps when aid is phased out. Finally, institutional constraints (such as weak capacity

Note: The main author of this box is Thierry Tressel.

to manage and monitor public expenditure, or even corruption) may limit the capacity to quickly absorb large amounts of aid effectively.

Another key macroeconomic concern arises when large aid flows are spent on goods and services produced in the domestic economy, which can push up the price of nontraded goods relative to the price of traded goods (the real exchange rate), resulting in a loss of competitiveness in export-oriented, high-value-added sectors. This phenomenon is often called Dutch disease. As an example, consider the case in which aid is spent on hiring skilled workers, such as nurses, doctors, and teachers. Because skilled workers are in short supply, their wages quickly go up. As a result, wages of educated people in manufacturing industries and other sectors also increase, hurting exporters who cannot pass on their higher costs to customers.

Rajan and Subramanian (2005) confirm that Dutch disease is a real concern by showing that in countries that received more aid in the 1980s and 1990s, export-oriented, labor-intensive manufacturing industries grew more slowly than other industries. Similarly, Prati and Tressel (2006) find that foreign aid inflows depress overall exports of poor countries, as Dutch disease would imply. They do not find, however, any negative effect of aid disbursed when countries experience large exogenous shocks (droughts, large negative commodity price shocks, hurricanes, or earthquakes) or during post-war reconstruction. This suggests that aid may help production recover from adverse events.

Policies to Mitigate the Side Effects of Aid

Country case studies find that aid-recipient countries were often reluctant to let the real exchange rate appreciate as aid flowed in (Berg and others, 2007). In some countries, the fiscal authority simply did not spend the aid in the year it was received, while the central bank accumulated foreign exchange reserves (Ethiopia and Ghana). In other countries, the fiscal authority increased spending in line with the surge in aid, while the monetary authority tried to prevent real exchange rate appreciation by sterilizing the monetary expansion associated with the increase in public spending (Mozambique, Tanzania, and Uganda).

Gradually phasing in a spending buildup so as to limit the strain on domestic capacity and sterilizing the monetary expansion associated with aid spending both amount to temporarily saving part of the aid in the form of international reserves and can mitigate Dutch disease problems and other side effects of aid. Indeed, Prati and Tressel (2006) show that these policy responses eased the aggregate demand and real appreciation pressures associated with aid inflows. The effectiveness of such policy responses may also explain why Berg and others (2007) do not find symptoms of Dutch disease in a small group of countries that have recently experienced aid surges.

However, policies aimed at redistributing aid resources over time for the purpose of managing the macroeconomic consequences of large aid flows pose specific challenges. In poor countries, shallow financial markets may make it difficult to execute sterilization operations in the bond markets and result in a burden on banks, for example, through higher reserve requirements. Sterilization policies could also lead to an undesired increase in interest rates and crowding out of private investment.

As a general principle, countries receiving aid should aim at spending it over time as part of their poverty reduction strategy. However, in the short term, saving part of volatile and unpredictable aid flows in the form of international reserves can be justified from both a public finance and a macroeconomic management perspective. First, from a public finance perspective, if a temporary spurt of aid is all spent when it arrives (as was often the case in the past), a subsequent sharp drop in aid receipts could prompt the need for either a costly retrenchment of spending or recourse to higher domestic financing of expenditures, which could lead to loss of monetary control and inflation (Celasun and Walliser, 2006). In contrast, saving part of temporary aid surges would help avoid

Box 2.3 *(concluded)*

excessive reliance on domestic financing and prevent an unsustainable buildup of expenditures. On the whole, effective medium-term budgeting requires that aid-recipient countries smooth recurrent expenditures, so that all programs undertaken are funded while providing for key lumpy expenditures (Heller, 2005). Finally, to prevent aid dependency, periods of sustained large flows should not diminish efforts to mobilize domestic revenues (Gupta, Powell, and Yang, 2006).

From a macroeconomic management perspective, saving part of temporary increases in aid flows reflects the need to smooth aggregate consumption and to balance demand against supply. Building reserve buffers to self-insure against future negative shocks is particularly important in countries that have low reserve coverage of imports and are subject to frequent exogenous shocks (such as terms-of-trade shocks and droughts). Saving part of aid to smooth spending paths may also be necessary when a country's absorptive capacity is weak and when there are risks of loss of competitiveness from Dutch disease.

In choosing aid spending and absorption paths, policymakers in recipient countries should take into account country specifics such as macroeconomic stability, current and projected improvements in absorptive capacity, the risks of Dutch disease, and debt sustainability. Given the challenges associated with achieving optimal aid spending paths through macroeconomic policy adjustments, donors would contribute to a more effective use of aid by committing to coordinated multiyear aid disbursements tailored to country-specific circumstances. In this perspective, the 2005 Paris Declaration on Aid Effectiveness is a welcome step in improving aid predictability.

More generally, to take full advantage of globalization, SSA countries must continue to build institutions that will help sustain improved macroeconomic management, push through governance and other reforms to strengthen poverty alleviation, and develop the infrastructure and business environment to foster the rising productivity and investment needed to sustain high growth even in the face of a less benign global environment. Many countries will need to develop more flexible exchange rate regimes and more active monetary policy management in response to greater trade and capital interlinkages with the rest of the world. South Africa provides a leading example on the continent of such management, and it is encouraging that other countries, such as Ghana, are moving or preparing to move in a similar direction to put in place inflation-targeting regimes with more actively floating currencies. It will also be important to be prudent in taking advantage of opportunities for external funding to make sure that projects are carefully chosen and that gains from official debt reduction are preserved.

Middle East: Balancing Cyclical and Long-Term Considerations in Fiscal Policy

The long spell of strong growth in the Middle East continues to be supported by high oil prices and robust domestic demand. Regional growth has been maintained at over 5 percent a year in the past four years, reaching 5.6 percent in 2006 (Table 2.8). Although investment in the oil sector stagnated in real terms because of increasing investment costs, GDP growth in oil-exporting countries was sustained by expansion in the non-oil sectors, pushed by rising government spending out of oil revenues, foreign capital inflows, and rapidly growing domestic private credit. A buildup of government spending on infrastructure and social projects, as well as investment programs to expand oil production and refining capacity, narrowed fiscal surpluses and external

Table 2.8. Selected Middle Eastern Countries: Real GDP, Consumer Prices, and Current Account Balance
(Annual percent change unless noted otherwise)

	Real GDP				Consumer Prices[1]				Current Account Balance[2]			
	2005	2006	2007	2008	2005	2006	2007	2008	2005	2006	2007	2008
Middle East	**5.4**	**5.6**	**5.9**	**5.9**	**6.9**	**7.5**	**10.8**	**9.2**	**19.4**	**19.7**	**16.7**	**16.0**
Oil exporters[3]	**5.6**	**5.4**	**5.7**	**5.6**	**6.7**	**8.4**	**11.0**	**9.7**	**22.3**	**22.7**	**19.2**	**18.5**
Iran, I.R. of	4.4	4.9	6.0	6.0	12.1	13.6	19.0	17.7	8.8	8.7	7.6	6.6
Saudi Arabia	6.1	4.3	4.1	4.3	0.7	2.2	3.0	3.0	28.5	27.4	22.2	20.1
Kuwait	10.0	5.0	3.5	4.8	4.1	2.8	2.6	2.6	40.5	43.0	37.8	35.3
Mashreq	**4.3**	**6.1**	**6.3**	**6.5**	**7.7**	**5.3**	**9.6**	**7.2**	**–2.3**	**–2.6**	**–2.4**	**–2.5**
Egypt	4.5	6.8	7.1	7.3	8.8	4.2	10.9	7.8	3.2	0.8	1.4	0.8
Syrian Arab Republic	3.3	4.4	3.9	3.7	7.2	10.0	7.0	7.0	–4.1	–6.1	–5.6	–6.6
Jordan	7.1	6.3	6.0	6.0	3.5	6.3	5.0	4.5	–17.9	–14.0	–12.6	–11.9
Lebanon	1.0	—	2.0	3.5	–0.7	5.6	3.5	2.5	–13.6	–6.2	–10.6	–9.4
Memorandum												
Israel	5.3	5.2	5.1	3.8	1.3	2.1	0.5	2.5	3.3	5.6	3.7	3.2

[1]Movements in consumer prices are shown as annual averages. December/December changes can be found in Table A7 in the Statistical Appendix.
[2]Percent of GDP.
[3]Includes Bahrain, Islamic Republic of Iran, Kuwait, Libya, Oman, Qatar, Saudi Arabia, Syrian Arab Republic, United Arab Emirates, and the Republic of Yemen.

current account surpluses, despite higher oil prices (Figure 2.9). Oil-importing countries, for their part, benefited from the favorable external environment and robust domestic demand, with growth rising to 6 percent in 2006 and early 2007. Growth remains strong and broad based in Egypt and Jordan, but the Lebanese economy is still weak in the aftermath of last year's military conflict.

Growth momentum should pick up near term, supported by high oil prices and expansionary fiscal policy. Regional economies are projected to expand by about 6 percent in both 2007 and 2008, with growth accelerating in the Islamic Republic of Iran and Egypt. Oil prices are forecast to remain near current high levels, but robust domestic demand is projected to lower current account surpluses in the region to 16 percent of GDP, down from almost 20 percent of GDP in 2006. Growth in oil-importing economies is expected to continue to outpace that in oil-exporting countries, supported by strong private and public consumption and investment growth. Risks appear broadly balanced. Slower global growth, increased financial market volatility, or regional geopolitical risks could hurt growth, but the strength of oil prices provides upside potential.

With resource utilization and import prices rising, inflation is accelerating (see Figure 2.9). In Saudi Arabia, inflation rose for the first time in a decade in 2006, although from very low levels. Inflation increases have also been moderate in Kuwait, given its open product and factor markets. In Egypt, inflation accelerated in 2006 and early 2007, owing to rising demand pressures and increases in administered prices (primarily fuel prices), as well as bird flu effects, but has been slowing in recent months, in part as a result of the tightening of the monetary stance in the second half of 2006. In the Islamic Republic of Iran, high inflation has become entrenched owing to an extended and significant policy stimulus.

Weakness of the U.S. dollar added to inflationary pressures in the Gulf Cooperation Council (GCC) countries. Most of these countries peg their currencies to the U.S. dollar, although in a surprise move in May 2007, Kuwait (one of the GCC members) abandoned the peg to the U.S. dollar in favor of pegging to an undisclosed currency basket and allowed its currency to adjust in line with movements in the basket.[11]

[11]By October 2, 2007, the cumulative appreciation of the Kuwaiti dinar was 3.4 percent.

Figure 2.9. Middle East: How Are Oil Revenues Used?

Governments increased investment in infrastructure and social projects, substituting oil revenues for debt financing. The twin fiscal and current account surpluses fell, and rising resource utilization pushed up inflation, despite moderating private credit growth.

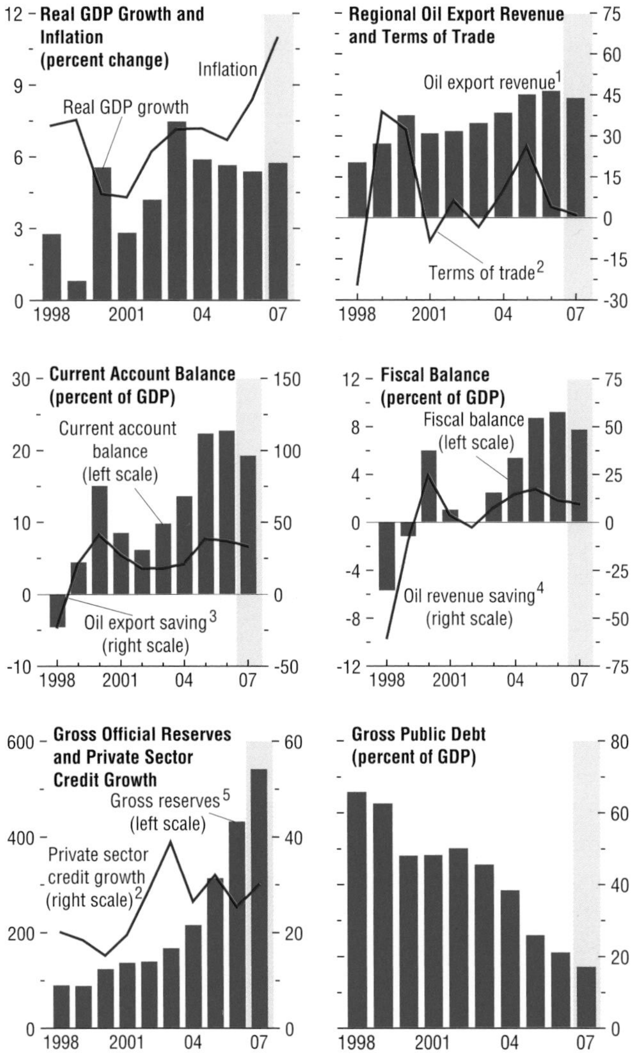

Sources: IMF, *International Financial Statistics;* and IMF staff estimates.
[1]Percent of GDP.
[2]Annual percent change.
[3]Oil export saving, expressed as percent, is calculated as the ratio of current account balance to oil exports.
[4]Oil revenue saving, expressed as percent, is calculated as the ratio of fiscal balance to fiscal oil revenue.
[5]Billions of U.S. dollars.

Kuwait's move came shortly after Oman's decision not to join the planned common-currency block in the region, at least not as a founding member, because it would not be able to meet all the requirements by the target date of 2010. Although these steps need not undermine the single-currency project, together with other economic developments, they would make it hard to meet the 2010 deadline for launching the single currency. The GCC countries also agreed that each central bank would decide on its own policies to control inflation. Inflationary pressures are expected to persist in the GCC countries as domestic demand expands in response to the positive terms-of-trade and wealth developments, and the equilibrium real exchange rate should appreciate as a result of these developments. The acceleration of imports associated with expansionary fiscal policy and rising investment is expected to lower the GCC countries' current account surpluses, thereby contributing to the resolution of global imbalances.

Against this backdrop, the challenge for fiscal policy in oil- and non-oil commodity-exporting countries is striking a balance between the long-term developmental objectives and cyclical considerations. With the outlook for oil and other commodity prices projected to remain strong, raising the trend of government spending would be warranted, as it would allow the terms-of-trade and wealth gains to be spent partly on addressing infrastructure and social needs, in line with long-term growth and diversification objectives. However, these considerations will have to be balanced against the shorter-term, cyclical need to maintain fiscal surpluses as a counterbalance to strong private demand growth in an environment of rapidly expanding domestic liquidity. Policymakers thus need to carefully calibrate the speed of implementing investment and social projects to the absorptive capacity of their economies, while strengthening market mechanisms to keep long-term inflation expectations anchored at appropriate levels and improving expenditure management to ensure the efficiency and effectiveness of public spending.

For exporters of oil and other commodities, whose fortunes are tied to commodity price fluctuations, the main challenge is to diversify toward non-oil sectors, while containing cyclical inflationary pressures.[12] Policymakers in oil-exporting countries (for example, Saudi Arabia, Kuwait, Qatar, and the United Arab Emirates) thus need to calibrate the speed of implementing large-scale projects to the absorptive capacity of the economy, while improving the flexibility of markets to keep long-term inflation expectations anchored at low levels and developing tools for managing liquidity. In some countries (Qatar and the United Arab Emirates), slowing the pace of fiscal spending and large investments under the public-private partnership arrangements may be considered a means of helping contain domestic demand. In the Islamic Republic of Iran, sizable fiscal adjustment and monetary tightening will help ease demand pressures and put inflation on a downward path.

In the structural policy area, the diversification strategy of oil exporters hinges on reforms to improve the business climate and make investment in non-oil sectors more attractive. Increasing the role of the private sector in the provision of services that up to now have been supplied by governments, opening government procurement and domestic sectors to competition, and lifting price controls would go a long way in this regard. More flexible employment procedures and measures facilitating labor mobility and human capital development would also help relieve labor supply bottlenecks and create job opportunities for the young and rapidly growing population.

These policies are germane to the oil-importing countries as well, which also share rapid population growth and the challenges of forestalling a further rise in unemployment. These economies have also been experiencing significant capital inflows, owing to ample regional and global liquidity as well as domestic privatization programs (Egypt). Maintaining macroeconomic stability in these circumstances requires tightening fiscal and, where appropriate, monetary policies, while strengthening the quality of supervision and regulation would help develop and enhance the efficiency and soundness of financial systems in the region.

[12]Non-oil sectors with potential for development in the Middle East include, among others, tourism, energy-intensive processing industries, and infrastructure development. Addressing supply constraints in oil production and refining would also benefit the region and the global economy.

References

Barker, Kate, 2004, "Delivering Stability: Securing Our Future Housing Needs," *Review of Housing Supply: Interim and Final Reports* (London: HM Treasury).

Benito, Andrew, Jamie Thompson, Matt Waldron, and Rob Wood, 2006, "House Prices and Consumer Spending," *Bank of England Quarterly Bulletin* (Summer), pp. 142–54.

Berg, Andrew, Shekhar Aiyar, Mumtaz Hussain, Shaun K. Roache, Tokhir N. Mirzoev, and Amber Mahone, 2007, *The Macroeconomics of Scaling Up Aid: Lessons from Recent Experience,* IMF Occasional Paper No. 253 (Washington: International Monetary Fund).

Blanchflower, David G., and Andrew J. Oswald, 1990, "The Wage Curve," NBER Working Paper No. 3181 (Cambridge, Massachusetts: National Bureau of Economic Research).

Bulíř, Aleš, and S. Javier Hamann, 2006, "Volatility of Development Aid: From the Frying Pan into the Fire?" IMF Working Paper 06/65 (Washington: International Monetary Fund).

Carroll, Christopher D., Misuzu Otsuka, and Jirka Slacalek, 2006, "How Large Is the Housing Wealth Effect? A New Approach," NBER Working Paper No. 12746 (Cambridge, Massachusetts: National Bureau of Economic Research).

Celasun, Oya, and Jan Walliser, 2006, "Predictability of Budget Aid: Recent Experiences," in *Budget Support as More Effective Aid? Recent Experiences and Emerging Lessons,* ed. by Stefan Koeberle, Zoran Stavreski, and Jan Walliser (Washington: World Bank).

———, forthcoming, "Predictability and Procyclicality of Aid: Do Fickle Donors Undermine Economic Development?" *Economic Policy.*

European Central Bank, 2007, *Monthly Bulletin* (January), pp. 63–75.

Girouard, Nathalie, Mike Kennedy, Paul van den Noord, and Christophe André, 2006, "Recent House Price Developments: The Role of Fundamentals," OECD Economics Department Working Paper No. 475 (Paris: Organization for Economic Cooperation and Development).

Gupta, Sanjeev, Robert Powell, and Yongzheng Yang, eds., 2006, *Macroeconomic Challenges of Scaling Up Aid to Africa: A Checklist for Practitioners* (Washington: International Monetary Fund).

Haas, François, and Natalia Tamirisa, 2007, "The Euro and the New Member States," in *Euro Area Policies: Selected Issues*, IMF Country Report No. 07/259 (Washington: International Monetary Fund), pp. 17–35.

Heller, Peter S., 2005, "'Pity the Finance Minister': Issues in Managing a Substantial Scaling Up of Aid Flows," IMF Working Paper 05/180 (Washington: International Monetary Fund).

Hilbers, Paul, Inci Ötker-Robe, and Ceyla Pazarbasioglu, 2007, "Analysis of and Policy Responses to Rapid Credit Growth," in *Rapid Credit Growth in Central and Eastern Europe: Endless Boom or Early Warning?* ed. by Charles Enoch and Inci Ötker-Robe (Houndmills, United Kingdom: Palgrave MacMillan and International Monetary Fund).

International Monetary Fund, 2007, "Sub-Saharan Africa's Emerging Export Pattern," in *Regional Economic Outlook: Sub-Saharan Africa,* April (Washington).

Klyuev, Vladimir, and Paul Mills, 2006, "Is Housing Wealth an 'ATM'?: The Relationship Between Household Wealth, Home Equity Withdrawal, and Saving Rates," IMF Working Paper 06/162 (Washington: International Monetary Fund).

Prati, Alessandro, and Thierry Tressel, 2006, "Aid Volatility and Dutch Disease: Is There a Role for Macroeconomic Policies?" IMF Working Paper 06/145 (Washington: International Monetary Fund).

Rajan, Raghuram G., and Arvind Subramanian, 2005, "What Undermines Aid's Impact on Growth?" IMF Working Paper 05/126 (Washington: International Monetary Fund).

Stavrev, Emil, 2007, "Growth and Inflation Dispersions in EMU: Reasons, the Role of Adjustment Channels, and Policy Implications," IMF Working Paper 07/167 (Washington: International Monetary Fund).

Swiston, Andrew, Martin Mühleisen, and Koshy Mathai, 2007, "Summary of U.S. Revenue Surprises: Are Happy Days Here to Stay?" in *United States: Selected Issues,* IMF Country Report No. 07/265 (Washington: International Monetary Fund), pp. 54–55.

Tamirisa, Natalia, and Deniz Igan, 2006, "Credit Growth and Bank Soundness in the New Member States," in *Czech Republic, Republic of Estonia, Hungary, Republic of Latvia, Republic of Lithuania, Republic of Poland, Slovak Republic, and Republic of Slovenia,* IMF Country Report No. 06/414 (Washington: International Monetary Fund).

Terrones, Marco, 2004, "What Explains the Recent Run-Up in House Prices?" *World Economic Outlook* (Washington), pp. 74–76.

CHAPTER 3

MANAGING LARGE CAPITAL INFLOWS

This chapter examines the policy responses to surges in private capital inflows in a group of emerging market countries and open advanced economies over the past two decades. The results suggest that fiscal restraint during periods of large capital inflows can help limit real currency appreciation and foster better growth outcomes in the aftermath of such episodes. Resisting nominal exchange rate appreciation through sterilized intervention is likely to be ineffective when the influx of capital is persistent. Tightening capital controls does not appear to deliver better outcomes.

The wave of capital flows sweeping through many emerging market economies since the early 2000s has brought renewed attention on how macroeconomic policies should respond to them (Figure 3.1). Although these flows are associated with ample global liquidity and favorable worldwide economic conditions, in many cases they are, at least in part, a reflection of strengthened macroeconomic policy frameworks and growth-enhancing structural reforms, and they help deliver the economic benefits of increased financial integration.[1] But the inflows also create important challenges for policymakers because of their potential to generate overheating, loss of competitiveness, and increased vulnerability to crisis.

Reflecting these concerns, policies in emerging market countries have responded to capital inflows in a variety of ways.[2] Whereas some countries have let exchange rates move upward, in many cases the monetary authorities have intervened heavily in foreign exchange markets to resist currency appreciation. To varying

Figure 3.1. Net Private Capital Inflows to Emerging Markets[1]

Net private capital inflows to emerging markets have accelerated since 2002 and, in U.S. dollar terms, are much larger than in the mid-1990s.

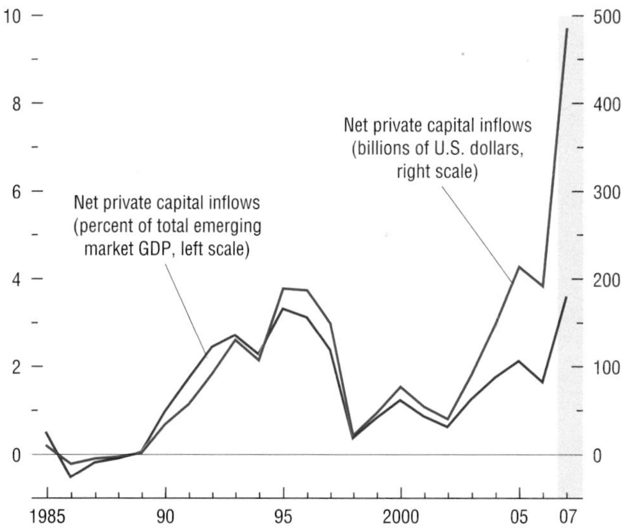

Sources: IMF, *Balance of Payments Statistics;* and IMF staff calculations.
[1]Values for 2007 are IMF staff projections.

Note: The main authors of this chapter are Roberto Cardarelli, Selim Elekdag, and M. Ayhan Kose, with support from Ben Sutton and Gavin Asdorian. Menzie Chinn and Carlos Végh provided consultancy support.

[1]See IMF (2007a).

[2]See IMF (2007b, 2007c) and World Bank (2006).

degrees, they have sought to neutralize the monetary impact of intervention through sterilization, with a view to forestalling an excessively rapid expansion of domestic demand. Controls on capital inflows have been introduced or tightened, and controls on outflows eased, to relieve upward pressure on exchange rates. Fiscal policies have also responded—in some cases, stronger revenue growth from buoyant activity has been harnessed to achieve better fiscal outcomes, although in many countries rising revenues have led to higher government spending.

For a number of emerging market countries, recent policy concerns mirror those in the first half of the 1990s, when renewed access to international capital markets in the wake of the resolution of the debt crisis resulted in a surge in the availability of external capital. An important lesson from that earlier period is that the policy choices made in response to the arrival of capital inflows may have an important bearing on macroeconomic outcomes, including the consequences of their abrupt reversal (Montiel, 1999).

Although a number of studies have examined the policy responses to capital inflows, they have focused mainly on the experience of a few countries during the 1990s. There have been fewer studies on recent episodes and fewer attempts at comprehensive cross-country examination of policy responses.[3] The main objective of this chapter is thus to review the experience with large capital inflows over the past two decades in a large number of emerging market and advanced economies, characterize the various policy responses to these experiences, and assess their macroeconomic implications. The chapter addresses the following questions:

- What policy challenges are created by surges of net private capital inflows?
- What policy measures were adopted in the past, and did they work? For example, did intervention and capital controls succeed in limiting real appreciation? Did these measures help mitigate the risk of sharp reversals of capital inflows? Does the fiscal policy response make a difference?

Four main lessons emerge from this analysis. First, countries that experience more volatile macroeconomic fluctuations—including a sharp reversal of inflows—tend to have higher current account deficits and experience stronger increases in both aggregate demand and the real value of the currency during the period of capital inflows. Second, episodes during which the decline in GDP growth following the surge in inflows was more moderate tend to be those in which the authorities exercised greater fiscal restraint during the inflow period, which helped contain aggregate demand and limit real appreciation. Third, countries resisting nominal exchange rate appreciation through intervention were generally not able to moderate real appreciation in the face of a persistent surge in capital inflows and faced more serious adverse macroeconomic consequences when the surge eventually stopped. Fourth, tightening capital controls has, in general, been associated neither with lower real appreciation nor with reduced vulnerability to a sharp reversal of inflows.

In practice, the appropriate policy response to large capital inflows depends on a variety of country-specific circumstances, including the nature of the underlying inflows (in particular, the extent to which they reflect domestic or external factors and the extent to which the inflows are expected to be persistent), the stage of the business cycle, and the fiscal policy situation. In addition, and as discussed in the October 2007 *Global Financial Stability Report*, the quality of domestic financial markets also matters. Nevertheless, the findings of this chapter provide helpful guidance on what has worked, and not worked, in the past.

One key implication is that the consequences of large capital inflows are of particular concern to countries with substantial current account deficits, such as many in emerging Europe,

[3]Examples of the first type of study are Calvo, Leiderman, and Reinhart (1994); Fernández-Arias and Montiel (1996); Glick (1998); Montiel (1999); Reinhart and Reinhart (1998); and Edwards (2000). There is an example of a cross-country analysis of policy responses to capital inflows in World Bank (1997).

and to countries with inflexible exchange rate regimes. Especially in the latter context, the most effective policy instrument available to attenuate these consequences is to maintain fiscal spending discipline in the face of buoyant revenues, rather than allowing procyclical growth of public spending. Moreover, countries that adopted a policy of resistance to exchange rate appreciation when the capital inflows started to arrive should consider moving to a more flexible exchange rate policy as the influx of capital is sustained.

Two Waves of Large Capital Inflows to Emerging Markets

There have been two great waves of private capital flows to emerging market countries in the past two decades (see Figure 3.1).[4] The first began in the early 1990s, then ended abruptly with the 1997–98 Asian crisis. The recent wave has been building since 2002, but has accelerated markedly recently, with flows in the first half of this year already far exceeding the total for 2006.

Looking at the nature and composition of the inflows reveals interesting differences between the current wave of capital inflows and the one in the 1990s. In particular, the current wave is taking place in the context of much stronger current account positions for most (but not all) emerging market countries and a substantial acceleration in the accumulation of foreign reserves (Figure 3.2). The surge in pri-

[4]The concept of "private" capital inflows adopted in this chapter is based on the nature of the recipient sector. That is, only changes in foreign assets and liabilities of the domestic private sector—as recorded in the IMF's Balance of Payments database—are taken into account, independently of the nature of the foreign counterpart. The main difference compared with a "source" concept of private inflows is the exclusion of sovereign borrowing (specifically, the changes in a government's assets and liabilities vis-à-vis the foreign private sector) and the inclusion of private borrowing from external official sources. Although this difference may be relevant for the early to mid-1990s, it is less likely to be relevant for the recent past, given the decline in sovereign borrowing and official lending.

Figure 3.2. Gross Private Flows, Current Account Balance, and Reserve Accumulation[1]
(Percent of total emerging market GDP)

For emerging markets as a whole, the surge in net private capital inflows since the early 2000s reflects a strong acceleration in gross inflows that has more than offset the pickup in gross outflows, and it has been accompanied by a current account surplus and a substantial accumulation of foreign reserves.

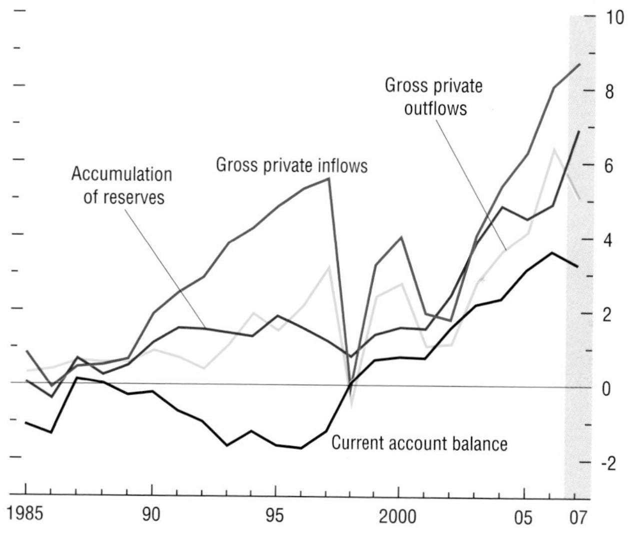

Sources: IMF, *Balance of Payments Statistics;* and IMF staff calculations.
[1]Values for 2007 are IMF staff projections.

Figure 3.3. Current Account Balance, Private Capital Inflows, and Reserve Accumulation by Region[1]
(Percent of regional GDP)

As a percent of GDP, net private capital inflows are currently below their mid-1990s peak in both Latin America and emerging Asia. However, they have reached historic highs in both emerging Europe and other emerging markets, where they are accompanied by current account deficits.

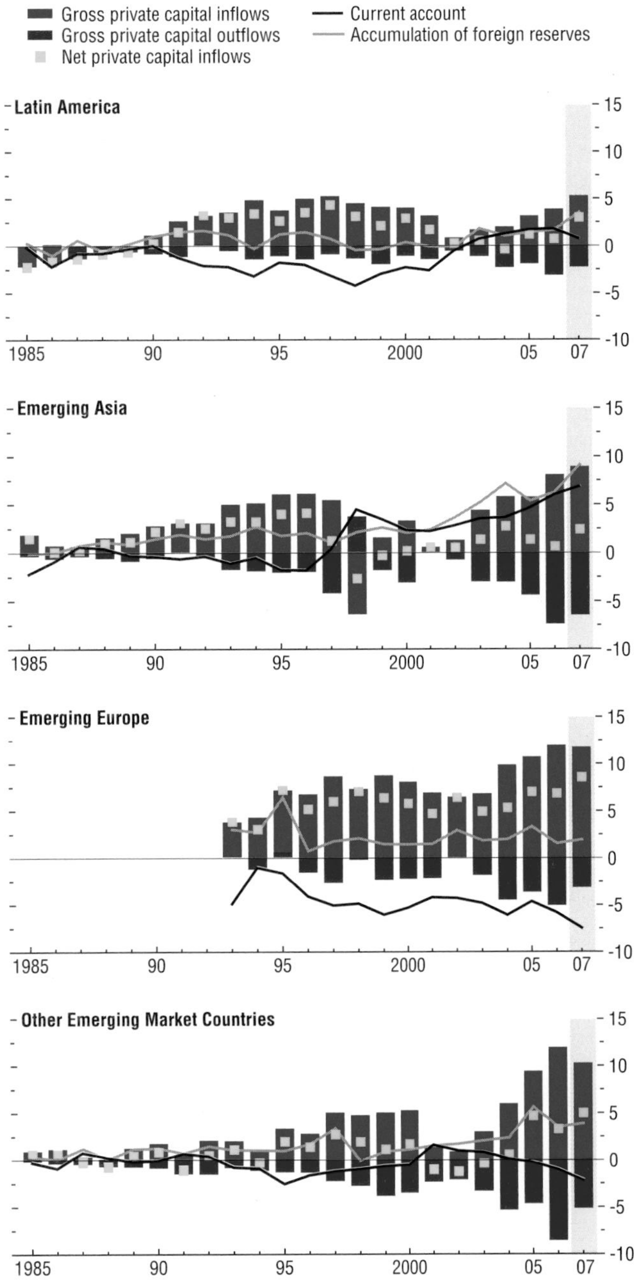

Sources: IMF, *Balance of Payments Statistics;* and IMF staff calculations.
[1]Values for 2007 are IMF staff projections.

vate capital inflows has also been accompanied by a sharp increase in outflows, in line with the global trend toward increasing diversification of international portfolios. Behind these aggregate trends are some distinctive regional patterns:

- In *Latin America,*[5] net private capital inflows, as a percentage of GDP, have picked up since 2004 and are projected to return to the 1990s levels during the course of this year (Figure 3.3). The surge in gross private capital inflows has been largely offset by the continued increase in gross private capital outflows—which reached historical highs in 2006. The increase in net private capital inflows coincided with a turnaround of the current account position of the region, from the large external deficit of the 1990s to a record-high surplus in 2006, resulting in a substantial accumulation of foreign reserves.
- In *emerging Asia,*[6] net private capital inflows have rebounded from their sharp reversal during the 1997–98 crisis. Gross capital inflows to the region have now returned to the historically high levels of the precrisis period, but private capital outflows—particularly portfolio flows—have accelerated strongly since the early 2000s, leaving net inflows well below their pre-crisis levels. For the region as a whole, large and growing current account surpluses have represented an even bigger source of foreign currency inflows, driving a massive accumulation of foreign reserves.
- In *emerging Europe and the Commonwealth of Independent States (CIS),*[7] net capital inflows

[5]This region includes Argentina, Brazil, Chile, Colombia, Costa Rica, Mexico, Paraguay, Peru, Uruguay, and Venezuela.

[6]This region includes China, Hong Kong SAR, India, Indonesia, Korea, Malaysia, Pakistan, the Philippines, Singapore, Thailand, and Vietnam.

[7]This region includes Bulgaria, Croatia, the Czech Republic, Estonia, Hungary, Latvia, Lithuania, Poland, Romania, Russia, the Slovak Republic, Slovenia, and Ukraine. Given Russia's large current account surplus, it is excluded from the figures describing the evolution of the regional balance of payments.

have been on a rising trend since the early 1990s, as opportunities created by entry into the European Union have propelled gross inflows to levels (as a share of GDP) that are unprecedented for emerging market countries in recent history. Unlike in other regions, though, net capital inflows have been accompanied by a deteriorating external position, with the current account deficit (excluding Russia) at about 6 percent of regional GDP in 2006.

- In *other emerging markets*,[8] net capital inflows have also accelerated strongly over the past three years, driven by the rebound of net private inflows to Turkey and South Africa after the reversal in the early 2000s. For this group of countries as a whole, the recent robust acceleration in gross inflows has more than offset the trend increase in gross outflows and has more than compensated for a current account deficit.

An important feature of the recent wave of net capital inflows to emerging markets—which differentiates it from the 1990s—is the predominance of net foreign direct investment (FDI) flows relative to net "financial" flows (portfolio and other flows) in all four regions (Figure 3.4). This reflects continued strength in FDI inflows, together with the rapid increase in financial outflows from emerging markets, which has largely offset the acceleration of financial inflows in most of these countries.

In sum, the recent cycle of capital inflows is different from the previous one, because it involves a larger set of countries; is underpinned by generally more solid current account positions (with the notable exception of emerging European countries); and is taking place in a more financially integrated world economy, in which significant financial outflows are at least partially offsetting the inflows of capital to emerging markets.

[8]This group of countries includes Albania, Algeria, Cyprus, Egypt, Israel, Malta, Morocco, South Africa, Tunisia, and Turkey. The latter two countries account for about two-thirds of regional GDP.

Figure 3.4. Net FDI and Non-FDI Inflows[1]
(Percent of regional GDP)

Net foreign direct investment (FDI) inflows account for most of the net private capital inflows in all regions.

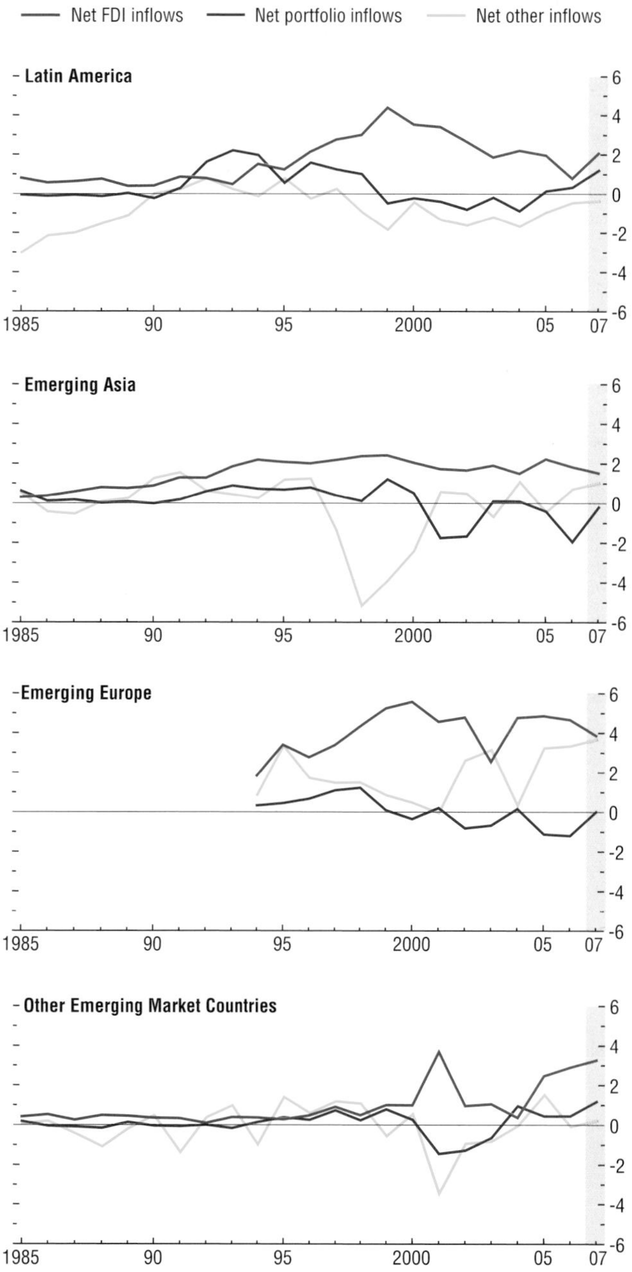

Sources: IMF, *Balance of Payments Statistics;* and IMF staff calculations.
[1]Values for 2007 are IMF staff projections.

Figure 3.5. Characteristics of Episodes of Large Net Private Capital Inflows

The total number of episodes of large net private capital inflows has sharply increased since early 2000, driven by the increase in the number of episodes in emerging Europe and the Commonwealth of Independent States (CIS) countries. Foreign direct investment (FDI) generally represents the largest share of total inflows during episodes.

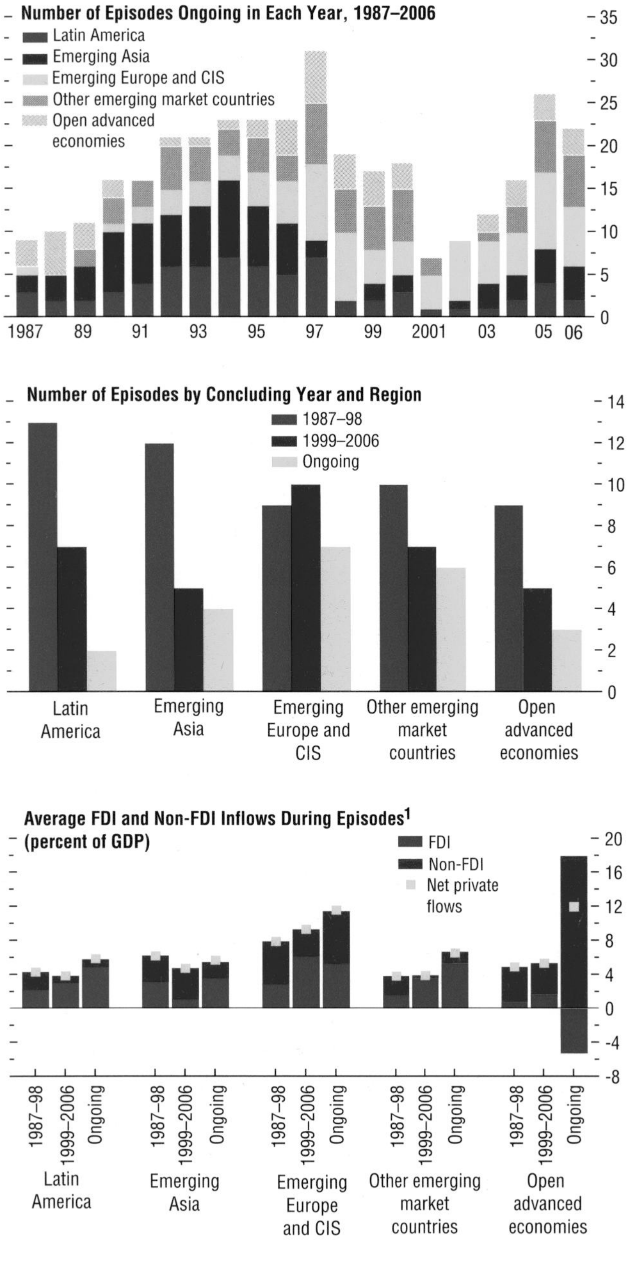

Sources: IMF, *Balance of Payments Statistics;* and IMF staff calculations.
[1]Medians across episodes.

Identifying Episodes of Large Capital Inflows

To systematically assess countries' experiences with large net capital inflows, characterize their policy responses, and gauge the effectiveness of these responses, this chapter uses a consistent set of criteria to identify episodes of large net private capital inflows to emerging market countries that have occurred over the past two decades. Such episodes are also identified for a group of open advanced economies to compare their experience with that of emerging markets.[9]

To identify these episodes, two criteria are used that account for both country- and region-specific dimensions.[10] The country-specific dimension of the episodes is captured by the following criterion: the ratio of net capital inflows to GDP for a particular country must be significantly (one standard deviation) larger than the trend of capital inflows to that country. The regional dimension is captured by the following criterion: capital inflows are significantly larger than a regional threshold (the 75th percentile of the distribution of the ratios of net private capital inflows to GDP of the countries in that region), even if they are not out of line with country-specific historical trends. An episode is defined as a year or string of years in which at least one of these criteria is met.

An important characteristic of these episodes is how they ended. In particular, an episode is considered to end "abruptly" if the ratio of net private capital inflows to GDP in the year after the episode terminates is more than 5 percentage points of GDP lower than at the end of the episode—closely following the definition of "sudden stops" in the literature (see Mauro and Becker, 2006). An episode is also considered to finish abruptly if its end coincides with a cur-

[9]This group includes Australia, Canada, Denmark, Iceland, New Zealand, Norway, Sweden, and Switzerland.

[10]See Appendix 3.1 for a complete list of the episodes and a more detailed description of the methodology used to identify them.

rency crisis, that is, with a steep depreciation of the exchange rate.[11]

Based on these criteria, 109 episodes of large net private capital inflows since 1987 were identified; 87 of these were completed by 2006. These episodes show several interesting patterns, broadly in line with the stylized facts discussed above:

- The incidence of episodes over time mirrors trends in net private capital inflows to emerging markets, with two waves of episodes of large capital inflows to emerging markets since the late 1980s—one in the mid-1990s and the recent one, starting in 2002 (Figure 3.5, upper panel).
- Episodes completed during the first wave (between 1987 and 1998) generally involved a smaller volume of flows relative to GDP, especially compared with episodes that are ongoing; but they lasted longer than those that ended between 1999 and 2006 (Table 3.1).
- Emerging Asian and Latin American countries dominated the first wave of episodes, whereas the more recent episodes have been concentrated more in emerging Europe and other emerging market countries (Figure 3.5, middle panel).
- More than one-third of the completed episodes ended with a sudden stop or a currency crisis (see Table 3.1), suggesting that abrupt endings are not a rare phenomenon.[12]
- Late and ongoing episodes are characterized by larger FDI flows, relative to the episodes completed in the 1990s (Figure 3.5, lower panel).

Table 3.1. Episodes of Large Net Private Capital Inflows—Summary Statistics

	Completed During 1987–98	Completed During 1999–2006	Ongoing	All Episodes
Number of episodes	53	34	22	109
Average size[1]	4.7	5.1	7.5	5.1
(percent of GDP)	(5.3)	(5.8)	(8.7)	(6.1)
Duration[1]	3.0	1.5	3.0	2.0
(in years)	(3.3)	(2.6)	(3.6)	(3.1)
No. of episodes that ended abruptly	26	14	. . .	40
In sudden stop	22	12	. . .	34
In currency crisis	10	3	. . .	13

Sources: IMF, *Balance of Payments Statistics;* and IMF staff calculations.
[1]Medians across episodes; mean in parentheses.

Policy Responses to Large Capital Inflows

Identifying Policy Responses

The influx of large capital inflows has induced policymakers to adopt a variety of measures to prevent overheating and real currency appreciation, and reduce the economy's vulnerability to a sharp reversal of the capital inflows. A key policy decision for countries facing large capital inflows is to what extent to resist pressures for the currency to appreciate by intervening in the foreign exchange market.[13]

One of the main motivations for intervention is the concern that massive and rapid capital inflows may induce steep exchange rate appreciation in a short period of time, damaging the competitiveness of export sectors and potentially reducing economic growth. Moreover, if net capital inflows occur in the context of a current account deficit, the real appreciation could exacerbate the external imbalance, heightening vulnerability to a sharp reversal of capital inflows. From a macroeconomic stabilization perspective, however, the accumulation of foreign reserves required to keep the exchange rate from appreciating may lead to excessively loose monetary conditions, thus creating the potential for overheating and financial system vulnerabilities. In this case, real appreciation could occur through higher inflation, rather than through an increase in nominal exchange rates.[14]

[11]A currency crisis is defined as in Frankel and Rose (1996)—a depreciation of at least 25 percent cumulative over a 12-month period, and at least 10 percentage points greater than in the preceding 12 months.

[12]In particular, of the 87 completed episodes, 34 ended with a sudden stop and 13 with a currency crisis. In seven episodes, a sudden stop coincided with a currency crisis.

[13]These issues are discussed, in the context of European transition economies, in Lane, Lipschitz, and Mourmouras (2002).

[14]Allowing the exchange rate to fluctuate could also discourage short-term speculative capital inflows, by introducing uncertainty on the changes in the value of the currency (see Calvo, Leiderman, and Reinhart, 1996).

The "impossible trinity" paradigm of open economy macroeconomics—the inability to simultaneously target the exchange rate, run an independent monetary policy, and allow full capital mobility—suggests that in the absence of direct capital controls, countries facing large capital inflows need to choose between nominal appreciation and inflation.[15] In practice, however, given that capital mobility is not perfect—even in the absence of direct capital controls—policymakers may have more scope to pursue intermediate options than this paradigm would suggest, and they have generally used the full menu of available measures.[16] When they have intervened to prevent exchange rate appreciation, they have often sought to sterilize the monetary impact of intervention through open market operations and other measures (such as increasing bank reserve requirements or transferring government deposits from the banking system to the central bank).[17] In some cases, policymakers have tried to restrict the net inflow of capital by imposing controls on capital inflows or by removing controls on capital outflows (Box 3.1).

Although the motives for sterilization are clear, its effectiveness is less so, and it can entail substantial costs. Because sterilization is designed to prevent a decline in interest rates, it maintains the incentives for continuing capital inflows, thus perpetuating the problem. Moreover, sterilization often implies quasi-fiscal costs, because it generally involves the central bank exchanging high-yield domestic assets for low-yield reserves. If sterilization is implemented by increasing unremunerated bank reserve requirements, this cost is shifted to the banking system, promoting disintermediation.

Fiscal policy is another instrument available to attenuate the effects of capital flows on aggregate demand and the real exchange rate during a surge of inflows and in its aftermath. Typically, fiscal policy in emerging markets receiving capital inflows is procylical, because a fast-growing economy generates revenues that feed higher government spending, thus aggravating overheating problems (see Kaminsky, Reinhart, and Végh, 2004; and Mendoza and Ostry, 2007). By contrast, greater restraint on expenditure growth has three benefits. First, by dampening aggregate demand during the period of high inflows, it allows lower interest rates and may therefore reduce incentives for inflows. Second, it alleviates the appreciating pressures on the exchange rate directly, given the bias of public spending toward nontraded goods (Calvo, Leiderman, and Reinhart, 1994). Third, to the extent that it helps address or forestall debt sustainability concerns, it may provide greater scope for a countercyclical fiscal response to cushion economic activity when the inflows stop. Although discretionary fiscal tightening during a period of capital inflows may be problematic because of political constraints and implementation lags, avoiding fiscal excesses—holding the line on spending—could nonetheless play an important stabilization role in this context.[18]

Measuring Policy Responses

For the purposes of this chapter, these policy choices are characterized using a set of

[15]For a general discussion of the impossible trinity paradigm, see Obstfeld and Taylor (2002).

[16]See Reinhart and Reinhart (1998); Montiel (1999); and World Bank (1997) for a survey of the theory behind policy responses to capital inflows and some empirical evidence.

[17]With perfect substitution between domestic and foreign assets, maintaining predetermined exchange rates would amount to giving up monetary autonomy, as suggested by the strict form of the impossible trinity. Under these circumstances, sterilization would be futile, because any uncovered interest rate differential would be quickly eliminated by international interest arbitrage. But because foreign and domestic assets are not perfect substitutes, interest rate differentials can and do persist.

[18]In particular, fiscal rules based on cyclically adjusted balances could help resist political and social pressures for additional spending in the face of large capital inflows. A relevant example is provided by Chile, which aims at achieving a cyclically adjusted fiscal surplus, with an additional adjuster to save excess copper revenues, thereby contributing to offset appreciation pressures on the currency (see IMF, 2007c).

Box 3.1. Can Capital Controls Work?

Capital controls are one of the more controversial choices available to policymakers during periods of large capital flows. Countries employ control measures to attain a variety of policy objectives, such as discouraging capital inflows to reduce upward pressures on the exchange rate, reducing the risk associated with the sudden reversal of inflows, and maintaining some degree of monetary policy independence. After a brief overview of the different types of capital controls and their measurement, this box examines the macroeconomic impact of capital controls during the large inflow episodes identified in the chapter, compares the results with the recent literature, and provides a summary of microeconomic distortions associated with capital controls.[1]

Capital Controls: Implementation and Measurement Issues

Although capital controls cover a wide range of measures regulating inflows and outflows of foreign capital, they generally take two broad forms: direct (or administrative) and indirect (or market based). Direct controls are associated with administrative measures, such as direct prohibitions and explicit limits on the volume of transactions. For example, Malaysia introduced a set of direct capital controls in 1998 that involved various quantitative restrictions on cross-border trade of its currency and credit transactions. Indirect capital controls include explicit or implicit taxation of financial flows and differential exchange rates for capital transactions. For example, in order to discourage capital inflows, Chile imposed an implicit tax in 1991 in the form of an unremunerated reserve requirement (URR) on specified inflows for up to one year. These controls were substantially relaxed in 1998.

Recently, to slow the rate of appreciation of their respective currencies, a number of countries have introduced controls on capital inflows. In December 2006, Thailand imposed a URR of 30 percent on most capital inflows, requiring them to be deposited with the central bank for one year. The scope of these controls has been substantially narrowed since their inception because of their adverse impact on market developments and investor confidence. In May 2007, Colombia introduced a package of measures, including a 40 percent URR on external borrowing to be held for six months in the central bank. At the same time, a new ceiling on the foreign exchange position of banks, counting gross positions in derivative markets, was established to limit circumvention of the URR and in response to growing concerns about banks' exposure to counterparty risk. Brazil, Kazakhstan, Korea, and India have also recently implemented other specific capital control measures.

The traditional approach to measuring capital controls is based on the IMF's *Annual Report on Exchange Arrangements and Exchange Restrictions* (AREAER), which provides information on different types of controls. Early work quantified the narrative descriptions in the AREAER by simply using a binary measure (Grilli and Milesi-Ferretti, 1995). More sophisticated approaches use finer measures of controls, but they still essentially summarize the information in the AREAER (Chinn and Ito, 2006; Edwards, 2005; Miniane, 2004; Mody and Murshid, 2005; and Quinn, 2003). With the expansion of the set of control categories and further refinements in the 1996 issue of the AREAER, it is now possible to distinguish between controls on inflows and those on outflows beginning in 1995 (IMF, 2007a).

Using these measures, a large body of literature has studied the macroeconomic and microeconomic implications of capital controls. However, it is worth noting up front that, irrespective of their type, it is a challenge to effec-

Note: The main authors of this box are Selim Elekdag and M. Ayhan Kose.

[1] This box focuses mainly on the implications of the temporary use of capital controls during periods of inflow surges in countries with fairly liberalized capital accounts. There is a large body of literature analyzing the growth and stability outcomes of capital controls for countries at different stages of the liberalization process (Kose and others, 2006).

Box 3.1 *(continued)*

tively quantify the extent of capital controls. In particular, it would be desirable to capture the degree of enforcement of capital controls. Moreover, the impact of a measure would depend on a broad assessment of the openness of the capital account.

Macroeconomic Implications

The literature assessing whether capital controls have attained their stated macroeconomic objectives is, at best, mixed. It is hard to draw a set of general results because most of the studies are based on country cases (Ariyoshi and others, 2000). Overall, the studies suggest that controls on inflows did not affect the volume of net flows in most countries, although it seems that the controls were able to temporarily tilt the composition toward longer maturities in a few cases (Chile after 1991; see Edwards and Rigobon, 2005).[2] Even in cases in which a narrow range of objectives were met, controls had only temporary effects as market participants eventually found ways to circumvent them.

What additional evidence can be derived from the study of capital inflow episodes in this chapter? Episodes characterized by tighter controls on inflows are associated with narrower current account deficits and lower net private inflows, including lower net FDI flows (first figure). Although stricter inflow controls are accompanied by lower post-inflow growth and a larger appreciation of the currency, these distinctions are not statistically significant. In contrast, inflation rates have been significantly higher in episodes with tighter controls.

Does having capital controls in place reduce vulnerability to financial crises and sudden stops? Episodes that ended in an abrupt reversal of net inflows do not seem to be associated with lower capital controls (second figure).[3] On the contrary, although the differences are not statistically significant, episodes that ended abruptly were associated with somewhat stricter inflow controls. Consistent with this finding, recent

Controls on Capital Inflows and Selected Macroeconomic Indicators[1]

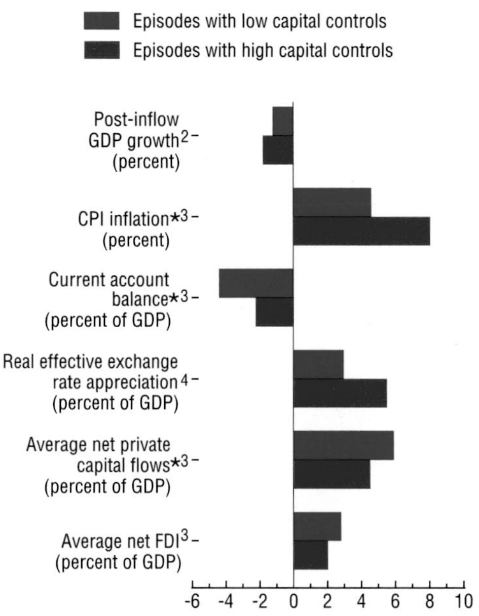

Sources: IMF, *Annual Report on Exchange Arrangements and Exchange Restrictions;* IMF, *Balance of Payments Statistics;* and IMF staff calculations.

[1]Values reported are medians for the two groups of episodes. Episodes with high (low) capital controls are those with above (below) median values of the capital controls index discussed in the text, where higher (lower) values indicate tighter (looser) regulation of inflows. The asterisk (*) indicates that the difference between medians is significant at a 10 percent confidence level or better.

[2]Average real GDP growth in the two years after an episode minus average during the episode.

[3]Average during the episode.

[4]Cumulative change during the episode.

[2]Moreover, stricter controls on outflows appeared to reduce net capital flows and allow more independent monetary policy in Malaysia after 1998, but there is little support for such outcomes in other countries (Magud and Reinhart, 2007).

[3]The evolution of capital controls is also examined using the full sample of episodes. The results suggest that there has not been any significant change in the median of capital controls during episodes relative to the periods before or after.

Endings of Episodes and Controls on Capital Inflows[1]

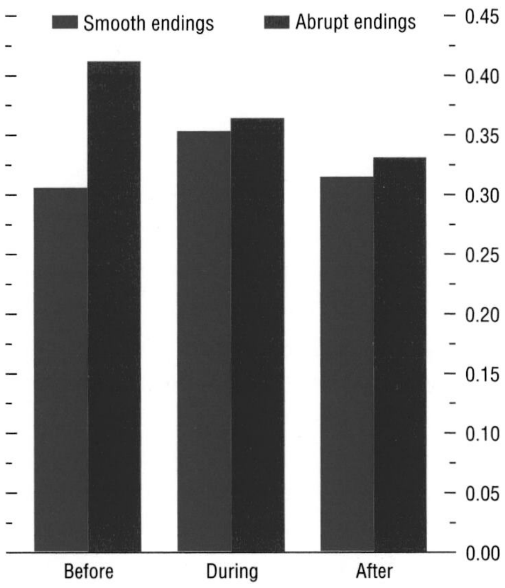

Sources: IMF, *Annual Report on Exchange Arrangements and Exchange Restrictions;* and IMF staff calculations.
[1]Median values across all completed episodes using the index of capital controls discussed in the text, where higher values indicate tighter regulation of inflows. "Before" denotes averages of the index in the two years before the episode. "After" denotes averages of the index in the two years after the episode.

studies also document that countries with capital controls are in fact more susceptible to crises (Glick, Guo, and Hutchison, 2006). This could be simply because of a "selection effect"—often it is countries with weaker macroeconomic fundamentals that put controls in place to insulate themselves from crises. However, these studies find that even after controlling for such effects, countries with controls have a higher likelihood of currency crises and sudden stops. Moreover, there seems to be little empirical evidence that the output costs of currency and banking crises are smaller in countries that restrict capital mobility (IMF, 2007a).

Another policy used by some countries to cope with large net inflows was the removal of controls on outflows. Evidence based on the wave of inflows during the 1990s suggests that elimination of controls on outflows has often led to larger inflows.[4] However, the study of episodes in this chapter suggests that in about 40 percent of episodes in which rising gross outflows offset gross inflows, countries indeed relaxed capital controls on outflows. Most of these episodes occurred during the past three years.

Microeconomic Implications

Although there is little evidence that capital controls are effective at achieving their macroeconomic objectives beyond a limited period, they are associated with substantial microeconomic costs, especially when they are sustained for a prolonged period of time (IMF, 2007a).[5]

- *Cost of capital.* Capital controls are estimated to make it more difficult and expensive for small firms to raise capital (Forbes, 2007a). Moreover, multinational affiliates located in countries with capital controls face local borrowing costs that are much higher than those of affiliates of the same parent company borrowing locally in countries without capital controls (Desai, Foley, and Hines, 2004).
- *Costs of distortions and reduced market discipline.* Economic behavior is likely to be distorted by capital controls, and resources are wasted in seeking to circumvent controls (Johnson and Mitton, 2003; and Forbes, 2007b).
- *Lower international trade.* Capital controls increase the cost of engaging in international trade, even for those firms that do not intend

[4]Liberalizing outflow restrictions may attract heavier inflows by sending a positive signal to markets and increasing investor confidence, and thereby fueling even larger inflows (Bartolini and Drazen, 1997), which is supported by evidence based on several countries (Reinhart and Reinhart, 1998).

[5]A full discussion of the costs and distortions stemming from capital controls is beyond the scope of this box. By analyzing the specific effects of capital controls on individual firms and/or sectors in a particular country, microeconomic studies are often able to produce more concrete results than those focusing on macroeconomic implications of controls.

Box 3.1 *(concluded)*

to evade them, because of expenses incurred to meet various inspection and reporting requirements associated with controls (Wei and Zhang, 2007).

In sum, although the macroeconomic impact of capital controls has been temporary at best, evidence suggests they have been associated with substantial microeconomic costs. While capital controls might have a role in certain cases, they should not be seen as a substitute for sound macroeconomic policies that include a prudent fiscal stance and a supporting exchange rate and monetary policy framework, as well as appropriate prudential measures.

quantitative indicators. The main indicators are as follows:

- *Exchange rate policy.* Exchange rate policy is characterized based on an index of "exchange market pressures" *(EMP),* which is a combination of movements in the exchange rate and international reserves.[19] In theory, for a pure float, the change in the exchange rate would correspond exactly to the index of exchange market pressures. At the other extreme, for a peg, the exchange rate would be constant, and fluctuations in *EMP* would be driven entirely by changes in reserves through intervention. Dividing the changes in foreign reserves by *EMP* yields a ratio measuring the proportion of exchange market pressures that are resisted through intervention. This ratio is then standardized to create an index of the degree of resistance to changes in exchange rates—hereafter called a "resistance index"—with values between 0 and 1, where values closer to 1 imply a greater degree of resistance to exchange rate fluctuations.
- *Sterilization policy.* The sterilization index captures the extent to which the monetary authorities are able to insulate domestic liquidity from foreign exchange market intervention. Specifically, it measures the degree to which the monetary authorities contracted domestic credit to offset the expansion of the monetary base associated with the accumulation of foreign reserves.[20] A value of the index equal to (or above) unity implies full sterilization, whereas a value of zero (or a negative value) represents no sterilization. Moreover, changes in nominal short-term interest rates will be considered as an alternative measure of the cyclical stance of monetary policy.[21]
- *Fiscal policy.* The cyclical stance of fiscal policy in response to large capital inflows is represented by the change in the growth of real noninterest government expenditure. Although it is possible to consider other measures of fiscal policy, such as government revenues and fiscal balances, these variables are more closely related to cyclical changes in the economy, and thus they generally give ambiguous indications about the cyclical stance of fiscal policy (Kaminsky, Reinhart, and Végh, 2004).[22]

[19]See Girton and Roper (1977). A more detailed description of the index is in Appendix 3.1.

[20]This index of sterilization thus follows the literature on the coefficient of sterilization (see, for example, Cavoli and Rajan, 2006; and Kwack, 2001).

[21]Clearly, movements in short-term interest rates can be seen as counterparts of changes in central banks' domestic assets and thus of the sterilization effort, with a decrease in central banks' domestic assets leading to an increase in interest rates. In practice, however, using the sterilization index as a measure of the monetary policy stance is complicated by the fact that the demand for money balances could be highly unstable, especially in countries with high and volatile inflation (Kaminsky, Reinhart, and Végh, 2004). Hence, an increase in the monetary base (low sterilization) may not reflect an expansionary monetary policy, but simply the accommodation of a higher demand for money.

[22]The cyclical component of the fiscal response to capital inflows is also calculated as the deviation of real government spending from its trend, obtained using the Hodrick-Prescott filter.

Figure 3.6. Exchange Market Pressure Index[1]

Exchange market pressures have increased since the early 2000s in all emerging market regions. Although exchange rates have generally been allowed to move, increased reserves point to an effort to limit nominal exchange rate appreciation.

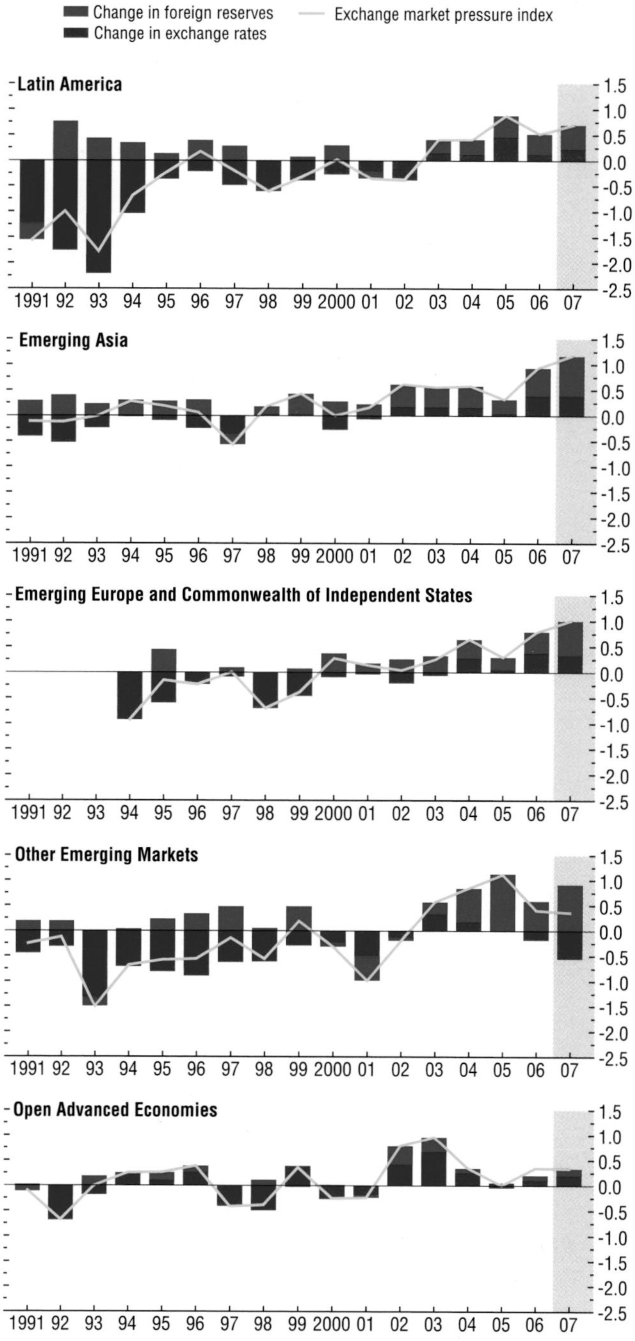

Sources: IMF, *International Financial Statistics;* and IMF staff calculations.
[1]Weighted average of country-specific exchange market pressure indices (using shares of regional GDP as weights). The exchange market pressure index is the weighted average of the annual change in foreign reserves and annual change in nominal bilateral exchange rate, using the inverse of their standard deviations as weights. See Appendix 3.1.

- *Capital controls.* The degree to which the authorities restrict net inflows of capital by imposing administrative controls on capital inflows is captured through an index based on the IMF's *Annual Report on Exchange Arrangements and Exchange Restrictions* (AREAER). The same source is used to construct a second index that measures the degree to which authorities react to the surge in capital inflows by liberalizing a variety of restrictions on capital outflows.[23]

Some Stylized Facts on Policy Responses

Recent years have seen substantial changes in the use of these various policy responses, compared with the 1990s. The recent wave of capital inflows has been associated with strong exchange market pressures in all regions, which have been resisted through the accumulation of foreign reserves while also allowing some upward movement in exchange rates (Figure 3.6). This pattern is significantly different from the earlier wave of net capital inflows, when, for most emerging market countries, pressures on exchange rates were negative, reflecting large current account deficits. During this wave, exchange rates typically depreciated. Emerging Asia was one region that experienced positive exchange market pressures over 1994–96, but these pressures were absorbed through reserve accumulation.

The fact that foreign exchange reserves increased during the 1990s may indicate an asymmetry in the response to exchange rate pressures, with a tendency to intervene to prevent the appreciation of the currency but not to stem a depreciation (except when the pressures became extreme in a financial crisis, as shown by the large reduction of reserves in 1997 in emerging Asia and, in 2001, in Latin America and other emerging markets). Over the past three years, there has been substantial exchange

[23]The IMF's AREAER has indices on nine different dimensions of capital controls, both on inflows and outflows, including controls on capital and money market instruments, on direct investment, and on personal capital movements. The indices used in this chapter are the average across these nine dimensions.

rate appreciation in the face of high and rising positive exchange market pressures, reflecting the trend toward increasing exchange rate flexibility in many countries, especially in emerging Asia. Nevertheless, the relatively high values of the resistance index over the recent past in all four emerging market regions considered in this chapter reflect a continued, widespread desire to limit the extent of exchange rate appreciation (Figure 3.7).

At the same time, the degree of sterilization has increased over the past few years in emerging Asia, and more moderately in Latin America and emerging Europe and the CIS (see Figure 3.7). The high values of the index in the early 1990s and the early 2000s—the beginning of the two waves of large capital inflows—suggest an aggressive sterilization effort when capital began to pour in. This index subsequently tapered off, perhaps indicating that as intervention continued, the authorities became increasingly conscious of its cost.[24]

The pattern of real government expenditure reveals that in the emerging market countries considered in this chapter, real government expenditure growth accelerated over the past few years, especially in Latin America and emerging Europe and the CIS (see Figure 3.7).

Finally, the indices of capital controls in emerging market regions suggest that controls on capital inflows have been relaxed since the late 1990s, although in the aggregate the changes have been relatively slow (see Figure 3.7). Emerging European and the CIS countries have relaxed these controls the most, with emerging Asian countries remaining quite restrictive. Restrictions on residents' capital outflows have also been progressively loosened in emerging Europe and the CIS, and other emerg-

[24]At the same time, the slight decline of the index over the past two decades could reflect both the increased degree of financial integration, which heightens the substitutability of domestic and foreign assets and thus makes sterilization less effective, and the increased demand for money balances from lower inflation and higher output growth, which reduced the need to sterilize the inflationary impact of the increase in reserves.

Figure 3.7. Evolution of Policy Indicators[1]

Real government expenditure growth and resistance to exchange market pressures have generally increased since the early 2000s, sterilization has tapered off over the past two years, and capital controls have been relaxed in most emerging markets.

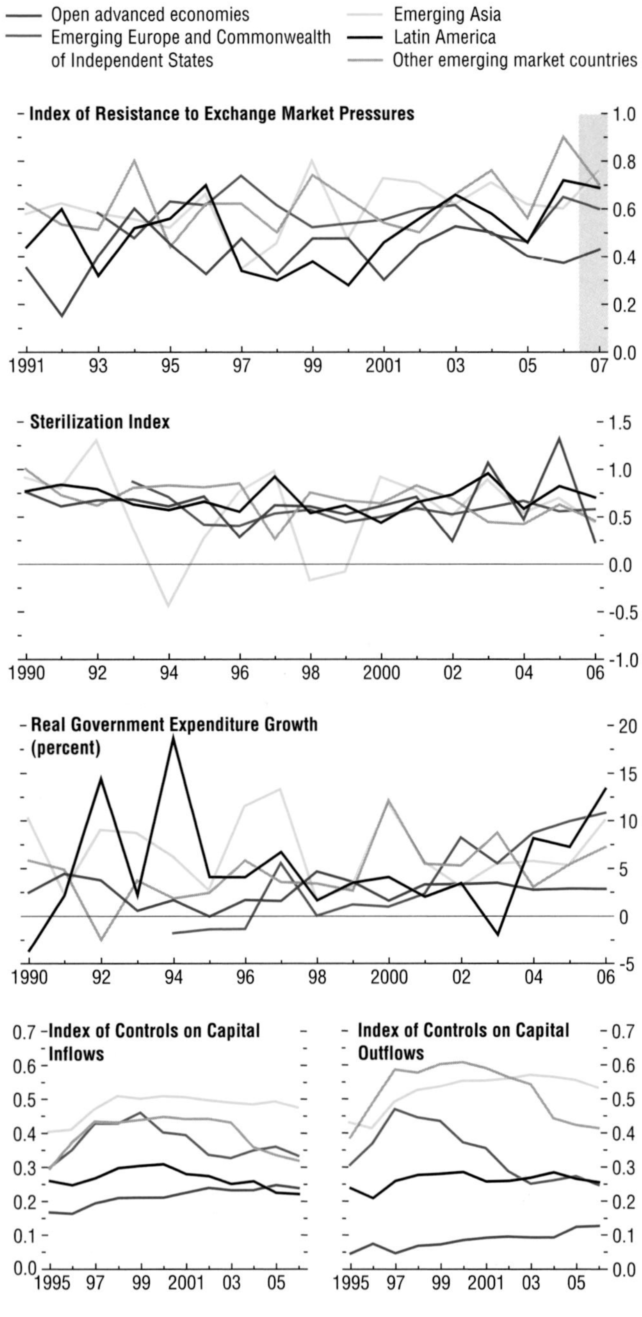

Sources: IMF, *Annual Report on Exchange Arrangements and Exchange Restrictions;* IMF, *International Financial Statistics;* and IMF staff calculations.
[1]Unweighted averages of country-specific indices.

ing market regions, and only more recently in emerging Asia and Latin America, which started from a relatively more open position.

Looking specifically at episodes of large capital inflows, the policy responses are characterized by the following general trends (Figure 3.8):[25]

- The resistance index tends to increase during an episode. This is especially the case for episodes completed before 1998 in which the increase in the index during the inflow period is statistically significant.[26]
- Sterilization does not tend to increase during an episode, relative to the two years before the episode. This result seems consistent with the temporary nature of the sterilization efforts during the episodes discussed above, as many countries were unable to sustain aggressive sterilization over the inflow periods, at least partly because of the associated quasi-fiscal costs.
- Real government expenditures tend to increase strongly as capital inflows surge, suggesting that fiscal policy has generally been procyclical.
- Controls on inward capital flows appear to have been tightened (even if not significantly so) during the episodes completed before 1998. By contrast, during the more recent and ongoing episodes, capital controls appear to have been eased, in line with the general trend toward increased financial integration and greater capital mobility (IMF, 2007a). For completed episodes, the

[25]For each episode, the averages of policy indicators over the years of the episode, the two years before its beginning, and the two years after its end are first estimated. Figures 3.8–3.13 report the medians across these averages.

[26]Although Figures 3.8–3.13 show medians across episodes, a statistical test (based on a chi-squared statistic) is also performed to determine whether the difference between the two medians is significant at a 10 percent confidence level or better. If the test is passed, it means that the difference between the medians reflects a genuine difference across the two groups of episodes. If the test fails, it means that the heterogeneity within the two groups of episodes is large, and thus the difference between the medians is not necessarily indicative of a genuine difference between the two classes of episodes.

Figure 3.8. Policy Indicators in the Episodes of Large Net Private Capital Inflows[1]

Both resistance to exchange market pressures and government expenditure growth have generally increased during completed episodes, while the extent of sterilization has not changed significantly. Controls on capital inflows and outflows seem to have been relaxed during ongoing episodes, even if the difference is not statistically significant.

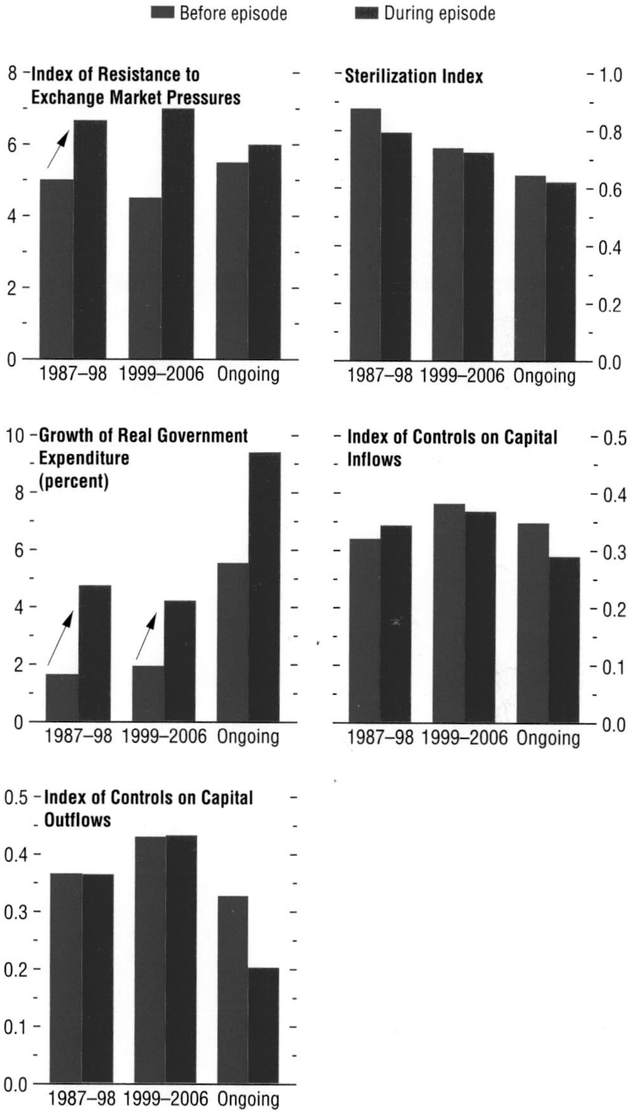

Sources: IMF, *Annual Report on Exchange Arrangements and Exchange Restrictions;* IMF, *International Financial Statistics;* and IMF staff estimates.

[1]Medians across episodes. "Before episode" denotes averages of the indicators in the two years before the episode. "During episode" denotes averages during the episode. The arrows indicate that the difference between medians is significant at a 10 percent confidence level or better. For example, in the top left panel, the average resistance indices during the episodes completed in 1987–98 are statistically significantly different from the average resistance indices in the two years before those episodes.

Figure 3.9. Selected Macroeconomic Variables: Averages During, Before, and After Episodes of Large Net Private Capital Inflows[1]

Episodes of large net private capital inflows are associated with increases in GDP growth, aggregate demand, and current account deficits, which are all reversed when the episodes end. The real exchange rate generally appreciates but inflation does not accelerate. While both foreign direct investment (FDI) and non-FDI inflows increase during the episodes, only the former decline significantly in the aftermath.

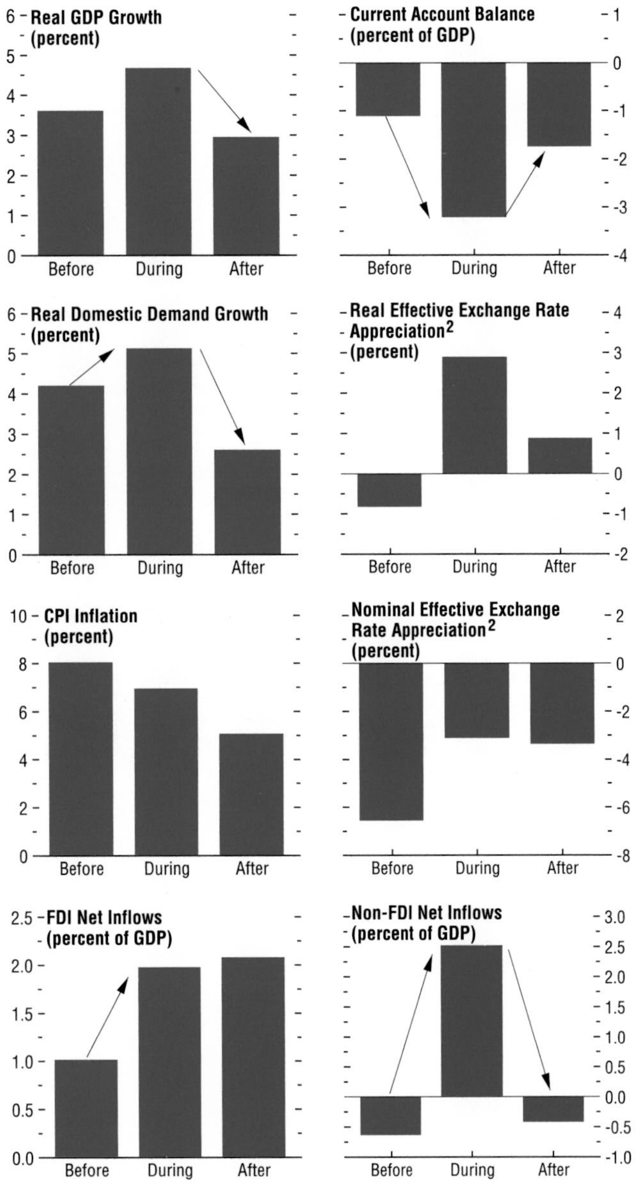

Sources: IMF, *Balance of Payments Statistics;* and IMF staff estimates.

[1]Medians across all completed episodes. "Before" denotes averages of the variables in the two years before the episodes. "After" denotes averages of the variables in the two years after the episodes. The arrows indicate that the difference between medians is significant at a 10 percent confidence level or better. For example, in the top left panel, the average real GDP growth in the two years after the episode is statistically significantly different from the average real GDP growth during the episodes.

[2]Cumulative change within periods.

surge of capital inflows has not coincided with a relaxation of controls on capital outflows. However, these restrictions appear to be less strict during the ongoing episodes (see Box 3.1).

Linking Macroeconomic Outcomes and Policy Responses

This section examines the macroeconomic consequences of the policy responses to large capital inflows. The analysis focuses especially on how successful these policies were in reducing the economy's vulnerability to an abrupt—and costly—end to the inflows.

A first step in this analysis is to examine the behavior of real GDP growth, real aggregate demand, the current account balance, and the real effective exchange rate before, during, and after the episodes (Figure 3.9). The main findings are as follows:

- Episodes of large capital inflows were associated with an acceleration of GDP growth, but afterward growth often dropped significantly.[27]
- Fluctuations in GDP growth have been accompanied by large swings in aggregate demand and in the current account balance, with a strong deterioration of the current account during the inflow period and a sharp reversal at the end.
- Consistent with the literature on capital outflows, the end of the inflow episodes typically entailed a sharp reversal of non-FDI flows, whereas FDI proved much more resilient (Becker, Jeanne, Mauro, Ostry, and Ranciere, 2007).[28]

[27]The post-inflow decline in GDP growth is significantly larger for episodes that end "abruptly." In these cases, average GDP growth in the two years after the end of the episodes tends to be about 3 percentage points lower than during the episode, and about 1 percentage point lower than during the two years before the episode. This suggests that for episodes ending abruptly, it may take some time to fully recover from the economic slowdown associated with the "hard landing."

[28]The stability of capital inflows vis-à-vis financial markets' depth and liquidity is discussed in Chapter 3 of the

- The surge in capital inflows also appears to be associated with a real effective exchange rate appreciation, but the lack of statistical significance in the difference between median appreciation before and during the surge in capital inflows reflects the considerable variation across country experience.
- The mechanism generating real appreciation during an episode has not, on average, been higher inflation. This reflects the fact that for a significant group of episodes, the surge in capital inflows occurred in the context of inflation stabilization plans.[29]

Avoiding a Hard Landing After the Inflows

In light of these findings, an important test of the effectiveness of policies during the inflow period is whether they helped a country achieve a soft landing, that is, a moderate decline in GDP growth after the inflows abated.

Episodes characterized by a sharper post-inflow decline in GDP growth tend to experience a faster acceleration in domestic demand, a sharper rise in inflation, and a larger real appreciation during the inflow period (Figure 3.10, upper panel). These episodes also lasted longer, as shown by the much higher cumulative size of the inflows.[30] Hence, the sharper post-inflow decline in GDP growth seems to be associated with persistent, expansionary capital inflows, which compound external imbalances and sow the seeds of the eventual sharp reversal.

From a policy perspective, it is striking that hard landings have also been associated with a

October 2007 *Global Financial Stability Report.*

[29]Examples are Peru 1992–97, Brazil 1994–96, Bulgaria 1992–93, and Latvia 1994–95. As noted in Calvo and Végh (1999), except for the behavior of inflation, exchange-rate-based inflation stabilization typically leads to the same outcome as an "exogenous" capital inflow, that is, a surge in capital inflows, a pickup in aggregate demand, and a larger real appreciation of the domestic currency that, together with larger current account deficits, sow the seeds of a much stronger decline in GDP growth at the end of an episode.

[30]Examples are Thailand 1988–96, Argentina 1992–94 and 1997–99, and Mexico 1990–94.

Figure 3.10. Post-Inflow GDP Growth, Selected Macroeconomic Variables, and Policy Indicators[1]

Episodes with the weakest post-inflow GDP growth are generally characterized by a stronger increase in aggregate demand, larger real appreciation, and greater size of inflows during the episode. They are also characterized by a strong increase in the cyclical component of government spending.

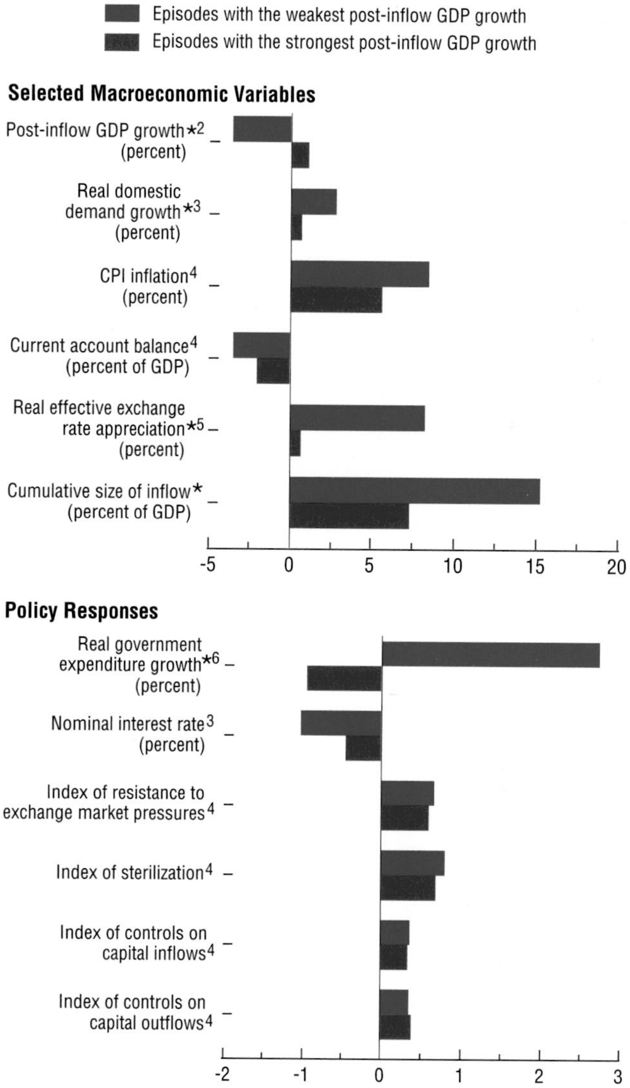

Sources: IMF, *Annual Report on Exchange Arrangements and Exchange Restrictions;* IMF, *Balance of Payments Statistics;* and IMF staff calculations.

[1]Values reported are medians for the two groups of episodes. Episodes with the weakest (strongest) post-inflow GDP growth are those with below (above) median difference between average GDP growth in the two years after the episode and the average during the episodes. The asterisk (*) indicates that the difference between medians is significant at a 10 percent confidence level or better.

[2]Average real GDP growth in the two years after episode minus average during episode.

[3]Average during episode minus average in the two years before the episode.

[4]Average during episode.

[5]Cumulative change during episode.

[6]Average deviations from trend of real government expenditures (excluding interest) during the episode minus average in the two years before the episode. The trend component of real government expenditure is obtained from a Hodrick-Prescott filter.

Table 3.2. Post-Inflow GDP Growth Regressions

Dependent Variable: Post-Inflow GDP Growth[1]	(1)	(2)	(3)	(4)	(5)
Real government expenditure growth[2]	–0.109 (0.015)**	–0.111 (0.014)**	–0.111 (0.014)**	–0.099 (0.027)**	–0.093 (0.040)**
Index of resistance to exchange market pressures[3]	–1.812 (0.114)	–2.090 (0.085)*	–2.086 (0.088)*	–2.147 (0.080)*	–2.282 (0.059)*
Post-inflow world GDP growth[1]	1.023 (0.017)**	0.836 (0.056)*	0.858 (0.071)*	0.875 (0.063)*	0.844 (0.076)*
Real U.S. Federal funds rate[4]		0.279 (0.165)	0.279 (0.170)	0.209 (0.294)	0.240 (0.226)
Post-inflow terms-of-trade change[1]			–0.013 (0.773)	–0.011 (0.827)	–0.024 (0.662)
Cumulative size of capital inflow				–0.049 (0.148)	–0.048 (0.157)
Sterilization index[3]					–0.981 (0.262)
Constant	0.093 (0.905)	0.260 (0.757)	0.265 (0.757)	1.100 (0.263)	1.854 (0.124)
Observations	69	69	69	69	69
Adjusted R-squared	0.133	0.138	0.125	0.187	0.188

Sources: IMF, *International Financial Statistics;* IMF, *Balance of Payments Statistics;* and IMF staff calculations.

Note: * and ** denote significance at the 10 percent and 5 percent level, respectively. Robust P-values are in parentheses.

[1]Average in the two years after the episode minus average during the episode.

[2]Average deviation from trend of real government expenditure (excluding interest) during the episode minus average in the two years before the episode.

[3]Average during the episode.

[4]Average during the episode minus average in the two years before the episode.

strong increase in government spending during the inflow period, whereas expenditure restraint helps reduce upward pressures on both aggregate demand and the real exchange rate and facilitates a soft landing (Figure 3.10, lower panel).[31] By contrast, a higher degree of resistance to exchange rate changes during the inflow period and a greater degree of sterilization were unable to prevent real appreciation and were generally unsuccessful in achieving a soft landing.

The results of cross-sectional regressions on the sample of events confirm the correlation between post-inflow GDP growth and the macroeconomic policies captured by the event analysis. In particular, Table 3.2 shows that countercyclical fiscal policy through expenditure restraint during episodes of large capital inflows is associated with a smaller post-inflow decline in GDP growth, even after controlling for other factors that may have had a role in this decline—such as changes in the terms of trade, world output growth, and the real U.S. Federal funds rate.[32] The regressions also present evidence indicating that greater resistance to exchange market pressures is associated with a sharper economic slowdown in the aftermath of the episodes.[33]

[31]The fiscal policy indicator reported in this and the figures that follow is the cyclical component of government spending. The same results are obtained using the growth in real government spending.

[32]These regressions do not control for the endogeneity of the variables and should therefore not be interpreted as indicating a causality relationship among them. Their only purpose is to analyze the correlation between the dependent and policy variables in a multivariate context.

[33]Moreover, episodes that ended with a sudden stop tend to have a sharper decline of GDP growth in the aftermath of the episode, and also tend to be associated with higher resistance to exchange market pressures—20 of the 34 episodes that ended with a sudden stop are characterized by a high (above median) value of the resistance index.

Containing Real Exchange Rate Appreciation

These findings suggest that a smaller real exchange rate appreciation in response to large capital inflows may help reduce an economy's vulnerability to a sharp and costly reversal. But what policies have been effective in containing upward pressure on the exchange rate?

Splitting the episodes between those with high (above-median) real appreciation and those with low (below-median) real appreciation offers a first attempt at answering this question.[34] Figure 3.11 reveals that greater real appreciation has been associated with stronger acceleration of CPI inflation, more sterilized intervention, and rising government expenditure. These results suggest that a policy of sterilized intervention is unlikely to prevent real appreciation and often tends to be associated with higher inflation. Moreover, in these episodes, a greater increase in nominal interest rates—that is, a more countercyclical monetary policy—is strongly associated with greater real appreciation, because higher returns on domestic assets end up attracting more capital inflows and fueling upward pressures on the currency. In contrast, countercyclical fiscal policy in the form of slower growth in government expenditure is again strongly associated with lower real appreciation. Finally, tighter controls on capital flows do not appear to be associated with lower real appreciation (see Box 3.1 for detailed results on the role of capital controls in the face of large capital inflows).

To assess the strength of these correlations, a cross-sectional regression was run on the sample of events. This relates the extent of real exchange rate appreciation during the period of capital inflows to the policy responses discussed in this chapter, along with other factors that may also lead to real appreciation—including the

[34]The correlation between the extent of real appreciation and macroeconomic policies is analyzed here only in the context of episodes during which inflation accelerated—43 of the total 109 episodes—because these are more likely to be driven by an exogenous shock to capital inflows, rather than by exchange-rate-based inflation stabilization programs.

Figure 3.11. Real Effective Exchange Rate Appreciation and Policy Responses When Inflation Accelerates[1]

Episodes with a high real currency appreciation are characterized by an increase in the cyclical component of government spending, a higher degree of sterilized intervention, and an increase in nominal interest rates.

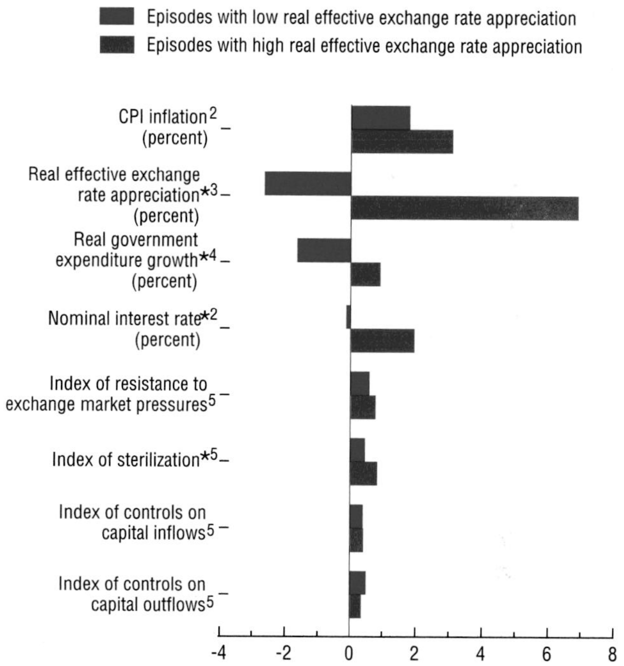

Sources: IMF, *Annual Report on Exchange Arrangements and Exchange Restrictions;* IMF, *Balance of Payments Statistics;* and IMF staff calculations.

[1]Values reported are medians for the two groups of episodes. Episodes with high (low) real effective exchange rate (REER) appreciation are those with above (below) median cumulative REER appreciation in the group of events for which CPI inflation accelerates during the episode. The asterisk (*) indicates that the difference between medians is significant at a 10 percent confidence level or better.

[2]Average during episode minus average in the two years before the episode.

[3]Cumulative change during episode.

[4]Average deviations from trend of real government expenditures (excluding interest) during the episode minus average in the two years before the episode. The trend component of real government expenditure is obtained from a Hodrick-Prescott filter.

[5]Average during episode.

Table 3.3. Real Exchange Rate Regressions

Dependent Variable: Real Effective Exchange Rate Appreciation[1]	(1)	(2)	(3)	(4)
Real government expenditure growth[2]	0.544 (0.003)***	0.396 (0.029)**	0.321 (0.071)*	0.307 (0.112)
Index of resistance to exchange market pressures[3]		–0.239 (0.953)	–0.256 (0.949)	–0.107 (0.979)
Output gap[4]		0.954 (0.050)**	0.715 (0.094)*	0.654 (0.130)
World GDP growth[4]		0.523 (0.704)	0.560 (0.701)	0.590 (0.687)
Real U.S. Federal funds rate[4]		0.492 (0.604)	1.606 (0.100)*	1.755 (0.078)*
Terms-of-trade change[4]		–0.019 (0.946)	–0.034 (0.891)	–0.038 (0.881)
Cumulative size of capital inflow			0.241 (0.083)*	0.249 (0.074)*
Sterilization index[3]				2.562 (0.289)
Constant	6.947 (0.000)***	5.013 (0.129)	1.123 (0.772)	–0.655 (0.884)
Observations	107	107	107	106
Adjusted R-squared	0.115	0.138	0.227	0.222

Sources: IMF, *International Financial Statistics;* IMF, *Balance of Payments Statistics;* and IMF staff calculations.
Note: *, **, and *** denote significance at the 10 percent, 5 percent, and 1 percent level, respectively. Robust P-values are in parentheses.
[1]Cumulative change during the episode.
[2]Average deviation from trend of real government expenditure (excluding interest) during the episode minus average in the two years before the episode.
[3]Average during the episode.
[4]Average during the episode minus average in the two years before the episode.

cumulative size of the inflows, movements in the terms of trade, and changes in the output gap. The results support the conclusion that a policy of resistance to exchange market pressures does not seem to be associated with lower real appreciation, while countercyclical fiscal policies have had the desired effect (Table 3.3).

Regional Differences and Two Particularly Relevant Cases

The importance of fiscal restraint in reducing the degree of real exchange rate appreciation and in smoothing GDP fluctuations in the periods surrounding the episodes is also borne out from a regional perspective. The regions with stronger real appreciation during the episodes, Latin America and emerging Europe and the CIS, also experienced larger increases in public expenditure in those periods (Figure 3.12). By contrast, the advanced economies that have followed more countercyclical fiscal policies and have refrained from resisting exchange market pressures appear to have experienced less real appreciation and smaller GDP growth fluctuations around the episodes.

It is also important to examine whether the policy responses and outcomes depend on the persistence of inflows and the current account position.

- Episodes that lasted less than two years display somewhat different patterns than longer episodes, with significantly larger resistance to exchange rate changes, less real appreciation, and better post-inflow GDP growth (Figure 3.13, upper panel). However, these results do not show that resistance is more effective in such cases, because during short inflow episodes higher resistance was not associated with significantly smaller real appreciation or better post-inflow growth (Figure 3.13, lower panel). This suggests that resisting exchange market pressures may be more feasible when facing transitory inflows, but it does not generate significantly better outcomes, at least when assessed over the entire duration of the episodes.[35] Moreover, in practice, it may be difficult for policymakers to identify ex ante when an episode of inflows will turn out to be temporary.[36]

- The fiscal policy response appears to have been less decisive in episodes associated with high balance of payments pressures (defined as an above-median sum of the current account and net private capital inflows). For such episodes, lower government spending growth is not associated with significantly lower real appreciation or better post-inflow GDP growth (Figure 3.14, upper panel). By contrast, fiscal spending restraint is associated with significantly better outcomes when the episodes are characterized by low balance of payments pressures (Figure 3.14, lower panel). This suggests that a countercyclical policy stance may be most important when inflows occur in the context of a large current account deficit.

Conclusions

The strong increase in net private capital inflows to emerging market economies over the past few years has restored the "capital inflows problem" to a prominent place in policy debates. The main objective of this chapter was to review the lessons from the experience of

[35]Because the empirical analysis in this chapter does not consider the transitional dynamics within the episodes, this finding does not necessarily exclude that sterilized intervention may be effective for short periods of time.

[36]Longer episodes are also characterized by higher (i.e., statistically significant) levels of capital controls, even if the difference is rather small.

Figure 3.12. Regional Dimension[1]

Regions with larger real currency appreciation (Latin America and emerging Europe) are also characterized by an increase in the cyclical component of government spending.

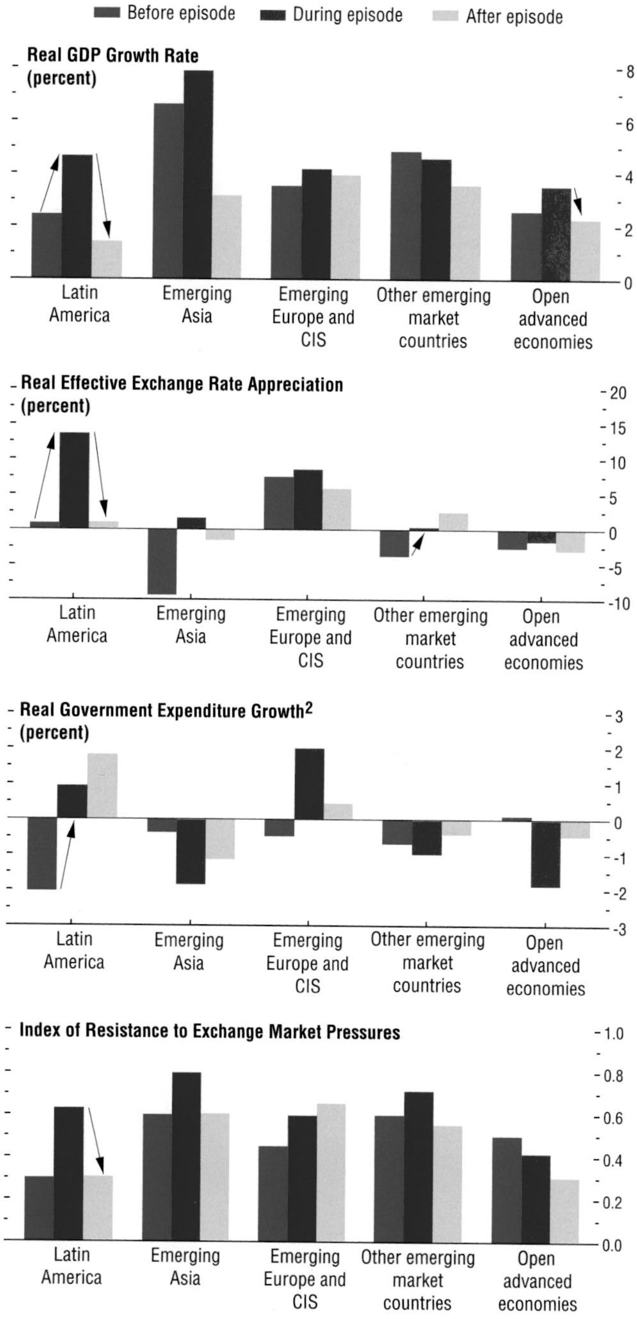

Sources: IMF, *International Financial Statistics;* and IMF staff calculations.

[1]Values reported are medians across completed episodes. CIS refers to the Commonwealth of Independent States.

[2]Average deviations from trend of real government expenditures (excluding interest) during the episode minus average in the two years before the episode. The trend component of real government expenditure is obtained from a Hodrick-Prescott filter.

Figure 3.13. Resistance to Exchange Market Pressures and Duration of Capital Inflow Episodes[1]

Shorter episodes are characterized by better post-inflow growth, lower appreciation, and higher resistance to exchange market pressures. Higher resistance, however, does not tend to be associated with significantly better outcomes during shorter episodes.

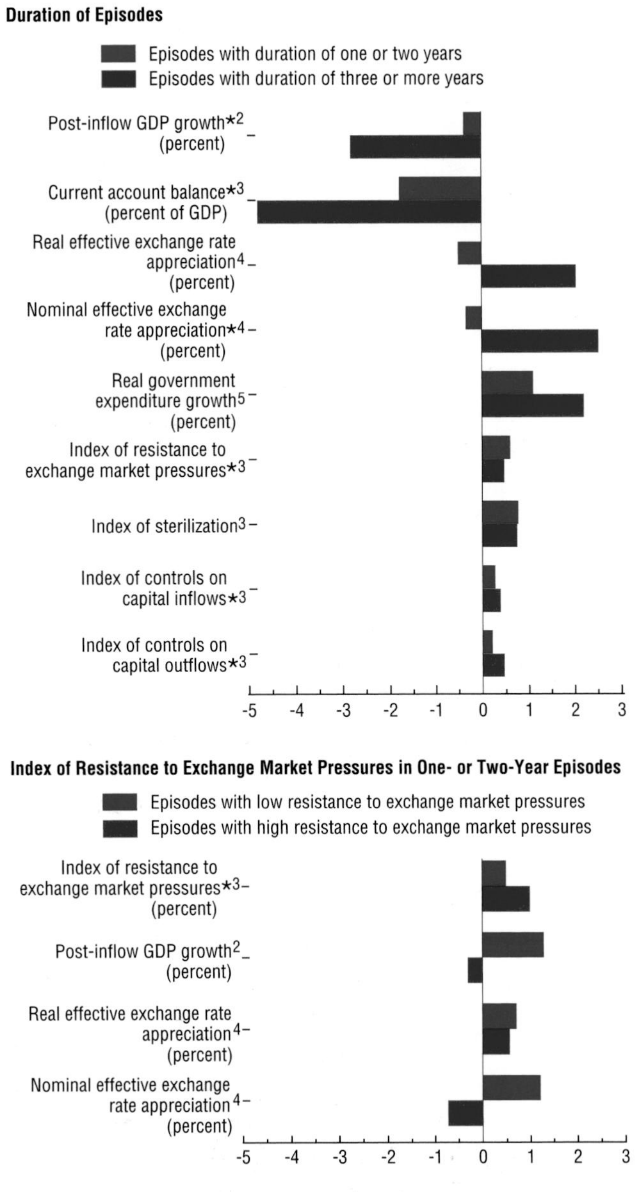

Sources: IMF, *Annual Report on Exchange Arrangements and Exchange Restrictions;* IMF, *Balance of Payments Statistics;* and IMF staff calculations.

[1]Values reported are medians for the two groups of episodes. The asterisk (*) indicates that the difference between medians is significant at a 10 percent confidence level or better.

[2]Average in the two years after an episode minus average during episode.

[3]Average during episode.

[4]Average during episode minus average in the two years before the episode.

[5]Average deviations from trend of real government expenditures (excluding interest) during the episode minus average in the two years before the episode. The trend component of real government expenditure is obtained from a Hodrick-Prescott filter.

large net private capital inflows over the past two decades, focusing especially on the macroeconomic consequences of the policy choices made in response to these inflows.

Although countries' responses to a surge of capital inflows depend on the specific nature of the inflows as well as on various aspects of their particular circumstances and objectives, some overall patterns nonetheless emerge from a systematic review of inflow episodes. First, countries with relatively high current account deficits have been more vulnerable to a sharp reversal of capital inflows, because they have been particularly affected by the increase in aggregate demand and the real appreciation of their currencies. Second, there is a clear policy message that public expenditure restraint during such episodes can contribute to both a lower real exchange rate appreciation and better post-inflow GDP growth performance. Third, a policy of resistance to nominal exchange rate appreciation has generally not been successful in preventing real appreciation and has often been followed by a sharper reversal of capital inflows, especially when these inflows have persisted for a longer time. Fourth, the chapter suggests that restrictions on capital inflows have in general not facilitated lower real appreciation and a soft landing at the end of an episode.

These findings imply that the stabilization challenges from large capital inflows are most serious for countries with substantial current account imbalances, which currently include many emerging European countries. The most effective tool available to policymakers to avoid overheating and output instability is likely to be fiscal restraint, especially in the context of relatively inflexible exchange rate policies. This chapter also suggests that even if a central bank initially intervenes to resist nominal exchange rate appreciation when capital inflows begin, this stance should be progressively relaxed if the inflows persist. This is because it becomes less likely that such a policy will succeed in preventing real appreciation and a painful end to the inflows.

In addition to the macroeconomic policy instruments discussed in this chapter, the authorities have other tools at their disposal, which have not been analyzed systematically—notably, financial supervision and regulation, but also a wider range of policies such as labor and product market reforms. The role of such policies in responding to capital inflows would be an important topic for future research.

Appendix 3.1. Event Analysis and Policy Indices: Methodologies and Data

The main author of this appendix is Roberto Cardarelli.

Event Analysis

Episodes of large net private capital inflows were identified based on the following methodology:

- For each country in the sample, a rolling, backward-looking Hodrick-Prescott (HP) filter (using the first five years of data and a smoothing coefficient λ equal to 1,000) was applied to annual net private capital inflows to GDP ratios (NPCIR).[37] For countries with insufficient time observations, the HP filter was applied to the whole time series of NPCIRs (with a λ equal to 100), rather than on a rolling basis.
- For a country *i*, which belongs to region *j*, a year *t* is an episode of "large capital inflow" if either
  - the deviation of the NPCIR from its trend at time *t* is larger than one historical standard deviation, and the NPCIR exceeds 1 percent of GDP, or
  - the NPCIR exceeds the 75th percentile of the distribution of NPCIRs for the region *j* over the whole sample.

Each episode begins in the first year in which one of these criteria is satisfied and continues

[37]See Gourinchas, Valdés, and Landerretche (2001) for a similar methodology.

Figure 3.14. Fiscal Policy and Balance of Payments Pressures[1]

Fiscal spending restraint is particularly important in the context of larger current account deficits (low balance of payments pressures).

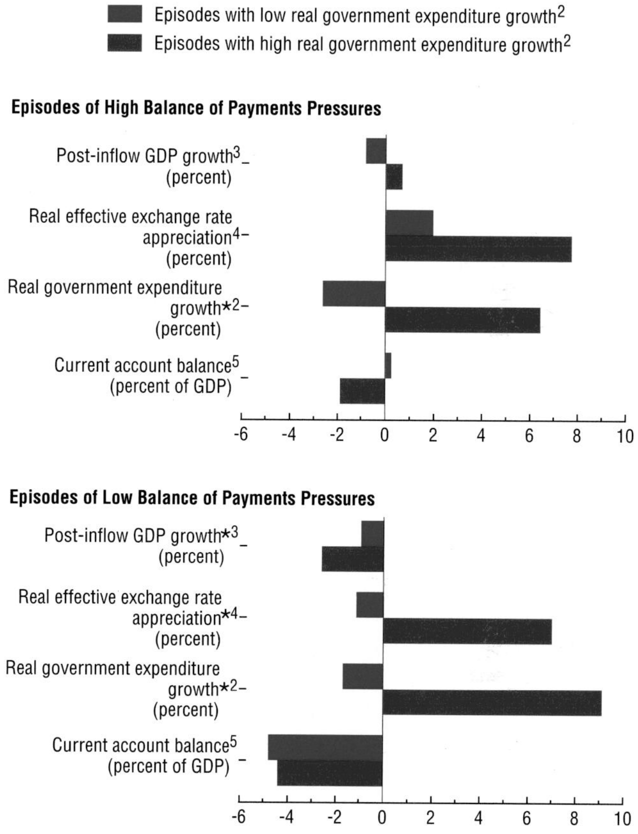

Sources: IMF, *Annual Report on Exchange Arrangements and Exchange Restrictions;* IMF, *Balance of Payments Statistics;* and IMF staff calculations.

[1]Values reported are medians for the two groups of episodes. Episodes with high (low) balance of payments pressures are those with above (below) median sum of current account and net private capital inflows, as a percent of GDP, on average during the episode. Episodes with low (high) real government expenditure growth are those with below (above) median government expenditure growth. The asterisk (*) indicates that the difference between medians is significant at a 10 percent confidence level or better.

[2]Average deviations from trend of real government expenditures (excluding interest) during the episode minus average in the two years before the episode. The trend component of real government expenditure is obtained from a Hodrick-Prescott filter.

[3]Average growth rate in the two years after an episode less average during the episode.

[4]Cumulative change of the real exchange rate index during the episode.

[5]Average during episode.

Table 3.4. List of Net Private Capital Inflow Episodes

Country	Duration	Cumulative Size (percent of GDP)	Country	Duration	Cumulative Size (percent of GDP)
Albania	1997	4.3	Malaysia	1989–96	79.1
Albania	2000	2.6	Malta	1993–2000	60.2
Argentina	1992–94	11.6	Malta	Ongoing since 2005	17.1
Argentina	1997–99	11	Mexico	1990–94	26.3
Australia	1988–90	16.8	Mexico	1997	6.2
Australia	1995–99	24.8	Mexico	2000	4.9
Australia	Ongoing since 2003	24.5	Morocco	1989–94	21
Brazil	1994–96	11.3	Morocco	1997–2001	22.7
Brazil	2000–01	7	New Zealand	1992	7
Bulgaria	1992–93	7.4	New Zealand	1995–97	19
Bulgaria	Ongoing since 1997	118.4	New Zealand	2000	5.9
Canada	1997–98	3.8	New Zealand	Ongoing since 2004	31.4
Chile	1988–97	70.5	Norway	1993	4.3
China	1993–95	12.6	Norway	1996–97	6.5
China	2004	5.6	Pakistan	1991–96	18.1
Colombia	1993–96	20.2	Pakistan	Ongoing since 2005	7.1
Colombia	2004–05	6	Paraguay	1994–97	10.1
Costa Rica	1987–92	16	Paraguay	2005	4.5
Costa Rica	1995	5.3	Peru	1992–97	39.6
Costa Rica	1999	6.1	Philippines	1987–97	59.6
Costa Rica	Ongoing since 2002	32.4	Poland	1995–2000	35
Croatia	1997–99	29.9	Romania	1990–93	9.5
Croatia	Ongoing since 2002	59	Romania	1996–98	14.2
Cyprus	1989–92	21.4	Romania	Ongoing since 2004	42.3
Cyprus	1997	3.3	Russia	2003	1.8
Cyprus	1999–2001	15.5	Russia	Ongoing since 2006	4.1
Cyprus	Ongoing since 2005	23.2	Singapore	1990–91	16.2
Czech Republic	1994–95	24	Slovak Republic	1996–98	31.4
Czech Republic	2000–02	26.3	Slovak Republic	2002	21.1
Denmark	1994	5.8	Slovak Republic	2005	14.2
Denmark	1997	5	Slovenia	1997	5
Denmark	1999	5.1	Slovenia	2001–02	14.7
Egypt	1992	2.8	South Africa	1995	3.3
Egypt	1997–98	8.2	South Africa	2000	1.8
Egypt	Ongoing since 2005	6.9	South Africa	Ongoing since 2004	12.4
Estonia	1996–98	38.6	Sweden	1988–90	15.2
Estonia	Ongoing since 2002	74.4	Sweden	1998–2000	14.4
Hong Kong SAR	1997	7.5	Thailand	1988–96	88.8
Hong Kong SAR	2000	2.5	Thailand	Ongoing since 2005	12.2
Hungary	1991–2000	75.3	Tunisia	1990–94	19.8
Hungary	2005	9.4	Tunisia	1998–99	6.3
Iceland	1996–2000	29.6	Tunisia	Ongoing since 2004	12.8
Iceland	Ongoing since 2003	77.1	Turkey	1992–93	4.4
India	1988–90	6.9	Turkey	1995–2000	15.3
India	1994	3.2	Turkey	Ongoing since 2003	25.7
India	Ongoing since 2002	18.3	Ukraine	2005	7.5
Indonesia	1990–96	26.3	Uruguay	1997	1.5
Israel	1995–97	17.4	Uruguay	2000	1.6
Korea	1990–96	18.9	Uruguay	Ongoing since 2005	12
Korea	1999–2000	4.7	Venezuela	1991–93	10.8
Korea	2003	3.4	Venezuela	1997–98	6.3
Latvia	1994–95	19.3	Vietnam	1994	9.1
Latvia	Ongoing since 2001	84.7	Vietnam	1999	10.1
Lithuania	1997–98	21	Vietnam	Ongoing since 2003	38.4
Lithuania	Ongoing since 2005	20.5			

Source: IMF staff calculations.

in subsequent years if the episode continues to meet these criteria.

According to this methodology, there could be two consecutive episodes of large inflows. However, sequences of episodes would make the identification of pre- and post-episode periods ambiguous. The following criteria are thus adopted to make sure that there is no episode of large capital inflows in the two years before each episode:

- if the end-year of an episode is immediately before the beginning year of another episode, then the two episodes are combined to form a single episode; and
- if there is only one year between the end of an episode and the beginning of another, that one year is included in the episode that combines the two episodes only if the NPCIR in that year is positive. If it is negative, the first episode is excluded.

Table 3.4 lists the episodes identified in this chapter, and Figure 3.15 shows an example using the case of Mexico.

The Exchange Market Pressure Index and the Index of Resistance

For a country i in year t, the exchange market pressure (EMP) index is defined as the weighted average of two components: (1) the percent change of the nominal exchange rate against a reference country in year t (an increase indicates an appreciation) and (2) the change in foreign reserves in year t. The weights are the inverse of the standard deviations of the two components, so as to ensure that none of them dominates the index:[38]

$$EMP_{i,t} = \frac{1}{\sigma_{\Delta \% er_{i,t}}} \Delta \% er_{i,t} + \frac{1}{\sigma_{\Delta res_{i,t}}} \Delta res_{i,t},$$

[38]Weymark (1995) uses model-consistent weights, and in particular weights that are based on the estimated interest rate elasticity of the demand for money. Pentecost, Van Hooydonk, and Van Poeck (2001) use principal component analysis to obtain the weights. This chapter follows Eichengreen, Rose, and Wyplosz (1996); Kaminsky and Reinhart (1999); and Van Poeck, Vanneste, and Veiner (2007), who use variance-smoothing weights.

Figure 3.15. Mexico: Identification of Large Net Private Capital Inflow Episodes

(Percent of GDP)

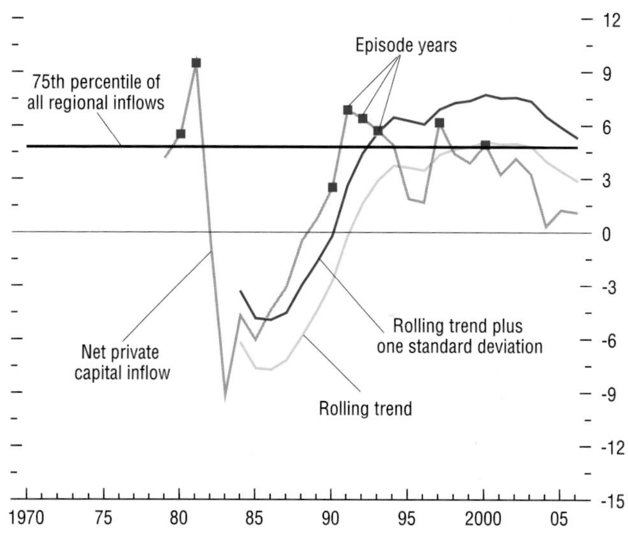

Sources: IMF, *Balance of Payments Statistics;* and IMF staff calculations.

where $\Delta\%er_{i,t}$ is the percentage year-over-year change of the nominal bilateral exchange rate of country *i* against a reference country, identified as in Levy-Yeyati and Sturzenegger (2005); $\Delta res_{i,t}$ is the change in country *i* central bank's net foreign assets (*NFA*) in year *t* normalized by the monetary base (*MB*) in year $t-1$; and $\sigma_{\Delta\%er}$ and $\sigma_{\Delta res}$ are the standard deviations of the two variables in year *t* (based on the monthly changes of exchange rates and foreign reserves in the region to which the country belongs):[39]

$$\Delta\%er_{i,t} = \frac{er_{i,t} - er_{i,t-1}}{er_{i,t-1}},\ \Delta res_{i,t} = \frac{NFA_{i,t} - NFA_{i,t-1}}{MB_{i,t-1}}.$$

Based on the *EMP* index, the resistance index is calculated as follows:

$$Resistance\ index_{i,t} = 1 - \frac{\Delta\%er_{i,t}}{\sigma_{\Delta\%er_{i,t}} EMP_{i,t}}.$$

While the index ranges from $-\infty$ to $+\infty$, its values are standardized between the interval 0 and 1.[40] When the index is equal to 0, it means that there is no resistance to exchange market pressures (either the exchange rate is allowed to float freely or a "leaning with the wind" policy is followed, which exacerbates, rather than relieves, the exogenous pressures on the exchange rate).[41] When the index is equal to 1, it denotes the maximum amount of resistance (either the exchange rate is prevented from moving at all or extreme forms of a "leaning against the wind" policy are followed, which makes the exchange rate move in the opposite direction to which it would have in the absence of intervention).[42] Intermediate values between 0 and 1 indicate the extent to which market pressures are relieved by intervention in the foreign exchange market.

The Sterilization Index

For country *i* and year *t*, the sterilization index is based on the coefficient β in the following annual ordinary least squares regression (using 12 monthly observations):

$$\Delta NDA_{i,t,m} = \alpha_{i,t} + \beta_{i,t}\Delta NFA_{i,t,m} + u_{i,t,m},$$

where $\Delta NDA_{i,t,m}$ is the monthly change in the country *i*'s central bank's net domestic assets during month *m* of year *t*. This index measures the central bank's effort to sterilize the effect of higher reserves on the monetary base, by reducing its stock of domestic assets. This has occurred generally through open market operations but also in several cases by transferring deposits of the government or pension funds, or the proceeds from privatization of public assets, from the banking system to the central bank.[43]

A value of β equal to –1 or lower implies full monetary sterilization, whereas a value of 0 represents no sterilization (values larger than –1 imply "oversterilization"). For simplicity, the slope coefficient is multiplied by –1, so that an estimated value of the sterilization index equal to 1 implies full sterilization, whereas a value of 0 represents no sterilization.

Although the chapter uses this index, a broader sterilization index is also estimated that reflects the central bank's effort to prevent an increase in the monetary base from causing an expansion of the money supply. This has occurred generally through an increase in the reserve requirements for the banking sec-

[39]Using regional—rather than country-specific—standard deviations avoids the risk that countries with barely significant changes in their exchange rate would result as having a flexible exchange rate policy because of the very small standard deviation of these changes.

[40]In particular, if the index is negative or 0, it is given the value of 0; if it is between 0 and 0.25, it is given the value of 0.2; if it is between 0.25 and 0.5, it is given the value of 0.4; if it is between 0.5 and 0.75, it is given the value of 0.6; if it is between 0.75 and 1, it is given the value of 0.8; and if it is 1 or above, it is given the value of 1.

[41]These are the cases in which the index would have negative values.

[42]These are the cases in which the index would have values larger than 1.

[43]When the authorities offset the purchase of foreign exchange by transferring government deposits from commercial banks to the central bank, the stock of the monetary base is unchanged, because they have exchanged a claim on the domestic banking sector for an external claim.

tor, which reduces the money multiplier. For a year t, this broader index is the coefficient δ in the annual regression based on 12 monthly observations:

$$\Delta M2_{i,t,m} = \alpha_{i,t} + \delta_{i,t}\Delta NFA_{i,t,m} + u_{i,t,m},$$

where $\Delta M2_{i,t,m}$ is the monthly change in country-i money supply (defined as $M2$) in year t and month m. In this case, a value of δ equal to 0 implies full monetary sterilization, whereas a value of 1 represents no sterilization. Results based on this broader index are consistent with those obtained using the narrower index and shown in the text. The results are available from the authors on request.

References

Ariyoshi, Akira, Karl Habermeier, Bernard Laurens, Inci Ötker-Robe, Jorge Iván Canales-Kriljenko, and Andrei Kirilenko, 2000, *Capital Controls: Country Experiences with Their Use and Liberalization.* IMF Occasional Paper No. 190 (Washington: International Monetary Fund).

Bartolini, Leonardo, and Allan Drazen, 1997, "Capital-Account Liberalization as a Signal," *American Economic Review,* Vol. 87, No. 1 (March), pp. 138–54.

Becker, Torbjörn I., Olivier Jeanne, Paulo Mauro, Jonathan D. Ostry, and Romain Ranciere, 2007, *Country Insurance: The Role of Domestic Policies,* IMF Occasional Paper No. 254 (Washington: International Monetary Fund).

Calvo, Guillermo A., Leonardo Leiderman, and Carmen M. Reinhart, 1994, "The Capital Inflows Problem: Concepts and Issues," *Contemporary Economic Policy,* Vol. 12, No. 3 (July), pp. 54–66.

———, 1996, "Inflows of Capital to Developing Countries in the 1990s," *Journal of Economic Perspectives,* Vol. 10 (Spring), pp. 123–39.

Calvo, Guillermo A., and Carlos A. Végh, 1999, "Inflation Stabilization and BOP Crises in Developing Countries," in *Handbook of Macroeconomics,* Vol. 1, ed. by John B. Taylor and Michael Woodford (Amsterdam: Elsevier), pp. 1531–614.

Cavoli, Tony, and Ramkishen S. Rajan, 2006, "Capital Inflows Problem in Selected Asian Economies in the 1990s Revisited: The Role of Monetary Sterilization," *Asian Economic Journal,* Vol. 20, No. 4, pp. 409–23.

Chinn, Menzie D., and Hiro Ito, 2006, "What Matters for Financial Development? Capital Controls, Institutions, and Interactions," *Journal of Development Economics,* Vol. 6, No. 1 (October), pp. 163–92.

Desai, Mihir A., C. Fritz Foley, and James R. Hines, Jr., 2004, "Capital Controls, Liberalizations, and Foreign Direct Investment," NBER Working Paper No. 10337 (Cambridge, Massachusetts: National Bureau of Economic Research).

Edwards, Sebastian, ed., 2000, *Capital Flows and the Emerging Economies: Theory, Evidence, and Controversies,* National Bureau of Economic Research Conference Report (Chicago: University of Chicago Press).

———, 2005, "Capital Controls, Sudden Stops, and Current Account Reversals," NBER Working Paper No. 11170 (Cambridge, Massachusetts: National Bureau of Economic Research).

———, and Roberto Rigobon, 2005, "Capital Controls, Exchange Rate Volatility and External Vulnerability," NBER Working Paper No. 11434 (Cambridge, Massachusetts: National Bureau of Economic Research).

Eichengreen, Barry, Andrew K. Rose, and Charles Wyplosz, 1996, "Contagious Currency Crises," NBER Working Paper No. 5681 (Cambridge, Massachusetts: National Bureau of Economic Research).

Fernández-Arias, Eduardo, and Peter J. Montiel, 1996, "The Surge in Capital Inflows to Developing Countries: An Analytical Overview," *World Bank Economic Review,* Vol. 10, No. 1, pp. 51–77.

Forbes, Kristin, 2007a, "One Cost of the Chilean Capital Controls: Increased Financial Constraints for Smaller Traded Firms," *Journal of International Economics,* Vol. 71, No. 2 (April), pp. 294–323.

———, 2007b, "The Microeconomic Evidence on Capital Controls: No Free Lunch," in *Capital Controls and Capital Flows in Emerging Economies: Policies, Practices, and Consequences,* ed. by Sebastian Edwards (Chicago: University of Chicago Press), pp. 171–99.

Frankel, Jeffrey, and Andrew Rose, 1996, "Currency Crashes in Emerging Markets: An Empirical Treatment," *Journal of International Economics,* Vol. 41, No. 3/4, pp. 351–66.

Girton, Lance, and Don Roper, 1977, "A Monetary Model of Exchange Market Pressure Applied to the Postwar Canadian Experience," *American Economic Review,* Vol. 67, No. 4, pp. 537–48.

Glick, Reuven, ed., 1998, *Managing Capital Flows and Exchange Rates: Perspectives from the Pacific Basin* (New York: Cambridge University Press).

———, Xueyan Guo, and Michael Hutchison, 2006, "Currency Crises, Capital Account Liberalization, and Selection Bias," *Review of Economics and Statistics*, Vol. 88, No. 4, pp. 698–714.

Gourinchas, Pierre Olivier, Rodrigo Valdés, and Oscar Landerretche, 2001, "Lending Booms: Latin America and the World," *Economia*, Vol. 1, No. 2 (Spring), pp. 41–63.

Grilli, Vittorio, and Gian Maria Milesi-Ferretti, 1995, "Economic Effects and Structural Determinants of Capital Controls," *Staff Papers*, International Monetary Fund, Vol. 42, No. 3, pp. 54–88.

International Monetary Fund, 2007a, "Reaping the Benefits of Financial Globalization," IMF Research Department discussion paper (Washington). Available via the Internet: www.imf.org/external/np/res/docs/2007/0607.htm.

———, 2007b, *Regional Economic Outlook: Asia and Pacific*, April (Washington).

———, 2007c, *Regional Economic Outlook: Western Hemisphere*, October (Washington).

Johnson, Simon, and Todd Mitton, 2003, "Cronyism and Capital Controls: Evidence from Malaysia," *Journal of Financial Economics*, Vol. 67, No. 2 (February), pp. 351–82.

Kaminsky, Graciela, L., and Carmen M. Reinhart, 1999, "The Twin Crises: The Causes of Banking and Balance of Payments Problems," *American Economic Review*, Vol. 89, No. 4, pp. 473–500.

———, and Carlos A. Végh, 2004, "When It Rains, It Pours: Procyclical Capital Flows and Macroeconomic Policies," in *NBER Macroeconomics Annual 2004*, ed. by Mark Gertler and Kenneth Rogoff (Cambridge, Massachusetts: MIT Press), pp. 11–53.

Kose M. Ayhan, Eswar Prasad, Kenneth Rogoff, and Shang-Jin Wei, 2006, "Financial Globalization: A Reappraisal," IMF Working Paper 06/189 (Washington: International Monetary Fund).

Kwack, Sung Yeung, 2001, "An Empirical Assessment of Monetary Policy Responses to Capital Inflows in East Asia before the Crisis," *International Economic Journal*, Vol. 15, No. 1, pp. 95–113.

Lane, Timothy D., Leslie Lipschitz, and Alex Mourmouras, 2002, "Capital Flows to Transition Economies: Master or Servant?" IMF Working Paper 02/11 (Washington: International Monetary Fund).

Levy-Yeyati, Eduardo, and Federico Sturzenegger, 2005, "Classifying Exchange Rate Regimes: Deeds vs. Words," *European Economic Review*, Vol. 49, No. 6 (August), pp. 1603–35.

Magud, Nicolas, and Carmen Reinhart, 2007, "Capital Controls: An Evaluation," in *Capital Controls and Capital Flows in Emerging Economies: Policies, Practices, and Consquences*, ed. by Sebastian Edwards (Chicago: University of Chicago Press), pp. 645–74.

Mauro, Paolo, and Torbjörn Becker, 2006, "Output Drops and the Shocks That Matter," IMF Working Paper 06/172 (Washington: International Monetary Fund).

Mendoza, Enrique G., and Jonathan D. Ostry, 2007, "International Evidence on Fiscal Solvency: Is Fiscal Policy 'Responsible'?" NBER Working Paper No. 12947 (Cambridge, Massachusetts: National Bureau of Economic Research).

Miniane, Jacques, 2004, "A New Set of Measures on Capital Account Restrictions," *Staff Papers*, International Monetary Fund, Vol. 51, No. 2, pp. 276–308.

Mody, Ashoka, and Antu Panini Murshid, 2005, "Growing Up With Capital Flows," *Journal of International Economics*, Vol. 65, No. 1 (January), pp. 249–66.

Montiel, Peter J., 1999, "Policy Responses to Volatile Capital Flows" (unpublished; Washington: World Bank). Available via the Internet: www.worldbank.org/research/interest/confs/past/papers15-16.htm.

Obstfeld, Maurice, and Alan Taylor, 2002, "Globalization and Capital Markets," NBER Working Paper No. 8846 (Cambridge, Massachusetts: National Bureau of Economic Research).

Pentecost, Eric J., Charlotte Van Hooydonk, and André Van Poeck, 2001, "Measuring and Estimating Exchange Market Pressure in the EU," *Journal of International Money and Finance*, Vol. 20, No. 3, pp. 401–18.

Quinn, Dennis, 2003, "Capital Account Liberalization and Financial Globalization, 1890–1999: A Synoptic View," *International Journal of Finance and Economics*, Vol. 8, No. 3, pp. 189–204.

Reinhart, Carmen M., and Vincent Reinhart, 1998, "Some Lessons for Policymakers Who Deal With the Mixed Blessing of Capital Inflows," in *Capital Flows and Financial Crises*, ed. by Miles Kahler (Ithaca, New York: Cornell University Press), pp. 93–127.

Van Poeck, André, Jacques Vanneste, and Maret Veiner, 2007, "Exchange Rate Regimes and Exchange Market Pressure in the New EU Member States," *Journal of Common Market Studies*, Vol. 45, No. 2, pp. 459–85.

Wei, Shang-Jin, and Zhiwei Zhang, 2007, "Collateral Damage: Exchange Controls and International Trade," IMF Working Paper 07/08 (Washington: International Monetary Fund).

Weymark, Diana N., 1995, "Estimating Exchange Market Pressure and the Degree of Exchange Market Intervention for Canada," *Journal of International Economics*, Vol. 39, pp. 273–95.

World Bank, 1997, *Private Capital Flows to Developing Countries: The Road to Financial Integration* (New York: Oxford University Press).

———, 2006, *Global Development Finance* (Washington).

CHAPTER 4

GLOBALIZATION AND INEQUALITY

This chapter examines the relationship between the rapid pace of trade and financial globalization and the rise in income inequality observed in most countries over the past two decades. The analysis finds that technological progress has had a greater impact than globalization on inequality within countries. The limited overall impact of globalization reflects two offsetting tendencies: whereas trade globalization is associated with a reduction in inequality, financial globalization—and foreign direct investment in particular—is associated with an increase in inequality. It should be emphasized that these findings are subject to a number of caveats related to data limitations, and it is particularly difficult to disentangle the effects of technology and financial globalization since they both work through processes that raise the demand for skilled workers. The chapter concludes that policies aimed at reducing barriers to trade and broadening access to education and credit can allow the benefits of globalization to be shared more equally.

The integration of the world economy through the progressive globalization of trade and finance has reached unprecedented levels, surpassing the pre–World War I peak. This new wave of globalization is having far-reaching implications for the economic well-being of citizens in all regions and among all income groups, and is the subject of active public debate. Previous issues of the *World Economic Outlook* have analyzed the impact of globalization on business cycle spillovers and labor markets (April 2007), on inflation (April 2006), and on external imbalances (April 2005). This chapter makes a further contribution to the study of globalization by examining the implications for inequality and the distribution of income within countries, with a focus on emerging market and developing countries (often referred to as developing economies in the remainder of the chapter).

The debate on the distributional effects of globalization is often polarized between two points of view. One school of thought argues that globalization leads to a rising tide of income, which raises all boats. Hence, even low-income groups come out as winners from globalization in absolute terms. This optimistic view has parallels with the Kuznets hypothesis from the development literature, which proposed that even though inequality might rise in the initial phases of industrial development, it eventually declined as the country's transition to industrialization was completed.[1] The opposing school argues that although globalization may improve overall incomes, the benefits are not shared equally among the citizens of a country, with clear losers in relative and possibly even absolute terms.[2] Moreover, widening income disparities may not only raise welfare and social concerns, but may also limit the drivers of growth because the opportunities created by the process of globalization may not be fully exploited.[3] The sustainability of globalization will also depend on maintaining broad support across the population, which could be adversely affected by rising inequality.

Against this background, this chapter addresses the broad question of how globalization affects the distribution of income within countries and the incomes of the poorest segment of the population in particular. The main

Note: The main authors of this chapter are Subir Lall, Florence Jaumotte, Chris Papageorgiou, and Petia Topalova, with support from Stephanie Denis and Patrick Hettinger. Nancy Birdsall and Gordon Hanson provided consultancy support.

[1]See Kuznets (1955) for the original formulation of this hypothesis.

[2]See *The Economist* (2000) and Forsyth (2000) for representative views.

[3]See Birdsall (2007) and World Bank (2006).

objectives are to (1) analyze the shifting patterns of globalization and income distribution over the past two decades, (2) identify the main channels through which increased trade and financial globalization affect the distribution of income within a country, and (3) offer policy suggestions in light of the evidence that would help countries take full advantage of the opportunities from globalization while also ensuring that the benefits from globalization are shared appropriately across the population.

This chapter aims to extend the considerable literature on globalization and inequality along several dimensions.[4] Unlike previous studies, which focus largely on trade globalization, this chapter also analyzes various channels of financial globalization to offer a more comprehensive view on the overall impact of globalization. Moreover, the chapter aims to explain changes in inequality over time across a broad range of countries, rather than explain average levels of inequality across a cross section of countries at a common point in time. The analysis also uses a new high-quality data set recently developed by the World Bank, applying a more consistent methodology than do most other studies that rely on multiple data sources of uneven quality. However, data issues remain a concern in any cross-country analysis of inequality, and the results of the estimations in all such analyses must be interpreted with some caution.

To anticipate the main conclusions, the available evidence does suggest that income inequality has risen across most countries and regions over the past two decades, although the data are subject to substantial limitations. Nevertheless, at the same time, average real incomes of the poorest segments of the population have increased across all regions and income groups. The analysis finds that increasing trade and financial globalization have had separately identifiable and opposite effects on income distribution. Trade liberalization and export growth are found to be associated with lower income inequality, whereas increased financial openness is associated with higher inequality. However, their combined contribution to rising inequality has been much lower than that of technological change, especially in developing countries. The spread of technology is, of course, itself related to increased globalization, but technological progress is nevertheless seen to have a separately identifiable effect on inequality.[5] The disequalizing impact of financial openness—mainly felt through foreign direct investment (FDI)—and technological progress appear to be working through similar channels by increasing the premium on higher skills, rather than limiting opportunities for economic advancement. Consistent with this, increased access to education is associated with more equal income distributions on average.

The next section reviews the evidence on both globalization and inequality over the past two decades, and how they have evolved across regions and income groups. The following section discusses the channels through which trade and financial globalization may be expected to influence inequality within countries and analyzes the empirical evidence to identify the main factors explaining changes in inequality. The concluding section offers some policy suggestions. Box 4.1 discusses in more detail the analytical and measurement issues arising from different methodologies used to collect and summarize inequality data across countries and regions. Box 4.2 looks in more detail at what might be learned from more in-depth analyses of individual country experiences and discusses how the conclusions of such studies do not easily lend themselves to generalization across countries.[6]

[4]See Goldberg and Pavcnik (2007) for a survey of theoretical and empirical research on the distributional effects of globalization in developing countries.

[5]Although much of the existing economic literature on globalization treats technological change as an exogenous variable, technological progress can also be viewed as potentially an additional channel through which globalization operates.

[6]See also Fishlow and Parker (1999) for a detailed analysis of the link between globalization and inequality in the United States.

Recent Trends in Inequality and Globalization

How Has Globalization Evolved?

World trade has grown five times in real terms since 1980, and its share of world GDP has risen from 36 percent to 55 percent over this period (Figure 4.1).[7] Trade integration accelerated in the 1990s, as former Eastern bloc countries integrated into the global trading system and as developing Asia—one of the most closed regions to trade in 1980—progressively dismantled barriers to trade. However, it is noteworthy that all groups of emerging market and developing countries, when aggregated by income group or by region, have been catching up with or surpassing high-income countries in their trade openness, reflecting the widespread convergence of low- and middle-income countries' trade systems toward the traditionally more open trading regimes in place in advanced economies.[8]

Financial globalization has also proceeded at a very rapid pace over the past two decades.[9] Total cross-border financial assets have more than doubled, from 58 percent of global GDP in 1990 to 131 percent in 2004. The advanced economies continue to be the most financially integrated, but other regions of the world have progressively increased their cross-border asset and liability positions (Figure 4.2). However, de jure measures of capital account openness present a mixed picture, with the newly industrialized Asian economies (NIEs) and developing economies showing little evidence of convergence to the more open capital account regimes in advanced economies,

Figure 4.1. Trade Globalization

(GDP-weighted average)

Trade globalization accelerated in the 1990s as countries of the former Eastern bloc integrated into the global trading system and developing Asia progressively dismantled barriers to trade.

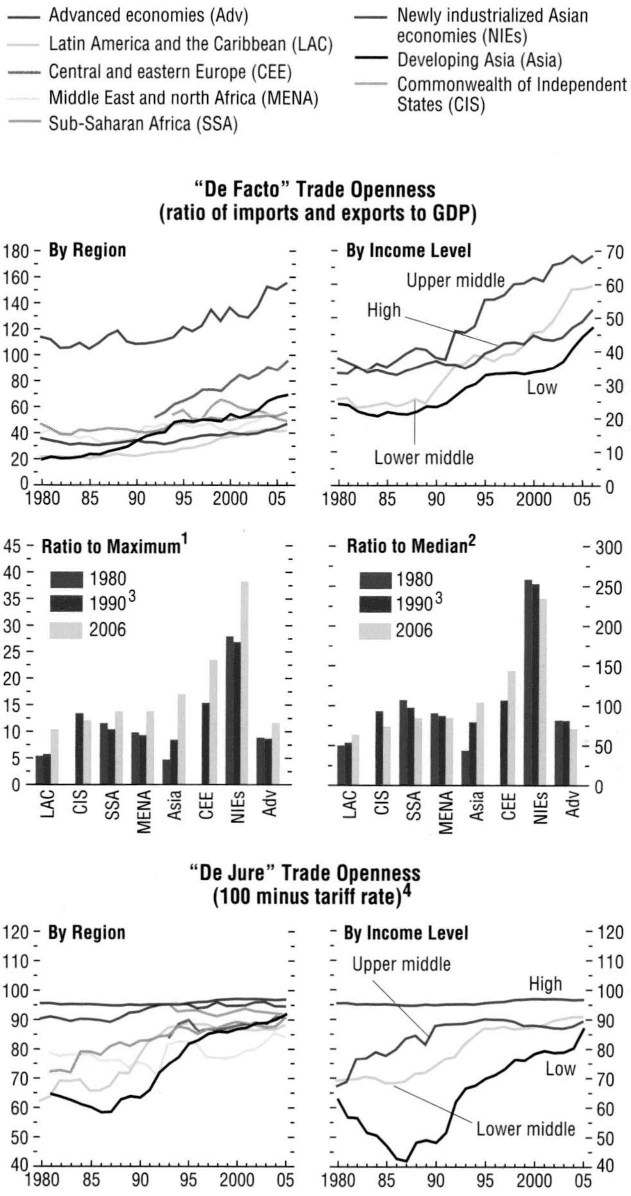

Source: IMF staff calculations.
[1]Maximum is the highest value in 2006 (Singapore).
[2]Median across countries for each year.
[3]Data series begin in 1994 for central and eastern Europe and the Commonwealth of Independent States.
[4]Tariff rate calculated as an average of the effective tariff rate (ratio of tariff revenue to import value) and of the average unweighted tariff rates.

[7]Oil exports and imports are excluded from the trade measures but not from overall GDP. The charts in the top panel of Figure 4.1 use GDP-weighted averages, but the trends over time are similar when using simple averages.

[8]Country compositions of the regional and income groups are documented in Appendix 4.1.

[9]For a comprehensive discussion of financial globalization and its implications, see IMF (2007).

Figure 4.2. Financial Globalization
(GDP-weighted average)

The advanced economies (including the NIEs) continue to have the largest amount of cross-border financial assets and liabilities, but other regions of the world have also progressively increased their cross-border asset and liability positions.

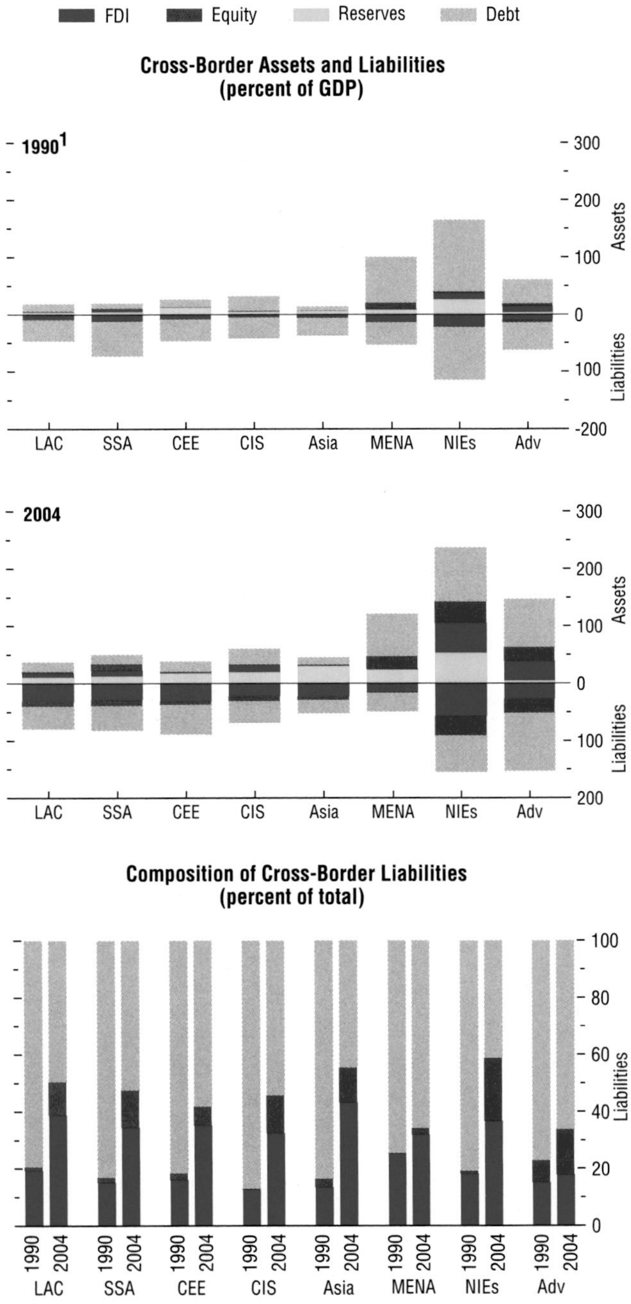

which have continued to liberalize further.[10] Of note, the share of FDI in total liabilities has risen across all emerging markets—from 17 percent of their total liabilities in 1990 to 38 percent in 2004—and far exceeds the share of portfolio equity liabilities, which rose from 2 percent to 11 percent of total liabilities over the same period. Reduced government borrowing needs have also contributed to changing liability structures, with the share of debt in total liabilities falling across all emerging market and developing country regions. Not surprisingly, the share of international reserves in cross-border assets has also risen, reflecting the accumulation of reserves among many emerging market and developing countries in recent years.

Has Income Distribution Within Countries Become Less Equal?

Cross-country comparisons of inequality are generally plagued by problems of poor reliability, lack of coverage, and inconsistent methodology.[11] Some of these issues are discussed in more detail in Box 4.1. This chapter relies on inequality data from the latest World Bank Povcal database constructed by Chen and Ravallion (2004, 2007) for a large number of developing countries. This database uses a more rigorous approach to filtering the individual income and consumption data for differences in quality than other commonly used databases, which rely on more mechanical approaches

[10]Both de facto and de jure measures have advantages and disadvantages, and are typically seen as complements rather than substitutes in empirical studies. See Kose and others (2006) for a discussion.

[11]Taking an alternative approach, Milanovic (2005b, 2006) and World Bank (2007) review patterns of global income inequality, that is, income inequality across the world's citizens, and their relation to globalization. Such studies typically conclude that global income inequality has declined with the increase in per capita incomes in developing countries that globalization has fostered. Policy implications within countries of such analysis are less clear. A related branch of research on cross-country income inequality focuses on the impact of globalization on growth.

to combine data from multiple sources.[12] The Povcal database has been supplemented with data from the Luxembourg Income Study (LIS) database, which provides high-quality coverage for advanced economies, and the resulting full sample allows for more accurate within- and cross-country comparisons than are available elsewhere. Given limitations of data availability, the analysis in this chapter uses inequality data based on both income and expenditure surveys. Mixing these two concepts makes a comparison of levels of inequality across countries and regions potentially misleading.[13] Given the difficulty in comparing inequality levels across countries, this section discusses them briefly and focuses instead on changes, whereas the empirical analysis relies solely on changes in inequality to avoid the biases inherent in level estimations.

Based on observed movements in Gini coefficients (the most widely used summary measure of inequality), inequality has risen in all but the low-income country aggregates over the past two decades, although there are significant regional and country differences (Figure 4.3).[14] While inequality has risen in developing Asia, emerging Europe, Latin America, the NIEs, and the advanced economies over the past two decades, it has declined in sub-Saharan Africa and the

[12]This database is available via the Internet at iresearch.worldbank.org/PovcalNet. Other databases include, for example, Deininger and Squire (1998) and the World Income Inequality Database (2005), which includes an update of the Deininger-Squire database; the Luxembourg Income Study; and a large number of data series from central statistical offices and research studies.

[13]See Deaton and Zaidi (2002) and Atkinson and Bourguignon (2000). Most advanced and Latin American economies construct inequality indices from income data, whereas most African and developing Asian countries use consumption data. World Bank (2006) illustrates how consumption-based Gini coefficients tend to show less inequality, in part because of government spending programs.

[14]The Gini coefficient is computed as the average difference between all pairs of incomes in a country, normalized by the mean (see Box 4.1). Other measures of inequality include decile and quintile ratios, the Atkinson index, and Theil's entropy measure.

Figure 4.2 *(concluded)*

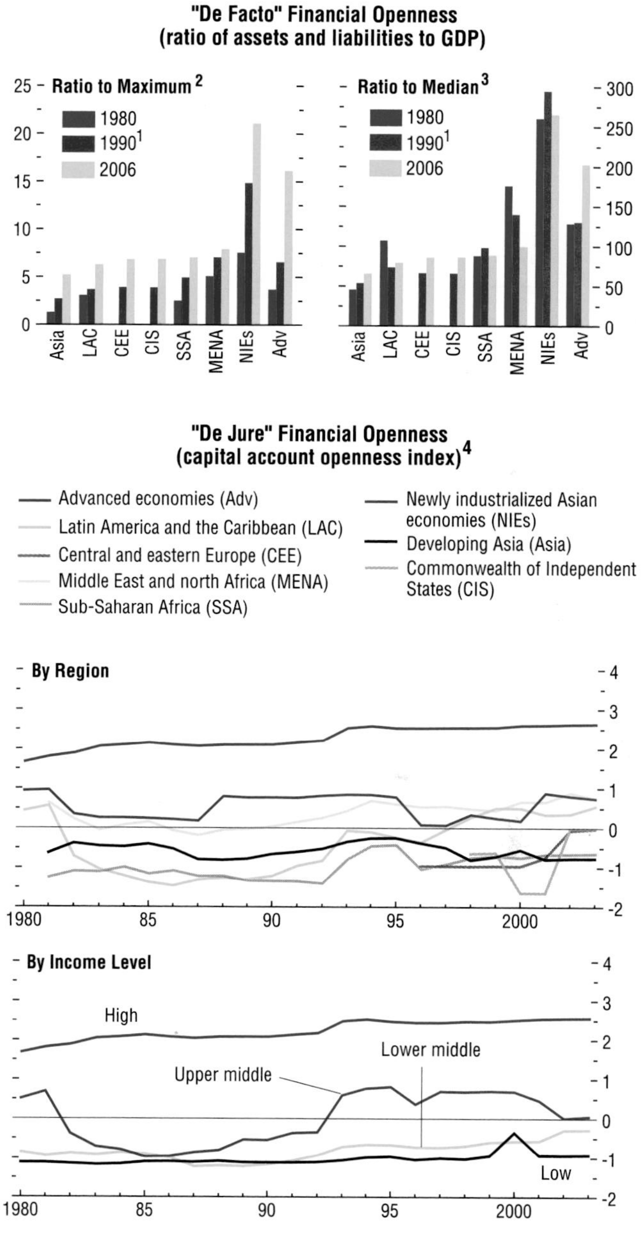

Sources: Chinn and Ito (2006); Lane and Milesi-Ferretti (2006); and IMF staff calculations.

[1]Data series begin in 1995 for central and eastern Europe and the Commonwealth of Independent States.

[2]Maximum is the highest value in 2004 (Ireland).

[3]Median across countries for each year.

[4]Index measuring a country's degree of capital account openness based on principal components extracted from disaggregated capital and current account restriction measures.

Figure 4.3. Cross-Country Trends in Inequality
(Gini coefficient)

Inequality has risen in developing Asia, central and eastern Europe, the NIEs, and the advanced economies, while falling in the Commonwealth of Independent States and, to a lesser extent, in sub-Saharan Africa.

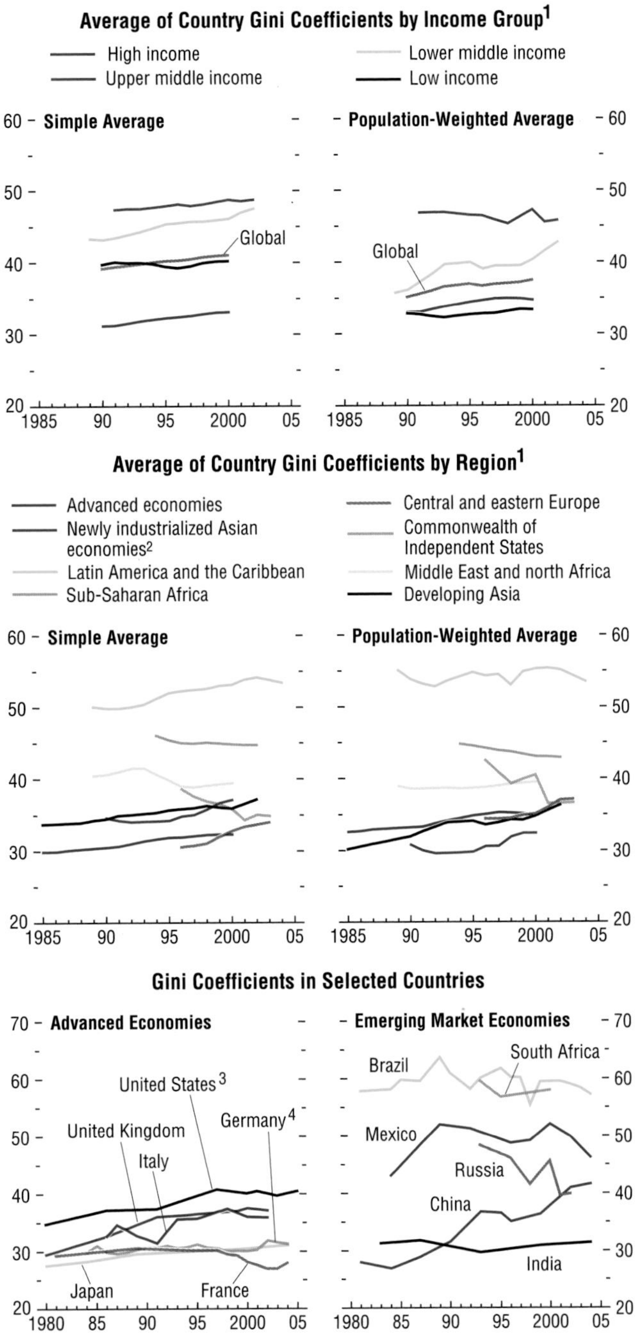

Sources: Choi (2006); Povcal database; WIDER database; and IMF staff calculations.
[1]Country coverage and years shown are limited to maintain constant country coverage. See Appendix 4.1.
[2]Excludes Hong Kong SAR due to data unavailability.
[3]Trends after 2000 are based on earnings data for full-time, year-round workers.
[4]Trends for pre-1992 are based on data for West Germany.

Commonwealth of Independent States (CIS).[15] This pattern remains broadly unchanged using population-weighted averages, except for emerging market countries in Latin America, as a result of the recent declines in inequality in Brazil and Mexico. Among the largest advanced economies, inequality appears to have declined only in France, whereas among the major emerging market countries, trends are more diverse, with sharply rising inequality in China, little change in India, and falling inequality in Brazil, Mexico, and Russia.[16] These overall measures of inequality do not, however, capture all country-specific characteristics of inequality within countries. As Box 4.2 illustrates, a different method of aggregation of rural and urban inequality in China leads to a substantially less sharp increase in overall inequality, whereas in India there is substantial variation in the experience of individual rural and urban districts despite the relatively small changes at the national level.

A more detailed picture of inequality is revealed by examining income shares for different country groups (Figure 4.4). Overall, changes in income shares by quintile (successive subsets with each containing 20 percent of the population) across regions and income levels mirror the evidence on inequality from Gini coefficients. However, the data show that rising Gini coefficients are explained largely by the increasing share of the richer quintiles

[15]Among the CIS countries, available evidence suggests that the sharp drop in inequality is partly a result of the reversal of the abrupt deterioration in income distribution during the initial stages of transition. See World Bank (2000), which suggests that inequality was substantially higher in the early 1990s in these countries.

[16]In a previous phase of (mainly trade) globalization, the East Asian economies grew rapidly during 1965–89, while income distribution either improved or did not worsen. In addition to active government policies and reforms such as land reforms, public housing, investments in health and rural infrastructure, and a manufacturing export-oriented growth strategy, investment in education is cited as an important factor explaining low average inequality (see Birdsall, Ross, and Sabot, 1995). However, data on inequality during this phase are highly tentative.

at the expense of middle quintiles, whereas the income share of the poorest quintile (1) changes little. Looking at average income levels across quintiles, per capita incomes have risen across virtually all regions for even the poorest quintiles (Figures 4.5 and 4.6). The exception is Latin America, where there was a small overall decline, driven mainly by the adverse impact of economic and financial crises on the poor in several countries. However, incomes have since recovered from post-crisis lows. In fact, consistent with the evidence from the Gini coefficients, the incomes of the poorest quintile have risen faster than those of other segments of the population in sub-Saharan Africa and the CIS countries, although from a very low base. Across all regions, the evidence therefore suggests that in an absolute sense the poor are no worse off (except in a few post-crisis economies), and in most cases significantly better off, during the most recent phase of globalization.

In summary, two broad facts emerge from the evidence. First, over the past two decades, income growth has been positive for all quintiles in virtually all regions and all income groups during the recent period of globalization. At the same time, however, income inequality has increased mainly in middle- and high-income countries, and less so in low-income countries. This recent experience seems to be a clear change in course from the general decline in inequality in the first half of the twentieth century, and the perception that East Asia's rapid growth during the 1960s and 1970s was achieved while maintaining inequality at relatively low levels. It must be emphasized, however, that comparison of inequality data across decades is fraught with difficulty, in view of numerous caveats about data accuracy and methodological comparability.

What Is the Impact of Globalization on Inequality?

Against this background, it is natural to ask how much of the rise in inequality seen in middle- and high-income countries in recent

Figure 4.4. Income Shares by Quintile

(Share of total income, population-weighted average)

Increasing inequality is largely explained by the increasing income share of the richest quintile at the expense of the middle quintiles, while there has been little change in the poorest quintile.

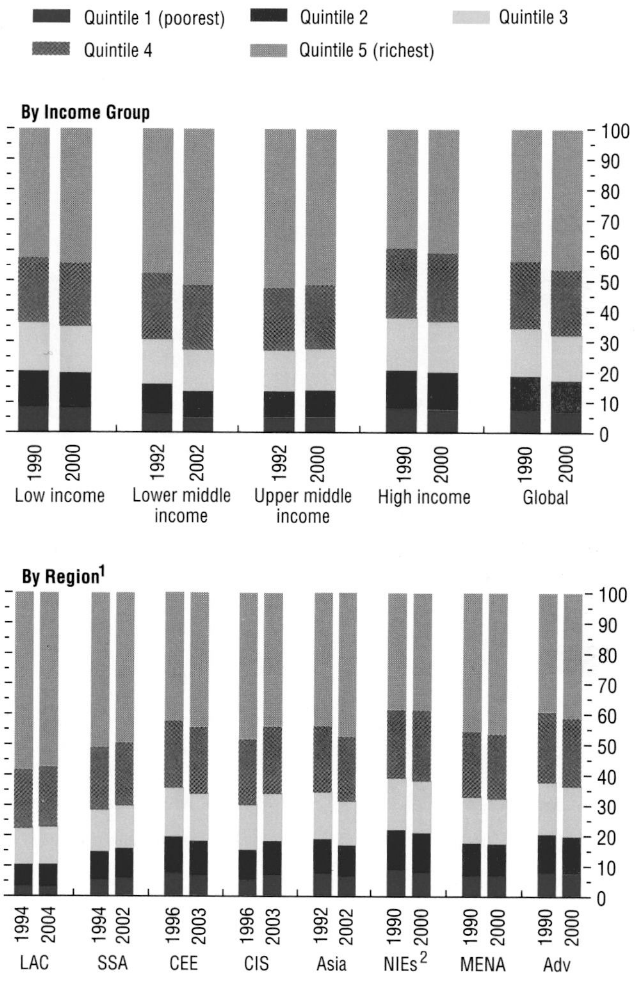

Sources: Choi (2006); Japanese Statistics Bureau; Povcal database; WIDER database; and IMF staff calculations.

[1] Data cover advanced economies (Adv), newly industrialized Asian economies (NIEs), developing Asia (Asia), Latin America and the Caribbean (LAC), sub-Saharan Africa (SSA), Middle East and north Africa (MENA), central and eastern Europe (CEE), and the Commonwealth of Independent States (CIS).

[2] Includes only Korea and Taiwan Province of China.

Figure 4.5. Per Capita Income by Quintile[1]
(2000 international dollars, population-weighted average)

Incomes have risen for all quintiles across all regions except for the poorest quintile in Latin America, related in part to the aftereffects of crises.

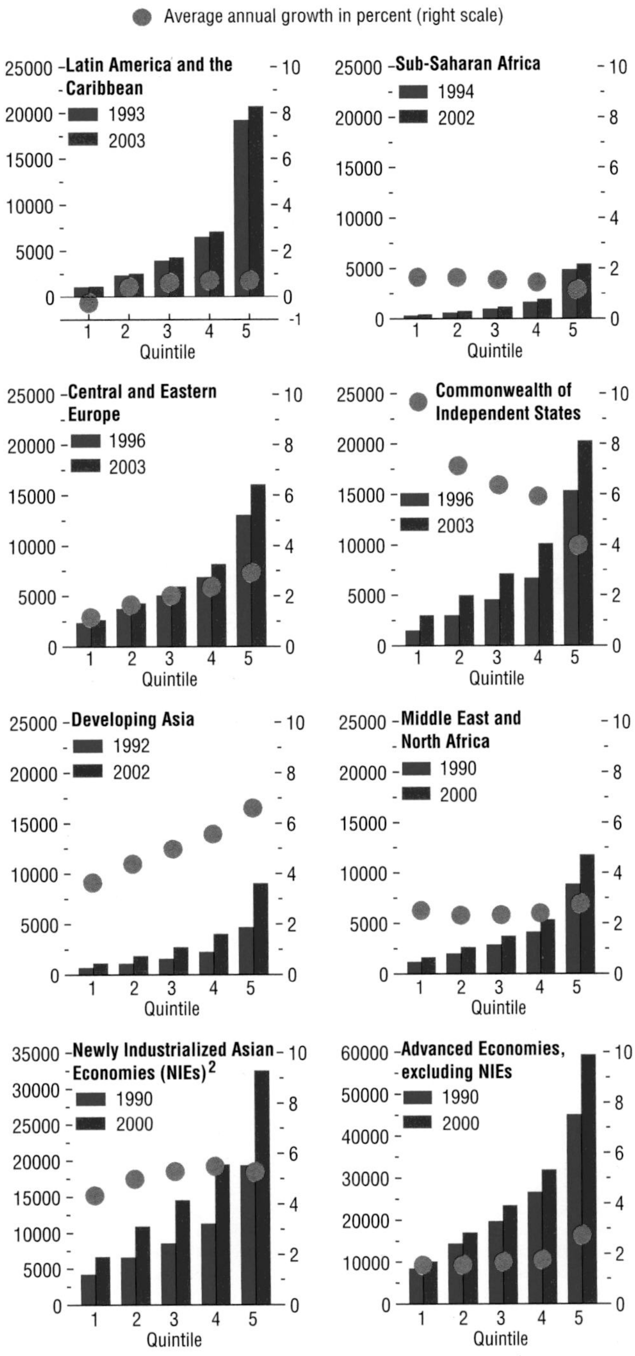

Sources: Choi (2006); Heston, Summers, and Aten (2006); Japanese Statistics Bureau; Povcal database; WIDER database; and IMF staff calculations.
[1]Income or consumption share data are applied to real GDP per capita levels from Penn World Tables to calculate per capita income by quintile. See Appendix 4.1.
[2]Includes only Korea and Taiwan Province of China.

decades can be attributed to increased globalization, and how much to other factors, such as the spread of technology and domestic constraints on equality of opportunity. This section first discusses the channels through which the globalization of trade and finance could affect the distribution of incomes within a country, setting the stage for the empirical analysis that follows.

Channels Through Which Globalization Affects Inequality

The principal analytical link between trade liberalization and income inequality provided by economic theory is derived from the Stolper-Samuelson theorem: it implies that in a two-country two-factor framework, increased trade openness (through tariff reduction) in a developing country where low-skilled labor is abundant would result in an increase in the wages of low-skilled workers and a reduction in the compensation of high-skilled workers, leading to a reduction in income inequality (see Stolper and Samuelson, 1941). After tariffs on imports are reduced, the price of the (importable) high-skill-intensive product declines and so does the compensation of the scarce high-skilled workers, whereas the price of the (exportable) low-skill-intensive good for which the country has relatively abundant factors increases and so does the compensation of low-skilled workers. For an advanced economy in which high-skill factors are relatively abundant, the reverse would hold, with an increase in openness leading to higher inequality.

An important extension of the basic model that weakens the dichotomy between advanced and developing economies in terms of distributional effects is the inclusion of "noncompeting" traded goods, that is, goods that are not produced in a country and are imported only as a result, for example, of very large differences in endowments across countries. Tariff reductions would reduce the prices of these goods—and therefore increase the effective real income of households—without affecting wages and prices

Figure 4.6. Per Capita Income by Quintile in Selected Countries[1]
(2000 international dollars)

Despite overall increases in inequality in middle- and high-income countries, there is substantial variation in the experience of individual countries.

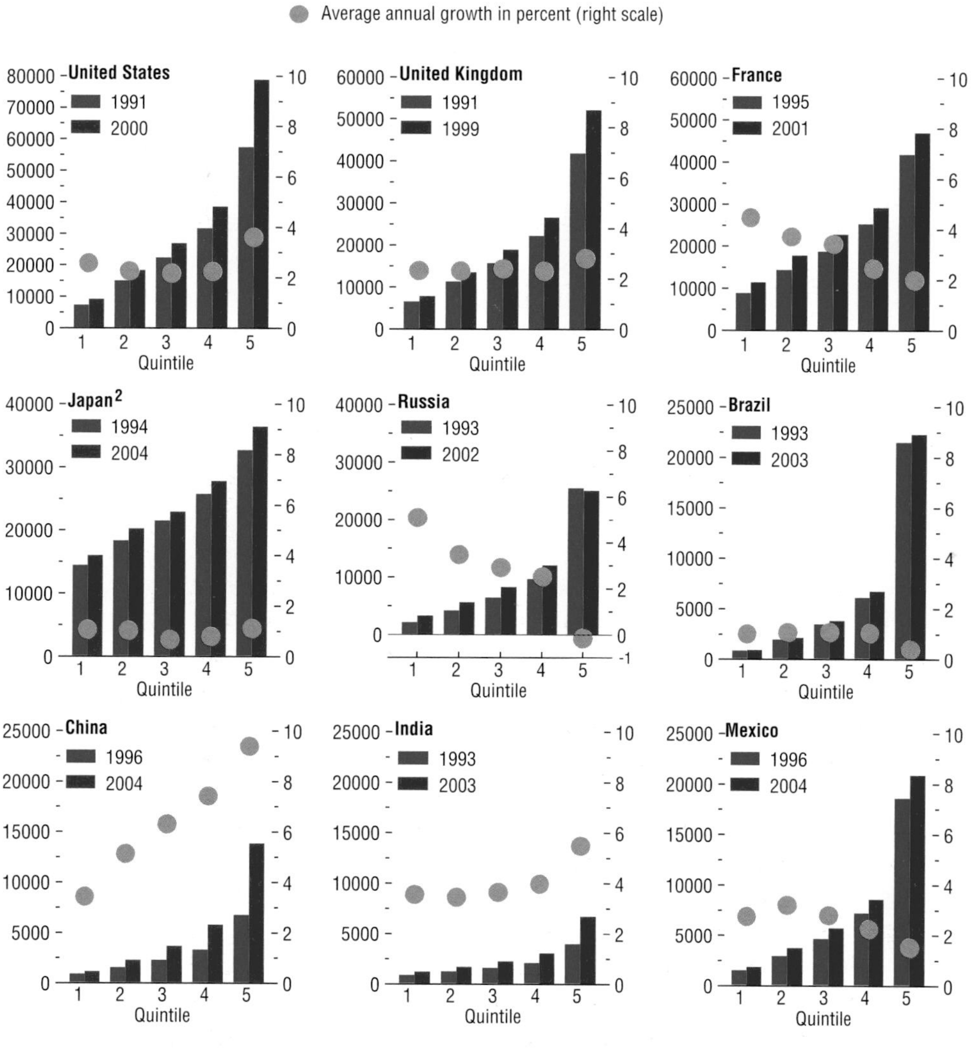

Sources: Heston, Summers, and Aten (2006); Japanese Statistics Bureau; Povcal database; WIDER database; and IMF staff calculations.
[1] Calculations are based on income share data except for India, Japan, Mexico, and Russia, where consumption share data are used. The income or consumption share data are applied to real GDP per capita levels from Penn World Tables to calculate per capita income by quintile. See Appendix 4.1.
[2] Based on household income share data.

Box 4.1. Measuring Inequality: Conceptual, Methodological, and Measurement Issues

Researchers on inequality employ several different measures, guided by the availability of underlying data and the focus of the research.[1] Of these, the Gini index is a commonly used summary measure of the income distribution of a country.[2] The Gini index captures the range between a perfectly egalitarian distribution in which all income is shared equally (a Gini coefficient of 0) and one where a single person has all the income (a coefficient of 1). Gini coefficients typically range from 0.20 to 0.65.

Despite the Gini index's widespread use, numerous conceptual, methodological, and definitional issues make it difficult to compare Gini indices across countries and over time.[3] One major source of variation is that some Gini indices are based on surveys of household consumption expenditure, whereas others are based on income surveys—a difference that can change a country's observed Gini index on the order of 0.15 point. In general, consumption-based Gini indices tend to show lower inequality and are more commonly used in developing countries in which higher rates of self-employment in business or agriculture (where income fluctuates throughout the year) make measurement of incomes difficult.[4] Consumption-based Gini indices are more common in Asia, sub-Saharan Africa, and, more recently, in central and emerging Europe and the Commonwealth of Independent States, whereas income Ginis are commonly used in advanced economies and Latin America.[5] Differences in definitions and survey methodologies further complicate the use of both consumption- and income-based Gini indices. Comparability of Gini indices based on consumption survey data can be limited as a result of differences in definitions of consumption; variation in the number of consumption items that are separately distinguished in surveys; whether survey participants record their consumption or are asked to recall their consumption in an interview; changes in the length of the recall period during which survey participants are asked to report their consumption; different methods used to impute housing, durables, and home production consumption; inconsistencies in the treatment of seasonality and the timing of surveys; underreporting or misleading reports of consumption of some items; and variation in respondents within a household. Income inequality data can also vary depending on whether the income is pre- or post-tax; whether and how in-kind income, imputed rents, and home production are included; and whether all income—including remittances, other transfers, and property income—or only wage earnings are captured.[6]

More general concerns with both types of Gini indices are that some surveys are not nationally representative and exclude rural populations, the military, students, or populations living in areas that are expensive or dangerous to survey. In addition, survey nonresponse and underreporting of income—which occurs more often in the high-income groups in a country—can skew income distributions, thereby underreporting inequality. Also, whether and how

Note: The main author of this box is Patrick Hettinger.

[1]Measures of inequality include, in addition to the Gini index, ratios of the average income of the richest to poorest segments of the population, the Atkinson index, the Theil entropy measure, and the mean logarithmic deviation of income.

[2]The Gini index is defined as $\frac{1}{2n^2\mu}\sum_{i=1}^{n}\sum_{j=1}^{n}|y_i - y_j|$, where μ is the mean income, y_i and y_j are the individually observed incomes, and n is the number of observed incomes.

[3]A general discussion of the difficulties in using the Gini index and data based on household surveys can be found in Deaton (2003); Ravallion (2003); and World Bank (2006).

[4]Among other causes, lower measures of consumption-based inequality can result from consumption smoothing across time and greater measurement error for incomes. See, for example, Ravallion and Chen (1996); and Meyer and Sullivan (2006).

[5]See, for example, Chen and Ravallion (2004).

[6]For most advanced economies in this study, post-tax income is used, although the components of income vary across countries. See Luxembourg Income Study data as provided in the World Income Inequality Database.

a survey adjusts for price-level differences between urban and rural areas can significantly alter distribution data.

Finally, there are differences between indicators of household and individual inequality. Household inequality measures, which were much more common before 1980, may show changing inequality over time merely as a result of changes in household size and composition. Adjusting inequality indicators to a per capita unit of analysis helps avoid this bias, and various methods have been adopted for making this adjustment.[7]

Although survey guidelines exist, they are not consistently applied over time and across countries, so that different surveys and even different survey rounds can produce different results.[8]

[7]For several examples of how measures are adjusted, see World Income Inequality Database (2005).

[8]See Canberra Group (2001); and Deaton and Zaidi (2002).

When comparing Gini indices, meticulous attention to concepts, definitions, and the details of survey methodology is required to improve comparability, and the World Bank's Povcal database goes further than other databases in doing this.[9] The database was created using primary data from nationally representative surveys with sufficiently comprehensive definitions of income or consumption. Attempts were made to ensure survey comparability over time within countries, although cross-country and within-country comparisons are still impaired because in many cases it was not possible to correct for differences in survey methods. Finally, measures are calculated consistently and on a per capita basis. For the econometric analysis in this study, using changes over time in Gini indices from this database rather than levels can address some of the major concerns regarding comparability of indices across countries.

[9]See Chen and Ravallion (2004).

of other traded goods.[17] If this noncompeting good is a large share of the consumption basket of poorer segments of society, a reduction in the tariff on the noncompeting good would reduce inequality in that country. More generally, in both advanced and developing economies, if tariffs are reduced for noncompeting goods that are not produced in a country but are consumed particularly by the poor, it would lead to lower inequality in both advanced and developing economies.

The implications of the Stolper-Samuelson theorem, in particular the ameliorating effects of trade liberalization on income inequality in developing countries, have generally not been verified in economy-wide studies.[18] A particular challenge has been to explain the increase in skill premium between skilled and unskilled workers observed in most developing countries. This has led to various alternative analytical approaches, including the introduction of (1) multiple countries where poor countries may also import low-skill-intensive goods from other poor countries and rich countries may similarly import high-skill-intensive goods from other rich countries; (2) a continuum of goods, implying that what is low-skill intensive in the advanced economy will be relatively high-skill intensive in a less-developed country (see Feenstra and Hanson, 1996); and (3) intermediate imported goods used for the skill-intensive product. However, these extensions have themselves presented additional challenges for empirical testing, and

[17]See, for example, Davis and Mishra (2007) for an overview of analytical and empirical approaches to the relationship between trade, inequality, and poverty.

[18]See Milanovic (2005a) for a survey of recent papers linking trade globalization to inequality, which notes that most papers find either no statistically significant relationship or a negative relationship between globalization and inequality.

Box 4.2. What Do Country Studies of the Impact of Globalization on Inequality Tell Us? Examples from Mexico, China, and India

A complementary approach to the cross-country analysis of the impact of globalization on inequality used in this chapter is to look in detail at particular country experiences (see Goldberg and Pavcnik, 2007). The advantage of country studies is that they focus on more detailed measures of inequality (that is, wage inequality) and at a finer level of disaggregation geographically or by sector. In addition, they also use more detailed data for other variables, such as tariffs and social policies. Given that globalization may affect inequality through different channels and at different speeds in different countries, country studies can provide important insights that cannot be gained in cross-country work and in which policies and outcomes can be more closely related.[1] The following overview of recent studies on Mexico, China, and India illustrates the usefulness as well as the limitations of country studies.[2]

Mexico

Mexico undertook far-reaching reforms between 1985 and 1994 that opened its economy to trade and capital flows. Over the same period, the earnings gap between high- and low-skilled workers began to widen, generating a substantial body of literature that examined whether this increasing gap was caused by the process of opening up.[3] In broad terms, researchers have found that the patterns of trade liberalization may have contributed to increasing the earnings gap. Hanson and Harrison (1999) find that trade protection was initially higher in less-skill-intensive sectors, and was reduced by more in these sectors during reform. If these tariff changes were passed through to changes in prices of goods, then the logic of the Stolper-Samuelson theorem would imply that the relative wage of skilled labor would have risen. Robertson (2004) finds evidence in support of this conclusion, with the relative price of skill-intensive goods in Mexico rising during 1987–94 and raising the relative wages of white-collar labor.

Other studies with a slightly different focus find that although globalization may have contributed to widening earnings inequality in Mexico, low-skilled workers have benefited in absolute terms as a result of the policy changes. Nicita (2004) shows that during the 1990s, tariff changes raised disposable income for all households, with richer households enjoying a 6 percent increase and poorer households enjoying a 2 percent increase, leading to a 3 percent reduction in the number of households in poverty. In a related work, Hanson (2007) finds that during the 1990s, individuals in regions more exposed to globalization enjoyed a 10 percent gain in labor income relative to individuals in regions less exposed to globalization, resulting in a reduction in poverty rates in high-exposure regions of 7 percent relative to low-exposure regions.

China

The dramatic increase in trade liberalization in China has been accompanied by a large fall in poverty rates, but also an increase in income inequality, with the overall Gini coefficient rising sharply from 0.28 in 1981 to 0.42 in 2004. The observed increase in overall inequality

Note: The main author of this box is Chris Papageorgiou, with contributions by Gordon Hanson and Petia Topalova.

[1]A limitation of most of these country studies is that they do not control explicitly for technological progress and, in some cases, for financial globalization, both of which were found in this chapter to play a key role. Another limitation is the use of a difference-in-difference methodology that does not capture the countrywide effect of globalization on inequality. While liberalization may have an overall effect of increasing or lowering inequality, this methodology tests whether this overall effect was unequal, and whether certain industries or regions benefited more from globalization than others.

[2]Studies that focus on the experiences of Colombia, Argentina, Brazil, Chile, and Hong Kong SAR are summarized in Goldberg and Pavcnik (2007).

[3]In 1988, urban workers at the 90th percentile had labor earnings that were 3.6 times those of workers at the 10th percentile. By 2004, the ratio had grown to 4.7 times, with large fluctuations in relative earnings around the Mexican peso crisis in 1994–95.

is mostly attributed to growing differences between rural and urban household incomes and uneven growth in incomes among urban households (see top panel of the figure, from Lin, Zhuang, and Yarcia, forthcoming). Focusing on inequality between 1988 and 1995, Wei and Wu (2007) also find that the aggregate inequality numbers may obscure a more subtle pattern of underlying changes. These authors examine the effect of trade globalization on Chinese income inequality using new methods and two unique data sets on 39 urban and 40 rural Chinese regions. The first data set allows examination of urban-rural income inequality and the second allows the examination of within-urban and within-rural inequality.[4] The authors employ a decomposition of the Theil index that combines the urban-rural, intra-urban, and intra-rural inequalities into an overall measure of income inequality, arguing that their Theil decomposition approach more accurately captures the unequal effects of the different components of overall inequality.[5]

China: Openness and Inequality in Urban and Rural Areas

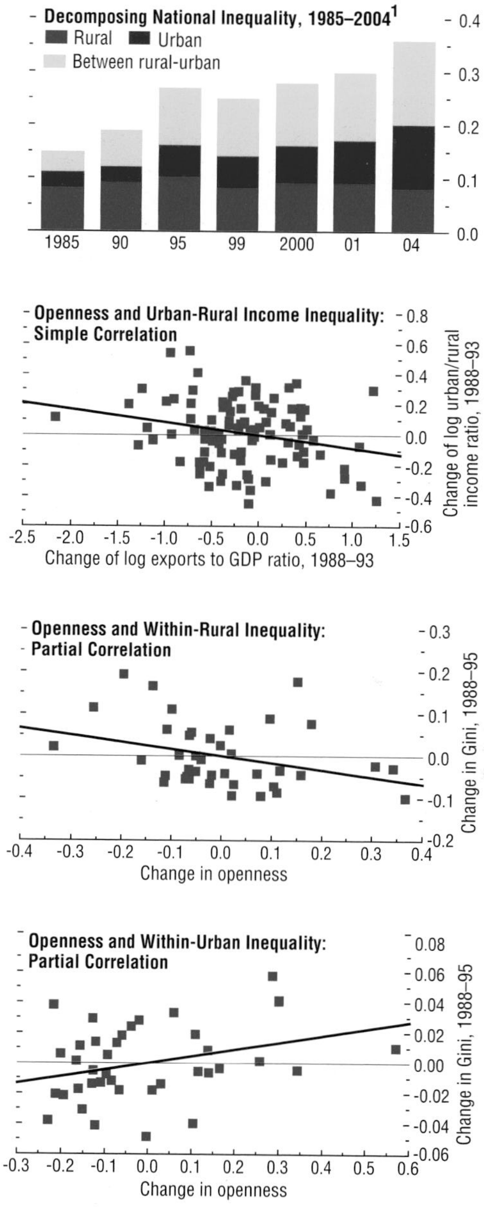

Sources: Lin, Zhuang, and Yarcia (forthcoming); and Wei and Wu (2007).

[1]Inequality is measured in terms of the Theil index and ranges from 0 to 1.

[4]The first data set comes from the *Urban Statistical Yearbook of China* and *Fifty Years of the Cities in New China: 1949–98*, both published by China's State Statistics Bureau. The second data set consists of two surveys of households conducted in 1988 and 1995 by international economists and the Economics Institute of the Chinese Academy of Social Sciences. The study relies on data from urban areas and rural counties administered by cities—an administrative arrangement specific to China—but not rural counties administered directly by prefectures.

[5]The Theil index is an alternative to the Gini coefficient. One of the advantages of the Theil index is that because it is the weighted sum of inequality within subgroups, it is easier to decompose. The particular decomposition of the Theil index used in Wei and Wu (2007, pp. 25–26) was proposed by Shorrocks (1980) and Mookherjee and Shorrocks (1982). More specifically, overall inequality is given by $I = V_r\lambda_r I_r + V_u\lambda_u I_u + V_r\lambda_r\log\lambda_r + V_u\lambda_u\log\lambda_u$, where V_r and V_u are the proportions of population living in rural and urban areas, respectively; λ_r and λ_u are the ratios of rural and urban average incomes to the overall national average income, respectively; and I_r and I_u are within-rural and within-urban Theil indices, respectively. The World Bank (1997) estimates that 75 percent of the change in the overall inequality is explained by urban-rural inequality during the period 1984–95.

Box 4.2 *(concluded)*

Illustrating the importance of the method of aggregation, the bottom three panels in the figure present correlations between trade openness and urban-rural inequality, within-rural inequality, and within-urban inequality. The authors' formal econometric analysis, consistent with the correlations in the figure, reveals that trade liberalization reduces urban-rural income inequality, leads to a relatively small increase in intra-urban inequality, and decreases intra-rural inequality. More important, summing up the three components of inequality, the authors estimate that increased openness modestly reduces overall inequality.[6]

This finding contrasts with the more widespread perception that trade liberalization has contributed to the rise in income inequality in China. A key lesson from this exercise is that the appropriate decomposition and measurement of income inequality across different regions can modify the observed effect of openness on income inequality in China.

The Chinese experience does not necessarily imply that the effect of trade liberalization on income inequality suggested by this methodology would be the same in other countries, given the diverse mechanisms through which globalization operates. Moreover, data limitations in many countries typically do not allow for the application of such a methodology.

India

India intensified reforms aimed at opening up its economy in the early 1990s, through reduction in tariffs and nontariff barriers, lowered barriers to foreign direct investment, and liberalization of restrictive domestic regulations. Kumar and Mishra (forthcoming) evaluate empirically the impact of the 1991 trade liberalization in India on industry wages.[7] The paper uses variations in industry wage premiums and trade policy across industries and over time. Industry wage premiums are defined as the portion of individual wages that accrues to the worker's industry affiliation after controlling for worker characteristics. Since different industries employ different proportions of skilled workers, changes in wage premiums translate into changes in the relative incomes of skilled and unskilled workers (see Pavcnik and others, 2004; and Goldberg and Pavcnik, 2005). The results suggest that reductions in tariffs were associated with increased wages within an industry, likely reflecting productivity increases. In addition, the study finds evidence that trade liberalization has led to decreased wage inequality between skilled and unskilled workers. This is consistent with the larger tariff reductions in sectors with a higher proportion of unskilled workers.

Other studies focus on the effect of tariff changes on income inequality at the district level. Topalova (2007) relates post-liberalization variations in industrial composition across districts to the degree of opening to foreign trade and FDI across industries.[8] Additional research applies a difference-in-difference methodology to investigate how consumption across the entire income distribution varied with the district's exposure to a decline in protection and the liberalization of FDI. Results from this work suggest that trade liberalization led to an increase in inequality, especially in urban districts, where the incomes of the richest and those with higher education rose substantially faster relative to households at the bottom of the income distribution. Although the estimates for the rural sample are not statistically significant, across all measures of inequality the point estimates imply that a decline in tariffs is associated with an increase in inequality. Moreover, there does not seem to be any relationship

[6]In related work using household survey data for 29 Chinese provinces for 1988–2001, Zhang and Wan (2006) find that trade liberalization increases the income share of the poor living in urban households.

[7]The data set combines microlevel data from the National Sample Survey Organisation with data on international trade protection for the years 1980–2000.

[8]This study uses consumption-based data from 360 districts (those in the 15–16 largest states in India) and for two time periods, 1987 and 1999. For a detailed explanation of the data and estimation method used, see Topalova (2007).

between FDI and inequality within a district in either the rural or the urban samples.

Conclusion

This box demonstrates how country studies can take advantage of more disaggregated and more detailed data to study the effects of globalization on inequality. However, no study can capture all aspects of this relationship, and each study focuses instead on some parameters of particular interest. In the case of Mexico, wage, rather than income, inequality was used to capture distributional disparities across regions. In the China example, decomposition between urban and rural inequality was shown to be fundamental in the estimation of the globalization-inequality relationship. In the India study, detailed import-tariff data across industries and districts were used as the measure of trade openness. The results from these case studies reveal a more intricate picture of the globalization-inequality interrelationship that cannot be captured in cross-country studies. The evidence broadly suggests that the mechanisms through which globalization affects inequality are country- and time-specific, reflecting the great heterogeneity of countries and the nature and timing of their trade reforms.

none has been consistently established.[19] This has led to explanations for rising skill premiums based on the notion that technological change is inherently skill biased, attributing the observed increases in inequality (including in advanced economies) to exogenous technology shocks. Any empirical estimation of the overall effects of globalization therefore needs to account explicitly for changes in technology in countries, in addition to standard trade-related variables.

An additional important qualification to the implications deriving from the Stolper-Samuelson theorem relates to its assumption that labor and capital are mobile within a country but not internationally. If capital can travel across borders, the implications of the theorem weaken substantially. This channel would appear to be most evident for FDI, which is often directed at high-skill sectors in the host economy.[20] Moreover, what appears to be relatively high-skill-intensive inward FDI for a less-developed country may appear to be relatively low-skill-intensive outward FDI for the advanced economy. An increase in FDI from advanced economies to developing economies could thus increase the relative demand for skilled labor in both countries, increasing inequality in both the advanced and the developing economy. The empirical evidence on these channels has provided mixed support for this view, with the impact of FDI seen as either negative, at least in the short run, or inconclusive.[21]

In addition to foreign direct investment, there are other important channels through which capital flows across borders, including cross-border bank lending, portfolio debt, and equity flows. Within this broader context, some have argued that greater capital account liberalization may increase access to financial resources for the poor, whereas others have suggested that by increasing the likelihood of financial crises, greater financial openness may disproportionately hurt the poor. [22] Some recent research has

[19]The level of aggregation of tariff data does not, for example, allow for clear identification of noncompeting imports in general and noncompeting intermediate goods in particular. Furthermore, in a multicountry setting with more than one low-skill-abundant country, it is unclear which goods are exportable and which are importable.

[20]See Cragg and Epelbaum (1996); and Behrman, Birdsall, and Székely (2003).

[21]See Behrman, Birdsall, and Székely (2003), who find negative effects in the short term in Latin America, and Milanovic (2005a), who suggests that the evidence from a wide sample of countries is inconclusive.

[22]See Agénor (2002) for a discussion of the channels through which financial integration may hurt the poor, and Fallon and Lucas (2002), who find that the evidence on the distributional effects of crises is not uniform.

Figure 4.7. Inequality Versus Globalization: Selected Countries[1]
(Change in indicators over last available 10 years; years indicated)

Changes in inequality do not have an obvious association with changes in trade or financial openness.

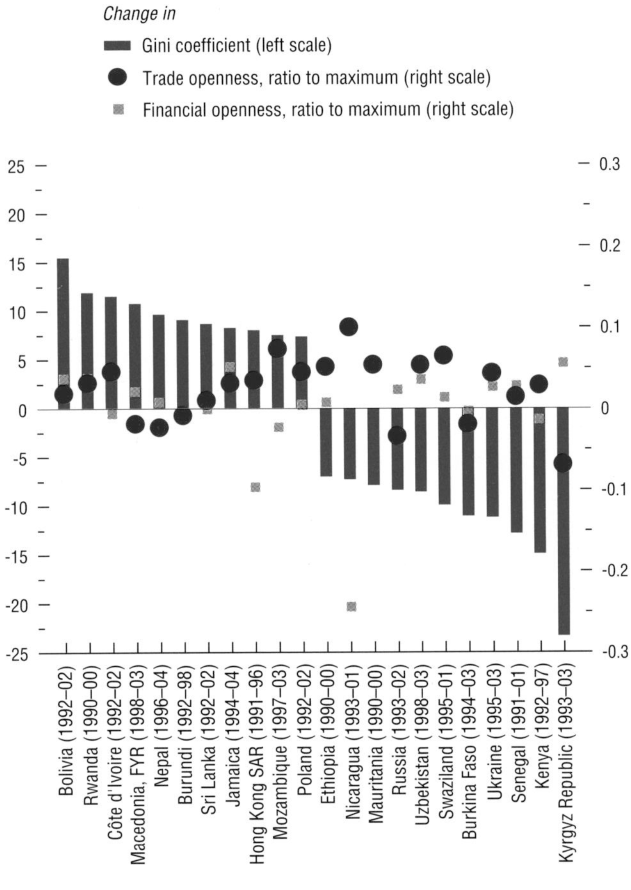

Sources: Lane and Milesi-Ferretti (2006); Povcal database; WIDER database; and IMF staff calculations.
[1]Sample includes the 11 countries with the greatest increase in Gini coefficient over the period, and the 11 countries with the greatest decrease.

found that the strength of institutions plays a crucial role: in the context of strong institutions, financial globalization may allow better consumption smoothing and lower volatility for the poor, but where institutions are weak, financial access is biased in favor of those with higher incomes and assets and the increase in finance from tapping global and not just domestic savings may further exacerbate inequality.[23] Thus, the composition of financial flows may matter, and the net impact may also be influenced by other factors, such as the quality of financial sector institutions.

In summary, analytical considerations suggest that any empirical analysis of the distributional consequences of globalization must take into account both trade and the various channels through which financial globalization operates, and also account for the separate impact of technological change. Moreover, against the background of real-world patterns of trade and financial flows, theory does not provide clear guidance on whether globalization affects inequality in advanced and developing economies differently.

An Empirical Investigation of Globalization and Inequality

Despite common perceptions, casual observation does not suggest an obvious association between changes in inequality across countries and changes in the degree to which countries have globalized over the same period (Figure 4.7). But this is perhaps not surprising, given the multiple channels through which such a relationship would operate and the variety of other factors that are also relevant. This chapter thus looks closely at cross-country data, relating changes in inequality to a broad set of variables that may affect income distribution,

[23]See Prasad and others (2007) for a discussion of lower volatility from financial globalization. While Demirgüç-Kunt and Levine (2007) argue that financial development is more positive for the poorest segment of the population, primarily through its positive effect on overall growth, Claessens and Perotti (forthcoming) find that the outcome can be different as most of the benefits of financial reforms are captured by a small elite.

including both variables that capture different aspects of globalization and other factors that can be important in determining how inequality changes in countries over time.

- One key factor is the role of technology. To the extent that technological change favors those with higher skills and exacerbates the "skills gap," it could adversely affect the distribution of income in both developing and advanced economies by reducing the demand for lower-skill activities and increasing the premium for higher-skill activities and returns on capital (see, for example, Birdsall, 2005; and the April 2007 issue of the *World Economic Outlook*). Technological development is measured in this study by the share of information and communications technology (ICT) capital in the total capital stock, which has risen rapidly over the past 20 years across all regions (Figure 4.8).
- A second important variable is access to education. For a given level of technology, greater access to education would be expected to reduce income inequality by allowing a greater share of the population to be engaged in high-skill activities. Educational opportunities have tended to increase across all regions, but with considerable cross-country variation.
- A third factor affecting income distribution is the sectoral share of employment. In developing countries, a move away from the agricultural sector to industry could be expected to improve the distribution of income by increasing the income of low-earning groups.[24] In this context, greater flexibility in labor markets that facilitates a move away from low-return occupations to those where opportunities are better can also be expected to improve the distribution of income (see Topalova, 2007).
- Another important variable that affects inequality is financial development, measured as the ratio of private credit to GDP. As discussed in the previous section, even though

[24]Similarly, increases in the relative productivity of agriculture might be expected to reduce income disparities by increasing the income of those employed in this sector.

Figure 4.8. Information and Communications Technology (ICT) Capital, Private Credit, Education, and Sectoral Employment Shares

Globalization is only one of the factors that have affected inequality. Rapid technological change, financial deepening, improvements in education, and the shift of employment away from agriculture are other significant developments with potentially important implications for inequality.

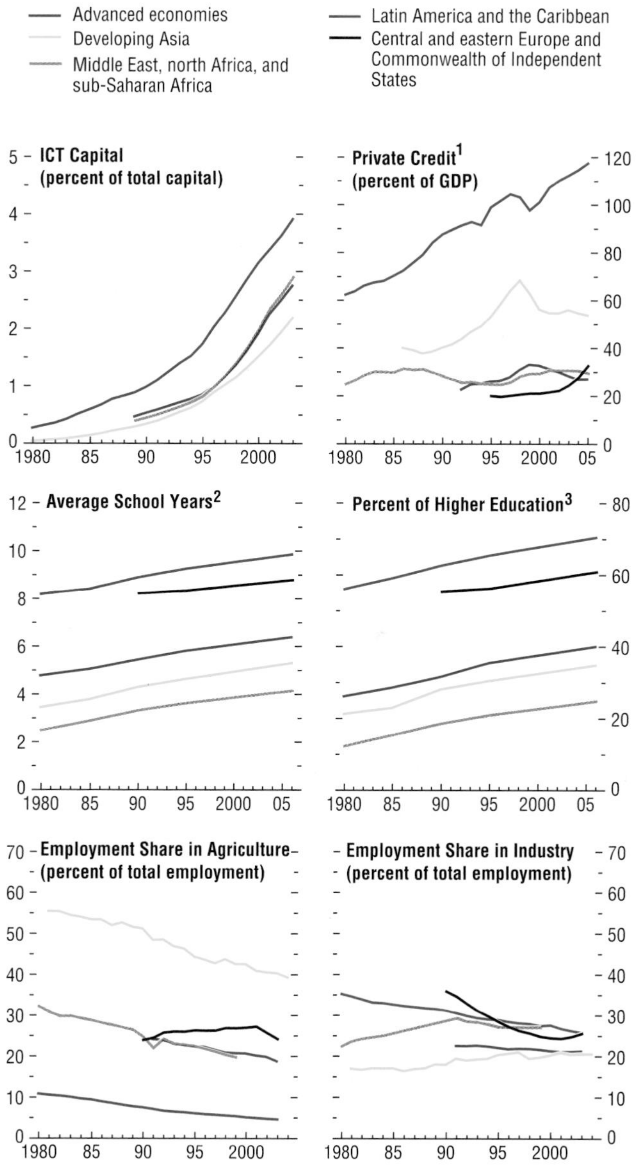

Sources: Barro and Lee (2000); Beck, Demirgüç-Kunt, and Levine (2000); Jorgenson and Vu (2005); and IMF staff calculations.
[1]Credit to the private sector by deposit money banks and other financial institutions.
[2]Average schooling years in total population 15 years and older.
[3]Percent of secondary school and higher education attained in total population 15 years and older.

Table 4.1. Determinants of the Gini Coefficient, Full Sample

(Dependent variable: natural logarithm of Gini)

	Summary Model (a)	Benchmark Model (b)	Sectoral Exports (c)	Sectoral Productivity (d)	Excluding Sectoral Employment Shares (e)
Trade globalization					
Ratio of exports and imports to GDP	–0.047				
	(1.50)				
Exports-to-GDP ratio		–0.057		–0.048	–0.056
		(2.56)**		(2.15)**	(2.41)**
Agricultural exports			–0.03		
			(2.49)**		
Manufacturing exports			–0.002		
			(0.10)		
Service exports			–0.006		
			(0.38)		
100 minus tariff rate	–0.002	–0.002	–0.003	–0.002	–0.003
	(2.27)**	(2.52)**	(2.71)***	(2.61)***	(2.50)**
Financial globalization					
Ratio of cross-border assets and liabilities to GDP	0.022				
	(1.24)				
Ratio of inward FDI stock to GDP		0.04	0.038	0.035	0.039
		(3.01)***	(3.06)***	(2.57)**	(2.96)***
Capital account openness index	0.002				
	(0.36)				
Control variables					
Share of ICT in total capital stock	0.047	0.031	0.027	0.030	0.033
	(2.79)***	(1.98)**	(1.62)	(2.03)**	(2.01)**
Credit to private sector (percent of GDP)	0.06	0.051	0.049	0.050	0.042
	(3.74)***	(3.49)***	(3.81)***	(3.54)***	(3.06)***
Population share with at least a secondary education	0.005	0.003	0.002	0.004	0.004
	(2.02)**	(1.47)	(0.77)	(1.82)*	(2.08)**
Average years of education	–0.355	–0.216	–0.182	–0.328	–0.359
	(1.91)*	(1.20)	(1.00)	(1.84)*	(1.91)*
Agriculture employment share	0.04	0.05	0.052		
	(1.67)*	(2.05)**	(2.21)**		
Industry employment share	–0.091	–0.095	–0.098		
	(2.40)**	(2.78)***	(2.26)**		
Relative labor productivity of agriculture				–0.037	
				(1.67)*	
Relative labor productivity of industry				0.128	
				(3.03)***	
Observations	288	288	284	279	288
Adjusted R-squared (within)	0.26	0.3	0.31	0.32	0.27

Source: IMF staff calculations.

Note: See Appendix 4.1. Heteroscedasticity-robust t-statistics are in parentheses; * denotes significance at the 10 percent level, ** denotes significance at the 5 percent level, and *** denotes significance at the 1 percent level. All explanatory variables are in natural logarithm, except the tariff measure, the capital account openness index, and the population share with at least a secondary education. The left- and right-hand-side variables are de-meaned using country-specific means (equivalent to doing a panel estimation with country fixed effects), and the equations include time dummies. The equations are estimated by ordinary least squares. FDI = foreign direct investment; ICT = information and communications technology.

financial development may reduce income inequality by increasing access to capital for the poor, this depends on the quality of institutions in a given country. In the context of weak institutions, the benefits of financial deepening may accrue disproportionately to the rich, further exacerbating initial inequality in access to finance.

The first stage of the empirical investigation looks at the relationship between summary measures of trade and financial openness and income inequality. This is followed by a more disaggregated analysis of the relationship between various components of trade and financial openness and inequality. Other explanatory variables included in the estimations are the share of ICT in a country's total capital stock, credit to the private sector, the average number of years of education and its distribution, and the share of employment in agriculture and industry. The analysis focuses on changes in inequality over time and controls for differences in levels across countries, using country fixed effects.[25] The model is estimated on a panel of 51 countries (of which 31 are emerging market and developing countries) over the period 1981–2003, with additional tests that split the sample between advanced and developing economies.[26]

The results indicate that the main factor driving the recent increase in inequality across countries has been technological progress. Based on the benchmark model, which is described in more detail in Appendix 4.1, technological progress alone explains most of the 0.45 percent average annual increase in the Gini coefficient from the early 1980s (Table 4.1, column b; and Figure 4.9).[27] Trade and financial globalization and financial deepening

Figure 4.9. Explaining Gini Coefficient Changes[1,2]

(Average annual percent change)

The disequalizing effect of globalization was larger in advanced economies, in part because of outward foreign direct investment, while in developing countries, and especially in developing Asia, technological change was the main contributor to the rise in inequality.

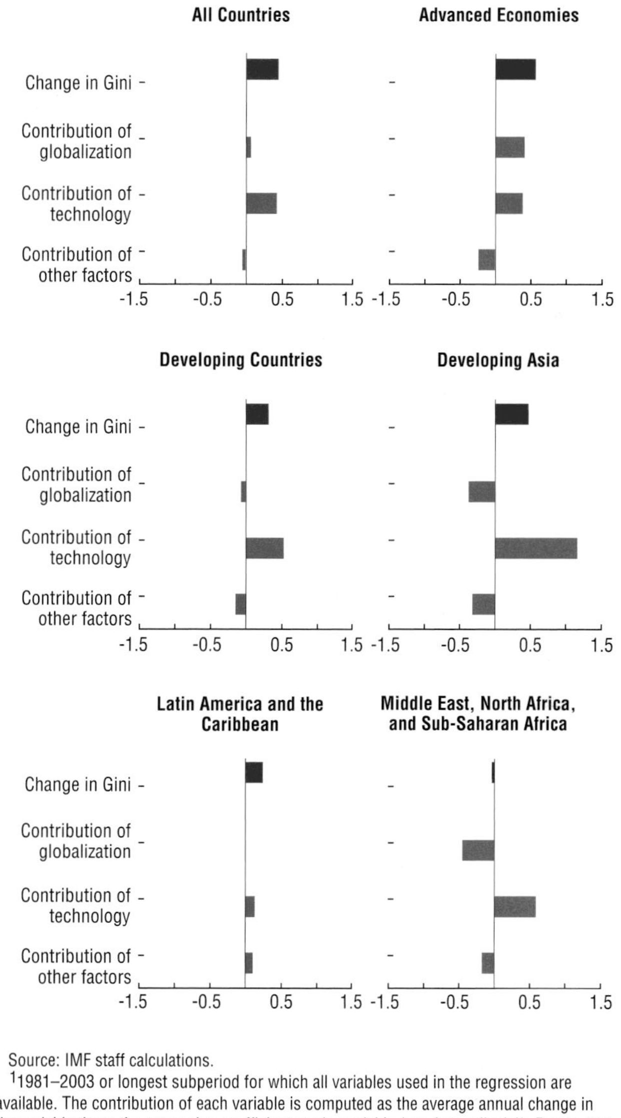

Source: IMF staff calculations.

[1]1981–2003 or longest subperiod for which all variables used in the regression are available. The contribution of each variable is computed as the average annual change in the variable times the regression coefficient on the variable (see Appendix 4.1). For the "All countries" panel, regression coefficients are taken from the full sample estimation in column (b) of Table 4.1. For the country group panels, regression coefficients are taken from Table 4.3, which provides group-specific estimates of the coefficients.

[2]See Figure 4.10 for the composition of the contribution of globalization. The contribution of other factors is the sum of the contributions of the ratio of credit to private sector to GDP, the education variables, the sectoral employment shares, and the residual.

[25]An additional advantage of focusing on within-country variation is to reduce the risk of omitted variable bias. The impact of common global shocks such as business cycles or growth spurts is excluded using time dummies.

[26]Since income and consumption surveys are not conducted annually, the estimations use an unbalanced panel with observations included only for years for which actual data are available. Moreover, given the smaller size of the samples for advanced and developing economies, the results on these subgroups are more tentative.

[27]The results are robust to including changes in GDP per capita as an explanatory variable. However, this variable was excluded in the reported estimations in order to estimate the full effects of the variables of interest, including their effect through higher overall growth. Other possible explanatory variables (democracy, constraints on the executive, flexibility of regulations, real exchange rate, and terms of trade) were initially included, but their effects were not robustly estimated. Comprehensive data on government social spending and transfers, migration, and remittances were not available across all countries, although these channels may potentially have important additional effects on the observed inequality outcomes.

Figure 4.10. Decomposition of Globalization Effects on Inequality[1]

(Average annual percent change)

Trade globalization has exerted an equalizing impact, while financial globalization, and foreign direct investment (FDI) in particular, has been associated with widening income disparities.

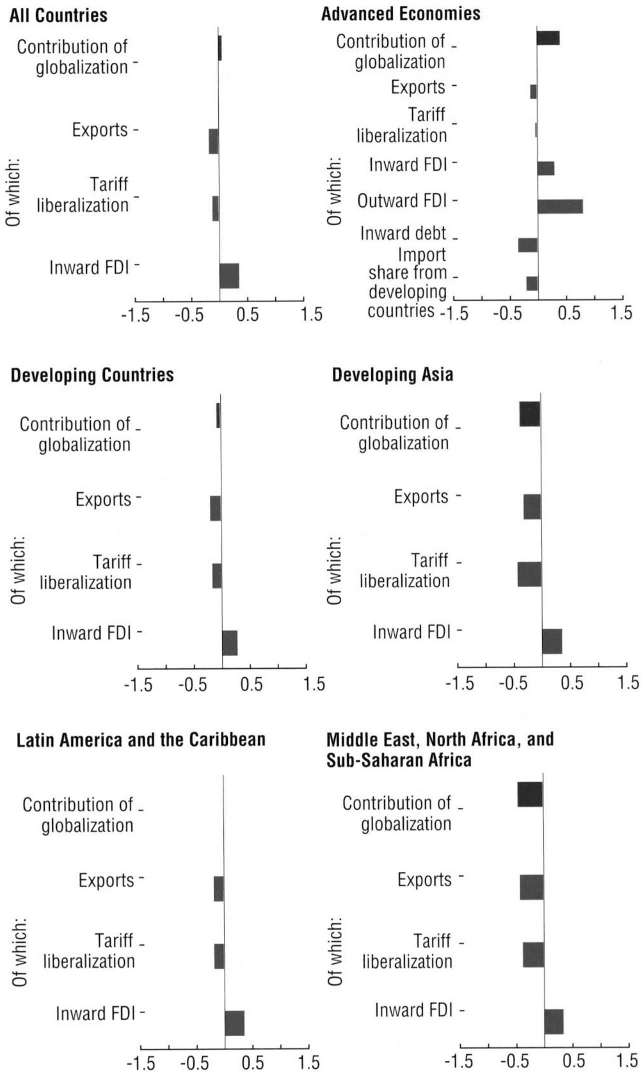

Source: IMF staff calculations.

[1]1981–2003 or longest subperiod for which all variables used in the regression are available. The contribution of each variable is computed as the average annual change in the variable times the regression coefficient on the variable (see Appendix 4.1). For the "All countries" panel, regression coefficients are taken from the full sample estimation in column (b) of Table 4.1. For the country group panels, regression coefficients are taken from Table 4.3, which provides group-specific estimates of the coefficients.

contributed a further 0.1 percent a year each to raising the Gini coefficient, offset by almost equivalent reductions in the Gini coefficient from increased access to education and a shift of employment away from agriculture.[28] The small net negative impact of globalization on inequality is a result of the opposing influences of different components of globalization: trade globalization has exerted an equalizing impact, whereas financial globalization (and FDI in particular) has been associated with widening income disparities over the period examined in this study (Figure 4.10).[29]

An analysis using more disaggregated data and estimating the regression coefficients for advanced and developing economies separately suggests that the impact of globalization on inequality varies across country groups. Among advanced economies, globalization has contributed somewhat more than technology to the 0.6 percent average annual increase in the Gini coefficient over the past two decades. Among developing countries, however, technology has been the main driving factor in the 0.3 percent annual average increase in the Gini coefficient; by contrast, globalization provided a small counterweight. These differences can be explained by changes in the channels of globalization across these two groups, with financial globaliza-

[28]The regression coefficient on education is imprecisely estimated in the benchmark model, a common problem in macroeconomic studies on the effect of education. However, microeconomic studies have generally been more successful in establishing the returns from investment in education, particularly for countries with lower per capita income and for primary education (see Psacharopoulos and Patrinos, 2004). The education variables applied in the regressions are from Barro and Lee (2000), as explained in Appendix 4.1.

[29]The reported results were confirmed for robustness in several ways. In order to address concerns that inequality may itself influence globalization variables, the export-to-GDP ratio and the ratio of the inward stock of FDI to GDP were instrumented using their lagged value, the export-weighted real GDP of trade partners (a measure of the demand for the country's exports), and an (inverse) distance-weighted sum of advanced economies' FDI assets (a measure of the supply of FDI). The results proved robust to endogeneity as well as to dropping one country at a time from the sample.

tion having expanded much more rapidly in advanced economies, and trade globalization having expanded more rapidly in developing economies.

Looking at the results in more detail, the positive effect of trade on reducing income inequality is particularly noticeable for agricultural exports, especially in developing countries where agriculture still employs a large share of the workforce (Table 4.1, column c).[30] Algeria, Brazil, Nicaragua, and Thailand are examples of countries where rising agricultural export shares have been associated with declining inequality—whereas the reverse has occurred in Bangladesh, Bolivia, Jamaica, and Sri Lanka (Figure 4.11). This conclusion is supported by evidence (see Table 4.1, column d) indicating that a rise in the relative productivity of agriculture is also associated with a reduction in inequality. A shift of underemployed agricultural workers away from agriculture to industry and services—which would raise the agricultural sector's productivity relative to the average of the economy—also tends to reduce inequality. The net impact of tariff reduction is also found to be positive in reducing income inequality.

For advanced economies, imports from developing countries are associated with a reduction in inequality.[31] This would be explained through the substitution of lower-paying low-end manufacturing jobs in advanced economies with higher-paying service sector jobs such as in retail.[32] A second channel could be that as noncompeting imported goods become more easily available at a lower price, the effective income of the poorer segment of the population in advanced economies rises if such goods are a

Figure 4.11. Inequality Versus Exports in Agriculture
(Change in log of indicators over last available 10 years; years indicated)

Growth in agricultural exports has contributed to reducing inequality in developing countries where agriculture still employs a large share of the workforce.

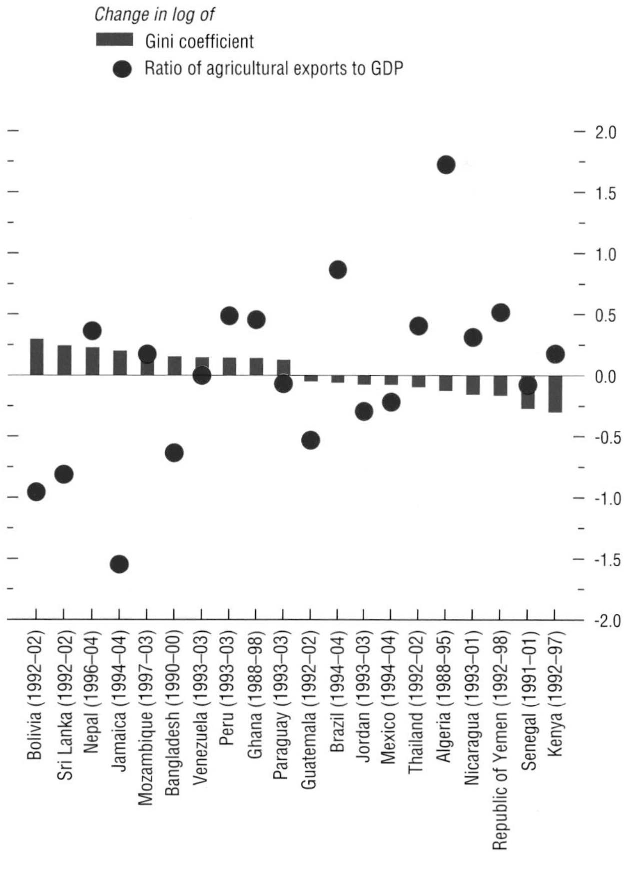

Sources: Povcal database; WIDER database; World Bank, World Development Indicators database (2007); and IMF staff calculations.

[30]The effects of agriculture, manufacturing, and service exports are statistically not significantly different from one another, but agricultural exports have the largest coefficient and are statistically significant.

[31]See Table 4.3 in Appendix 4.1 for econometric estimations.

[32]See Overholt (2003) for a discussion of substitution between manufacturing and service sector jobs in the United States.

Figure 4.12. Foreign Direct Investment Stock by Sector

(Share of total inward foreign direct investment stock)

The composition of inward foreign direct investment in both advanced economies and developing countries has been more concentrated in the high-skill sectors, including high/medium-high-technology manufacturing and the knowledge-intensive service sector.

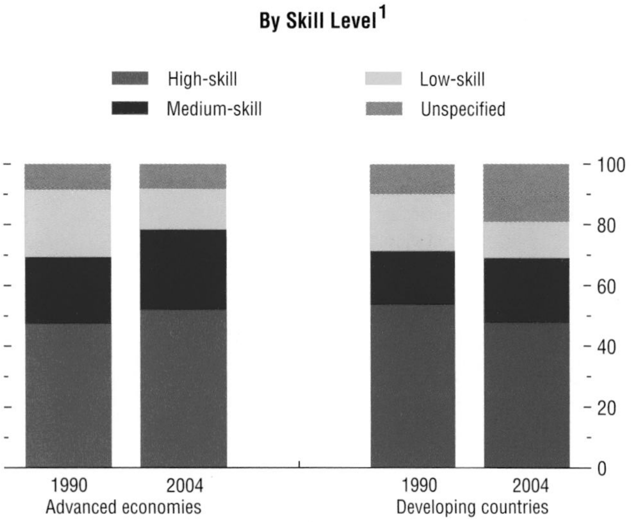

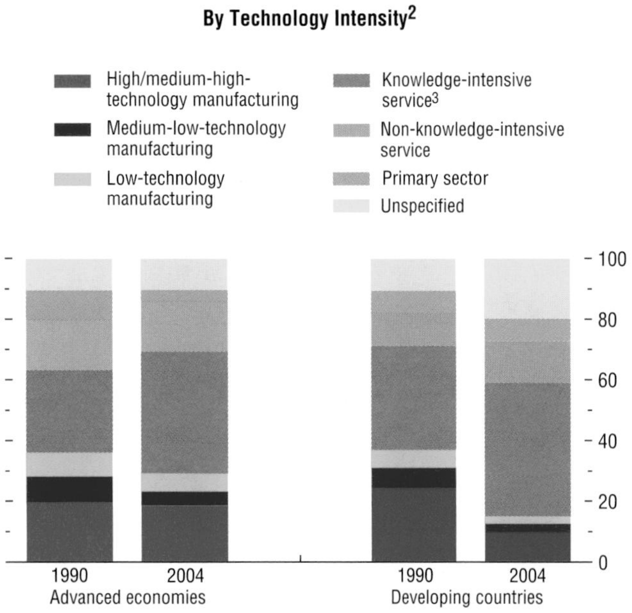

Sources: UNCTAD, *World Investment Report 2006*; and IMF staff calculations.
[1]Skill level as defined in Appendix 5.1 in the *World Economic Outlook* (April 2007).
[2]Technology intensity as defined by the Organization for Economic Cooperation and Development.
[3]Includes finance; business activities; education; health and social services; and transport, storage, and communications.

greater share of their consumption than for the richer segment.[33]

Financial globalization, and especially FDI, appears to be associated with higher inequality. While it is inward FDI that exacerbates inequality in developing countries, in advanced economies there is an additional negative effect from outward FDI. This finding is consistent with evidence that FDI tends to take place in more skill- and technology-intensive sectors (from the point of view of the host country), increasing the relative demand for skilled workers in both advanced and developing economies (Figure 4.12). This is, however, an average effect over the sample period. The impact of FDI can be expected to vary by sector and dissipate over time as workers acquire skills and education.

The finding that investment in technological advances has a disequalizing impact is consistent with the view that new technology, in both advanced and developing economies, increases the premium on skills and automates relatively low-skill inputs (see Birdsall, 2007). Just as FDI increases the rewards for higher-value-added activities, technological progress also creates greater demands for those with higher skills. In advanced economies, the use of technology is widespread in both manufacturing and services, raising the skills premium in a substantial portion of the economy. Among developing countries, the effect of technological progress is stronger in Asia than in Latin America, possibly reflecting the greater share of technology-intensive manufacturing in Asia (Figure 4.13). Despite the distinct and separate effect of technology on inequality that is found in the data, it remains important to keep in mind that the spread of technology and increasing globalization are not independent—technological advances have helped deepen trade and financial linkages between countries, while globalization has helped spread the use of technology.

[33]Income-based Gini coefficients often do not use different price deflators for rich and poor segments and are thus typically not able to capture this effect.

The evidence that domestic financial deepening adversely affects inequality is consistent with the notion that although overall financial depth is associated with higher growth, a disproportionately larger share of financial flows accrues to those with higher endowments and income that can serve as collateral.[34] As a result, the already better-off segments of the population are better able to invest in human and physical capital and increase their income.

To gain further insight into the impact of globalization on inequality, the empirical model was also estimated using the income shares of the five quintiles of the population as dependent variables (Table 4.2). Most of the results from the preceding analysis are confirmed, although the estimates at the quintile level are less precise for tariff liberalization and technological progress. In line with the changes observed in the income shares of quintiles (see Figure 4.4), the effects on the bottom four quintiles are qualitatively similar and in the opposite direction from that on the richest quintile.

Export growth is associated with a rise in the income shares of the bottom four quintiles and a decrease in the share of the fifth (that is, the richest) quintile. Similarly, a reduction in the share of agricultural employment (which raises the sector's productivity of labor) is also associated with a rise in the income share of the bottom four quintiles, whereas it has the opposite effect on the income share of the richest quintile. The benefits of tariff reduction are mostly concentrated in the income shares of the three bottom quintiles, offset by a decrease in the income share of the top quintile. In contrast, financial globalization, technological progress, and greater financial deepening benefit mainly the income share of the richest 20 percent of the population.

Across the whole sample of countries, technological progress is seen to be the main driver

[34]There was no evidence of a threshold effect by income level for this result, suggesting that the type of financial system—that is, based on relationship or arm's-length transaction—may be a more important determinant of equality of access to finance (see the September 2006 issue of the *World Economic Outlook*).

Figure 4.13. Inequality and Technology, 1981–2003[1]

Partial correlations by country group suggest that the disequalizing impact of technology was particularly strong in Asia, and was less powerful in Latin America and the Caribbean.

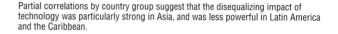

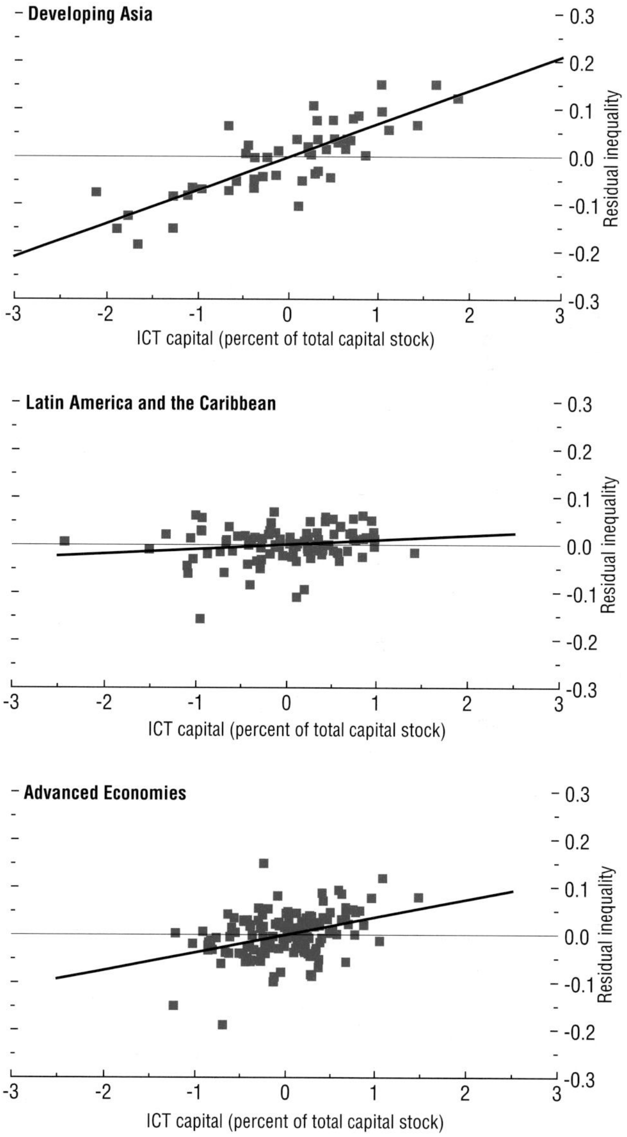

Source: IMF staff calculations.
[1]Correlation between information and communications technology (ICT) capital and residual inequality (i.e., inequality not explained by other regressors), based on the regression in column (b) of Table 4.3, allowing a specific coefficient on this variable for each country group (see Appendix 4.1).

Table 4.2. Estimation of the Benchmark Model Using Quintiles' Income Shares, Full Sample
(Dependent variable: income share of the quintile)

	Quintile 1	Quintile 2	Quintile 3	Quintile 4	Quintile 5	Test All Coefficients Equal to Zero (*p*-value)
Exports-to-GDP ratio	0.439	0.631	0.690	0.492	–2.220	
	(2.47)**	(3.52)***	(3.68)***	(2.58)***	(3.57)***	0.02**
100 minus tariff rate	0.021	0.020	0.017	0.013	–0.070	
	(2.16)**	(2.04)**	(1.67)*	(1.32)	(2.12)**	0.28
Ratio of inward FDI stock to GDP	–0.400	–0.385	–0.326	–0.163	1.241	
	(3.91)***	(3.74)***	(3.02)***	(1.48)	(3.47)***	0***
Share of ICT in total capital stock	–0.177	–0.223	–0.218	–0.207	0.830	
	(1.32)	(1.65)*	(1.54)	(1.44)	(1.77)*	0.59
Credit to private sector (percent of GDP)	–0.373	–0.625	–0.709	–0.437	2.136	
	(3.30)***	(5.47)***	(5.94)***	(3.59)***	(5.39)***	0***
Population share with at least a secondary education	–0.035	–0.025	–0.028	–0.003	0.094	
	(1.76)*	(1.26)	(1.31)	(0.16)	(1.35)	0.14
Average years of education	1.844	1.041	1.020	0.128	–3.99	
	(1.11)	(0.62)	(0.58)	(0.07)	(0.69)	0.80
Agriculture employment share	–0.460	–0.789	–0.981	–0.568	2.777	
	(1.76)*	(2.98)***	(3.55)***	(2.02)**	(3.02)***	0***
Industry employment share	1.081	0.866	0.603	0.084	–2.623	
	(3.07)***	(2.43)**	(1.62)	(0.22)	(2.12)**	0.09*
Observations	271	271	271	271	271	
R-squared (within)	0.34	0.36	0.33	0.18	0.35	

Source: IMF staff calculations.
Note: See Appendix 4.1. *t*-statistics are in parentheses; * denotes significance at the 10 percent level, ** denotes significance at the 5 percent level, and *** denotes significance at the 1 percent level. All explanatory variables are in natural logarithm, except the tariff measure and the population share with at least a secondary education. The left- and right-hand-side variables are de-meaned using country-specific means (equivalent to doing a panel estimation with country fixed effects), and the equations include time dummies. The equations are estimated jointly using the seemingly unrelated regressions estimator. FDI = foreign direct investment; ICT = information and communications technology.

of the fall in the income share of the bottom quintile and the rise of the income share of the top quintile (Figure 4.14). Globalization has contributed only moderately to net changes in income shares because the beneficial effects of export growth and tariff reductions for all but the richest quintile have substantially offset the disequalizing impact of inward FDI. Although the income shares of the four bottom quintiles have declined overall, it is important to note that the average levels of income within these quintiles have been rising, as technological progress, financial deepening, and globalization have been important drivers of overall growth (see Figures 4.5 and 4.6).[35] Average income levels in the bottom four quintiles have, however, grown at a lower rate than in the top quintile. The important exceptions to this general pattern are sub-Saharan Africa and the Commonwealth of Independent States.[36] In these regions, income levels in the lower quintiles have grown faster than for the top quintile.

Conclusions and Policy Implications

Inequality has been rising in countries across all income levels, except those classified as low income. Underlying these trends, the income share of the richest quintile has risen, whereas

[35]See IMF (2007) for an analysis of the positive effects of financial globalization on growth, and Levine (2004) for a survey of research concluding that financial deepening has a positive impact on growth.

[36]Available evidence suggests that rising exports and tariff liberalization have been the major factor contributing to the reduction in inequality observed in sub-Saharan Africa, offset partially by the effect of technology and, to a lesser extent, FDI (see Figures 4.9 and 4.10).

the shares of the remaining quintiles have declined. This chapter finds that, subject to the limitations imposed by the availability of data, technological progress has made the biggest contribution to rising income inequality over the past two decades. Globalization has had a much smaller disequalizing impact overall, reflecting the offsetting positive impact of trade globalization and a negative impact from FDI. In advanced economies, rising imports from developing countries are associated with declining income inequality, whereas in developing economies, both rising agricultural exports and tariff liberalization have contributed to improving income distribution. Foreign direct investment has on average had a disequalizing impact on the distribution of income over the sample period, as higher FDI inflows have increased the demand for skilled labor, whereas outward FDI in advanced economies has reduced the demand for relatively lower-skilled workers in these countries. Among other factors, financial deepening has also had a moderately negative impact on income distribution, whereas greater access to education and a shift in employment from agriculture to industry and services have supported improved distribution of income.

Thus, contrary to popular concerns, trade globalization is not found to have a negative impact on income distribution in either developing or advanced economies. Moreover, the positive role found for agricultural exports in improving distributional outcomes suggests the importance of reforms in developing countries to support growth of this sector. At the same time, greater liberalization of access for agricultural exports from developing countries to advanced economies' markets would support a more equal distribution of income in both developing and advanced economies.

Although FDI is associated with greater income inequality over the period of this study, it is associated with higher growth overall, and the result basically reflects an increase in the returns from acquiring higher skills. The impact of FDI may also vary by sector. Nevertheless, it might be expected that over a longer time

Figure 4.14. Explaining the Change in Income Share of Top and Bottom Quintiles[1,2]

(Average annual change, in percentage points)

Across all countries, technological progress is the main driver of the fall in the income share of the bottom quintile and of the rise in the income share of the top quintile.

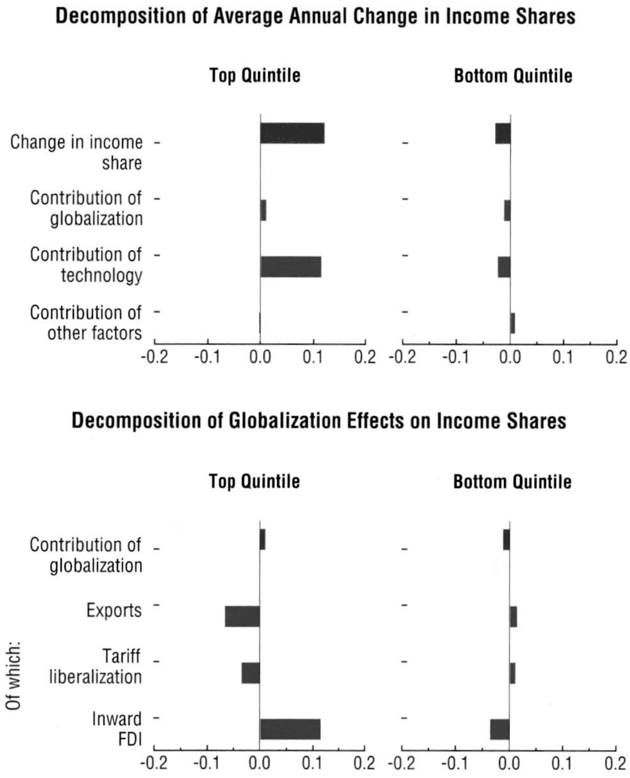

Source: IMF staff calculations.

[1]1981–2003 or longest subperiod for which all variables used in the regression are available. The contribution of each variable is computed as the average annual change in the variable times the regression coefficient on the variable (see Appendix 4.1). Regression coefficients are taken from Table 4.2.

[2]The contribution of globalization is the sum of the contributions of the export-to-GDP ratio, the tariff rate, and the ratio of inward FDI stock to GDP. The contribution of other factors is the sum of the contributions of the ratio of credit to private sector to GDP, the education variables, the sectoral employment shares, and the residual.

horizon, the disequalizing effects of FDI will dissipate as the increased demand for education and skills is met with improved supply.[37] The appropriate policy response is therefore not to suppress FDI or technological change, but to make increased access to education a priority. This would allow less-skilled and low-income groups to capitalize on the opportunities from both technological progress and the ongoing process of globalization, thereby shortening the length of time over which FDI has a disequalizing impact.

Finally, financial deepening in and of itself increases growth, but appears to have a disequalizing impact because of the unequal access to finance between rich and poor segments of the population. Policy reforms aimed at broadening access to finance, such as by improving institutions that promote pro-poor lending, could help improve the overall distribution of income, even as finance broadly continues to support overall growth.

The analysis presented in this chapter suggests that there are some common factors that can explain the broad patterns of inequality across countries and regions. However, individual country circumstances vary. The substantial literature analyzing inequality in individual countries underscores the need to understand the regional and sectoral dimensions of inequality and its relationship with globalization, and individual country circumstances with respect to the structure of the economy. Policies will therefore need to be calibrated to specific country circumstances to ensure that the maximum benefits of globalization for growth and poverty reduction can be realized.

Appendix 4.1. Data Sources and Methods

The main authors of this appendix are Florence Jaumotte, Stephanie Denis, and Patrick Hettinger.

Variable Definitions and Data Sources

This section provides further details on the construction of the variables and the data sources used in this chapter. The data cover 143 countries during 1980–2006, with the number of observations varying by country and variable.

Gini Index and Quintile Income Shares

The primary source for the Gini index (also known as the Gini coefficient) and income share data (referring to individual inequality, unless mentioned otherwise) is the World Bank Povcal database. For Mexico and Poland, the consumption-based Gini indices and quintile income shares were extrapolated historically for the period prior to 1992—for which only income-based measures are available—by assuming that the changes in consumption-based measures are identical to the observed changes in income-based measures that are available for that period. A similar process was applied to Peru's data prior to 1990, applying the changes in the observed consumption-based measures for earlier years to the income-based Gini index available from 1990 onward. For Argentina and Uruguay, the data cover only urban areas because of the high rate of urbanization in these two countries. For China and India, data with full country coverage (combining urban and rural data from the World Bank Povcal database) were provided by Shaohua Chen of the World Bank.[38]

When Povcal data were not available (mainly for advanced economies), the data from the Luxembourg Income Study were used, as provided in the World Income Inequality Database, Version 2.0b, May 2007 (WIDER). These data are mostly available only until 2000. The following other sources were also used to increase coverage for advanced economies: data for Australia are from the Australian Bureau of Statistics; data for Germany are from the Deutsches Institüt für

[37]Evidence for the temporary nature of the disequalizing effects of FDI for Latin America is presented in Behrman, Birdsall, and Székely (2003).

[38]The Gini indices for China and India account for the difference in cost of living between rural and urban areas, whereas the income shares for these two countries do not.

Wirtschaftsforschung; data for France are from the European Commission; household inequality data for Hong Kong SAR are from the Hong Kong Census and Statistics; household inequality data for Singapore are from Ong Whee Sze (2002); household Gini index data for Japan are from Shirahase (2001); income share data for Japan measuring household consumption inequality and excluding agricultural households are from the Family Income and Expenditure Survey provided by the Japanese Statistics Bureau (all included in WIDER); and household inequality data for Korea were provided by Professor Kyungsoo Choi of the Korea Development Institute.

These data were interpolated to create regional and income group averages in the figures, and the regressions used only actual observations.[39]

Per Capita Income per Quintile

Average income for quintiles is calculated using the quintile income-share data and real GDP per capita (in 2000 international dollars, chain-series) from the Penn World Tables Version 6.2, by Heston, Summers, and Aten (2006). Quintile income shares are multiplied by the GDP per capita variable and multiplied by 5 to arrive at the average income per quintile, as follows:

$$\frac{Y_1}{Pop_1} = \left(\frac{Y_1}{Y}\right)\left(\frac{Y}{Pop}\right)\left(\frac{1}{0.2}\right),$$

where Y_1 denotes the total income of quintile 1, Pop_1 is population in quintile 1, Y is economy-wide income, and Pop is economy-wide population.

Trade Globalization

De facto trade openness is calculated as the sum of imports and exports of (non-oil) goods and services over GDP. The data are from the World Economic Outlook database (April 2007). Sectoral trade data on agriculture, manufacturing, and services are from the World Bank's World Development Indicators database (April 2007).

De jure trade openness is calculated as 100 minus the tariff rate, which is an average of the effective tariff rate (tariff revenue/import value) and of the average unweighted tariff rate. The data are from a database prepared by IMF staff. Each component of the implied 100 minus tariff rate is interpolated linearly for countries with data gaps less than or equal to seven missing observations between 1980 and 2004. When data for either component (the effective tariff rate or the average unweighted tariff rate) are shorter than for the other, the shorter series is extrapolated using the growth rate of the longer series.[40] Finally, for countries with only one of the two components, only the available one is used.

Financial Globalization

De facto financial openness is calculated as the sum of total cross-border assets and liabilities over GDP. Data on financial globalization are from the "External Wealth of Nations Mark II" created by Lane and Milesi-Ferretti (2006). The components of de facto financial openness in percent of GDP include (for both assets and liabilities) (1) FDI, (2) portfolio equity, (3) debt, (4) financial derivatives, and (5) total reserves minus gold (assets only).

De jure financial openness refers to the capital account openness index (KAOPEN) from

[39]The data for some advanced economies were extended for the purpose of the charts. For Germany, the Gini index was extended prior to 1992 using trends in West German data. For France, the Gini index was extended prior to 1994 using trends from LIS data. For the United States, trends after 2000 were based on earnings data from the Current Population Survey for full-time, year-round workers. For Great Britain, trends after 1999 were extended using data from the Institute for Fiscal Studies. For Italy, trends after 2000 were extended using data from Brandolini (2004). For Japan, a longer Gini index series was used from the National Survey of Family Income and Expenditure.

[40]For some countries, longer data were available for the ratio of trade revenue to trade value (which covaried closely with the other two measures), and these were used to extend the effective tariff rate and/or the average unweighted tariff rate.

Chinn and Ito (2006). The index is based on principal components extracted from disaggregated capital and current account restriction measures in the IMF's *Annual Report on Exchange Arrangements and Exchange Restrictions.*

Capital Stock and ICT Capital

Fajnzylber and Lederman (1999) is the source of the capital stock series for the entire economy. This data set extends the capital stock series estimated by Nehru and Dhareshwar (1993) by adding the annual flow of gross fixed capital formation and assuming a 4 percent depreciation rate of the preexisting stock of capital. Fajnzylber and Lederman (1999) was further updated to recent years using the same methodology.

Jorgensen and Vu (2005) provides series on IT investment using national expenditure data for computer hardware, software, and telecommunications equipment. A perpetual inventory method applies varying depreciation rates to estimate the IT capital stock. This method assumes a geometric depreciation rate of 31.5 percent and a service life of seven years for computer hardware, 31.5 percent and five years for software, and 11 percent and 11 years for telecommunications equipment.

Private Credit

Each country's financial depth is estimated by its ratio of credit to the private sector by deposit money banks and other financial institutions to GDP. The source is the Financial Structure database prepared by Beck, Demirgüç-Kunt, and Levine (2000) and revised in March 2007. Data for China are based on IMF staff calculations.

Education

Data on educational attainment of the population ages 15 and older are from the Barro-Lee (2000) data set. The series used are the average schooling years in the population, and the share of the population with secondary and/or higher education. For the years between 1980 and 2000, the data (available every five years) are interpolated linearly for each country, and for the years 2001–06, the data are extrapolated linearly.

Sectoral Employment

Data on employment shares in agriculture and industry are from the World Bank's World Development Indicators database (April 2006). The shares are interpolated linearly for countries with data gaps of seven or fewer missing observations between 1980 and 2005. For Bolivia, data are from the International Labor Organization's LABORSTA database for 1988–2001 and from the Instituto Nacional de Estadística for 2002–05. For Ecuador, data for 1988–2005 are from the International Labor Organization's LABORSTA database. For Morocco, data for 1999–2002 are from the Direction de la Politique Economique Générale. For Paraguay, data for 1991–2005 are from the Departamento de Cuentas Nacionales y Mercado Interno, Gerencia de Estudios Económicos. For China, data for 1980–2004 are from the National Bureau of Statistics. For India, data for 1980–2004 are taken from the National Sample Survey Organisation. For Taiwan Province of China, data for 1980–2005 are from the CEIC database.

Aggregations by Region and Income Level

Charts showing aggregates by region and income level use the following:

- the *World Economic Outlook* analytical classification, as listed in Table F of the Statistical Appendix; and
- the classification by income from the World Bank's World Development Indicators database (April 2007). The economies are divided among income groups according to 2005 gross national income per capita, calculated using the World Bank Atlas method. The groups are low income, \$875 or less; lower-middle income, \$876–\$3,465; upper-middle income, \$3,466–\$10,725; and high income, \$10,726 or more. Taiwan Province of China is included in the high-income group.

In regional and income group averages, a maximum number of countries was included in each group, subject to data availability and to the constraint that country coverage is uniform throughout the period.[41] Countries with fewer than 1 million people in 2006 were dropped from the sample.

In Figures 4.1 and 4.2 relative trade and financial openness are measured by taking the ratio to the median across all countries for each year and the ratio to maximum across all countries in 2004 for financial openness and 2006 for trade openness. To avoid discontinuity in country coverage over time, it is assumed in the calculation of the median that in the 1980s and early 1990s, trade openness for countries in the former Soviet Union equaled Russia's trade openness, and that these countries were financially closed.

Econometric Methodology

The model relates the Gini index to measures of globalization and a number of control variables, chosen based on a review of the literature in this area. The following equation is adopted as the basic specification for the analysis:

$$ln(GINI) = \alpha_1 + \alpha_2\, ln\left(\frac{X+M}{Y}\right) + \alpha_3(100 - TARIFF)$$

$$+ \alpha_4\, ln\left(\frac{A+L}{Y}\right) + \alpha_5 KAOPEN$$

$$+ \alpha_6\, ln\left(\frac{K_{ICT}}{K}\right) + \alpha_7\, ln\left(\frac{CREDIT}{Y}\right)$$

$$+ \alpha_8\, POPSH + \alpha_9\, lnH + \alpha_{10}\, ln\left(\frac{E_{AGR}}{E}\right)$$

$$+ \alpha_{11}\, ln\left(\frac{E_{IND}}{E}\right) + \varepsilon,$$

where X and M are non-oil exports and imports, Y is GDP, $TARIFF$ is the average tariff rate, A and L are cross-border financial assets and liabilities, $KAOPEN$ is the capital account openness index, K_{ICT} is ICT capital, K is capital, $CREDIT$ is credit to the private sector by deposit money banks and other financial institutions, $POPSH$ is the share of population ages 15 and older with secondary or higher education, H is average years of education in the population ages 15 and older, E_{AGR} and E_{IND} are employment in agriculture and industry, and E is total employment. This summary model is then augmented by disaggregating into finer components the summary measures of de facto trade and financial globalization. The component model makes a distinction between non-oil exports and imports for trade globalization, while allowing different effects of various categories of financial liabilities (FDI, portfolio equity, and debt) and of the stock of FDI assets. The latter, which is closely associated with offshore outsourcing, may be particularly relevant to measure the impact of globalization on inequality in advanced economies, whereas its value is minimal for most emerging market and developing countries.

For the estimation, the left- and right-hand-side variables are de-meaned using country-specific means in order to focus on within-country changes instead of cross-country-level differences (this is equivalent to doing a panel estimation with fixed country effects). Time dummies are also introduced to capture common global shocks. The model is estimated using ordinary least squares (OLS) with heteroscedasticity-consistent standard errors. Using the logarithm of the Gini index (rather than the Gini index itself) makes this bounded variable behave more like a normally distributed variable and hence makes it more amenable to OLS estimation. The robustness of the results

[41]For example, in the inequality charts, the approximate population represented for each region is 93 percent in advanced economies excluding NIEs (77 percent for income share and income per capita charts); 92 percent in NIEs (87 percent for income share and income per capita charts); 94 percent in Latin America and the Caribbean; 63 percent in sub-Saharan Africa; 90 percent in central and eastern Europe; 92 percent in the Commonwealth of Independent States; 57 percent in the Middle East and North Africa; and 94 percent in developing Asia. The approximate population represented in each income group is as follows: 91 percent in the high-income group (84 percent for income share and income per capita charts); 82 percent in the upper-middle-income group; 87 percent in the lower-middle-income group; and 79 percent in the low-income group. For the global indicator, approximately 82 percent of the world population is represented.

Table 4.3. Determinants of the Gini Coefficient, Regional Heterogeneity
(Dependent variable: natural logarithm of Gini)

	Advanced Versus Developing Economies (a)	Regional Technology Effect (b)
Common model		
Exports-to-GDP ratio	−0.063	−0.071
	(2.23)**	(3.17)***
100 minus tariff rate	−0.002	−0.004
	(2.24)**	(3.53)***
Ratio of inward FDI stock to GDP	0.031	0.041
	(2.28)**	(3.03)***
Share of ICT in total capital stock	0.035	0.037
	(2.12)**	(2.11)**
Credit to private sector (percent of GDP)	0.058	0.041
	(3.94)***	(3.29)***
Population share with at least a secondary education	0.001	0.002
	(0.35)	(0.82)
Average years of education	−0.1	−0.124
	(0.54)	(0.65)
Agriculture employment share	0.074	0.052
	(2.59)**	(2.31)**
Industry employment share	−0.09	−0.139
	(2.23)**	(3.96)***
Additional variables for advanced economies		
Share of imports from developing economies	0.018	
	(0.57)	
Share of imports from developing economies * dummy for advanced economies	−0.104	
	(2.20)**	
Ratio of inward debt stock to GDP	0.014	
	(0.78)	
Ratio of inward debt stock to GDP * dummy for advanced economies	−0.083	
	(2.65)***	
Ratio of outward FDI stock to GDP	0	
	(0.31)	
Ratio of outward FDI stock to GDP * dummy for advanced economies	0.069	
	(2.68)***	
Different regional technology effect		
Share of ICT in total capital stock * dummy for developing Asia		0.033
		(1.99)**
Share of ICT in total capital stock * dummy for Latin America and the Caribbean		−0.028
		(1.91)*
Observations	282	282
Adjusted R-squared (within)	0.32	0.35

Source: IMF staff calculations.
Note: Heteroscedasticity-robust t-statistics are in parentheses; * denotes significance at the 10 percent level, ** denotes significance at the 5 percent level, and *** denotes significance at the 1 percent level. All explanatory variables are in natural logarithm, except the tariff measure and the population share with at least a secondary education. The left- and right-hand-side variables are demeaned using country-specific means (equivalent to doing a panel estimation with country fixed effects), and the equations include time dummies. The equations are estimated by ordinary least squares. FDI = foreign direct investment; ICT = information and communications technology.

was also tested using a logistic transformation of the Gini index (making the variable completely unbounded). The sample of countries for which all variables used in the regressions were available consists of 51 countries, of which 20 are advanced economies and 31 are developing economies. Based on data availability, the following countries are included:

- advanced economies: Australia, Austria, Belgium, Canada, Denmark, Finland, France, Germany, Ireland, Israel, Italy, Japan, Korea, the Netherlands, Norway, Singapore, Spain, Sweden, the United Kingdom, and the United States; and
- developing economies: Argentina, Bangladesh, Bolivia, Brazil, Chile, China, Costa Rica, Ecuador, Egypt, El Salvador, Ghana, Guatemala, Honduras, India, Indonesia, the Islamic Republic of Iran, Kenya, Malaysia, Mexico, Pakistan, Panama, Paraguay, Peru, the Philippines, Sri Lanka, Thailand, Turkey, Uganda, Uruguay, Venezuela, and Zambia.

The results of the estimation using the full sample of advanced and developing economies are reported in the text. Three globalization variables have statistically significant effects on inequality: the ratio of non-oil exports to GDP, the indicator of tariff liberalization, and the ratio of FDI liabilities to GDP. The model, including these three variables as well as all the controls, is referred to as the benchmark model. As described in footnote 29 of the main text, the robustness of this specification was tested in various ways, including by instrumenting for the ratio of non-oil exports to GDP and the ratio of FDI liabilities to GDP.

Additional Results: Heterogeneity Across Country Groups

The analysis in this section explores the possibility of heterogeneous effects of globalization, technological progress, and other variables across country groups; the results are, however, more tentative, because the number of observations used for identification of group-specific effects is much smaller. The first obvious distinction of interest is between advanced and developing economies, as defined in the *World Economic Outlook*. The starting model is the component model, described earlier, with an additional complexity: two additional variables are included that measure the share of exports destined for developing countries and the share of imports originating in these countries (this variable was not significant when the full sample was used). While maintaining common time dummies, interaction terms between the other regressors and a dummy for advanced economies are included to measure the difference between the effects for advanced economies and the estimated average effect for the full sample. A joint test that all the differences are zero is rejected, mostly as a result of different effects (for advanced and developing economies) of the ratio of FDI assets to GDP and, to a lesser extent, of the ratio of debt liabilities to GDP and the share of imports originating in developing countries (Table 4.3).[42] While these three variables are insignificant for the full sample (and particularly for developing countries), they are significantly different from zero for advanced economies. The estimation indicates that FDI assets increase inequality in advanced economies, while debt and the share of imports from developing countries contribute to reduce it (Figure 4.15).

Another distinction of interest is between different developing regions: the two main developing regions represented in the sample are developing Asia and Latin America (only a few African and Middle Eastern countries are included because of data limitations). Due to the even smaller sample sizes involved for these subgroups, the estimation starts from the benchmark model and allows a differential impact by developing region (developing Asia, Latin America, and other) only for the globalization

[42]The effects of exports, tariffs, and FDI liabilities on inequality are statistically insignificant for advanced economies; however, the hypothesis that these coefficients are not statistically significantly different from those for the full sample cannot be rejected.

Figure 4.15. Inequality, Import Share from Developing Countries, Inward Debt, and Outward Foreign Direct Investment (FDI), 1981–2003[1]

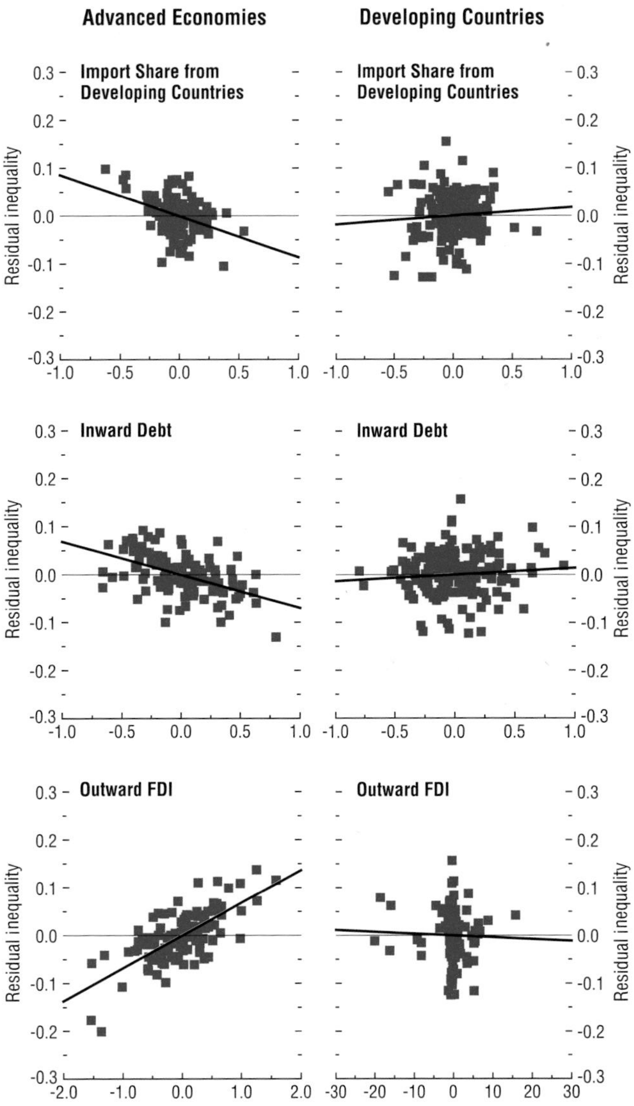

Source: IMF staff calculations.
[1]Correlation between the variable of interest (the share of imports from developing countries, inward debt, or outward FDI) and residual inequality (i.e., inequality not explained by other regressors), based on the regression in column (a) of Table 4.3, allowing a specific coefficient on these variables for each country group.

and technological progress variables. A joint test that all differences are zero is rejected, because of the different effect of technological progress in developing Asia and Latin America. The disequalizing effect of technological progress is stronger in Asia than on average in the full sample and weaker in Latin America (actually insignificantly different from zero) (see Table 4.3). This may reflect the greater share of technology-intensive manufacturing in Asia than in Latin America.

Partial Correlations and Decompositions of Gini Index Changes

The partial correlation between the Gini index and a variable *X* is the simple correlation between the variable *X* and residual inequality (that is, inequality not explained by other regressors, or the sum of the regression residual and the product of the variable *X* and its coefficient).

The contributions of the various factors to the change in the Gini index shown in the main text are calculated as the average annual change in the respective variable multiplied by the corresponding coefficient estimate. The averages across country groups are weighted by the number of years covered for each country, so that countries with a longer period of observation receive more weight in these averages.

Contributions for the full sample of countries ("All countries" panel of Figures 4.9 and 4.10) are based on the estimation of the benchmark model for the full sample of countries as reported in Table 4.1. Partial correlations and contributions for country groups use the estimates allowing coefficient heterogeneity across country groups as reported in Table 4.3.

References

Agénor, Pierre-Richard, 2002, "Does Globalization Hurt the Poor?" World Bank Working Paper No. 2922 (Washington: World Bank).

Atkinson, Anthony B., and François Bourguignon, 2000, "Introduction: Income Distribution and Economics," in *Handbook of Income Distribution*, Vol. 1, ed. by Anthony Atkinson and François Bourguignon (Amsterdam: Elsevier).

Barro, Robert J., and Jong-Wha Lee, 2000, "International Data on Educational Attainment: Updates and Implications," CID Working Paper No. 042 (Cambridge, Massachusetts: Center for International Development).

Beck, Thorsten, Asli Demirgüç-Kunt, and Ross Levine, 2000 (revised: March 20, 2007), "A New Database on Financial Development and Structure," *World Bank Economic Review*, Vol. 14, No. 3, pp. 597–605. Available via the Internet: www.econ.worldbank.org/staff/tbeck.

Behrman, Jere R., Nancy Birdsall, and Miguel Székely, 2003, "Economic Policy and Wage Differentials in Latin America," Working Paper No. 29 (Washington: Center for Global Development).

Birdsall, Nancy, 2005, "The World Is Not Flat: Inequality and Injustice in Our Global Economy," United Nations University—World Institute for Development Economics Research (WIDER) Lecture 9 (Helsinki: WIDER).

———, 2007, Discussion of *The Impact of Globalization on the World's Poor*, ed. by Machiko Nissanke and Erik Thorbecke, WIDER Book Launch, Brookings Institution, Washington, May 16.

———, David Ross, and Richard Sabot, 1995, "Inequality and Growth Reconsidered: Lessons from East Asia," *World Bank Economic Review*, Vol. 9, No. 3, pp. 477–508.

Brandolini, A., 2004, "Income Inequality and Poverty in Italy: A Statistical Compendium" (unpublished; Rome: Banca d'Italia).

Canberra Group, 2001, *Final Report and Recommendations* (Ottawa: Canberra Group, Expert Group on Household Income Statistics).

Chen, Shaohua, and Martin Ravallion, 2004, "How Have the World's Poorest Fared Since the Early 1980s?" *World Bank Research Observer*, Vol. 19, No. 2, pp. 141–69.

———, 2007, "Absolute Poverty Measures for the Developing World, 1981–2004," World Bank Policy Research Working Paper No. 4211 (Washington: World Bank).

Chinn, Menzie, and Hiro Ito, 2006, "What Matters for Financial Development? Capital Controls, Institutions, and Interactions," *Journal of Development Economics*, Vol. 81, No. 1, pp. 163–92. Available via the Internet: www.web.pdx.edu/~ito.

Claessens, Stijn, and Enrico C. Perotti, forthcoming, "Finance and Inequality: Channels and Evidence," *Journal of Comparative Economics.*

Cragg, Michael I., and Mario Epelbaum, 1996, "Why Has Wage Dispersion Grown in Mexico? Is It the Incidence of Reforms or the Growing Demand for Skills?" *Journal of Development Economics,* Vol. 51, No. 1, pp. 99–116.

Davis, Donald R., and Prachi Mishra, 2007, "Stolper-Samuelson Is Dead: And Other Crimes of Both Theory and Data," in *Globalization and Poverty,* ed. by Ann Harrison (Chicago: University of Chicago Press), pp. 87–107.

Deaton, Angus, 2003, "Measuring Poverty in a Growing World (or Measuring Growth in a Poor World)," NBER Working Paper No. 9822 (Cambridge, Massachusetts: National Bureau of Economic Research).

———, and Salman Zaidi, 2002, "Guidelines for Constructing Consumption Aggregates for Welfare Analysis," LSMS Working Paper No. 135 (Washington: World Bank).

Deininger, Klaus, and Lyn Squire, 1998, "New Ways of Looking at Old Issues: Inequality and Growth," *Journal of Development Economics,* Vol. 57, No. 2, pp. 259–87.

Demirgüç-Kunt, Asli, and Ross Levine, 2007, "Finance and Opportunity: Financial Systems and Intergenerational Persistence of Relative Incomes" (unpublished; Washington: World Bank).

Fajnzylber, Pablo, and Daniel Lederman, 1999, "Economic Reforms and Total Factor Productivity Growth in Latin America and the Caribbean (1950–95)—An Empirical Note," Policy Research Working Paper No. 2114 (Washington: World Bank).

Fallon, Peter R., and Robert E.B. Lucas, 2002, "The Impact of Financial Crises on Labor Markets, Household Incomes, and Poverty: A Review of Evidence," *The World Bank Research Observer,* Vol. 17, No. 1, pp. 21–45.

Feenstra, Robert C., and Gordon H. Hanson, 1996, "Globalization, Outsourcing, and Wage Inequality," *American Economic Review,* Vol. 86, No. 2, pp. 240–45.

Fishlow, Albert, and Karen Parker, eds., 1999, *Growing Apart: The Causes and Consequences of Global Wage Inequality* (New York: Council on Foreign Relations Press).

Forsyth, Justin, 2000, "Growth and Poor," Letters to the Editor, *The Economist* (June 10–17), p. 6.

Goldberg, Pinelopi K., and Nina Pavcnik, 2005, "Trade, Wages, and the Political Economy of Trade Protection: Evidence from the Colombian Trade Reforms," *Journal of International Economics,* Vol. 66, No. 1, pp. 75–105.

———, 2007, "Distributional Effects of Globalization in Developing Countries," *Journal of Economic Literature,* Vol. 45 (March), pp. 39–82.

Hanson, Gordon H., 2007, "Globalization, Labor Income, and Poverty in Mexico," in *Globalization and Poverty,* ed. by Ann Harrison (Chicago: University of Chicago Press), pp. 417–56.

———, and Ann E. Harrison, 1999, "Trade Liberalization and Wage Inequality in Mexico," *Industrial and Labor Relations Review,* Vol. 52, No. 2, pp. 271–88.

Heston, Alan, Robert Summers, and Bettina Aten, 2006, Penn World Table Version 6.2, Center for International Comparisons of Production, Income and Prices at the University of Pennsylvania (September).

International Monetary Fund, 2007, "Reaping the Benefits of Financial Globalization" (Washington: International Monetary Fund). Available via the Internet: www.imf.org/external/np/res/docs/2007/0607.htm.

Jorgenson, Dale W., and Khuong Vu, 2005, "Information Technology and the World Economy," *Scandinavian Journal of Economics,* Vol. 107 (December), pp. 631–50.

Kose M. Ayhan, Eswar Prasad, Kenneth Rogoff, and Shang-Jin Wei, 2006, "Financial Globalization: A Reappraisal," NBER Working Paper No. 12484 (Cambridge, Massachusetts: National Bureau of Economic Research).

Kumar, Utsav, and Prachi Mishra, forthcoming, "Trade Liberalization and Wage Inequality: Evidence from India," *Review of Development Economics.*

Kuznets, Simon, 1955, "Economic Growth and Income Inequality," *American Economic Review,* Vol. 45 (March), pp. 1–28.

Lane, Philip R., and Gian Maria Milesi-Ferretti, 2006, "The External Wealth of Nations Mark II: Revised and Extended Estimates of Foreign Assets and Liabilities, 1970–2004," IMF Working Paper 06/69 (Washington: International Monetary Fund).

Levine, Ross, 2004, "Finance and Growth: Theory and Evidence," NBER Working Paper No. 10766 (Cambridge, Massachusetts: National Bureau of Economic Research).

Lin, T., J. Zhuang, and D. Yarcia, forthcoming, "China's Inequality: Evidence from Group Income Data, 1985–2004," ERD Working Paper Series (Manila: Asian Development Bank, Economics and Research Department).

Meyer, Bruce, and James Sullivan, 2006, "Three Decades of Consumption and Income Poverty," National Poverty Center Working Paper Series No. 06–35 (Ann Arbor: University of Michigan, National Poverty Center).

Milanovic, Branko, 2005a, "Can We Discern the Effect of Globalization on Income Distribution? Evidence from Household Surveys," *The World Bank Economic Review*, Vol. 19, pp. 21–44.

———, 2005b, *World Apart: Measuring International and Global Inequality* (Princeton, New Jersey: Princeton University Press).

———, 2006, "Global Income Inequality: What It Is and Why It Matters," *World Economics*, Vol. 7, No. 1.

Mookherjee, Dilip, and Anthony F. Shorrocks, 1982, "A Decomposition Analysis of the Trend in U.K. Income Inequality," *Economic Journal*, Vol. 92 (December), pp. 886–902.

National Sample Survey Organisation, 1983–88, 1993–94, 1999–2000, "Employment and Unemployment Schedule 10.0" (New Delhi: Ministry of Statistics and Program Implementation, Government of India).

Nehru, Vikram, and Ashok Dhareshwar, 1993, "A New Database on Physical Capital Stock: Sources, Methodology and Results," *Rivista de Analisis Economico*, Vol. 8, No. 1, pp. 37–59.

Nicita, Alessandro, 2004, "Who Benefited from Trade Liberalization in Mexico? Measuring the Effects on Household Welfare," World Bank Policy Research Working Paper No. 3265 (Washington: World Bank).

Overholt, William, 2003, "Exposing the Myths," RAND Corporation. Available via the Internet: www.rand.org/commentary/111703SCMP.html.

Pavcnik, Nina, Andreas Blom, Pinelopi Goldberg, and Norbert Schady, 2004, "Trade Liberalization and Industry Wage Structure: Evidence from Brazil," *The World Bank Economic Review*, Vol. 18, No. 3, pp. 319–44.

Prasad, Eswar, Kenneth Rogoff, Shang-Jin Wei, and Ayhan Kose, 2007, "Financial Globalization, Growth, and Volatility in Developing Countries," in *Globalization and Poverty*, ed. by Ann Harrison (Chicago: University of Chicago Press), pp. 457–516.

Psacharopoulos, George, and Harry Anthony Patrinos, 2004, "Returns to Investment in Education: A Further Update," *Education Economics*, Vol. 12 (August), pp. 111–34.

Ravallion, Martin, 2003, "The Debate on Globalization, Poverty, and Inequality: Why Measurement Matters," World Bank Policy Research Working Paper No. 3038 (Washington: World Bank).

———, and Shaohua Chen, 1996, "What Can New Survey Data Tell Us About Recent Changes in Distribution and Poverty?" World Bank Policy Research Working Paper No. 1694 (Washington: World Bank).

Robertson, Raymond, 2004, "Relative Prices and Wage Inequality: Evidence from Mexico," *Journal of International Economics*, Vol. 64, No. 2, pp. 387–409.

Shorrocks, Anthony F., 1980, "The Class of Additively Decomposable Inequality Measures," *Econometrica*, Vol. 48, No. 3, pp. 613–25.

State Statistics Bureau, 1988–1995, *Urban Statistical Yearbook of China* (various volumes) (Beijing: Xinhua Press).

———, 1999, *Fifty Years of the Cities in New China: 1949–1998* (Beijing: China Statistics Publishing House).

Stolper, Wolfgang F., and Paul A. Samuelson, 1941, "Protection and Real Wages," *Review of Economic Studies*, Vol. 9 (November), pp. 58–73.

The Economist, 2000, "Growth Is Good" (May 27).

Topalova, Petia, 2007, "Trade Liberalization, Poverty, and Inequality: Evidence from Indian Districts," in *Globalization and Poverty*, ed. by Ann Harrison (Chicago: University of Chicago Press).

United Nations Conference on Trade and Development, 2006, *World Investment Report 2006*, "FDI from Developing and Transition Economies: Implications for Development," Annex Table A.I.2. Available via the Internet: www.unctad.org/wir.

United Nations University—World Institute for Development Economics Research (WIDER), 2005, World Income Inequality Database (Helsinki: WIDER).

Wei, Shang-Jin, and Yi Wu, 2007, "Openness and Inequality: Evidence from Within China" (unpublished; Washington: International Monetary Fund).

World Bank, 1997, *Sharing Rising Incomes—Disparities in China* (Washington).

———, 2000, "A Look at Income Inequality," in

Making Transition Work for Everyone: Poverty and Inequality in Europe and Central Asia (Washington), pp. 139–77.

———, 2006, *World Development Report 2006: Equity and Development* (Washington).

———, 2007, "Income Distribution, Inequality, and Those Left Behind," in *Global Economic Prospects: Managing the Next Wave of Globalization* (Washington), pp. 67–99.

Zhang, Yin, and Guanghua Wan, 2006, "Globalization and the Urban Poor in China," United Nations University—World Institute for Development Economics Research (WIDER) Paper No. 2006/42 (Helsinki: WIDER).

CHAPTER 5

THE CHANGING DYNAMICS OF THE GLOBAL BUSINESS CYCLE

World growth in recent years has been much more rapid than at any time since the oil price surges of the 1970s. This growth is being shared across countries to an unprecedented degree. Moreover, output volatility in most countries and regions has significantly declined. This chapter analyzes these changes in business cycle characteristics and finds that the increasing stability and the associated increase in the durability of expansions largely reflect sources that are likely to prove persistent. In particular, improvements in the conduct of monetary and fiscal policy, as well as in broader institutional quality, have all reduced output volatility. The prospects for future stability should, however, not be taken for granted. Low average volatility does not mean that the business cycle is dead. The abrupt end to the period of strong and sustained growth in the 1960s and early 1970s provides a useful cautionary lesson about what can happen if policies do not adjust to tackle emerging risks in a timely manner.

From 2004 to the present, the world economy has enjoyed its strongest period of sustained growth since the late 1960s and early 1970s, while inflation has remained at low levels. Not only has recent global growth been high but the expansion has also been broadly shared across countries. The volatility of growth has fallen, which may seem especially surprising because the more volatile emerging market and developing countries account for a rising share of the global economy.

How much of the recent performance of the global economy is a result of good policies, solid institutions, and structural changes, and how much is pure "good luck"? Can policymakers be confident that output volatility will remain low and that the current global expansion will continue for a long time? Or is the recent stability likely to come to an end?

This chapter aims to shed light on these questions in two separate ways. First, it compares the current global growth cycle with earlier periods, including the 1960s—a previous era of strong growth and low volatility. Second, the chapter analyzes the sources of differences, both across countries and over time, in business cycle characteristics such as output volatility and the length of expansions. It follows the recent literature on the "Great Moderation" in the U.S. economy, but extends the analysis to a global context. Further, it focuses on determining to what extent policy actions have helped to bring about an enduring reduction in volatility so as to make expansions more durable.

This chapter finds that, in important ways, the global economy has recently displayed greater stability than observed even in the 1960s. In particular, the volatility of output has declined in most countries, and growth is more broadly shared across countries than previously observed. Further, the chapter suggests that the increase in the durability of expansions largely reflects sources that are likely to prove persistent, including improvements in the conduct of monetary and fiscal policy, as well as in broader institutional quality.

The prospects for future stability, however, should not be taken for granted. Low average volatility does not rule out occasional recessions. More broadly, the abrupt end to the period of strong and stable growth in the 1960s and early 1970s provides a cautionary tale of what can happen if policies do not respond to risks and new challenges in the global economic system as they arise. The Bretton Woods system of fixed exchange rate parities worked well for an extended period. In the end, however, it did not prove sufficiently resilient as imbalances from

Note: The main authors of this chapter are Martin Sommer and Nikola Spatafora, with support from Angela Espiritu and Allen Stack. Massimiliano Marcellino provided consultancy support.

Figure 5.1. World Growth Has Been Strong and Stable[1]

World growth is very high compared with the past three decades. However, the strength of the current expansion does not appear unusual compared with the 1950s and 1960s. That said, the low dispersion of detrended growth across countries is unprecedented. World output volatility has been falling since its peak during the 1970s and, for a median country, output volatility is now one-third lower than in the 1960s.

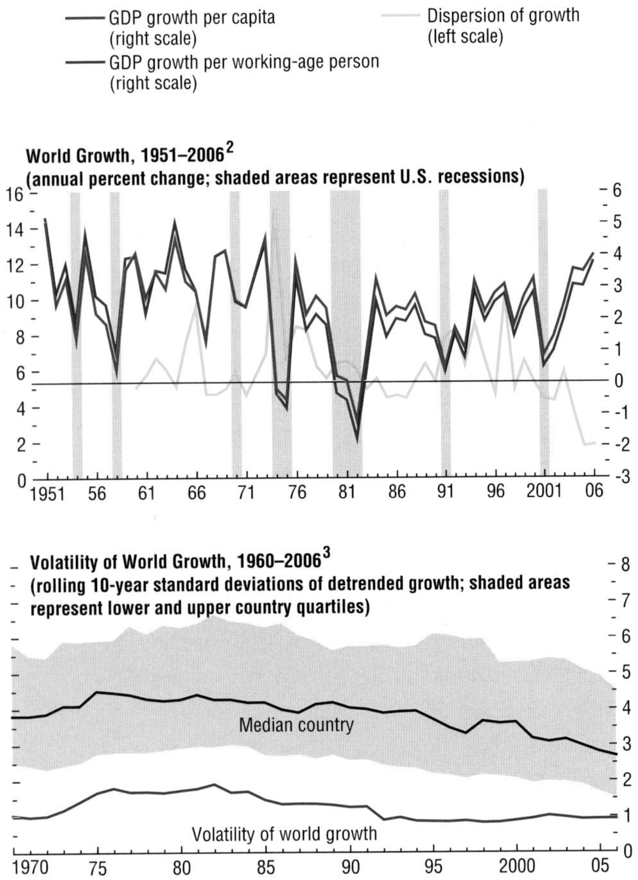

Sources: Heston, Summers, and Aten (2006); Maddison (2007); United Nations, Population Prospects: The 2004 Revision Population database; World Bank, World Development Indicators database (2007); and IMF staff calculations.

[1]See Appendix 5.1 for information on country group composition.

[2]Growth of world real GDP per capita and working-age person aggregated using purchasing-power-parity weights. Dispersion of growth is measured as the standard deviation of detrended GDP growth across countries. Shading represents U.S. recessions identified from annual real GDP per capita series. See Appendix 5.1 for details.

[3]Volatility in 1970 is calculated as the standard deviation of detrended growth over 1961–70, and so on.

expansionary fiscal and monetary policies in the United States led to overheating and eventual inflation—even before the first oil price shock of 1973–74. The 1970s subsequently turned out to be the decade of weakest growth in the post–World War II period.

Global Business Cycles: A Historical Perspective

The global economy is now in its fifth year of strong expansion. As noted above, the world growth rate is very high compared with the past three decades. Compared with earlier post–World War II cycles, however, the strength of the current expansion is not unusual. During the 1960s, world growth (expressed as growth in purchasing power parity (PPP)-weighted GDP per working-age person, to account for demographic shifts) averaged 3.4 percent, slightly above the 3.2 percent outcome over the past three years.[1] That said, one feature of the current expansion is clearly unique, even compared with the 1960s—strong growth is being shared by most countries, as evidenced by the unusually low dispersion of growth (relative to trend) across countries (Figure 5.1). In other words, virtually all countries are doing well.

As with growth rates, the length of the current expansion has not reached historical highs. The present world cycle is only half the length of those in the 1980s and 1990s. Similarly, in the United States, the current cyclical expansion has not matched the long expansions of the previous two decades (Figure 5.2). In the major European economies and Japan, the length of the current expansion stacks up well against those

[1]Expressed in per capita terms, current world growth is actually higher than in the 1960s—over the past three years, average world per capita growth was 3.6 percent, compared with 3.3 percent during the 1960s. The comparison of per capita growth rates between the two periods is influenced, however, by particularly strong population growth in the 1960s and slowing population growth thereafter. Since demographic shifts are typically very slow, the distinction between calculations using per capita and per working-age-person terms is unimportant for the chapter's analysis of business cycle duration and volatility.

of the recent decades, although the expansions were on average much longer in the 1950s and 1960s, supported by high trend growth.[2]

A comparison of business cycles over the past century points to a secular increase in the length of expansions and a decrease in the amount of time economies spend in recessions.[3] In advanced economies, deep recessions have virtually disappeared in the post–World War II period. That said, the 1970s represented a temporary break from the trend of ever-longer expansions in moderately growing advanced economies. In part, this reflected unprecedented oil supply disruptions and the productivity slowdown, but in part also monetary policy mistakes.[4]

[2]In this chapter, expansions are defined as periods of nonnegative growth of real GDP per capita. Analogously, recessions are defined as periods of falling real GDP per capita. Most analysis in this chapter therefore adopts the concept of the "classical" business cycle as discussed in, for example, Artis, Marcellino, and Proietti (2004) and Harding and Pagan (2001)—see Appendix 5.1 for details. Expansions are identified using annual data and in per capita terms to allow for broad comparisons across countries and over time. Expansions based on quarterly data would likely be shorter for many countries. There are also notable differences in cyclical behavior within regions: for example, the United Kingdom has not experienced a recession since 1991 based on this chapter's definition of business cycles.

[3]The stabilization of post–World War II business cycles relative to the pre-war period has been attributed to a number of factors, including higher average growth rates; lower share of commodity-linked sectors; introduction of deposit insurance, which reduced the number of banking panics; and the pursuit of macroeconomic stabilization policies—although at times policy mistakes destabilized output (Romer, 1999). In the academic literature, there is a vigorous debate about the quality of pre-war GDP data and the nature of pre-war cycles; see Balke and Gordon (1989); Diebold and Rudebusch (1992); and Romer (1989) for a detailed discussion.

[4]See Romer and Romer (2002) and DeLong (1997) for a discussion of U.S. monetary policy during the 1970s. Broadly, monetary policy was too accommodative during the period, partly reflecting unrealistically low estimates of the natural rate of unemployment. The eventual tightening of monetary policy in response to double-digit inflation caused a recession in the early 1980s. Orphanides (2003b) suggests that incomplete real-time information about the economy may have increased the likelihood of policy mistakes in the 1970s, especially in the period of difficult-to-observe productivity slowdown.

Figure 5.2. Expansions in Historical Perspective[1]

(Years; current cycle includes expected outcome for 2007)

As in the case of growth, the length of the current expansion has generally not yet reached historical highs. In China and India, long expansions driven by rapid growth are comparable with the post–World War II experience of some European economies, Japan, and the newly industrialized Asian economies (NIEs). In the key economies of Africa, Latin America, and the Middle East, performance was mixed during the 1980s and 1990s, but the current expansions of these economies are the longest in three decades.

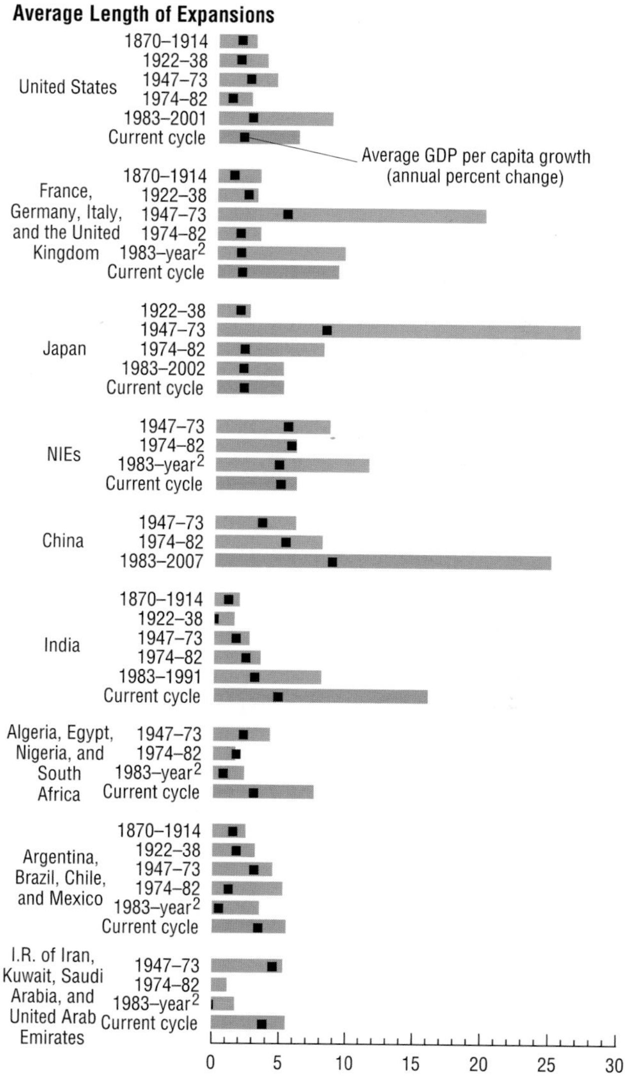

Sources: Heston, Summers, and Aten (2006); Maddison (2007); World Bank, World Development Indicators database (2007); and IMF staff estimates.

[1]Expansions are defined as periods with nonnegative annual real GDP per capita growth. See Appendix 5.1 for details. Data for country groups refer to group medians. The current cycle includes the expected outcome for 2007.

[2]The period starting in 1983 ends as follows: Europe: France (1993), Germany (2003), Italy (2005), and the United Kingdom (1991); NIEs: Hong Kong SAR (2001), Korea (1998), Singapore (2003), and Taiwan Province of China (2001); Africa: Algeria (2002), Egypt (1997), Nigeria (2004), and South Africa (1992); Latin America: Argentina, Brazil, Mexico (2002), and Chile (1999); and Middle East: I.R. of Iran (2001), Kuwait (2002), Saudi Arabia (2002), and the United Arab Emirates (1998).

Figure 5.3. Recessions in Historical Perspective[1]

In advanced economies, deep recessions have almost disappeared in the post–World War II period, although advanced economies spent a considerable amount of time in recessions during 1974–82 owing to supply shocks, productivity slowdowns, and policy swings. In moderately growing emerging market and developing countries, the frequency of recessions has been significantly higher than in the advanced economies, despite some improvements over the past couple of decades.

Average Length and Share of Time Spent in Recessions

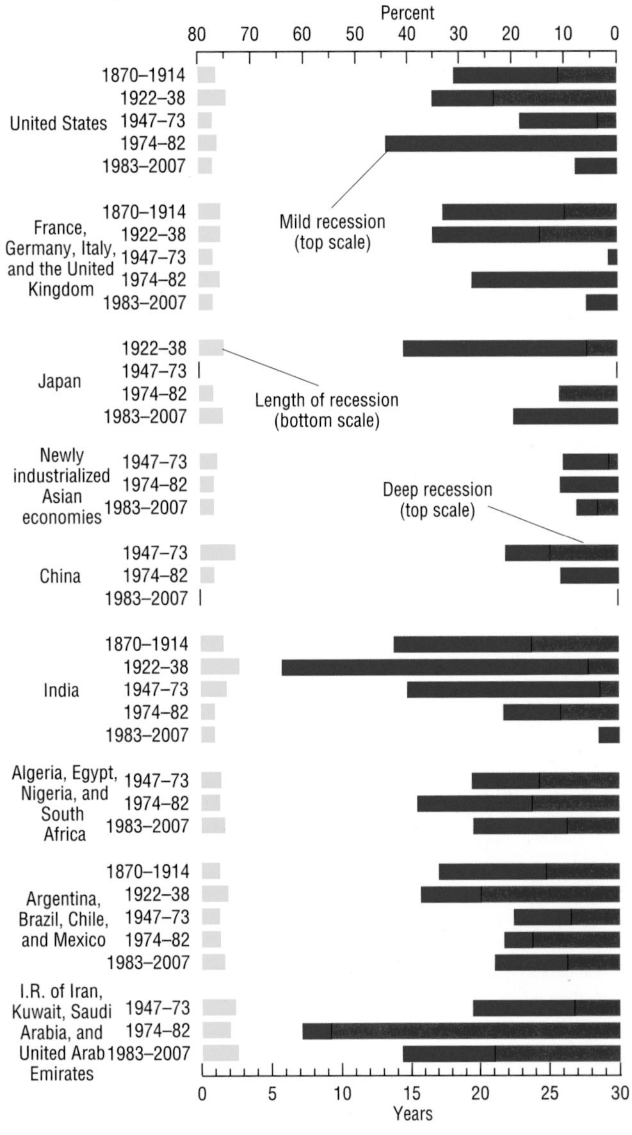

Sources: Heston, Summers, and Aten (2006); Maddison (2007); World Bank, World Development Indicators database (2007); and IMF staff estimates.
[1]Recessions are defined as periods with negative annual real GDP per capita growth. See Appendix 5.1 for details. Deep recessions are defined as recessions with a cumulative output loss greater than 3 percent. Data for country groups refer to group medians.

In emerging market and developing countries, the long-term trend toward improved business cycle dynamics has been more mixed. In Asia, the current long expansions in China and India are strikingly similar to the sustained post-war expansions in western Europe, Japan, and the newly industrialized Asian economies (NIEs). By contrast, the four largest Latin American economies have not seen an increase in the durability of expansions since the 1970s, owing to recurrent fiscal and currency crises. Likewise, the share of time these economies have spent in recessions has not declined (Figure 5.3). Average improvements among the four largest African and Middle Eastern economies have until recently been fairly modest. On the upside, the current expansions in developing regions are the longest in three decades.

At the country level, past expansions have ended for a variety of reasons, including unsustainable fiscal or external imbalances, monetary policy tightening in the face of rising inflation, cross-country spillovers, commodity and asset price swings, and associated financial squeezes.[5] Many of the same factors also tended to slow down world growth, especially when causing a recession in the United States or reducing growth in a broad group of countries. It is important to recognize that some of the factors triggering recessions were at times considered "new." For instance, the currency crises in some Asian economies (for example, in Indonesia and Korea in 1997) were linked to financial and external vulnerabilities that were not well identified beforehand and whose importance was not well understood.[6] Clearly, the task of maintaining expansions requires policymakers to adapt because the process of trade and financial globalization may have generated new risks and

[5]See Chapter 3 in the April 2002 *World Economic Outlook;* Dell'Ariccia, Detragiache, and Rajan (2005); and Fuhrer and Schuh (1998).

[6]Policymakers later responded to these crises through major improvements in financial sector surveillance, including through the IMF–World Bank Financial Sector Assessment Programs. See Ito (2007) for a discussion of the Asian currency crisis.

vulnerabilities—for example, the losses associated with highly leveraged investments in the U.S. subprime mortgage market have created distress in the banking sector in many advanced economies, raising concerns about a possible credit crunch (see Chapter 1). Looking beyond the most recent market developments, the policy debate has also focused on the potential risks arising from global imbalances or the linkages between monetary and prudential policies and sustained asset price booms. For example, White (2006) suggests that successful inflation targeting may have led to increased vulnerability of economies to an excessive buildup of asset prices.

Has the World Economy Become More Stable?

One important business cycle characteristic is output volatility. Together with the trend growth rate, volatility determines the amount of time that economies spend in expansions or recessions. The volatility of global growth, as measured by the rolling 10-year standard deviation of world GDP growth (PPP weighted), has fallen progressively since its 1970s peak.[7] The standard deviation of world output growth over the past 10 years has been 0.9 percent, which is only slightly lower than during the 1960s—another period of strong and sustained growth. This outcome at the aggregate level, however, masks a more substantial, one-third reduction in volatility at the country level between the 1960s and the present—the standard deviation of median country growth declined from 3.8 percent to 2.7 percent (see Figure 5.1). The different degrees of volatility moderation at the world and country levels arise because growth outcomes were less correlated across countries in the 1960s owing to more limited trade and financial linkages. Output fluctuations of individual countries therefore tended to offset one another to a greater degree during the 1960s.[8]

The evolution of output volatility over time can be broken down into several phases. In advanced economies, volatility was high in the 1950s, partly as a result of the boom-and-bust cycle associated with the Korean War and the rapid, but volatile, post-war reconstruction phase in Europe and Japan (Figure 5.4; output volatility during the 1950s is captured by the data point for 1960). Volatility declined during the 1960s, but it rose again in the 1970s as a result of oil supply disruptions and stop-go macroeconomic policies. After the disinflation of the early 1980s, volatility in advanced economies began to fall in a sustained way and is currently only about one-half of that seen during the 1960s.

Volatility has also fallen over time in emerging market and developing countries, although this decline occurred much later than in advanced economies. Looking at the performance of developing regions by decades, output volatility varied greatly during the 1960s,[9] with some countries, such as those in Latin America, experiencing a relatively stable period, while others, notably China, experienced high volatility.[10] Oil shocks, increases in other commodity prices, and spillovers from advanced economies increased output volatility in most emerging market and developing countries during the 1970s. Unlike in the advanced economies, however, volatility stayed high or increased further during the 1980s and much of the 1990s as

[7]The 10-year window was chosen because the length of a typical cycle in advanced economies increased to about 10 years during the 1980s and 1990s.

[8]See Box 4.3 in the April 2007 *World Economic Outlook.*

[9]Data limitations do not allow a comprehensive analysis of volatility in developing countries in the 1950s. Specifically, volatility of growth cannot be reliably calculated for many countries in Africa, Asia, and the Middle East because the available GDP data are often interpolations among infrequent benchmark estimates and, therefore, annual growth rates tend to be smoothed. In Latin America (for which more accurate data are available), output volatility was higher than in advanced economies during the decade (see Figure 5.4).

[10]The extremely high volatility of the Chinese economy was, to a large extent, caused by the Great Leap Forward economic plan and the Cultural Revolution (launched in 1958 and 1966, respectively).

Figure 5.4. Volatility of Growth in the Main World Regions[1]

(Rolling 10-year standard deviations of detrended growth—year 1960 represents volatility over 1951–60)

Advanced economies quickly stabilized after the oil shocks of the 1970s. Their volatility is now about one-half of their levels in the 1960s. Output stabilization was more gradual and modest in emerging market and developing countries, as many economies experienced debt, currency, and banking crises.

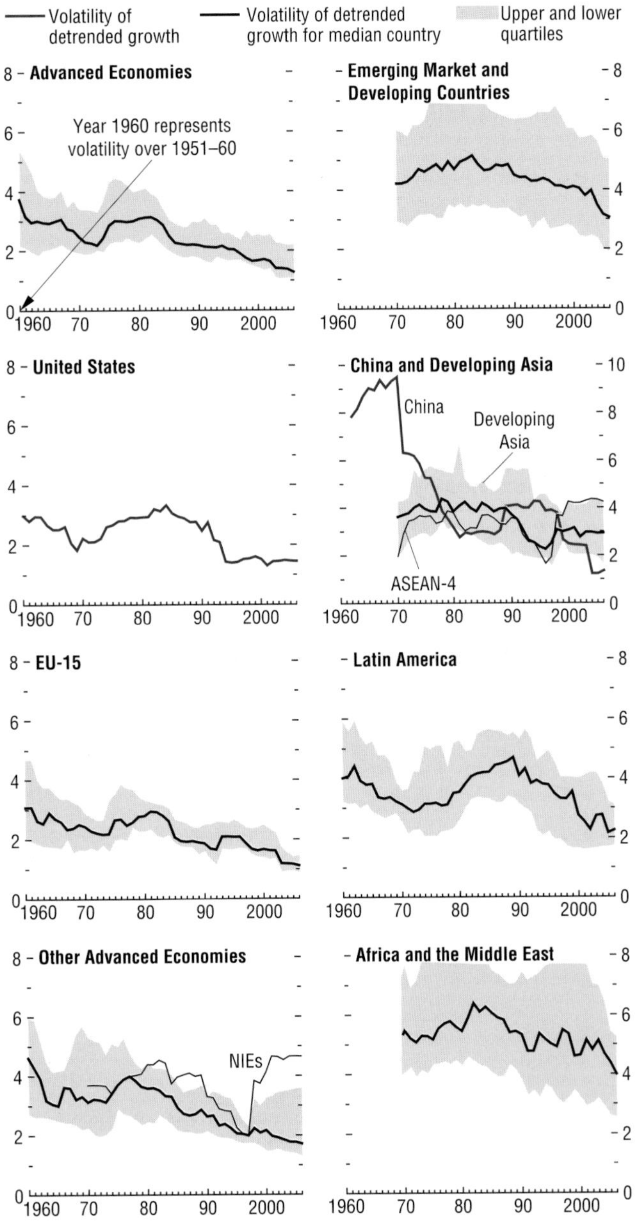

Sources: Heston, Summers, and Aten (2006); Maddison (2007); World Bank, World Development Indicators database (2007); and IMF staff calculations.

[1]Volatility in 1960 is calculated as the standard deviation of detrended growth over 1951–60, and so on. For some regions, volatility measures covering the 1950s are not shown due to the lack of accurate data on annual growth. See Appendix 5.1 for information on country group composition.

countries were buffeted by debt crises (especially in Latin America and Africa) and banking and currency crises (in Asia, central and eastern Europe, and Latin America). Some countries also experienced high volatility during their transition from centrally planned to market economies.[11] Despite a big decline in recent years, the output volatility in developing economies continues to be significantly higher than in advanced economies, partly as a result of structural differences, such as the greater weight of agriculture or commodity-related sectors. The median standard deviation of annual growth is currently 3 percent in emerging market and developing countries compared with 1¼ percent in advanced economies.

Volatility decompositions suggest that most of the past changes in the volatility of world growth can be attributed to advanced economies, especially the United States (Figure 5.5).[12] That said, falling output volatility in China contributed noticeably to the lower volatility of world growth during 1996–2006 compared with 1983–95.

[11]In central and eastern Europe, deep recessions associated with the transition from centrally planned to market economies generated very large output volatility during the 1990s. Countries of the former Soviet Union are not included in the analysis because many variables for these countries are not readily available for the period prior to the 1990s. See Chapter 2 in the April 2005 *World Economic Outlook* for a detailed discussion of output volatility in developing countries.

[12]Decompositions of volatility in this section are carried out using the volatility of aggregate world growth, given the computational difficulties of decomposing changes in median values. As a result, the decompositions cannot fully reflect the decline in country-specific volatility between the 1960s and today. Volatility is calculated over four periods (1960–73, 1974–82, 1983–95, and 1996–2006), with years 1973 and 1983 broadly representing the main breaks in the volatility of world growth since 1960. Owing to data limitations, world volatility is not calculated for the 1950s. The contribution of the United States to the changes in world output volatility appears larger than the contribution of the EU-15, because the EU-15 aggregate removes some of the country-specific volatility. In the past, U.S. output volatility was similar to the EU-15 median (see Figure 5.4). To simplify the analysis, the volatility decompositions are calculated using headline rather than per capita growth. However, volatilities of headline and per capita growth tend to be similar for most countries.

Despite the fact that emerging market and developing countries tend to be more volatile than advanced economies, their growing weight has so far not pushed world output volatility higher, mostly because output volatility in China is now as low as in advanced economies.[13]

Figure 5.5 also suggests that the comovement (covariance) of growth across countries is an important factor affecting volatility of world output. The simultaneity of growth decelerations after the oil price shocks of the 1970s illustrates how rising covariance can at times magnify the impact of country volatility on the volatility of world growth. Growing trade and financial integration of economies, especially within regions, has also tended to strengthen cross-country output spillovers (Box 5.1).[14] In particular, the lower volatility of output in the United States contributed a significant portion of the decline in world volatility between the 1960–73 and 1996–2006 periods, but the greater stability of the United States and most other advanced economies was offset largely by the increasing correlation between country growth rates. This increasing correlation can also be seen as reflecting the regional nature of currency crises in emerging markets in the late 1990s and the global slowdown following the bursting of the information technology bubble in 2000.

Further decompositions of world output volatility by expenditure components show that consumption and investment volatility have both shifted significantly over time (Figure 5.6). The rise in overall volatility during 1974–82 was to a large extent due to the rise in investment volatility. This finding is intuitively appealing because

[13]If the current world volatility were recalculated using country weights from the 1960s, it would be almost the same as the world volatility calculated using the current weights. However, if the country volatility from the 1960s were combined with the current country weights, the standard deviation of world growth would increase from 0.9 percent (the actual outcome for 1996–2006) to 1.5 percent. This result reflects mostly the significant decline of volatility in China and, to a more limited extent, in other developing economies since the 1960s.

[14]See also Chapter 4 in the April 2007 *World Economic Outlook*.

Figure 5.5. Decomposition of Changes in World Output Volatility by Region[1]

(Variance of real GDP growth)

Volatility of world growth was particularly high during 1974–82, a period characterized by oil supply disruptions and policy swings. At the aggregate level, the moderation of world volatility has been fairly small compared with 1960–73, although since then many countries have experienced significant reductions in volatility (see Figure 5.4). Greater trade and financial integration have increased the correlation of growth across countries, and this has largely offset the decline of volatility at the country level. Most of the past changes in world output volatility can be attributed to advanced economies, especially the United States.

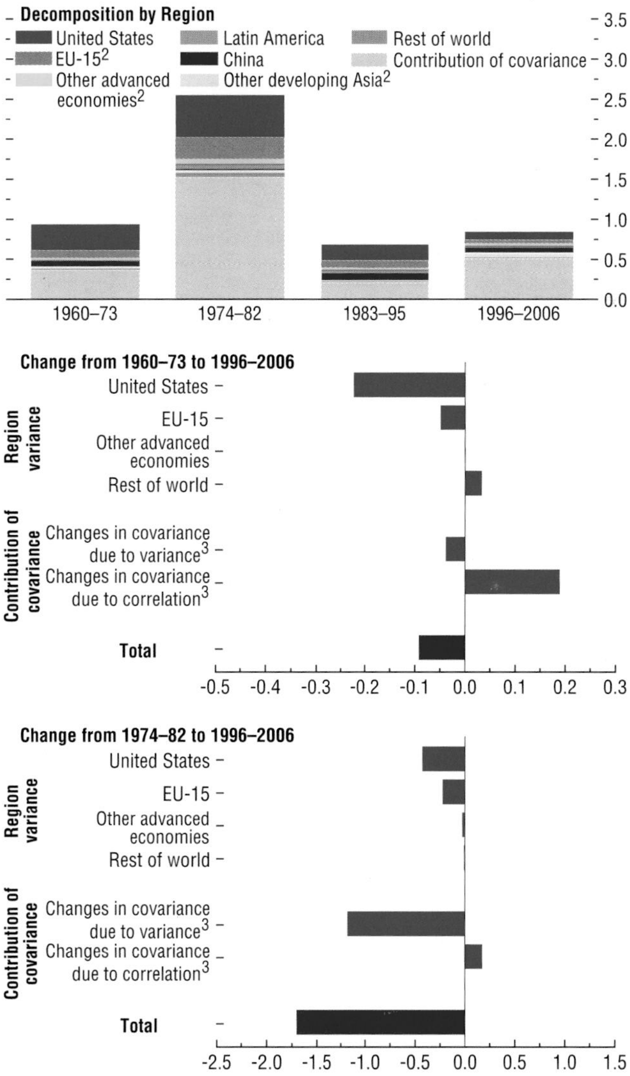

Sources: Heston, Summers, and Aten (2006); Maddison (2007); World Bank, World Development Indicators database (2007); and IMF staff calculations.

[1]Volatility is measured as the variance of real purchasing-power-parity-weighted GDP growth over a period. Given data limitations, world output volatility cannot be reliably calculated for the 1950s.

[2]See Appendix 5.1 for details on country groupings.

[3]Contributions of covariance to the changes in output volatility were decomposed into contributions due to changes in the variance of regions and changes in the correlation among them. See Appendix 5.1 for details.

Figure 5.6. Decomposition of Changes in World Output Volatility by Expenditure Component[1]

(Variance of real GDP growth)

Consumption and investment volatility have both shifted significantly over time. The rise in overall volatility during 1974–82 was, to a large extent, due to the rise in investment volatility, as supply disruptions, shifts in productivity trends, and policy swings induced volatility in investment plans. The mild decline in world output volatility from the 1960s to the present is mostly attributable to the lower volatility of consumption.

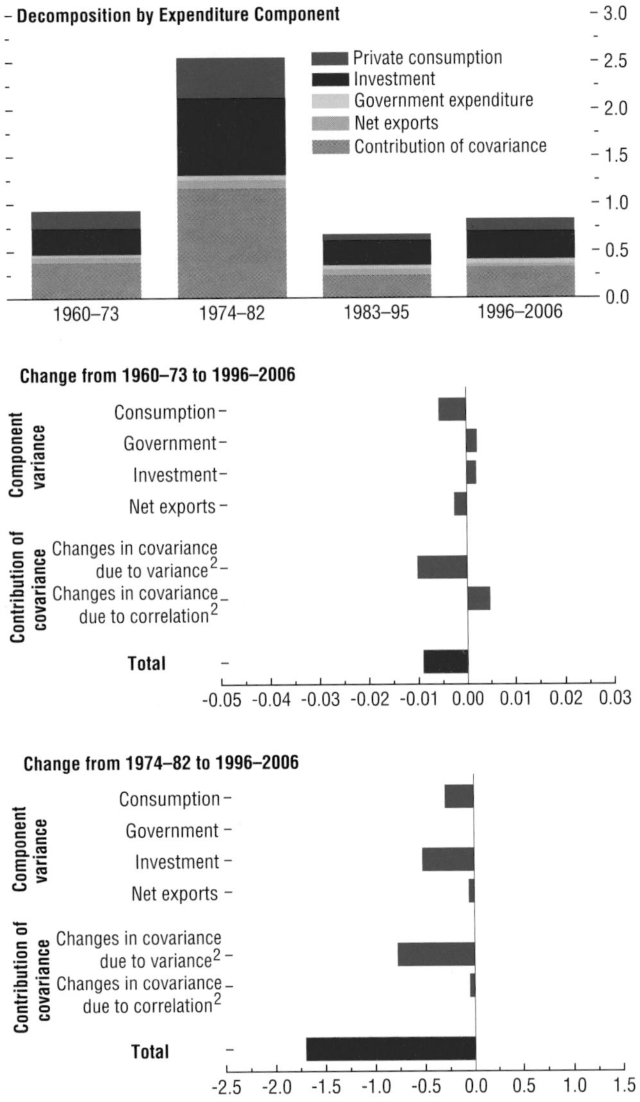

Sources: Heston, Summers, and Aten (2006); World Bank, World Development Indicators database (2007); and IMF staff calculations.

[1]Volatility is measured as the variance of real purchasing-power-parity-weighted GDP growth over a period. Given data limitations, world output volatility cannot be reliably calculated for the 1950s.

[2]Contributions of covariance to the changes in output volatility were decomposed into contributions due to changes in the variance of expenditure components and changes in the correlation among them. See Appendix 5.1 for details.

the period was characterized by repeated supply disruptions, shifts in productivity trends, and policy swings, all of which induced volatility in the expected profitability of investment plans. Nevertheless, the decline in world output volatility from the 1960s to the present is attributable mostly to lower volatility of consumption rather than investment. Some of this latter result is certainly driven by the nature of events unfolding over the past decade, including a significant reduction of investment in post-crisis and post-bubble economies. Indeed, volatility of investment was somewhat lower during 1983–95 compared with the past decade. The finding, however, suggests that any explanations for the current output stability need to include factors that affect consumer behavior, such as the rising availability of financing to smooth consumption over time.[15]

Looking in more detail at the United States (Figure 5.7), the decline in output volatility since the 1960s has indeed been driven largely by consumer behavior (through a variety of channels, including lower volatility of consumer spending, residential investment, and lower correlation between consumption and investment) and by the government.[16] The role of inventory investment in explaining the reduction in U.S. output volatility between 1960–73 and 1996–2006 is surprisingly limited,[17]

[15]Dynan, Elmendorf, and Sichel (2006) make a similar point about consumption volatility in the context of U.S. data. While the aggregate world data do not identify government expenditures as the major source of output volatility, fiscal policy in the form of, for instance, procyclical spending or excessive debt accumulation has been a significant driver of output volatility in many countries (see the next section). These country-specific effects, however, disappear in the aggregate world data.

[16]During the 1960s, government expenditures increased U.S. output volatility through volatile defense spending associated with the Vietnam War.

[17]Several studies have highlighted the contribution of improved inventory management techniques and lower volatility of inventory investment to the reduction of *quarterly* output volatility in the United States since the 1980s (McConnell and Perez-Quiros, 2000; and Kahn, McConnell, and Perez-Quiros, 2002). However, the role of inventories is greatly diminished in the annual data, especially when considering volatility changes between

although—for the same reasons as at the world level—the lower volatilities of inventories and business fixed investment have contributed to the moderation of U.S. output volatility relative to the 1970s.

Looking forward, the performance of emerging market and developing countries will be increasingly important for the stability of the world economy. In 2006, these economies accounted for over 40 percent of global GDP, two-thirds of world GDP growth (using PPP weights), and about one-third of world trade (at market exchange rates). China and India alone now account for one-fifth of the world PPP-adjusted GDP, up from 10 percent in 1990. The output paths of China and India have broadly followed the output paths of other economies that experienced rapid expansions earlier, although China has been able to maintain extremely high growth for a longer period of time than Japan and the NIEs (including Korea), the previous best performers during the growth takeoff episodes (Figure 5.8). Interestingly, the volatility trajectories of rapidly growing economies have also been similar. Initially, these economies tended to exhibit much higher volatility than world growth. As the economies diversified away from volatile sectors such as agriculture and the policy frameworks improved, their output volatility started to converge to the world average. But these historical comparisons also offer some cautionary tales. Brazil and Mexico were not able to sustain high growth as structural rigidities became binding, and fiscal and currency crises increased volatility in these economies for an extended period. Although the NIEs managed to sustain rapid

the 1960s and today. From a policy perspective, changes in the quarterly fluctuations of inventory investment may not have important welfare implications unless these have a significant longer-lived impact on, for example, consumption growth—which appears unlikely. Another aspect influencing the interpretation of any volatility studies based on quarterly data is that components of quarterly national accounts tend to suffer from much greater measurement error than annual data; for example, Sommer (2007) documents that measurement errors make up a nontrivial fraction of quarterly consumption growth.

Figure 5.7. Decomposition of Changes in U.S. Output Volatility[1]

(Variance of real GDP growth)

The decline in U.S. output volatility since the 1960s has been driven largely by consumer behavior, including through lower volatility of consumer spending, residential investment, and the lower correlation between consumption and investment. Lower volatility of government spending also explains some of the volatility moderation between 1960–73 and 1996–2006.

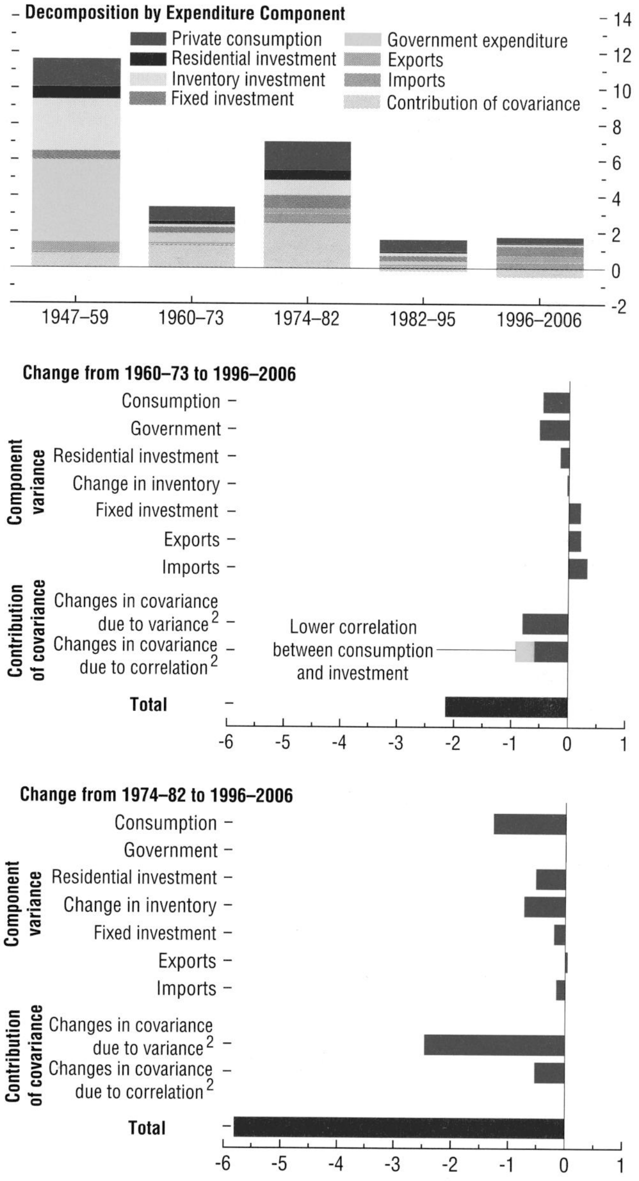

Sources: U.S. Bureau of Economic Analysis; and IMF staff calculations.
[1]Volatility is measured as the variance of real GDP growth over a period.
[2]Contributions of covariance to the changes in output volatility were decomposed into contributions due to changes in the variance of expenditure components and changes in the correlation among them. See Appendix 5.1 for details.

Figure 5.8. Volatility Patterns in Rapidly Growing Economies[1]

(Growth takeoff begins in time t = 0 *on the x-axis)*

The growth paths of China and India have broadly followed the patterns of earlier rapid expansions, although China has been able to sustain strong growth for the longest period of time. Volatility of rapidly growing economies has tended to converge gradually to the world average. However, unaddressed vulnerabilities can trigger recessions or outright crises associated with large increases in volatility, such as in Brazil, Mexico, and Korea.

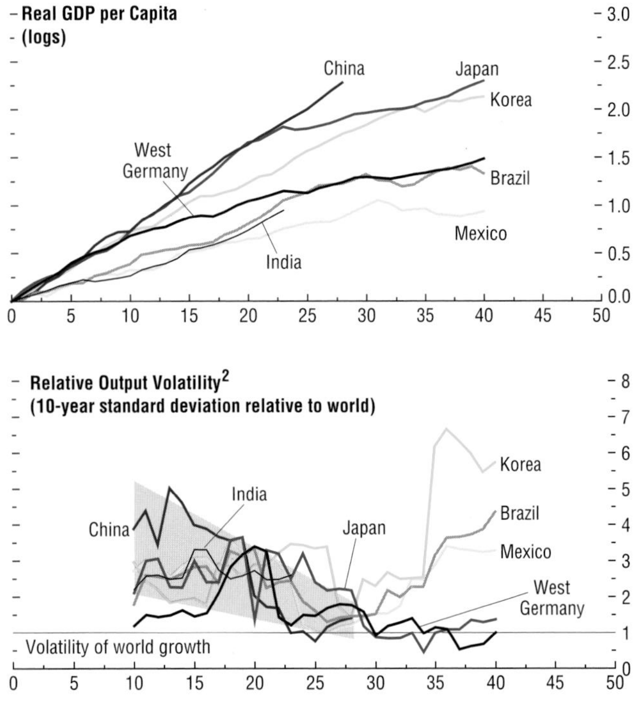

Sources: Heston, Summers, and Aten (2006); Maddison (2007); World Bank, World Development Indicators database (2007); and IMF staff calculations.

[1]Growth takeoff is dated as follows: 1950 for Brazil, 1979 for China, 1984 for India, 1950 for Japan, 1963 for Korea, 1950 for Mexico, and 1950 for West Germany. See Appendix 5.1 for details.

[2]Relative output volatility is defined as the ratio of the rolling 10-year standard deviation of detrended country growth divided by the 10-year standard deviation of detrended world growth over the same period.

growth, expansions in most NIEs did not prove resilient to the Asian crisis and volatility sharply increased. All these experiences suggest that policymakers cannot take the good times for granted and need to continuously identify and address vulnerabilities.

What Is Driving the Moderation of the Global Business Cycle?

What underlying factors explain the differences, both across countries and over time, in output volatility and in the duration of expansions? And are they likely to persist? There has been considerable analysis of the decline in output volatility in the United States since the 1970s (the Great Moderation debate),[18] but work on other advanced economies and on emerging market and developing countries is more limited.[19] Given the growing importance of developing countries in the global economy, this section looks at the broader canvas.

Specifically, the analysis considers a sample of nearly 80 countries, including both advanced and developing economies over the period 1970–2005, and employs a variety of econometric techniques. It examines the determinants of the volatility of detrended output as well as of four other closely related business cycle characteristics: the share of output lost to recessions and slowdowns, the average length of expansions, the share of time spent in recessions, and the probability of economic expansion for a given country in any given year.[20]

In line with the existing literature, the analysis encompasses a broad range of variables that

[18]See, for instance, Kim and Nelson (1999); Blanchard and Simon (2001); and Arias, Hansen, and Ohanian (2006). Bernanke (2004) provides an overview.

[19]See Dijk, Osborn, and Sensier (2002); Artis, Krolzig, and Toro (2004); and Cecchetti, Flores-Lagunes, and Krause (2006a). Summers (2005) provides an overview.

[20]See Appendix 5.1 for further details. Berg, Ostry, and Zettelmeyer (2006), focusing on trend growth rather than on cyclical fluctuations, use a probability model to analyze the determinants of a different but complementary concept: the length of "growth spells" (that is, periods of significantly higher growth than previously observed).

Box 5.1. Major Economies and Fluctuations in Global Growth

Over the past five years, the world economy has enjoyed the highest growth since the early 1970s, despite a significant slowing of the U.S. economy since 2006 and, earlier, a sluggish recovery in the euro area and Japan. Some observers have argued that the apparently reduced spillovers could mean that the world economy has become more robust to disturbances in major economies, partly because, with new poles such as China and India, there are more sources of growth to pick up the slack.

At the same time, however, the scope for cross-country spillovers from disturbances in major economies has increased with rapidly rising cross-border trade and financial linkages, which could at least partly offset these economies' declining share of global trade growth. Against this background, this box compares recent patterns of business cycle comovement for China and India with those of major industrial countries and analyzes the impact of disturbances in major economies on global growth in a general framework.[1]

Turning first to the experience with international business cycle comovement, the first table reports the extent of output correlations between major economies and different regions for 1960–73 (a period with limited cross-border linkages and, unlike the 1970s and early 1980s, no large global disturbances) and 1996–2006, a period with rapidly rising cross-border linkages.[2] Three findings stand out.

- Business cycle comovement with the new poles indeed increased in the second period compared with the first one. The rise is particularly evident for China. Increased comovement with the new poles is particularly noticeable for countries in Latin America and emerging Asia.
- In industrial countries, comovement with the United States and Germany increased sharply between 1960–73 and 1996–2006, whereas it decreased with Japan.
- In other emerging market and developing countries, and particularly in Latin America, comovement with the United States and Japan increased.

Using the correlations as rough approximations for cross-border spillover effects of disturbances, the results suggest that a disturbance to growth in China could now have substantial spillover effects on some emerging market and developing countries, although the effects on industrial countries would be considerably smaller.

Overall, the picture that emerges is one of increasing business cycle comovement, first, among industrial countries and, second, among China and emerging market economies in Latin America and Asia. In contrast, business cycle comovement between industrial countries and other emerging market and developing countries has risen by less.

Output Comovement with Major Economies, by Region[1]

(Averages by region)

	United States	Germany	Japan	India	China
All countries					
1960–73	0.00	0.07	0.03	0.03	0.07
1996–2006	0.24	0.23	0.23	0.06	0.20
Industrial countries					
1960–73	0.07	0.35	0.25	0.08	0.05
1996–2006	0.54	0.74	0.03	0.04	0.14
Latin America					
1960–73	0.02	0.09	0.05	0.02	0.13
1996–2006	0.26	0.28	0.44	0.15	0.43
Emerging Asia					
1960–73	–0.04	0.08	0.05	–0.07	0.16
1996–2006	0.17	0.06	0.49	0.06	0.25
Africa					
1960–73	–0.05	0.04	–0.02	0.05	0.03
1996–2006	0.11	0.03	0.16	0.05	0.16

Source: IMF staff calculations.

[1]The table reports regional averages of bilateral correlation coefficients with the major economy indicated. Correlations are based on annual growth rates. The regional classification of countries follows that used in Chapter 2.

Note: The main author of this box is Thomas Helbling.

[1]The box draws on Chapter 4 of the April 2007 *World Economic Outlook*.

[2]See Box 4.3 in the April 2007 *World Economic Outlook* on the measurement of international business cycle synchronization. The comparison between the 1960s and more recent periods follows Kose, Otrok, and Whiteman (2005).

Box 5.1 *(concluded)*

What are the main factors determining the impact of disturbances in a major economy on international business cycles and ultimately global growth? Three seem particularly relevant.[3] First, the size of a country's GDP matters, both directly, through its own impact on global growth, and indirectly, through the impact on other countries. For given trade shares, a larger importer will have a greater effect on other countries' external demand (or, in other words, export exposure) as a percent of GDP. In this regard, China has now surpassed most major industrial countries in terms of its share in global GDP and global imports, whereas India's economic size is still relatively small. More generally, the total share of the largest 10 economies has remained broadly unchanged since the early 1970s, in terms of both global GDP and world imports.[4] From this perspective, the scope for other major economies to pick up the slack from another one has thus not changed significantly.

A second factor is the extent of a country's cross-border trade and financial linkages. Numerous empirical studies have found that business cycle comovement tends to rise in tandem with trade and financial linkages.[5] The generally higher comovement among industrial economies, for example, is partly related to more intensive linkages among them, with other variables, such as similarity in stages of development or per capita income, also playing a role. Regarding the new poles, China's trade linkages with other emerging market and developing countries have risen rapidly (see second table), especially in Asia but also elsewhere, which partly explains the rising cyclical comovement reported in the first table.[6] With their rising trade linkages with the new poles, other emerging market and developing countries now trade relatively less with the major industrial countries, suggesting that emerging markets have become *relatively* less dependent on advanced economies. As a share of GDP, however, the total trade of emerging market and developing countries with major industrial countries has increased, partly driving the rising output correlations between these two groups.

The depth of financial linkages among emerging market and developing economies, and between these economies and industrial countries, remains well below the levels found among industrial countries. This helps explains why, on average, business cycle comovement among advanced economies still exceeds the correlations for the other pairings (see first table). Limited financial linkages notwithstanding, emerging market countries have faced common fluctuations in general external financing

Exports to Major Economies, by Region
(In percent of total exports; averages by region)

	Exports to				
	United States	Germany	Japan	India	China
Exports from					
All countries[1]					
1973	17.5	7.4	6.1	0.5	0.8
2006	16.0	5.3	3.8	2.3	6.0
Industrial countries					
1973	12.5	11.6	4.3	0.3	0.5
2006	11.9	12.6	2.9	0.8	2.9
Latin America					
1973	37.8	7.4	4.0	0.1	0.3
2006	27.6	1.7	1.6	0.4	2.6
Emerging Asia					
1973	15.1	3.5	15.0	0.7	1.3
2006	11.9	4.1	6.9	5.9	8.6
Africa					
1973	11.1	7.1	3.5	0.6	1.1
2006	10.3	3.4	2.7	3.3	8.7

Sources: IMF, *Direction of Trade Statistics;* and IMF staff calculations.
[1]90 countries.

[3]See Canova and Dellas (1993); and Baxter and King (1999).

[4]Although the composition of this group has remained unchanged, relative sizes within the group have changed substantially, with those of China and India increasing and those of major industrial countries decreasing.

[5]See, among others, Frankel and Rose (1998); Imbs (2004, 2006); and Baxter and Kouparitsas (2005).

[6]See Moneta and Rüffer (2006).

conditions. Indeed, financial contagion and the attendant financial crises during the late 1990s may be one factor behind the increased business cycle comovement among emerging market countries.[7]

Third, the nature of disturbances plays an important role. Disturbances in a major economy tend to have limited cross-border spillover effects if they are specific to the country or if they are transmitted primarily through trade channels.

- Regarding the reach of disturbances, past episodes with large declines in growth across countries at the same time were characterized by common disturbances that were either truly global in nature (e.g., abrupt oil price changes) or were correlated across countries (e.g., disinflationary policies during the early 1980s).[8]
- As for the limited effects of disturbances transmitted through trade channels, the main reason is that, except for countries in the same region, the effects on external demand are usually small in terms of overall demand. In contrast, spillovers tend to be larger if asset price and/or confidence channels are involved. In this respect, with the continued dominant role of the United States in global financial markets, cross-border spillovers from financial shocks in the United States remain a particular concern.[9]

Against this backdrop, the broad decoupling of Japan from other industrial countries in the late 1990s is not surprising because developments in the Japanese economy at the time were country specific—protracted adjustment after a major asset price boom-bust cycle—with limited apparent global financial market impact.[10] Similarly, because the current U.S. slowdown has been driven by sector-specific developments—primarily in housing but also in manufacturing—with limited impact on broader asset markets until very recently, the spillover effects on growth in other countries outside the region have generally remained small so far.

In sum, the seemingly limited impact of disturbances in major economies on global growth in the current episode to date reflects a number of factors, including the nature of the slowdown in the United States. The new poles likely have played a role as well, primarily through the direct impact of their high growth rates on global growth and their impact on commodity prices (which has benefited many emerging market and developing countries), but also through their impact on growth in emerging Asia and Latin America. Nevertheless, with financial markets around the world now being affected by the fallout from U.S. subprime mortgage difficulties, a broader growth slowdown cannot be ruled out.

[7]See also Kose, Otrok, and Prasad (forthcoming).
[8]See the April 2007 *World Economic Outlook*.
[9]See, among others, Bayoumi and Swiston (2007); and Ehrmann, Fratzscher, and Rigobon (2005).
[10]See, for example, Helbling and Bayoumi (2003); and Stock and Watson (2005).

could explain changes in business cycle characteristics (see Appendix 5.1 for details). The variables include the following:

- *Institutional quality.* Broadly understood, this can increase a country's capacity to reconcile internal political differences. In turn, greater political stability and continuity in policymaking may foster economic stability and sustainability. More specifically, weak institutions may render adjustment to major economic shocks more difficult and, in the extreme, may encourage coups and revolutions.[21]

[21]Institutional quality is captured here by a measure of constraints on the political executive. Among other advantages, this variable is available for a broad sample of countries and for extended periods; it also seems less prone to endogeneity problems than other indicators, such as the ICRG risk measures. See Acemoglu and others (2003); and Satyanath and Subramanian (2004) for a fuller discussion of this variable and of how institutions in general may affect volatility.

Figure 5.9. Some Determinants of Differences in Business Cycle Characteristics[1]

(Unweighted averages)

Monetary policy improved substantially in advanced economies after the 1970s; more recently, significant improvements have occurred in emerging market and developing countries as well. Since the 1980s, the volatility of fiscal policy has declined in most advanced economies, institutional quality has increased in most emerging market and developing countries, and terms-of-trade volatility has declined sharply in both advanced economies and developing countries. For all these variables, advanced economies score more favorably than emerging market and developing countries.

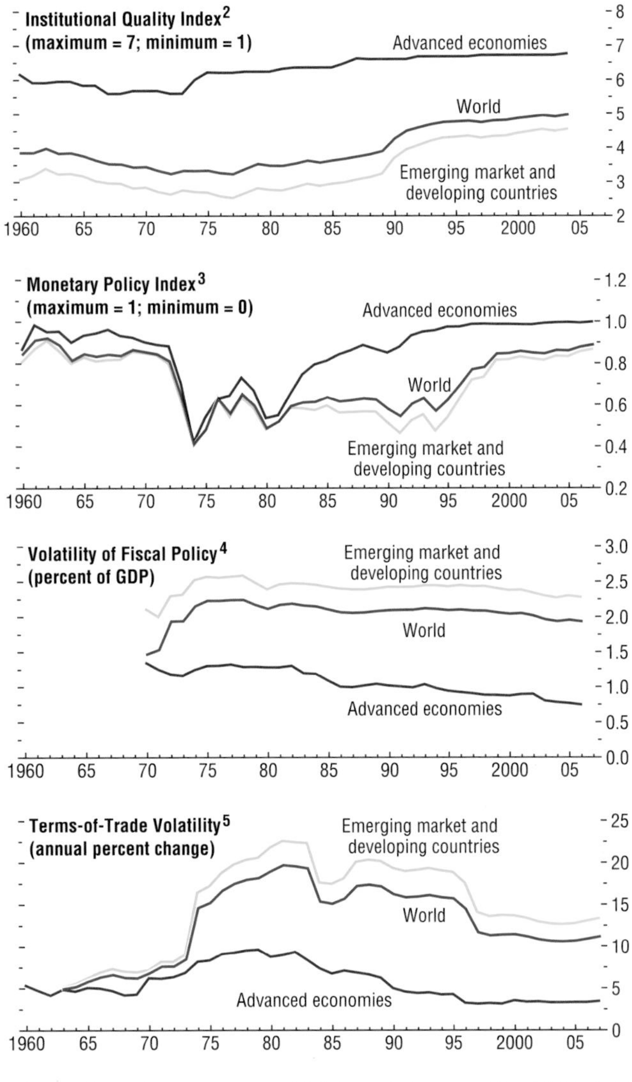

Sources: Heston, Summers, and Aten (2006); Marshall, Jaggers, and Gurr (2004); World Bank, World Development Indicators database (2007); and IMF staff calculations.

[1]See Appendix 5.1 for information on country group composition.

[2]Measured using the "executive constraint" variable from Marshall, Jaggers, and Gurr's Polity IV data set.

[3]Defined as $\exp[-0.005 * (\text{inflation} - 2\%)^2]$.

[4]Defined as the rolling 10-year standard deviation of cyclically adjusted government consumption as a percent of GDP.

[5]Defined as the rolling 10-year standard deviation of the annual percent change in the terms of trade.

- *The quality of macroeconomic policies.* In part, this is assessed through an index measuring the success of the monetary framework in maintaining low inflation (see Box 5.2 for an assessment of the extent to which better monetary policies and more flexible markets have muted the business cycle in the United States).[22] In addition, more stable fiscal policy can help dampen, or at least not amplify, output fluctuations; in this context, the analysis focuses on the volatility of cyclically adjusted government expenditures.[23] As mentioned above, external vulnerabilities have in the past also brought expansions to a premature end. Therefore, the impact of large current account deficits (defined here as a deficit exceeding 5 percent of GDP) is also analyzed.
- *Structural features.* For instance, a better-developed financial infrastructure (measured using the ratio of private sector credit to GDP) may enable greater smoothing of both consumption and investment plans.[24] Other structural factors, including changes in the sectoral composition of output, improved inventory management techniques in the wake of the information technology revolution, more flexible labor and product markets, and a general opening up to international trade, may have smoothed fluctuations and reduced inflationary bottlenecks.[25] Clearly, many of the above factors are not just reducing susceptibility to

[22]The role of monetary policy is emphasized in Clarida, Galí, and Gertler (2000); and Cecchetti, Flores-Lagunes, and Krause (2006b). Importantly, globalization may have strengthened policymakers' incentives to maintain low inflation, especially in developing economies—see Box 3.1 in the April 2006 *World Economic Outlook.*

[23]See Fatás and Mihov (2003); and Chapter 2 in the April 2005 *World Economic Outlook.*

[24]See Easterly, Islam, and Stiglitz (2000); Kose, Prasad, and Terrones (2003); Barrell and Gottschalk (2004); and Dynan, Elmendorf, and Sichel (2006).

[25]On the impact of sectoral changes, see Dalsgaard, Elmeskov, and Park (2002); of inventory management, see footnote 17; of product-market regulation, see Kent, Smith, and Holloway (2005); and of globalization, see Chapter 3 in the April 2006 *World Economic Outlook.* Neither inventory management techniques nor labor and product-market flexibility are captured in this analysis, owing to data limitations.

Table 5.1. Cross-Sectional Regressions

	Output Volatility	Lost Output	Length of Expansion	Time in Recessions
Broad institutions	**−0.18***	−0.02	0.19	**−1.08***
Financial development[1]	**−1.99***	**−0.18***	**0.39****	**−3.30****
Monetary policy quality	0.07	−0.70	**3.33***	**−18.27****
Fiscal policy volatility	**0.58***	**0.30****	−0.72	0.58
Current account deficit	0.39	−0.03	**−1.49*****	**12.24*****
R^2	0.49	0.50	0.49	0.65

Source: IMF staff calculations.

Note: number of countries = 78. Sample covers the period 1970–2005. Statistically significant coefficients are in boldface; *, **, and *** denote significance at the 10 percent, 5 percent, and 1 percent level, respectively. Other controls include trade openness, terms-of-trade volatility, exchange rate flexibility, and share of agriculture in GDP.

[1]To allow for nonlinearities, regressions employ both the level and the square of financial development; the joint coefficient presented represents the marginal value, evaluated at the sample mean.

Table 5.2. Panel and Probit Regressions

	Output Volatility	Probability of Being in an Expansion
Broad institutions	−0.07	−0.00
Financial development[1]	0.22	−0.11
Monetary policy quality	**−2.39*****	**0.22*****
Fiscal policy volatility	**0.61***	**−0.04****
Current account deficit	−0.17	0.01
Trade openness	−0.61	**0.11*****
Terms-of-trade volatility	0.05	−0.00
R^2	0.27	0.08
Number of countries	78	78
Number of observations	299	1,824

Source: IMF staff calculations.

Note: Results for "output volatility" are based on a panel fixed-effects regression, estimated using decade-average values over 1960–2005. Results for "probability of being in an expansion" are based on a probit regression, estimated using annual data over 1960–2005. Statistically significant coefficients are in boldface; *, **, and *** denote significance at the 10 percent, 5 percent, and 1 percent level, respectively. Other controls include exchange rate flexibility and share of agriculture in GDP.

[1]To allow for nonlinearities, regressions employ both the level and the square of financial development; the joint coefficient presented represents the marginal value, evaluated at the sample mean.

both demand and supply shocks but are also raising trend productivity growth rates, which will also reduce the risk of an output decline.

- *Supply shocks,* including in particular oil-supply disruptions. These are widely understood to have played an important role in driving previous business cycles.[26] They are represented here by the volatility of the external terms of trade.

As shown in Figure 5.9, the combination of a more challenging environment and inadequacies in monetary policy frameworks helped bring about poor inflationary performance in the 1970s (see Box 5.2). However, monetary policy improved substantially in advanced economies starting in the 1980s. More recently, significant improvements have also occurred in emerging market and developing countries. Also, since the 1980s, the volatility of fiscal policy has declined in most advanced economies, broad institutional quality has increased in most emerging market and developing countries, and terms-of-trade volatility has declined sharply in both advanced and developing economies. For all these variables, advanced economies score more favorably than emerging market and developing countries.

More formally, both cross-sectional analysis (Table 5.1) and panel and probit regressions (Table 5.2) suggest the following broad findings:[27]

- Greater *institutional quality* is associated with lower volatility and less time spent in recessions. This effect is statistically significant in the cross section.
- *Financial deepening* significantly dampens all aspects of business cycle volatility in the cross-sectional analysis. However, there is strong evidence that this impact diminishes once a country attains a certain level of financial development. The influence of this variable, just as with institutional quality, is more

[26]For instance, Stock and Watson (2005), using a structural vector autoregression methodology, conclude that "the widespread reduction in volatility [since the 1970s] is in large part associated with a reduction in the magnitude of the common international shocks." Similarly, Ahmed, Levin, and Wilson (2004) emphasize the role of "good luck" in driving recent U.S. macroeconomic stability. See also Stock and Watson (2003).

[27]In the absence of a structural econometric model of the business cycle, care should be taken in interpreting these correlations as indicating causality, even though instruments are employed for both institutional quality and fiscal policy volatility.

Box 5.2. Improved Macroeconomic Performance—Good Luck or Good Policies?

As discussed in the main text, output volatility has declined significantly in recent years across the main advanced economies. This box discusses how much of the lower volatility in the United States can be attributed to, respectively, better monetary policies, structural changes to the economy, and smaller shocks (potentially reflecting "good luck"). To do so, it uses a structural model of the U.S. economy that can statistically identify macroeconomic shocks and structural changes, and can simulate counterfactual monetary policies that would have been more effective at stabilizing the economy than actual policies. This analysis also provides some perspective on the important policy question of whether output volatility is likely to remain low in the future.

The main result is that sustainable improvements in monetary policy account for about one-third of the reduction in the volatility of U.S. output and inflation between the pre-1984 and the post-1984 period. This contrasts sharply with a study by Stock and Watson (2003), who find that monetary policy has not played a significant role in reducing output variability.

U.S. Inflation and Output Volatility: Data and Model-Based Results
(Percent)

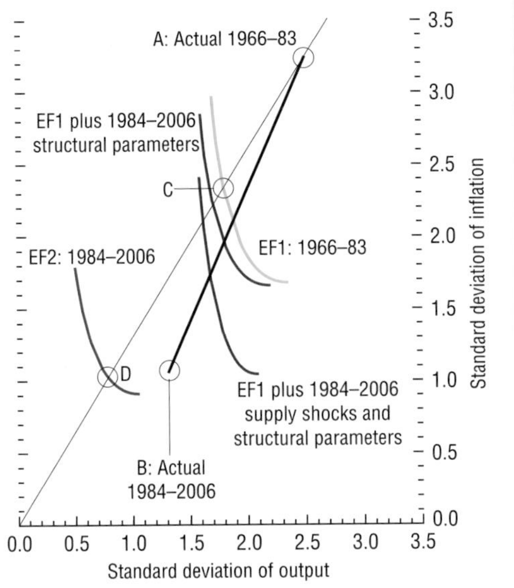

Sources: Haver Analytics; and IMF staff calculations.

Performance of Monetary Policy Has Improved Considerably

The figure plots the actual volatility of U.S. inflation and detrended output during 1966–83 (point A) and 1984–2006 (point B).[1] This experience can be compared with what model-based estimates suggest could have been achieved by following an optimal monetary policy rule, represented by the efficiency frontiers EF1 and EF2.[2] Specifically, the efficiency frontier EF1 represents the best possible combinations of inflation and output volatility that could have been achieved by the Federal Reserve during 1966–83, had it followed a monetary policy rule that adjusted interest rates sufficiently to stabilize inflation and output outcomes. Note

Note: The authors of this box are Michael Kumhof and Douglas Laxton, with support from Susanna Mursula.

[1]The volatility of the output gap and of inflation are defined in this box as the standard deviation of, respectively, the output gap and the year-on-year percent change in the CPI. All estimates are based on quarterly data.

[2]The efficiency frontiers are constructed in two steps. First, a structural monetary model of the U.S. economy is used to estimate the distribution of a set of eight macroeconomic shocks over the period 1966–83 (EF1) or 1984–2006 (EF2); the model is documented in Juillard and others (2006). Second, the estimated coefficients of the model's interest rate reaction function are replaced by optimal coefficients that minimize a weighted sum of standard deviations of inflation and output; the functional form of this monetary policy rule is adopted from Orphanides (2003a). This procedure is repeated for a variety of different relative weights of inflation and output, and in each case the realized standard deviations are recorded as one point on the efficiency frontier.

that this model-based frontier is downward sloping—policymakers face a trade-off between inflation volatility and output volatility. This trade-off arises because when the economy is hit by, for instance, an oil-price shock, the Federal Reserve must decide whether to tighten monetary policy to keep inflation within a narrow range while temporarily tolerating a decline in output or to accept higher inflation so as to achieve more stable output. Similarly, the efficiency frontier EF2 represents the best possible combinations of inflation and output volatility that could have been achieved by the Federal Reserve during 1984–2006. It has shifted inward considerably relative to EF1 (mostly reflecting smaller shocks, as discussed below).

Crucially, the model suggests that there is a significant difference between actual performance at point A and what could have been achieved during 1966–83, as represented by the set of points along EF1. This indicates that suboptimal monetary policy played a major role during that period in increasing both inflation and output volatility. In contrast, over 1984–2006, U.S. monetary policy became much more credible, adjusting the policy rate more aggressively in response to underlying inflationary pressures.[3] This achieved outcomes closer to the efficiency frontier.

The figure examines the role of monetary policy and other factors in reducing output and inflation volatility. The contribution of monetary policy to better performance of the U.S. economy is calculated as $(AB - CD)/AB$, where AB represents the total decline in volatility between 1966–83 and 1984–2006 and CD reflects the portion of this change unrelated to monetary policy. This calculation suggests that around one-third of the reduction in output volatility was a result of better monetary policies.

[3]For empirical evidence on the role of monetary policy credibility in changing the persistence of the inflation process in OECD countries, see Laxton and N'Diaye (2002).

Role of Structural Changes and Shocks

The inward shift of the efficiency frontier since 1984 reflects a combination of changed structural characteristics of the economy and smaller shocks. To illustrate this, the figure shows two alternative frontiers for the 1966–83 period that are generated by the model under two different sets of assumptions. First, the pre-1984 estimates of structural parameters of the economy are replaced with post-1984 estimates. Clearly, changes in the structural characteristics of the economy can account for only a small part of the estimated inward shift of the efficiency frontier. Second, the pre-1984 model is modified using post-1984 values for both structural parameters and the distributions of supply shocks (e.g., productivity shocks and oil price hikes). Unsurprisingly, the frontier EF1 shifts mainly downward because, in the short run, supply shocks have a stronger effect on inflation than on output. The difference between this frontier and the post-1984 frontier EF2 represents the contribution of demand shocks (for instance, smaller shocks to private consumption and investment demand, and/or greater stability in the conduct of fiscal policy). The role of demand factors in explaining reduced output volatility since 1984 is much larger than the role of supply shocks. This finding is consistent with the traditional interpretation of business cycles as being mostly demand driven.[4]

Conclusions

Monetary policy has clearly improved the economy's performance by keeping it closer to the efficiency frontier, and this gain is not likely to disappear. What is less certain is whether the frontier itself will stay where it is, that is, whether supply and demand shocks will continue to be small. As discussed in Chapter 1, there are a number of important risks facing the global economy that could increase volatility going forward.

[4]See Juillard and others (2006) and the references cited therein.

Figure 5.10. Contribution to Outcome Differences

(Dependent variable and total difference in percentage points on the x-axis, and percent of total difference on the y-axis unless otherwise indicated)

More stable monetary and fiscal policies in advanced economies than in emerging market and developing countries play a large part in explaining their lower volatility and longer expansions. Much of the remaining difference reflects advanced economies' better institutional quality. Improvements in monetary policy and lower terms-of-trade volatility account for much of the reduction in output volatility over time.

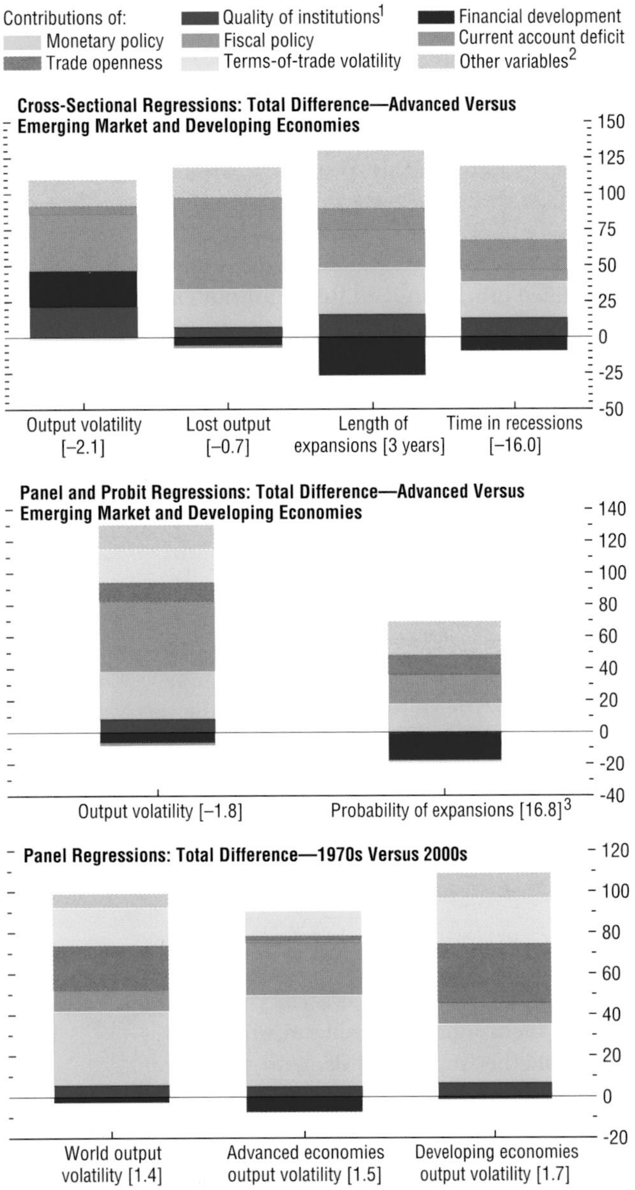

Sources: Beck, Demirgüç-Kunt, and Levine (2007); Heston, Summers, and Aten (2006); Maddison (2007); Marshall, Jaggers, and Gurr (2004); Reinhart and Rogoff (2004); Wacziarg and Welch (2003); World Bank, World Development Indicators database (2007); and IMF staff calculations (see Appendix 5.1 for details).

[1]Initial values for the cross-sectional and panel regressions.

[2]See Tables 5.1 and 5.2 for the list of "other variables."

[3]The y-axis indicates the probability of an expansion in percentage points.

difficult to detect in the panel regressions, because financial development tends to be a relatively slow-moving variable.

- The impact of the quality of *monetary and fiscal policy* is sometimes difficult to disentangle. That said, in the cross section, better monetary policy is associated with longer expansions, whereas volatility in fiscal policy is associated with output volatility. Better monetary and fiscal policies are both associated in the panel with smaller output fluctuations. Further, they are also associated with a higher probability of being in an expansion.
- There is some evidence that large *external deficits* can bring expansions to a premature end (in the cross section), and that periods with lower *terms-of-trade volatility* tend to have lower output volatility (in the panel).

The results imply that more stable monetary and fiscal policies in advanced economies play a large part in explaining lower volatility and longer expansions in advanced economies, when compared with emerging market and developing countries (Figure 5.10). Part of the remaining difference reflects advanced economies' better institutional quality. Their lower terms-of-trade volatility also plays a role. In a similar vein, better monetary policy, more stable fiscal policy, and greater trade openness in advanced economies all help to increase their probability of being and remaining in an expansion, relative to emerging market and developing countries (see Figure 5.10).

The results can also be applied to explain the large reduction in average volatility between the 1970s and the current decade, both for the world as a whole and for advanced and developing economies separately. Improvements in monetary policy account for much of the reduction in volatility over time (see Figure 5.10). A significant portion of the remainder reflects improved fiscal policy (in advanced economies), and trade liberalization and institutional improvements (in emerging market and developing countries). Lower terms-of-trade volatility than observed in the 1970s does have an important, but certainly not a dominant, role to play.

This is consistent with the finding, expressed in Box 5.2, that policy mistakes were an important contributor to the volatility observed in the 1970s.[28]

Conclusions

The current global expansion certainly stands out in comparison with the experience of the past three decades, but it is not unprecedented. In recent years, output growth has been much more rapid than observed at any time since the oil shocks of the 1970s. Compared with the 1960s, however, neither the strength nor the length of the current expansion appears exceptional. That said, rapid growth has been shared across countries more broadly than in the past, and output volatility in most countries and regions has been significantly lower than during the 1960s.

Advanced economies in particular have improved their performance since the 1970s, and they have typically experienced long expansions. Output stabilization in emerging market and developing countries has been more gradual and modest, with certain regions experiencing deep and sometimes recurrent crises. Over time, greater trade and financial integration have increased the covariance of growth across countries, and therefore at the world level output volatility is only slightly lower than in the 1960s.

This chapter finds that the increasing stability of economies and the associated increase in the durability of expansions largely reflect sources that are likely to prove persistent. In particular, improvements in the conduct of monetary and fiscal policy, as well as in broader institutional quality, are all robustly associated with smaller fluctuations in output, both over time and across countries. Reductions in terms-of-trade volatility have played an important, but not dominant, role.

The prospects for future stability should nevertheless not be overstated. The process of globalization continues to present policymakers with new challenges, as reflected in the difficulties in managing volatile capital flows, increasing exposure of investors to developments in overseas financial markets, and the uncertainties associated with large global current account imbalances. The recent return of interest rates to more neutral levels in most major advanced economies, the corrections of asset prices in some countries, and the current rise in risk premiums and tightening of credit market conditions may also test the strength of the current expansion. Overconfidence in the ability of the current policy framework to deliver stability indefinitely would certainly not be warranted. Although the business cycle has changed for the better, policymakers must remember that it has not disappeared.

Appendix 5.1. Data and Methods

The main authors of this appendix are Martin Sommer and Nikola Spatafora, with support from Angela Espiritu and Allen Stack. Massimiliano Marcellino provided consultancy support.

Expansions are defined as periods of nonnegative growth of real GDP per capita. Analogously, *recessions* are defined as periods of negative growth. Most of the analysis in this chapter therefore adopts the concept of "classical" business cycles as discussed in, for example, Artis, Marcellino, and Proietti (2004) and Harding and Pagan (2001).[29] Expansions are identi-

[28]Caution is needed in interpreting these results as indicating a small role for "good luck" in recent years. The panel regressions involve relatively large error terms, which may partly reflect temporary shocks. That said, the estimated equations do a very good job in matching the average business cycle characteristics for broad country groups.

[29]Harding and Pagan (2001) review various alternative business cycle definitions and their implications for business cycle properties. Business cycle research on advanced economies has typically used headline GDP series to determine the timing of expansions and recessions. This chapter, however, also analyzes many emerging market and developing countries with high population growth rates. To ease cross-country comparisons, the chapter therefore defines business cycles using per capita output growth.

fied using annual data and in per capita terms to allow for broad comparisons across countries and over time. Expansions based on quarterly data would likely be shorter for many countries. For the United States, the identified recessions broadly match those reported by the National Bureau of Economic Research, with the exception of the 1960 recession, which cannot be identified from annual data.

Volatility Decompositions

For the purposes of volatility decompositions, GDP growth at time t, y_t, is first expressed as the sum of growth contributions by regions or expenditure component, *Cont:*

$$y_t = (GDP_t/GDP_{t-1} - 1) * 100 = \sum_{i=1}^{n} Cont_{t,i},$$

where $n = 4$ in the case of decomposition of world volatility by expenditure components and $n = 7$ in the cases of decomposition of world growth by regions and decomposition of U.S. output volatility by expenditure components. The contributions to world growth are calculated from the data sources described below. For the United States, the contributions to growth are reported directly by the Bureau of Economic Analysis. To simplify analysis, the volatility decompositions are not calculated on a per capita basis—however, volatilities of headline and per capita growth tend to be similar for most countries.

Volatility decompositions in the top panels of Figures 5.5, 5.6, and 5.7 are calculated using the standard formula:

$$var\, y_t = \sum_{i=1}^{n} var(Cont_{t,i}) + \sum_{\substack{i=1,j=1 \\ \text{and } t\neq j}}^{n} cov(Cont_{t,i}, Cont_{t,j}),$$

where *var* and *cov* denote the variance and covariance operators. The volatility decompositions are computed over four periods (1960–73, 1974–82, 1983–95, and 1996–2006), with years 1973 and 1983 broadly representing the main breaks in the volatility of world growth since 1960. Given data limitations, world volatility is not calculated for the 1950s. The year 1996 was selected as an additional breakpoint to facilitate analysis of volatility over the past decade (in advanced economies, the length of the typical cycle increased to about 10 years during the 1980s and 1990s).

The change in output volatility from period B to period A is decomposed as follows:

$$\begin{aligned} var^A y_t - var^B y_t &= \sum_{i=1}^{n}\{var^A(Cont_{t,i}) - var^B(Cont_{t,i})\} \\ &+ \sum_{\substack{i=1,j=1 \\ \text{and } t\neq j}}^{n} \{std^A(Cont_{t,i})\, std^A(Cont_{t,j}) \\ &- std^B(Cont_{t,i})\, std^B(Cont_{t,j})\} corr^B(Cont_{t,i}, Cont_{t,j}) \\ &+ \sum_{\substack{i=1,j=1 \\ \text{and } t\neq j}}^{n} std^A(Cont_{t,i})\, std^A(Cont_{t,j}) \{corr^A(Cont_{t,i}, Cont_{t,j}) \\ &- corr^B(Cont_{t,i}, Cont_{t,j})\}, \end{aligned}$$

where *std* and *corr* are the standard deviation and correlation operators. The first term in the equation above is the change in the volatility of regions or expenditure components and corresponds to "region variance" and "component variance" in the middle and bottom panels of Figures 5.5, 5.6, and 5.7. The second and third terms in the equation reflect the "contribution of covariance" in the figures. Specifically, the second term is the contribution of covariance to the decline in output volatility because of the lower standard deviations of growth contributions (note that these standard deviations enter as pairs and therefore cannot be assigned to individual regions or expenditure components). The third term is the contribution of covariance to the change in output volatility that occurred as a result of the change in the correlation of growth contributions among regions or expenditure components. The contribution of covariance is split into these two terms because changes in the volatility of components do not necessarily have the same sign as the changes in the correlation among components—see, for example, the middle and bottom panels of Figure 5.5—with interesting economic implications, as discussed in the main text.

In Figure 5.8 ("Volatility Patterns in Rapidly Growing Economies"), the beginning of the rapid growth period is identified as follows: initially, the first available year is identified in which the five-year moving average of real GDP growth (1) exceeds 5 percent, and (2) remains above 5 percent for at least two years. Subsequently, the beginning of the takeoff is identified within the five-year window before this year.

Econometric Analysis

The econometric analysis (Tables 5.1 and 5.2) considers the following dependent variables:

- *output volatility:* defined as the standard deviation of detrended GDP growth per capita. Detrending is carried out using the Hodrick-Prescott (HP) filter;
- *share of output that is lost to recessions and slowdowns:* defined as the cumulative sum of all below-trend outputs, divided by the cumulative sum of all outputs. Detrending is again carried out using the HP filter; and
- *average length of expansions; share of time spent in recessions; whether a country is in an expansion in any given year:* expansions and recessions are defined as described at the start of this appendix.

Explanatory variables employed in the analysis include the following:

- *Broad institutions:* measured using the "executive constraint" variable from Marshall, Jaggers, and Gurr's Polity IV data set (2004).[30] This variable is instrumented using country- and period-specific initial values. The variable follows a seven-category scale, with higher values denoting better checks and balances in place on the executive branch of the government. A score of one indicates that the executive branch has unlimited authority in decision making; a score of seven represents the highest possible degree of accountability to another group of at least equal power, such as a legislature.
- *Financial development:* measured using the ratio of private sector credit by banks and other financial institutions to GDP. Data are from Beck, Demirgüç-Kunt, and Levine's Financial Development and Structure database (2007).[31] To allow for nonlinearities, regressions employ both the level and the square of this variable; the joint coefficient presented represents the marginal value, evaluated at the sample mean.
- *Quality of monetary policy:* the index is defined as exp[–0.005 * (inflation – 2 percent)^2]. This measure of price stability rapidly deteriorates once inflation rises above 10 percent. For instance, the index equals 1 when inflation equals 2 percent, roughly ¾ when inflation equals 10 percent, and 0.2 when inflation equals 20 percent. The index moves only slightly in response to short-term inflation fluctuations, such as those stemming from oil price changes, so long as the initial inflation level is low. Although this variable is clearly influenced by factors other than the quality of monetary policy, it is nevertheless correlated with other proxies for the quality of the institutional setup behind monetary policy, over the more limited sample for which the latter are available.[32]
- *Volatility of fiscal policy:* measured as the rolling 10-year standard deviation of cyclically adjusted government expenditure to GDP, following the country-specific, instrumental-variable estimation procedure set out in Fatás and Mihov (2003).[33] The government expenditure data are from the World Bank's World

[30]For more details on the Polity IV database, see www.cidcm.umd.edu/polity.

[31]For more details on the Financial Development and Structure database, see www.worldbank.org.

[32]For instance, a cross-sectional regression of the monetary policy index on a measure of the turnover of central bank governors yields a *t*-statistic of 5.5 and an R^2 of 0.24. The analogous fixed-effects panel regression yields a *t*-statistic of 4.0 and an R^2 of 0.10.

[33]Using government expenditures, rather than the government balance, minimizes endogeneity concerns that stem from difficulties in cyclical adjustment. As discussed in Fatás and Mihov (2003, p. 11), "There are both theoretical considerations and empirical estimates that support the idea that spending (excluding transfers) does not react contemporaneously to the cycle. On the other hand, there is plenty of evidence that the budget deficit is automatically affected by changes in macroeconomic conditions and therefore more subject to endogeneity problems."

Development Indicators database (2007)[34] when available and the IMF's World Economic Outlook database otherwise.

- *Large current account deficit:* this indicator equals 1 when the current account deficit exceeds 5 percent of GDP; the indicator equals zero otherwise. Data are from the IMF's World Economic Outlook database when available and the World Bank's World Development Indicators database (2007) otherwise.
- *Trade openness:* the Wacziarg and Welch (2003) index is based on average tariff rates, average nontariff barriers, the average parallel market premium for foreign exchange, the presence of export marketing boards, and the presence of a socialist economic system. The variable is equal to zero prior to liberalization and 1 from the beginning of liberalization.[35]
- *Exchange rate flexibility:* measured based on the Reinhart-Rogoff coarse index of de facto exchange rate flexibility, collapsed to a three-value indicator (where 1 denotes a fixed or pegged exchange rate regime, 2 denotes an intermediate regime, and 3 denotes a free float). The Reinhart-Rogoff classification takes into account the existence in some economies of dual rates or parallel markets, and it uses the volatility of market-determined exchange rates to statistically classify an exchange rate regime.[36]
- *Share of agriculture in GDP:* the data are from the World Bank's, World Development Indicators database (2007).

All cross-sectional regressions are estimated using average values over the period 1970–2003.[37] Panel regressions are estimated using all available decade-average observations, starting in 1960, and use fixed effects. Probit regressions are estimated using annual data, starting in 1960.

Figure 5.10 is constructed as follows. First, each regression is estimated using the whole sample. Then the sample is split into advanced economies versus emerging market and developing countries, and mean values of the dependent and explanatory variables are calculated for each subsample. For each explanatory variable, the difference in its mean value across subsamples is multiplied by the relevant coefficient (estimated using the whole sample). This yields the contribution of the relevant explanatory variable to the (mean) difference of the dependent variable between advanced and other economies. Finally, and analogously, the above procedure is repeated, but with the sample split by decade (rather than into advanced versus other economies). This yields the contribution of each explanatory variable to the (mean) difference of the dependent variable between decades.

Other Data Sources

- *Real GDP and its components.* Data on an aggregate and per capita basis are from (1) Heston, Summers, and Aten's Penn World Tables Version 6.2 (2006);[38] (2) the World Bank's World Development Indicators database (2007); (3) the IMF's World Economic Outlook database; and (4) Maddison (2007).[39] Data from these sources are spliced multiplicatively together in the order in which they are numbered to produce the longest time series possible. Most of the data, however, are from the Penn World Tables, with data for 2007 based on projections from the IMF's World Economic Outlook database. Data from Maddison are available only for total GDP and GDP per capita.[40] Given the ongoing discussion about the accuracy of pre–World War II data (see Box 5.3), the analysis of pre-war data is con-

[34]For more details on the World Development Indicators data, see www.worldbank.org.

[35]For more details on the openness variable, see www.papers.nber.org/papers/w10152.pdf.

[36]For more details on the Reinhart-Rogoff index, see www.wam.umd.edu/~creinhar/Links.html.

[37]The robustness of the conclusions was also checked by estimating the regressions separately over the subperiods 1970–83 and 1984–2003.

[38]For more details on the Penn World Tables Version 6.2, see www.pwt.econ.upenn.edu.

[39]For more details, see www.ggdc.net/Maddison.

[40]See Johnson and others (2007) for a discussion of how GDP data vary across data sets, including across different versions of the Penn World Tables.

Box 5.3. New Business Cycle Indices for Latin America: A Historical Reconstruction

Important insights into the roots of business cycle volatility can be gained from long-run data spanning a variety of policy regimes and institutional settings. Yet there is a striking dearth of systematic work along these lines for most countries outside North America and western Europe.

A main obstacle to this line of research has been limited or patently unreliable historical GDP data for developing countries. Although the work of Maddison (1995, 2003) has been useful in making long-run data more easily accessible to macroeconomists, important deficiencies remain in the pre–World War II data reported by Maddison. For most developing countries, these data are either provided only for sparse benchmark years or compiled directly from secondary sources relying on a very limited set of macroeconomic variables and often using disparate methodologies to build up GDP estimates. As discussed below, this procedure can be misleading.

This box summarizes a new methodology for real GDP reconstruction laid out in Aiolfi, Catão, and Timmerman (2006; ACT henceforth), and compares the estimates for four Latin American countries (Argentina, Brazil, Chile, and Mexico) with those reported by Maddison (2007). Underpinning this new methodology is the idea that a cross section of economic variables shares a common factor structure. That is, fluctuations in any individual economic variables (such as industrial production, investment, and so on) stem from the combination of a common factor that affects all individual economic variables in an economy (that is, "a tide that raises all boats") plus an idiosyncratic (that is, sector- or variable-specific) component. Recent time-series techniques allow a sounder formalization of this classical factor approach, and recent studies have used it for forecasting purposes. ACT argue that such dynamic factor models can be also suitable for "backcasting" purposes, notably in the reconstruction of aggregate indices of economic activity. A critical requirement is the availability of a broad set of variables that is both heterogeneous enough and comprises individual series that bear a close relation to aggregate cyclical behavior. Natural candidates include investment, government revenues and expenditures, and sectoral output, as well as external trade and a host of financial variables for which there are data stretching far back in time. A main advantage of such a methodology is its relative robustness to errors in the measurement of individual variables—a problem deemed particularly severe in developing country statistics. Provided that such measurement errors are largely idiosyncratic, the resulting estimates will be far less sensitive to the effects of such errors than the usual procedure of adding up sectoral output indices to estimate an aggregate GDP, where each of these individual indices is measured with substantial idiosyncratic error.

The ACT backcasting methodology consists of three steps. First, all individual series are made stationary by detrending—a standard procedure in factor model estimation. Second, common factors are extracted from the cross section of stationary series. The third step consists of projecting the extracted factors on real GDP by an ordinary least squares regression confined to the period for which real GDP data are judged to be sufficiently reliable (usually sometime after World War II). Although the resulting indices track actual GDP very closely over this latter "in-sample" period (yielding very high R^2s and t-ratios), the methodology's reliance on coefficient stability over a period spanning several decades could potentially be criticized. However, Stock and Watson (2002) show that such common factor estimates are consistent even under temporal instability in the individual time series, provided this instability averages out in the construction

Note: The main author of this box is Luis Catão.

Box 5.3 *(concluded)*

of the factors. In addition, ACT postulate a variety of structural stability tests and find that the respective backcasting estimates are remarkably robust to those tests. As a further robustness check, ACT also apply this backcasting method to U.S. data, comparing the resulting estimates with those of Romer (1989) and Balke and Gordon (1989), which are viewed as reasonably reliable gauges of U.S. pre–World War II GDP. ACT find that the proposed backcasting method gauges well the timing and magnitude of U.S. pre–World War II cycles, particularly when compared with the Balke and Gordon series.

How do these estimates differ from those previously found in the literature, including those reported in Maddison (1995, 2003)? Although the average volatility of output gaps over the time periods used in the main text is fairly comparable across data sets, the differences can be very dramatic at other times. Indeed, ACT show that some differences in the interpretation of historical episodes are startling. For instance, the Maddison-compiled index for Brazil shows a much deeper downturn in the wake of the 1891 Barings crisis (see figure), but this is very likely an artifact, arising because the index relies almost exclusively on foreign trade information and ignores indicators more tightly related to domestic production. Conversely, Maddison's (2003) real GDP figures for Mexico portray a remarkable output stability for the revolution years 1911–20, when it is well known from a variety of other indicators and historical narratives that output plunged during at least the height of the revolutionary disruptions in 1914–17.

Overall, these results indicate that extending this reconstruction methodology to other developing countries should prove worthwhile. Such an extension should enable us to better answer key questions about the historical evolution of world business cycles and the role of institutions and policy regimes therein.

Historical Output Gap Estimates: Differences Between Previous and New Estimates
(Percent)

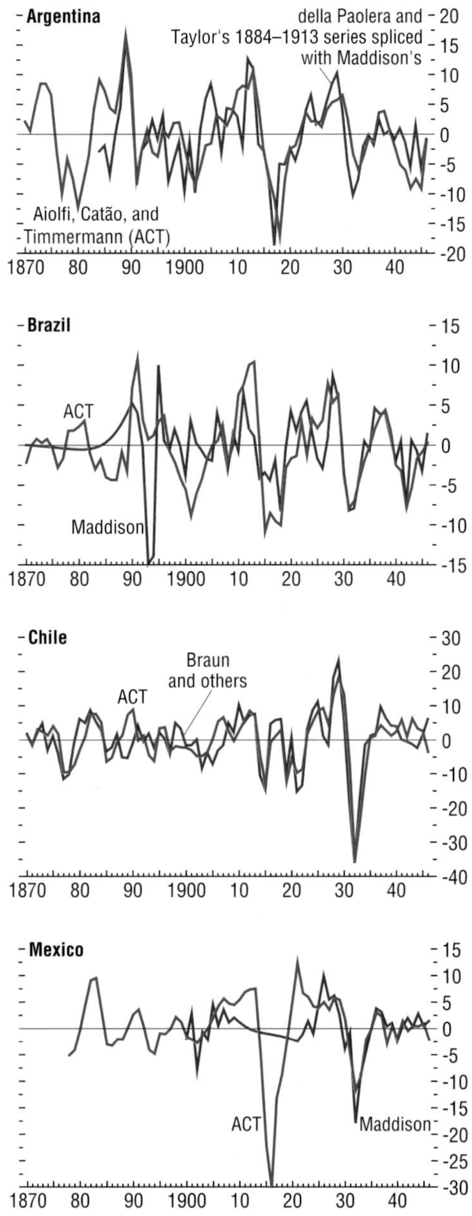

Sources: Aiolfi, Catão, and Timmermann (2006); Braun and others (2000); della Paolera and Taylor (2003); and Maddison (1995, 2003).

fined to the average length of expansions and recessions for a selected group of countries (Figures 5.2 and 5.3).

- *Working-age population.* Interpolated five-year working-age population data are from the United Nations' Population Prospects: The 2004 Revision Population database.[41] Working-age population is defined as people between ages 15 and 64.

Country Coverage

The chapter covers 133 advanced economies and emerging market and developing countries. The countries are presented in the chapter as part of the following economic and regional groupings (the number of countries is in parentheses):

- *advanced economies* (28): Japan and the United States plus the following countries:
  - *EU-15:* Austria, Belgium, Denmark, Finland, France, Germany, Greece, Ireland, Italy, Luxembourg, the Netherlands, Portugal, Spain, Sweden, and the United Kingdom;
  - *newly industrialized Asian economies* (4): Hong Kong SAR, Korea, Singapore, and Taiwan Province of China; and
  - *other advanced economies* (7): Australia, Canada, Iceland, Israel, New Zealand, Norway, and Switzerland; and
- *emerging market and developing countries* (105): China and India plus the following countries:
  - *Africa* (49): Algeria, Angola, Benin, Botswana, Burkina Faso, Burundi, Cameroon, Cape Verde, Central African Republic, Chad, Comoros, Democratic Republic of the Congo, Republic of Congo, Côte d'Ivoire, Djibouti, Egypt, Equatorial Guinea, Ethiopia, Gabon, The Gambia, Ghana, Guinea, Guinea-Bissau, Kenya, Lesotho, Madagascar, Malawi, Mali, Mauritania, Mauritius, Morocco, Mozambique, Namibia, Niger, Nigeria, Rwanda, São Tomé and Príncipe, Senegal, Seychelles, Sierra Leone, South Africa, Sudan, Swaziland, Tanzania, Togo, Tunisia, Uganda, Zambia, and Zimbabwe;
  - *central and eastern Europe* (8): Albania, Bulgaria, Czech Republic, Hungary, Poland, Romania, Slovak Republic, and Turkey (countries of the former Soviet Union are not included in the analysis because many variables for these countries are not readily available for the period prior to the 1990s);
  - *developing Asia* (13): Bangladesh, Cambodia, Indonesia, Kiribati, Lao People's Democratic Republic, Malaysia, Nepal, Pakistan, Philippines, Sri Lanka, Thailand, Tonga, and Vietnam;
  - *Latin America* (21): Argentina, Bolivia, Brazil, Chile, Colombia, Costa Rica, Dominican Republic, Ecuador, El Salvador, Guatemala, Haiti, Honduras, Jamaica, Mexico, Nicaragua, Panama, Paraguay, Peru, Trinidad and Tobago, Uruguay, and Venezuela; and
  - *Middle East* (12): Bahrain, Islamic Republic of Iran, Jordan, Kuwait, Lebanon, Libya, Oman, Qatar, Saudi Arabia, Syrian Arab Republic, United Arab Emirates, and Republic of Yemen.

[41]For more details, see esa.un.org/unpp.

References

Acemoglu, Daron, Simon Johnson, James Robinson, and Yunyong Thaicharoen, 2003, "Institutional Causes, Macroeconomic Symptoms: Volatility, Crises and Growth," *Journal of Monetary Economics*, Vol. 50, No. 1, pp. 49–123.

Ahmed, Shaghil, Andrew Levin, and Beth Anne Wilson, 2004, "Recent U.S. Macroeconomic Stability: Good Policies, Good Practices, or Good Luck?" *The Review of Economics and Statistics*, Vol. 86, No. 3, pp. 824–32.

Aiolfi, Marco, Luis Catão, and Allan Timmermann, 2006, "Common Factors in Latin America's Business Cycles," IMF Working Paper 06/49 (Washington: International Monetary Fund).

Arias, Andres, Gary D. Hansen, and Lee E. Ohanian, 2006, "Why Have Business Cycle Fluctuations Become Less Volatile?" NBER Working Paper No. 12079 (Cambridge, Massachusetts: National Bureau of Economic Research).

Artis, Michael, Hans-Martin Krolzig, and Juan Toro, 2004, "The European Business Cycle," *Oxford Economic Papers*, Vol. 56 (January), pp. 1–44.

Artis, Michael, Massimiliano Marcellino, and Tommaso Proietti, 2004, "Dating Business Cycles: A Methodological Contribution with an Application to the Euro Area," *Oxford Bulletin of Economics and Statistics*, Vol. 66, No. 4, pp. 537–65.

Balke, Nathan S., and Robert J. Gordon, 1989, "The Estimation of Prewar Gross National Product: Methodology and New Evidence," *Journal of Political Economy*, Vol. 97, No. 1, pp. 38–92.

Barrell, Ray, and Sylvia Gottschalk, 2004, "The Volatility of the Output Gap in the G7," *National Institute Economic Review*, Vol. 188 (April), pp. 100–107.

Baxter, Marianne, and Robert G. King, 1999, "Measuring Business Cycles: Approximate Band-Pass Filters for Economic Time Series," *Review of Economics and Statistics*, Vol. 81 (November), pp. 575–93.

Baxter, Marianne, and Michael A. Kouparitsas, 2005, "Determinants of Business Cycle Comovement: A Robust Analysis," *Journal of Monetary Economics*, Vol. 52 (January), pp. 113–57.

Bayoumi, Tamim, and Andrew Swiston, 2007, "The Ties That Bind: Measuring International Bond Spillovers Using the Inflation-Indexed Bond Yields," IMF Working Paper 07/128 (Washington: International Monetary Fund).

Beck, Thorsten, Asli Demirgüç-Kunt, and Ross Levine, 2000 (revised: March 21, 2007), "A New Database on Financial Development and Structure," *World Bank Economic Review*, Vol. 14 (September), pp. 597–605. Available via the Internet: www.econ.worldbank.org/staff/tbeck.

Berg, Andy, Jonathan D. Ostry, and Jeromin Zettelmeyer, 2006, "What Makes Growth Sustained?" (unpublished; Washington: International Monetary Fund).

Bernanke, Ben S., 2004, "The Great Moderation," remarks at the meetings of the Eastern Economic Association, Washington, February 20.

Blanchard, Olivier, and John Simon, 2001, "The Long and Large Decline in U.S. Output Volatility," *Brookings Papers on Economic Activity: 1*, pp. 135–64.

Braun, Juan, Matías Braun, Ignacio Briones, José Diaz, Rolf Lüders, and Gert Wagner, 2000, "Economia Chilena 1810–1995: Estadistícas Históricas," Working Paper No. 187 (Santiago: Catholic University of Chile, Instituto de Economía).

Canova, Fabio, and Harris Dellas, 1993, "Trade Interdependence and the International Business Cycle," *Journal of International Economics*, Vol. 34 (February), pp. 23–47.

Cecchetti, Stephen G., Alfonso Flores-Lagunes, and Stefan Krause, 2006a, "Assessing the Sources of Changes in the Volatility of Real Growth," NBER Working Paper No. 11946 (Cambridge, Massachusetts: National Bureau of Economic Research).

———, 2006b, "Has Monetary Policy Become More Efficient? A Cross-Country Analysis," *The Economic Journal*, Vol. 116 (April), pp. 408–33.

Clarida, Richard, Jordi Galí, and Mark Gertler, 2000, "Monetary Policy Rules and Macroeconomic Stability: Evidence and Some Theory," *Quarterly Journal of Economics*, Vol. 115, No. 1, pp. 147–80.

Dalsgaard, Thomas, Jørgen Elmeskov, and Cyn-Young Park, 2002, "Ongoing Changes in the Business Cycle—Evidence and Causes," SUERF Studies No. 20 (Vienna: Société Universitaire Européenne de Recherches Financières).

Dell'Ariccia, Giovanni, Enrica Detragiache, and Raghuram Rajan, 2005, "The Real Effect of Banking Crises," IMF Working Paper 05/63 (Washington: International Monetary Fund).

della Paolera, Gerardo, and Alan Taylor, 2003, *A New Economic History of Argentina* (New York: Cambridge University Press).

DeLong, J. Bradford, 1997, "America's Peacetime Inflation: The 1970s," in *Reducing Inflation: Motivation and Strategy*, ed. by Christina D. Romer and David H. Romer (Chicago: University of Chicago Press), pp. 247–76.

Diebold, Francis X., and Glenn D. Rudebusch, 1992, "Have Postwar Economic Fluctuations Been Stabilized?" *The American Economic Review*, Vol. 82, No. 4, pp. 993–1005.

Dijk, Dick van, Denise R. Osborn, and Marianne Sensier, 2002, "Changes in Variability of the Business Cycle in the G7 Countries," Econometric Institute Report EI 282 (Rotterdam: Erasmus University, Econometric Institute).

Dynan, Karen E., Douglas W. Elmendorf, and Daniel E. Sichel, 2006, "Can Financial Innovation Help to Explain the Reduced Volatility of Economic Activity?" *Journal of Monetary Economics*, Vol. 53 (January), pp. 123–50.

Easterly, William, Roumeen Islam, and Joseph Stiglitz, 2000, "Shaken and Stirred: Explaining Growth Volatility," in *Annual Bank Conference on Development Economics* (Washington: World Bank).

Ehrmann, Michael, Marcel Fratzscher, and Roberto Rigobon, 2005, "Stocks, Bonds, Money Markets, and

Exchange Rates: Measuring International Financial Transmission," NBER Working Paper No. 11166 (Cambridge, Massachusetts: National Bureau of Economic Research).

Fatás, Antonio, and Ilian Mihov, 2003, "The Case for Restricting Fiscal Policy Discretion," *Quarterly Journal of Economics*, Vol. 118, No. 4, pp. 1419–47.

Frankel, Jeffrey A., and Andrew K. Rose, 1998, "The Endogeneity of the Optimum Currency Area Criteria," *Economic Journal*, Vol. 108 (July), pp. 1009–25.

Fuhrer, Jeffrey, and Scott Schuh, 1998, "Beyond Shocks: What Causes Business Cycles? An Overview," *New England Economic Review* (November/December), pp. 3–24.

Harding, Don, and Adrian Pagan, 2001, "Extracting, Analysing and Using Cyclical Information," MPRA Paper No. 15 (Munich: University Library of Munich).

Helbling, Thomas, and Tamim Bayoumi, 2003, "Are They All in the Same Boat? The 2000–2001 Growth Slowdown and the G-7 Business Cycle Linkages," IMF Working Paper 03/46 (Washington: International Monetary Fund).

Heston, Alan, Robert Summers, and Bettina Aten, 2006, Penn World Table Version 6.2, Center for International Comparisons of Production, Income and Prices at the University of Pennsylvania (September).

Imbs, Jean, 2004, "Trade, Finance, Specialization, and Synchronization," *The Review of Economics and Statistics*, Vol. 86 (August), pp. 723–34.

———, 2006, "The Real Effects of Financial Integration," *Journal of International Economics*, Vol. 68 (March), pp. 296–324.

Ito, Takatoshi, 2007, "Asian Currency Crisis and the International Monetary Fund, 10 Years Later: Overview," *Asian Economic Policy Review*, Vol. 2, pp. 16–49.

Johnson, Simon, Will Larson, Chris Papageorgiou, and Arvind Subramanian, 2007, "When the Facts Change: Shifting GDP Data and Their Implications" (unpublished; Washington: International Monetary Fund).

Juillard, Michel, Philippe Karam, Douglas Laxton, and Paolo Pesenti, 2006, "Welfare-Based Monetary Policy Rules in an Estimated DSGE Model of the US Economy," ECB Working Paper No. 613 (Frankfurt: European Central Bank).

Kahn, James A., Margaret M. McConnell, and Gabriel Perez-Quiros, 2002, "On the Causes of the Increased Stability of the U.S. Economy," *Economic Policy Review*, Vol. 8, No. 1, pp. 183–202.

Kent, Christopher, Kylie Smith, and James Holloway, 2005, "Declining Output Volatility: What Role for Structural Change?" Research Discussion Paper No. 2005-08 (Sydney: Reserve Bank of Australia, Economic Group).

Kim, Chang-Jin, and Charles R. Nelson, 1999, "Has the U.S. Economy Become More Stable? A Bayesian Approach Based on a Markov-Switching Model of the Business Cycle," *The Review of Economics and Statistics*, Vol. 81 (November), pp. 608–16.

Kose, M. Ayhan, Christopher Otrok, and Eswar Prasad, forthcoming, "Twin Peaks in Global Business Cycle Convergence," IMF Working Paper (Washington: International Monetary Fund).

Kose, M. Ayhan, Christopher Otrok, and Charles Whiteman, 2005, "Understanding the Evolution of World Business Cycles," IMF Working Paper 05/211 (Washington: International Monetary Fund).

Kose, M. Ayhan, Eswar Prasad, and Marco Terrones, 2003, "Financial Integration and Macroeconomic Volatility," IMF Working Paper 03/50 (Washington: International Monetary Fund).

Laxton, Douglas, and Papa N'Diaye, 2002, "Monetary Policy Credibility and the Unemployment-Inflation Trade-Off: Some Evidence from 17 Industrial Countries," IMF Working Paper 02/220 (Washington: International Monetary Fund).

Maddison, Angus, 1995, *Monitoring the World Economy* (Paris: Organization for Economic Cooperation and Development).

———, 2003, *The World Economy: Historical Statistics* (Paris: Organization for Economic Cooperation and Development).

———, 2007, World Population, GDP and Per Capita GDP, 1–2003 AD data set. Available via the Internet: www.ggdc.net/Maddison.

Marshall, Monty, Keith Jaggers, and Ted Robert Gurr, 2004, Polity IV data set. Available via the Internet: www.cidcm.umd.edu/polity.

McConnell, Margaret M., and Gabriel Perez-Quiros, 2000, "Output Fluctuations in the United States: What Has Changed Since the Early 1980s?" *American Economic Review*, Vol. 90, No. 5, pp. 1464–76.

Moneta, Fabio, and Rasmus Rüffer, 2006, "Business Cycle Synchronisation in East Asia," ECB Working Paper No. 671 (Frankfurt: European Central Bank).

Orphanides, Athanasios, 2003a, "Historical Monetary Policy Analysis and the Taylor Rule," *Journal of Monetary Economics*, Vol. 50 (July), pp. 983–1022.

———, 2003b, "Monetary Policy Evaluation with Noisy Information," *Journal of Monetary Economics*, Vol. 50 (April), pp. 605–31.

Reinhart, Carmen, and Kenneth Rogoff, 2004, "The Modern History of Exchange Rate Arrangements: A Reinterpretation," *Quarterly Journal of Economics*, Vol. 119 (February), pp. 1–48.

Romer, Christina D., 1989, "The Prewar Business Cycle Reconsidered: New Estimates of Gross National Product, 1869–1908," *Journal of Political Economy*, Vol. 97 (February), pp. 1–37.

———, 1999, "Changes in Business Cycles: Evidence and Explanations," *Journal of Economic Perspectives*, Vol. 13, No. 2, pp. 23–44.

———, and David H. Romer, 2002, "The Evolution of Economic Understanding and Postwar Stabilization Policy," in *Rethinking Stabilization Policy* (Federal Reserve Bank of Kansas City), pp. 11–78.

Satyanath, Shanker, and Arvind Subramanian, 2004, "What Determines Long-Run Macroeconomic Stability? Democratic Institutions," IMF Working Paper 04/215 (Washington: International Monetary Fund).

Sommer, Martin, 2007, "Habit Formation and Aggregate Consumption Dynamics," *The B.E. Journal of Macroeconomics—Advances*, Vol. 7, No. 1, Article 21. Available via the Internet: www.bepress.com/bejm/vol7/iss1/art21.

Stock, James H., and Mark W. Watson, 2002, "Macroeconomic Forecasting Using Diffusion Indexes," *Journal of Business and Economic Statistics*, Vol. 20, pp. 147–62.

———, 2003, "Has the Business Cycle Changed and Why?" in *NBER Macroeconomics Annual 2002* (Cambridge, Massachusetts: MIT Press), pp. 159–218.

———, 2005, "Understanding Changes in International Business Cycle Dynamics," *Journal of the European Economic Association*, Vol. 3 (September), pp. 968–1006.

Summers, Peter M., 2005, "What Caused the Great Moderation? Some Cross-Country Evidence," *Economic Review* (Third Quarter) (Federal Reserve Bank of Kansas City), pp. 5–32.

Wacziarg, Romain, and Karen Horn Welch, 2003, "Trade Liberalization and Growth: New Evidence," NBER Working Paper No. 10152 (Cambridge, Massachusetts: National Bureau of Economic Research).

White, William R., 2006, "Procyclicality in the Financial System: Do We Need a New Macrofinancial Stabilisation Framework?" BIS Working Paper No. 193 (Basel: Bank for International Settlements).

World Bank, 2007, *World Development Indicators* (Washington: World Bank).

IMF EXECUTIVE BOARD DISCUSSION OF THE OUTLOOK, SEPTEMBER 2007

The following remarks by the Acting Chair were made at the conclusion of the Executive Board's discussion of the World Economic Outlook *on September 24, 2007.*

Global Prospects and Policies

Executive Directors welcomed the continued strong growth of the global economy in the first half of 2007, while emphasizing that downside risks to the near-term outlook have increased in the face of the ongoing financial market disturbances. They expected global growth in the period ahead to be slower than previously forecast in the July update, although the severity of the slowdown is difficult to predict given the uncertainties regarding the magnitude and duration of the financial stress. Directors were generally of the view that the global economy's strong fundamentals and the continued robust growth of emerging market and other developing economies will cushion the impact of the disturbances. In light of this, many Directors agreed that while the situation was still evolving, at this point the degree of the slowdown seemed likely to be relatively modest and agreed with the staff's baseline forecast. However, a number of Directors cautioned that the slowdown in growth could be more severe.

Directors acknowledged that at the current juncture, the global outlook remains exceptionally uncertain. A number of Directors saw heightened risks of prolonged financial market instability and a broad credit retrenchment, with the possibility of further financial contagion and declining confidence that could weaken the global growth environment. In particular, further downward pressure on house prices in the United States may cause steeper declines in residential investment and consumption growth, with consequently more severe spillovers to the rest of the world. In addition, the risks faced by some countries may be compounded by the rapid appreciation of their currencies. Some emerging market countries with large current account deficits could be particularly at risk from more restricted availability of external financing. Some Directors also stressed that the possibility of a disorderly unwinding of global imbalances remains an important concern. Others saw little risk of a disorderly unwinding.

Against this backdrop, Directors underscored the importance of sound policies and continued vigilance. They saw the task of restoring orderly conditions in financial markets as the immediate policy priority, and generally endorsed the actions by central banks in the major advanced economies to address the continuing squeeze in liquidity. At the same time, they emphasized that it is important to avoid perceptions that central banks will automatically respond to financial distress by taking action to curtail losses, which could raise moral hazard and reduce credit discipline. A number of Directors viewed the repricing of risks and tightening of credit standards as a return toward greater market discipline after a prolonged period of excessive risk-taking in certain market segments. Directors believed that an important lesson to be learned from the financial market turbulence is the need to ensure effective financial regulation, which will call for greater transparency and improved awareness of financial risks.

Directors noted that a slower pace of growth is likely to moderate pressures on capacity and resources, which will help reduce inflationary pressure. At the same time, tight commodities markets and rising food prices will remain important sources of price pressures, especially if growth continues to be strong in emerging markets. Directors agreed that in setting the monetary stance, central banks should focus on achieving price stability in the medium term, and continue to carefully assess the inflation outlook in light of the envisaged downside risks to growth.

Looking toward the medium term, Directors underlined the importance of actions to strengthen the foundations for sustained high growth. Many countries will need to pursue ambitious medium-term fiscal consolidation plans to address rising pressures on health and social security spending. They will also need to advance key reforms—including further liberalizing financial and service sectors in advanced countries and improving infrastructure and the business environment in emerging and developing countries—in order to take full advantage of the opportunities provided by globalization and technological advances.

Directors welcomed the analysis of the role that better monetary and fiscal policies, stronger institutions, and financial development have played over the past two decades in reducing the volatility of economic growth. Some Directors noted that fewer exogenous shocks and the rise of the emerging market economies may have contributed to lower volatility. Directors emphasized, however, that the lower volatility of growth does not mean that future stability should be taken for granted. Policymakers will need to stand ready to adapt to changing circumstances, particularly in light of the increased risk of spillover effects associated with the more synchronized business cycles across countries.

Advanced Economies

Most Directors agreed that the risks to the short-term outlook in the United States are firmly on the downside, given the financial market turmoil, weak housing market, softening labor market, and declining productivity growth. They emphasized that the current financial market turmoil could broaden, and a more protracted housing downturn could put pressure on household finances and consumption. They accordingly considered the downward revision in the growth forecast for 2008 to be reasonable. With inflation pressures declining and inflation expectations remaining well anchored, Directors saw room for monetary policy to help cushion the downside risks to the outlook. Directors were encouraged by the recent fiscal overperformance, while stressing that a more ambitious medium-term program of fiscal consolidation will be needed to guarantee long-term fiscal sustainability.

Directors welcomed the relatively strong performance of the euro area economy, but cautioned that the balance of risks to near-term growth has shifted to the downside because of slowing growth in the United States and the financial market turmoil. They noted that the European Central Bank continues to monitor developments closely to ensure inflation objectives are met. Directors welcomed the progress made toward fiscal consolidation, but felt that more ambitious efforts will be necessary given the strength of the cyclical upswing and the looming pressures from population aging. Directors also noted that the euro area's long-term prospects will hinge on its success in accelerating productivity and employment growth, and improving structural flexibility. Enhancing the contestability of services markets will help boost productivity in these sectors, while steps to strengthen incentives to work and improve wage flexibility will be key elements in labor and product market reforms.

Directors noted that after two quarters of very strong growth, the Japanese economy contracted in the second quarter of 2007, driven by a drop in investment and weaker consumption growth. The outlook remains mixed, as growth could be dampened by the recent financial market turmoil and yen appreciation. Directors supported the Bank of Japan's accommodative monetary stance, and suggested that monetary tightening should await clear signs that inflation is moving decisively higher and that risks from recent financial market volatility are waning. Directors were encouraged by the considerable progress made in reducing the fiscal deficit in recent years, but urged a more ambitious fiscal agenda to lower the public debt ratio and meet the challenge of population aging.

Emerging Market and Other Developing Countries

Directors believed that large foreign exchange inflows in emerging market and other developing countries could continue to complicate macroeconomic management in the coming years. They stressed that the nature of the inflows—including their composition and terms—and country circumstances will determine the appropriate policy response to large capital inflows in individual cases. Many Directors agreed that fiscal restraint and increasing exchange rate flexibility, complemented by capital account liberalization, can be helpful in attenuating the impact of these inflows. A number of Directors, however, noted that fiscal adjustment may not always be feasible or effective, and that sustained exchange rate appreciation could cause difficulties. These Directors suggested that temporary capital controls, while not a first-best measure, might be a practical way to deal with capital flows in certain cases, as a useful supplement to macroeconomic policies. A number of Directors considered it important to distinguish between short-term and long-term capital flows, as the policy implications would be different. Directors agreed that fostering financial development and strengthening financial regulation and supervision are also important in the face of capital inflows.

Directors expected growth in emerging market countries in Asia to remain strong, led by China and India. Most Directors viewed the balance of risks as being tilted to the downside, particularly because of the U.S. economic slowdown. Some Directors, however, believed that the risks to growth and inflation in China are on the upside in the absence of additional monetary tightening and more flexible exchange rate management. Against the background of continuing large current account surpluses in many countries in the region, several Directors emphasized that greater exchange rate flexibility and measures to boost domestic demand would help reduce the reliance on export-led growth.

Directors welcomed the favorable economic performance and the reduced external vulnerability in Latin America, which reflect stronger policy frameworks, improved debt management, and development of domestic capital markets. At the same time, they observed that growth remains subject to risks arising from the close trade and financial linkages with the United States and the dependence on commodity exports. They emphasized the importance of reforms to foster investment and productivity growth. Directors noted that in recent years Latin American countries have experienced large foreign exchange flows. They welcomed the greater exchange rate flexibility in many countries that has helped to contain inflation in the face of these inflows.

Directors welcomed the continued rapid economic convergence of emerging Europe, supported by robust productivity growth, but expressed concern about overheating in some countries. They observed that the recent financial market turbulence has heightened concerns about the vulnerability of some countries in the region to reversals of capital flows, especially given the heavy reliance on foreign-currency borrowing and the potential for spillover effects. In this context, Directors underscored the importance of prudent macroeconomic policies, structural reforms to improve economic flexibility, and vigilant bank supervision.

Directors observed that economic activity in the Commonwealth of Independent States continues to expand rapidly, supported by high commodity prices and large capital inflows. Growth prospects appear to be generally positive, although global credit retrenchment has affected the outlook in some countries. Directors welcomed the region's ability to attract large inflows of foreign private capital, but underscored that limited exchange rate flexibility in many countries has resulted in upward price pressures. They saw a need for more flexible exchange rates, and for continued efforts to strengthen institutions, the business climate, and bank regulation and supervision.

Directors were encouraged by the sustained expansion in sub-Saharan Africa, which is being led by high commodity prices, improved policy implementation, reforms to strengthen the business environment, and debt reduction. Growth is expected to accelerate in a number of countries in 2008 as new oil projects come on stream. Sustaining the growth performance and promoting export diversification will require continued macroeconomic stability and a vibrant private sector, supported by further trade liberalization, improved market access for regional exports, and fulfillment of aid commitments by advanced economies.

In the Middle East, high oil prices have supported buoyant growth and strong external and fiscal balances in oil-exporting countries, and are expected to continue to do so in the near term. At the same time, Directors noted that resource utilization and import prices are rising, leading to inflationary pressures in many oil-exporting and oil-importing countries. The challenge for fiscal policy in oil-exporting countries is to strike the right balance between using the oil revenues to pursue long-term development objectives and exercising restraint in the short term to counterbalance strong private demand growth. While welcoming the ongoing buildup of investment in the petroleum sector in a number of oil-exporting countries, Directors underscored the importance of continuing to foster private investment in both the oil and the non-oil sectors of these economies.

Multilateral and Other Issues

Directors welcomed the analysis of the relationship between globalization and inequality, while noting the importance of interpreting the results in the context of individual country circumstances. Most Directors accepted the two main findings of the study: first, that technological change is more important than globalization in explaining rising inequality in many countries; and, second, that contrary to popular belief, trade liberalization appears to reduce inequality while financial globalization appears to increase it. Directors cautioned that the solution to rising inequality would be not to restrict foreign direct investment, but rather to strengthen education to ensure that workers have the appropriate skills in the emerging "knowledge-based" global economy. Labor market reforms will be needed to ensure that jobs are created flexibly in the most dynamic sectors. Also, social safety nets should be enhanced to provide greater protection for those who may be adversely affected by globalization, and policies will be needed to increase the availability of finance to the poor.

Directors emphasized that multilateral action to ensure a smooth unwinding of global imbalances remains a critical task. During the Fund's Multilateral Consultation, the participants indicated their policy plans that are consistent with the strategy endorsed by the IMFC for reducing global imbalances. These comprise steps to boost national saving in the United States, including fiscal consolidation; further progress on growth-enhancing reforms in Europe; further structural reforms, including fiscal consolidation, in Japan; reforms to boost domestic demand in emerging Asia, together with greater exchange rate flexibility in a number of surplus countries; and increased spending consistent with absorptive capacity and macroeconomic stability in oil-producing countries. Full implementation of these policy plans is needed to reduce imbalances while sustaining growth. While Directors acknowledged that there has been some progress toward realignment of major world currencies, they noted the staff's analysis that the U.S. dollar is still overvalued and that the yen, the renminbi, and the currencies of the oil-exporting countries are still undervalued relative to their medium-term fundamentals.

Directors expressed concern about the continued lack of progress with the Doha multilateral trade round, and the risk that this would encourage protectionist measures. They expressed hope that countries would find a way to re-energize the process of multilateral trade liberalization. Directors also agreed that global issues such as climate change and energy security would also require a multilateral approach.

STATISTICAL APPENDIX

The Statistical Appendix presents historical data, as well as projections. It comprises five sections: Assumptions, What's New, Data and Conventions, Classification of Countries, and Statistical Tables.

The assumptions underlying the estimates and projections for 2007–08 and the medium-term scenario for 2009–12 are summarized in the first section. The second section presents a brief description of changes to the database and statistical tables. The third section provides a general description of the data and of the conventions used for calculating country group composites. The classification of countries in the various groups presented in the *World Economic Outlook* is summarized in the fourth section.

The last, and main, section comprises the statistical tables. Data in these tables have been compiled on the basis of information available through end-September 2007. The figures for 2007 and beyond are shown with the same degree of precision as the historical figures solely for convenience; because they are projections, the same degree of accuracy is not to be inferred.

Assumptions

Real effective *exchange rates* for the advanced economies are assumed to remain constant at their average levels during the period August 22 to September 19, 2007. For 2007 and 2008, these assumptions imply average U.S. dollar/SDR conversion rates of 1.520 and 1.538, U.S. dollar/euro conversion rates of 1.35 and 1.37, and yen/U.S. dollar conversion rates of 118.4 and 115.0, respectively.

It is assumed that the *price of oil* will average $68.52 a barrel in 2007 and $75.00 a barrel in 2008.

Established *policies* of national authorities are assumed to be maintained. The more specific policy assumptions underlying the projections for selected advanced economies are described in Box A1.

With regard to *interest rates*, it is assumed that the London interbank offered rate (LIBOR) on six-month U.S. dollar deposits will average 5.2 percent in 2007 and 4.4 percent in 2008, that three-month euro deposits will average 4.0 percent in 2007 and 4.1 percent in 2008, and that six-month Japanese yen deposits will average 0.9 percent in 2007 and 1.1 percent in 2008.

With respect to *introduction of the euro*, on December 31, 1998, the Council of the European Union decided that, effective January 1, 1999, the irrevocably fixed conversion rates between the euro and currencies of the member states adopting the euro are as follows.

1 euro	= 13.7603	Austrian schillings
	= 40.3399	Belgian francs
	= 1.95583	Deutsche mark
	= 5.94573	Finnish markkaa
	= 6.55957	French francs
	= 340.750	Greek drachma[1]
	= 0.787564	Irish pound
	= 1,936.27	Italian lire
	= 40.3399	Luxembourg francs
	= 2.20371	Netherlands guilders
	= 200.482	Portuguese escudos
	= 239.640	Slovenian tolars[2]
	= 166.386	Spanish pesetas

See Box 5.4 in the October 1998 *World Economic Outlook* for details on how the conversion rates were established.

[1]The conversion rate for Greece was established prior to inclusion in the euro area on January 1, 2001.

[2]The conversion rate for Slovenia was established prior to inclusion in the euro area on January 1, 2007.

Box A1. Economic Policy Assumptions Underlying the Projections for Selected Economies

The short-term ***fiscal policy assumptions*** used in the *World Economic Outlook* are based on officially announced budgets, adjusted for differences between the national authorities and the IMF staff regarding macroeconomic assumptions and projected fiscal outturns. The medium-term fiscal projections incorporate policy measures that are judged likely to be implemented. In cases where the IMF staff has insufficient information to assess the authorities' budget intentions and prospects for policy implementation, an unchanged structural primary balance is assumed, unless otherwise indicated. Specific assumptions used in some of the advanced economies follow (see also Tables B5–B7 in the Statistical Appendix for data on fiscal and structural balances).[1]

United States. The fiscal projections are based on the administration's FY2008 budget and Mid-Session Review (February and July, 2007). Adjustments are made to account for differences in macroeconomic projections as well as staff assumptions about (1) additional defense spending based on analysis by the Congressional Budget Office; (2) slower compression in the growth rate of discretionary spending; and (3) continued AMT relief beyond FY2008. The projections also assume that proposed Medicare savings are achieved only in part, and that personal retirement accounts are not introduced.

Japan. The medium-term fiscal projections assume that expenditure and revenue of the general government (excluding social security) are adjusted in line with the current government target to achieve primary fiscal balance (excluding social security) by FY2011.

Germany. Projections reflect the fiscal measures announced in the 2005 government's coalition agreement, 2007 Stability and Growth Pact, the 2008 budget, and 2009–2011 financial plan for the central government. Specifically, projections include the increase in indirect taxes due to the VAT rate increase in 2007, as well as a loss in direct tax revenue due to corporate income tax reform implementation in 2008.

France. The fiscal projections for 2007 are based on the initial budget law and incorporate the impact of the July 2007 tax package. Medium-term projections reflect the authorities' latest official tax revenue forecast, including the impact of the recent tax measures, but assume different spending and nontax revenue profiles, consistent with an unchanged policy assumption. All fiscal projections are adjusted for the IMF staff's macroeconomic assumptions.

Italy. For 2007, the deficit projection is based on the IMF staff's assessment of this year's budget, adjusted for recent developments, including the additional expenditure package adopted in the summer of 2007. In addition, it is assumed that revenue overperformance relative to the official projections in the medium-term economic and budget plan of June (also known as DPEF) would not be spent. For the medium term, staff projects its own "current policies" scenario, defined as a constant structural primary balance net of one-off measures.

United Kingdom. The fiscal projections are based on information provided in the 2007 Budget Report. Additionally, the projections incorporate the most recent statistical releases from the Office for National Statistics, including provisional budgetary outturns through the first quarter of 2007.

Canada. Projections use the baseline forecast in the 2007 Budget for FY2007/08–2008/09 and the 2006 Economic and Fiscal Update for

[1]The output gap is actual less potential output, as a percent of potential output. Structural balances are expressed as a percent of potential output. The structural budget balance is the budgetary position that would be observed if the level of actual output coincided with potential output. Changes in the structural budget balance consequently include effects of temporary fiscal measures, the impact of fluctuations in interest rates and debt-service costs, and other noncyclical fluctuations in the budget balance. The computations of structural budget balances are based on IMF staff estimates of potential GDP and revenue and expenditure elasticities (see the October 1993 *World Economic Outlook*, Annex I). Net debt is defined as gross debt less financial assets of the general government, which include assets held by the social security insurance system. Estimates of the output gap and of the structural balance are subject to significant margins of uncertainty.

FY2009/10–2010/11. The staff forecast incorporates the most recent data releases from Statistics Canada, including provincial and territorial budgetary outturns through the first quarter of 2007.

Australia. The fiscal projections through the fiscal year 2010/11 are based on the budget published in May 2007. For the remainder of the projection period, the IMF staff assumes unchanged policies.

Austria. Fiscal figures for 2006 are based on the authorities' estimated outturn. Projections for 2007 and beyond are IMF staff projections based on current policies in place.

Brazil. The fiscal projections for 2007 are based on the information provided in the 2007 budget and recent budget execution decrees, with some adjustments made by the IMF staff. For the remainder of the projection period, the IMF staff assumes unchanged policies, except for a further increase in public investment in line with the authorities' intentions.

Belgium. The projections for 2007 are based on the information provided in the 2007 Budget Report. For 2007, the projection excludes one-off measures not explicitly outlined in the budget (representing 0.3 percent of GDP). For the remainder of the projection period, the IMF staff assumes unchanged policies.

China. Projections for 2007 are based on the authorities' budget released in March, with some adjustment for the IMF staff's definition for overall budget balance. For 2008, IMF staff projections assume that the deficit will be held roughly constant at its projected 2008 level (just under 1 percent of GDP), which is broadly in line with the authorities' budget plans.

Denmark. Projections for 2007 are aligned with the latest official projections and budget. For 2008–12, the projections incorporate the June 2006 welfare agreement as well as key features of the prior medium-term fiscal plan.

Greece. Projections are based on the 2007 budget, the latest Stability Program, and other forecasts provided by the authorities. According to preliminary estimates by the European Commission, the revision of gross national income could lead to a permanent increase of Greece's contribution to the EU budget of less than ¼ percent of GDP, as well as to a one-off payment of arrears of such a contribution of about ¾ percent of GDP, which could accrue to the 2007 balance. These possible contributions are not reflected in the staff projections.

Hong Kong SAR. Fiscal projections for 2007–10 are consistent with the authorities' medium-term strategy as outlined in the FY2007–08 budget, with projections for 2011–12 based on the assumptions underlying the IMF staff's medium-term macroeconomic scenario.

India. Projections for 2007 are based on the authorities' budget, with some adjustment for the IMF staff's assumptions. For the remainder of the projection period, the IMF staff assumes unchanged policies.

Korea. Projections for 2007 are based on the authorities' budget, with some adjustment for the IMF staff's assumptions. For 2008–12, projections are in line with the authorities' budget plans.

Mexico. Fiscal projections for 2007 build on the authorities' budget. Projections for 2008 and beyond are based on the IMF staff calculations in line with the Federal Government Fiscal Responsibility Law.

Netherlands. The fiscal projections build on the 2006 and 2007 budgets, the latest Stability Program, and other forecasts provided by the authorities.

New Zealand. The fiscal projections through the fiscal year 2010/11 are based on the 2007/08 budget released in May 2007. For the remainder of the projection period, the IMF staff assumes unchanged policies. The New Zealand fiscal account switched to new GAAP standards beginning in the 2006/07 fiscal year, with no comparable historical data.

Portugal. Fiscal projections through 2010 are based on the IMF staff's assessment of the 2007 budget and the authorities' revised projections presented in April 2007, which updated the current Stability Program. In subsequent years, the fiscal projections assume maintaining the primary balance excluding age-related expenditures.

Box A1 *(concluded)*

Singapore. For FY2007/08, expenditure projections are based on budget numbers, while revenue projections reflect IMF staff estimates of the impact of new policy measures, including an increase in the goods and services tax. Medium-term revenue projections assume that capital gains on fiscal reserves will be included in investment income.

Spain. Fiscal projections through 2009 are based on the 2007 budget and the 2008 draft budget policies outlined in the authorities' updated Stability Program 2006–09, information from recent statistical releases, and official announcements. In subsequent years, the fiscal projections assume unchanged policies.

Sweden. The fiscal projections are based on information provided in the budget presented on October 16, 2006. Additionally, the projections incorporate the most recent statistical releases from Statistics Sweden, including provisional budgetary outturns through December 2006.

Switzerland. Projections for 2007–12 are based on IMF staff calculations, which incorporate measures to restore balance in the Federal accounts and strengthen social security finances.

Monetary policy assumptions are based on the established policy framework in each country. In most cases, this implies a nonaccommodative stance over the business cycle: official interest rates will therefore increase when economic indicators suggest that inflation will rise above its acceptable rate or range, and they will decrease when indicators suggest that prospective inflation will not exceed the acceptable rate or range, that prospective output growth is below its potential rate, and that the margin of slack in the economy is significant. On this basis, the LIBOR on six-month U.S. dollar deposits is assumed to average 5.2 percent in 2007 and 4.4 percent in 2008 (see Table 1.1). The projected path reflects the assumption prevailing in financial markets that the Federal Reserve will cut interest rates in late 2007 and early 2008. The rate on three-month euro deposits is assumed to average 4.0 percent in 2007 and 4.1 percent in 2008. The interest rate on six-month Japanese yen deposits is assumed to average 0.9 percent in 2007 and 1.1 percent in 2008.

What's New

The following changes have been made to streamline the Statistical Appendix of the *World Economic Outlook.* Starting with this issue, the printed version of the *World Economic Outlook* will carry only Part A Tables in the Statistical Appendix section.

Part A contains Tables 1, 2, 3, 6, 7, 8, 11, 20, 25, 26, 31, 35, 43, and 44 from the previous issues of the *World Economic Outlook*; Tables 1.2 and 1.3, which used to be in the main text of the report; and a new table on private capital flows. Tables in Part A present summary data for both advanced economies and emerging market and developing countries in the categories of Output, Inflation, Financial Policies, Foreign Trade, Current Account Transactions, Balance of Payments and External Financing, Flow of Funds, and Medium-Term Baseline Scenario.

Part B of the Statistical Appendix contains the remaining tables. The complete Statistical Appendix, which includes both Part A and Part B Tables, will be available only via the Internet at www.imf.org/external/pubs/ft/weo/2007/02/index.htm.

Data and Conventions

Data and projections for 182 countries form the statistical basis for the *World Economic Outlook* (the World Economic Outlook database). The data are maintained jointly by the IMF's Research Department and area departments, with the latter regularly updating country projections based on consistent global assumptions.

Although national statistical agencies are the ultimate providers of historical data and definitions, international organizations are also involved in statistical issues, with the objective of harmonizing methodologies for the national compilation of statistics, including the analytical frameworks, concepts, definitions, classifications, and valuation procedures used in the production of economic statistics. The World Economic Outlook database reflects information from both national source agencies and international organizations.

The comprehensive revision of the standardized *System of National Accounts 1993 (SNA),* the IMF's *Balance of Payments Manual, Fifth Edition (BPM5),* the *Monetary and Financial Statistics Manual (MFSM),* and the *Government Finance Statistics Manual 2001 (GFSM 2001)* represented important improvements in the standards of economic statistics and analysis.[3] The IMF was actively involved in all these projects, particularly the *Balance of Payments, Monetary and Financial Statistics,* and *Government Finance Statistics* manuals, which reflects the IMF's special interest in countries' external positions, financial sector stability, and public sector fiscal positions. The process of adapting country data to the new definitions began in earnest when the manuals were released. However, full concordance with the manuals is ultimately dependent on the provision by national statistical compilers of revised country data, and hence the *World Economic Outlook* estimates are still only partially adapted to these manuals.

In line with recent improvements in standards of reporting economic statistics, several countries have phased out their traditional *fixed-base-year* method of calculating real macroeconomic variables levels and growth by switching to a *chain-weighted* method of computing aggregate growth. Recent dramatic changes in the structure of these economies have obliged these countries to revise the way in which they measure real GDP levels and growth. Switching to the chain-weighted method of computing aggregate growth, which uses current price information, allows countries to measure GDP growth more accurately by eliminating upward biases in new data.[4] Currently, real macroeconomic data for Albania, Australia, Austria, Azerbaijan, Belgium, Canada, the Czech Republic, Cyprus, Denmark, the euro area, Finland, France, Georgia, Germany, Greece, Iceland, Ireland, Italy, Japan, Kazakhstan, Lithuania, Luxembourg, Malta, the Netherlands, New Zealand, Norway, Poland, Portugal, Russia, Slovenia, Spain, Sweden, Switzerland, the United Kingdom, and the United States are based on chain-weighted methodology. However, data before 1996 (Albania), 1995 (Belgium), 1995 (Cyprus), 1995 (Czech Republic), 1995 (euro area), 1991 (Germany), 2000 (Greece), 1994 (Kazakhstan), 1990 (Iceland), 1995 (Ireland), 1994 (Japan), 1995 (Luxembourg), 2000 (Malta), 1995 (Poland), 1995 (Russia), 1995 (Slovenia), and 1995 (Spain) are based on unrevised national accounts and subject to revision in the future.

The members of the European Union have adopted a harmonized system for the compilation of the national accounts, referred to as ESA 1995. All national accounts data from 1995 onward are presented on the basis of the new system. Revision by national authorities of data prior to 1995 to conform to the new system has progressed but has, in some cases, not been completed. In such cases, historical *World Economic Outlook* data have been carefully adjusted to avoid breaks in the series. Users of EU national accounts data prior to 1995 should nevertheless exercise caution until such time as

[3]Commission of the European Communities, International Monetary Fund, Organization for Economic Cooperation and Development, United Nations, and World Bank, *System of National Accounts 1993* (Brussels/Luxembourg, New York, Paris, and Washington, 1993); International Monetary Fund, *Balance of Payments Manual, Fifth Edition* (Washington, 1993); International Monetary Fund, *Monetary and Financial Statistics Manual* (Washington, 2000); and International Monetary Fund, *Government Finance Statistics Manual* (Washington, 2001).

[4]Charles Steindel, 1995, "Chain-Weighting: The New Approach to Measuring GDP," *Current Issues in Economics and Finance* (Federal Reserve Bank of New York), Vol. 1 (December).

the revision of historical data by national statistical agencies has been fully completed. See Box 1.2, "Revisions in National Accounts Methodologies," in the May 2000 *World Economic Outlook.*

Composite data for country groups in the *World Economic Outlook* are either sums or weighted averages of data for individual countries. Unless otherwise indicated, multiyear averages of growth rates are expressed as compound annual rates of change.[5] Arithmetically weighted averages are used for all data except inflation and money growth for the other emerging market and developing country group, for which geometric averages are used. The following conventions apply.

- Country group composites for exchange rates, interest rates, and the growth rates of monetary aggregates are weighted by GDP converted to U.S. dollars at market exchange rates (averaged over the preceding three years) as a share of group GDP.
- Composites for other data relating to the domestic economy, whether growth rates or ratios, are weighted by GDP valued at purchasing power parities (PPPs) as a share of total world or group GDP.[6]
- Composites for data relating to the domestic economy for the euro area (13 member countries throughout the entire period unless otherwise noted) are aggregates of national source data using weights based on 1995 European currency unit (ECU) exchange rates.
- Composite unemployment rates and employment growth are weighted by labor force as a share of group labor force.
- Composites relating to the external economy are sums of individual country data after conversion to U.S. dollars at the average market exchange rates in the years indicated for balance of payments data and at end-of-year market exchange rates for debt denominated in currencies other than U.S. dollars. Composites of changes in foreign trade volumes and prices, however, are arithmetic averages of percentage changes for individual countries weighted by the U.S. dollar value of exports or imports as a share of total world or group exports or imports (in the preceding year).

For central and eastern European countries, external transactions in nonconvertible currencies (through 1990) are converted to U.S. dollars at the implicit U.S. dollar/ruble conversion rates obtained from each country's national currency exchange rate for the U.S. dollar and for the ruble.

All data refer to calendar years, except for the following countries, which refer to fiscal years: Australia (July/June), Bangladesh (July/June), Egypt (July/June), Ethiopia (July/June), Islamic Republic of Iran (March/February), Mauritius (July/June), Myanmar (April/March), Nepal (July/June), New Zealand (July/June), Pakistan (July/June), Samoa (July/June), and Tonga (July/June).

Classification of Countries

Summary of the Country Classification

The country classification in the *World Economic Outlook* divides the world into two major groups: advanced economies, and other emerging market and developing countries.[7] Rather than being based on strict criteria, economic or otherwise, this classification has evolved over time with the objective of facilitating analysis by providing a reasonably meaningful organization

[5]Averages for real GDP and its components, employment, per capita GDP, inflation, factor productivity, trade, and commodity prices are calculated based on compound annual rate of change, except for the unemployment rate, which is based on simple arithmetic average.

[6]See Box A2 of the April 2004 *World Economic Outlook* for a summary of the revised PPP-based weights and Annex IV of the May 1993 *World Economic Outlook.* See also Anne-Marie Gulde and Marianne Schulze-Ghattas, "Purchasing Power Parity Based Weights for the *World Economic Outlook,*" in *Staff Studies for the World Economic Outlook* (International Monetary Fund, December 1993), pp. 106–23.

[7]As used here, the term "country" does not in all cases refer to a territorial entity that is a state as understood by international law and practice. It also covers some territorial entities that are not states, but for which statistical data are maintained on a separate and independent basis.

Table A. Classification by *World Economic Outlook* Groups and Their Shares in Aggregate GDP, Exports of Goods and Services, and Population, 2006[1]

(Percent of total for group or world)

	Number of Countries	GDP		Exports of Goods and Services		Population	
		Advanced economies	World	Advanced economies	World	Advanced economies	World
Advanced economies	**30**	**100.0**	**52.0**	**100.0**	**67.7**	**100.0**	**15.3**
United States		37.8	19.7	14.6	9.8	30.7	4.7
Euro area	13	28.2	14.7	42.8	28.7	32.2	4.9
Germany		7.4	3.9	13.3	8.9	8.4	1.3
France		5.6	2.9	6.1	4.1	6.3	1.0
Italy		5.2	2.7	5.2	3.5	6.0	0.9
Spain		3.5	1.8	3.3	2.2	4.5	0.7
Japan		12.1	6.3	7.4	5.0	13.1	2.0
United Kingdom		6.2	3.2	6.9	4.6	6.2	0.9
Canada		3.4	1.7	4.7	3.1	3.3	0.5
Other advanced economies	13	12.4	6.4	23.6	15.8	14.5	2.2
Memorandum							
Major advanced economies	7	77.6	40.4	58.2	39.1	73.9	11.3
Newly industrialized Asian economies	4	6.5	3.4	13.8	9.3	8.4	1.3
		Other emerging market and developing countries	World	Other emerging market and developing countries	World	Other emerging market and developing countries	World
Other emerging market and developing countries	**143**	**100.0**	**48.0**	**100.0**	**32.9**	**100.0**	**84.7**
Regional groups							
Africa	48	7.0	3.4	7.7	2.5	15.3	12.9
Sub-Sahara	45	5.4	2.6	5.8	1.9	13.9	11.8
Excluding Nigeria and South Africa	43	2.9	1.4	2.8	0.9	10.3	8.7
Central and eastern Europe	14	7.1	3.4	13.1	4.3	3.4	2.9
Commonwealth of Independent States[2]	13	8.0	3.8	10.1	3.3	5.2	4.4
Russia		5.4	2.6	6.9	2.3	2.6	2.2
Developing Asia	23	56.3	27.0	38.7	12.7	61.9	52.4
China		31.4	15.1	22.0	7.2	24.2	20.5
India		13.1	6.3	4.1	1.3	20.5	17.4
Excluding China and India	21	11.7	5.6	12.6	4.1	17.1	14.5
Middle East	13	5.9	2.8	14.5	4.8	4.3	3.6
Western Hemisphere	32	15.7	7.6	15.9	5.2	10.0	8.5
Brazil		5.4	2.6	3.3	1.1	3.4	2.9
Mexico		3.7	1.8	5.5	1.8	1.9	1.6
Analytical groups							
By source of export earnings							
Fuel	23	13.3	6.4	26.5	8.7	10.9	9.2
Nonfuel	120	86.7	41.6	73.5	24.1	89.1	75.5
of which, primary products	21	1.7	0.8	2.2	0.7	4.1	3.5
By external financing source							
Net debtor countries	121	54.1	26.0	48.4	15.9	64.8	54.9
of which, official financing	34	6.1	2.9	3.8	1.2	14.0	11.8
Net debtor countries by debt-servicing experience							
Countries with arrears and/or rescheduling during 2001–05	51	10.2	4.9	7.6	2.5	19.0	16.1
Other net debtor countries	70	43.9	21.1	40.8	13.4	45.8	38.8
Other groups							
Heavily indebted poor countries	30	2.0	1.0	1.2	0.4	8.3	7.0
Middle East and north Africa	19	7.8	3.8	16.6	5.5	6.4	5.4

[1]The GDP shares are based on the purchasing-power-parity (PPP) valuation of country GDPs. The number of countries comprising each group reflects those for which data are included in the group aggregates.

[2]Mongolia, which is not a member of the Commonwealth of Independent States, is included in this group for reasons of geography and similarities in economic structure.

Table B. Advanced Economies by Subgroup

Major Currency Areas	Other Subgroups					
	Euro area		Newly industrialized Asian economies	Major advanced economies	Other advanced economies	
United States	Austria	Ireland	Hong Kong SAR[1]	Canada	Australia	Korea
Euro area	Belgium	Italy	Korea	France	Cyprus	New Zealand
Japan	Finland	Luxembourg	Singapore	Germany	Denmark	Norway
	France	Netherlands	Taiwan Province of China	Italy	Hong Kong SAR[1]	Singapore
	Germany	Portugal		Japan	Iceland	Sweden
	Greece	Slovenia		United Kingdom	Israel	Switzerland
		Spain		United States		Taiwan Province of China

[1]On July 1, 1997, Hong Kong was returned to the People's Republic of China and became a Special Administrative Region of China.

of data. Table A provides an overview of these standard groups in the *World Economic Outlook,* showing the number of countries in each group and the average 2006 shares of groups in aggregate PPP-valued GDP, total exports of goods and services, and population.

A few countries are currently not included in these groups, either because they are not IMF members and their economies are not monitored by the IMF or because databases have not yet been fully developed. Because of data limitations, group composites do not reflect the following countries: the Islamic Republic of Afghanistan, Bosnia and Herzegovina, Brunei Darussalam, Eritrea, Iraq, Liberia, Serbia, Somalia, and Timor-Leste. Cuba and the Democratic People's Republic of Korea are examples of countries that are not IMF members, whereas San Marino, among the advanced economies, and Aruba, Marshall Islands, Federated States of Micronesia, Palau, and the Republic of Montenegro, among the developing countries, are examples of economies for which databases have not been completed.

General Features and Composition of Groups in the *World Economic Outlook* Classification

Advanced Economies

The 30 advanced economies are listed in Table B. The seven largest in terms of GDP—the United States, Japan, Germany, France, Italy, the United Kingdom, and Canada—constitute the subgroup of *major advanced economies,* often referred to as the Group of Seven (G-7) countries. The 13 members of the *euro area* and the four *newly industrialized Asian economies* are also distinguished as subgroups. Composite data shown in the tables for the euro area cover the current members for all years, even though the membership has increased over time.

In 1991 and subsequent years, data for *Germany* refer to west Germany *and* the eastern Länder (that is, the former German Democratic Republic). Before 1991, economic data were not available on a unified basis or in a consistent manner. Hence, in tables featuring data expressed as annual percent change, these apply to west Germany in years up to and including 1991, but to unified Germany from 1992 onward. In general, data on national accounts and domestic economic and financial activity through 1990 cover west Germany only, whereas data for the central government and balance of payments apply to west Germany through June 1990 and to unified Germany thereafter.

Table C. European Union

Austria	Finland	Latvia	Romania
Belgium	France	Lithuania	Slovak Republic
Bulgaria	Germany	Luxembourg	Slovenia
Cyprus	Greece	Malta	Spain
Czech Republic	Hungary	Netherlands	Sweden
Denmark	Ireland	Poland	United Kingdom
Estonia	Italy	Portugal	

Table D. Middle East and North Africa Countries

Algeria	Jordan	Morocco	Syrian Arab Republic
Bahrain	Kuwait	Oman	Tunisia
Djibouti	Lebanon	Qatar	United Arab Emirates
Egypt	Libya	Saudi Arabia	Yemen, Rep. of
Iran, I.R. of	Mauritania	Sudan	

Table C lists the member countries of the European Union, not all of which are classified as advanced economies in the *World Economic Outlook.*

Other Emerging Market and Developing Countries

The group of other emerging market and developing countries (143 countries) includes all countries that are not classified as advanced economies.

The *regional breakdowns* of other emerging market and developing countries—*Africa, central and eastern Europe, Commonwealth of Independent States, developing Asia, Middle East, and Western Hemisphere*—largely conform to the regional breakdowns in the IMF's *International Financial Statistics.* In both classifications, Egypt and the Libyan Arab Jamahiriya are included in the *Middle East* region rather than in Africa. In addition, the *World Economic Outlook* sometimes refers to the regional group of Middle East and North Africa countries, also referred to as the MENA countries, whose composition straddles the Africa and Middle East regions. This group is defined as the Arab League countries plus the Islamic Republic of Iran (see Table D).

Other emerging market and developing countries are also classified according to *analytical criteria.* The analytical criteria reflect countries' composition of export earnings and other income from abroad; exchange rate arrangements; a distinction between net creditor and net debtor countries; and, for the net debtor countries, financial criteria based on external financing sources and experience with external debt servicing. The detailed composition of other emerging market and developing countries in the regional and analytical groups is shown in Tables E and F.

The analytical criterion, by *source of export earnings,* distinguishes between categories: *fuel* (Standard International Trade Classification—SITC 3) and *nonfuel* and then focuses on *nonfuel primary products* (SITC 0, 1, 2, 4, and 68).

The financial criteria focus on *net creditor countries, net debtor countries,* and *heavily indebted poor countries (HIPCs).* Net debtor countries are

Table E. Other Emerging Market and Developing Countries by Region and Main Source of Export Earnings

	Fuel	Nonfuel, of Which Primary Products
Africa	Algeria Angola Congo, Rep. of Equatorial Guinea Gabon Nigeria Sudan	Botswana Burkina Faso Burundi Chad Congo, Dem. Rep. of Guinea Guinea-Bissau Malawi Mauritania Namibia Niger Sierra Leone Zambia Zimbabwe
Commonwealth of Independent States	Azerbaijan Russia Turkmenistan	Mongolia Tajikistan Uzbekistan
Developing Asia		Papua New Guinea Solomon Islands
Middle East	Bahrain Iran, I.R. of Kuwait Libya Oman Qatar Saudi Arabia Syrian Arab Republic United Arab Emirates Yemen, Rep. of	
Western Hemisphere	Ecuador Trinidad and Tobago Venezuela	Chile Suriname

Note: Mongolia, which is not a member of the Commonwealth of Independent States, is included in this group for reasons of geography and similarities in economic structure.

Table F. Other Emerging Market and Developing Countries by Region, Net External Position, and Heavily Indebted Poor Countries

	Net External Position		Heavily Indebted Poor Countries
	Net creditor	Net debtor[1]	
Africa			
Maghreb			
Algeria	*		
Morocco		*	
Tunisia		*	
Sub-Sahara			
South Africa		*	
Horn of Africa			
Djibouti		*	
Ethiopia		•	*
Sudan		*	
Great Lakes			
Burundi		•	*
Congo, Dem. Rep. of		*	*
Kenya		*	
Rwanda		•	*
Tanzania		•	*
Uganda		*	*
Southern Africa			
Angola		*	
Botswana	*		
Comoros		•	
Lesotho		*	
Madagascar		•	*
Malawi		•	*
Mauritius		*	
Mozambique, Rep. of		*	*
Namibia	*		
Seychelles		*	
Swaziland		*	
Zambia		*	*
Zimbabwe		*	
West and Central Africa			
Cape Verde		*	
Gambia, The		*	*
Ghana		•	*
Guinea		*	*
Mauritania		*	*
Nigeria	*		
São Tomé and Príncipe		*	*
Sierra Leone		•	*
CFA franc zone			
Benin		*	*
Burkina Faso		•	*
Cameroon		*	*
Central African Republic		•	
Chad		*	*
Congo, Rep. of		•	*
Côte d'Ivoire		*	
Equatorial Guinea		*	
Gabon		•	
Guinea-Bissau		*	*
Mali		*	*
Niger		•	*
Senegal		*	*
Togo		•	
Central and eastern Europe			
Albania		*	
Bulgaria		*	
Croatia		*	
Czech Republic		*	
Estonia		*	
Hungary		*	
Latvia		*	
Lithuania		*	
Macedonia, FYR		*	
Malta		*	
Poland		*	
Romania		*	
Slovak Republic		*	
Turkey		*	
Commonwealth of Independent States[2]			
Armenia		*	
Azerbaijan		*	
Belarus		*	
Georgia		*	
Kazakhstan		*	
Kyrgyz Republic		*	
Moldova		*	
Mongolia		•	
Russia	*		
Tajikistan		•	
Turkmenistan	*		
Ukraine	*		
Uzbekistan	*		
Developing Asia			
Bhutan		•	
Cambodia		•	
China	*		
Fiji		*	
Indonesia		*	
Kiribati	*		
Lao PDR		*	
Malaysia	*		
Myanmar		*	
Papua New Guinea		*	
Philippines		*	
Samoa		*	
Solomon Islands		•	
Thailand		*	
Tonga		•	
Vanuatu		*	
Vietnam		•	
South Asia			
Bangladesh		•	
India		*	
Maldives		*	
Nepal		•	
Pakistan		•	
Sri Lanka		•	

Table F *(concluded)*

	Net External Position: Net creditor	Net External Position: Net debtor[1]	Heavily Indebted Poor Countries
Middle East			
Bahrain	*		
Iran, I.R. of	*		
Kuwait	*		
Libya	*		
Oman	*		
Qatar	*		
Saudi Arabia	*		
United Arab Emirates	*		
Yemen, Rep. of	*		
Mashreq			
Egypt		*	
Jordan		*	
Lebanon		*	
Syrian Arab Republic		*	
Western Hemisphere			
Mexico		*	
South America			
Argentina		*	
Brazil		*	
Bolivia		•	*
Chile		*	
Colombia		*	
Ecuador		*	
Paraguay		•	
Peru		•	
Uruguay		•	
Venezuela	*		
Central America			
Costa Rica		*	
El Salvador		•	
Guatemala		*	
Honduras		*	*
Nicaragua		*	*
Panama		*	
The Caribbean			
Antigua and Barbuda		*	
Bahamas, The		*	
Barbados		*	
Belize		*	
Dominica		*	
Dominican Republic		•	
Grenada		•	
Guyana		*	*
Haiti		*	*
Jamaica		*	
St. Kitts and Nevis		*	
St. Lucia		*	
St. Vincent and the Grenadines		•	
Suriname		*	
Trinidad and Tobago	*		

[1]Dot instead of star indicates that the net debtor's main external finance source is official financing.
[2]Mongolia, which is not a member of the Commonwealth of Independent States, is included in this group for reasons of geography and similarities in economic structure.

further differentiated on the basis of two additional financial criteria: by *official external financing* and by *experience with debt servicing*.[8] The HIPC group comprises the countries considered by the IMF and the World Bank for their debt initiative, known as the HIPC Initiative, with the aim of reducing the external debt burdens of all the eligible HIPCs to a "sustainable" level in a reasonably short period of time.[9]

[8]During 2001–05, 51 countries incurred external payments arrears or entered into official or commercial bank debt-rescheduling agreements. This group of countries is referred to as *countries with arrears and/or rescheduling during 2001–05*.

[9]See David Andrews, Anthony R. Boote, Syed S. Rizavi, and Sukwinder Singh, *Debt Relief for Low-Income Countries: The Enhanced HIPC Initiative*, IMF Pamphlet Series, No. 51 (Washington: International Monetary Fund, November 1999).

List of Tables

Output

Inflation

Financial Policies

Foreign Trade

Current Account Transactions

Balance of Payments and External Financing

Flow of Funds

Medium-Term Baseline Scenario

Table A1. Summary of World Output[1]

(Annual percent change)

	Ten-Year Averages											
	1989–98	1999–2008	1999	2000	2001	2002	2003	2004	2005	2006	2007	2008
World	**3.2**	**4.4**	**3.8**	**4.8**	**2.5**	**3.1**	**4.0**	**5.3**	**4.8**	**5.4**	**5.2**	**4.8**
Advanced economies	**2.7**	**2.6**	**3.5**	**4.0**	**1.2**	**1.6**	**1.9**	**3.2**	**2.5**	**2.9**	**2.5**	**2.2**
United States	3.0	2.6	4.4	3.7	0.8	1.6	2.5	3.6	3.1	2.9	1.9	1.9
Euro area	. . .	2.1	3.0	3.8	1.9	0.9	0.8	2.0	1.5	2.8	2.5	2.1
Japan	2.0	1.5	–0.1	2.9	0.2	0.3	1.4	2.7	1.9	2.2	2.0	1.7
Other advanced economies[2]	3.2	3.5	4.7	5.3	1.7	3.2	2.5	4.1	3.2	3.7	3.7	3.1
Other emerging market and developing countries	**3.8**	**6.5**	**4.1**	**6.0**	**4.3**	**5.1**	**6.7**	**7.7**	**7.5**	**8.1**	**8.1**	**7.4**
Regional groups												
Africa	2.2	4.8	2.8	3.2	4.3	3.6	4.7	5.8	5.6	5.6	5.7	6.5
Central and eastern Europe	1.1	4.4	0.5	4.9	0.2	4.5	4.8	6.7	5.6	6.3	5.8	5.2
Commonwealth of Independent States[3]	. . .	7.1	5.2	9.0	6.3	5.3	7.9	8.4	6.6	7.7	7.8	7.0
Developing Asia	7.3	8.1	6.5	7.0	6.0	7.0	8.3	8.8	9.2	9.8	9.8	8.8
Middle East	4.5	4.9	1.9	5.4	3.0	4.0	6.6	5.6	5.4	5.6	5.9	5.9
Western Hemisphere	3.1	3.3	0.3	3.9	0.5	0.3	2.4	6.0	4.6	5.5	5.0	4.3
Memorandum												
European Union	2.0	2.5	3.0	3.9	2.1	1.4	1.5	2.7	2.0	3.2	3.0	2.5
Analytical groups												
By source of export earnings												
Fuel	–0.3	6.0	3.0	7.1	4.3	4.0	6.9	7.3	6.7	6.7	7.0	6.9
Nonfuel	4.6	6.6	4.3	5.9	4.2	5.2	6.6	7.8	7.6	8.4	8.3	7.5
of which, primary products	2.5	3.7	0.6	1.6	2.9	2.8	3.6	6.1	5.1	4.2	5.2	5.3
By external financing source												
Net debtor countries	3.4	5.0	2.8	4.7	2.4	3.4	4.8	6.5	6.2	6.9	6.5	6.1
of which, official financing	4.1	5.4	3.9	4.6	3.5	3.9	4.7	6.5	7.1	7.1	6.7	6.5
Net debtor countries by debt-servicing experience												
Countries with arrears and/or rescheduling during 2001–05	3.4	4.7	1.1	3.2	2.5	1.6	5.2	6.9	7.2	6.8	6.8	6.4
Memorandum												
Median growth rate												
Advanced economies	3.0	2.9	4.1	4.0	1.9	1.7	1.9	3.7	3.0	3.3	3.4	2.6
Other emerging market and developing countries	3.3	4.7	3.4	4.2	3.6	3.5	4.7	5.4	5.4	5.8	5.6	5.4
Output per capita												
Advanced economies	2.0	2.0	2.9	3.4	0.6	1.0	1.3	2.6	2.0	2.4	2.0	1.7
Other emerging market and developing countries	2.2	5.2	2.7	4.6	2.9	3.7	5.4	6.4	6.2	6.9	6.8	6.2
World growth based on market exchange rates	**2.5**	**3.1**	**3.1**	**4.1**	**1.5**	**1.9**	**2.6**	**3.9**	**3.3**	**3.8**	**3.5**	**3.3**
Value of world output in billions of U.S. dollars												
At market exchange rates	26,246	40,909	30,925	31,775	31,559	32,834	36,882	41,452	44,745	48,245	53,352	57,323
At purchasing power parities	32,232	56,697	42,039	45,010	47,227	49,474	52,510	56,782	61,259	66,229	70,807	75,632

[1]Real GDP.

[2]In this table, "other advanced economies" means advanced economies excluding the United States, euro area countries, and Japan.

[3]Mongolia, which is not a member of the Commonwealth of Independent States, is included in this group for reasons of geography and similarities in economic structure.

Table A2. Advanced Economies: Real GDP and Total Domestic Demand

(Annual percent change)

	Ten-Year Averages												Fourth Quarter[1]		
	1989–98	1999–2008	1999	2000	2001	2002	2003	2004	2005	2006	2007	2008	2006	2007	2008
Real GDP															
Advanced economies	**2.7**	**2.6**	**3.5**	**4.0**	**1.2**	**1.6**	**1.9**	**3.2**	**2.5**	**2.9**	**2.5**	**2.2**	**3.0**	**2.3**	**2.3**
United States	3.0	2.6	4.4	3.7	0.8	1.6	2.5	3.6	3.1	2.9	1.9	1.9	2.6	2.0	2.0
Euro area	. . .	2.1	3.0	3.8	1.9	0.9	0.8	2.0	1.5	2.8	2.5	2.1	3.3	2.0	2.2
Germany	2.5	1.5	1.9	3.1	1.2	—	–0.3	1.1	0.8	2.9	2.4	2.0	3.9	1.7	1.7
France	1.9	2.1	3.3	3.9	1.9	1.0	1.1	2.5	1.7	2.0	1.9	2.0	2.1	2.2	1.8
Italy	1.6	1.4	1.9	3.6	1.8	0.3	—	1.2	0.1	1.9	1.7	1.3	2.8	0.9	1.4
Spain	2.8	3.6	4.7	5.0	3.6	2.7	3.1	3.3	3.6	3.9	3.7	2.7	4.0	3.0	2.9
Netherlands	3.1	2.3	4.7	3.9	1.9	0.1	0.3	2.2	1.5	3.0	2.6	2.5	2.9	2.6	2.5
Belgium	2.3	2.2	3.3	3.9	0.7	1.4	1.0	2.8	1.4	3.0	2.6	1.9	3.0	2.3	2.0
Austria	2.7	2.3	3.3	3.4	0.8	0.9	1.2	2.3	2.0	3.3	3.3	2.5	3.3	3.3	2.0
Finland	1.6	3.4	3.9	5.0	2.6	1.6	1.8	3.7	2.9	5.0	4.3	3.0	6.6	1.9	5.8
Greece	1.9	4.1	3.4	4.5	4.5	3.9	4.9	4.7	3.7	4.3	3.9	3.6	4.4	3.5	4.1
Portugal	3.6	1.7	3.9	3.9	2.0	0.8	–0.7	1.5	0.5	1.3	1.8	1.8	1.6	1.9	1.9
Ireland	6.4	6.0	10.7	9.1	5.9	6.4	4.3	4.3	5.9	5.7	4.6	3.0	4.8	2.1	8.8
Luxembourg	4.9	4.8	8.4	8.4	2.5	3.8	1.3	3.6	4.0	6.2	5.4	4.2	5.9	4.4	3.8
Slovenia	. . .	4.3	5.4	4.1	3.1	3.7	2.8	4.4	4.1	5.7	5.4	3.8	6.0	6.7	5.0
Japan	2.0	1.5	–0.1	2.9	0.2	0.3	1.4	2.7	1.9	2.2	2.0	1.7	2.5	1.3	1.9
United Kingdom	2.0	2.7	3.0	3.8	2.4	2.1	2.8	3.3	1.8	2.8	3.1	2.3	3.2	2.9	2.2
Canada	2.1	3.1	5.5	5.2	1.8	2.9	1.9	3.1	3.1	2.8	2.5	2.3	1.9	2.8	2.5
Korea	5.9	5.5	9.5	8.5	3.8	7.0	3.1	4.7	4.2	5.0	4.8	4.6	4.0	5.2	4.3
Australia	3.3	3.4	4.4	3.4	2.1	4.1	3.1	3.7	2.8	2.7	4.4	3.8	3.0	4.6	3.5
Taiwan Province of China	6.8	4.0	5.7	5.8	–2.2	4.6	3.5	6.2	4.1	4.7	4.1	3.8	4.0	3.5	4.3
Sweden	1.4	3.1	4.5	4.3	1.1	2.0	1.7	4.1	2.9	4.2	3.6	2.8	3.8	4.5	2.3
Switzerland	1.4	1.8	1.3	3.6	1.2	0.4	–0.2	2.5	2.4	3.2	2.4	1.6	2.9	1.9	1.8
Hong Kong SAR	3.8	5.3	4.0	10.0	0.6	1.8	3.2	8.6	7.5	6.9	5.7	4.7	7.2	4.7	6.4
Denmark	2.2	2.0	2.6	3.5	0.7	0.5	0.4	2.1	3.1	3.5	1.9	1.5	3.7	1.7	1.5
Norway	3.5	2.6	2.0	3.3	2.0	1.5	1.0	3.9	2.7	2.8	3.5	3.8	2.9	3.9	3.4
Israel	5.1	3.7	2.9	8.9	–0.4	–0.6	2.3	5.2	5.3	5.2	5.1	3.8	3.8	6.8	3.6
Singapore	7.8	5.8	7.2	10.1	–2.4	4.2	3.1	8.8	6.6	7.9	7.5	5.8	6.6	7.1	6.2
New Zealand	2.1	3.3	4.3	3.9	2.7	5.2	3.5	4.4	2.7	1.6	2.8	2.3	2.1	2.1	2.9
Cyprus	4.7	3.7	4.8	5.0	4.0	2.0	1.8	4.2	3.9	3.8	3.8	3.7	3.6	3.7	4.1
Iceland	1.9	3.4	4.1	4.3	3.9	–0.1	2.7	7.6	7.2	2.6	2.1	–0.1	2.5	5.3	–0.1
Memorandum															
Major advanced economies	2.5	2.2	3.1	3.6	1.0	1.2	1.8	2.9	2.3	2.6	2.1	1.9	2.7	1.9	1.9
Newly industrialized Asian economies	6.1	5.0	7.5	7.9	1.2	5.5	3.2	5.9	4.7	5.3	4.9	4.4	4.5	4.8	4.7
Real total domestic demand															
Advanced economies	**2.7**	**2.6**	**4.1**	**4.0**	**1.1**	**1.7**	**2.1**	**3.3**	**2.5**	**2.7**	**2.2**	**2.1**	**. . .**	**. . .**	**. . .**
United States	3.1	2.9	5.3	4.4	0.9	2.2	2.8	4.1	3.1	2.8	1.4	1.6	2.1	1.6	1.8
Euro area	. . .	2.1	3.6	3.3	1.2	0.4	1.5	1.9	1.7	2.6	2.1	2.4	2.5	2.0	2.3
Germany	2.3	0.8	2.7	2.2	–0.5	–2.0	0.6	–0.2	0.3	1.9	1.2	2.4	0.7	2.6	1.8
France	1.6	2.5	3.8	4.3	1.8	1.1	1.7	3.2	2.3	2.4	1.5	2.7	1.9	3.1	2.2
Italy	1.4	1.6	3.2	2.8	1.6	1.3	0.9	1.1	0.3	1.6	1.9	1.4	2.9	1.8	1.0
Spain	2.6	4.6	6.9	5.8	4.2	3.2	3.8	4.8	5.1	4.9	4.3	2.8	5.1	3.8	3.0
Japan	2.0	1.2	—	2.4	1.0	–0.4	0.8	1.9	1.7	1.4	1.2	1.6	1.9	0.7	2.0
United Kingdom	2.0	3.1	4.2	3.9	2.9	3.1	2.8	3.8	1.6	3.0	3.4	2.3	3.6	3.1	2.1
Canada	1.8	3.8	4.2	4.8	1.2	3.2	4.6	4.3	5.1	4.4	3.2	3.2	3.5	4.0	2.8
Other advanced economies	4.2	3.6	5.5	5.4	0.4	3.8	1.5	4.5	3.3	3.5	4.4	3.5	. . .	. . .	. . .
Memorandum															
Major advanced economies	2.5	2.3	3.8	3.7	1.1	1.3	2.1	3.1	2.3	2.5	1.6	1.9	2.1	1.9	1.9
Newly industrialized Asian economies	6.2	3.9	8.0	7.6	—	4.5	0.3	4.6	2.6	3.5	4.6	4.0	4.0	4.9	2.8

[1]From fourth quarter of preceding year.

Table A3. Advanced Economies: Components of Real GDP

(Annual percent change)

	Ten-Year Averages											
	1989–98	1999–2008	1999	2000	2001	2002	2003	2004	2005	2006	2007	2008
Private consumer expenditure												
Advanced economies	**2.7**	**2.7**	**4.1**	**3.9**	**2.3**	**2.2**	**1.9**	**2.8**	**2.5**	**2.5**	**2.6**	**2.3**
United States	3.0	3.3	5.1	4.7	2.5	2.7	2.8	3.6	3.2	3.1	2.9	2.2
Euro area	. . .	1.9	3.4	3.1	2.0	0.8	1.2	1.6	1.5	1.8	1.6	2.1
Germany	2.5	0.9	3.0	2.4	1.9	–0.8	0.1	0.2	–0.1	1.0	–0.1	1.9
France	1.6	2.6	3.5	3.6	2.6	2.4	2.0	2.5	2.2	2.0	2.1	2.7
Italy	1.8	1.3	2.5	2.4	0.7	0.2	1.0	0.7	0.6	1.5	1.8	1.4
Spain	2.4	3.8	5.0	5.6	3.7	2.8	2.9	4.2	4.2	3.8	3.3	2.2
Japan	2.3	1.2	1.0	0.7	1.6	1.1	0.4	1.6	1.6	0.9	1.7	1.8
United Kingdom	2.2	3.1	4.5	4.6	3.0	3.5	2.9	3.4	1.5	2.1	3.0	2.4
Canada	2.1	3.5	3.8	4.0	2.3	3.6	3.0	3.4	3.8	4.2	4.1	3.1
Other advanced economies	4.2	3.6	5.9	5.6	2.6	3.8	1.1	3.4	3.2	3.2	3.7	3.2
Memorandum												
Major advanced economies	2.6	2.5	3.8	3.5	2.2	2.0	2.0	2.7	2.3	2.3	2.3	2.1
Newly industrialized Asian economies	6.1	4.0	8.2	7.3	3.2	5.1	–0.2	2.4	3.3	3.4	3.8	3.6
Public consumption												
Advanced economies	**1.8**	**2.2**	**2.8**	**2.5**	**2.8**	**3.3**	**2.3**	**1.7**	**1.5**	**1.8**	**1.9**	**1.7**
United States	1.0	2.1	3.1	1.7	3.1	4.3	2.5	1.5	0.8	1.4	1.6	1.4
Euro area	. . .	1.9	1.9	2.3	2.0	2.4	1.8	1.3	1.3	1.9	2.0	1.8
Germany	1.8	0.8	1.2	1.4	0.5	1.5	0.4	–1.5	0.5	0.9	1.8	1.2
France	1.7	1.7	1.4	1.9	1.2	1.9	2.0	2.3	0.9	1.4	2.0	2.0
Italy	—	1.5	1.3	2.3	3.6	2.1	2.0	1.6	1.5	–0.3	0.3	0.8
Spain	3.7	4.9	4.0	5.3	3.9	4.5	4.8	6.3	5.5	4.8	5.1	4.4
Japan	2.8	2.2	4.2	4.3	3.0	2.4	2.3	1.9	1.7	0.4	0.8	1.0
United Kingdom	1.0	2.8	3.7	3.1	2.4	3.5	3.5	3.2	2.7	2.1	1.9	2.5
Canada	0.9	2.8	2.1	3.1	3.9	2.5	3.1	2.5	2.2	3.3	2.5	2.5
Other advanced economies	3.9	2.6	1.9	2.1	3.1	3.6	2.2	1.8	2.6	3.1	3.3	2.5
Memorandum												
Major advanced economies	1.4	2.0	2.8	2.3	2.7	3.2	2.3	1.5	1.2	1.2	1.5	1.5
Newly industrialized Asian economies	5.9	2.9	0.8	2.4	3.5	4.4	2.5	1.8	2.9	3.7	4.7	2.8
Gross fixed capital formation												
Advanced economies	**3.4**	**2.6**	**5.6**	**5.0**	**–0.8**	**–1.5**	**2.1**	**4.6**	**4.1**	**4.2**	**1.8**	**1.4**
United States	4.6	2.2	8.2	6.1	–1.7	–3.5	3.2	6.1	5.8	2.6	–2.4	–1.3
Euro area	. . .	2.9	6.3	5.0	0.5	–1.5	1.2	2.3	2.6	5.0	4.8	3.3
Germany	2.9	1.4	4.7	3.0	–3.6	–6.1	–0.3	–0.2	1.0	6.1	6.0	3.8
France	1.3	3.7	8.3	7.2	2.4	–1.7	2.2	3.6	4.0	3.7	3.9	3.3
Italy	1.1	2.2	3.6	6.4	2.5	4.0	–1.7	1.6	–0.5	2.3	2.3	2.0
Spain	3.4	5.9	10.4	6.6	4.8	3.4	5.9	5.1	6.9	6.8	5.8	3.0
Japan	0.9	0.4	–0.8	1.2	–0.9	–4.9	–0.5	1.4	2.4	3.4	0.7	1.9
United Kingdom	2.6	3.6	3.0	2.7	2.6	3.6	1.1	5.9	1.5	8.2	5.6	2.1
Canada	1.7	5.4	7.3	4.7	4.0	1.6	6.2	7.7	8.5	7.2	3.4	4.0
Other advanced economies	5.6	3.9	2.9	7.1	–4.6	3.8	2.8	7.4	4.3	5.2	6.8	4.0
Memorandum												
Major advanced economies	3.1	2.2	5.6	4.8	–0.6	–2.5	1.8	4.3	4.1	3.8	0.5	0.7
Newly industrialized Asian economies	8.2	3.6	2.9	10.9	–6.2	2.6	2.5	8.1	1.8	3.6	6.2	4.8

Table A3 *(concluded)*

	Ten-Year Averages 1989–98	Ten-Year Averages 1999–2008	1999	2000	2001	2002	2003	2004	2005	2006	2007	2008
Final domestic demand												
Advanced economies	**2.5**	**2.5**	**4.1**	**3.7**	**1.8**	**1.4**	**2.1**	**2.9**	**2.6**	**2.7**	**2.1**	**1.9**
United States	3.0	2.9	5.4	4.5	1.8	1.8	2.8	3.8	3.3	2.7	1.7	1.4
Euro area	. . .	2.1	3.7	3.3	1.7	0.6	1.3	1.6	1.6	2.6	2.2	2.1
Germany	2.4	1.0	3.0	2.3	0.4	–1.5	0.1	–0.2	0.3	2.0	1.5	2.2
France	1.6	2.5	3.9	3.9	2.2	1.4	2.1	2.7	2.2	2.2	2.1	2.7
Italy	1.3	1.5	2.5	3.1	1.6	1.3	0.6	1.1	0.5	1.3	1.6	1.4
Spain	3.2	4.5	6.6	6.6	4.1	2.9	3.8	4.7	4.6	4.9	4.3	3.1
Japan	2.0	1.2	1.1	1.4	1.2	–0.2	0.5	1.6	1.8	1.4	1.3	1.7
United Kingdom	2.0	3.1	4.1	4.0	2.8	3.5	2.7	3.7	1.8	3.1	3.2	2.4
Canada	1.8	3.8	4.2	4.0	2.9	3.0	3.7	4.1	4.5	4.7	3.6	3.2
Other advanced economies	4.4	3.4	4.3	5.4	0.9	3.7	1.7	3.9	3.3	3.6	4.4	3.3
Memorandum												
Major advanced economies	2.4	2.4	4.0	3.6	1.7	1.3	2.0	2.8	2.4	2.4	1.8	1.8
Newly industrialized Asian economies	6.6	3.7	5.5	7.6	0.7	4.3	0.9	3.6	2.9	3.5	4.6	3.8
Stock building[1]												
Advanced economies	**—**	**—**	**–0.2**	**0.1**	**–0.6**	**—**	**0.1**	**0.2**	**–0.1**	**0.1**	**–0.2**	**0.1**
United States	0.1	—	—	–0.1	–0.9	0.4	—	0.4	–0.2	0.1	–0.3	0.1
Euro area	. . .	—	–0.1	—	–0.4	–0.3	0.2	0.2	0.1	—	–0.1	0.2
Germany	—	–0.1	–0.2	–0.1	–0.9	–0.6	0.5	—	0.1	–0.1	–0.4	0.2
France	—	–0.1	–0.1	0.5	–0.4	–0.3	–0.3	0.6	—	0.2	–0.6	–0.1
Italy	—	0.1	0.1	–0.2	0.1	—	0.1	–0.1	–0.2	1.2	0.2	—
Spain	–0.1	—	0.2	–0.1	–0.1	—	–0.1	—	–0.1	0.1	—	—
Japan	—	—	–1.0	1.0	–0.2	–0.3	0.2	0.3	–0.1	0.1	–0.1	—
United Kingdom	—	—	0.2	–0.1	0.1	–0.3	0.2	0.1	–0.1	–0.2	0.2	–0.1
Canada	—	—	0.1	0.8	–1.7	0.2	0.8	0.1	0.3	–0.2	–0.4	0.1
Other advanced economies	–0.1	0.1	0.9	—	–0.5	0.1	–0.1	0.5	—	–0.1	—	0.2
Memorandum												
Major advanced economies	—	—	–0.2	0.1	–0.6	0.1	0.1	0.3	–0.1	0.1	–0.2	0.1
Newly industrialized Asian economies	–0.3	0.2	2.1	–0.1	–0.7	0.2	–0.5	0.9	–0.2	—	–0.1	0.1
Foreign balance[1]												
Advanced economies	**—**	**–0.1**	**–0.6**	**–0.1**	**—**	**–0.2**	**–0.4**	**–0.3**	**–0.2**	**—**	**0.3**	**0.1**
United States	–0.1	–0.4	–1.0	–0.9	–0.2	–0.7	–0.4	–0.7	–0.2	–0.1	0.4	0.3
Euro area	. . .	0.1	–0.5	0.5	0.7	0.5	–0.6	0.2	–0.2	0.2	0.3	–0.1
Germany	0.2	0.7	–0.8	1.0	1.7	2.0	–0.8	1.3	0.5	1.1	1.3	–0.3
France	0.3	–0.3	–0.4	–0.5	0.1	–0.1	–0.7	–0.9	–0.7	–0.5	0.4	–0.2
Italy	0.2	–0.2	–1.2	0.8	0.2	–1.0	–0.8	0.1	–0.3	0.2	–0.1	–0.1
Spain	–0.2	–0.9	–1.7	–0.4	–0.2	–0.6	–0.8	–1.7	–1.6	–1.2	–0.9	–0.3
Japan	0.1	0.4	–0.1	0.5	–0.8	0.7	0.7	0.8	0.3	0.8	0.8	—
United Kingdom	0.1	–0.4	–1.0	–0.1	–0.5	–1.1	–0.1	–0.6	—	–0.2	–0.4	—
Canada	0.3	–0.6	1.4	0.6	0.7	–0.1	–2.5	–1.0	–1.7	–1.4	–0.6	–0.8
Other advanced economies	—	0.7	0.4	0.8	0.8	0.2	1.2	0.7	0.9	1.2	0.2	0.6
Memorandum												
Major advanced economies	—	–0.1	–0.7	–0.2	—	–0.2	–0.4	–0.2	–0.2	0.1	0.4	0.1
Newly industrialized Asian economies	–0.2	1.4	0.3	0.5	1.1	1.0	2.9	2.0	2.4	2.4	0.8	1.0

[1]Changes expressed as percent of GDP in the preceding period.

Table A4. Other Emerging Market and Developing Countries—by Country: Real GDP[1]

(Annual percent change)

	Average 1989–98	1999	2000	2001	2002	2003	2004	2005	2006	2007	2008
Africa	**2.2**	**2.8**	**3.2**	**4.3**	**3.6**	**4.7**	**5.8**	**5.6**	**5.6**	**5.7**	**6.5**
Algeria	1.7	3.2	2.2	2.6	4.7	6.9	5.2	5.1	3.6	4.8	5.2
Angola	0.3	3.2	3.0	3.1	14.5	3.3	11.2	20.6	18.6	23.1	27.2
Benin	4.1	5.3	4.9	6.2	4.5	3.9	3.1	2.9	3.8	4.0	5.3
Botswana	6.5	7.2	8.3	4.9	5.7	6.2	6.3	3.8	2.6	5.0	5.2
Burkina Faso	4.5	7.4	1.8	6.6	4.7	8.0	4.6	7.1	5.9	6.0	6.1
Burundi	–1.0	–1.0	–0.9	2.1	4.4	–1.2	4.8	0.9	5.1	3.5	5.8
Cameroon[2]	–0.3	4.4	4.2	4.5	4.0	4.0	3.7	2.0	3.8	3.8	5.3
Cape Verde	5.5	11.9	7.3	6.1	5.3	4.7	4.4	5.8	6.5	6.9	7.5
Central African Republic	0.2	3.6	1.8	0.3	–0.6	–7.6	1.3	2.2	3.8	4.0	4.3
Chad	3.5	–0.7	–0.9	11.7	8.5	14.7	33.6	7.9	0.5	1.5	4.1
Comoros	0.9	1.9	1.4	3.3	4.1	2.5	–0.2	4.2	1.2	1.0	3.0
Congo, Dem. Rep. of	–5.3	–4.3	–6.9	–2.1	3.5	5.8	6.6	6.5	5.1	6.5	8.4
Congo, Rep. of	3.0	–2.6	7.6	3.8	4.6	0.8	3.5	7.8	6.1	3.7	7.3
Côte d'Ivoire	3.8	1.8	–4.6	—	–1.6	–1.7	1.6	1.8	0.9	1.7	3.8
Djibouti	–1.7	3.0	0.5	2.0	2.6	3.2	3.0	3.2	4.8	4.8	5.7
Equatorial Guinea	26.9	24.1	13.5	61.9	18.8	11.6	31.7	6.7	–5.2	10.1	8.1
Eritrea	. . .	—	–13.1	9.2	0.6	3.9	2.0	4.8	2.0	1.3	1.3
Ethiopia	1.9	6.0	5.9	7.7	1.2	–3.5	13.1	10.2	9.0	10.5	9.6
Gabon	4.8	–8.9	–1.9	2.1	–0.3	2.4	1.1	3.0	1.2	4.8	4.2
Gambia, The	4.0	6.4	5.5	5.8	–3.2	6.9	7.0	5.1	6.5	7.0	6.0
Ghana	4.3	4.4	3.7	4.2	4.5	5.2	5.6	5.9	6.2	6.3	6.9
Guinea	4.2	4.5	2.9	3.8	4.2	1.2	2.7	3.3	2.2	1.5	5.1
Guinea-Bissau	0.2	7.6	7.5	0.2	–7.1	–0.6	2.2	3.2	2.7	2.5	2.1
Kenya	2.3	2.4	0.6	4.7	0.3	2.8	4.6	5.8	6.1	6.4	6.5
Lesotho	4.9	–0.3	2.0	1.8	2.8	2.7	4.2	2.9	7.2	4.9	5.2
Liberia	. . .	. . .	29.3	2.9	3.7	–31.3	2.6	5.3	7.8	9.4	10.4
Madagascar	1.5	4.7	4.7	6.0	–12.7	9.8	5.3	4.6	4.9	6.5	7.3
Malawi	3.7	3.5	0.8	–4.1	1.9	4.2	5.0	2.3	7.9	5.5	5.2
Mali	5.9	3.0	–3.2	12.1	4.3	7.2	2.4	6.1	5.3	5.2	4.8
Mauritania	2.2	6.7	1.9	2.9	1.1	5.6	5.2	5.4	11.4	0.9	4.4
Mauritius	5.9	4.6	7.2	4.2	1.5	3.8	4.7	3.1	3.5	4.7	4.7
Morocco	2.8	0.5	1.8	7.6	3.3	6.1	5.2	2.4	8.0	2.5	5.9
Mozambique, Rep. of	5.0	7.5	1.9	13.1	8.2	7.9	7.5	6.2	8.5	7.0	7.0
Namibia	3.7	3.4	3.5	2.4	6.7	3.5	6.6	4.2	4.6	4.8	4.6
Niger	1.9	–0.6	–1.4	7.1	3.0	4.5	–0.8	7.4	5.2	5.6	5.4
Nigeria	3.4	1.5	5.4	3.1	1.5	10.7	6.0	7.2	5.6	4.3	8.0
Rwanda	–1.8	7.6	6.0	6.7	9.4	0.9	4.0	6.0	5.3	4.5	4.6
São Tomé and Príncipe	1.3	2.5	0.4	3.1	11.6	6.8	4.8	5.4	7.0	6.0	6.0
Senegal	2.5	6.3	3.2	4.6	0.7	6.7	5.8	5.3	2.1	5.1	5.7
Seychelles	5.7	1.9	4.3	–2.3	1.2	–5.9	–2.9	1.2	5.3	6.1	5.9
Sierra Leone	–6.6	–8.1	3.8	18.2	27.4	9.5	7.4	7.3	7.4	7.4	7.0
South Africa	1.4	2.4	4.2	2.7	3.7	3.1	4.8	5.1	5.0	4.7	4.2
Sudan	2.6	3.1	8.4	6.2	5.4	7.1	5.1	8.6	11.8	11.2	10.7
Swaziland	4.2	3.5	2.6	1.6	2.9	2.9	2.1	2.3	2.1	1.0	1.0
Tanzania	3.1	3.5	5.1	6.2	7.2	5.7	6.7	6.7	6.2	7.1	7.5
Togo	1.7	2.6	–1.0	–2.3	–0.2	5.2	2.3	1.2	2.0	2.9	3.5
Tunisia	4.6	6.1	4.7	5.0	1.7	5.6	6.0	4.0	5.4	6.0	6.2
Uganda	6.1	8.3	5.3	4.8	6.9	4.4	5.7	6.7	5.4	6.2	6.5
Zambia	–1.2	2.2	3.6	4.9	3.3	5.1	5.4	5.2	5.9	6.0	6.2
Zimbabwe	2.9	–3.6	–7.3	–2.7	–4.4	–10.4	–3.8	–5.3	–4.8	–6.2	–4.5

Table A4 *(continued)*

	Average 1989–98	1999	2000	2001	2002	2003	2004	2005	2006	2007	2008
Central and eastern Europe[3]	**1.1**	**0.5**	**4.9**	**0.2**	**4.5**	**4.8**	**6.7**	**5.6**	**6.3**	**5.8**	**5.2**
Albania	–0.5	10.1	7.3	7.0	2.9	5.7	5.9	5.5	5.0	6.0	6.0
Bosnia and Herzegovina	. . .	9.5	5.2	3.6	5.0	3.5	6.1	5.0	6.0	5.8	6.5
Bulgaria	–5.6	2.3	5.4	4.1	4.5	5.0	6.6	6.2	6.1	6.0	5.9
Croatia	. . .	–0.9	2.9	4.4	5.6	5.3	4.3	4.3	4.8	5.6	4.7
Czech Republic	—	1.3	3.6	2.5	1.9	3.6	4.6	6.5	6.4	5.6	4.6
Estonia	. . .	0.3	10.8	7.7	8.0	7.2	8.3	10.2	11.2	8.0	6.0
Hungary	–0.2	4.2	5.2	4.1	4.4	4.2	4.8	4.2	3.9	2.1	2.7
Latvia	. . .	4.7	6.9	8.0	6.5	7.2	8.7	10.6	11.9	10.5	6.2
Lithuania	. . .	–1.5	4.1	6.6	6.9	10.3	7.3	7.6	7.5	8.0	6.5
Macedonia, FYR	. . .	4.3	4.5	–4.5	0.9	2.8	4.1	4.1	3.0	5.0	5.0
Malta	. . .	. . .	–1.0	–1.6	2.6	–0.3	0.1	3.3	3.3	3.2	2.6
Serbia	. . .	–18.0	4.5	4.8	4.2	2.5	8.4	6.2	5.7	6.0	5.0
Poland	2.5	4.5	4.3	1.2	1.4	3.9	5.3	3.6	6.1	6.6	5.3
Romania	–2.9	–1.2	2.1	5.7	5.1	5.2	8.5	4.1	7.7	6.3	6.0
Slovak Republic	. . .	0.3	0.7	3.2	4.1	4.2	5.4	6.0	8.3	8.8	7.3
Turkey	4.3	–4.7	7.4	–7.5	7.9	5.8	8.9	7.4	6.1	5.0	5.3
Commonwealth of Independent States[3,4]	**. . .**	**5.2**	**9.0**	**6.3**	**5.3**	**7.9**	**8.4**	**6.6**	**7.7**	**7.8**	**7.0**
Russia	. . .	6.4	10.0	5.1	4.7	7.3	7.2	6.4	6.7	7.0	6.5
Excluding Russia	. . .	2.4	6.7	9.1	6.6	9.3	11.0	6.9	9.8	9.4	8.1
Armenia	. . .	3.3	6.0	9.6	13.2	14.0	10.5	14.0	13.3	11.1	10.0
Azerbaijan	. . .	11.4	6.2	6.5	8.1	10.5	10.4	24.3	31.0	29.3	23.2
Belarus	. . .	3.4	5.8	4.7	5.0	7.0	11.4	9.3	9.9	7.8	6.4
Georgia	. . .	3.0	1.9	4.7	5.5	11.1	5.9	9.6	9.4	11.0	9.0
Kazakhstan	. . .	2.7	9.8	13.5	9.8	9.3	9.6	9.7	10.7	8.7	7.8
Kyrgyz Republic	. . .	3.7	5.4	5.3	–0.0	7.0	7.0	–0.2	2.7	7.5	7.0
Moldova	. . .	–3.4	2.1	6.1	7.8	6.6	7.4	7.5	4.0	5.0	5.0
Mongolia	–0.3	3.2	3.9	1.9	1.8	5.4	13.3	7.6	8.6	8.5	7.5
Tajikistan	. . .	3.7	8.3	10.2	9.1	10.2	10.6	6.7	7.0	7.5	8.0
Turkmenistan	. . .	16.5	18.6	20.4	15.8	17.1	14.7	9.0	9.0	10.0	10.0
Ukraine	. . .	–0.2	5.9	9.2	5.2	9.6	12.1	2.7	7.1	6.7	5.4
Uzbekistan	. . .	4.3	3.8	4.2	4.0	4.2	7.7	7.0	7.3	8.8	7.5

Table A4 *(continued)*

	Average 1989–98	1999	2000	2001	2002	2003	2004	2005	2006	2007	2008
Developing Asia	**7.3**	**6.5**	**7.0**	**6.0**	**7.0**	**8.3**	**8.8**	**9.2**	**9.8**	**9.8**	**8.8**
Afghanistan, Rep. of	. . .	. . .	. . .	. . .	28.6	15.7	8.0	14.0	7.5	13.0	8.4
Bangladesh	4.7	5.4	5.6	4.8	4.8	5.8	6.1	6.3	6.4	5.8	6.0
Bhutan	4.7	7.9	7.6	7.2	10.0	7.6	6.8	6.9	11.0	22.4	7.8
Brunei Darussalam	. . .	3.1	2.9	2.7	3.9	2.9	0.5	0.4	5.1	1.9	2.3
Cambodia	. . .	12.1	8.8	8.1	6.6	8.5	10.3	13.3	10.8	9.5	7.7
China	9.6	7.6	8.4	8.3	9.1	10.0	10.1	10.4	11.1	11.5	10.0
Fiji	3.8	8.9	–1.4	2.0	3.2	1.1	5.4	0.7	3.6	–3.1	1.9
India	5.7	6.9	5.4	3.9	4.5	6.9	7.9	9.0	9.7	8.9	8.4
Indonesia	4.8	0.8	5.4	3.6	4.5	4.8	5.0	5.7	5.5	6.2	6.1
Kiribati	2.7	7.3	3.9	1.7	5.8	1.4	–2.9	–0.2	5.8	2.5	1.6
Lao PDR	6.6	7.3	5.8	5.7	5.9	6.1	6.4	7.1	7.6	7.1	7.6
Malaysia	7.4	6.1	8.9	0.3	4.4	5.5	7.2	5.2	5.9	5.8	5.6
Maldives	6.7	7.2	4.8	3.5	6.5	8.5	9.5	–4.5	19.1	5.5	4.5
Myanmar	5.3	10.9	13.7	11.3	12.0	13.8	13.6	13.6	12.7	5.5	4.0
Nepal	4.8	4.5	6.1	5.6	0.1	3.9	4.7	3.1	2.8	2.5	4.0
Pakistan	4.1	3.7	4.3	2.0	3.2	4.8	7.4	7.7	6.9	6.4	6.5
Papua New Guinea	4.2	1.9	–2.5	–0.1	–0.2	2.2	2.7	3.4	2.6	5.2	4.0
Philippines	3.0	3.4	6.0	1.8	4.4	4.9	6.4	4.9	5.4	6.3	5.8
Samoa	2.4	2.1	3.7	7.1	4.4	1.6	3.3	5.4	2.3	3.0	3.5
Solomon Islands	4.8	–0.5	–14.3	–9.0	–1.6	6.4	8.0	5.0	6.1	5.4	4.2
Sri Lanka	5.0	4.3	6.0	–1.5	4.0	6.0	5.4	6.0	7.4	6.5	6.5
Thailand	5.8	4.4	4.8	2.2	5.3	7.1	6.3	4.5	5.0	4.0	4.5
Timor-Leste, Dem. Rep. of	. . .	. . .	15.5	16.5	–6.7	–6.2	0.3	2.3	–2.9	27.4	3.8
Tonga	1.4	2.3	5.4	2.6	3.0	3.2	1.4	2.3	1.3	–3.5	0.8
Vanuatu	4.4	–3.2	2.7	–2.6	–7.4	3.2	5.5	6.8	5.5	5.0	4.0
Vietnam	7.7	4.8	6.8	6.9	7.1	7.3	7.8	8.4	8.2	8.3	8.2
Middle East	**4.5**	**1.9**	**5.4**	**3.0**	**4.0**	**6.6**	**5.6**	**5.4**	**5.6**	**5.9**	**5.9**
Bahrain	4.8	4.3	5.2	4.6	5.2	7.2	5.6	7.8	7.6	6.8	6.5
Egypt	3.7	6.1	5.4	3.5	3.2	3.2	4.1	4.5	6.8	7.1	7.3
Iran, I.R. of	5.5	1.9	5.1	3.7	7.5	7.2	5.1	4.4	4.9	6.0	6.0
Iraq	. . .	. . .	. . .	. . .	. . .	. . .	. . .	. . .	. . .	. . .	. . .
Jordan	2.7	3.4	4.3	5.3	5.8	4.2	8.6	7.1	6.3	6.0	6.0
Kuwait	2.7	–1.8	4.7	0.2	3.0	16.5	10.5	10.0	5.0	3.5	4.8
Lebanon	–0.1	–0.8	1.7	4.5	3.3	4.1	7.4	1.0	—	2.0	3.5
Libya	–1.1	1.1	3.4	5.9	1.4	5.9	5.0	6.3	5.6	9.2	6.9
Oman	5.2	–0.2	5.5	7.5	2.6	2.0	5.4	5.8	5.9	6.0	6.3
Qatar	4.1	5.5	10.9	6.3	3.2	6.3	17.7	9.2	10.3	14.2	14.1
Saudi Arabia	3.1	–0.7	4.9	0.5	0.1	7.7	5.3	6.1	4.3	4.1	4.3
Syrian Arab Republic	5.3	–3.1	2.3	3.7	5.9	1.1	2.8	3.3	4.4	3.9	3.7
United Arab Emirates	6.6	3.1	12.4	1.7	2.6	11.9	9.7	8.2	9.4	7.7	6.6
Yemen, Rep. of	. . .	3.8	6.2	3.8	3.9	3.7	4.0	4.6	4.0	3.6	4.3

Table A4 *(concluded)*

	Average 1989–98	1999	2000	2001	2002	2003	2004	2005	2006	2007	2008
Western Hemisphere	**3.1**	**0.3**	**3.9**	**0.5**	**0.3**	**2.4**	**6.0**	**4.6**	**5.5**	**5.0**	**4.3**
Antigua and Barbuda	3.5	4.9	3.3	1.5	2.0	4.3	5.2	5.5	12.2	3.8	1.8
Argentina	3.8	–3.4	–0.8	–4.4	–10.9	8.8	9.0	9.2	8.5	7.5	5.5
Bahamas, The	1.6	4.0	1.9	0.8	2.3	1.4	1.8	2.5	3.4	3.1	4.0
Barbados	0.7	0.4	2.3	–2.6	0.6	2.0	4.8	4.1	3.9	4.2	2.7
Belize	6.5	8.7	13.0	5.0	5.1	9.3	4.6	3.5	5.8	4.1	3.0
Bolivia	4.3	0.4	2.5	1.7	2.5	2.7	4.2	4.0	4.6	4.0	5.4
Brazil	2.0	0.3	4.3	1.3	2.7	1.1	5.7	2.9	3.7	4.4	4.0
Chile	7.5	–0.4	4.5	3.5	2.2	4.0	6.0	5.7	4.0	5.9	5.0
Colombia	3.6	–4.2	2.9	1.5	1.9	3.9	4.9	4.7	6.8	6.6	4.8
Costa Rica	5.1	8.2	1.8	1.1	2.9	6.4	4.3	5.9	8.2	6.0	5.0
Dominica	2.3	1.6	1.3	–4.2	–5.1	0.1	3.0	3.3	4.0	3.2	2.8
Dominican Republic	4.2	8.1	8.1	3.6	4.4	–1.9	2.0	9.3	10.7	8.0	4.5
Ecuador	2.9	–6.3	2.8	5.3	4.2	3.6	8.0	6.0	3.9	2.7	3.4
El Salvador	4.6	3.4	2.2	1.7	2.3	2.3	1.9	3.1	4.2	4.2	3.8
Grenada	3.6	7.3	7.0	–4.2	1.2	6.4	–6.5	12.8	0.7	3.0	4.0
Guatemala	3.8	3.7	2.5	2.4	3.9	2.5	3.2	3.5	4.9	4.8	4.3
Guyana	3.9	3.0	–1.3	2.3	1.1	–0.7	1.6	–1.9	5.1	5.6	4.6
Haiti	–0.6	2.6	1.3	–0.6	–0.5	0.2	–2.6	0.4	2.2	3.2	4.3
Honduras	3.4	–1.9	5.7	2.6	2.7	3.5	5.0	4.1	6.0	5.4	3.4
Jamaica	1.2	1.0	0.7	1.5	1.1	2.3	1.0	1.4	2.5	1.4	2.0
Mexico	3.4	3.8	6.6	—	0.8	1.4	4.2	2.8	4.8	2.9	3.0
Nicaragua	2.3	7.0	4.1	3.0	0.8	2.5	5.3	4.4	3.7	4.2	4.7
Panama	5.8	3.9	2.7	0.6	2.2	4.2	7.5	6.9	8.1	8.5	8.8
Paraguay	3.2	–1.5	–3.3	2.1	—	3.8	4.1	2.9	4.3	5.0	4.0
Peru	1.6	0.9	3.0	0.2	5.0	4.0	5.1	6.7	7.6	7.0	6.0
St. Kitts and Nevis	4.3	3.9	6.5	1.7	–0.3	–1.2	7.3	4.4	4.0	4.0	4.1
St. Lucia	3.5	3.9	0.1	–3.7	0.8	3.1	4.5	3.8	5.0	3.5	4.3
St. Vincent and the Grenadines	3.4	3.6	2.0	–0.1	3.2	2.8	6.8	2.2	6.9	4.4	6.2
Suriname	0.8	–0.9	–0.1	6.8	2.6	6.0	8.1	5.5	5.8	5.3	4.0
Trinidad and Tobago	3.0	8.0	6.9	4.2	7.9	14.4	8.8	8.0	12.0	6.0	5.8
Uruguay	3.6	–2.8	–1.4	–3.4	–11.0	2.2	11.8	6.6	7.0	5.2	3.8
Venezuela	2.1	–6.0	3.7	3.4	–8.9	–7.8	18.3	10.3	10.3	8.0	6.0

[1]For many countries, figures for recent years are IMF staff estimates. Data for some countries are for fiscal years.

[2]The percent changes in 2002 are calculated over a period of 18 months, reflecting a change in the fiscal year cycle (from July–June to January–December).

[3]Data for some countries refer to real net material product (NMP) or are estimates based on NMP. For many countries, figures for recent years are IMF staff estimates. The figures should be interpreted only as indicative of broad orders of magnitude because reliable, comparable data are not generally available. In particular, the growth of output of new private enterprises of the informal economy is not fully reflected in the recent figures.

[4]Mongolia, which is not a member of the Commonwealth of Independent States, is included in this group for reasons of geography and similarities in economic structure.

Table A5. Summary of Inflation

(Percent)

	Ten-Year Averages											
	1989–98	1999–2008	1999	2000	2001	2002	2003	2004	2005	2006	2007	2008
GDP deflators												
Advanced economies	**3.2**	**1.7**	**0.9**	**1.5**	**1.9**	**1.6**	**1.7**	**2.0**	**2.0**	**2.1**	**1.9**	**1.6**
United States	2.5	2.3	1.4	2.2	2.4	1.7	2.1	2.9	3.2	3.2	2.6	1.7
Euro area	. . .	1.9	1.0	1.5	2.4	2.6	2.2	2.0	1.9	1.9	2.0	1.9
Japan	0.9	–1.1	–1.3	–1.7	–1.2	–1.5	–1.6	–1.1	–1.3	–0.9	–0.6	0.1
Other advanced economies[1]	4.0	1.9	1.1	2.0	2.0	1.8	2.1	2.1	1.9	1.9	1.9	2.0
Consumer prices												
Advanced economies	**3.5**	**2.0**	**1.4**	**2.2**	**2.1**	**1.5**	**1.8**	**2.0**	**2.3**	**2.3**	**2.1**	**2.0**
United States	3.3	2.7	2.2	3.4	2.8	1.6	2.3	2.7	3.4	3.2	2.7	2.3
Euro area[2]	. . .	2.1	1.1	2.1	2.4	2.3	2.1	2.1	2.2	2.2	2.0	2.0
Japan	1.5	–0.2	–0.3	–0.8	–0.7	–0.9	–0.3	—	–0.3	0.3	—	0.5
Other advanced economies	4.0	1.9	1.1	1.8	2.1	1.7	1.8	1.7	2.1	2.1	2.1	2.2
Other emerging market and developing countries[3]	**50.3**	**6.2**	**10.2**	**7.0**	**6.5**	**5.7**	**5.7**	**5.4**	**5.2**	**5.1**	**5.9**	**5.3**
Regional groups												
Africa[3]	28.4	8.1	10.8	12.6	11.4	8.0	7.8	5.5	6.6	6.3	6.6	6.0
Central and eastern Europe	63.4	11.3	23.7	23.1	19.7	14.9	9.2	6.1	4.9	5.0	5.1	4.1
Commonwealth of Independent States[4]	. . .	17.7	69.1	24.1	19.9	13.4	11.9	10.3	12.1	9.4	8.9	8.3
Developing Asia	9.7	3.3	2.5	1.8	2.7	2.0	2.5	4.1	3.6	4.0	5.3	4.4
Middle East	11.4	6.7	6.6	4.0	3.8	5.3	6.2	7.2	6.9	7.5	10.8	9.2
Western Hemisphere	134.2	7.1	8.3	7.6	6.1	8.9	10.6	6.5	6.3	5.4	5.3	5.8
Memorandum												
European Union	11.5	2.4	2.2	3.1	3.0	2.5	2.2	2.3	2.3	2.3	2.3	2.3
Analytical groups												
By source of export earnings												
Fuel	74.1	13.0	36.2	13.9	13.5	11.7	11.3	9.6	9.9	8.7	9.2	8.6
Nonfuel[3]	46.5	5.2	6.6	6.0	5.5	4.8	4.9	4.8	4.5	4.5	5.5	4.8
of which, primary products	80.7	12.8	25.5	30.9	25.2	9.0	6.9	4.0	8.4	7.8	7.5	6.1
By external financing source												
Net debtor countries[3]	55.8	7.1	10.3	8.7	8.0	7.9	7.0	5.3	6.0	6.3	6.0	5.3
of which, official financing	27.7	5.9	5.5	3.9	4.1	3.7	5.9	7.4	7.3	7.0	7.5	6.8
Net debtor countries by debt-servicing experience[3]												
Countries with arrears and/or rescheduling during 2001–05	45.1	10.0	13.4	9.7	10.6	13.0	9.6	6.8	9.5	10.8	8.7	8.3
Memorandum												
Median inflation rate												
Advanced economies	3.1	2.1	1.4	2.7	2.6	2.2	2.1	1.9	2.2	2.2	2.0	2.1
Other emerging market and developing countries[3]	10.3	4.7	4.0	4.0	4.7	3.3	4.1	4.5	5.5	5.6	6.1	5.0

[1]In this table, "other advanced economies" means advanced economies excluding the United States, euro area countries, and Japan.

[2]Based on Eurostat's harmonized index of consumer prices.

[3]Excludes Zimbabwe.

[4]Mongolia, which is not a member of the Commonwealth of Independent States, is included in this group for reasons of geography and similarities in economic structure.

Table A6. Advanced Economies: Consumer Prices

(Annual percent change)

	Ten-Year Averages												End of Period		
	1989–98	1999–2008	1999	2000	2001	2002	2003	2004	2005	2006	2007	2008	2006	2007	2008
Consumer prices															
Advanced economies	**3.5**	**2.0**	**1.4**	**2.2**	**2.1**	**1.5**	**1.8**	**2.0**	**2.3**	**2.3**	**2.1**	**2.0**	**2.0**	**2.4**	**1.9**
United States	3.3	2.7	2.2	3.4	2.8	1.6	2.3	2.7	3.4	3.2	2.7	2.3	2.5	3.3	2.2
Euro area[1]	. . .	2.1	1.1	2.1	2.4	2.3	2.1	2.1	2.2	2.2	2.0	2.0	1.9	2.2	2.0
Germany	2.6	1.6	0.6	1.4	1.9	1.4	1.0	1.8	1.9	1.8	2.1	1.8	1.4	1.9	1.7
France	2.2	1.8	0.6	1.8	1.8	1.9	2.2	2.3	1.9	1.9	1.6	1.8	1.7	2.1	1.8
Italy	4.5	2.2	1.7	2.6	2.3	2.6	2.8	2.3	2.2	2.2	1.9	1.9	2.1	1.9	1.9
Spain	4.8	3.1	2.2	3.5	2.8	3.6	3.1	3.1	3.4	3.6	2.5	2.8	2.7	2.9	2.5
Netherlands	2.2	2.4	2.0	2.3	5.1	3.8	2.2	1.4	1.5	1.7	2.0	2.2	1.7	2.0	2.2
Belgium	2.2	2.0	1.1	2.7	2.4	1.6	1.5	1.9	2.5	2.3	1.8	1.8	2.1	1.8	1.8
Austria	2.3	1.7	0.5	2.0	2.3	1.7	1.3	2.0	2.1	1.7	1.9	1.9	1.5	2.2	1.9
Finland	2.6	1.6	1.3	2.9	2.7	2.0	1.3	0.1	0.8	1.3	1.5	1.8	1.2	1.5	1.8
Greece	12.0	3.2	2.1	2.9	3.7	3.9	3.4	3.0	3.5	3.3	3.0	3.2	3.2	3.3	3.0
Portugal	6.7	2.9	2.2	2.8	4.4	3.7	3.3	2.5	2.1	3.0	2.5	2.4	2.5	2.5	2.4
Ireland	2.5	3.2	2.5	5.2	4.0	4.7	4.0	2.3	2.2	2.7	2.5	2.1	3.0	2.5	2.0
Luxembourg	2.5	2.3	1.0	3.2	2.7	2.1	2.0	2.2	2.5	2.7	2.2	2.2	2.3	2.6	2.0
Slovenia	. . .	5.1	6.2	8.8	8.4	7.5	5.6	3.6	2.5	2.5	3.2	3.1	2.8	3.8	2.4
Japan	1.5	–0.2	–0.3	–0.8	–0.7	–0.9	–0.3	—	–0.3	0.3	—	0.5	0.3	—	0.5
United Kingdom[1]	3.7	1.6	1.3	0.9	1.2	1.3	1.4	1.3	2.0	2.3	2.4	2.0	2.8	2.1	2.0
Canada	2.5	2.2	1.7	2.7	2.5	2.3	2.7	1.8	2.2	2.0	2.2	1.9	1.3	2.6	2.1
Korea	6.2	2.7	0.8	2.3	4.1	2.8	3.5	3.6	2.8	2.2	2.6	2.7	2.1	3.0	2.7
Australia	3.1	3.0	1.5	4.5	4.4	3.0	2.8	2.3	2.7	3.5	2.3	2.8	3.3	2.9	2.4
Taiwan Province of China	3.3	0.8	0.2	1.3	—	–0.2	–0.3	1.6	2.3	0.6	1.2	1.5	0.7	1.7	1.5
Sweden	4.1	1.6	0.5	1.3	2.7	1.9	2.3	1.0	0.8	1.5	1.9	2.0	1.4	2.0	2.0
Switzerland	2.6	1.0	0.8	1.6	1.0	0.6	0.6	0.8	1.2	1.0	1.0	1.0	0.6	1.5	0.8
Hong Kong SAR	8.3	–0.7	–3.9	–3.7	–1.6	–3.0	–2.6	–0.4	0.9	2.0	2.0	3.2	2.3	3.7	1.5
Denmark	2.3	2.1	2.5	2.9	2.4	2.4	2.1	1.2	1.8	1.9	1.9	2.0	1.8	1.9	2.0
Norway	2.7	2.0	2.3	3.1	3.0	1.3	2.5	0.4	1.6	2.3	0.8	2.5	2.2	1.2	2.6
Israel	12.7	2.0	5.2	1.1	1.1	5.7	0.7	–0.4	1.3	2.1	0.5	2.5	–0.1	2.8	2.0
Singapore	2.2	0.9	—	1.3	1.0	–0.4	0.5	1.7	0.5	1.0	1.7	1.7	0.8	2.6	1.2
New Zealand	2.7	2.3	–0.1	2.6	2.6	2.6	1.7	2.3	3.0	3.4	2.4	2.7	2.7	3.0	2.5
Cyprus	4.1	2.6	1.6	4.1	2.0	2.8	4.1	2.3	2.6	2.5	2.0	2.4	1.8	2.0	2.4
Iceland	5.8	4.4	3.4	5.1	6.6	4.8	2.1	3.2	4.0	6.8	4.8	3.3	7.0	3.8	3.0
Memorandum															
Major advanced economies	2.9	1.9	1.4	2.1	1.9	1.3	1.7	2.0	2.3	2.3	2.1	1.9	1.9	2.3	1.8
Newly industrialized Asian economies	5.3	1.6	—	1.2	1.9	1.0	1.5	2.4	2.3	1.6	2.0	2.3	1.6	2.7	2.1

[1]Based on Eurostat's harmonized index of consumer prices.

Table A7. Other Emerging Market and Developing Countries—by Country: Consumer Prices[1]

(Annual percent change)

	Average											End of Period		
	1989–98	1999	2000	2001	2002	2003	2004	2005	2006	2007	2008	2006	2007	2008
Africa	**28.4**	**10.8**	**12.6**	**11.4**	**8.0**	**7.8**	**5.5**	**6.6**	**6.3**	**6.6**	**6.0**	**7.2**	**6.5**	**5.6**
Algeria	18.0	2.6	0.3	4.2	1.4	2.6	3.6	1.6	2.5	4.5	4.3	4.4	4.4	4.2
Angola	397.8	248.2	325.0	152.6	108.9	98.3	43.6	23.0	13.3	11.9	8.9	12.2	10.0	8.0
Benin	7.2	0.3	4.2	4.0	2.4	1.5	0.9	5.4	3.8	3.0	2.8	5.3	2.9	2.9
Botswana	11.3	7.8	8.5	6.6	8.0	9.2	7.0	8.6	11.6	7.0	7.0	8.5	7.4	6.5
Burkina Faso	4.4	–1.1	–0.3	4.7	2.3	2.0	–0.4	6.4	2.4	0.5	2.0	1.5	0.5	2.0
Burundi	14.4	3.4	24.3	9.3	–1.3	10.7	8.0	13.6	2.7	5.3	5.7	9.1	5.4	4.0
Cameroon[2]	4.8	2.9	0.8	2.8	6.3	0.6	0.3	2.0	5.1	2.0	2.7	2.4	4.3	0.9
Cape Verde	7.3	4.3	–2.4	3.7	1.9	1.2	–1.9	0.4	5.4	2.5	2.3	6.2	0.2	3.0
Central African Republic	3.7	–1.4	3.2	3.8	2.3	4.4	–2.2	2.9	6.7	3.1	2.3	7.2	3.1	1.7
Chad	4.5	–8.4	3.8	12.4	5.2	–1.8	–5.4	7.9	7.9	3.0	3.0	3.0	21.0	0.8
Comoros	2.9	1.1	5.9	5.6	3.6	3.7	4.5	3.0	3.4	3.0	3.0	1.7	3.0	3.0
Congo, Dem. Rep. of	790.1	284.9	550.0	357.3	25.3	12.8	4.0	21.4	13.2	17.5	8.8	18.2	12.0	8.0
Congo, Rep. of	5.9	3.1	0.4	0.8	3.1	1.5	3.6	2.5	4.8	7.0	5.0	8.2	5.0	3.0
Côte d'Ivoire	5.7	0.7	2.5	4.4	3.1	3.3	1.5	3.9	2.5	2.5	3.0	2.0	3.0	3.0
Djibouti	4.5	0.2	1.6	1.8	0.6	2.0	3.1	3.1	3.5	3.5	3.5	3.5	3.5	3.5
Equatorial Guinea	6.7	0.4	4.8	8.8	7.6	7.3	4.2	5.7	4.5	6.1	5.7	3.8	6.1	5.5
Eritrea	. . .	8.4	19.9	14.6	16.9	22.7	25.1	12.5	17.3	22.7	25.2	17.7	25.6	25.5
Ethiopia	7.6	4.8	6.2	–5.2	–7.2	15.1	8.6	6.8	12.3	17.8	15.9	11.6	17.7	15.1
Gabon	5.7	–0.7	0.5	2.1	0.2	2.1	0.4	—	4.0	5.5	3.0	6.4	4.5	2.7
Gambia, The	5.8	3.8	0.9	4.5	8.6	17.0	14.2	3.2	1.4	5.0	4.5	1.4	5.0	4.0
Ghana	28.1	12.4	25.2	32.9	14.8	26.7	12.6	15.1	10.9	9.4	8.8	10.5	9.0	8.3
Guinea	3.2	4.6	6.8	5.4	3.0	12.9	17.5	31.4	34.7	23.4	13.8	39.1	15.0	10.0
Guinea-Bissau	44.1	–2.1	8.6	3.3	3.3	–3.5	0.8	3.4	2.0	3.0	2.6	3.2	2.8	2.5
Kenya	16.2	5.8	10.0	5.8	2.0	9.8	11.6	10.3	14.5	6.9	7.2	15.6	5.3	7.2
Lesotho	11.7	8.6	6.1	6.9	12.5	7.3	5.0	3.4	6.1	6.6	6.4	6.4	6.9	6.1
Liberia	. . .	. . .	5.3	12.1	14.2	10.3	3.6	6.9	7.2	11.2	9.0	8.9	9.5	8.5
Madagascar	16.5	8.1	10.7	6.9	16.2	–1.1	14.0	18.4	10.8	10.1	6.9	10.9	7.7	6.0
Malawi	25.8	44.8	29.6	27.2	14.9	9.6	11.6	12.3	9.0	7.0	6.0	10.1	8.2	7.5
Mali	3.9	–1.2	–0.7	5.2	5.0	–1.3	–3.1	6.4	1.9	2.5	2.5	2.5	2.5	2.5
Mauritania	5.5	3.6	6.8	7.7	5.4	5.3	10.4	12.1	6.2	7.6	7.3	8.9	7.9	6.0
Mauritius	8.8	6.9	4.2	5.3	6.5	3.9	4.7	4.9	5.5	10.7	7.5	7.6	10.0	7.0
Morocco	4.7	0.7	1.9	0.6	2.8	1.2	1.5	1.0	3.3	2.5	2.0	3.3	2.5	2.0
Mozambique, Rep. of	36.2	2.9	12.7	9.1	16.8	13.5	12.6	6.4	13.2	6.4	5.7	9.4	5.5	5.3
Namibia	10.9	8.6	9.3	9.3	11.3	7.2	4.1	2.3	5.1	6.3	5.9	6.0	6.6	5.5
Niger	4.6	–2.3	2.9	4.0	2.7	–1.8	0.4	7.8	0.1	—	2.0	0.4	0.9	2.0
Nigeria	33.0	6.6	6.9	18.0	13.7	14.0	15.0	17.8	8.3	5.3	7.4	8.5	6.0	8.0
Rwanda	16.7	–2.4	3.9	3.4	2.0	7.4	12.0	9.2	8.8	8.2	5.0	11.9	5.0	5.0
São Tomé and Príncipe	42.8	11.0	11.0	10.0	10.1	9.9	13.8	17.2	23.6	16.6	11.4	23.3	13.5	9.5
Senegal	4.0	0.8	0.7	3.0	2.3	—	0.5	1.7	2.1	5.4	2.9	3.9	4.1	2.5
Seychelles	1.6	6.3	6.3	6.0	0.2	3.3	3.9	0.9	–0.4	4.4	12.9	0.8	9.8	14.3
Sierra Leone	45.2	34.1	–0.9	2.6	–3.7	7.5	14.2	12.1	9.5	10.8	10.2	8.3	11.0	9.4
South Africa	10.8	5.2	5.4	5.7	9.2	5.8	1.4	3.4	4.7	6.6	6.2	5.8	6.9	5.6
Sudan	81.5	16.0	8.0	4.9	8.3	7.7	8.4	8.5	7.2	8.0	6.5	15.7	7.0	6.0
Swaziland	9.7	5.9	7.2	7.5	11.7	7.4	3.4	4.8	5.3	6.8	6.3	5.5	6.6	5.6
Tanzania	22.5	9.0	6.2	5.1	4.6	4.4	4.1	4.4	7.3	5.6	5.0	6.7	5.0	5.0
Togo	5.9	–0.1	1.9	3.9	3.1	–0.9	0.4	6.8	2.2	3.2	3.0	1.6	3.3	3.0
Tunisia	5.3	2.7	2.3	2.0	2.7	2.7	3.6	2.0	4.5	3.0	3.0	3.3	3.0	3.0
Uganda	26.4	0.2	5.8	4.5	–2.0	5.7	5.0	8.0	6.6	7.5	5.1	7.2	6.6	4.9
Zambia	78.5	26.8	26.1	21.7	22.2	21.4	18.0	18.3	9.1	11.3	5.7	8.2	9.0	5.0
Zimbabwe[3]	23.8	58.0	55.6	73.4	133.2	365.0	350.0	237.8	1,016.7	16,170.2	. . .	1,281.1	137,873.1	. . .

Table A7 *(continued)*

	Average 1989–98	1999	2000	2001	2002	2003	2004	2005	2006	2007	2008	End of Period 2006	End of Period 2007	End of Period 2008
Central and eastern Europe[4]	**63.4**	**23.7**	**23.1**	**19.7**	**14.9**	**9.2**	**6.1**	**4.9**	**5.0**	**5.1**	**4.1**	**5.1**	**4.7**	**3.8**
Albania	34.6	0.4	—	3.1	5.2	2.3	2.9	2.4	2.4	2.5	3.3	2.5	3.1	3.0
Bosnia and Herzegovina	...	2.9	5.0	3.2	0.3	0.5	0.3	3.6	7.5	2.5	1.9	...	...	...
Bulgaria	111.1	2.6	8.2	7.5	5.8	2.3	6.1	5.0	7.3	8.2	7.9	6.5	11.9	3.8
Croatia	...	4.0	4.6	3.8	1.7	1.8	2.0	3.3	3.2	2.3	2.8	2.0	2.7	2.8
Czech Republic	13.9	2.3	3.8	4.7	1.8	0.1	2.8	1.8	2.5	2.9	4.4	1.8	4.0	4.5
Estonia	...	3.3	4.0	5.8	3.6	1.3	3.0	4.1	4.4	6.0	7.0	5.1	7.2	5.7
Hungary	22.7	10.0	9.8	9.2	5.3	4.6	6.8	3.6	3.9	7.6	4.5	6.5	5.9	3.7
Latvia	...	2.4	2.6	2.5	1.9	2.9	6.2	6.7	6.5	9.0	8.9	6.8	9.7	8.3
Lithuania	...	1.5	1.1	1.6	0.3	–1.1	1.2	2.7	3.8	5.2	4.6	4.5	5.0	4.2
Macedonia, FYR	...	–0.3	6.4	5.5	2.2	1.2	–0.4	0.5	3.2	2.0	3.0	3.0	3.5	2.5
Malta	3.0	2.3	3.0	2.5	2.6	1.9	2.7	2.5	2.6	0.6	2.0	0.8	1.3	1.9
Poland	70.4	7.3	10.1	5.5	1.9	0.8	3.5	2.1	1.0	2.2	2.7	1.4	2.7	3.1
Romania	102.7	45.8	45.7	34.5	22.5	15.3	11.9	9.0	6.6	4.3	4.8	4.9	4.5	4.8
Serbia	...	41.1	70.0	91.8	19.5	11.7	10.1	17.3	12.7	6.4	8.8	6.6	9.0	7.5
Slovak Republic	...	10.6	12.0	7.1	3.3	8.5	7.5	2.8	4.4	2.4	2.0	4.2	2.0	2.0
Turkey	75.6	64.9	55.0	54.2	45.1	25.3	8.6	8.2	9.6	8.2	4.6	9.7	6.0	4.0
Commonwealth of Independent States[4,5]	...	**69.1**	**24.1**	**19.9**	**13.4**	**11.9**	**10.3**	**12.1**	**9.4**	**8.9**	**8.3**	**9.3**	**8.8**	**8.0**
Russia	...	85.7	20.8	21.5	15.8	13.7	10.9	12.7	9.7	8.1	7.5	9.0	8.0	7.0
Excluding Russia	...	35.8	32.5	16.3	8.2	8.1	9.0	10.9	8.9	10.4	10.3	9.9	10.6	10.0
Armenia	...	0.6	–0.8	3.1	1.1	4.7	7.0	0.6	2.9	3.7	4.9	5.2	4.0	4.5
Azerbaijan	...	–8.5	1.8	1.5	2.8	2.2	6.7	9.7	8.4	16.6	17.0	11.4	20.0	15.0
Belarus	...	293.7	168.6	61.1	42.6	28.4	18.1	10.3	7.0	8.1	10.0	6.6	9.7	10.2
Georgia	...	19.1	4.0	4.7	5.6	4.8	5.7	8.3	9.2	8.5	8.1	8.8	9.3	7.0
Kazakhstan	...	8.4	13.3	8.4	5.9	6.4	6.9	7.6	8.6	8.6	7.8	8.4	8.8	7.2
Kyrgyz Republic	...	35.9	18.7	6.9	2.1	3.1	4.1	4.3	5.6	7.0	7.0	5.1	8.5	7.0
Moldova	...	39.3	31.3	9.8	5.3	11.7	12.5	11.9	12.7	11.2	8.9	14.1	10.0	8.0
Mongolia	...	7.6	11.6	5.6	0.9	5.1	8.3	12.7	5.1	6.7	7.2	6.0	7.5	7.0
Tajikistan	...	27.5	32.9	38.6	12.2	16.4	7.2	7.3	10.0	9.9	12.6	12.5	9.0	8.0
Turkmenistan	...	23.5	8.0	11.6	8.8	5.6	5.9	10.7	8.2	6.5	9.0	7.2	6.0	12.5
Ukraine	...	22.7	28.2	12.0	0.8	5.2	9.0	13.5	9.0	11.5	10.8	11.6	11.0	10.6
Uzbekistan	...	29.1	25.0	27.3	27.3	11.6	6.6	10.0	14.2	12.2	9.8	11.4	11.0	10.0

Table A7 *(continued)*

	Average											End of Period		
	1989–98	1999	2000	2001	2002	2003	2004	2005	2006	2007	2008	2006	2007	2008
Developing Asia	**9.7**	**2.5**	**1.8**	**2.7**	**2.0**	**2.5**	**4.1**	**3.6**	**4.0**	**5.3**	**4.4**	**4.1**	**5.7**	**3.9**
Afghanistan, Rep. of	. . .	. . .	. . .	. . .	5.1	24.1	13.2	12.3	5.1	8.3	7.6	4.8	8.5	7.0
Bangladesh	6.6	6.2	2.5	1.9	3.7	5.4	6.1	7.0	6.5	7.2	6.3	7.5	6.8	5.9
Bhutan	10.0	6.8	4.0	3.4	2.5	2.1	4.6	5.3	5.0	4.9	4.7	5.3	4.8	4.5
Brunei Darussalam	. . .	—	1.2	0.6	–2.3	0.3	0.9	1.1	0.2	1.2	1.2	. . .	. . .	. . .
Cambodia	. . .	4.0	–0.8	0.2	3.3	1.2	3.8	5.9	4.7	6.5	5.5	2.8	6.5	5.5
China	9.4	–1.4	0.4	0.7	–0.8	1.2	3.9	1.8	1.5	4.5	3.9	2.0	5.7	3.5
Fiji	4.6	2.0	1.1	4.3	0.8	4.2	2.8	2.4	2.5	5.5	4.5	3.1	7.0	2.5
India	9.7	4.7	4.0	3.8	4.3	3.8	3.8	4.2	6.1	6.2	4.4	6.7	4.9	4.0
Indonesia	12.2	20.7	3.8	11.5	11.8	6.8	6.1	10.5	13.1	6.3	6.2	6.6	6.5	5.7
Kiribati	3.8	1.8	0.4	6.0	3.2	2.5	–1.9	–0.5	–0.2	0.2	1.0	–0.2	0.2	1.0
Lao PDR	18.3	128.4	23.2	9.3	10.6	15.5	10.5	7.2	6.8	4.0	4.5	4.7	4.1	4.4
Malaysia	3.7	2.7	1.6	1.4	1.8	1.1	1.4	3.0	3.6	2.1	2.4	3.1	2.2	2.4
Maldives	8.8	3.0	–1.2	0.7	0.9	–2.8	6.3	3.3	3.7	7.0	7.0	5.0	7.0	6.0
Myanmar	28.3	10.9	–1.7	34.5	58.1	24.9	3.8	10.7	25.7	36.9	27.5	38.7	35.0	20.0
Nepal	9.5	11.4	3.4	2.4	2.9	4.8	4.0	4.5	8.0	6.5	5.3	8.3	5.6	5.3
Pakistan	9.9	5.7	3.6	4.4	2.5	3.1	4.6	9.3	7.9	7.8	7.0	7.6	7.0	6.5
Papua New Guinea	7.6	14.9	15.6	9.3	11.8	14.7	2.1	1.7	2.3	3.0	4.8	–1.0	6.3	4.8
Philippines	10.1	6.4	4.0	6.8	2.9	3.5	6.0	7.6	6.2	3.0	4.0	4.3	4.1	3.2
Samoa	5.5	0.8	–0.2	1.9	7.4	4.3	7.9	7.8	3.2	2.6	3.0	2.2	2.3	2.3
Solomon Islands	11.3	8.0	6.9	7.6	9.3	10.0	6.9	7.3	8.1	6.3	7.3	7.5	7.0	6.7
Sri Lanka	11.9	4.0	1.5	12.1	10.2	2.6	7.9	10.6	9.5	17.0	11.5	17.9	13.0	11.0
Thailand	5.5	0.3	1.6	1.7	0.6	1.8	2.8	4.5	4.6	2.0	2.0	3.5	2.3	1.2
Timor-Leste, Dem. Rep. of	. . .	. . .	63.6	3.6	4.8	7.0	3.2	1.8	4.1	5.4	3.9	6.7	5.4	3.9
Tonga	4.4	3.9	5.3	6.9	10.4	11.1	11.7	9.7	7.0	5.9	5.3	6.4	5.6	5.4
Vanuatu	3.8	2.2	2.5	3.7	2.0	3.0	1.4	1.2	1.6	2.5	3.0	2.5	2.5	3.5
Vietnam	26.9	4.1	–1.6	–0.4	4.0	3.2	7.7	8.3	7.5	7.3	7.6	6.6	8.0	7.3
Middle East	**11.4**	**6.6**	**4.0**	**3.8**	**5.3**	**6.2**	**7.2**	**6.9**	**7.5**	**10.8**	**9.2**	**9.4**	**9.9**	**9.3**
Bahrain	1.1	–1.3	–0.7	–1.2	–0.5	1.7	2.3	2.6	2.9	2.9	2.7	2.9	2.8	2.7
Egypt	12.3	3.7	2.8	2.4	2.4	3.2	8.1	8.8	4.2	10.9	7.8	7.2	8.5	7.9
Iran, I.R. of	23.3	20.1	12.6	11.4	15.8	15.6	15.2	12.1	13.6	19.0	17.7	16.6	19.0	17.7
Iraq	. . .	. . .	. . .	. . .	. . .	. . .	. . .	. . .	. . .	. . .	. . .	. . .	. . .	. . .
Jordan	7.4	0.6	0.7	1.8	1.8	1.6	3.4	3.5	6.3	5.0	4.5	7.5	4.3	3.3
Kuwait	3.6	3.1	1.6	1.4	0.8	1.0	1.3	4.1	2.8	2.6	2.6	3.6	2.6	2.6
Lebanon	31.9	0.2	–0.4	–0.4	1.8	1.3	1.7	–0.7	5.6	3.5	2.5	7.2	2.0	3.0
Libya	6.4	2.6	–2.9	–8.8	–9.9	–2.1	–2.2	2.0	3.4	16.2	6.9	7.2	16.2	6.9
Oman	1.7	0.5	–1.2	–0.8	–0.3	0.2	0.7	1.9	3.2	3.8	3.5	3.5	3.6	3.2
Qatar	3.0	2.2	1.7	1.4	0.2	2.3	6.8	8.8	11.8	12.0	10.0	. . .	. . .	. . .
Saudi Arabia	1.4	–1.3	–1.1	–1.1	0.2	0.6	0.4	0.7	2.2	3.0	3.0	2.9	3.0	3.0
Syrian Arab Republic	9.1	–3.7	–3.9	3.4	–0.5	5.8	4.4	7.2	10.0	7.0	7.0	11.9	–3.2	5.0
United Arab Emirates	3.6	2.1	1.4	2.7	2.9	3.2	5.0	6.2	9.3	8.0	6.4	. . .	. . .	. . .
Yemen, Rep. of	37.7	8.0	10.9	11.9	12.2	10.8	12.5	11.7	18.2	12.5	12.1	16.5	13.2	11.0

Table A7 *(concluded)*

	Average 1989–98	1999	2000	2001	2002	2003	2004	2005	2006	2007	2008	End of Period 2006	2007	2008
Western Hemisphere	**134.2**	**8.3**	**7.6**	**6.1**	**8.9**	**10.6**	**6.5**	**6.3**	**5.4**	**5.3**	**5.8**	**5.0**	**5.4**	**5.7**
Antigua and Barbuda	3.8	0.6	–0.6	–0.4	2.4	2.0	2.0	2.1	1.8	3.2	2.0	0.0	3.2	2.0
Argentina	125.4	–1.2	–0.9	–1.1	25.9	13.4	4.4	9.6	10.9	9.5	12.6	9.8	10.0	13.0
Bahamas, The	3.2	1.3	1.6	2.0	2.2	3.0	0.9	2.2	1.8	2.4	2.4	2.3	2.6	2.4
Barbados	3.4	1.5	2.4	2.6	–1.2	1.6	1.4	6.0	7.3	5.5	3.6	5.6	5.7	2.3
Belize	2.1	–1.3	0.7	1.2	2.2	2.6	3.1	3.7	4.3	3.3	3.3	3.0	3.5	3.0
Bolivia	11.7	2.2	4.6	1.6	0.9	3.3	4.4	5.4	4.3	8.5	13.3	5.0	10.4	16.0
Brazil	456.2	4.9	7.1	6.8	8.4	14.8	6.6	6.9	4.2	3.6	3.9	3.1	4.0	4.0
Chile	12.9	3.3	3.8	3.6	2.5	2.8	1.1	3.1	3.4	3.9	4.1	2.6	5.5	3.0
Colombia	23.6	10.9	9.2	8.0	6.3	7.1	5.9	5.0	4.3	5.5	4.6	4.5	5.0	4.3
Costa Rica	17.4	10.0	11.0	11.3	9.2	9.4	12.3	13.8	11.5	9.1	6.9	9.4	9.0	6.0
Dominica	2.9	1.2	0.9	1.6	0.1	1.6	2.4	1.6	2.6	2.2	2.0	1.6	1.5	1.5
Dominican Republic	17.4	6.5	7.7	8.9	5.2	27.4	51.5	4.2	7.6	5.8	4.2	5.0	6.0	4.0
Ecuador	40.6	52.2	96.1	37.7	12.6	7.9	2.7	2.1	3.3	2.1	2.3	2.9	2.3	2.3
El Salvador	12.2	0.5	2.3	3.7	1.9	2.1	4.5	3.7	4.6	4.4	3.7	4.9	4.0	3.5
Grenada	2.8	0.6	2.1	1.7	1.1	2.2	2.3	3.5	3.8	2.4	2.0	1.7	2.0	2.0
Guatemala	15.3	5.2	6.0	7.3	8.1	5.6	7.6	9.1	6.6	6.2	6.1	5.8	6.0	6.0
Guyana	28.9	7.5	6.1	2.7	5.3	6.0	4.7	6.9	6.7	9.6	3.3	4.2	8.0	5.0
Haiti	20.8	8.7	13.7	14.2	9.9	39.3	21.2	15.8	14.2	9.0	7.8	12.4	8.0	7.5
Honduras	19.3	11.6	11.0	9.7	7.7	7.7	8.1	8.8	5.6	6.9	9.0	5.3	8.0	9.0
Jamaica	27.8	6.0	8.1	7.0	7.1	10.5	13.5	15.3	8.6	6.6	10.1	5.8	8.9	8.9
Mexico	20.4	16.6	9.5	6.4	5.0	4.5	4.7	4.0	3.6	3.9	4.2	4.1	3.6	3.6
Nicaragua	154.7	7.2	9.9	4.7	4.0	6.5	8.5	9.6	9.1	8.2	7.3	9.5	7.3	7.0
Panama	1.0	1.3	1.4	0.3	1.0	0.6	0.5	2.9	2.5	3.8	3.6	2.2	4.4	3.6
Paraguay	18.1	6.8	9.0	7.3	10.5	14.2	4.3	6.8	9.6	7.6	3.9	12.5	5.0	3.0
Peru	201.6	3.5	3.8	2.0	0.2	2.3	3.7	1.6	2.0	1.5	2.3	1.1	2.7	2.0
St. Kitts and Nevis	3.7	3.4	2.1	2.1	2.1	2.3	2.2	3.4	8.5	5.2	3.2	8.4	4.0	2.5
St. Lucia	3.3	3.5	3.7	5.4	–0.3	1.0	1.5	3.9	2.4	2.5	2.9	–0.6	2.5	2.9
St. Vincent and the Grenadines	3.3	1.0	0.2	0.8	0.8	0.2	3.0	3.7	3.0	6.1	4.1	4.8	5.8	3.2
Suriname	59.7	98.7	58.6	39.8	15.5	23.0	9.1	9.9	11.3	4.6	4.3	4.7	4.5	4.0
Trinidad and Tobago	6.7	3.4	3.6	5.5	4.2	3.8	3.7	6.9	8.3	8.5	7.5	9.1	8.0	7.0
Uruguay	53.1	5.7	4.8	4.4	14.0	19.4	9.2	4.7	6.4	8.0	6.8	6.4	8.3	6.0
Venezuela	52.1	23.6	16.2	12.5	22.4	31.1	21.7	16.0	13.7	18.0	19.0	17.0	17.0	21.0

[1]In accordance with standard practice in the *World Economic Outlook,* movements in consumer prices are indicated as annual averages rather than as December/December changes during the year, as is the practice in some countries. For many countries, figures for recent years are IMF staff estimates. Data for some countries are for fiscal years. In this table, Africa excludes Zimbabwe.

[2]The percent changes in 2002 are calculated over a period of 18 months, reflecting a change in the fiscal year cycle (from July–June to January–December).

[3]Given recent trends, it is not possible to forecast inflation with any degree of precision and consequently no projection for 2008 is shown.

[4]For many countries, inflation for the earlier years is measured on the basis of a retail price index. Consumer price indices with a broader and more up-to-date coverage are typically used for more recent years.

[5]Mongolia, which is not a member of the Commonwealth of Independent States, is included in this group for reasons of geography and similarities in economic structure.

Table A8. Major Advanced Economies: General Government Fiscal Balances and Debt[1]

(Percent of GDP)

	Average 1991–2000	2001	2002	2003	2004	2005	2006	2007	2008	2012
Major advanced economies										
Actual balance	–3.0	–1.7	–4.0	–4.8	–4.2	–3.5	–2.7	–2.4	–2.6	–2.1
Output gap[2]	—	0.5	–0.5	–1.0	–0.4	–0.5	–0.2	–0.4	–0.8	—
Structural balance[2]	–2.8	–1.9	–3.8	–4.3	–4.0	–3.3	–2.6	–2.2	–2.3	–2.1
United States										
Actual balance	–2.2	–0.4	–3.8	–4.8	–4.4	–3.6	–2.6	–2.6	–2.9	–2.6
Output gap[2]	—	0.7	–0.4	–0.6	—	0.2	0.3	–0.5	–1.2	—
Structural balance[2]	–2.2	–0.7	–3.7	–4.6	–4.3	–3.7	–2.7	–2.4	–2.5	–2.6
Net debt	49.4	35.6	38.4	41.4	43.2	44.2	44.1	45.0	46.7	51.0
Gross debt	65.4	53.7	56.1	59.4	60.4	60.9	60.2	60.8	62.2	65.8
Euro area										
Actual balance	–3.8	–1.9	–2.6	–3.1	–2.9	–2.6	–1.6	–0.9	–1.1	–0.8
Output gap[2]	–0.1	1.3	0.1	–1.0	–1.0	–1.4	–0.6	–0.3	–0.2	—
Structural balance[2]	–3.3	–2.2	–2.5	–2.6	–2.4	–1.9	–1.2	–0.8	–0.9	–0.7
Net debt	56.9	58.5	58.5	59.8	60.3	60.9	58.9	57.0	55.9	51.6
Gross debt	69.2	68.3	68.2	69.3	69.7	70.4	68.6	66.6	65.4	60.5
Germany[3]										
Actual balance	–2.2	–2.8	–3.7	–4.0	–3.8	–3.4	–1.6	–0.2	–0.5	–0.5
Output gap[2]	0.2	1.3	–0.2	–1.7	–2.0	–2.4	–1.0	–0.1	0.2	—
Structural balance[2,4]	–2.0	–2.6	–2.9	–3.0	–2.9	–2.5	–1.2	–0.4	–0.7	–0.5
Net debt	43.6	52.1	54.3	57.7	60.0	61.7	60.2	58.1	56.9	54.6
Gross debt	52.4	57.9	59.6	62.8	64.7	66.3	66.0	63.7	62.3	59.4
France										
Actual balance	–3.8	–1.5	–3.1	–4.1	–3.6	–3.0	–2.5	–2.5	–2.7	–1.3
Output gap[2]	–1.4	1.0	—	–0.9	–0.5	–0.8	–0.9	–1.2	–1.3	—
Structural balance[2,4]	–2.9	–2.1	–3.1	–3.4	–3.1	–2.7	–1.9	–1.7	–2.0	–1.2
Net debt	42.8	48.2	49.1	53.2	55.3	57.0	54.4	53.6	53.7	50.8
Gross debt	52.0	56.9	58.8	62.9	65.0	66.7	64.1	63.3	63.4	60.5
Italy										
Actual balance	–6.3	–3.1	–2.9	–3.5	–3.5	–4.2	–4.4	–2.1	–2.3	–2.5
Output gap[2]	–0.7	1.4	0.5	–0.7	–0.7	–1.9	–1.3	–0.8	–0.7	—
Structural balance[2,4]	–6.0	–3.8	–3.9	–3.3	–3.4	–3.5	–3.9	–1.8	–2.0	–2.5
Net debt	108.3	105.2	102.1	101.5	100.9	103.1	103.1	101.7	101.1	98.4
Gross debt	113.8	108.7	105.6	104.3	103.8	106.2	106.8	105.3	104.7	102.0
Japan										
Actual balance	–3.8	–6.3	–8.0	–8.0	–6.2	–4.8	–4.1	–3.9	–3.8	–2.9
Excluding social security	–5.6	–6.5	–7.9	–8.1	–6.6	–5.1	–4.1	–3.8	–3.9	–3.8
Output gap[2]	–0.1	–1.4	–2.3	–2.3	–1.2	–1.0	–0.5	–0.2	–0.2	—
Structural balance[2]	–3.8	–5.7	–7.0	–7.0	–5.7	–4.5	–4.0	–3.8	–3.8	–2.9
Excluding social security	–5.6	–6.2	–7.3	–7.6	–6.3	–4.9	–4.0	–3.8	–3.8	–3.8
Net debt	31.7	66.3	72.6	76.5	82.7	84.0	87.1	89.8	92.1	95.0
Gross debt	100.2	151.7	160.9	167.2	178.1	191.4	193.1	194.4	194.9	189.6
United Kingdom										
Actual balance	–3.4	0.9	–1.8	–3.5	–3.4	–3.3	–2.7	–2.5	–2.3	–1.4
Output gap[2]	–0.6	0.6	–0.1	–0.1	0.5	–0.2	–0.2	0.2	–0.1	—
Structural balance[2]	–2.3	–0.1	–1.9	–3.0	–3.6	–3.2	–2.7	–2.5	–2.2	–1.3
Net debt	34.0	32.5	32.5	34.2	35.9	37.8	38.5	38.4	38.5	37.8
Gross debt	39.6	38.1	37.7	39.0	40.5	42.4	43.1	43.0	43.1	42.5
Canada										
Actual balance	–3.6	0.7	–0.1	–0.1	0.8	1.6	1.0	0.9	0.9	0.6
Output gap[2]	4.1	0.3	0.2	–0.7	–0.3	0.2	0.3	0.2	–0.2	—
Structural balance[2]	–3.4	0.4	–0.2	0.2	0.9	1.5	0.9	0.9	1.0	0.5
Net debt	61.0	43.7	42.6	38.6	34.4	30.1	27.6	25.1	23.2	16.7
Gross debt	105.2	91.5	89.4	85.2	80.2	78.4	73.5	68.4	64.7	51.3

Note: The methodology and specific assumptions for each country are discussed in Box A1 in the Statistical Appendix.

[1]Debt data refer to end of year. Debt data are not always comparable across countries.

[2]Percent of potential GDP.

[3]Beginning in 1995, the debt and debt-service obligations of the Treuhandanstalt (and of various other agencies) were taken over by the general government. This debt is equivalent to 8 percent of GDP, and the associated debt service to ½ to 1 percent of GDP.

[4]Excludes one-off receipts from the sale of mobile telephone licenses (the equivalent of 2.5 percent of GDP in 2000 for Germany, 0.1 percent of GDP in 2001 and 2002 for France, and 1.2 percent of GDP in 2000 for Italy). Also excludes one-off receipts from sizable asset transactions, in particular 0.5 percent of GDP for France in 2005.

Table A9. Summary of World Trade Volumes and Prices

(Annual percent change)

	Ten-Year Averages											
	1989–98	1999–2008	1999	2000	2001	2002	2003	2004	2005	2006	2007	2008
Trade in goods and services												
World trade[1]												
Volume	6.7	6.7	5.8	12.2	0.2	3.5	5.5	10.8	7.5	9.2	6.6	6.7
Price deflator												
In U.S. dollars	0.2	3.4	–1.6	–0.4	–3.5	1.2	10.4	9.5	5.7	4.8	7.0	2.4
In SDRs	0.1	2.2	–2.4	3.2	—	–0.6	2.1	3.6	5.9	5.2	3.6	1.2
Volume of trade												
Exports												
Advanced economies	6.7	5.6	5.6	11.7	–0.6	2.3	3.3	9.0	5.8	8.2	5.4	5.3
Other emerging market and developing countries	7.6	9.3	3.7	13.8	2.7	7.0	11.1	14.6	11.1	11.0	9.2	9.0
Imports												
Advanced economies	6.4	5.7	8.0	11.7	–0.6	2.7	4.1	9.3	6.1	7.4	4.3	5.0
Other emerging market and developing countries	7.0	10.1	0.6	13.7	3.3	6.3	10.5	16.7	12.1	14.9	12.5	11.3
Terms of trade												
Advanced economies	—	–0.3	–0.3	–2.6	0.3	0.8	1.0	–0.1	–1.6	–0.9	0.2	–0.2
Other emerging market and developing countries	–0.9	2.4	4.2	6.0	–2.4	0.6	0.9	3.0	5.7	4.7	0.2	1.0
Trade in goods												
World trade[1]												
Volume	6.8	6.8	5.6	12.8	–0.5	3.7	6.4	10.9	7.4	9.3	6.3	6.9
Price deflator												
In U.S. dollars	0.1	3.7	–1.2	0.4	–3.7	0.6	9.9	10.0	6.4	5.4	7.4	2.4
In SDRs	—	2.4	–1.9	4.0	–0.3	–1.1	1.7	4.0	6.6	5.9	3.9	1.2
World trade prices in U.S. dollars[2]												
Manufactures	0.5	3.1	–2.7	–5.3	–3.4	2.1	14.3	9.5	3.7	3.8	7.9	2.8
Oil	–1.2	19.1	37.5	57.0	–13.8	2.5	15.8	30.7	41.3	20.5	6.6	9.5
Nonfuel primary commodities	–2.2	5.8	–7.2	4.8	–4.9	1.7	6.9	18.5	10.3	28.4	12.2	–6.7
Food	–1.5	2.8	–12.6	2.5	0.2	3.4	5.2	14.3	–0.3	9.9	8.7	–0.5
Beverages	0.3	–1.0	–21.3	–15.1	–16.1	16.5	4.9	3.0	21.0	6.3	2.9	–3.4
Agricultural raw materials	–0.3	2.4	1.2	4.4	–4.9	1.8	3.7	5.5	1.6	10.1	3.5	–1.8
Metals	–4.5	11.8	–1.1	12.2	–9.8	–2.7	12.2	36.1	26.4	56.5	17.9	–12.0
World trade prices in SDRs[2]												
Manufactures	0.4	1.8	–3.4	–1.8	0.1	0.4	5.7	3.6	3.9	4.2	4.4	1.6
Oil	–1.3	17.6	36.4	62.8	–10.7	0.8	7.1	23.6	41.6	21.0	3.2	8.2
Nonfuel primary commodities	–2.3	4.5	–7.9	8.6	–1.5	—	–1.2	12.1	10.5	29.0	8.6	–7.8
Food	–1.6	1.5	–13.3	6.2	3.8	1.6	–2.8	8.1	–0.1	10.4	5.2	–1.6
Beverages	0.2	–2.2	–21.9	–12.0	–13.1	14.6	–3.0	–2.5	21.3	6.7	–0.4	–4.5
Agricultural raw materials	–0.4	1.2	0.4	8.3	–1.5	—	–4.1	–0.2	1.8	10.6	0.1	–2.9
Metals	–4.6	10.4	–1.9	16.3	–6.6	–4.4	3.7	28.8	26.7	57.2	14.1	–13.0
World trade prices in euros[2]												
Manufactures	1.1	1.0	2.2	9.3	–0.3	–3.1	–4.5	–0.4	3.5	2.9	0.3	1.0
Oil	–0.7	16.7	44.4	81.3	–11.1	–2.8	–3.3	18.9	41.0	19.5	–0.8	7.6
Nonfuel primary commodities	–1.6	3.7	–2.6	20.9	–1.9	–3.5	–10.8	7.8	10.0	27.4	4.4	–8.3
Food	–1.0	0.7	–8.2	18.3	3.3	–1.9	–12.2	3.9	–0.5	9.0	1.1	–2.2
Beverages	0.9	–3.0	–17.3	–2.0	–13.5	10.5	–12.4	–6.3	20.8	5.4	–4.3	–5.1
Agricultural raw materials	0.3	0.4	6.3	20.6	–1.9	–3.5	–13.4	–4.1	1.4	9.2	–3.8	–3.5
Metals	–4.0	9.5	3.8	29.6	–6.9	–7.8	–6.3	23.8	26.2	55.3	9.7	–13.5

Table A9 *(concluded)*

	Ten-Year Averages											
	1989–98	1999–2008	1999	2000	2001	2002	2003	2004	2005	2006	2007	2008
Trade in goods												
Volume of trade												
Exports												
Advanced economies	6.6	5.5	5.1	12.5	–1.5	2.3	3.9	8.7	5.5	8.7	4.7	5.4
Other emerging market and developing countries	7.4	9.2	3.4	13.9	2.2	7.3	12.0	14.3	10.9	11.0	9.0	8.8
Fuel exporters	3.9	4.8	–0.3	7.1	0.6	2.5	11.7	8.6	5.8	3.9	3.3	5.8
Nonfuel exporters	8.8	10.8	4.4	16.0	2.8	8.9	12.1	16.2	12.7	13.9	11.5	10.1
Imports												
Advanced economies	6.6	5.9	8.3	12.3	–1.5	3.0	5.0	9.6	6.1	7.8	3.9	5.1
Other emerging market and developing countries	7.1	10.0	–0.2	14.1	3.1	6.6	12.1	17.2	12.2	12.5	12.4	11.7
Fuel exporters	1.4	11.1	–10.4	10.8	16.0	7.7	9.8	16.5	18.0	14.0	17.4	14.8
Nonfuel exporters	8.9	9.8	1.9	14.7	0.9	6.4	12.6	17.3	11.1	12.1	11.4	11.1
Price deflators in SDRs												
Exports												
Advanced economies	–0.2	1.5	–3.1	0.5	–0.1	–0.9	2.6	3.2	3.8	3.9	4.3	1.1
Other emerging market and developing countries	0.8	5.6	4.2	14.9	–1.0	—	1.5	7.6	14.2	10.6	3.6	2.0
Fuel exporters	—	12.9	20.6	43.8	–7.3	1.0	4.4	17.1	33.0	17.5	2.9	5.0
Nonfuel exporters	1.0	3.1	–0.1	6.0	1.4	–0.4	0.5	4.4	7.6	7.7	3.9	0.6
Imports												
Advanced economies	–0.5	1.9	–2.9	3.7	–0.6	–1.9	1.3	3.4	5.9	5.2	3.8	1.2
Other emerging market and developing countries	1.7	2.9	–0.7	6.8	1.4	–0.7	0.2	4.4	7.4	6.7	3.8	0.7
Fuel exporters	1.9	2.2	–3.3	1.9	0.3	1.2	0.6	4.2	7.1	7.2	3.0	–0.1
Nonfuel exporters	1.6	3.1	–0.2	7.7	1.6	–1.1	0.1	4.4	7.5	6.7	3.9	0.8
Terms of trade												
Advanced economies	0.3	–0.4	–0.2	–3.1	0.5	1.0	1.2	–0.2	–2.0	–1.2	0.4	–0.2
Other emerging market and developing countries	–0.9	2.6	4.9	7.5	–2.3	0.7	1.3	3.1	6.4	3.6	–0.2	1.3
Regional groups												
Africa	–1.4	5.1	8.0	13.1	–3.5	0.3	2.7	4.4	14.3	9.5	–0.1	3.6
Central and eastern Europe	–0.4	—	–1.8	–2.3	3.6	1.0	–0.4	1.2	–0.6	–1.7	0.9	0.3
Commonwealth of Independent States[3]	–2.3	7.1	7.0	23.7	–2.5	–2.3	10.4	12.4	14.7	9.2	–0.1	1.0
Developing Asia	–0.1	–0.9	–1.2	–4.3	—	0.7	—	–2.1	–1.3	–0.7	–0.3	0.3
Middle East	–2.1	10.2	32.4	39.8	–8.2	2.0	–0.2	10.8	24.7	5.8	–0.3	5.2
Western Hemisphere	–0.5	3.0	2.7	7.8	–4.4	1.2	3.3	5.5	5.6	8.8	0.7	–0.4
Analytical groups												
By source of export earnings												
Fuel exporters	–1.9	10.5	24.7	41.2	–7.5	–0.2	3.8	12.3	24.2	9.5	–0.1	5.0
Nonfuel exporters	–0.6	—	—	–1.6	–0.1	0.7	0.4	—	0.1	1.0	—	–0.2
Memorandum												
World exports in billions of U.S. dollars												
Goods and services	5,423	11,382	7,092	7,889	7,617	7,995	9,310	11,282	12,822	14,697	16,786	18,334
Goods	4,325	9,148	5,629	6,348	6,074	6,351	7,425	9,023	10,296	11,893	13,581	14,854
Average oil price[4]	–1.2	19.1	37.5	57.0	–13.8	2.5	15.8	30.7	41.3	20.5	6.6	9.5
In U.S. dollars a barrel	18.20	42.33	18.0	28.2	24.3	25.0	28.9	37.8	53.4	64.3	68.5	75.0
Export unit value of manufactures[5]	0.5	3.1	–2.7	–5.3	–3.4	2.1	14.3	9.5	3.7	3.8	7.9	2.8

[1]Average of annual percent change for world exports and imports.

[2]As represented, respectively, by the export unit value index for the manufactures of the advanced economies; the average of U.K. Brent, Dubai, and West Texas Intermediate crude oil prices; and the average of world market prices for nonfuel primary commodities weighted by their 1995–97 shares in world commodity exports.

[3]Mongolia, which is not a member of the Commonwealth of Independent States, is included in this group for reasons of geography and similarities in economic structure.

[4]Average of U.K. Brent, Dubai, and West Texas Intermediate crude oil prices.

[5]For the manufactures exported by the advanced economies.

Table A10. Summary of Balances on Current Account

(Billions of U.S. dollars)

	1999	2000	2001	2002	2003	2004	2005	2006	2007	2008
Advanced economies	**–107.9**	**–265.7**	**–204.5**	**–211.1**	**–208.9**	**–220.6**	**–431.6**	**–508.8**	**–499.8**	**–550.2**
United States	–299.8	–417.4	–384.7	–459.6	–522.1	–640.2	–754.9	–811.5	–784.3	–788.3
Euro area[1]	28.6	–37.0	8.0	47.3	42.9	109.3	27.9	0.9	–21.2	–48.8
Japan	114.5	119.6	87.8	112.6	136.2	172.1	165.7	170.4	195.9	195.1
Other advanced economies[2]	48.8	69.1	84.4	88.6	134.1	138.3	129.7	131.3	109.9	91.8
Memorandum										
Newly industrialized Asian economies	57.1	38.9	48.1	55.5	80.0	83.9	79.8	87.6	90.9	87.0
Other emerging market and developing countries	**–19.3**	**86.4**	**40.8**	**78.4**	**146.3**	**211.5**	**438.2**	**596.0**	**593.3**	**623.6**
Regional groups										
Africa	–14.2	8.1	0.9	–6.8	–1.8	1.0	16.4	28.9	–0.5	7.8
Central and eastern Europe	–25.8	–31.8	–16.0	–23.9	–37.4	–59.7	–61.9	–88.1	–119.2	–134.3
Commonwealth of Independent States[3]	23.8	48.3	33.1	30.2	35.9	63.5	88.3	98.4	77.2	57.7
Developing Asia	38.3	38.1	36.5	64.6	82.9	89.2	163.8	278.1	389.2	445.7
Middle East	15.1	71.7	40.0	30.3	59.0	96.7	196.7	233.8	227.0	247.1
Western Hemisphere	–56.4	–48.0	–53.8	–15.9	7.7	20.9	34.9	44.9	19.5	–0.4
Memorandum										
European Union	–15.8	–84.2	–27.3	19.1	20.9	62.9	–30.0	–95.3	–167.3	–217.7
Analytical groups										
By source of export earnings										
Fuel	40.0	151.3	84.9	65.0	109.3	184.3	348.4	423.1	367.0	380.6
Nonfuel	–59.3	–64.9	–44.1	13.5	37.0	27.2	89.8	172.9	226.3	242.9
of which, primary products	–0.9	–1.5	–3.1	–4.1	–2.6	0.6	0.3	9.1	10.5	5.8
By external financing source										
Net debtor countries	–92.3	–94.1	–73.8	–35.2	–31.2	–70.1	–94.0	–96.4	–169.3	–207.0
of which, official financing	–8.7	–6.6	–4.6	–2.3	0.1	–1.7	–4.6	–7.6	–15.6	–18.7
Net debtor countries by debt-servicing experience										
Countries with arrears and/or rescheduling during 2001–05	–19.0	–8.4	–10.2	7.7	11.2	–2.6	–7.7	5.8	–13.6	–15.1
World[1]	**–127.2**	**–179.3**	**–163.7**	**–132.7**	**–62.6**	**–9.1**	**6.6**	**87.2**	**93.5**	**73.3**
Memorandum										
In percent of total world current account transactions	–0.9	–1.1	–1.1	–0.8	–0.3	—	—	0.3	0.3	0.2
In percent of world GDP	–0.4	–0.6	–0.5	–0.4	–0.2	—	—	0.2	0.2	0.1

[1]Reflects errors, omissions, and asymmetries in balance of payments statistics on current account, as well as the exclusion of data for international organizations and a limited number of countries. Calculated as the sum of the balance of individual euro area countries. See "Classification of Countries" in the introduction to this Statistical Appendix.

[2]In this table, "other advanced economies" means advanced economies excluding the United States, euro area countries, and Japan.

[3]Mongolia, which is not a member of the Commonwealth of Independent States, is included in this group for reasons of geography and similarities in economic structure.

Table A11. Advanced Economies: Balance on Current Account

(Percent of GDP)

	1999	2000	2001	2002	2003	2004	2005	2006	2007	2008
Advanced economies	**–0.4**	**–1.0**	**–0.8**	**–0.8**	**–0.7**	**–0.7**	**–1.3**	**–1.4**	**–1.3**	**–1.4**
United States	–3.2	–4.3	–3.8	–4.4	–4.8	–5.5	–6.1	–6.2	–5.7	–5.5
Euro area[1]	0.4	–0.6	0.1	0.7	0.5	1.1	0.3	—	–0.2	–0.4
Germany	–1.3	–1.7	—	2.0	1.9	4.3	4.6	5.0	5.4	5.1
France	3.1	1.6	1.9	1.4	0.8	0.1	–1.1	–1.2	–1.6	–1.8
Italy	0.7	–0.5	–0.1	–0.8	–1.3	–0.9	–1.5	–2.4	–2.3	–2.2
Spain	–2.9	–4.0	–3.9	–3.3	–3.5	–5.3	–7.4	–8.6	–9.8	–10.2
Netherlands	3.8	1.9	2.4	2.5	5.5	8.5	7.7	8.6	7.4	6.7
Belgium	7.9	4.0	3.4	4.6	4.1	3.5	2.6	2.0	2.5	2.5
Austria	–3.2	–2.5	–1.9	0.3	–0.2	1.7	2.1	3.2	3.7	3.7
Finland	5.9	8.7	9.6	10.1	6.4	7.7	4.9	5.2	5.0	5.0
Greece	–5.4	–6.8	–6.3	–5.6	–5.6	–5.0	–6.4	–9.6	–9.7	–9.6
Portugal	–8.5	–10.2	–9.9	–8.1	–6.1	–7.7	–9.7	–9.4	–9.2	–9.2
Ireland	0.2	–0.4	–0.6	–1.0	—	–0.6	–3.5	–4.2	–4.4	–3.3
Luxembourg	10.7	13.2	8.8	11.6	8.0	11.8	11.1	10.6	10.5	10.3
Slovenia	–3.3	–2.7	0.2	1.0	–0.8	–2.7	–1.9	–2.5	–3.4	–3.1
Japan	2.6	2.6	2.1	2.9	3.2	3.7	3.6	3.9	4.5	4.3
United Kingdom	–2.4	–2.6	–2.2	–1.6	–1.3	–1.6	–2.5	–3.2	–3.5	–3.6
Canada	0.3	2.7	2.3	1.7	1.2	2.3	2.0	1.6	1.8	1.2
Korea	5.5	2.4	1.7	1.0	2.0	4.1	1.9	0.7	0.1	–0.4
Australia	–5.3	–3.8	–2.0	–3.8	–5.4	–6.0	–5.8	–5.5	–5.7	–5.6
Taiwan Province of China	2.7	2.8	6.3	8.6	9.6	5.6	4.5	6.8	6.8	7.1
Sweden	4.2	4.1	4.4	5.1	7.3	6.9	7.0	7.2	6.0	5.7
Switzerland	11.0	12.3	7.8	8.3	12.9	12.9	13.5	15.1	15.8	15.0
Hong Kong SAR	6.3	4.1	5.9	7.6	10.4	9.5	11.4	10.8	11.2	9.5
Denmark	1.9	1.4	3.1	2.5	3.4	3.1	3.8	2.4	1.3	1.3
Norway	5.6	15.0	16.1	12.6	12.3	12.7	15.5	16.4	14.6	15.1
Israel	–1.4	–0.8	–1.1	–0.9	1.2	2.4	3.3	5.6	3.7	3.2
Singapore	17.4	11.6	14.0	13.7	24.2	20.1	24.5	27.5	27.0	25.4
New Zealand	–6.2	–5.1	–2.8	–3.9	–4.3	–6.4	–8.6	–8.7	–8.5	–8.6
Cyprus	–1.7	–5.3	–3.3	–3.7	–2.2	–5.0	–5.6	–5.9	–5.5	–5.6
Iceland	–6.8	–10.2	–4.3	1.5	–4.8	–9.8	–16.1	–27.3	–11.6	–6.0
Memorandum										
Major advanced economies	–0.9	–1.6	–1.4	–1.4	–1.5	–1.4	–2.0	–2.2	–1.9	–1.9
Euro area[2]	–0.5	–1.5	–0.3	0.8	0.4	0.8	—	–0.2	–0.1	–0.3
Newly industrialized Asian economies	5.8	3.5	4.7	5.1	6.9	6.5	5.5	5.6	5.4	4.9

[1]Calculated as the sum of the balances of individual euro area countries.

[2]Corrected for reporting discrepancies in intra-area transactions.

Table A12. Other Emerging Market and Developing Countries—by Country: Balance on Current Account
(Percent of GDP)

	1999	2000	2001	2002	2003	2004	2005	2006	2007	2008
Africa	**–3.2**	**1.8**	**0.2**	**–1.4**	**–0.3**	**0.1**	**2.0**	**3.1**	**—**	**0.6**
Algeria	—	16.7	12.8	7.6	13.0	13.1	20.7	25.6	19.4	18.4
Angola	–27.5	8.7	–16.0	–1.3	–5.2	3.5	16.8	23.3	7.6	10.7
Benin	–7.3	–7.7	–6.4	–8.4	–8.3	–7.2	–6.2	–6.4	–6.3	–6.1
Botswana	11.0	8.8	9.9	3.3	5.6	2.9	14.4	19.3	20.6	10.0
Burkina Faso	–10.5	–12.3	–11.2	–9.9	–8.9	–10.4	–11.4	–10.3	–11.4	–10.9
Burundi	–5.0	–8.6	–4.6	–3.5	–4.6	–8.1	–9.6	–12.0	–14.2	–11.4
Cameroon	–3.5	–1.4	–3.6	–5.1	–1.8	–3.8	–3.3	–0.7	–1.5	–3.1
Cape Verde	–13.7	–10.9	–10.6	–11.1	–11.1	–14.3	–3.4	–6.5	–12.6	–16.7
Central African Republic	–1.6	–1.3	–1.7	–1.6	–2.1	–1.8	–6.5	–3.8	–3.4	–4.3
Chad	–13.5	–20.5	–35.4	–95.2	–47.2	–12.0	–5.5	–6.3	–1.0	–3.1
Comoros	–6.8	1.7	3.0	–1.4	–3.1	–2.9	–3.4	–5.6	–3.7	–4.8
Congo, Dem. Rep. of	–2.6	–4.0	–4.0	–1.6	1.0	–2.4	–10.6	–7.5	–8.1	–10.9
Congo, Rep. of	–17.2	7.9	–5.6	0.6	1.5	2.0	11.2	12.8	4.9	6.8
Côte d'Ivoire	–1.4	–2.8	–0.6	6.7	2.1	1.6	0.2	3.0	2.6	1.3
Djibouti	–4.3	–9.6	–3.4	–1.6	3.4	–1.3	1.2	–8.9	–14.5	–18.8
Equatorial Guinea	–29.5	–15.7	–40.8	0.1	–33.3	–21.9	–5.5	4.4	3.4	6.3
Eritrea	–17.9	0.5	4.2	7.4	7.6	5.6	0.4	–2.1	–3.7	–1.9
Ethiopia	–6.7	–4.2	–3.0	–4.7	–1.4	–4.2	–6.8	–10.4	–5.9	–3.0
Gabon	8.4	19.7	11.0	6.8	9.5	11.2	20.2	19.7	15.2	16.7
Gambia, The	–2.8	–4.1	–3.3	–3.6	–7.1	–11.0	–25.5	–19.8	–21.8	–18.6
Ghana	–11.6	–8.4	–5.3	0.5	1.7	–2.7	–7.0	–9.7	–9.7	–7.7
Guinea	–6.9	–6.4	–2.7	–2.5	–3.4	–5.8	–4.5	–5.9	–8.7	–12.0
Guinea-Bissau	–13.3	–5.6	–22.1	–10.7	–2.8	3.1	–7.3	–12.2	–12.7	–5.0
Kenya	–1.8	–2.3	–3.1	2.2	–0.2	0.1	–0.8	–2.4	–3.7	–5.1
Lesotho	–23.6	–18.0	–12.4	–19.4	–12.3	–5.5	–7.0	4.4	1.6	0.7
Liberia	. . .	–20.2	–17.1	1.0	–14.1	–5.6	–9.4	–28.3	–24.3	–43.4
Madagascar	–5.6	–5.6	–1.3	–6.0	–4.9	–9.1	–10.9	–8.6	–19.7	–23.5
Malawi	–8.3	–5.3	–6.8	–12.9	–7.2	–7.3	–11.6	–6.2	–3.0	–2.9
Mali	–8.5	–10.0	–10.4	–3.1	–6.2	–8.4	–8.3	–4.9	–4.5	–4.7
Mauritania	–2.5	–9.0	–11.7	3.0	–13.6	–34.6	–47.2	–1.3	–6.8	–7.0
Mauritius	–1.6	–1.5	3.4	5.7	2.4	0.8	–3.5	–5.3	–8.8	–7.6
Morocco	–0.4	–1.3	4.3	3.6	3.2	1.7	2.4	3.4	0.7	0.2
Mozambique, Rep. of	–22.0	–18.2	–19.4	–19.3	–15.1	–8.6	–10.7	–7.8	–9.1	–8.8
Namibia	6.9	10.5	1.5	4.4	5.1	9.5	7.2	15.0	18.5	12.8
Niger	–6.5	–6.2	–4.8	–6.3	–8.3	–7.8	–9.4	–8.6	–11.0	–10.8
Nigeria	–8.4	11.7	4.5	–11.7	–2.7	5.3	9.3	12.2	1.8	6.0
Rwanda	–7.7	–5.0	–5.9	–6.7	–7.8	–3.0	–3.2	–7.5	–7.3	–6.5
São Tomé and Príncipe	–15.7	–17.5	–16.4	–13.9	–11.4	–13.8	–19.4	–45.9	–41.2	–42.0
Senegal	–4.8	–6.6	–4.4	–5.7	–6.1	–6.1	–7.8	–10.1	–9.6	–9.8
Seychelles	–19.8	–7.3	–23.4	–16.3	6.4	–0.3	–27.6	–23.2	–30.4	–32.4
Sierra Leone	–7.9	–8.8	–6.3	–2.0	–4.8	–5.8	–7.1	–5.7	–6.7	–10.0
South Africa	–0.5	–0.1	0.3	0.8	–1.1	–3.2	–4.0	–6.5	–6.7	–6.4
Sudan	–8.8	–8.2	–12.5	–10.3	–7.8	–6.5	–10.7	–14.7	–10.7	–8.5
Swaziland	–2.6	–5.4	–4.5	4.8	6.5	3.1	1.6	1.6	0.2	–1.1
Tanzania	–9.9	–5.3	–5.0	–6.8	–4.7	–3.9	–4.5	–8.6	–10.6	–10.8
Togo	–3.4	–9.0	–9.3	–5.4	–4.2	–3.0	–5.3	–6.0	–6.4	–6.3
Tunisia	–2.2	–4.2	–5.1	–3.5	–2.9	–2.0	–1.1	–2.3	–2.6	–2.7
Uganda	–9.4	–7.1	–3.8	–4.9	–5.8	–1.2	–2.1	–4.1	–2.4	–6.3
Zambia	–13.7	–18.2	–19.9	–15.3	–14.8	–11.8	–10.0	0.5	–0.5	–2.0
Zimbabwe[1]	2.8	0.4	–0.3	–0.6	–2.9	–8.3	–11.2	–4.0	–0.9	. . .

Table A12 *(continued)*

	1999	2000	2001	2002	2003	2004	2005	2006	2007	2008
Central and eastern Europe	**–4.4**	**–5.3**	**–2.7**	**–3.5**	**–4.5**	**–5.9**	**–5.2**	**–6.6**	**–7.3**	**–7.5**
Albania	2.2	–3.6	–3.6	–7.1	–5.3	–3.9	–6.5	–5.9	–7.4	–6.5
Bosnia and Herzegovina	–8.3	–7.5	–13.3	–19.1	–20.9	–19.7	–21.7	–11.5	–15.3	–15.0
Bulgaria	–5.0	–5.6	–5.6	–2.4	–5.5	–6.6	–12.0	–15.8	–20.3	–19.0
Croatia	–7.1	–2.5	–3.6	–8.3	–6.1	–5.1	–6.4	–7.8	–8.4	–8.8
Czech Republic	–2.4	–4.7	–5.3	–5.7	–6.3	–5.2	–1.6	–3.1	–3.4	–3.5
Estonia	–4.4	–5.4	–5.2	–10.6	–11.3	–12.3	–10.0	–15.5	–16.9	–15.9
Hungary	–7.8	–8.4	–6.0	–7.0	–7.9	–8.4	–6.8	–6.5	–5.6	–5.1
Latvia	–8.9	–4.8	–7.6	–6.6	–8.2	–12.9	–12.6	–21.1	–25.3	–27.3
Lithuania	–11.0	–5.9	–4.7	–5.2	–6.9	–7.7	–7.1	–10.9	–14.0	–12.6
Macedonia, FYR	–2.7	–1.9	–7.2	–9.4	–3.3	–7.7	–1.3	–0.4	–2.8	–5.9
Malta	–3.7	–12.5	–3.8	2.7	–2.8	–6.3	–8.0	–6.1	–9.4	–8.2
Poland	–7.4	–5.8	–2.8	–2.5	–2.1	–4.2	–1.7	–2.3	–3.7	–5.1
Romania	–4.1	–3.7	–5.5	–3.3	–5.8	–8.4	–8.7	–10.3	–13.8	–13.2
Serbia	–4.1	–1.7	–2.4	–7.9	–7.0	–11.7	–8.5	–11.5	–14.7	–15.0
Slovak Republic	–4.8	–3.3	–8.3	–8.0	–6.0	–7.8	–8.6	–8.3	–5.3	–4.5
Turkey	–0.7	–5.0	2.4	–0.8	–3.3	–5.2	–6.2	–7.9	–7.5	–7.0
Commonwealth of Independent States[2]	**8.2**	**13.6**	**8.0**	**6.5**	**6.3**	**8.2**	**8.8**	**7.6**	**4.8**	**3.0**
Russia	12.6	18.0	11.1	8.4	8.2	10.1	11.1	9.7	5.9	3.3
Excluding Russia	–0.9	1.5	–0.8	0.9	0.4	2.2	1.6	1.0	1.2	1.9
Armenia	–16.6	–14.6	–9.5	–6.2	–6.8	–4.5	–3.9	–1.4	–4.0	–4.2
Azerbaijan	–13.1	–3.5	–0.9	–12.3	–27.8	–29.8	1.3	15.7	31.4	39.9
Belarus	–1.6	–2.7	–3.2	–2.1	–2.4	–5.2	1.6	–4.1	–7.9	–8.1
Georgia	–10.0	–7.9	–6.4	–8.4	–9.3	–12.2	–9.8	–13.8	–15.7	–15.2
Kazakhstan	–0.2	3.0	–5.4	–4.2	–0.9	0.8	–1.8	–2.2	–2.2	–1.1
Kyrgyz Republic	–14.5	–4.3	–1.5	–4.0	–2.2	4.9	3.2	–6.6	–17.9	–15.1
Moldova	–5.8	–7.6	–1.7	–4.0	–6.6	–2.3	–10.3	–12.0	–8.0	–7.3
Mongolia	–5.8	–5.0	–6.6	–8.5	–6.8	1.5	1.3	7.0	2.1	–18.0
Tajikistan	–0.9	–1.6	–4.9	–3.5	–1.3	–3.9	–2.5	–2.9	–11.6	–12.6
Turkmenistan	–14.8	8.2	1.7	6.7	2.7	0.6	5.1	15.3	13.0	12.5
Ukraine	5.3	4.7	3.7	7.5	5.8	10.6	2.9	–1.5	–3.5	–6.2
Uzbekistan	–1.0	1.8	–1.0	1.2	8.7	10.1	13.6	18.8	21.1	21.0

Table A12 *(continued)*

	1999	2000	2001	2002	2003	2004	2005	2006	2007	2008
Developing Asia	**1.8**	**1.7**	**1.5**	**2.4**	**2.8**	**2.6**	**4.1**	**5.9**	**6.9**	**7.0**
Afghanistan, Rep. of	. . .	. . .	. . .	–3.7	3.0	3.7	0.5	–1.4	–1.4	–2.4
Bangladesh	–0.9	–1.4	–0.9	0.3	0.3	–0.3	—	1.2	1.3	0.8
Bhutan	–4.2	–9.7	–11.2	–13.6	–12.5	–20.1	–14.9	4.4	10.3	6.6
Brunei Darussalam	33.7	48.6	51.5	42.5	49.6	47.9	56.0	55.2	55.2	55.9
Cambodia	–5.0	–2.8	–1.2	–2.4	–3.6	–2.2	–4.2	–2.0	–2.8	–4.4
China	1.4	1.7	1.3	2.4	2.8	3.6	7.2	9.4	11.7	12.2
Fiji	–3.8	–5.7	–3.3	–1.6	–3.6	–11.0	–10.8	–20.0	–22.8	–21.3
India	–0.7	–1.0	0.3	1.4	1.5	0.1	–1.0	–1.1	–2.1	–2.6
Indonesia	3.7	4.8	4.3	4.0	3.5	0.6	0.1	2.7	1.6	1.2
Kiribati	16.5	–1.2	22.0	10.7	12.5	–3.0	–39.9	–37.9	–50.7	–51.7
Lao PDR	–4.0	–10.6	–8.2	–7.2	–8.1	–14.3	–20.2	–13.3	–22.9	–21.1
Malaysia	15.9	9.4	8.3	8.4	12.7	12.6	15.3	17.2	14.4	13.3
Maldives	–13.4	–8.2	–9.4	–5.6	–4.6	–16.5	–35.8	–40.7	–40.5	–36.6
Myanmar	–5.9	–0.8	–2.4	0.2	–1.0	2.4	3.7	7.2	6.9	4.8
Nepal	4.3	3.2	4.5	4.2	2.4	2.7	2.0	2.2	2.5	2.4
Pakistan	–2.6	–0.3	0.4	3.9	4.9	1.8	–1.4	–3.9	–4.9	–4.9
Papua New Guinea	2.8	8.5	6.5	–1.0	4.5	2.2	3.9	5.3	7.8	4.0
Philippines	–3.8	–2.9	–2.5	–0.5	0.4	1.9	2.0	4.3	3.8	2.6
Samoa	2.0	1.0	0.1	–1.1	–1.0	0.5	2.4	–6.2	–6.2	–1.0
Solomon Islands	4.3	–10.6	–10.9	–10.2	–2.5	3.1	–24.2	–26.5	–40.0	–27.5
Sri Lanka	–3.6	–6.5	–1.1	–1.4	–0.4	–3.2	–2.8	–5.0	–5.1	–4.8
Thailand	10.2	7.6	4.4	3.7	3.4	1.7	–4.5	1.6	3.7	2.2
Timor-Leste, Dem. Rep. of	2.1	–60.2	–52.8	–37.2	–25.4	30.4	83.6	118.2	149.7	172.2
Tonga	–0.6	–6.2	–9.5	5.1	–3.1	4.2	–2.6	–8.2	–10.5	–19.0
Vanuatu	–4.9	2.0	2.0	–9.7	–10.7	–7.3	–10.0	–8.0	–13.2	–13.7
Vietnam	4.5	2.3	1.6	–1.9	–4.9	–3.4	–0.9	–0.3	–3.2	–3.2
Middle East	**2.7**	**11.4**	**6.3**	**4.8**	**8.3**	**11.7**	**19.4**	**19.7**	**16.7**	**16.0**
Bahrain	–0.3	10.6	3.0	–0.4	2.3	4.0	11.9	12.8	17.2	15.2
Egypt	–1.9	–1.2	—	0.7	2.4	4.3	3.2	0.8	1.4	0.8
Iran, I.R. of	6.3	13.0	5.2	3.1	0.6	0.9	8.8	8.7	7.6	6.6
Iraq	. . .	. . .	. . .	. . .	. . .	. . .	. . .	. . .	. . .	. . .
Jordan	5.0	0.7	–0.1	5.6	11.6	—	–17.9	–14.0	–12.6	–11.9
Kuwait	16.8	38.9	23.9	11.2	19.7	30.6	40.5	43.0	37.8	35.3
Lebanon	–19.0	–17.2	–19.3	–14.2	–13.2	–15.5	–13.6	–6.2	–10.6	–9.4
Libya	14.0	32.2	13.3	3.3	21.5	24.3	41.6	48.1	29.9	30.7
Oman	–2.9	15.5	9.8	6.9	3.9	1.2	8.7	8.4	4.1	7.1
Qatar	12.5	23.2	27.3	21.9	25.3	22.4	33.4	31.0	33.8	35.7
Saudi Arabia	0.3	7.6	5.1	6.3	13.1	20.7	28.5	27.4	22.2	20.1
Syrian Arab Republic	1.6	5.2	5.7	7.2	0.8	–3.2	–4.1	–6.1	–5.6	–6.6
United Arab Emirates	1.6	17.3	9.5	5.0	8.6	10.0	18.3	22.0	22.6	23.0
Yemen, Rep. of	7.2	13.8	6.8	4.1	1.5	1.6	3.8	3.2	–2.9	–0.6

Table A12 *(concluded)*

	1999	2000	2001	2002	2003	2004	2005	2006	2007	2008
Western Hemisphere	**–3.1**	**–2.4**	**–2.8**	**–0.9**	**0.4**	**1.0**	**1.4**	**1.5**	**0.6**	**—**
Antigua and Barbuda	–3.1	–3.2	–8.0	–11.5	–12.9	–8.3	–11.9	–16.5	–14.2	–10.7
Argentina	–4.2	–3.2	–1.4	8.9	6.3	2.1	1.9	2.5	0.9	0.4
Bahamas, The	–5.1	–10.4	–11.6	–7.8	–8.6	–5.4	–14.3	–25.4	–21.1	–16.5
Barbados	–5.9	–5.7	–4.4	–6.8	–6.3	–12.4	–12.5	–8.4	–8.6	–8.5
Belize	–10.1	–20.3	–21.9	–17.7	–18.2	–14.8	–14.4	–2.0	–3.0	–3.1
Bolivia	–5.9	–5.3	–3.4	–4.1	1.0	3.8	6.5	11.7	15.1	9.9
Brazil	–4.3	–3.8	–4.2	–1.5	0.8	1.8	1.6	1.2	0.8	0.3
Chile	0.1	–1.2	–1.6	–0.9	–1.1	2.2	1.1	3.6	3.7	2.3
Colombia	0.8	0.9	–1.3	–1.7	–1.2	–0.9	–1.5	–2.1	–3.9	–3.5
Costa Rica	–3.8	–4.3	–3.7	–5.1	–5.0	–4.3	–4.8	–4.9	–4.8	–5.0
Dominica	–20.3	–23.2	–22.0	–16.1	–15.3	–20.3	–34.7	–22.8	–20.0	–22.6
Dominican Republic	–2.4	–5.1	–3.4	–3.7	6.0	6.1	–1.4	–3.2	–3.4	–2.3
Ecuador	4.6	5.3	–3.2	–4.8	–1.5	–1.7	0.8	3.6	2.4	2.5
El Salvador	–1.9	–3.3	–1.1	–2.8	–4.7	–4.0	–4.6	–4.7	–4.9	–5.0
Grenada	–14.1	–21.5	–26.6	–32.0	–32.3	–12.4	–24.7	–23.9	–28.5	–25.1
Guatemala	–6.2	–6.1	–6.7	–5.9	–4.7	–5.1	–5.1	–5.2	–5.1	–4.7
Guyana	–8.1	–14.1	–15.7	–13.4	–8.8	–6.2	–15.5	–17.5	–19.7	–17.0
Haiti	–0.7	–1.2	–1.9	–1.3	–1.6	–1.5	1.8	0.6	2.1	1.5
Honduras	–4.4	–3.9	–4.1	–3.1	–4.0	–6.0	–0.9	–1.6	–5.5	–5.0
Jamaica	–3.9	–4.9	–10.7	–10.3	–9.4	–5.8	–11.2	–11.1	–10.9	–10.8
Mexico	–2.9	–3.2	–2.8	–2.2	–1.4	–1.0	–0.6	–0.3	–0.7	–1.1
Nicaragua	–24.9	–20.1	–19.4	–17.7	–15.7	–12.6	–14.9	–15.8	–15.8	–16.3
Panama	–10.1	–5.9	–1.5	–0.8	–4.5	–7.5	–5.0	–3.8	–5.4	–6.6
Paraguay	–2.3	–2.3	–4.1	1.8	2.3	2.0	0.1	–2.0	–0.2	–0.3
Peru	–3.4	–2.8	–2.1	–1.9	–1.5	—	1.4	2.8	1.3	1.1
St. Kitts and Nevis	–22.4	–21.0	–32.0	–39.1	–34.9	–20.2	–22.6	–28.8	–30.7	–29.7
St. Lucia	–16.6	–13.4	–15.7	–15.1	–19.7	–10.9	–17.1	–32.2	–20.1	–18.2
St. Vincent and the Grenadines	–20.6	–7.1	–10.4	–11.5	–20.8	–25.1	–24.0	–26.4	–26.7	–29.9
Suriname	–19.0	–3.8	–15.2	–5.6	–10.8	–4.1	–10.8	5.0	2.4	–1.7
Trinidad and Tobago	0.5	6.6	5.9	1.6	8.8	13.0	23.8	25.6	19.7	17.2
Uruguay	–2.4	–2.8	–2.9	3.2	–0.5	0.3	—	–2.4	–2.8	–2.8
Venezuela	2.2	10.1	1.6	8.2	14.1	13.8	17.8	15.0	7.8	4.1

[1]Given recent trends, it is not possible to forecast nominal GDP with any precision and consequently no projection for 2008 is shown.

[2]Mongolia, which is not a member of the Commonwealth of Independent States, is included in this group for reasons of geography and similarities in economic structure.

Table A13. Emerging Market and Developing Countries: Net Capital Flows[1]

(Billions of U.S. dollars)

	Average 1996–98	1999	2000	2001	2002	2003	2004	2005	2006	2007	2008
Emerging Market and Developing Countries											
Private capital flows, net[2]	167.0	74.4	72.1	80.6	90.1	168.3	239.4	271.1	220.9	495.4	291.3
Private direct investment, net	142.2	177.5	170.0	185.9	154.7	164.4	191.5	262.7	258.3	302.2	293.9
Private portfolio flows, net	61.7	64.0	12.5	–79.8	–91.3	–11.7	21.1	23.3	–111.9	20.6	–93.1
Other private capital flows, net	–36.7	–166.8	–110.6	–25.8	26.0	14.5	25.1	–17.0	73.6	171.0	88.8
Official flows, net[3]	10.8	18.2	–32.3	0.1	–2.7	–48.7	–67.2	–146.4	–165.8	–132.1	–141.2
Change in reserves[4]	–67.8	–98.1	–137.6	–122.6	–195.4	–359.7	–509.2	–595.3	–754.2	–1085.3	–887.1
Memorandum											
Current account[5]	–70.9	36.4	124.2	87.5	133.0	227.7	298.3	522.4	691.7	689.9	715.8
Africa											
Private capital flows, net[2]	6.5	8.9	1.6	7.1	5.4	7.0	17.2	26.5	17.3	42.1	45.9
Private direct investment, net	5.8	8.6	7.8	23.2	13.5	17.2	16.8	24.2	20.4	27.1	27.7
Private portfolio flows, net	5.0	9.1	–1.8	–7.9	–1.6	–0.5	5.3	3.7	17.9	11.7	14.9
Other private capital flows, net	–4.3	–8.8	–4.4	–8.1	–6.6	–9.7	–4.9	–1.4	–20.9	3.3	3.3
Official flows, net[3]	4.9	4.0	1.2	1.4	3.7	2.5	–0.1	–6.4	–11.7	5.5	5.5
Change in reserves[4]	–5.0	–0.6	–13.6	–10.3	–5.8	–11.6	–31.9	–43.4	–54.7	–52.1	–63.0
Central and eastern Europe											
Private capital flows, net[2]	27.1	35.7	38.5	10.9	53.8	53.7	75.3	116.1	122.4	140.5	145.5
Private direct investment, net	14.8	22.5	24.0	24.0	24.1	17.5	36.2	51.7	67.2	68.6	68.4
Private portfolio flows, net	1.7	5.3	3.0	0.4	1.7	6.4	26.3	18.9	7.7	5.8	17.0
Other private capital flows, net	10.7	8.2	11.3	–13.8	27.2	28.7	11.1	43.4	46.6	64.6	58.3
Official flows, net[3]	–0.5	–2.4	1.6	6.0	–7.5	–5.1	–6.6	–8.3	–4.9	–3.0	–3.1
Change in reserves[4]	–8.9	–12.1	–6.0	–3.0	–18.4	–12.9	–14.5	–47.0	–22.7	–27.1	–23.2
Commonwealth of Independent States											
Private capital flows, net[2]	–5.7	–13.3	–27.4	7.1	15.8	18.3	7.6	34.4	58.8	82.4	42.8
Private direct investment, net	5.5	4.7	2.3	4.9	5.2	5.4	13.0	11.4	22.7	12.8	24.5
Private portfolio flows, net	2.2	–0.9	–10.0	–1.2	0.4	–0.5	8.1	–3.1	12.7	13.8	6.1
Other private capital flows, net	–13.3	–17.1	–19.7	3.3	10.3	13.4	–13.6	26.2	23.4	55.8	12.3
Official flows, net[3]	–1.0	–1.8	–5.8	–4.9	–10.4	–8.9	–7.3	–22.2	–29.6	–5.3	–5.5
Change in reserves[4]	5.4	–6.5	–20.4	–14.4	–15.1	–32.7	–54.8	–77.2	–129.1	–153.3	–94.0
Emerging Asia[6]											
Private capital flows, net[2]	41.0	–2.9	5.9	23.3	24.4	65.3	146.8	83.3	40.5	157.2	5.1
Private direct investment, net	56.0	71.4	60.8	53.1	53.4	70.2	66.9	107.0	102.0	97.7	94.1
Private portfolio flows, net	16.0	54.1	19.7	–50.1	–60.0	7.9	11.8	–13.5	–120.8	–26.7	–146.1
Other private capital flows, net	–31.0	–128.3	–74.6	20.3	31.1	–12.9	68.1	–10.2	59.3	86.2	57.1
Official flows, net[3]	4.2	6.5	–1.7	–13.0	3.0	–17.8	–13.2	–21.0	–22.5	–17.0	–17.6
Change in reserves[4]	–45.3	–84.8	–59.4	–85.8	–154.7	–236.0	–340.1	–288.9	–373.9	–624.0	–519.7
Middle East[7]											
Private capital flows, net[2]	13.3	–4.7	–8.9	–6.9	–20.7	1.7	–22.1	–24.5	–28.1	–10.6	4.5
Private direct investment, net	6.9	4.2	4.9	12.3	9.6	17.7	10.1	18.1	17.9	24.1	23.4
Private portfolio flows, net	2.0	–8.5	0.1	–13.3	–16.8	–14.9	–14.7	–10.7	–15.7	–3.6	10.5
Other private capital flows, net	4.4	–0.5	–13.9	–5.9	–13.4	–1.1	–17.5	–31.9	–30.3	–31.1	–29.4
Official flows, net[3]	–0.2	7.5	–20.9	–14.3	–9.5	–23.7	–31.3	–58.1	–78.7	–111.9	–121.0
Change in reserves[4]	–8.2	–0.8	–31.2	–11.0	–3.1	–33.4	–45.7	–106.5	–125.3	–115.9	–136.1
Western Hemisphere											
Private capital flows, net[2]	84.7	50.7	62.4	39.1	11.5	22.2	14.5	35.3	9.9	83.7	47.5
Private direct investment, net	53.1	66.1	70.2	68.4	49.0	36.3	48.6	50.4	28.0	71.9	55.8
Private portfolio flows, net	34.9	4.9	1.5	–7.6	–14.9	–10.2	–15.8	28.1	–13.7	19.4	4.5
Other private capital flows, net	–3.3	–20.2	–9.3	–21.6	–22.6	–3.9	–18.2	–43.1	–4.4	–7.6	–12.7
Official flows, net[3]	3.4	4.4	–6.7	24.9	18.1	4.4	–8.6	–30.5	–18.4	–0.4	0.6
Change in reserves[4]	–5.8	6.6	–7.0	1.9	1.6	–33.0	–22.3	–32.4	–48.6	–113.0	–51.1
Memorandum											
Fuel exporting countries											
Private capital flows, net[2]	–4.1	–25.6	–47.3	–9.1	–15.2	5.7	–24.8	–14.0	–18.0	34.6	15.4
Other countries											
Private capital flows, net[2]	171.1	100.0	119.4	89.6	105.3	162.5	264.1	285.1	238.9	460.7	275.9

[1]Net capital flows comprise net direct investment, net portfolio investment, and other long- and short-term net investment flows, including official and private borrowing. In this table, Hong Kong SAR, Israel, Korea, Singapore, and Taiwan Province of China are included.
[2]Because of data limitations, flows listed under "private capital flows, net" may include some official flows.
[3]Excludes grants and includes overseas investments of official investment agencies.
[4]A minus sign indicates an increase.
[5]The sum of the current account balance, net private capital flows, net official flows, and the change in reserves equals, with the opposite sign, the sum of the capital account and errors and omissions. For regional current account balances, see Table A10 of the Statistical Appendix.
[6]Consists of developing Asia and the newly industrialized Asian economies.
[7]Includes Israel.

Table A14. Emerging Market and Developing Countries: Private Capital Flows[1]

(Billions of U.S. dollars)

	Average 1996–98	1999	2000	2001	2002	2003	2004	2005	2006	2007	2008
Emerging Market and Developing Countries											
Private capital flows, net	167.0	74.4	72.1	80.6	90.1	168.3	239.4	271.1	220.9	495.4	291.3
Inflow	324.0	202.9	315.7	163.8	174.1	418.4	632.0	809.3	1,111.2	1,336.8	1,259.1
Outflow	–148.3	–137.8	–243.3	–89.4	–83.6	–254.1	–394.4	–538.6	–890.1	–841.5	–967.8
Africa											
Private capital flows, net	6.5	8.9	1.6	7.1	5.4	7.0	17.2	26.5	17.3	42.1	45.9
Inflow	16.2	21.8	10.3	19.4	16.3	21.4	29.7	40.8	56.0	65.8	75.1
Outflow	–5.9	–12.9	–8.7	–12.3	–11.0	–14.4	–12.5	–14.3	–38.6	–23.7	–29.2
Central and eastern Europe											
Private capital flows, net	27.1	35.7	38.5	10.9	53.8	53.7	75.3	116.1	122.4	140.5	145.5
Inflow	29.3	44.1	48.5	19.9	55.0	64.2	104.6	136.2	169.6	171.3	166.1
Outflow	–1.2	–8.0	–9.8	–8.9	–1.0	–10.2	–29.3	–19.6	–46.7	–30.5	–20.4
Commonwealth of Independent States[2]											
Private capital flows, net	–5.7	–13.3	–27.4	7.1	15.8	18.3	7.6	34.4	58.8	82.4	42.8
Inflow	16.7	2.8	–2.7	10.9	22.5	46.1	67.1	114.5	163.3	180.2	152.8
Outflow	–1.1	–16.1	–24.7	–3.8	–6.7	–27.8	–59.5	–80.0	–104.4	–97.8	–110.0
Emerging Asia[3]											
Private capital flows, net	41.0	–2.9	5.9	23.3	24.4	65.3	146.8	83.3	40.5	157.2	5.1
Inflow	124.3	51.0	136.2	47.5	66.1	209.9	309.1	366.6	508.0	641.0	641.5
Outflow	–74.8	–63.2	–130.3	–29.8	–41.7	–149.1	–164.1	–285.5	–468.0	–484.3	–636.9
Middle East[4]											
Private capital flows, net	13.3	–4.7	–8.9	–6.9	–20.7	1.7	–22.1	–24.5	–28.1	–10.6	4.5
Inflow	23.9	–5.8	38.2	–3.5	–10.6	31.1	57.3	64.3	111.4	105.5	115.3
Outflow	–10.6	1.1	–47.1	–3.5	–10.1	–29.3	–79.3	–88.8	–139.5	–116.1	–110.8
Western Hemisphere											
Private capital flows, net	84.7	50.7	62.4	39.1	11.5	22.2	14.5	35.3	9.9	83.7	47.5
Inflow	113.5	89.0	85.2	69.6	24.7	45.6	64.3	86.9	103.0	173.0	108.3
Outflow	–10.4	–38.3	–22.8	–30.5	–13.3	–23.4	–49.7	–51.6	–93.1	–89.2	–60.8

[1]Private capital flows comprise direct investment, portfolio investment, and other long- and short-term investment flows. In this table, Hong Kong SAR, Israel, Korea, Singapore, and Taiwan Province of China are included.

[2]Mongolia, which is not a member of the Commonwealth of Independent States, is included in this group for reasons of geography and similarities in economic structure.

[3]Consists of developing Asia and the newly industrialized Asian economies.

[4]Includes Israel.

Table A15. Other Emerging Market and Developing Countries: Reserves[1]

	1999	2000	2001	2002	2003	2004	2005	2006	2007	2008
					Billions of U.S. dollars					
Other emerging market and developing countries	**713.3**	**802.5**	**897.5**	**1,075.0**	**1,398.2**	**1,850.9**	**2,341.4**	**3,044.0**	**4,094.6**	**4,942.5**
Regional groups										
Africa	42.1	54.2	64.4	72.0	90.3	126.3	160.3	215.0	267.2	330.1
Sub-Sahara	29.3	35.2	35.6	36.1	40.0	62.4	83.1	114.7	138.5	173.2
Excluding Nigeria and South Africa	17.3	19.0	18.8	22.5	26.1	32.1	36.1	49.3	59.3	73.8
Central and eastern Europe	90.6	92.7	93.0	123.9	151.8	174.7	204.7	227.4	254.5	277.7
Commonwealth of Independent States[2]	16.5	33.2	43.9	58.1	92.4	148.5	214.5	343.5	496.8	590.8
Russia	9.1	24.8	33.1	44.6	73.8	121.5	176.5	284.0	419.5	500.8
Excluding Russia	7.4	8.4	10.8	13.5	18.6	27.0	38.0	59.6	77.3	90.0
Developing Asia	307.7	320.7	379.5	496.2	669.7	933.9	1,155.3	1,478.0	2,068.0	2,548.8
China	158.3	168.9	216.3	292.0	409.2	615.5	822.5	1,069.5	1,559.5	1,969.5
India	33.2	38.4	46.4	68.2	99.5	127.2	132.5	163.7	201.7	231.4
Excluding China and India	116.2	113.4	116.9	136.0	161.1	191.2	200.3	244.8	306.8	347.9
Middle East	113.5	146.1	157.9	163.9	198.3	246.7	351.1	476.0	591.1	726.9
Western Hemisphere	143.0	155.7	158.8	160.7	195.6	220.8	255.5	304.1	417.1	468.2
Brazil	23.9	31.5	35.8	37.7	49.1	52.8	53.6	85.6	175.1	206.9
Mexico	31.8	35.5	44.8	50.6	59.0	64.1	74.1	73.1	80.3	86.2
Analytical groups										
By source of export earnings										
Fuel	125.7	190.3	214.5	230.2	305.8	428.1	619.4	894.8	1,178.1	1,450.8
Nonfuel	587.6	612.2	683.1	844.8	1,092.4	1,422.8	1,722.0	2,149.2	2,916.6	3,491.7
of which, primary products	24.7	25.5	24.3	25.7	26.8	28.3	31.0	38.7	43.0	47.5
By external financing source										
Net debtor countries	404.6	423.1	446.3	529.9	648.5	750.5	832.6	1,002.6	1,257.1	1,408.6
of which, official financing	28.8	28.4	32.2	36.9	47.9	54.1	60.4	74.1	92.1	103.2
Net debtor countries by debt-servicing experience										
Countries with arrears and/or rescheduling during 2001–05	72.8	76.0	68.0	75.7	89.9	101.8	115.7	143.9	186.7	216.2
Other groups										
Heavily indebted poor countries	9.6	10.2	10.9	13.3	16.0	19.2	20.3	26.0	30.4	34.8
Middle East and north Africa	126.7	165.5	187.1	200.6	249.7	312.5	430.7	578.3	721.8	886.4

Table A15 *(concluded)*

	1999	2000	2001	2002	2003	2004	2005	2006	2007	2008
	Ratio of reserves to imports of goods and services[3]									
Other emerging market and developing countries	**46.3**	**44.7**	**49.5**	**55.3**	**60.5**	**62.8**	**66.4**	**72.5**	**81.5**	**86.7**
Regional groups										
Africa	31.2	39.2	45.5	47.0	48.4	53.6	57.2	66.5	68.2	75.6
Sub-Sahara	28.7	33.6	33.3	31.3	28.1	34.7	38.1	44.9	45.7	51.6
Excluding Nigeria and South Africa	30.2	33.2	31.1	35.4	34.6	34.0	31.2	37.8	38.6	42.1
Central and eastern Europe	38.8	34.6	34.9	41.2	39.4	34.8	35.2	32.3	29.1	27.8
Commonwealth of Independent States[2]	17.6	30.5	34.3	40.9	52.6	65.2	76.9	97.7	110.7	111.9
Russia	17.2	40.6	44.6	52.9	71.5	93.0	107.4	135.6	150.6	149.5
Excluding Russia	18.1	17.5	20.0	23.4	25.6	27.8	33.2	41.9	45.4	46.6
Developing Asia	58.6	49.1	58.3	68.1	74.5	79.5	81.8	89.0	105.8	114.8
China	83.3	67.4	79.7	89.0	91.1	101.5	115.5	125.4	153.5	170.1
India	52.9	52.6	65.0	90.0	107.1	97.0	72.5	71.5	69.6	67.5
Excluding China and India	42.6	34.5	37.9	41.8	45.1	43.8	38.7	42.3	47.3	48.4
Middle East	64.1	75.6	78.7	74.2	78.0	77.7	90.7	101.4	108.2	117.1
Western Hemisphere	38.0	35.9	37.3	40.5	47.6	44.8	43.8	44.2	51.5	52.1
Brazil	37.6	43.5	49.2	61.1	77.2	65.9	54.8	71.1	117.1	121.5
Mexico	20.4	18.6	24.2	27.3	31.4	29.8	30.5	26.3	25.4	24.8
Analytical groups										
By source of export earnings										
Fuel	48.2	66.1	67.9	65.7	74.4	82.5	96.4	113.9	121.2	128.7
Nonfuel	45.9	40.6	45.6	53.1	57.5	58.5	59.8	63.0	71.9	76.3
of which, primary products	62.2	60.1	57.7	59.2	54.9	45.7	41.3	46.3	45.2	45.4
By external financing source										
Net debtor countries	39.9	36.4	39.1	45.0	47.7	43.9	40.7	41.4	43.5	43.3
of which, official financing	30.4	27.1	31.1	34.7	39.8	37.2	34.3	34.9	37.8	37.7
Net debtor countries by debt-servicing experience										
Countries with arrears and/or rescheduling during 2001–05	43.0	40.5	37.1	43.0	45.0	40.5	36.5	39.8	44.3	45.9
Other groups										
Heavily indebted poor countries	27.1	28.5	29.1	32.8	35.3	34.3	30.3	33.6	34.9	36.0
Middle East and north Africa	59.7	72.0	78.4	76.4	82.5	82.4	93.8	105.4	111.3	120.3

[1]In this table, official holdings of gold are valued at SDR 35 an ounce. This convention results in a marked underestimate of reserves for countries that have substantial gold holdings.

[2]Mongolia, which is not a member of the Commonwealth of Independent States, is included in this group for reasons of geography and similarities in economic structure.

[3]Reserves at year-end in percent of imports of goods and services for the year indicated.

Table A16. Summary of Sources and Uses of World Saving

(Percent of GDP)

	Averages										Average
	1985–92	1993–2000	2001	2002	2003	2004	2005	2006	2007	2008	2009–12
World[1]											
Saving	22.8	22.2	21.3	20.5	20.9	21.9	22.5	23.3	23.6	23.8	24.3
Investment	22.5	22.5	21.5	20.9	21.1	22.0	22.4	23.0	23.3	23.6	24.5
Advanced economies											
Saving	22.3	21.7	20.4	19.2	19.1	19.8	19.7	20.0	19.9	19.7	19.8
Investment	22.8	21.9	20.8	19.9	19.9	20.5	20.9	21.4	21.1	21.1	21.4
Net lending	–0.5	–0.2	–0.4	–0.7	–0.8	–0.7	–1.2	–1.3	–1.2	–1.4	–1.6
Current transfers	–0.4	–0.5	–0.5	–0.6	–0.6	–0.6	–0.7	–0.7	–0.7	–0.7	–0.6
Factor income	–0.2	—	0.7	0.2	0.2	0.5	0.5	0.5	0.4	0.2	—
Resource balance	—	0.4	–0.5	–0.4	–0.4	–0.5	–1.0	–1.2	–0.9	–0.9	–1.0
United States											
Saving	16.7	16.8	16.4	14.2	13.3	13.8	14.0	14.1	13.3	12.8	13.0
Investment	19.3	19.4	19.1	18.4	18.4	19.4	19.9	20.0	18.8	18.3	18.6
Net lending	–2.6	–2.7	–2.8	–4.2	–5.1	–5.5	–6.0	–5.9	–5.5	–5.5	–5.6
Current transfers	–0.4	–0.6	–0.5	–0.6	–0.6	–0.7	–0.7	–0.7	–0.7	–0.5	–0.5
Factor income	–0.2	–0.2	1.3	0.5	0.1	0.5	0.5	0.5	0.4	—	–0.5
Resource balance	–2.0	–1.9	–3.6	–4.0	–4.5	–5.2	–5.7	–5.7	–5.2	–5.0	–4.6
Euro area											
Saving	. . .	21.4	21.3	20.8	20.8	21.6	21.1	21.6	21.9	21.9	22.1
Investment	. . .	21.1	21.0	20.0	20.1	20.4	20.8	21.6	22.0	22.2	22.6
Net lending	. . .	0.4	0.2	0.8	0.7	1.2	0.4	0.1	–0.2	–0.4	–0.5
Current transfers[2]	–0.5	–0.7	–0.8	–0.7	–0.8	–0.8	–0.9	–0.9	–1.0	–1.0	–1.0
Factor income[2]	–0.3	–0.4	–0.6	–0.9	–0.8	–0.2	–0.3	–0.2	–0.5	–0.6	–0.7
Resource balance[2]	1.0	1.6	1.5	2.3	2.1	2.1	1.5	1.2	1.3	1.2	1.0
Germany											
Saving	24.0	20.7	19.5	19.3	19.3	21.3	21.7	22.8	23.7	23.7	23.1
Investment	21.5	21.7	19.5	17.3	17.4	17.1	17.1	17.8	18.3	18.6	18.9
Net lending	2.5	–1.0	—	2.0	1.9	4.3	4.6	5.0	5.4	5.1	4.2
Current transfers	–1.6	–1.5	–1.3	–1.3	–1.3	–1.3	–1.3	–1.2	–1.4	–1.3	–1.3
Factor income	0.9	–0.1	–0.5	–0.8	–0.7	0.6	0.9	1.0	1.0	1.0	1.0
Resource balance	3.2	0.5	1.8	4.1	3.9	5.0	4.9	5.2	5.9	5.4	4.5
France											
Saving	20.7	20.1	22.0	20.3	19.7	19.7	19.1	19.8	19.6	19.1	19.7
Investment	21.0	18.5	20.0	19.0	18.9	19.5	20.2	21.0	21.1	20.9	21.2
Net lending	–0.3	1.6	1.9	1.4	0.8	0.1	–1.1	–1.2	–1.6	–1.8	–1.5
Current transfers	–0.6	–0.8	–1.1	–1.0	–1.1	–1.1	–1.3	–1.2	–1.0	–1.0	–1.0
Factor income	–0.3	0.3	1.5	0.6	0.8	1.1	1.2	1.1	0.6	0.6	0.6
Resource balance	0.6	2.1	1.6	1.7	1.1	0.1	–1.0	–1.1	–1.2	–1.5	–1.1
Italy											
Saving	20.3	21.1	20.5	20.4	19.4	19.9	19.1	18.8	19.3	19.7	20.4
Investment	22.2	19.5	20.6	21.1	20.7	20.8	20.6	21.2	21.6	22.0	22.5
Net lending	–1.9	1.5	–0.1	–0.8	–1.3	–0.9	–1.5	–2.4	–2.3	–2.2	–2.1
Current transfers	–0.3	–0.5	–0.5	–0.4	–0.5	–0.6	–0.6	–0.8	–0.6	–0.6	–0.6
Factor income	–1.7	–1.2	–0.9	–1.2	–1.3	–1.1	–1.0	–0.9	–0.9	–0.9	–0.9
Resource balance	0.1	3.2	1.4	0.8	0.6	0.7	—	–0.7	–0.8	–0.7	–0.6
Japan											
Saving	33.6	30.0	26.9	25.9	26.1	26.8	27.0	28.0	28.6	28.4	28.0
Investment	30.8	27.5	24.8	23.1	22.8	23.0	23.4	24.1	24.1	24.1	24.2
Net lending	2.8	2.5	2.1	2.9	3.2	3.7	3.6	3.9	4.6	4.3	3.8
Current transfers	–0.1	–0.2	–0.2	–0.1	–0.2	–0.2	–0.2	–0.2	–0.3	–0.2	–0.2
Factor income	0.7	1.1	1.7	1.7	1.7	1.9	2.3	2.7	3.1	2.9	3.2
Resource balance	2.3	1.5	0.6	1.3	1.7	2.0	1.5	1.4	1.7	1.6	0.8
United Kingdom											
Saving	16.9	16.2	15.6	15.8	15.7	15.9	15.0	14.8	15.0	15.0	15.2
Investment	19.4	17.5	17.7	17.4	17.1	17.5	17.5	18.0	18.5	18.5	19.0
Net lending	–2.5	–1.3	–2.2	–1.6	–1.3	–1.6	–2.5	–3.2	–3.5	–3.6	–3.8
Current transfers	–0.7	–0.9	–0.7	–0.9	–0.9	–0.9	–1.0	–0.9	–0.9	–0.9	–1.0
Factor income	–0.1	0.4	1.2	2.2	2.2	2.2	2.1	1.4	0.8	0.7	0.6
Resource balance	–1.7	–0.8	–2.7	–2.9	–2.6	–3.0	–3.6	–3.7	–3.4	–3.3	–3.4
Canada											
Saving	18.0	18.7	22.2	21.0	21.2	22.9	23.8	24.2	24.2	24.1	24.7
Investment	21.0	19.4	19.2	19.3	20.0	20.7	21.7	22.5	22.4	23.0	23.7
Net lending	–3.0	–0.7	3.0	1.7	1.2	2.3	2.0	1.6	1.8	1.2	1.0
Current transfers	–0.2	—	0.1	—	—	—	–0.1	—	—	—	—
Factor income	–3.3	–3.4	–2.8	–2.6	–2.5	–1.9	–1.6	–0.8	–0.9	–0.7	–0.7
Resource balance	0.5	2.7	5.7	4.3	3.7	4.2	3.7	2.5	2.8	1.9	1.6

Table A16 *(continued)*

	Averages										Average
	1985–92	1993–2000	2001	2002	2003	2004	2005	2006	2007	2008	2009–12
Newly industrialized Asian economies											
Saving	35.4	33.5	30.0	29.8	31.6	32.9	31.6	31.6	31.5	31.1	30.7
Investment	29.1	30.7	25.3	24.7	24.7	26.4	25.8	25.9	26.1	26.2	26.8
Net lending	6.3	2.9	4.6	5.1	6.9	6.5	5.8	5.7	5.4	4.9	3.9
Current transfers	0.1	–0.3	–0.6	–0.7	–0.7	–0.7	–0.7	–0.7	–0.8	–0.8	–0.8
Factor income	1.2	0.6	0.8	0.6	1.0	0.7	0.4	0.5	0.7	0.5	0.6
Resource balance	5.0	2.5	4.5	5.1	6.7	6.6	6.0	5.9	5.4	5.1	4.1
Other emerging market and developing countries[1]											
Saving	24.5	24.1	24.7	26.0	27.9	29.7	31.4	32.6	33.2	33.8	34.3
Investment	25.0	25.2	24.1	24.8	25.9	27.3	27.2	27.8	29.1	30.0	31.2
Net lending	–2.5	–1.2	0.6	1.2	2.0	2.4	4.2	4.8	4.1	3.8	3.0
Current transfers	0.4	0.9	1.2	1.4	1.6	1.6	1.6	1.6	1.4	1.3	1.2
Factor income	–2.0	–1.5	–2.0	–2.0	–2.0	–2.1	–1.9	–1.9	–1.5	–1.2	–0.7
Resource balance	–0.5	–0.5	1.4	1.8	2.4	2.9	4.5	5.1	4.2	3.7	2.5
Memorandum											
Acquisition of foreign assets	0.8	3.6	3.3	3.6	5.9	7.1	9.1	10.3	11.4	9.8	8.0
Change in reserves	0.2	1.0	1.5	2.3	3.8	4.8	5.1	5.7	7.2	5.1	4.6
Regional groups											
Africa[1]											
Saving	18.4	18.0	21.2	20.2	21.7	22.7	24.2	26.0	24.5	25.3	24.3
Investment	20.4	20.0	20.8	21.5	21.6	22.6	22.2	22.8	24.5	24.6	25.2
Net lending	–2.0	–2.0	0.4	–1.2	—	0.1	2.0	3.1	—	0.7	–0.9
Current transfers	2.3	2.5	3.0	3.1	3.1	3.2	3.1	2.9	3.0	2.8	2.6
Factor income	–4.3	–3.9	–4.4	–4.8	–4.6	–5.1	–5.7	–5.3	–5.4	–5.4	–4.0
Resource balance	0.1	–0.6	1.8	0.4	1.5	2.0	4.7	5.5	2.5	3.4	0.4
Memorandum											
Acquisition of foreign assets	0.2	1.9	6.1	2.9	3.8	4.5	5.8	7.8	6.5	7.0	5.6
Change in reserves	0.3	1.0	2.4	1.3	2.0	4.6	5.3	6.0	5.1	5.4	3.9
Central and eastern Europe											
Saving	27.0	20.8	19.2	19.0	18.4	18.7	18.7	18.2	18.7	19.5	21.2
Investment	27.6	23.9	22.0	22.5	22.9	24.5	23.9	24.6	25.5	26.3	27.1
Net lending	–0.6	–3.0	–2.7	–3.5	–4.5	–5.8	–5.1	–6.4	–6.8	–6.8	–5.9
Current transfers	1.5	1.9	1.9	1.8	1.7	1.6	1.7	1.7	1.5	1.5	1.6
Factor income	–1.5	–1.0	–1.3	–1.6	–2.0	–2.9	–2.6	–2.7	–2.4	–2.1	–2.3
Resource balance	–0.6	–3.9	–3.3	–3.8	–4.1	–4.5	–4.2	–5.3	–5.9	–6.3	–5.3
Memorandum											
Acquisition of foreign assets	1.0	2.4	1.7	3.4	2.3	3.5	5.1	5.3	3.1	2.2	2.2
Change in reserves	–0.6	2.1	0.5	2.7	1.6	1.4	4.0	1.7	1.7	1.3	1.3
Commonwealth of Independent States[3]											
Saving	. . .	24.1	29.8	26.6	27.5	29.6	29.6	28.6	27.0	25.5	22.5
Investment	. . .	21.6	21.9	20.2	21.2	21.4	21.0	21.2	22.2	22.6	23.5
Net lending	. . .	2.5	7.9	6.4	6.3	8.3	8.6	7.4	4.8	3.0	–1.0
Current transfers	. . .	0.5	0.5	0.6	0.6	0.5	0.6	0.6	0.6	0.4	0.4
Factor income	. . .	–2.1	–1.7	–2.0	–2.8	–2.1	–2.9	–3.6	–2.6	–2.1	–1.7
Resource balance	. . .	4.0	9.1	7.9	8.4	9.9	11.0	10.5	6.8	4.6	0.3
Memorandum											
Acquisition of foreign assets	. . .	4.1	6.9	5.5	11.6	14.4	15.4	16.5	14.5	9.6	5.9
Change in reserves	. . .	0.8	3.5	3.3	5.7	7.1	7.7	10.0	9.6	4.9	2.6

Table A16 *(continued)*

	Averages 1985–92	Averages 1993–2000	2001	2002	2003	2004	2005	2006	2007	2008	Average 2009–12
Developing Asia											
Saving	27.8	33.1	31.6	33.6	36.5	38.4	41.1	43.5	45.3	46.7	48.5
Investment	30.7	33.2	30.1	31.2	33.8	35.8	36.9	37.6	38.4	39.8	41.2
Net lending	–2.9	–0.1	1.5	2.4	2.8	2.6	4.1	5.9	6.9	7.0	7.3
Current transfers	0.8	1.2	1.7	1.9	2.1	2.0	2.1	2.1	1.9	1.7	1.4
Factor income	–2.0	–1.3	–1.8	–1.6	–1.1	–1.0	–0.7	–0.6	–0.3	–0.2	0.2
Resource balance	–1.7	–0.1	1.6	2.1	1.8	1.6	2.7	4.4	5.4	5.5	5.7
Memorandum											
Acquisition of foreign assets	1.5	6.2	3.2	5.2	6.2	7.3	9.8	11.7	15.2	14.2	12.3
Change in reserves	0.6	1.6	2.4	4.2	5.5	7.5	5.9	6.9	10.5	7.5	7.7
Middle East											
Saving	16.8	24.2	27.6	27.6	31.3	34.8	41.5	42.1	43.0	43.5	40.4
Investment	23.2	22.6	21.4	23.0	23.0	23.0	22.2	22.4	26.4	27.6	29.0
Net lending	–6.4	1.6	6.2	4.6	8.3	11.7	19.3	19.6	16.6	15.9	11.4
Current transfers	–3.3	–3.0	–2.5	–2.5	–2.2	–1.9	–1.7	–1.8	–1.8	–1.6	–1.5
Factor income	2.0	2.9	1.4	0.4	0.1	0.3	1.0	1.9	2.1	2.5	3.7
Resource balance	–5.1	1.7	7.4	6.8	10.4	13.4	20.0	19.5	16.3	15.0	9.2
Memorandum											
Acquisition of foreign assets	—	3.4	5.2	2.7	12.8	16.9	22.7	24.1	21.1	20.5	15.4
Change in reserves	–0.4	0.8	1.8	0.6	4.6	5.5	10.3	10.5	8.5	8.8	6.5
Western Hemisphere											
Saving	19.0	17.1	16.5	17.8	18.7	20.8	21.0	21.7	21.5	21.4	20.6
Investment	19.1	20.0	19.5	18.7	18.2	19.8	19.6	20.2	20.9	21.5	21.5
Net lending	–0.1	–3.0	–3.0	–0.9	0.5	1.0	1.4	1.6	0.6	—	–0.9
Current transfers	0.8	0.9	1.4	1.7	2.0	2.1	2.0	2.0	1.9	1.8	1.8
Factor income	–2.5	–2.5	–3.2	–3.1	–3.3	–3.3	–3.1	–3.1	–2.6	–2.3	–2.0
Resource balance	1.7	–1.3	–1.2	0.5	1.7	2.2	2.5	2.6	1.3	0.5	–0.7
Memorandum											
Acquisition of foreign assets	0.5	1.8	1.9	1.2	2.9	2.8	2.9	3.1	5.3	2.3	1.4
Change in reserves	0.4	0.4	–0.1	–0.1	1.8	1.1	1.3	1.7	3.3	1.4	0.8
Analytical groups											
By source of export earnings											
Fuel											
Saving	27.4	24.9	30.3	28.4	30.6	33.6	37.9	37.8	36.0	35.1	31.3
Investment	29.1	22.6	22.8	22.8	22.5	22.8	21.9	22.0	24.5	25.0	26.1
Net lending	–1.7	2.3	7.5	5.6	8.1	10.8	16.0	15.8	11.5	10.1	5.2
Current transfers	–1.4	–2.0	–1.9	–1.8	–1.4	–1.1	–0.9	–0.9	–0.9	–0.9	–0.8
Factor income	—	–0.7	–1.1	–2.0	–2.5	–2.3	–2.2	–2.0	–1.5	–1.2	–0.2
Resource balance	–0.2	5.0	10.5	9.4	12.0	14.3	19.1	18.7	13.9	12.1	6.2
Memorandum											
Acquisition of foreign assets	0.6	3.7	6.6	3.3	11.8	14.4	18.6	18.8	16.8	14.2	9.9
Change in reserves	–0.2	0.4	2.7	1.1	5.0	6.9	9.6	10.4	9.0	7.3	4.8
Nonfuel[1]											
Saving	23.2	23.9	23.5	25.5	27.3	28.7	29.7	31.2	32.4	33.4	35.2
Investment	24.4	25.7	24.4	25.2	26.7	28.3	28.6	29.4	30.3	31.4	32.8
Net lending	–1.7	–1.9	–0.9	0.3	0.7	0.4	1.1	1.8	2.1	2.0	2.4
Current transfers	1.1	1.4	1.9	2.1	2.3	2.2	2.2	2.2	2.1	2.0	1.8
Factor income	–1.9	–1.7	–2.2	–2.0	–1.9	–2.0	–1.8	–1.8	–1.5	–1.2	–0.9
Resource balance	–0.7	–1.6	–0.5	0.2	0.3	0.2	0.7	1.4	1.5	1.3	1.5
Memorandum											
Acquisition of foreign assets	0.8	3.6	2.6	3.7	4.6	5.4	6.6	8.0	10.0	8.5	7.5
Change in reserves	0.3	1.2	1.2	2.6	3.6	4.3	4.0	4.4	6.7	4.5	4.6

Table A16 *(concluded)*

	Averages										Average
	1985–92	1993–2000	2001	2002	2003	2004	2005	2006	2007	2008	2009–12
By external financing source											
Net debtor countries[1]											
Saving	21.0	19.6	18.4	19.7	20.7	21.5	21.6	22.3	22.7	23.2	23.8
Investment	23.1	22.4	20.4	20.5	21.4	22.8	23.1	23.6	24.6	25.4	26.2
Net lending	–2.1	–2.7	–2.0	–0.9	–0.6	–1.3	–1.5	–1.3	–1.9	–2.2	–2.4
Current transfers	1.4	1.8	2.4	2.6	2.8	2.7	2.8	2.8	2.6	2.5	2.4
Factor income	–2.7	–2.7	–2.5	–2.5	–2.5	–2.8	–2.9	–2.9	–2.6	–2.4	–2.2
Resource balance	–0.9	–2.6	–1.8	–1.0	–0.9	–1.2	–1.4	–1.2	–1.9	–2.2	–2.7
Memorandum											
Acquisition of foreign assets	0.6	1.7	1.9	2.4	3.1	3.0	3.2	4.4	4.5	2.8	2.1
Change in reserves	0.3	0.9	0.4	1.6	2.1	1.6	1.9	2.4	3.1	1.7	1.2
Official financing											
Saving	15.0	16.8	18.9	19.8	21.2	21.0	21.5	21.7	21.3	21.8	22.0
Investment	18.2	20.4	20.0	20.5	21.2	21.2	21.9	22.7	23.8	24.5	24.7
Net lending	–3.2	–3.6	–1.1	–0.7	—	–0.2	–0.4	–1.0	–2.5	–2.7	–2.7
Current transfers	3.1	4.5	5.7	6.3	6.8	6.8	7.3	7.5	7.5	7.3	7.1
Factor income	–0.3	–2.1	–2.2	–2.6	–2.8	–3.0	–2.9	–3.3	–3.5	–2.9	–2.4
Resource balance	–6.0	–6.0	–4.7	–4.5	–3.9	–3.9	–4.7	–5.2	–6.5	–7.1	–7.4
Memorandum											
Acquisition of foreign assets	–0.5	0.9	1.9	1.8	5.0	3.2	3.2	3.1	4.9	3.2	2.7
Change in reserves	0.2	0.3	0.4	0.4	2.9	1.7	1.4	2.4	2.8	1.6	1.2
Net debtor countries by debt-servicing experience											
Countries with arrears and/or rescheduling during 2001–05[1]											
Saving	16.2	19.4	16.6	20.0	22.1	20.5	20.9	23.1	22.0	22.4	22.0
Investment	22.6	22.9	18.5	18.4	20.2	20.5	21.3	22.2	22.7	23.3	24.1
Net lending	–6.4	–3.5	–1.9	1.7	1.9	—	–0.4	0.9	–0.8	–0.9	–2.1
Current transfers	1.4	1.9	2.9	3.9	4.0	3.8	4.4	4.1	4.0	3.8	3.5
Factor income	–6.1	–3.0	–4.4	–4.3	–3.7	–4.5	–4.3	–3.9	–4.3	–4.5	–3.8
Resource balance	–1.7	–2.4	–0.4	2.0	1.6	0.6	–0.4	0.7	–0.5	–0.2	–1.8
Memorandum											
Acquisition of foreign assets	0.4	2.0	–0.1	3.3	3.8	2.3	2.1	3.3	3.6	2.4	1.4
Change in reserves	0.2	0.6	–1.6	0.7	2.2	1.6	1.7	2.4	3.2	2.0	1.2

Note: The estimates in this table are based on individual countries' national accounts and balance of payments statistics. Country group composites are calculated as the sum of the U.S. dollar values for the relevant individual countries. This differs from the calculations in the April 2005 and earlier *World Economic Outlooks*, where the composites were weighted by GDP valued at purchasing power parities as a share of total world GDP. For many countries, the estimates of national saving are built up from national accounts data on gross domestic investment and from balance-of-payments-based data on net foreign investment. The latter, which is equivalent to the current account balance, comprises three components: current transfers, net factor income, and the resource balance. The mixing of data source, which is dictated by availability, implies that the estimates for national saving that are derived incorporate the statistical discrepancies. Furthermore, error omissions and asymmetries in balance of payments statistics affect the estimates for net lending; at the global level, net lending, which in theory would be zero, equals the world current account discrepancy. Notwithstanding these statistical shortcomings, flow of funds estimates, such as those presented in these tables, provide a useful framework for analyzing development in saving and investment, both over time and across regions and countries.

[1]Excludes Zimbabwe.

[2]Calculated from the data of individual euro area countries.

[3]Mongolia, which is not a member of the Commonwealth of Independent States, is included in this group for reasons of geography and similarities in economic structure.

Table A17. Summary of World Medium-Term Baseline Scenario

	Eight-Year Averages		Four-Year Average					Four-Year Average
	1989–96	1997–2004	2005–08	2005	2006	2007	2008	2009–12
	Annual percent change unless otherwise noted							
World real GDP	**3.1**	**3.8**	**5.1**	**4.8**	**5.4**	**5.2**	**4.8**	**5.1**
Advanced economies	2.7	2.7	2.5	2.5	2.9	2.5	2.2	2.6
Other emerging market and developing countries	3.7	5.3	7.8	7.5	8.1	8.1	7.4	7.3
Memorandum								
Potential output								
Major advanced economies	2.6	2.4	2.3	2.3	2.3	2.3	2.3	2.3
World trade, volume[1]	**6.6**	**6.5**	**7.5**	**7.5**	**9.2**	**6.6**	**6.7**	**7.2**
Imports								
Advanced economies	6.1	6.2	5.7	6.1	7.4	4.3	5.0	5.6
Other emerging market and developing countries	7.4	7.6	12.7	12.1	14.9	12.5	11.3	11.0
Exports								
Advanced economies	6.6	5.7	6.2	5.8	8.2	5.4	5.3	5.5
Other emerging market and developing countries	7.4	8.6	10.1	11.1	11.0	9.2	9.0	9.8
Terms of trade								
Advanced economies	–0.1	–0.0	–0.6	–1.6	–0.9	0.2	–0.2	0.0
Other emerging market and developing countries	–0.2	0.6	2.9	5.7	4.7	0.2	1.0	–0.4
World prices in U.S. dollars								
Manufactures	2.2	0.0	4.5	3.7	3.8	7.9	2.8	1.7
Oil	4.1	8.0	18.7	41.3	20.5	6.6	9.5	–2.2
Nonfuel primary commodities	–0.4	–0.1	10.3	10.3	28.4	12.2	–6.7	–6.8
Consumer prices								
Advanced economies	4.0	1.8	2.2	2.3	2.3	2.1	2.0	2.1
Other emerging market and developing countries[2]	62.1	7.9	5.4	5.2	5.1	5.9	5.3	4.4
Interest rates (in percent)								
Real six-month LIBOR[3]	3.2	2.1	2.0	0.5	2.1	2.6	2.7	3.2
World real long-term interest rate[4]	4.1	2.7	2.0	1.3	1.7	2.4	2.7	2.8
	Percent of GDP							
Balances on current account								
Advanced economies	–0.1	–0.5	–1.3	–1.3	–1.4	–1.3	–1.4	–1.6
Other emerging market and developing countries	–1.6	0.5	4.2	4.1	4.8	4.0	3.7	1.6
Total external debt								
Other emerging market and developing countries	33.6	37.3	26.5	28.5	27.0	25.7	24.7	12.6
Debt service								
Other emerging market and developing countries	4.6	6.3	4.9	5.7	5.7	4.4	4.0	2.1

[1]Data refer to trade in goods and services.

[2]Excludes Zimbabwe.

[3]London interbank offered rate on U.S. dollar deposits less percent change in U.S. GDP deflator.

[4]GDP-weighted average of 10-year (or nearest maturity) government bond rates for the United States, Japan, Germany, France, Italy, the United Kingdom, and Canada.

WORLD ECONOMIC OUTLOOK AND *STAFF STUDIES FOR THE WORLD ECONOMIC OUTLOOK*, SELECTED TOPICS, 2000–2007

I. Methodology—Aggregation, Modeling, and Forecasting

	World Economic Outlook
Revised Purchasing Power Parity Based Weights for the *World Economic Outlook*	May 2000, Box A1
The Global Current Account Discrepancy	October 2000, Chapter I, Appendix II
How Well Do Forecasters Predict Turning Points?	May 2001, Box 1.1
The Information Technology Revolution: Measurement Issues	October 2001, Box 3.1
Measuring Capital Account Liberalization	October 2001, Box 4.1
The Accuracy of *World Economic Outlook* Growth Forecasts: 1991–2000	December 2001, Box 3.1
On the Accuracy of Forecasts of Recovery	April 2002, Box 1.2
The Global Current Account Discrepancy and Other Statistical Problems	September 2002, Box 2.1
The Global Economy Model	April 2003, Box 4.3
How Should We Measure Global Growth?	September 2003, Box 1.2
Measuring Foreign Reserves	September 2003, Box 2.2
The Effects of Tax Cuts in a Global Fiscal Model	April 2004, Box 2.2
How Accurate Are the Forecasts in the *World Economic Outlook*?	April 2006, Box 1.3
Drawing the Line Between Personal and Corporate Savings	April 2006, Box 4.1
Measuring Inequality: Conceptual, Methodological, and Measurement Issues	October 2007, Box 4.1
New Business Cycle Indices for Latin America: A Historical Reconstruction	October 2007, Box 5.3

II. Historical Surveys

	World Economic Outlook
The World Economy in the Twentieth Century	May 2000, Chapter V
The Monetary System and Growth During the Commercial Revolution	May 2000, Box 5.2
The Great Depression	April 2002, Box 3.2
Historical Evidence on Financial Crises	April 2002, Box 3.3
A Historical Perspective on Booms, Busts, and Recessions	April 2003, Box 2.1
Institutional Development: The Influence of History and Geography	April 2003, Box 3.1
External Imbalances Then and Now	April 2005, Box 3.1
Long-Term Interest Rates from a Historical Perspective	April 2006, Box 1.1
Recycling Petrodollars in the 1970s	April 2006, Box 2.2

	Staff Studies for the World Economic Outlook
Globalization and Growth in the Twentieth Century *Nicholas Crafts*	May 2000
The International Monetary System in the (Very) Long Run *Barry Eichengreen and Nathan Sussman*	May 2000

III. Economic Growth—Sources and Patterns

	World Economic Outlook
How Can the Poorest Countries Catch Up?	May 2000, Chapter IV
Trends in the Human Development Index	May 2000, Box 5.1
Productivity Growth and IT in the Advanced Economies	October 2000, Chapter II
Transition: Experience and Policy Issues	October 2000, Chapter III
Business Linkages in Major Advanced Countries	October 2001, Chapter II
How Do Macroeconomic Fluctuations in the Advanced Countries Affect the Developing Countries?	October 2001, Chapter II
Confidence Spillovers	October 2001, Box 2.1
Channels of Business Cycle Transmission to Developing Countries	October 2001, Box 2.2
The Information Technology Revolution	October 2001, Chapter III
Has the IT Revolution Reduced Output Volatility?	October 2001, Box 3.4
The Impact of Capital Account Liberalization on Economic Performance	October 2001, Box 4.2
How Has September 11 Influenced the Global Economy?	December 2001, Chapter II
The Long-Term Impact of September 11	December 2001, Box 2.1
Is Wealth Increasingly Driving Consumption?	April 2002, Chapter II
Recessions and Recoveries	April 2002, Chapter III
Was It a Global Recession?	April 2002, Box 1.1
How Important Is the Wealth Effect on Consumption?	April 2002, Box 2.1
A Household Perspective on the Wealth Effect	April 2002, Box 2.2
Measuring Business Cycles	April 2002, Box 3.1
Economic Fluctuations in Developing Countries	April 2002, Box 3.4
How Will Recent Falls in Equity Markets Affect Activity?	September 2002, Box 1.1
Reversal of Fortune: Productivity Growth in Europe and the United States	September 2002, Box 1.3
Growth and Institutions	April 2003, Chapter III
Is the New Economy Dead?	April 2003, Box 1.2
Have External Anchors Accelerated Institutional Reform in Practice?	April 2003, Box 3.2
Institutional Development: The Role of the IMF	April 2003, Box 3.4
How Would War in Iraq Affect the Global Economy?	April 2003, Appendix 1.2
How Can Economic Growth in the Middle East and North Africa Region Be Accelerated?	September 2003, Chapter II
Recent Changes in Monetary and Financial Conditions in the Major Currency Areas	September 2003, Box 1.1
Accounting for Growth in the Middle East and North Africa	September 2003, Box 2.1
Managing Increasing Aid Flows to Developing Countries	September 2003, Box 1.3
Fostering Structural Reforms in Industrial Countries	April 2004, Chapter III
How Will Demographic Change Affect the Global Economy?	September 2004, Chapter III
HIV/AIDS: Demographic, Economic, and Fiscal Consequences	September 2004, Box 3.3
Implications of Demographic Change for Health Care Systems	September 2004, Box 3.4
Workers' Remittances and Economic Development	April 2005, Chapter II
Output Volatility in Emerging Market and Developing Countries	April 2005, Chapter II
How Does Macroeconomic Instability Stifle Sub-Saharan African Growth?	April 2005, Box 1.5
How Should Middle Eastern and Central Asian Oil Exporters Use Their Oil Revenues?	April 2005, Box 1.6

Why Is Volatility Harmful?	April 2005, Box 2.3
Building Institutions	September 2005, Chapter III
Return on Investment in Industrial and Developing Countries	September 2005, Box 2.2
The Use of Specific Levers to Reduce Corruption	September 2005, Box 3.2
Examining the Impact of Unrequited Transfers on Institutions	September 2005, Box 3.3
The Impact of Recent Housing Market Adjustments in Industrial Countries	April 2006, Box 1.2
Awash With Cash: Why Are Corporate Savings So High?	April 2006, Chapter IV
The Global Implications of an Avian Flu Pandemic	April 2006, Appendix 1.2
Asia Rising: Patterns of Economic Development and Growth	September 2006, Chapter III
Japan's Potential Output and Productivity Growth	September 2006, Box 3.1
The Evolution and Impact of Corporate Governance Quality in Asia	September 2006, Box 3.2
Decoupling the Train? Spillovers and Cycles in the Global Economy	April 2007, Chapter 4
Spillovers and International Business Cycle Synchronization: A Broader Perspective	April 2007, Box 4.3
What Risks Do Housing Markets Pose for Global Growth?	October 2007, Box 2.1
Climate Change: Economic Impact and Policy Responses	October 2007, Appendix 1.2
The Discounting Debate	October 2007, Box 1.7
Taxes Versus Quantities Under Uncertainty (Weitzman, 1974)	October 2007, Box 1.8
Experience with Emissions Trading in the European Union	October 2007, Box 1.9
The Changing Dynamics of the Global Business Cycle	October 2007, Chapter 5
Major Economies and Fluctuations in Global Growth	October 2007, Box 5.1
Improved Macroeconomic Performance—Good Luck or Good Policies?	October 2007, Box 5.2

IV. Inflation and Deflation; Commodity Markets

	World Economic Outlook
Cycles in Nonfuel Commodity Prices	May 2000, Box 2.2
Booms and Slumps in the World Oil Market	May 2000, Box 2.3
Commodity Prices and Commodity Exporting Countries	October 2000, Chapter II
Developments in the Oil Markets	October 2000, Box 2.2
The Decline of Inflation in Emerging Markets: Can It Be Maintained?	May 2001, Chapter IV
The Global Slowdown and Commodity Prices	May 2001, Chapter I, Appendix 1
Why Emerging Market Countries Should Strive to Preserve Lower Inflation	May 2001, Box 4.1
Is There a Relationship Between Fiscal Deficits and Inflation?	May 2001, Box 4.2
How Much of a Concern Is Higher Headline Inflation?	October 2001, Box 1.2
Primary Commodities and Semiconductor Markets	October 2001, Chapter I, Appendix 1
Can Inflation Be Too Low?	April 2002, Box 2.3
Could Deflation Become a Global Problem?	April 2003, Box 1.1
Housing Markets in Industrial Countries	April 2004, Box 1.2
Is Global Inflation Coming Back?	September 2004, Box 1.1
What Explains the Recent Run-Up in House Prices?	September 2004, Box 2.1
Will the Oil Market Continue to Be Tight?	April 2005, Chapter IV
Should Countries Worry About Oil Price Fluctuations?	April 2005, Box 4.1

V. Fiscal Policy

VI. Monetary Policy; Financial Markets; Flow of Funds

U.S. Monetary Policy and Sovereign Spreads in Emerging Markets	October 2000, Box 2.1
Impact of the Global Technology Correction on the Real Economy	May 2001, Chapter II
Inflation Targeting in Emerging Market Economies: Implementation and Challenges	May 2001, Box 4.3
Financial Market Dislocations and Policy Responses After the September 11 Attacks	December 2001, Box 2.2
Investor Risk Appetite	December 2001, Box 2.3
Monetary Policy in a Low Inflation Era	April 2002, Chapter II
The Introduction of Euro Notes and Coins	April 2002, Box 1.3
Cross-Country Determinants of Capital Structure	September 2002, Box 2.3
When Bubbles Burst	April 2003, Chapter II
How Do Balance Sheet Vulnerabilities Affect Investment?	April 2003, Box 2.3
Identifying Asset Price Booms and Busts	April 2003, Appendix 2.1
Are Foreign Exchange Reserves in Asia Too High?	September 2003, Chapter II
Reserves and Short-Term Debt	September 2003, Box 2.3
Are Credit Booms in Emerging Markets a Concern?	April 2004, Chapter IV
How Do U.S. Interest and Exchange Rates Affect Emerging Markets' Balance Sheets?	April 2004, Box 2.1
Does Financial Sector Development Help Economic Growth and Welfare?	April 2004, Box 4.1
Adjustable- or Fixed-Rate Mortgages: What Influences a Country's Choices?	September 2004, Box 2.2
What Are the Risks from Low U.S. Long-Term Interest Rates?	April 2005, Box 1.2
Regulating Remittances	April 2005, Box 2.2
Financial Globalization and the Conduct of Macroeconomic Policies	April 2005, Box 3.3
Monetary Policy in a Globalized World	April 2005, Box 3.4
Does Inflation Targeting Work in Emerging Markets?	September 2005, Chapter IV
A Closer Look at Inflation Targeting Alternatives: Money and Exchange Rate Targets	September 2005, Box 4.1
How Has Globalization Affected Inflation?	April 2006, Chapter III
The Impact of Petrodollars on U.S. and Emerging Market Bond Yields	April 2006, Box 2.3
Globalization and Inflation in Emerging Markets	April 2006, Box 3.1
Globalization and Low Inflation in a Historical Perspective	April 2006, Box 3.2
Exchange Rate Pass-Through to Import Prices	April 2006, Box 3.3
Trends in the Financial Sector's Profits and Savings	April 2006, Box 4.2
How Do Financial Systems Affect Economic Cycles?	September 2006, Chapter 4
Financial Leverage and Debt Deflation	September 2006, Box 4.1
Financial Linkages and Spillovers	April 2007, Box 4.1
Macroeconomic Conditions in Industrial Countries and Financial Flows to Emerging Markets	April 2007, Box 4.2
What Is Global Liquidity?	October 2007, Box 1.4
Macroeconomic Implications of Recent Market Turmoil: Patterns From Previous Episodes	October 2007, Box 1.2
	Staff Studies for the World Economic Outlook
Capital Structure and Corporate Performance Across Emerging Markets	September 2002, Chapter II

VII. Labor Markets, Poverty, and Inequality

VIII. Exchange Rate Issues

IX. External Payments, Trade, Capital Movements, and Foreign Debt

	World Economic Outlook
The Global Current Account Discrepancy	October 2000, Chapter I, Appendix II
Trade Integration and Sub-Saharan Africa	May 2001, Chapter II
Sustainability of the U.S. External Current Account	May 2001, Box 1.2
Reducing External Balances	May 2001, Chapter I, Appendix 2
The World Trading System: From Seattle to Doha	October 2001, Chapter II
International Financial Integration and Economic Performance: Impact on Developing Countries	October 2001, Chapter IV
Potential Welfare Gains From a New Trade Round	October 2001, Box 2.3
Critics of a New Trade Round	October 2001, Box 2.4
Foreign Direct Investment and the Poorer Countries	October 2001, Box 4.3
Country Experiences with Sequencing Capital Account Liberalization	October 2001, Box 4.4
Contagion and Its Causes	December 2001, Chapter I, Appendix
Capital Account Crises in Emerging Market Countries	April 2002, Box 3.5
How Have External Deficits Adjusted in the Past?	September 2002, Box 2.2
Using Prices to Measure Goods Market Integration	September 2002, Box 3.1
Transport Costs	September 2002, Box 3.2
The Gravity Model of International Trade	September 2002, Box 3.3
Vertical Specialization in the Global Economy	September 2002, Box 3.4
Trade and Growth	September 2002, Box 3.5
How Worrisome Are External Imbalances?	September 2002, Chapter II
How Do Industrial Country Agricultural Policies Affect Developing Countries?	September 2002, Chapter II
Trade and Financial Integration	September 2002, Chapter III
Risks to the Multilateral Trading System	April 2004, Box 1.3
Is the Doha Round Back on Track?	September 2004, Box 1.3
Regional Trade Agreements and Integration: The Experience with NAFTA	September 2004, Box 1.4
Trade and Financial Integration in Europe: Five Years After the Euro's Introduction	September 2004, Box 2.5
Globalization and External Imbalances	April 2005, Chapter III
The Ending of Global Textile Trade Quotas	April 2005, Box 1.3
What Progress Has Been Made in Implementing Policies to Reduce Global Imbalances?	April 2005, Box 1.4
Measuring a Country's Net External Position	April 2005, Box 3.2
Global Imbalances: A Saving and Investment Perspective	September 2005, Chapter II
Impact of Demographic Change on Saving, Investment, and Current Account Balances	September 2005, Box 2.3
How Will Global Imbalances Adjust?	September 2005, Appendix 1.2
Oil Prices and Global Imbalances	April 2006, Chapter II
How Much Progress Has Been Made in Addressing Global Imbalances?	April 2006, Box 1.4
The Doha Round After the Hong Kong SAR Meetings	April 2006, Box 1.5
Capital Flows to Emerging Market Countries: A Long-Term Perspective	September 2006, Box 1.1

X. Regional Issues

XI. Country-Specific Analyses

World Economic and Financial Surveys

This series (ISSN 0258-7440) contains biannual, annual, and periodic studies covering monetary and financial issues of importance to the global economy. The core elements of the series are the *World Economic Outlook* report, usually published in April and September, the semiannual *Global Financial Stability Report,* and the semiannual Regional Economic Outlooks published by the IMF's area departments. Occasionally, studies assess international trade policy, private market and official financing for developing countries, exchange and payments systems, export credit policies, and issues discussed in the *World Economic Outlook.* Please consult the IMF *Publications Catalog* for a complete listing of currently available World Economic and Financial Surveys.

World Economic Outlook: A Survey by the Staff of the International Monetary Fund

The *World Economic Outlook,* published twice a year in English, French, Spanish, and Arabic, presents IMF staff economists' analyses of global economic developments during the near and medium term. Chapters give an overview of the world economy; consider issues affecting industrial countries, developing countries, and economies in transition to the market; and address topics of pressing current interest.

Annual subscription: $94.00
Published twice yearly. Paperback.
ISSN: 0256-6877. **Stock# WEOSEA**
Available in English, French, Spanish, and Arabic.

Global Financial Stability Report

The *Global Financial Stability Report,* published twice a year, examines trends and issues that influence world financial markets. It focuses on current market conditions, highlighting issues of financial imbalances, and of a structural nature, that could pose risks to financial market stability and sustained market access by emerging market borrowers. The report is designed to deepen understanding of international capital flows, which play a critical role as an engine of world economic growth.

Annual subscription: $94.00
Published twice yearly. Paperback. **Stock# GFSREA**

Regional Economic Outlooks

These in-depth studies of the Asia and Pacific, Europe, Middle East and Central Asia, sub-Saharan Africa, and Western Hemisphere regions drill down to specific regional economic and financial developments and trends—bringing the unique resources, experience, and perspective of the IMF to bear. While near-term responses to exogenous shocks, policies for growth, and the effectiveness of financial policies get center-stage examination, the reports also consider vulnerabilities and opportunities developing in the wings.

Individual copies of the Regional Economic Outlooks are available at $31.00 (academic rate: $26.00). Please visit www.imfbookstore.org/REOs or contact publications@imf.org for further information on all REO subscription packages.

Emerging Local Securities and Derivatives Markets

by Donald Mathieson, Jorge E. Roldos, Ramana Ramaswamy, and Anna Ilyina

The volatility of capital flows since the mid-1990s has sparked an interest in the development of local securities and derivatives markets. This report examines the growth of these markets in emerging market countries and the key policy issues that have arisen as a result.

$42.00 (academic rate: $35.00); paper.
2004. ISBN 1-58906-291-4. **Stock# WEOEA0202004.**

Official Financing: Recent Developments and Selected Issues

by a staff team in the Policy Development and Review Department led by Martin G. Gilman and Jian-Ye Wang

This study provides information on official financing for developing countries, with the focus on low-income countries. It updates the 2001 edition and reviews developments in direct financing by official and multilateral sources.

$42.00 (academic rate: $35.00); paper.
2003. ISBN 1-58906-228-0. **Stock# WEOEA0132003.**
2001. ISBN 1-58906-038-5. **Stock# WEOEA0132001.**

Exchange Arrangements and Foreign Exchange Markets: Developments and Issues

by a staff team led by Shogo Ishii

This study updates developments in exchange arrangements during 1998–2001. It also discusses the evolution of exchange rate regimes based on de facto policies since 1990, reviews foreign exchange market organization and regulations in a number of countries, and examines factors affecting exchange rate volatility.

ISSN 0258-7440
$42.00 (academic rate: $35.00)
March 2003. ISBN 1-58906-177-2. **Stock# WEOEA0192003.**

Available by series subscription or single title (including back issues); academic rate available only to full-time university faculty and students. For earlier editions please inquire about prices.

The IMF *Catalog of Publications* is available on-line at the Internet address listed below.

Please send orders and inquiries to:
International Monetary Fund, Publication Services, 700 19th Street, N.W.
Washington, D.C. 20431, U.S.A.
Tel.: (202) 623-7430 Telefax: (202) 623-7201
E-mail: publications@imf.org
Internet: http://www.imf.org/external/pubind.htm